Real Applications

Eye On Boxes apply theory to important issues and problems that shape our global society and individual decisions.

New to the Fifth Edition are *Eye On* boxes that answer the chapter-opening questions.

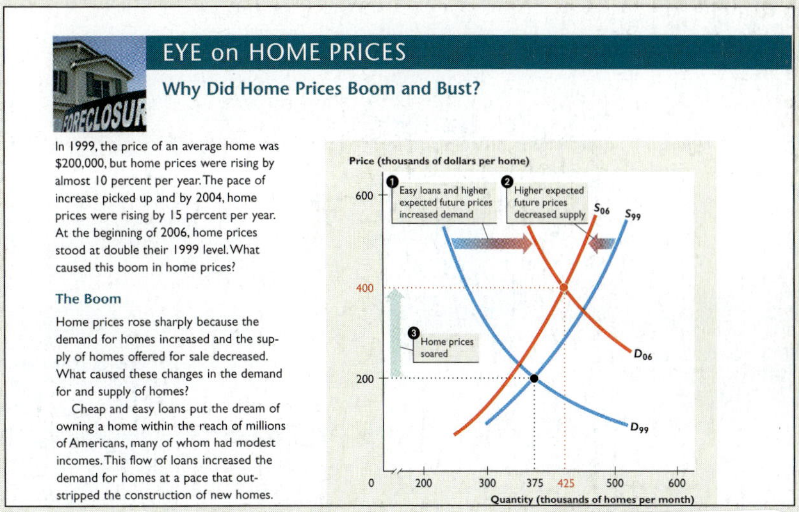

EYE on HOME PRICES

Why Did Home Prices Boom and Bust?

In 1999, the price of an average home was $200,000, but home prices were rising by almost 10 percent per year. The pace of increase picked up and by 2004, home prices were rising by 15 percent per year. At the beginning of 2006, home prices stood at double their 1999 level. What caused this boom in home prices?

The Boom

Home prices rose sharply because the demand for homes increased and the supply of homes offered for sale decreased. What caused these changes in the demand for and supply of homes?

Cheap and easy loans put the dream of owning a home within the reach of millions of Americans, many of whom had modest incomes. This flow of loans increased the demand for homes at a pace that outstripped the construction of new homes.

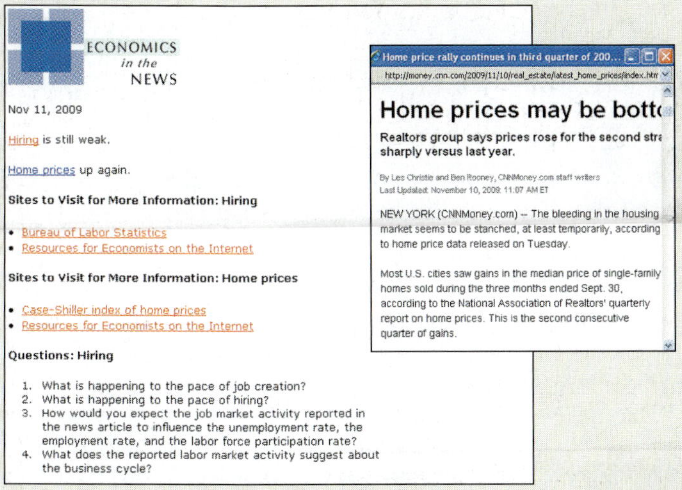

ECONOMICS in the NEWS

Nov 11, 2009

Hiring is still weak.

Home prices up again.

Sites to Visit for More Information: Hiring

- Bureau of Labor Statistics
- Resources for Economists on the Internet

Sites to Visit for More Information: Home prices

- Case-Shiller index of home prices
- Resources for Economists on the Internet

Questions: Hiring

1. What is happening to the pace of job creation?
2. What is happening to the pace of hiring?
3. How would you expect the job market activity reported in the news article to influence the unemployment rate, the employment rate, and the labor force participation rate?
4. What does the reported labor market activity suggest about the business cycle?

Home price rally continues in third quarter of 200...

http://money.cnn.com/2009/11/10/real_estate/latest_home_prices/index.htm

Home prices may be bott

Realtors group says prices rose for the second stra sharply versus last year.

By Les Christie and Ben Rooney, CNNMoney.com staff writers
Last Updated: November 10, 2009: 11:07 AM ET

NEW YORK (CNNMoney.com) -- The bleeding in the housing market seems to be stanched, at least temporarily, according to home price data released on Tuesday.

Most U.S. cities saw gains in the median price of single-family homes sold during the three months ended Sept. 30, according to the National Association of Realtors' quarterly report on home prices. This is the second consecutive quarter of gains.

Economics in the News

myeconlab

To keep you informed about the latest economic news, each day the authors upload two relevant news articles: a microeconomic topic and a macroeconomic topic. Each article includes discussion questions, links to additional online resources, and references to related textbook chapters.

Practice and Guided Tutorials

myeconlab

An end-of-chapter problem based on the chapter-opening issue gives students further practice.

All of the Checkpoint problems are in MyEconLab and available for self-assessment or instructor assignment.

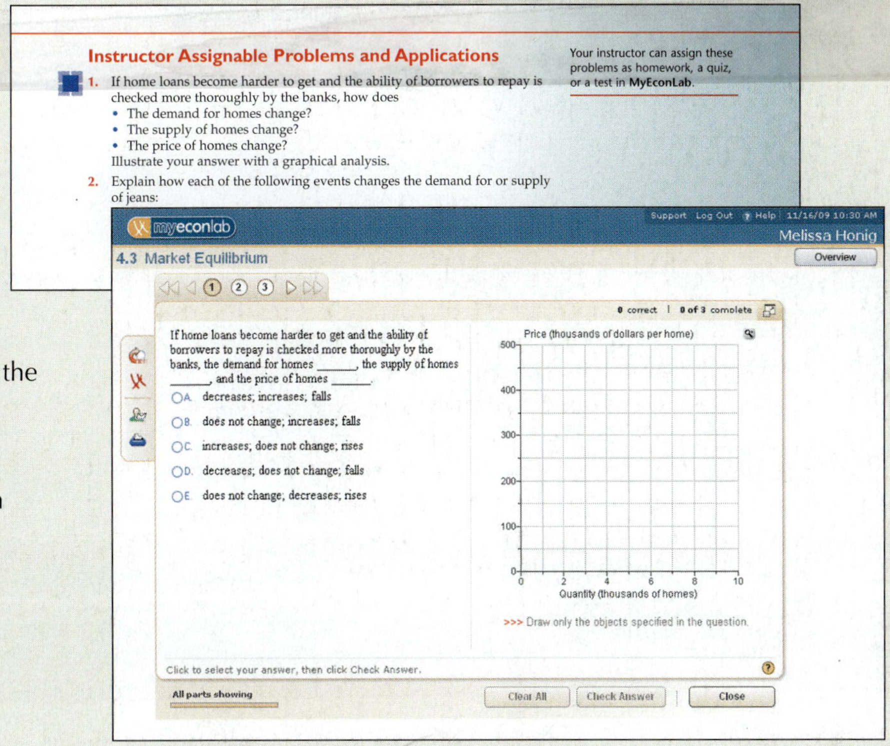

Instructor Assignable Problems and Applications

Your instructor can assign these problems as homework, a quiz, or a test in **MyEconLab**.

1. If home loans become harder to get and the ability of borrowers to repay is checked more thoroughly by the banks, how does
   - The demand for homes change?
   - The supply of homes change?
   - The price of homes change?

   Illustrate your answer with a graphical analysis.
2. Explain how each of the following events changes the demand for or supply of jeans:

Foundations of

MACROECONOMICS

Robin Bade

Michael Parkin

University of Western Ontario

FIFTH EDITION

Addison-Wesley

Boston Columbus Indianapolis New York San Francisco Upper Saddle River
Amsterdam Cape Town Dubai London Madrid Milan Munich Paris Montreal Toronto
Delhi Mexico City Sao Paulo Sydney Hong Kong Seoul Singapore Taipei Tokyo

Editor in Chief Donna Battista
Senior Acquisitions Editor Adrienne D'Ambrosio
Development Editor Deepa Chungi
Supplements Editor Alison Eusden
Director of Media Susan Schoenberg
Content Lead for MyEconLab Noel Lotz
Senior Media Producer Melissa Honig
Executive Marketing Manager Lori DeShazo
Marketing Assistant Justin Jacob
Managing Editor Nancy Fenton
Art Director, Cover Linda Knowles
Cover Designer Anthony Saizon
Copyeditor Catherine Baum
Technical Illustrator Richard Parkin
Senior Manufacturing Buyer Carol Melville
Project Management, Page Makeup, Design
Elm Street Publishing Services

Cover photographs (clockwise from top left): © Shigeki Fujiwara/Sebun Photo/Getty Images; © Joel W. Rogers/Corbis; © Vector Images.com; © OJO Images/Getty Images

Text and photo credits appear on page C–1, which constitutes a continuation of the copyright page.

Library of Congress Cataloging-in-Publication Data
Bade, Robin.
Foundations of Macroeconomics / Robin Bade, Michael Parkin.--5th ed.
p. cm.
Includes index.
ISBN 0-13-612583-2
1. Economics. I. Parkin, Michael, 1939– II. Title
HB171.5 .B155 2010
330—dc21

2009050138

2 3 4 5 6 7 8 9 10—CRK—13 12 11 10

Addison-Wesley
is an imprint of

PEARSON

www.pearsonhighered.com

ISBN-13: 978-0-13-612583-9
ISBN-10: 0-13-612583-2

To Erin, Tessa, Jack, Abby, and Sophie

About the Authors

Robin Bade was an undergraduate at the University of Queensland, Australia, where she earned degrees in mathematics and economics. After a spell teaching high school math and physics, she enrolled in the Ph.D. program at the Australian National University, from which she graduated in 1970. She has held faculty appointments at the University of Edinburgh in Scotland, at Bond University in Australia, and at the Universities of Manitoba, Toronto, and Western Ontario in Canada. Her research on international capital flows appears in the *International Economic Review* and the *Economic Record*.

Robin first taught the principles of economics course in 1970 and has taught it (alongside intermediate macroeconomics and international trade and finance) most years since then. She developed many of the ideas found in this text while conducting tutorials with her students at the University of Western Ontario.

Michael Parkin studied economics in England and began his university teaching career immediately after graduating with a B.A. from the University of Leicester. He learned the subject on the job at the University of Essex, England's most exciting new university of the 1960s, and at the age of 30 became one of the youngest full professors. He is a past president of the Canadian Economics Association and has served on the editorial boards of the *American Economic Review* and the *Journal of Monetary Economics*. His research on macroeconomics, monetary economics, and international economics has resulted in more than 160 publications in journals and edited volumes, including the *American Economic Review*, the *Journal of Political Economy*, the *Review of Economic Studies*, the *Journal of Monetary Economics*, and the *Journal of Money, Credit, and Banking*. He is author of the best-selling textbook, *Economics* (Addison-Wesley), now in its Ninth Edition.

Robin and Michael are a wife-and-husband duo. Their most notable joint research created the Bade-Parkin Index of central bank independence and spawned a vast amount of research on that topic. They don't claim credit for the independence of the new European Central Bank, but its constitution and the movement toward greater independence of central banks around the world were aided by their pioneering work. Their joint textbooks include *Macroeconomics* (Prentice-Hall), *Modern Macroeconomics* (Pearson Education Canada), and *Economics: Canada in the Global Environment*, the Canadian adaptation of Parkin, *Economics* (Addison-Wesley). They are dedicated to the challenge of explaining economics ever more clearly to an ever-growing body of students.

Music, the theater, art, walking on the beach, and five fast-growing grandchildren provide their relaxation and fun.

MACROECONOMICS Brief Contents

Contents

PART 2 MONITORING THE MACROECONOMY

PART 4 THE MONEY ECONOMY

PART 5 ECONOMIC FLUCTUATIONS

Preface

Students know that throughout their lives they will make economic decisions and be influenced by economic forces. They want to understand the economic principles that can help them navigate these forces and guide their decisions. *Foundations of Macroeconomics* is our attempt to satisfy this want.

The response to our earlier editions from hundreds of colleagues across the United States and throughout the world tells us that most of you agree with our view that to achieve its goals, the principles course must do four things well. It must

- Motivate with compelling issues and questions;
- Focus on core ideas;
- Steer a path between an overload of detail and too much left unsaid;
- Encourage and aid learning by doing.

The *Foundations* icon with its four blocks (on the cover and throughout the book) symbolizes this four-point approach that has guided all our choices in writing this text and creating its comprehensive teaching and learning supplements.

WHAT'S NEW IN THE FIFTH EDITION

The evolving U.S. and global economies provide a rich display of economic forces in action through which students can be motivated to discover the economic way of thinking. The global financial crisis and slump, ongoing tensions that result from globalization and international outsourcing, the continued spectacular expansion of China and India in the information-age economy, relentless pressure on the federal budget from the demands of an aging population and increased defense and homeland security expenditures, a falling dollar, and an ongoing U.S. international deficit and ever-growing national and international debt are just a few of these interest-arousing events. All of them feature at the appropriate points in our new edition, and the text and examples are all thoroughly updated to reflect the most recently available data and events.

Every chapter contains many small changes, all designed to enhance clarity and currency. We have also made some major changes that we now describe.

FEATURE CHANGES

Each chapter opens with a photograph and a question about an issue that the chapter addresses. An *Eye On* box answers the question and an end-of-chapter problem (also in the instructor-assignable section of MyEconLab) makes the issues available for homework or quiz assignment. This feature enables the student to get the point of the chapter quickly; it ties the chapter together; and it enables the instructor to focus on a core issue in class and for practice.

Checkpoint Practice Problems and end-of-chapter problems now include mini case studies from recent news stories. These problems feature in MyEconLab: some for student practice and some reserved for instructor homework and test assignments.

■ Major Content Changes

Questions about the economic way of thinking (Did greed cause the global economic slump?); offshoring and outsourcing (Who makes the iPhone?); opportunity cost (Is wind power free?), and demand and supply (Why did home prices boom and bust?) are the motivating questions and features of *Eye On* boxes and end-of-chapter problems in the four introductory chapters.

We reorganized Chapter 2, but did not change its overall content. Chapter 4 has two new demand and supply application boxes on the markets for automobiles and wheat.

The macroeconomic events and debates of 2008 and 2009 permeate the macro chapters, all of which have been radically updated and revised. Policy features at every possible opportunity throughout these chapters.

How do we track the booms and busts of the business cycle? How long does it take to find a job? How do we measure the changing value of money? Why do Americans earn and produce more than Europeans? Why are some nations rich and others poor? What created the global financial crisis? How does the Fed create money? What causes inflation? What causes the business cycle? Can we have low unemployment and low inflation? Did fiscal stimulus end the recession? Did the Fed save us from another Great Depression? Why is our dollar sinking? These are the motivating questions and features of *Eye On* boxes and end-of-chapter problems in the fourteen macro chapters.

Chapter 5 now has a section that defines the business cycle and its phases and compares the NBER's method of dating the turning points with the message that real GDP gives for the onset of the 2008–2009 recession.

We reversed the order of the chapters on "Jobs and Unemployment" (6) and "The CPI and the Cost of Living" (7) to emphasize the importance of unemployment today. The unemployment chapter now explains the six alternative measures of unemployment and the idea of marginal labor force attachment. The chapter also has an improved explanation of the linkage between fluctuations in unemployment around the natural rate and the output gap. The CPI chapter now includes an explanation of the core inflation rate.

The chapter on "Finance, Saving, and Investment" (10) incorporates default risk as a factor influencing the supply of loanable funds and explains why lending dried up during the financial crisis. The chapter also examines the issue of crowding out in the face of a large fiscal deficit.

The two money chapters, "The Monetary System" (11) and "Money, Interest, and Inflation" (12), are revised to explain the extraordinary policy actions undertaken by the Fed following the collapse of Lehman Brothers. The chapters look at the enormous increase in the monetary base and corresponding increase in banks' desired reserves as they coped with enhanced default risk.

We also revised the two policy chapters, "Fiscal Policy" (16) and "Monetary Policy" (17), to include the major actions of 2008 and 2009. The fiscal policy chapter is restructured to begin with an account of the cracks in the consensus and the public debate on the merits of fiscal stimulus in recession. The chapter then examines discretionary and automatic fiscal stimulus and the challenges facing the conduct of discretionary policies. In 2009, the effect of automatic stimulus was vastly greater than the discretionary stimulus initiated by Congress. The monetary policy chapter contrasts the orderly near rule-based policies before 2008 with the radical and aggressive countercyclical actions since 2008.

Chapter 18 (International Trade Policy) is entirely new. It explains the sources and distribution of the gains and losses from international trade and government intervention in global markets through tariffs, import quotas, and other trade policy actions. This chapter uses the demand and supply model and may be covered at any time after chapter 4. By covering this topic early in the course, it becomes possible to discuss issues of major concern to students today.

THE FOUNDATIONS VISION

■ Focus on Core Concepts

Each chapter of *Foundations* concentrates on a manageable number of main ideas (most commonly three or four) and reinforces each idea several times throughout the chapter. This patient, confidence-building approach guides students through unfamiliar terrain and helps them to focus their efforts on the most important tools and concepts of our discipline.

■ Many Learning Tools for Many Learning Styles

Foundations' integrated print and electronic package builds on the basic fact that students have a variety of learning styles. In MyEconLab, students have a powerful tool at their fingertips: They can complete all Checkpoint problems online, work interactive graphs, assess their skills by taking Practice Tests, receive a personalized Study Plan, and step through Guided Solutions.

■ Diagrams That Tell the Whole Story

We developed the style of our diagrams with extensive feedback from faculty focus group participants and student reviewers. All of our figures make consistent use of color to show the direction of shifts and contain detailed, numbered captions designed to direct students' attention step-by-step through the action. Because beginning students of economics are often apprehensive about working with graphs, we have made a special effort to present material in as many as three ways—with graphs, words, and tables—in the same figure. In an innovation that seems necessary, but is to our knowledge unmatched, nearly all of the information supporting a figure appears on the same page as the figure itself. No more flipping pages back and forth!

Real-World Connections That Bring Theory to Life

Students learn best when they can see the purpose of what they are studying, apply it to illuminate the world around them, and use it in their lives.

Eye On boxes, and *Eye On* features offer fresh new examples to help students see that economics is everywhere. Current and recent events appear in *Eye On the U.S. Economy* boxes; we place current U.S. economic events in global and historical perspectives in our *Eye on the Global Economy* and *Eye on the Past* boxes; and we show how students can use economics in day-to-day decisions in *Eye On Your Life* boxes.

The new *Eye On* boxes that build off of the chapter-opening question help students see the economics behind key issues facing our world and highlight a major aspect of the chapter's story.

ORGANIZATION

We have organized the sequence of material and chapters in what we think is the most natural order in which to cover the material. But we recognize that there are alternative views on the best order. We have kept this fact and the need for flexibility firmly in mind throughout the text. Many alternative sequences work, and the Flexibility Chart on pp. xxvii—xxix explains the alternatives that we believe work well.

MYECONLAB

MyEconLab's powerful assessment and tutorial system works hand-in-hand with *Foundations*. With comprehensive homework, quiz, test, and tutorial options, instructors can manage all assessment needs in one program.

- All of the Checkpoint and Chapter Checkpoint Problems and Applications are assignable and automatically graded in MyEconLab.
- Extra problems and applications, including algorithmic, draw-graph, and numerical exercises are available for student practice, or instructor assignment.
- Test Item File questions are available for assignment as homework.
- The Custom Exercise Builder allows instructors the flexibility of creating their own problems for assignment.
- The powerful Gradebook records each student's performance and time spent on the Tests and Study Plan and generates reports by student or by chapter.
- Economics in the News is a turn-key solution to bringing daily news into the classroom. Updated daily during the academic year, the authors upload two relevant articles (one micro, one macro) and provide discussion questions.
- A comprehensive suite of ABC news videos, which address current topics such as education, energy, Federal Reserve policy, and business cycles, is available for classroom use. Video-specific exercises are available for instructor assignment.

We are the authors of the MyEconLab content for *Foundations of Macroeconomics* and have worked hard to ensure that it is tightly integrated with the book's content and vision. A more detailed walk-through of the student benefits and features of MyEconLab can be found on pp. xxx–xxxi. For more information, visit the online demonstration at www.myeconlab.com.

SUPPORT MATERIALS FOR INSTRUCTORS AND STUDENTS

Foundations of Macroeconomics is accompanied by the most comprehensive set of teaching and learning tools ever assembled. Each component of our package is organized by Checkpoint topic for a tight, seamless integration with both the textbook and the other components. In addition to authoring the MyEconLab and PowerPoint content, we have helped in the reviewing and revising of the Study Guide, Solutions Manual, Instructor's Manual, and Test Item Files to ensure that every element of the package achieves the consistency that students and teachers need.

■ Study Guide

Mark Rush of the University of Florida has prepared the Study Guide, which is available in both print and electronic formats. It provides an expanded Chapter Checklist that enables the student to break the learning tasks down into smaller, bite-sized pieces; self-test materials; and additional practice problems. The Study Guide has been carefully coordinated with the text, MyEconLab, and the Test Item Files.

■ Solutions Manual

The Solutions Manual, written by Mark Rush, contains the solutions to all the Checkpoint Practice Problems and Chapter Checkpoint Problems and Applications. It is available for download in Word and PDF formats.

■ Instructor's Manual

The Instructor's Manual, written by Luke Armstrong and edited by Mark Rush, contains chapter outlines and road maps, additional exercises with solutions, and a virtual encyclopedia of suggestions on how to enrich class presentation and use class time efficiently. The fifth edition is enhanced with a Chapter Lecture which incorporates lively Lecture Launchers to enrich your presentation, Landmines that point out potential stumbling blocks, and additional teaching tips, creating one comprehensive lecture resource. The Instructor's Manual has been updated to reflect changes in the main text as well as infused with a fresh and intuitive approach to teaching this course. It is available for download in Word and PDF formats.

■ Three Test Item Files and TestGen

More than 6,000 multiple-choice, numerical, fill-in-the-blank, short answer, essay, and integrative questions make up the three Test Item Files that support *Foundations of Macroeconomics*. While these questions continue to build on more than one Checkpoint or more than one chapter, this edition's Test Item Files now feature a linear progression through the text, which will enable instructors to easily view, pick and choose questions for homework and exams. Mark Rush reviewed and edited questions from two dedicated principles instructors to form one of the most comprehensive testing systems on the market. Our questions were written by Carol Dole (Jacksonville University) and Buffie Schmidt (Augusta State University). The entire set of questions is available for download in Word, PDF, and TestGen formats.

All three Test Item Files are available in test generator software (TestGen with QuizMaster). TestGen's graphical interface enables instructors to view, edit, and add questions; transfer questions to tests; and print different forms of tests. Instructors also have the option to reformat tests with varying fonts and styles, margins, and headers and footers, as in any word-processing document. Search and sort features let the instructor quickly locate questions and arrange them in a preferred order. QuizMaster, working with your school's computer network, automatically grades the exams, stores the results on disk, and allows the instructor to view and print a variety of reports.

PowerPoint Resources

We have created the PowerPoint resources based on our 15 years of experience using this tool in our own classrooms. Three types of PowerPoint presentations are available:

- Lecture notes with full-color, animated figures and tables from the textbook
- Figures and tables from the textbook. All of the textbook figures are animated for step-by-step walk-through.
- Clicker-enabled slides for your Personal Response System. The slides consist of 10 multiple choice questions from the Study Guide for each chapter. You can use these in class to encourage active learning.

Instructor's Resource CD-ROM

This CD-ROM contains the Instructor's Manual, Solutions Manual, and Test Item Files in Word and PDF formats. It also contains the Computerized Test Item Files (with a TestGen program installer) and Powerpoint Resources. It is compatible with both Windows and Macintosh operating systems.

For your convenience, all instructor resources are also available online via our centralized supplements Web site, the Instructor Resource Center (www.pearsonhighered.com/irc). For access or more information, contact your local Pearson representative or request access online at the Instructor Resource Center.

CourseSmart

CourseSmart goes beyond traditional expectations by providing instant, online access to the textbooks and course materials you need at a lower cost to students. And, even as students save money, you can save time and hassle with a digital textbook that allows you to search the most relevant content at the very moment you need it. Whether it's evaluating textbooks or creating lecture notes to help students with difficult concepts, CourseSmart can make life a little easier. See how when you visit www.coursesmart.com.

ACKNOWLEDGMENTS

Working on a project such as this one generates many debts that can never be repaid. But they can be acknowledged, and it is a special pleasure to be able to do so here and to express our heartfelt thanks to each and every one of the following long list, without whose contributions we could not have produced *Foundations*.

Mark Rush again coordinated, managed, and contributed to our Study Guide, Solutions Manual, Instructor's Manual, and Test Item Files. He assembled, polished, wrote, and rewrote these materials to ensure their close consistency with the text. He and we were in constant contact as all the elements of our text and package came together. Mark also made many valuable suggestions for improving the text and the Checkpoint Problems. His contribution went well beyond that of a reviewer, and his effervescent sense of humor kept us all in good spirits along the way.

Working closely with Mark, Luke Armstrong wrote content for the Instructor's Manual. Carol Dole and Buffie Schmidt authored new questions for the Test Item Files.

The ideas that ultimately became *Foundations* began to form over dinner at the Andover Inn in Andover, Massachusetts, with Denise Clinton and Sylvia Mallory. We gratefully acknowledge Sylvia's role not only at the birth of this project but also in managing its initial development team. Denise has been our ongoing inspiration for more than 10 years. She is the most knowledgeable economics editor in the business, and we are privileged to have the benefit of her enormous experience.

The success of *Foundations* owes much to its outstanding Sponsoring Editor, Adrienne D'Ambrosio. Adrienne's acute intelligence and sensitive understanding of the market have helped sharpen our vision of this text and package. Her value-added on this project is huge. It has been, and we hope it will for many future editions remain, a joy to work with her.

Deepa Chungi, Development Editor, and Rachel Mattison, Project Manager, ensured that we were provided with outstanding and timely reviews and gave our draft chapters a careful and helpful read and edit. They also managed the extensive photo research for this edition.

Linda Knowles created the new impressive cover design and converted the raw ideas of our brainstorms into an outstandingly designed text.

Susan Schoenberg, Media Director, Melissa Honig, Senior Media Producer, and Noel Lotz, MyEconLab Content Lead have set a new standard for online learning and teaching resources. Building on the pioneering work of Michelle Neil, Susan worked creatively to improve our technology systems. Melissa managed the building of MyEconLab, and Noel provided reviews of the content. They have all been sources of high energy, good sense, and level-headed advice and quickly found creative solutions to all our technology problems.

Nancy Fenton, our ever cheerful, never stressed Managing Editor, worked with a talented team at Elm Street Publishing Services, Project Editor Heather Johnson, and designer, art coordinator, and typesetter Debbie Kubiak. Our copy editor, Catherine Baum, gave our work a thorough review and helpful polish, and our proofreader ensured the most error-free text we have yet produced.

Laura Murphy and Alison Eusden did an excellent job coordinating the development and production of our print and PowerPoint supplements.

Our Executive Marketing Manager, Lori DeShazo, has been a constant source of good judgment and sound advice on content and design issues ranging over the entire package from text to print and electronic supplements. Dave Theisen reviewed our previous edition and gave excellent advice (much of which we have taken) on areas that needed adjusting to achieve the clarity that we seek.

Richard Parkin, our technical illustrator, created the figures in the text, the dynamic figures in the eText, and the animated figures in the PowerPoint presentations and contributed many ideas to improve the clarity of our illustrations.

Laurel Davies provided painstakingly careful work on MyEconLab questions and acted as one of its accuracy checkers.

Jeannie Gillmore, our personal assistant, worked closely with us in creating MyEconLab exercises and guided solutions. Jane McAndrew, economics librarian at the University of Western Ontario, went the extra mile on many occasions to help us track down the data and references we needed.

Finally, our reviewers, whose names appear on the following pages, have made an enormous contribution to this text and MyEconLab resources. Once again we find ourselves using superlatives, but they are called for. In the many texts that we've written, we've not seen reviewing of the quality that we enjoyed on this revision. It has been a pleasure (if at times a challenge) to respond constructively to their many excellent suggestions.

Robin Bade
Michael Parkin
London, Ontario, Canada
robin@econ100.com
michael.parkin@uwo.ca

Foundations of Macroeconomics: Flexibility Chart

1. Getting Started
The questions and way of thinking that define economics.

1. Appendix: Making and Using Graphs
Good for students with a fear of graphs.

2. The U.S. and Global Economies
Describes 'what,' 'how,' and 'for whom' in the U.S. and global economies and introduces the circular flows that arise from interactions.

3. The Economic Problem
Carefully paced and complete first look at the fundamental economic problem. Includes the distinction between absolute advantage and an explanation of why comparative advantage is the source of the gains from trade.

4. Demand and Supply
Carefully paced and complete explanation of this core topic with painstaking emphasis on the distinction between a change demand (supply) and a change in the quantity demanded (supplied).

We cover all the standard topics of the principles curriculum and we do so in the order that has increasingly found favor among teachers.

A powerful case can be made for teaching the subject in the order in which we present it here, but we recognize that there is a range of opinion about sequencing, and we have structured our text so that it works well if other sequences are preferred. This table provides a guide to the flexibility that we've built into our text.

Deciding the order in which to teach the components of economics involves a tradeoff between building foundations and getting to policy issues early in the course. There is little disagreement that the place to begin is with production possibilities and demand and supply. We provide a carefully paced and thoroughly modern treatment of these topics.

5. GDP: A Measure of Total Production of Income
Explains expenditure and income approaches to measuring real GDP and the uses and limitations of real GDP. An appendix explains the chained-dollar measure of real GDP.

6. Jobs and Unemployment
Describes labor market measures and trends and the link between unemployment and real GDP.

7. The CPI and the Cost of Living
Emphasizes the interpretation and use of the CPI and the measurement of real variables.

The macro course divides naturally into five parts: (1) measurement, (2) the real economy in the long run, (3) the money economy in the long run, (4) fluctuations, and (5) policy issues.

These parts can be covered in sequence or in several alternative ways.

After Chapter 7, it is possible to jump to either Chapter 13 (Aggregate Supply and Aggregate Demand), or Chapter 14 (Aggregate Expenditure Multiplier), or Chapter 15 (The Short-Run Policy Tradeoff).

It is also possible to jump straight to the money chapters (Chapters 11 and 12).

Most of the content of Chapter 16 (Fiscal Policy) and Chapter 17 (Monetary Policy) can be covered after doing Chapters 11, 12, and 13.

8. Potential GDP and the Natural Unemployment Rate
Explains how potential GDP and the natural unemployment rate are determined.

9. Economic Growth
Explains the sources of economic growth and the policies that might speed it.

10. Finance, Saving, and Investment
Describes the financial markets and institutions and explains how saving, investment, and the real interest rate are determined and influenced by the government budget deficit (or surplus).

These chapters explain the real economy in the long run—classical macro. They may be studied after Chapters 13–15, but we think they work better at this point in the course.

At full employment, the real economy is influenced by only real variables, and the price level is proportional to the quantity of money. This idea has been incredibly productive in advancing our understanding of both the full-employment economy and the business cycle. By having a firm understanding of the forces that determine potential GDP, the student better appreciates the more complex interactions of real and monetary factors that bring economic fluctuations. The student also sees that the long-term trends in our economy play a larger role in determining our standard of living and cost of living than do the fluctuations around those trends.

Even if you defer Chapters 9 and 10, it is a good plan to cover Chapter 8.1 "Potential GDP" at this point.

11. The Monetary System
Defines money and describes its functions. Describes the banking system and the Fed and explains how the Fed influences the quantity of money.

12. Money, Interest, and Inflation
Explains the demand for money and how the supply of and demand for money determine the nominal interest rate in the short run and the price level and inflation rate in the long run.

These chapters explain the money economy in the long run and the short run. They may be studied after Chapters 13 and 14.

13. Aggregate Supply and Aggregate Demand
A carefully paced but comprehensive account of the AS-AD model and its use in understanding the business cycle. This chapter may be studied before Chapter 8.

14. Aggregate Expenditure Multiplier
The Keynesian cross model. If you don't want to explain in detail how unplanned inventory changes set off a multiplier process, you may omit this chapter.

15. The Short-Run Policy Tradeoff
An explanation of the sources of the short-run tradeoff and the forces that keep shifting it.

Chapters 13–15 explain economic fluctuations (interactions between the real and monetary sectors) using the ideas of aggregate supply and aggregate demand, and optionally the aggregate expenditure model and the Phillips curve.

16. Fiscal Policy

Explains how fiscal policy is made, discusses the effectiveness of fiscal stabilization policy, and discusses the supply-side effects on potential GDP and economic growth. Section 16.1 can be studied at any point. Chapter 13 is prerequisite for section 16.2.

17. Monetary Policy

Explains how monetary policy is made and its effects on inflation and real GDP. Includes a discussion of alternative approaches to monetary policy. Chapters 11, 12, and 13 are prerequisites. Chapters 8 and 10 are prerequisites for section 17.2.

18. International Trade Policy

Explains how markets work when an economy trades with the world. Explains the effects of tariffs and import quotas and assesses arguments for protection. Chapter 4 is the only prerequisite.

19. International Finance

The balance of payments section can be studied anytime after Chapter 5 and the exchange rate section can be studied anytime after Chapter 4.

Policy runs through all the macro chapters. Macro *is* policy. Chapters 16 and 17 pull together all the policy issues and explain the decision-making institutions, the policy choices, and the debates surrounding them.

Chapters 18 and 19 extend the policy discussion to the open economy—international trade policy, the balance of payments, and the exchange rate. With a bit of care and imagination, parts of these chapters can be covered earlier in the course.

MyEconLab provides

The Power of Practice

MyEconLab is the perfect tool for assigning homework, quizzes, and tests and for encouraging hands-on learning-by-doing.

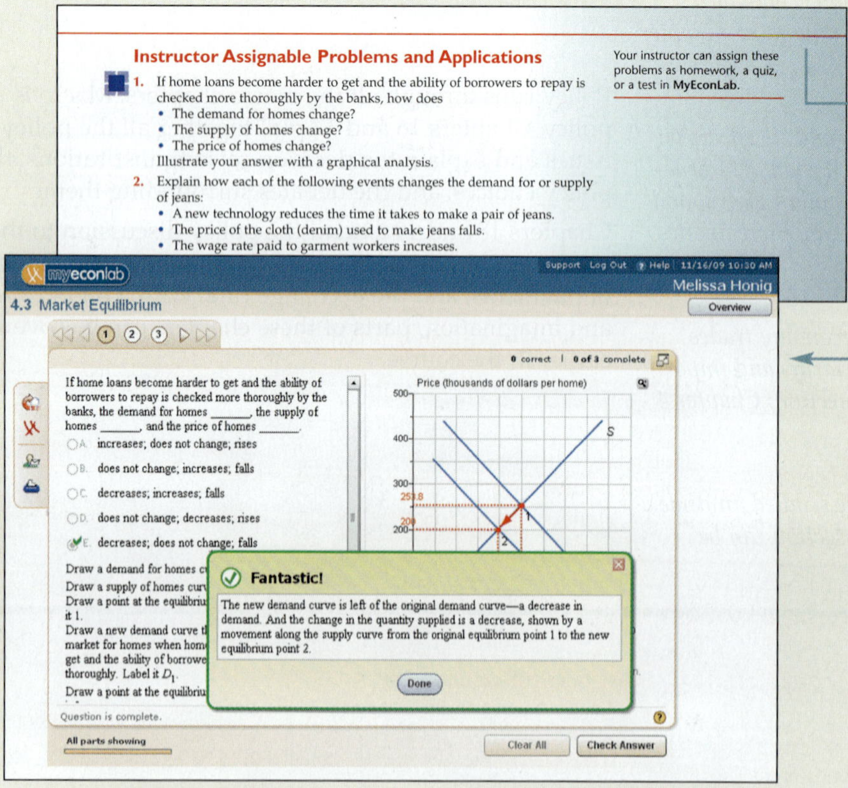

Auto-graded Assignments

MyEconLab comes with preloaded assignments all of which are automatically graded and that include all the Instructor Assignable Problems and Applications in the textbook.

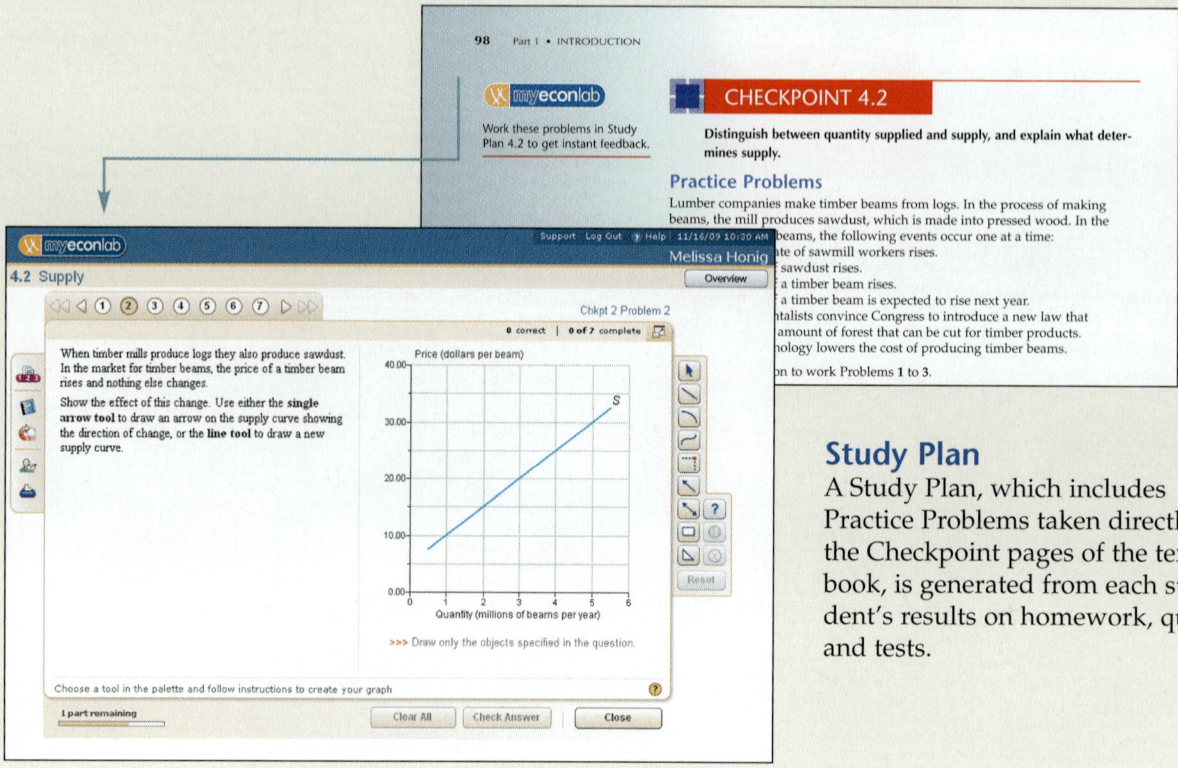

Study Plan

A Study Plan, which includes Practice Problems taken directly from the Checkpoint pages of the textbook, is generated from each student's results on homework, quizzes, and tests.

Unlimited Practice

Many Study Plan and instructor Assignable exercises contain algorithms to ensure that students get as much practice as they need. As students work Study Plan or Homework exercises, instant feedback guides them toward understanding. When students work a Quiz or Test, feedback is provided only when the instructor chooses to make it available.

Learning Resources

To further reinforce understanding, Study Plan and Homework problems link to four learning resources:

- A step-by-step Guided Solution [Helps students break down a problem much the same way as an instructor would do during office hours];
- The eText page on which the topic of the exercise is explained [Promotes reading the text when further explanation is needed];
- An animated graph with audio narration [Caters to a variety of learning styles];
- A graphing tool [Encourages students to draw and manipulate graphs and deepen their understanding by illustrating economic relationships and ideas].

Student Testimonials

"It was very helpful to get instant feedback. Sometimes I would get lost reading the book, and these individual problems would help me focus and see if I understood the concepts."

—Student, Temple University

"The guided solutions really helped me when I didn't understand the problem."

—Student, University of Central Florida

"I really like the way MyEconLab took me through the graphs step-by-step."

—Student, Stephen F. Austin State University

myeconlab

Reviewers

Seemi Ahmad, Dutchess Community College
William Aldridge, Shelton State Community College
Rashid B. Al-Hmoud, Texas Tech University
Neil Alper, Northeastern University
Nejat Anbarci, Deakin University
Luke A. Armstrong, Lee College
Ali Ataiifar, Delaware County Community College
John Baffoe-Bonnie, Pennsylvania State University, Delaware County Campus
A. Paul Ballantyne, University of Colorado
Sue Bartlett, University of South Florida
Klaus Becker, Texas Tech University
William K. Bellinger, Dickinson College
John Bethune, Barton College
Gautam Bhattacharya, University of Kansas
Gerald W. Bialka, University of North Florida
David Bivin, Indiana University–Purdue University at Indianapolis
Geoffrey Black, Boise State University
Carey Anne Borkoski, Arundel Community College
Jurgen Brauer, Augusta State University
Greg Brock, Georgia Southern University
Barbara Brogan, Northern Virginia Community College
Bruce C. Brown, California State Polytechnic University, Pomona
Christopher Brown, Arkansas State University
Brian Buckley, Clemson University
Donald Bumpass, Sam Houston State University
Seewoonundun Bunjun, East Stroudsburg University
Nancy Burnett, University of Wisconsin at Oshkosh
James L. Butkiewicz, University of Delaware
Barbara Caldwell, Saint Leo University
Bruce Caldwell, University of North Carolina, Greensboro
Joseph Calhoun, Florida State University
Robert Carlsson, University of South Carolina
Shawn Carter, Jacksonville State University
Regina Cassady, Valencia Community College
Jack Chambless, Valencia Community College
Joni Charles, Southwest Texas State University
Anoshua Chaudhuri, San Francisco State University
Robert Cherry, Brooklyn College
Chi-Young Choi, University of New Hampshire
Paul Cichello, Xavier University
Quentin Ciolfi, Brevard Community College
Jim Cobbe, Florida State University
John Cochran, University of Chicago
Mike Cohick, Collin County Community College
Ludovic Comeau, De Paul University
Carol Conrad, Cerro Coso Community College
Christopher Cornell, Vassar College
Richard Cornwall, University of California, Davis
Kevin Cotter, Wayne State University

Tom Creahan, Morehead State University
Elizabeth Crowell, University of Michigan at Dearborn
Susan Dadres, Southern Methodist University
Troy Davig, College of William and Mary
Jeffrey Davis, ITT Technical Institute (Utah)
Lewis Davis, Union College
Dennis Debrecht, Carroll College
Al DeCooke, Broward Community College
Vince DiMartino, University of Texas at San Antonio
Vernon J. Dobis, Minnesota State University–Moorhead
Carol Dole, Jacksonville University
Kathleen Dorsainvil, American University
John Dorsey, University of Maryland, College Park
Amrik Singh Dua, Mt. San Antonio College
Marie Duggan, Keene State College
David Eaton, Murray State University
Kevin J. Egan, University of Toledo
Harold W. Elder, University of Alabama
Harry Ellis, University of North Texas
Stephen Ellis, North Central Texas College
Carl Enomoto, New Mexico State University
Chuen-mei Fan, Colorado State University
Elena Ermolenko Fein, Oakton Community College
Gary Ferrier, University of Arkansas
Rudy Fichtenbaum, Wright State University
Donna K. Fisher, Georgia Southern University
Kaya Ford, Northern Virginia Community College
Robert Francis, Shoreline Community College
Roger Frantz, San Diego State University
Amanda S. Freeman, Kansas State University
Marc Fusaro, East Carolina University
Arthur Friedberg, Mohawk Valley Community College
Julie Gallaway, Southwest Missouri State University
Byron Gangnes, University of Hawaii
Gay Garesché, Glendale Community College
Neil Garston, California State University, Los Angeles
Lisa Geib-Gunderson, University of Maryland
Linda Ghent, Eastern Illinois University
Soma Ghosh, Bridgewater State College
Kirk Gifford, Ricks College
Scott Gilbert, Southern Illinois University–Carbondale
Maria Giuili, Diablo Valley Community College
Mark Gius, Quinnipiac College
Randall Glover, Brevard Community College
Stephan Gohmann, University of Louisville
Richard Gosselin, Houston Community College
John Graham, Rutgers University
Patricia E. Graham, University of Northern Colorado
Warren Graham, Tulsa Community College
Osman Gulseven, North Carolina State University
Jang-Ting Guo, University of California, Riverside

Dennis Hammett, University of Texas at El Paso
Leo Hardwick, Macomb Community College
Mehdi Haririan, Bloomsburg University
Paul Harris, Camden County Community College
Mark Healy, William Rainey Harper College
Rey Hernandez-Julian, Metropolitan State College of Denver
Gus Herring, Brookhaven College
Michael Heslop, Northern Virginia Community College
Steven Hickerson, Mankato State University
Frederick Steb Hipple, East Tennessee State University
Andy Howard, Rio Hondo College
Yu Hsing, Southeastern Louisiana University
Greg Hunter, California State Polytechnic University, Pomona
Matthew Hyle, Winona State University
Todd Idson, Boston University
Harvey James, University of Hartford
Russell Janis, University of Massachusetts at Amherst
Jay A. Johnson, Southeastern Louisiana University
Ted Joyce, City University of New York, Baruch College
Jonathan D. Kaplan, California State University, Sacramento
Arthur Kartman, San Diego State University
Chris Kauffman, University of Tennessee
Diane Keenan, Cerritos College
Brian Kench, University of Tampa
John Keith, Utah State University
Kristen Keith, University of Toledo
Joe Kerkvliet, Oregon State University
Gary Kikuchi, University of Hawaii at Manoa
Douglas Kinnear, Colorado State University
Morris Knapp, Miami Dade Community College
Steven Koch, Georgia Southern University
Kate Krause, University of New Mexico
Stephan Kroll, California State University, Sacramento
Joyce Lapping, University of Southern Maine
Tom Larson, California State University, Los Angeles
Robert Lemke, Florida International University
J. Mark Leonard, University of Nebraska at Omaha
Tony Lima, California State University, Hayward
Kenneth Long, New River Community College
Noel Lotz, Middle Tennessee State University
Marty Ludlum, Oklahoma City Community College
Brian Lynch, Lake Land College
Michael Machiorlatti, Oklahoma City Community College
Roger Mack, De Anza College
Michael Magura, University of Toledo
Mark Maier, Glendale College
Svitlana Maksymenko, University of Pittsburgh
Paula Manns, Atlantic Cape Community College
Dan Marburger, Arkansas State University
Kathryn Marshall, Ohio State University
John V. Martin, Boise State University

Drew E. Mattson, Anoka-Ramsey Community College
Stephen McCafferty, Ohio State University
Thomas McCaleb, Florida State University
Katherine S. McCann, University of Delaware
William McLean, Oklahoma State University
Diego Mendez-Carbajo, Illinois Wesleyan University
Evelina Mengova, California State University, Fullerton
Thomas Meyer, Patrick Henry Community College
Meghan Millea, Mississippi State University
Michael Milligan, Front Range Community College
Jenny Minier, University of Miami
David Mitchell, Valdosta State University
Dr. Carl B. Montano, Lamar University
William Mosher, Clark University
Mike Munoz, Northwest Vista College
Kevin Murphy, Oakland University
Ronald Nate, Brigham Young University, Idaho
Michael Nelson, Texas A&M University
Rebecca Neumann, University of Wisconsin—Milwaukee
Charles Newton, Houston Community College Southwest
Melinda Nish, Salt Lake Community College
Lee Nordgren, Indiana University at Bloomington
Norman P. Obst, Michigan State University
Inge O'Connor, Syracuse University
William C. O'Connor, Western Montana College–University of Montana
Fola Odebunmi, Cypress College
Charles Okeke, College of Southern Nevada
Lydia M. Ortega, St. Philip's College
P. Marcelo Oviedo, Iowa State University
Jennifer Pate, Ph.D., Loyola Marymount University
Sanjay Paul, Elizabethtown College
Ken Peterson, Furman University
Tim Petry, North Dakota State University
Charles Pflanz, Scottsdale Community College
Jonathon Phillips, North Carolina State University
Basharat Pitafi, Southern Illinois University
Paul Poast, Ohio State University
Greg Pratt, Mesa Community College
Fernando Quijano, Dickinson State University
Andy Radler, Butte Community College
Ratha Ramoo, Diablo Valley College
Karen Reid, University of Wisconsin, Parkside
Mary Rigdon, University of Texas, Austin
Helen Roberts, University of Illinois at Chicago
Greg Rose, Sacramento City College
Barbara Ross, Kapi'olani Community College
Jeffrey Rous, University of North Texas
June Roux, Salem Community College
Udayan Roy, Long Island University
Nancy C. Rumore, University of Louisiana–Lafayette
Mark Rush, University of Florida

Joseph Santos, South Dakota State University
Roland Santos, Lakeland Community College
Mark Scanlan, Stephen F. Austin State University
Ted Scheinman, Mount Hood Community College
Buffie Schmidt, Augusta State University
Jerry Schwartz, Broward Community College
Gautam Sethi, Bard College
Margaret Anne Shannon, Georgia Southern University
Virginia Shingleton, Valparaiso University
Steven S. Shwiff, Texas A & M University—Commerce
Charles Sicotte, Rock Valley College
Issoufou Soumaila, Texas Tech University
Martin Spechler, Indiana University
Stela Stefanova, University of Delaware
John Stiver, University of Connecticut
Richard W. Stratton, The University of Akron
Terry Sutton, Southeast Missouri State University
Janet M. Thomas, Bentley College
Donna Thompson, Brookdale Community College
James Thorson, Southern Connecticut State University
Marc Tomljanovich, Colgate University
Cynthia Royal Tori, Valdosta State University
Ngoc-Bich Tran, San Jacinto College South
Nora Underwood, University of California, Davis
Jogindar S. Uppal, State University of New York
Va Nee L. Van Vleck, California State University, Fresno
Victoria Vernon, Empire State College / SUNY
Christian Weber, Seattle University
Ethel Weeks, Nassau Community College
Jack Wegman, Santa Rosa Junior College
Jason White, Northwest Missouri State University
Benjamin Widner, Colorado State University
Barbara Wiens-Tuers, Pennsylvania State University, Altoona
Katherine Wolfe, University of Pittsburgh
William Wood, James Madison University
Ben Young, University of Missouri, Kansas City
Michael Youngblood, Rock Valley College
Bassam Yousif, Indiana State University
Sourushe Zandvakili, University of Cincinnati
Inske Zandvliet, Brookhaven College
Joachim Zietz, Middle Tennessee State University
Armand Zottola, Central Connecticut State University

Did greedy Wall Street bankers cause the global economic slump?

The banks incurred huge losses and their executives received fat bonuses and flew to Washington in private jets to ask for handouts from taxpayers. But did they *cause* the global financial crisis?

1

Getting Started

CHAPTER CHECKLIST

When you have completed your study of this chapter, you will be able to

1. Define economics and explain the kinds of questions that economists try to answer.
2. Explain the core ideas that define the economic way of thinking.

1.1 DEFINITION AND QUESTIONS

Wall Street bankers might be greedy, but they are not alone. We all want more than we can get. We want good health and long lives. We want spacious and comfortable homes. We want running shoes and jet skis. We want the time to enjoy our favorite sports, video games, novels, music, and movies; to travel to exotic places; and just to hang out with friends. Human wants exceed the resources available to satisfy them, and this fact is the source of all economic questions and problems.

Scarcity

Scarcity
The condition that arises because wants exceed the ability of resources to satisfy them.

Our inability to satisfy all our wants is called **scarcity**. The ability of each of us to satisfy our wants is limited by the time we have, the incomes we earn, and the prices we pay for the things we buy. These limits mean that everyone has unsatisfied wants. The ability of all of us as a society to satisfy our wants is limited by the productive resources that exist. These resources include the gifts of nature, our labor and ingenuity, and the tools and equipment that we have made.

Everyone, poor and rich alike, faces scarcity. A student wants Beyonce's latest CD and a paperback but has only $10.00 in his pocket. He faces scarcity. Brad Pitt wants to spend a week in New Orleans discussing plans for his new eco-friendly housing and he also wants to spend the week promoting his new movie. He faces scarcity. The U.S. government wants to increase defense spending and cut taxes. It faces scarcity. An entire society wants improved health care, an Internet connection in every classroom, an ambitious space exploration program, clean lakes and rivers, and so on. Society faces scarcity.

Faced with scarcity, we must make choices. We must choose among the available alternatives. The student must choose the CD or the paperback. Brad Pitt must choose New Orleans or promoting his new movie. The government must choose defense or tax cuts. And society must choose among health care, computers, space exploration, the environment, and so on. Even parrots face scarcity!

Not only do I want a cracker—we all want a cracker!

Economics Defined

Economics is the social science that studies the choices that individuals, businesses, governments, and entire societies make as they cope with *scarcity*, the *incentives* that influence those choices, and the arrangements that coordinate them.

Economics
The social science that studies the choices that individuals, businesses, governments, and entire societies make as they cope with *scarcity*, the *incentives* that influence those choices, and the arrangements that coordinate them.

The subject is extremely broad and touches all aspects of our lives. To get beyond this definition of economics, you need to understand the kinds of questions that economists try to answer and the way they think and go about seeking those answers.

We begin with some key economic questions. Although the scope of economics is broad and the range of questions that economists address is equally broad, two big questions provide a useful summary of the scope of economics:

- How do choices end up determining *what, how,* and *for whom* goods and services get produced?
- When do choices made in the pursuit of *self-interest* also promote the *social interest*?

What, How, and For Whom?

Goods and services are the objects and actions that people value and produce to satisfy human wants. Goods are *objects* that satisfy wants. Running shoes and ketchup are examples. Services are *actions* that satisfy wants. Haircuts and rock concerts are examples. We produce a dazzling array of goods and services that range from necessities such as food, houses, and health care to leisure items such as DVD players and roller coaster rides.

Goods and services
The objects (goods) and the actions (services) that people value and produce to satisfy human wants.

In a California vineyard a machine and a few workers do the same job as a hundred grape pickers in France.

What?

What determines the quantities of corn we grow, homes we build, and health-care services we produce? Sixty years ago, 25 percent of Americans worked on a farm. That number has shrunk to less than 3 percent today. Over the same period, the number of people who produce goods—in mining, construction, and manufacturing—has also shrunk, from 30 percent to 20 percent. The decrease in farming and the production of goods is matched by an increase in the production of services. How will these quantities change in the future as ongoing changes in technology make an ever-wider array of goods and services available to us?

How?

How are goods and services produced? In a vineyard in France, basket-carrying workers pick the annual grape crop by hand. In a vineyard in California, a huge machine and a few workers do the same job that a hundred grape pickers in France do. Look around you and you will see many examples of this phenomenon—the same job being done in different ways. In some stores, checkout clerks key in prices. In others, they use a laser scanner. One farmer keeps track of his livestock feeding schedules and inventories by using paper-and-pencil records, while another uses a personal computer. GM hires workers to weld auto bodies in some of its plants and uses robots to do the job in others.

Why do we use machines in some cases and people in others? Do mechanization and technological change destroy more jobs than they create? Do they make us better off or worse off?

For Whom?

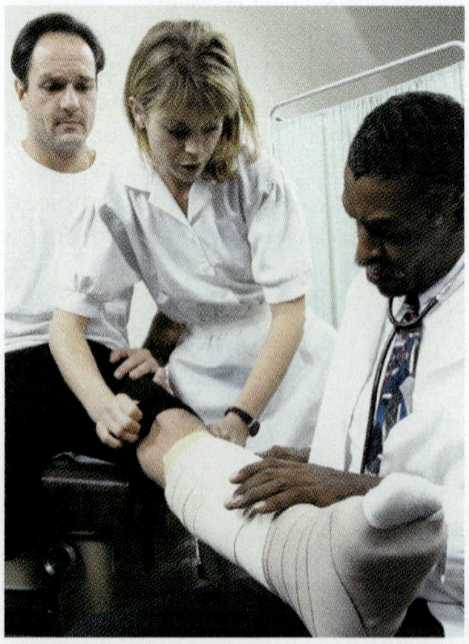

A doctor gets more of the goods and services produced than a nurse or a medical assistant gets.

For whom are goods and services produced? The answer to this question depends on the incomes that people earn and the prices they pay for the goods and services they buy. At given prices, a person who has a high income is able to buy more goods and services than a person who has a low income. Doctors earn much higher incomes than do nurses and medical assistants, so doctors get more of the goods and services produced than nurses and medical assistants get.

You probably know about many other persistent differences in incomes. Men, on the average, earn more than women. Whites, on the average, earn more than minorities. College graduates, on the average, earn more than high school graduates. Americans, on the average, earn more than Europeans, who in turn earn more, on the average, than Asians and Africans. But there are some significant exceptions. The people of Japan and Hong Kong now earn an average income similar to that of Americans. And there is a lot of income inequality throughout the world.

What determines the incomes we earn? Why do doctors earn larger incomes than nurses? Why do men earn more, on average, than women? Why do college graduates earn more, on average, than high school graduates? Why do Americans earn more, on average, than Africans?

Economics explains how the choices that individuals, businesses, and governments make and the interactions of those choices end up determining *what*, *how*, and *for whom* goods and services get produced. In answering these questions, we have a deeper agenda in mind. We're not interested in just knowing how many DVD players get produced, how they get produced, and who gets to enjoy them. We ultimately want to know the answer to the second big economic question that we'll now explore.

■ When Is the Pursuit of Self-Interest in the Social Interest?

Every day, you and 300 million other Americans, along with 6.8 billion people in the rest of the world, make economic choices that result in *"what," "how,"* and *"for whom"* goods and services are produced.

Are the goods and services produced, and the quantities in which they are produced, the right ones? Do the scarce resources get used in the best possible way? Do the goods and services that we produce go to the people who benefit most from them?

Self-Interest and the Social Interest

Self-interest
The choices that are best for the individual who makes them.

Social interest
The choices that are best for society as a whole.

Choices that are the best for the individual who makes them are choices made in the pursuit of **self-interest**. Choices that are the best for society as a whole are said to be in the **social interest**. The social interest has two dimensions: *efficiency* and *equity*. We'll explore these concepts in later chapters. For now, think of efficiency as being achieved by baking the biggest possible pie, and think of equity as being achieved by sharing the pie in the fairest possible way.

You know that your own choices are the best ones for you—or at least you *think* they're the best at the time that you make them. You use your time and other resources in the way that makes most sense to you. But you don't think much about how your choices affect other people. You order a home delivery pizza because you're hungry and want to eat. You don't order it thinking that the delivery person or the cook needs an income. You make choices that are in your self-interest—choices that you think are best for you.

When you act on your economic decisions, you come into contact with thousands of other people who produce and deliver the goods and services that you decide to buy or who buy the things that you sell. These people have made their own decisions—what to produce and how to produce it, whom to hire or whom to work for, and so on.

Like you, everyone else makes choices that they think are best for them. When the pizza delivery person shows up at your home, he's not doing you a favor. He's earning his income and hoping for a good tip.

Could it be possible that when each one of us makes choices that are in our own best interest—our self-interest—it turns out that these choices are also the best for society as a whole—in the social interest?

Much of the rest of this book helps you to learn what economists know about this question and its answer. To help you start thinking about the question, we're going to illustrate it with seven topics that generate heated discussion in today's world. You're already at least a little bit familiar with each one of them. They are

- Financial crisis and global slump
- Globalization and international outsourcing
- The information-age economy
- Disappearing rainforests and fish stocks
- Water shortages
- Climate change
- A Social Security time bomb

Financial Crisis and Global Slump

Most years, production increases and the standard of living rises. But sometimes production shrinks, jobs are lost, and incomes fall. In the United States, production has fallen, briefly, ten times since World War II, but in the world as a whole, it has fallen only once: in 2009. The global recession of 2009 is so widespread and severe that it is being called a global slump.

The collapse of credit and falling home prices were at the epicenter of the global slump of 2009.

Early warning signs became apparent to some farsighted observers in 2005 when U.S. home prices had increased to twice their 1999 level. This price explosion looked like a bubble that was about to burst. And burst it did in 2006. With falling home prices in 2007, people started to walk away from their mortgage debts and foreclosures increased. Banks that had been eager to lend were now in a bigger financial hole than the people to whom they had made loans. Bank lending dried up.

With credit hard to get, consumers and businesses cut back their spending, production slowed, and layoffs started to climb. The situation became so alarming that people began to compare 2009 with 1929, the year that saw the start of the *Great Depression,* what turned out to be a decade in which unemployment climbed to more than 20 percent of the labor force.

During the 1930s, the longest lines were for jobs.

Financial crisis and its consequences illustrate well the distinction and tension between self-interest and the social interest. The bankers that were eager to lend to home buyers between 2000 and 2006 were pursuing their self-interest (what has been called greed). Borrowers and homebuyers also acted in what they saw as their self-interest. When the home price bubble burst and a struggling homebuyer defaulted on loan repayments, that person, too, was acting in her or his self-interest. And when the bank foreclosed on a borrower, that too was done in the pursuit of self-interest. But when all these self-interested actions are combined, the consequences are an outcome that is clearly not in the social interest.

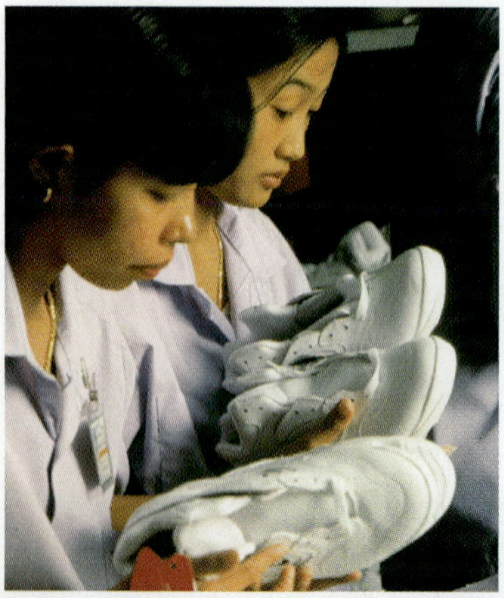

Workers in Asia make our shoes.

Globalization and International Outsourcing

Globalization and international outsourcing—the expansion of international trade and the production of components and services by firms in other countries—has been going on for centuries. But during the 1990s, its pace accelerated as advances in microchips, satellites, and fiber-optic cables lowered the cost of communication. A phone call, a video-conference, or a face-to-face meeting involving people who live 10,000 miles apart has become an everyday and easily affordable event.

This explosion of communication has globalized production decisions. When Nike produces more sports shoes, people in China, Indonesia, or Malaysia get more work. When Steven Spielberg wants an animation sequence for a new movie, programmers in New Zealand write the code. And when China Airlines wants a new airplane, Americans who work for Boeing build it.

The number of jobs in manufacturing and routine services is shrinking in the United States and Europe and expanding in India, China, and other Asian economies. And production is growing more rapidly in Asia than in the United States and Europe. China is already the world's second largest economy, and if the current trends continue, it will become the largest economy during the 2020s.

But globalization is leaving some people behind. The nations of Africa and parts of South America are not sharing in the prosperity that globalization is bringing to other parts of the world.

Is globalization in the social interest, or does it benefit some at the expense of others? The owners of multinational firms clearly benefit from lower production costs. So do the consumers of low-cost imported goods and services. But don't displaced American workers lose? And doesn't even the worker in Malaysia, who sews your new running shoes for a few cents an hour, also lose?

The computer chip has transformed our lives.

The Information-Age Economy

The 1980s and 1990s were years of extraordinary economic change that have been called the *Information Revolution*. This name suggests a parallel with the *Industrial Revolution* of the years around 1800 and the *Agricultural Revolution* of 12,000 years ago.

The changes that occurred during the last 25 years were based on one major technology: the microprocessor or computer chip. Gordon Moore of Intel predicted that the number of transistors that could be placed on one integrated chip would double every 18 months (Moore's law). This prediction turned out to be remarkably accurate.

The spin-offs from faster and cheaper computing have been widespread. Telecommunications became much faster and cheaper, music and movie recording became more realistic and cheaper, millions of routine tasks that previously required human decision and action were automated. You encounter these automated tasks every day when you check out at the supermarket, use an ATM, or call a government department or large business. All the new products and processes and the low-cost computing power that made them possible were produced by people who made choices in the pursuit of self-interest. They did not result from any grand design or government plan.

When Gordon Moore set up Intel and started making chips, he wasn't thinking how much easier it would be for you to turn in your essay on time if you had a faster PC. When Bill Gates quit Harvard to set up Microsoft, he wasn't trying to create the best operating system and improve people's computing experience. Moore and Gates and thousands of other entrepreneurs were in hot pursuit of the big payoffs that many of them achieved. Yet their actions did make many other people better off. They advanced the social interest.

But could more have been done? Were resources used in the best possible way during the information revolution? Did Intel make the best possible chips and sell them in the right quantities for the right prices? Or was the quality of the chips too low and the price too high? And what about Microsoft? Did Bill Gates have to be paid almost $50 billion to produce the successive generations of Windows and Word? Were these programs developed in the social interest?

Disappearing Rainforests and Fish Stocks

Tropical rainforests in South America, Africa, and Asia support the lives of 30 million species of plants, animals, and insects—approaching 50 percent of all species on the planet. The Amazon rainforest alone converts about 1 trillion pounds of carbon dioxide into oxygen each year. These rainforests also provide us with the ingredients for many goods including soaps, mouthwashes, shampoos, food preservatives, rubber, nuts, and fruits.

Logging is destroying the world's rainforests ...

Yet tropical rainforests cover less than two percent of the Earth's surface and are heading for extinction. Logging, cattle ranching, mining, oil extraction, hydroelectric dams, and subsistence farming are destroying the equivalent of two football fields every second, or an area larger than New York City every day. At the current rate of destruction, almost all the tropical rainforest ecosystems will be gone by 2030.

A similar problem confronts the world's fish resources. Advances in fishing technology have lowered the cost of fishing and increased the daily catch. Every day, fishing boats scoop up 250,000 tons of fish. Almost 50 percent of the catch is wasted.

... and overfishing is depleting the world's fish stocks.

Of the 267 fish species used as food, 70 percent are overfished, which means that they are heading toward extinction. Some species such as Atlantic Cod and Blue Fin Tuna are near extinction. The stock of Atlantic Cod has fallen by 90 percent in the past 45 years. Fish can be farmed. But fish farming brings its own problems of waste management and pollution.

Each one of us makes economic choices that are in our self-interest to consume products, some of which are destroying our rainforests and others of which are killing our fish resources. But it seems that our self-interested choices are damaging the social interest. If they are, what can be done to change the incentives we face and change our behavior?

Water Shortages

The world is awash with water—it is our most abundant resource. But 97 percent of it is seawater. Another 2 percent is frozen in glaciers and ice. The 1 percent of the Earth's water that is available for human consumption would be sufficient if only it were in the right places. Finland, Canada, and a few other places have more water than they can use, but Australia, Africa, and California (and many other places) could use much more water than they can get.

Water is abundant but clean water is scarce.

Some people pay less for water than others. California farmers, for example, pay less than California households. Some of the highest prices for water are faced by people in the poorest countries who must either buy from a water dealer's truck or carry water in buckets over many miles.

In the United States, water is provided by public enterprises. In the United Kingdom, private companies deliver the water.

In India and Bangladesh, plenty of rain falls, but it falls during a short wet season and the rest of the year is dry. Dams could help to reduce the shortage in the dry season but too few have been built in those countries.

Are we managing our water resources properly? Are the decisions that each of us makes in our self-interest to use, conserve, and transport water also in the social interest?

Human activity is raising the Earth's temperature.

Climate Change

The Earth is getting hotter and the ice at the two poles is melting. Since the late nineteenth century, the Earth's surface temperature has increased about 1 degree Fahrenheit, and close to a half of that increase occurred over the past 25 years. While these changes are small, particularly when viewed against the temperature fluctuations associated with Ice Ages, they are large enough to have a lot of people worried.

Most climate scientists believe that the current warming has come at least in part from human economic activity—from self-interested choices—and that, if left unchecked, the warming will bring large future economic costs.

As part of an attempt to slow global warming, an international meeting in Japan in 1997 led to the Kyoto Protocol, an agreement that seeks legally binding emissions cuts for the industrialized nations. But the Protocol does not impose limits on the poorer developing nations. Almost the entire world signed onto Kyoto. But the United States and Australia refused to do so. They argue that the agreement does too little to address the global warming problem and that their own independent efforts will make a more effective contribution.

Are the choices that each of us makes to use energy damaging the social interest? What needs to be done to make our choices serve the social interest? Would the United States signing onto the Kyoto Protocol serve the social interest? What other measures must be introduced?

A Social Security time bomb is ticking as benefits grow faster than contributions.

A Social Security Time Bomb

Every year since 2001, the U.S. government has run a budget deficit. On the average, the government has spent \$1.6 billion a day more than it has received in taxes. The government's debt has increased each day by that amount. Over the nine years from 2001 through 2009, government debt has increased by \$5.3 trillion. Your personal share of this debt is \$18,000.

Also, since 2000, Americans bought goods and services from the rest of the world in excess of what foreigners bought from the United States to the tune of \$4.8 trillion. To pay for these goods and services, Americans borrowed from the rest of the world.

These large deficits are just the beginning of an even bigger problem. From about 2019 onwards, the retirement and health-care benefits to which older Americans are entitled are going to cost increasingly more than the current Social Security taxes can cover. With no changes in taxes or benefit rates, the deficit and debt will swell ever higher.

Deficits and the debts they create cannot persist indefinitely, and debts must somehow be repaid. They will most likely be repaid by you, not by your parents. When we make our voter choices and our choices to buy from or sell to the rest of the world, we pursue our self-interest. Do our choices damage the social interest?

CHECKPOINT 1.1

Define economics and explain the kinds of questions that economists try to answer.

myeconlab

Work these problems in Study Plan 1.1 to get instant feedback.

Practice Problems

1. Economics studies choices that arise from one fact. What is that fact?
2. Provide three examples of wants in the United States today that are especially pressing but not satisfied.
3. Here are three news headlines. Find in these headlines examples of the *what*, *how*, and *for whom* questions: "With more research, we will cure cancer"; "A good education is the right of every child"; "The government must cut its budget deficit by raising taxes."
4. How does a new Starbucks in Beijing, China, influence self-interest and the social interest?
5. How does Facebook influence self-interest and the social interest?
6. **Job losses slow dramatically**

   In May, 2009, 345,000 U.S. jobs disappeared, fewer than the 504,000 jobs that disappeared in April. The jobs lost in May were spread across the economy: in manufacturing, construction, retail, and professional services. But 9.1 million part-time workers said that they are working part-time jobs because they could not find full-time work or their employers had shortened their hours.

   Source: CNN Money, June 5, 2009

   Describe the change in May 2009 in *What* and *For whom* goods and services were produced in the United States. Is the decision to work part-time a decision made in self-interest or the social interest? Is an employer's decision to shorten work hours a decision made in self-interest or the social interest?

Guided Solutions to Practice Problems

1. The fact is scarcity—human wants exceed the resources available.
2. Security from international terrorism, cleaner air in our cities, better public schools. (You can perhaps think of some more.)
3. More research is a *how* question, and a cure for cancer is a *what* question. Good education is a *what* question, and every child is a *for whom* question. The government's raising taxes is a *for whom* question.
4. Decisions made by Starbucks are in Starbucks' self-interest but they serve the self-interest of its customers and so contribute to the social interest.
5. Facebook serves the self-interest of its investors, users, and advertisers. It also serves the social interest by enabling people to share information.
6. With job losses spread across the economy, the decrease in goods and services produced by most sectors slowed. So the change in What goods and services were produced was widespread. For whom goods and services were produced also changed. Job losers and new part-time workers earned lower incomes than in April, so they received fewer goods and services. A person's decision to work part-time is usually a self-interested decision—they want to earn an income. The employer's decision is in self-interest if the decision is to "save his or her own job," but if it is "to share" the job loss, the decision might be in the social interest.

1.2 THE ECONOMIC WAY OF THINKING

The definition of economics and the kinds of questions that economists try to answer give you a flavor of the scope of economics. But they don't tell you how economists *think* about these questions and how they go about seeking answers to them. You're now going to see how economists approach their work.

We'll break this task into three parts. First, we'll explain the core ideas that economists constantly and repeatedly use to frame their view of the world. These ideas will soon have you thinking like an economist. Second, we'll explain the distinction between the micro and macro views of the economic world. Finally, we'll look at economics both as a social science and as a policy tool that governments, businesses, and *you* can use.

Core Economic Ideas

Five core ideas summarize the economic approach or economic way of thinking about the choices that must be made to cope with scarcity:

- People make *rational choices* by comparing costs and benefits.
- *Cost* is what you *must* give up to get something.
- *Benefit* is what you gain when you get something and is measured by what you *are willing to* give up to get it.
- A rational choice is made on the *margin.*
- Choices respond to *incentives.*

Rational Choice

Rational choice
A choice that uses the available resources to best achieve the objective of the person making the choice.

The most basic idea of economics is that in making choices, people act rationally. A **rational choice** is one that uses the available resources to best achieve the objective of the person making the choice.

Only the wants and preferences of the person making a choice are relevant to determine its rationality. For example, you might like chocolate ice cream more than vanilla ice cream, but your friend prefers vanilla. So it is rational for you to choose chocolate and for your friend to choose vanilla.

A rational choice might turn out not to have been the best choice after the event. A farmer might decide to plant wheat rather than soybeans. Then, when the crop comes to market, the price of soybeans might be much higher than the price of wheat. The farmer's choice was rational when it was made, but subsequent events made it less profitable than the alternative choice.

The idea of rational choice provides an answer to the first economic question: What goods and services will get produced and in what quantities? The answer is: Those that people rationally choose to buy.

But how do people choose rationally? Why have most people chosen to buy Microsoft's Windows operating system rather than another? Why do more people today choose to drink bottled water and sports energy drinks than did in the past? Why has the U.S. government chosen to fund the building of an interstate highway system and not an interstate high-speed railroad system?

We make rational choices by comparing *costs* and *benefits.* But economists think about costs and benefits in a special and revealing way. Let's look at the economic concepts of cost and benefit.

Cost: What You *Must* Give Up

The **opportunity cost** of something is the best thing that you must give up to get it. No matter what you choose to do, you make a choice among many alternatives. But only one of these alternatives is the *best alternative* that you gave up. And it is the best alternative—the highest-valued alternative forgone—that is the opportunity cost of the thing that you choose to do.

Opportunity cost
The opportunity cost of something is the best thing you *must* give up to get it.

We use the term *opportunity cost* to emphasize that when we make a choice in the face of scarcity, we give up an opportunity to do something else. You can quit school right now, or you can remain in school. Suppose that if you quit school, the best job you can get is at FedEx Kinko's, where you can earn $10,000 during the year. The opportunity cost of remaining in school includes the things that you could have bought with this $10,000. The opportunity cost also includes the value of the leisure time that you must forgo to study.

Opportunity cost of the thing you get is *only* the best alternative forgone. It does not include all the expenditures that you make. For example, your expenditure on tuition is part of the opportunity cost of being in school. But your meal plan and rent are not. Whether you're in school or working, you must eat and have somewhere to live. So the cost of your school meal plan and your rent are *not* part of the opportunity cost of being in school.

Also, past expenditures that cannot be reversed are not part of opportunity cost. Suppose you've paid your term's tuition and it is nonrefundable. If you now contemplate quitting school, the paid tuition is irrelevant. It is called a sunk cost. A **sunk cost** is a previously incurred and irreversible cost. Whether you remain in school or quit school, the tuition that you've paid is not part of the opportunity cost of remaining in school.

Sunk cost
A previously incurred and irreversible cost.

Benefit: Gain Measured by What You *Are Willing to* Give Up

The **benefit** of something is the gain or pleasure that it brings. Benefit is how a person *feels* about something. For example, you might be anxious to get the latest game for Nintendo Wii. It will bring you a large benefit. And you might have almost no interest in a Yo Yo Ma CD of Vivaldi's cello concertos. It will bring you a small benefit.

Benefit
The benefit of something is the gain or pleasure that it brings.

For these students, the opportunity cost of being in school is worth bearing.

For the full-time fast-food worker, the opportunity cost of remaining in school is too high.

Economists measure the benefit of something by what a person *is willing to* give up to get it. You can buy a DVD or magazines. The magazines that you are willing to give up to get a DVD measure the benefit that you get from a DVD.

On the Margin

Margin
A choice on the margin is a choice that is made by comparing *all* the relevant alternatives systematically and incrementally.

Margin means "border" or "edge." You can think of a choice on the margin as one that adjusts the borders or edges of a plan to determine the best course of action. Making a choice on the **margin** means comparing *all* the relevant alternatives systematically and incrementally.

For example, you must choose how to divide the next hour between studying and texting your friends. To make this choice, you must evaluate the costs and benefits of the alternative possible allocations of your next hour. You choose on the margin by considering whether you will be better off or worse off if you spend an extra few minutes studying or an extra few minutes texting.

The margin might involve a small change, as it does when you're deciding how to divide an hour between studying and texting friends. Or it might involve a large change, as it does, for example, when you're deciding whether to remain in school for another year. Attending school for part of the year is no better (and might be worse) than not attending at all. So you likely will want to commit the entire year to school or to something else. But you still choose on the margin. It is just that the marginal change is now a change for one year rather than a change for a few minutes.

Marginal Cost

Marginal cost
The opportunity cost that arises from a one-unit increase in an activity. The marginal cost of something is what you *must* give up to get *one additional* unit of it.

The opportunity cost of a one-unit increase in an activity is called **marginal cost**. Marginal cost of something is what you *must* give up to get *one additional* unit of it. Think about your marginal cost of going to the movies for a third time in a week. Your marginal cost of seeing the movie is what you must give up to see that one additional movie. It is *not* what you give up to see all three movies. The reason is that you've already given up something for two movies, so you don't count this cost as resulting from the decision to see the third movie.

The marginal cost of any activity increases as you do more of it. You know that going to the movies decreases your study time and lowers your grade. Suppose that seeing a second movie in a week lowers your grade by five percentage points. Seeing a third movie will lower your grade by more than five percentage points. Your marginal cost of moviegoing is increasing.

Marginal Benefit

Marginal benefit
The benefit that arises from a one-unit increase in an activity. The marginal benefit of something is *measured* by what you *are willing* to give up to get *one additional* unit of it.

The benefit of a one-unit increase in an activity is called **marginal benefit**. Marginal benefit is what you gain when you get *one more* unit of something. But the marginal benefit of something is *measured* by what you *are willing* to give up to get that *one additional* unit of it.

A fundamental feature of marginal benefit is that it diminishes. Think about your marginal benefit from movies. If you've been studying hard and haven't seen a movie this week, your marginal benefit from seeing your next movie is large. But if you've been on a movie binge this week, you now want a break and your marginal benefit from seeing your next movie is small.

Because the marginal benefit of a movie decreases as you see more movies, you are willing to give up less to see one more movie. For example, you know that going to the movies decreases your study time and lowers your grade. You pay for seeing a movie with a lower grade. You might be willing to give up ten percentage points to see your first movie in a week, but you won't be willing to take such a big hit on your grade to see a second movie in a week. Your willingness to pay to see a movie is decreasing.

Making a Rational Choice

So, will you go to the movies for that third time in a week? If the marginal cost is less than the marginal benefit, your rational choice will be to see the third movie. If the marginal cost exceeds the marginal benefit, your rational choice will be to spend the evening studying. As long as the marginal benefit exceeds or equals the marginal cost, our choice is rational and our scarce resources are used to make us as well off as possible.

Responding to Incentives

The choices we make depend on the incentives we face. An **incentive** is a reward or a penalty—a "carrot" or a "stick"—that encourages or discourages an action. We respond positively to "carrots" and negatively to "sticks." The carrots are marginal benefits; the sticks are marginal costs. A change in marginal benefit or a change in marginal cost changes the incentives that we face and leads us to change our actions.

Incentive
A reward or a penalty—a "carrot" or a "stick"—that encourages or discourages an action.

Most students believe that the payoff from studying just before a test is greater than the payoff from studying a month before a test. In other words, as a test date approaches, the marginal benefit of studying increases and the incentive to study becomes stronger. For this reason, we observe an increase in study time and a decrease in leisure pursuits during the last few days before a test. And the more important the test, the greater is this effect.

A change in marginal cost also changes incentives. For example, suppose that last week, you found your course work easy and you scored 100 percent on your practice quizzes. You figured that the marginal cost of taking an evening off to enjoy a movie was low and that your grade on the next test would not suffer, so you had a movie feast. But this week the going has gotten tough. You're just not getting it, and your practice test scores are low. If you take off even one evening, your grade on next week's test will suffer. The marginal cost of seeing a movie is now high so you decide to give the movies a miss.

A central idea of economics is that by observing *changes in incentives*, we can predict how *choices change*.

Changes in marginal benefit and marginal cost change the incentive to study or to enjoy a movie.

EYE on WALL STREET

Did Greedy Wall Street Bankers Cause the Global Slump?

The President has expressed outrage at the bonuses paid to the Wall Street bankers at the center of the economic slump. Isn't Wall Street greed the source of our economic problems?

Most economists would answer "No." Greed is an expression (an extreme one) of self-interest. We all act in our self-interest. Greed is persistent: It isn't something that comes and goes, and regulated greed can be a force for good.

The problem in recent years is that financial technology has outpaced financial regulation. A challenge for the President's economic team is to figure out and sell to Congress the regulations that will harness greed and restore financial strength and stability.

President Obama and his economic team:
Christina Romer Timothy Geithner Larry Summers

The Micro and Macro Views of the World

Economics has two major parts: microeconomics (or micro) and macroeconomics (or macro).

Microeconomics

Microeconomics
The study of the choices that individuals and businesses make and the way these choices interact and are influenced by governments.

Microeconomics is the study of the choices that individuals and businesses make and the way these choices interact and are influenced by governments. Some examples of microeconomic questions are: Will you buy a flat screen or traditional television? Will Nintendo sell more units of Wii if it cuts the price? Will a cut in the income tax rate encourage people to work longer hours? Will a hike in the gas tax lead to more hybrid or smaller automobiles? Are MP3 downloads killing CDs?

Macroeconomics

Macroeconomics
The study of the aggregate (or total) effects on the national economy and the global economy of the choices that individuals, businesses, and governments make.

Macroeconomics is the study of the aggregate (or total) effects on the national economy and the global economy of the choices that individuals, businesses, and governments make. Some examples of macroeconomic questions are: Why did production and jobs expand so slowly in the United States in the early 2000s? Why are incomes growing much faster in China and India than in the United States? Why did production and incomes stagnate in Japan in the 1990s? Why are Americans borrowing more than $2 billion a day from the rest of the world?

Economics as Social Science

As social scientists, economists seek to discover how the economic world works. In pursuit of this goal, like all scientists, they distinguish between two types of statements:

- Positive statements
- Normative statements

Positive Statements

Positive statements are about what *is*. They say what is currently believed about the way the world operates. A positive statement might be right or wrong, but we can test a positive statement by checking it against the facts. "Our planet is warming because of the amount of coal that we're burning" is a positive statement. "A rise in the minimum wage will bring more teenage unemployment" is another positive statement. Each statement might be right or wrong, and it can be tested.

A central task of economists is to test positive statements about how the economic world works and to weed out those that are wrong. Economics first got off the ground in the late 1700s (see *Eye on the Past* on p. 17), so economics is a young subject compared with, for example, physics, and much remains to be discovered.

Normative Statements

Normative statements are statements about what *ought to be*. These statements depend on values and cannot be tested. The statement "We ought to cut back on our use of coal" is a normative statement. "The minimum wage should not be increased" is another normative statement. You may agree or disagree with either of these statements, but you can't test them. They express an opinion, but they don't assert a fact that can be checked. They are not economics.

Unscrambling Cause and Effect

Economists are especially interested in positive statements about cause and effect. Are computers getting cheaper because people are buying them in greater quantities? Or are people buying computers in greater quantities because they are getting cheaper? Or is some third factor causing both the price of a computer to fall and the quantity of computers bought to increase? These are examples of positive statements that economists want to test, but such testing can be difficult.

The central idea that economists (and all scientists) use to unscramble cause and effect is *ceteris paribus*. ***Ceteris paribus*** is a Latin term (often abbreviated as *cet. par.*) that means "other things being equal" or "if all other relevant things remain the same." Ensuring that other things are equal is crucial in many activities, including athletic events. All successful attempts to make scientific progress use this device. By changing one factor at a time and holding all the other relevant factors constant, we isolate the factor of interest and are able to investigate its effects in the clearest possible way.

In economics, we observe the outcomes of the simultaneous operation of many factors. Consequently, it is hard to sort out the effects of each individual factor and to compare the effects with what a model predicts. To cope with this problem, economists use natural experiments, statistical investigations, and economic experiments.

Ceteris paribus
Other things remaining the same (often abbreviated as *cet. par.*).

In track and field, other things are equal.

A natural experiment is a situation that arises in the ordinary course of economic life in which the one factor of interest is different and other things are equal (or similar). For example, Canada has higher unemployment benefits than the United States, but the people in the two nations are similar. So to study the effect of unemployment benefits on the unemployment rate, economists might compare the United States with Canada.

Correlation
The tendency for the values of two variables to move together in a predictable and related way.

A statistical investigation looks for a **correlation**—a tendency for the values of two variables to move together (either in the same direction or in opposite directions) in a predictable and related way. For example, cigarette smoking and lung cancer are correlated. Sometimes a correlation shows a causal influence of one variable on the other. For example, smoking causes lung cancer. But sometimes the direction of causation is hard to determine.

An economic experiment puts people in a decision-making situation and varies the influence of one factor at a time to discover how they respond.

Economics as Policy Tool

Economics is useful, and you don't have to be an economist to think like one and to use the insights of economics as a policy tool. The subject provides a way of approaching problems in all aspects of our lives:

- Personal
- Business
- Government

Personal Economic Policy

Should you take out a student loan? Should you get a weekend job? Should you buy a used car or a new one? Should you rent an apartment or take out a loan and buy a condominium? Should you pay off your credit card balance or make just the minimum payment? How should you allocate your time between study, working for a wage, caring for family members, and having fun? How should you allocate your time between studying economics and your other subjects? Should you leave school after getting a bachelor's degree or should you go for a masters or a professional qualification?

All these questions involve a marginal benefit and a marginal cost. Although some of the numbers might be hard to pin down, you will make more solid decisions if you approach these questions with the tools of economics.

Business Economic Policy

Should Sony make only flat panel televisions and stop making conventional ones? Should Texaco get more oil and gas from the Gulf of Mexico or from Alaska? Should Palm outsource its online customer services to India or run the operation from California? Should Marvel Studios produce *Spider-Man 4*, a sequel to *Spider-Man 3*? Can Microsoft compete with Google in the search engine business? Can eBay compete with the surge of new Internet auction services? Is Alex Rodriguez really worth $33,000,000 to the New York Yankees?

Like personal economic questions, these business questions involve the evaluation of a marginal benefit and a marginal cost. Some of the questions require a broader investigation of the interactions of individuals and businesses. But again, by approaching these questions with the tools of economics and by hiring economists as advisers, businesses can make better decisions.

EYE on the PAST

Adam Smith and the Birth of Economics as a Social Science

Many people had written about economics before Adam Smith, but he made economics a social science.

Born in 1723 in Kirkcaldy, a small fishing town near Edinburgh, Scotland, Smith was the only child of the town's customs officer. Lured from his professorship (he was a full professor at 28) by a wealthy Scottish duke who gave him a pension of £300 a year—ten times the average income at that time—Smith devoted ten years to writing his masterpiece, *An Inquiry into the Nature and Causes of the Wealth of Nations,* published in 1776.

Why, Adam Smith asked in that book, are some nations wealthy while others are poor? He was pondering these questions at the height of the Industrial Revolution. During these years, new technologies were applied to the manufacture of textiles, iron, transportation, and agriculture.

Adam Smith answered his questions by emphasizing the role of the division of labor and free markets. To illustrate his argument, he used the example of a pin factory. He guessed that one person, using the hand tools available in the 1770s, might make 20 pins a day. Yet, he observed, by using those same hand tools but breaking the process into a number of individually small operations in which people specialize—by the division of labor—ten people could make a staggering 48,000 pins a day. One draws out the wire, another straightens it, a third cuts it, a fourth points it, a fifth grinds it. Three specialists make the head, and a fourth attaches it. Finally, the pin is polished and packaged.

But a large market is needed to support the division of labor: One factory employing ten workers would need to sell more than 15 million pins a year to stay in business!

Government Economic Policy

How can California balance its budget? Should the federal government cut taxes or raise them? How can the tax system be simplified? Should people be permitted to invest their Social Security money in stocks that they pick themselves? Should Medicaid and Medicare be extended to the entire population? Should there be a special tax to penalize corporations that send jobs overseas? Should cheap foreign imports of furniture and textiles be limited? Should the farms that grow tomatoes and sugar beets receive a subsidy? Should water be transported from Washington and Oregon to California?

These government policy questions call for decisions that involve the evaluation of a marginal benefit and a marginal cost and an investigation of the interactions of individuals and businesses. Yet again, by approaching these questions with the tools of economics, governments can make better decisions.

Notice that all the policy questions we've just posed involve a blend of the positive and the normative. Economics can't help with the normative part—the objective. But for a given objective, economics provides a method of evaluating alternative solutions. That method is to evaluate the marginal benefits and marginal costs and to find the solution that brings the greatest available gain.

myeconlab

Work these problems in Study Plan 1.2 to get instant feedback.

CHECKPOINT 1.2

Explain the core ideas that define the economic way of thinking.

Practice Problems

Every week, Kate plays tennis for two hours, and her grade on each math test is 70 percent. Last week, after playing for two hours, Kate considered playing for another hour. She decided to play for another hour and cut her study time by one hour. But last week, her math grade fell to 60 percent. Use this information to work Problems **1** to **5**.

1. What was Kate's opportunity cost of the third hour of tennis?
2. Given that Kate played the third hour, what can you conclude about her marginal benefit and marginal cost of the second hour of tennis?
3. Was Kate's decision to play the third hour of tennis rational?
4. Did Kate make her decision on the margin?
5. Check the local media and find an example of a positive statement and an example of a normative statement.
6. Provide two examples of positive statements and two examples of normative statements.
7. Provide an example of economics as a personal policy tool.

Guided Solutions to Practice Problems

1. Kate's opportunity cost of the third hour of tennis was the drop in her grade of ten-percentage points.
2. The marginal benefit from the second hour of tennis must have exceeded the marginal cost of the second hour because Kate chose to play the third hour.
3. If marginal benefit exceeded marginal cost, Kate's decision was rational.
4. Kate made her decision on the margin because she considered the benefit and cost of one additional hour.
5. "The Butterfly House must be kept near 80 degrees at all times, or butterflies won't fly" is a positive statement because it can be tested against the facts.

   "Flex-time, which allows employees to shift their work hours over a two-week period, will allow workers to better meet family needs" is a normative statement because it cannot be tested.
6. Positive statements are statements that can be tested by looking at the data. Examples are (1) On 7 June 2009, the price of gas is highest in Michigan and lowest in South Carolina. (2) College tuition in 2010 will be the same as in 2009.

   Normative statements are statements that cannot be tested: (1) Most cities don't have enough open green space and trees. (2) The workweek ought to be cut to 30 hours for all workers.
7. You are offered the chance to take a weekend cruise at a reduced price. Should you take it? What is the opportunity cost of the cruise? What is the best alternative you would forgo if you took the cruise? Perhaps you have a test next week. If you took the cruise, you'd forgo valuable study time and possibly receive a lower grade. What would be the marginal benefit from the cruise? Which is larger: Opportunity cost or marginal benefit?

CHAPTER SUMMARY

Key Points

1 Define economics and explain the kinds of questions that economists try to answer.

- Economics is the social science that studies the choices that we make as we cope with scarcity and the incentives that influence and reconcile our choices.
- The first big question of economics is: How do the choices that people make end up determining *what, how,* and *for whom* goods and services are produced?
- The second big question is: When do choices made in the pursuit of *self-interest* also promote the *social interest*?

2 Explain the core ideas that define the economic way of thinking.

- Five core ideas define the economic way of thinking:
  1. People make *rational* choices by comparing costs and benefits.
  2. Cost is what you *must* give up to get something.
  3. Benefit is what you gain when you get something and is measured by what you *are willing to* give up to get it.
  4. A rational choice is made on the *margin.*
  5. Choices respond to *incentives.*
- Microeconomics is the study of individual choices and interactions, and macroeconomics is the study of the national economy and global economy.
- Economists try to understand how the economic world works by testing positive statements using natural experiments, statistical investigations, and economic experiments.
- Economics is a tool for personal, business, and government decisions.

Key Terms

Benefit, 11
Ceteris paribus, 15
Correlation, 16
Economics, 3
Goods and services, 3
Incentive, 13
Macroeconomics, 14
Margin, 12
Marginal benefit, 12
Marginal cost, 12
Microeconomics, 14
Opportunity cost, 11
Rational choice, 10
Scarcity, 2
Self-interest, 4
Social interest, 4
Sunk cost, 11

myeconlab

Work these problems in Chapter 1 Study Plan to get instant feedback.

CHAPTER CHECKPOINT

Study Plan Problems and Applications

1. Provide three examples of scarcity that illustrate why even the 691 billionaires in the world face scarcity.

Use the following information to work Problems 2 to 5.

Spider-Man 3 was the most successful movie of 2007, with world-wide box office receipts of $891 million. The movie might have cost more to make than any film in Hollywood history. Sony put the budget at $260 million, with additional marketing costs of about $120 million. Creating a successful movie brings pleasure to millions, generates work for thousands, and makes a few rich.

2. What contribution does a movie like *Spider-Man 3* make to coping with scarcity? When you buy a ticket to see a movie in a theater, are you buying a good or a service?
3. Who decides whether a movie is going to be a blockbuster? How do you think the creation of a blockbuster movie influences what, how, and for whom goods and services are produced?
4. What are some of the marginal costs and marginal benefits that the producer of a movie faces?
5. Suppose that Tobey Maguire had been offered a bigger and better part in another movie and that to hire him for *Spider-Man 3*, the producer had to double Tobey's pay. What incentives would have changed? How might the changed incentives have changed the choices that people made?
6. Arnold Schwarzenegger chose politics over making movies such as a sequel to *Terminator 3*. In making his decision to run for governor of California, did he make his choice on the margin? Was his choice rational? Did he face an opportunity cost? If so, what might have been some of the components of his opportunity cost?
7. Pam, Pru, and Pat are deciding how they will celebrate the New Year. Pam prefers to take a cruise, is happy to go to Hawaii, but does not want to go skiing. Pru prefers to go skiing, is happy to go to Hawaii, but does not want to take a cruise. Pat prefers to go to Hawaii or to take a cruise but does not want to go skiing. Their decision is to go to Hawaii. Is this decision rational? What is the opportunity cost of the trip to Hawaii for each of them? What is the benefit that each gets?
8. Label each of the news items as a positive or a normative statement:
   - The Poor Pay Too Much for Housing
   - The Number of Farms Decreased over the Last 50 Years
   - Pets Killed for Food in Zimbabwe
   - Imports from China Swamping U.S. Department Stores
   - Rural Population Constant over the Past Decade
9. Explain the *ceteris paribus* assumption and why economists use it. Give an example of when you would use the *ceteris paribus* assumption.

Instructor Assignable Problems and Applications

Your instructor can assign these problems as homework, a quiz, or a test in **MyEconLab**.

1. Suppose a person gets a loan from a bank to buy a new home.
   - Are the borrower and the bank pursuing self-interest, the social interest, or both?
   - If the borrower can't afford to keep up the payments and defaults, is the borrower pursuing self-interest, the social interest, or both?
   - If the bank forecloses on the delinquent borrower, is the bank pursuing self-interest, the social interest, or both?
2. On Friday May 14, 2009, the following headlines appeared in *The Wall Street Journal*. Classify each headline as a signal that the news article is about a microeconomic topic or a macroeconomic topic. Explain your answers.
   - US Set to Rethink Fed's Role
   - Wal-Mart Makes Electronics Push
   - VW, Porsche Take Break in Talks
   - Economists Foresee Protracted Recovery
3. Think about each of the following situations and explain how they affect incentives and might change the choices that people make:
   - A hurricane hits Central Florida.
   - The World Series begins tonight but a thunderstorm warning is in effect for the area in which the stadium is located.
   - The price of a personal computer falls to $50.
   - Political instability in the Middle East sends the price of gas to $5 a gallon.
4. Think about the following news items and label each as involving a *what, how,* or *for whom* question:
   - Today, most stores use computers to keep their inventory records, whereas 20 years ago most stores used paper records.
   - Health-care professionals and drug companies recommend that Medicaid drug rebates be made available to everyone in need.
   - A doubling of the gas tax might lead to a better public transit system.
5. Your school decides to increase the intake of new students next year. To make its decision, what economic concepts would it have considered? Would the school have used the "economic way of thinking" in reaching its decision? Would the school have made its decision on the margin?
6. Provide two examples of monetary and two examples of non-monetary incentives, a carrot and a stick of each, that government policies use to influence behavior.
7. Does the decision to make a blockbuster movie mean that some other more desirable activities get fewer resources than they deserve? Is your answer a positive or a normative? Explain your answer.
8. Provide two examples of economics being used as a tool by each of a student, a business, and a government. Classify your examples as dealing with microeconomic topics and macroeconomic topics.
9. Find in the media one example of economics being used as a tool by each of a person, a business, and a government to make a decision.

Use the following information to work Problems 10 to 16.

Hundreds line up for 5 p.m. Eminem ticket giveaway

Hundreds of Eminem fans lined up today for a chance to get a free ticket to the Detroit rapper's secret concert. Despite the fact that tickets would not be released before 5 p.m., people lined up all day.

Source: *Detroit Free Press*, May 18, 2009

Eminem announced on MySpace that he planned to release his new album *Relapse*— first album in 5 years—on the same day as his free concert in Detroit.

10. Eminem is giving away tickets to his show in a 1,500-seat theater in Detroit. What is free and what is scarce? Explain your answer.
11. What do you think Eminem's incentive is to give a free show?
12. Did Eminem make his decision to give a free concert in self-interest or in the social interest? Explain.
13. Because all the tickets were free, was the marginal benefit from the concert zero? Explain your answer.
14. For the people who scored tickets, is the concert really free? If not, explain why not?
15. Did the people who lined up but missed out on getting tickets incur any costs? What sort of a cost? Explain.
16. Was Eminem's decision to give a free concert a rational choice?

Use the following information to work Problems 17 to 21.

Report: Obama will drive up miles-per-gallon requirements

The Obama administration will announce sweeping revision of auto-emission and fuel-economy standards in the same package, which will require automakers to boost overall fuel economy to 35.5 miles per gallon by 2016, notching up 5% each year from 2012, to limit the amount of carbon dioxide cars can emit.

Source: *USA Today*, May 18, 2009

17. What are two benefits of the new miles-per-gallon requirements?
18. What are two benefits of the new auto-emission standards?
19. Are the benefits you listed in Problems 17 and 18 benefits in someone's self-interest or in the social interest?
20. What costs associated with the new miles-per-gallon requirements arise from decisions made in self-interest and in the social interest?
21. What costs associated with the new auto-emission standards arise from decisions made in self-interest and in the social interest?

APPENDIX: MAKING AND USING GRAPHS

When you have completed your study of this appendix, you will be able to

1. Interpret a scatter diagram, a time-series graph, and a cross-section graph.
2. Interpret the graphs used in economic models.
3. Define and calculate slope.
4. Graph relationships among more than two variables.

Basic Idea

A graph represents a quantity as a distance and enables us to visualize the relationship between two variables. To make a graph, we set two lines called *axes* perpendicular to each other, like those in Figure A1.1. The vertical line is called the *y*-axis, and the horizontal line is called the *x*-axis. The common zero point is called the *origin.* In Figure A1.1, the *x*-axis measures temperature in degrees Fahrenheit. A movement to the right shows an increase in temperature, and a movement to the left shows a decrease in temperature. The *y*-axis represents ice cream consumption, measured in gallons per day.

To make a graph, we need a value of the variable on the *x*-axis and a corresponding value of the variable on the *y*-axis. For example, if the temperature is 40°F, ice cream consumption is 5 gallons a day at point *A* in Figure A1.1. If the temperature is 80°F, ice cream consumption is 20 gallons a day at point *B* in Figure A1.1. Graphs like that in Figure A1.1 can be used to show any type of quantitative data on two variables.

FIGURE A1.1

Making a Graph

myeconlab Animation

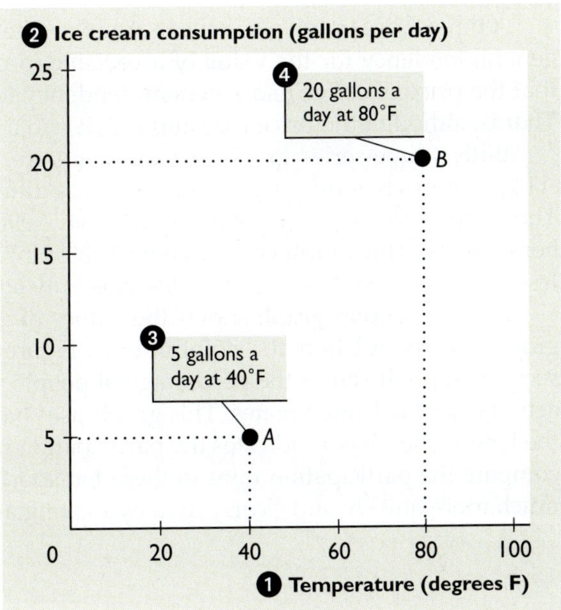

All graphs have axes that measure quantities as distances.

❶ The horizontal axis (*x*-axis) measures temperature in degrees Fahrenheit. A movement to the right shows an increase in temperature.

❷ The vertical axis (*y*-axis) measures ice cream consumption in gallons per day. A movement upward shows an increase in ice cream consumption.

❸ Point *A* shows that 5 gallons of ice cream are consumed on a day when the temperature is 40°F.

❹ Point *B* shows that 20 gallons of ice cream are consumed on a day when the temperature is 80°F.

Interpreting Data Graphs

Scatter diagram
A graph of the value of one variable against the value of another variable.

A **scatter diagram** is a graph of the value of one variable against the value of another variable. It is used to reveal whether a relationship exists between two variables and to describe the relationship. Figure A1.2 shows two examples.

Figure A1.2(a) shows the relationship between expenditure and income. Each point shows expenditure per person and income per person in the United States in a given year from 1999 to 2009. The points are "scattered" within the graph. The label on each point shows its year. The point marked 04 shows that in 2004, income per person was $28,990 and expenditure per person was $27,400. This scatter diagram reveals that as income increases, expenditure also increases.

Figure A1.2(b) shows the relationship between the percentage of Americans who own a cell phone and the average monthly cell phone bill. This scatter diagram reveals that as the cost of using a cell phone falls, the number of cell phones increases.

Time-series graph
A graph that measures time on the x-axis and the variable or variables in which we are interested on the y-axis.

A **time-series graph** measures time (for example, months or years) on the x-axis and the variable or variables in which we are interested on the y-axis. Figure A1.2(c) shows an example. In this graph, time (on the x-axis) is measured in years, which run from 1979 to 2009. The variable that we are interested in is the price of coffee, and it is measured on the y-axis.

A time-series graph conveys an enormous amount of information quickly and easily, as this example illustrates. It shows when the value is

1. High or low. When the line is a long way from the x-axis, the price is high, as it was in 2008. When the line is close to the x-axis, the price is low, as it was in 1993.
2. Rising or falling. When the line slopes upward, as in 1994, the price is rising. When the line slopes downward, as in 1998, the price is falling.
3. Rising or falling quickly or slowly. If the line is steep, then the price is rising or falling quickly. If the line is not steep, the price is rising or falling slowly. For example, the price rose quickly in 1994 and slowly in 1984. The price fell quickly in 1998 and slowly in 2003.

Trend
A general tendency for the value of a variable to rise or fall over time.

A time-series graph also reveals whether the variable has a trend. A **trend** is a general tendency for the value of a variable to rise or fall over time. You can see that the price of coffee had a general tendency to rise from 1979 to the late 1990s. That is, although the price rose and fell, it had a general tendency to rise.

With a time-series graph, we can compare different periods quickly. Figure A1.2(c) shows that the period after 1990 was different from the period before 1990. The price of coffee jumped during the early 1990s and remained high for a number of years. This graph conveys a wealth of information, and it does so in much less space than we have used to describe only some of its features.

Cross-section graph
A graph that shows the values of an economic variable for different groups in a population at a point in time.

A **cross-section graph** shows the values of an economic variable for different groups in a population at a point in time. Figure A1.2(d) is an example of a cross-section graph. It shows the percentage of people who participate in selected sports activities in the United States. This graph uses bars rather than dots and lines, and the length of each bar indicates the participation rate. Figure A1.2(d) enables you to compare the participation rates in these ten sporting activities. And you can do so much more quickly and clearly than by looking at a list of numbers.

FIGURE A1.2

Data Graphs

myeconlab Animation

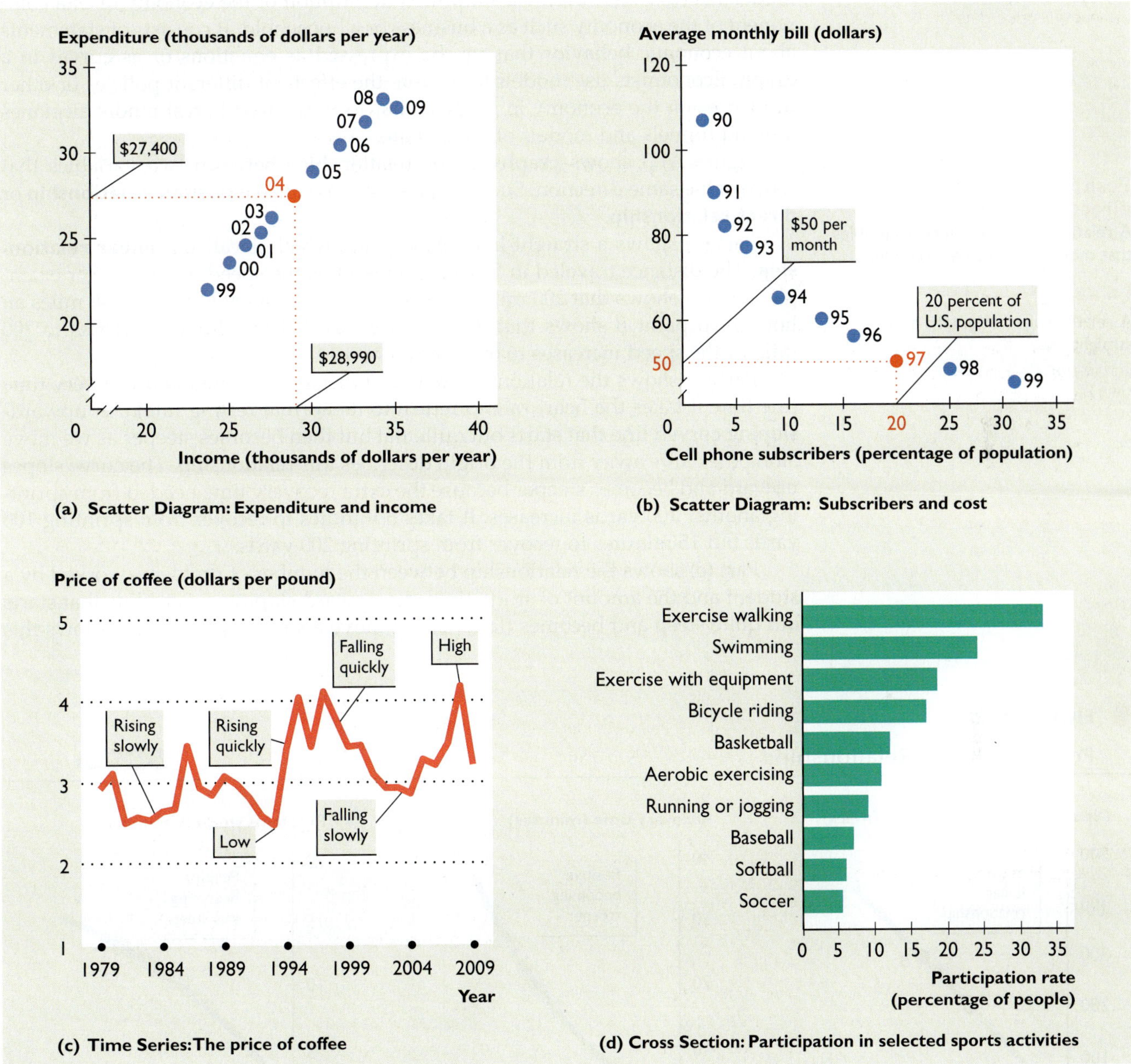

A scatter diagram reveals the relationship between two variables. In part (a), as income increases, expenditure almost always increases. In part (b), as the monthly cell phone bill falls, the percentage of people who own a cell phone increases.

A time-series graph plots the value of a variable on the *y*-axis against time on the *x*-axis. Part (c) plots the price of coffee each year from 1979 to 2009. The graph shows when the price of coffee was high and low, when it increased and decreased, and when it changed quickly and changed slowly.

A cross-section graph shows the value of a variable across the members of a population. Part (d) shows the participation rate in the United States in each of ten sporting activities.

Interpreting Graphs Used in Economic Models

We use graphs to show the relationships among the variables in an economic model. An *economic model* is a simplified description of the economy or of a component of the economy such as a business or a household. It consists of statements about economic behavior that can be expressed as equations or as curves in a graph. Economists use models to explore the effects of different policies or other influences on the economy in ways similar to those used to test model airplanes in wind tunnels and models of the climate.

Positive relationship or direct relationship
A relationship between two variables that move in the same direction.

Linear relationship
A relationship that graphs as a straight line.

Figure A1.3 shows graphs of the relationships between two variables that move in the same direction. Such a relationship is called a **positive relationship** or **direct relationship**.

Part (a) shows a straight-line relationship, which is called a **linear relationship**. The distance traveled in 5 hours increases as the speed increases. For example, point *A* shows that 200 miles are traveled in 5 hours at a speed of 40 miles an hour. And point *B* shows that the distance traveled in 5 hours increases to 300 miles if the speed increases to 60 miles an hour.

Part (b) shows the relationship between distance sprinted and recovery time (the time it takes the heart rate to return to its normal resting rate). An upward-sloping curved line that starts out quite flat but then becomes steeper as we move along the curve away from the origin describes this relationship. The curve slopes upward and becomes steeper because the extra recovery time needed from sprinting another 100 yards increases. It takes 5 minutes to recover from sprinting 100 yards but 15 minutes to recover from sprinting 200 yards.

Part (c) shows the relationship between the number of problems worked by a student and the amount of study time. An upward-sloping curved line that starts out quite steep and becomes flatter as we move away from the origin shows this

FIGURE A1.3
Positive (Direct) Relationships

myeconlab Animation

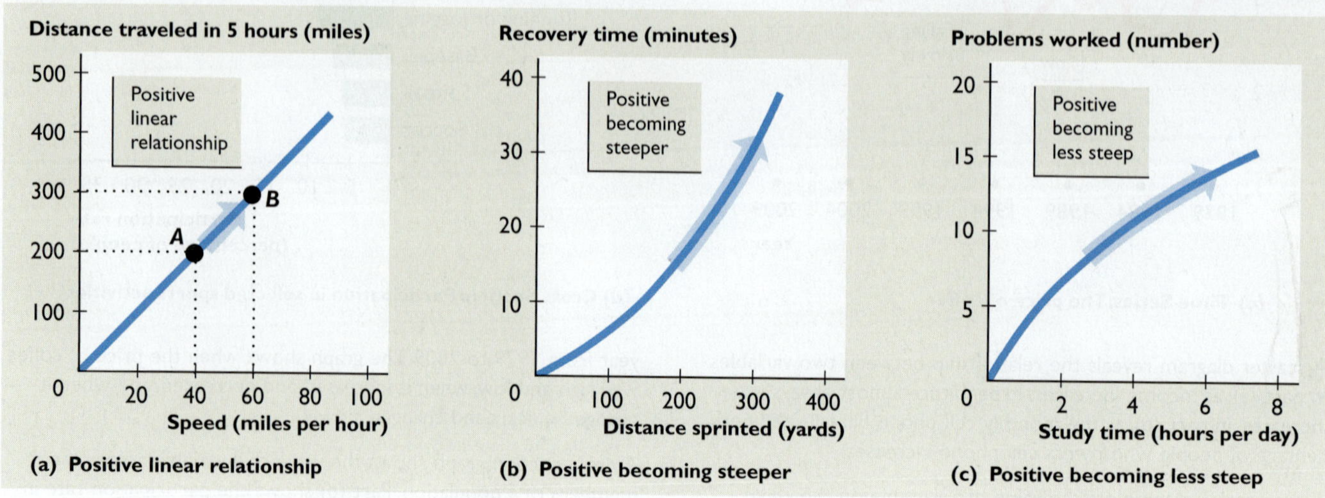

Part (a) shows that as speed increases, the distance traveled in a given number of hours increases along a straight line.

Part (b) shows that as the distance sprinted increases, recovery time increases along a curve that becomes steeper.

Part (c) shows that as study time increases, the number of problems worked increases along a curve that becomes less steep.

relationship. Study time becomes less effective as you increase the hours worked and become more tired.

Figure A1.4 shows relationships between two variables that move in opposite directions. Such a relationship is called a **negative relationship** or **inverse relationship**.

Negative relationship or inverse relationship
A relationship between two variables that move in opposite directions.

Part (a) shows the relationship between the number of hours spent playing squash and the number of hours spent playing tennis when the total number of hours available is five. One extra hour spent playing tennis means one hour less playing squash and vice versa. This relationship is negative and linear.

Part (b) shows the relationship between the cost per mile traveled and the length of a journey. The longer the journey, the lower is the cost per mile. But as the journey length increases, the fall in the cost per mile becomes smaller. This feature of the relationship is shown by the fact that the curve slopes downward, starting out steep at a short journey length and then becoming flatter as the journey length increases. This relationship arises because some of the costs, such as auto insurance, are fixed, and as the journey length increases, the fixed costs are spread over more miles.

Part (c) shows the relationship between the amount of leisure time and the number of problems worked by a student. Increasing leisure time produces an increasingly large reduction in the number of problems worked. This relationship is a negative one that starts out with a gentle slope at a small number of leisure hours and becomes steeper as the number of leisure hours increases. This relationship is a different view of the idea shown in Figure A1.3(c).

Many relationships in economic models have a maximum or a minimum. For example, firms try to make the largest possible profit and to produce at the lowest possible cost. Figure A1.5 shows relationships that have a maximum or a minimum.

FIGURE A1.4

Negative (Inverse) Relationships

myeconlab Animation

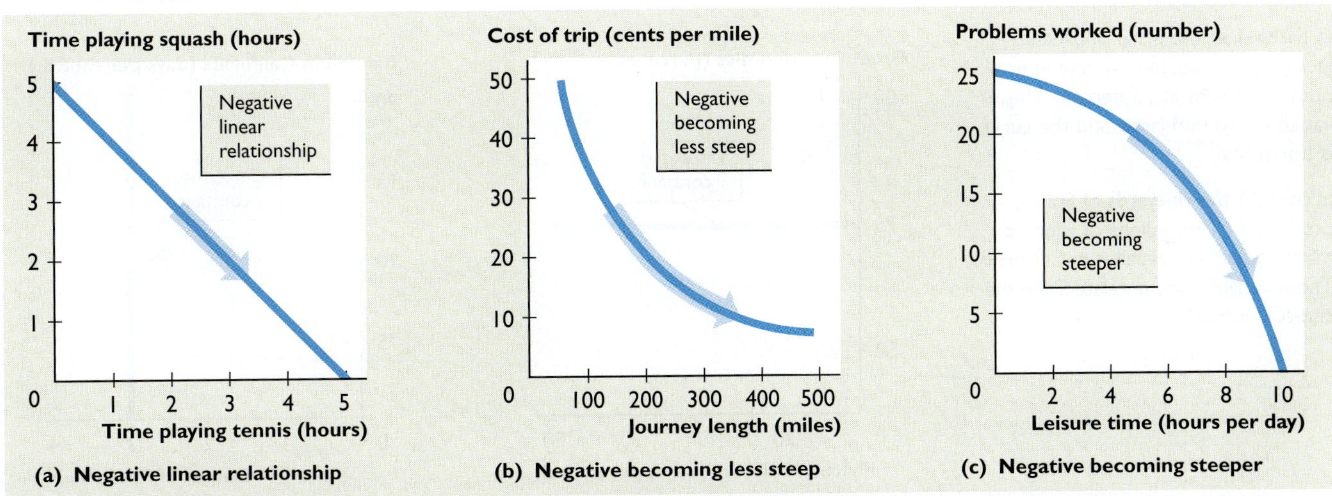

Part (a) shows that as the time playing tennis increases, the time playing squash decreases along a straight line.

Part (b) shows that as the journey length increases, the cost of the trip falls along a curve that becomes less steep.

Part (c) shows that as leisure time increases, the number of problems worked decreases along a curve that becomes steeper.

FIGURE A1.5

Maximum and Minimum Points

myeconlab Animation

In part (a), as the rainfall increases, the curve ❶ slopes upward as the yield per acre rises, ❷ is flat at point *A*, the maximum yield, and then ❸ slopes downward as the yield per acre falls.

In part (b), as the speed increases, the curve ❶ slopes downward as the cost per mile falls, ❷ is flat at the minimum point *B*, and then ❸ slopes upward as the cost per mile rises.

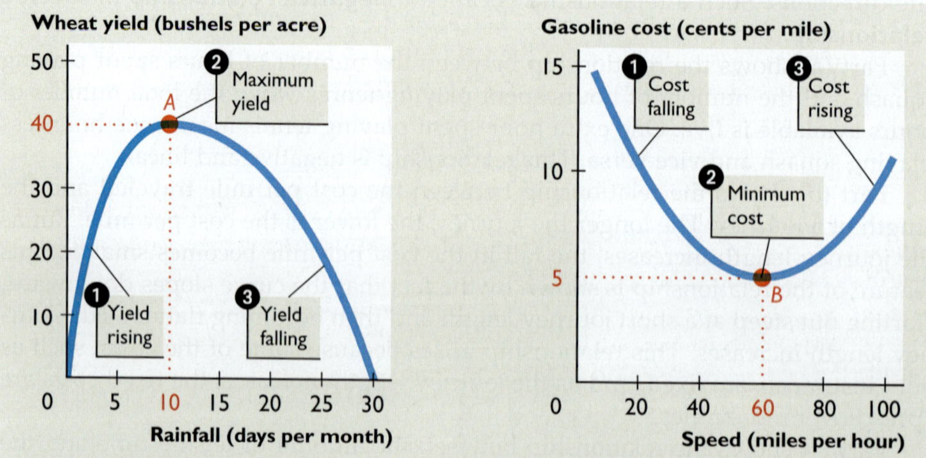

(a) Relationship with a maximum

(b) Relationship with a minimum

Part (a) shows a relationship that starts out sloping upward, reaches a maximum, and then slopes downward. Part (b) shows a relationship that begins sloping downward, falls to a minimum, and then slopes upward.

Finally, there are many situations in which, no matter what happens to the value of one variable, the other variable remains constant. Sometimes we want to show two variables that are unrelated in a graph. Figure A1.6 shows two graphs in which the variables are unrelated.

FIGURE A1.6

Variables That Are Unrelated

myeconlab Animation

In part (a), as the price of bananas increases, the student's grade in economics remains at 75 percent. These variables are unrelated, and the curve is horizontal.

In part (b), the vineyards of France produce 3 billion gallons of wine no matter what the rainfall is in California. These variables are unrelated, and the curve is vertical.

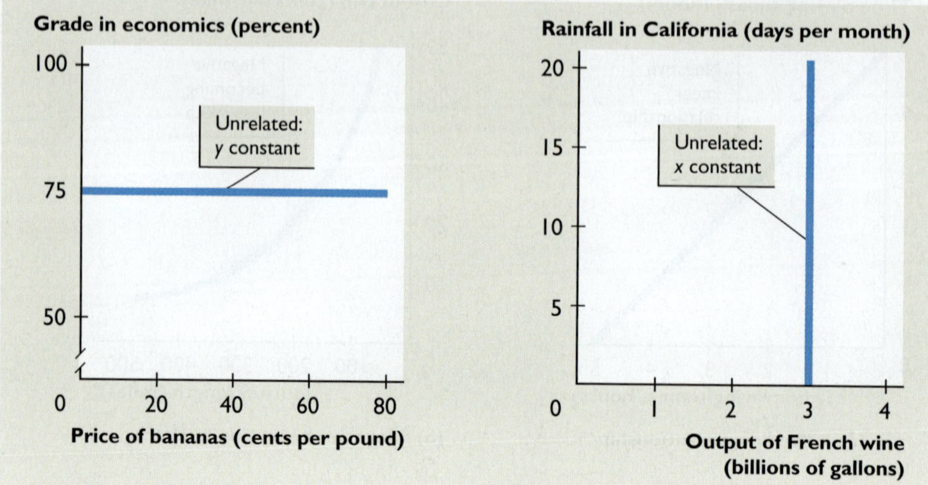

(a) Unrelated: *y* constant

(b) Unrelated: *x* constant

The Slope of a Relationship

We can measure the influence of one variable on another by the slope of the relationship. The **slope** of a relationship is the change in the value of the variable measured on the y-axis divided by the change in the value of the variable measured on the x-axis. We use the Greek letter Δ (delta) to represent "change in." So Δy means the change in the value of y, and Δx means the change in the value of x. The slope of the relationship is

$$\Delta y \div \Delta x.$$

Slope
The change in the value of the variable measured on the y-axis divided by the change in the value of the variable measured on the x-axis.

If a large change in y is associated with a small change in x, the slope is large and the curve is steep. If a small change in y is associated with a large change in x, the slope is small and the curve is flat.

Figure A1.7 shows you how to calculate slope. The slope of a straight line is the same regardless of where on the line you calculate it—the slope is constant. In part (a), when x increases from 2 to 6, y increases from 3 to 6. The change in x is 4—that is, Δx is 4. The change in y is 3—that is, Δy is 3. The slope of that line is 3/4. In part (b), when x increases from 2 to 6, y *decreases* from 6 to 3. The change in y is *minus* 3—that is, Δy is -3. The change in x is plus 4—that is, Δx is 4. The slope of the curve is $-3/4$.

In part (c), we calculate the slope at a point on a curve. To do so, place a ruler on the graph so that it touches point A and no other point on the curve, then draw a straight line along the edge of the ruler. The slope of this straight line is the slope of the curve at point A. This slope is 3/4.

FIGURE A1.7

Calculating Slope

myeconlab Animation

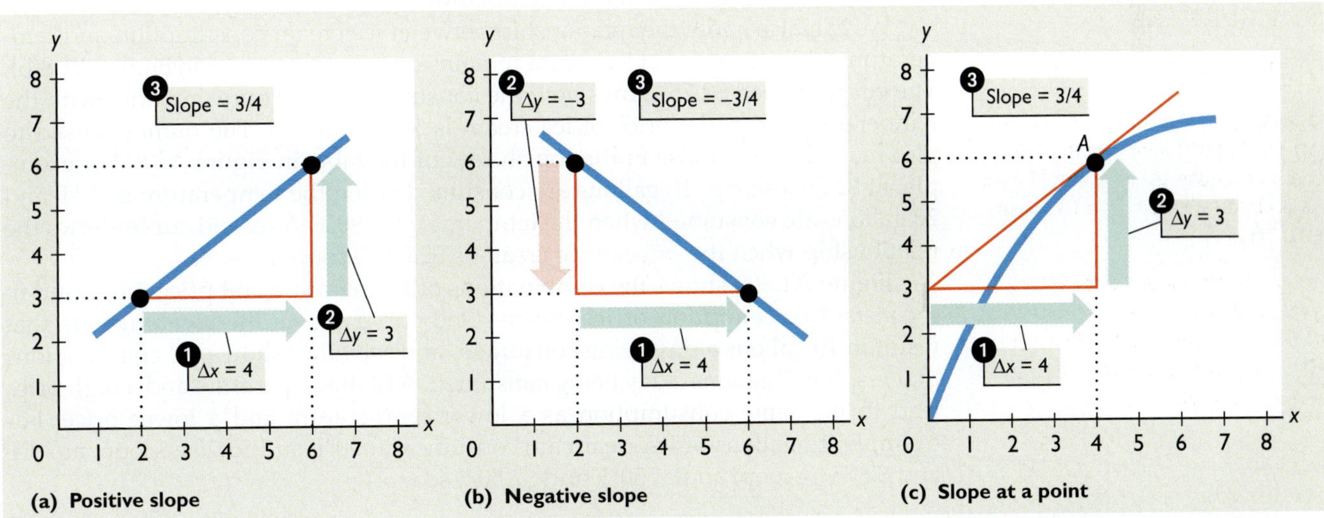

In part (a), ❶ when Δx is 4, ❷ Δy is 3, so ❸ the slope ($\Delta y \div \Delta x$) is 3/4.

In part (b), ❶ when Δx is 4, ❷ Δy is -3, so ❸ the slope ($\Delta y \div \Delta x$) is $-3/4$.

In part (c), the slope of the curve at point A equals the slope of the red line. ❶ When Δx is 4, ❷ Δy is 3, so ❸ the slope ($\Delta y \div \Delta x$) is 3/4.

Relationships Among More Than Two Variables

All the graphs that you have studied so far plot the relationship between two variables as a point formed by the x and y values. But most of the relationships in economics involve relationships among many variables, not just two. For example, the amount of ice cream consumed depends on the price of ice cream and the temperature. If ice cream is expensive and the temperature is low, people eat much less ice cream than when ice cream is inexpensive and the temperature is high. For any given price of ice cream, the quantity consumed varies with the temperature; and for any given temperature, the quantity of ice cream consumed varies with its price.

Figure A1.8 shows a relationship among three variables. The table shows the number of gallons of ice cream consumed per day at various temperatures and ice cream prices. How can we graph these numbers?

To graph a relationship that involves more than two variables, we use the *ceteris paribus* assumption.

Ceteris Paribus

The Latin phrase *ceteris paribus* means "other things remaining the same." Every laboratory experiment is an attempt to create *ceteris paribus* and isolate the relationship of interest. We use the same method to make a graph.

Figure A1.8(a) shows an example. This graph shows what happens to the quantity of ice cream consumed when the price of ice cream varies while the temperature remains constant. The curve labeled 70°F shows the relationship between ice cream consumption and the price of ice cream if the temperature is 70°F. The numbers used to plot that curve are those in the first and fourth columns of the table in Figure A1.8. For example, if the temperature is 70°F, 10 gallons are consumed when the price is \$2.75 a scoop and 18 gallons are consumed when the price is \$2.25 a scoop. The curve labeled 90°F shows the relationship between consumption and the price when the temperature is 90°F.

We can also show the relationship between ice cream consumption and temperature while the price of ice cream remains constant, as shown in Figure A1.8(b). The curve labeled \$2.75 shows how the consumption of ice cream varies with the temperature when the price of ice cream is \$2.75 a scoop. The numbers used to plot that curve are those in the fourth row of the table in Figure A1.8. For example, at \$2.75 a scoop, 10 gallons are consumed when the temperature is 70°F and 20 gallons are consumed when the temperature is 90°F. A second curve shows the relationship when the price of ice cream is \$2.00 a scoop.

Figure A1.8(c) shows the combinations of temperature and price that result in a constant consumption of ice cream. One curve shows the combinations that result in 10 gallons a day being consumed, and the other shows the combinations that result in 7 gallons a day being consumed. A high temperature and a high price lead to the same consumption as a lower temperature and a lower price. For example, 10 gallons of ice cream are consumed at 90°F and \$3.25 a scoop, at 70°F and \$2.75 a scoop, and at 50°F and \$2.50 a scoop.

With what you've learned about graphs in this Appendix, you can move forward with your study of economics. There are no graphs in this textbook that are more complicated than the ones you've studied here.

FIGURE A1.8

Graphing a Relationship Among Three Variables

myeconlab Animation

Price (dollars per scoop)	Ice cream consumption (gallons per day)			
	30°F	50°F	70°F	90°F
2.00	12	18	25	50
2.25	10	12	18	37
2.50	7	10	13	27
2.75	5	7	10	20
3.00	3	5	7	14
3.25	2	3	5	10
3.50	1	2	3	6

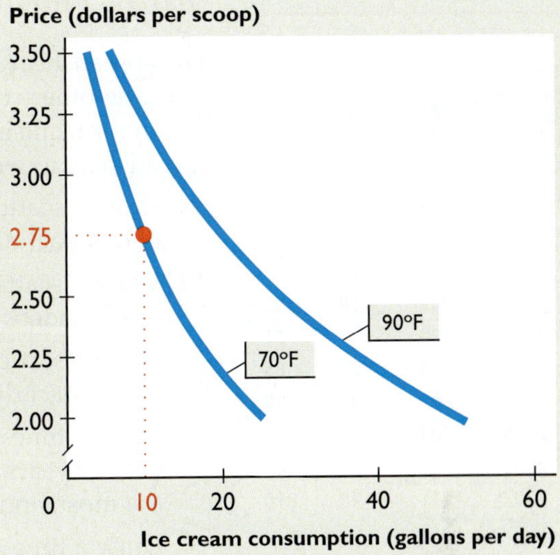

(a) Price and consumption at a given temperature

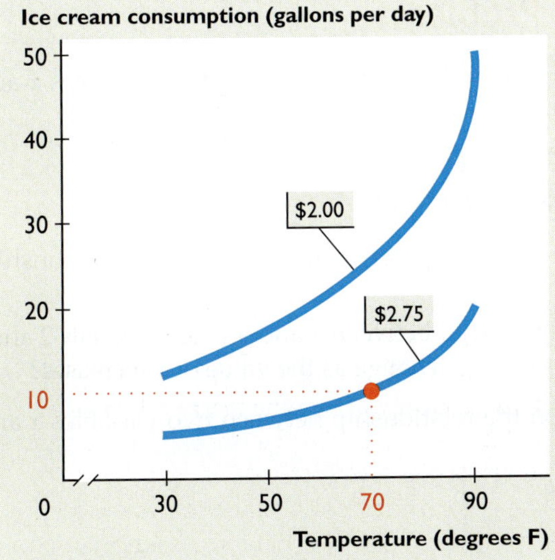

(b) Temperature and consumption at a given price

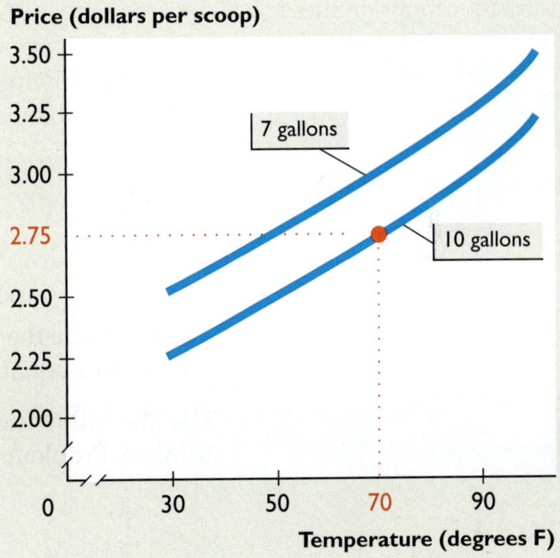

(c) Temperature and price at a given consumption

The table tells us how many gallons of ice cream are consumed at different prices and different temperatures. For example, if the price is $2.75 a scoop and the temperature is 70°F, 10 gallons of ice cream are consumed. This set of values is highlighted in the table and each part of the figure.

Part (a) shows the relationship between price and consumption when temperature is held constant. One curve holds temperature at 90°F, and the other at 70°F.

Part (b) shows the relationship between temperature and consumption when price is held constant. One curve holds the price at $2.75 a scoop, and the other at $2.00 a scoop.

Part (c) shows the relationship between temperature and price when consumption is held constant. One curve holds consumption at 10 gallons a day, and the other at 7 gallons a day.

myeconlab

Work these problems in Chapter 1 Study Plan to get instant feedback.

TABLE 1

	A	B	C	D
1	1996	779	17	3
2	1997	753	19	4
3	1998	847	27	7
4	1999	939	20	12
5	2000	943	18	19
6	2001	882	18	31
7	2002	803	15	51
8	2003	746	20	85
9	2004	767	33	139
10	2005	705	34	367
11	2006	620	23	586
12	2007	511	28	810

APPENDIX CHECKPOINT

Study Plan Problems

The spreadsheet in Table 1 provides data on the U.S. economy: Column A is the year; the other columns are quantities sold in millions per year of compact discs (column B), music videos (column C), and singles downloads (column D). Use this spreadsheet to work Problems 1 to 5.

1. Draw a scatter diagram to show the relationship between the quantities sold of compact discs and music videos. Describe the relationship.
2. Draw a scatter diagram to show the relationship between quantities sold of music videos and singles downloads. Describe the relationship.
3. Draw a scatter diagram to show the relationship between the quantities sold of compact discs and singles downloads. Describe the relationship.
4. Draw a time-series graph of quantity of compact discs sold. Say in which year or years the quantity sold (a) was highest, (b) was lowest, (c) increased the most, and (d) decreased the most. If the data show a trend, describe it.
5. Draw a time-series graph of the quantity of music videos sold. Say in which year or years the quantity sold (a) was highest, (b) was lowest, (c) decreased the most, and (d) decreased the least. If the data show a trend, describe it.

Your instructor can assign these problems as homework, a quiz, or a test in **MyEconLab**.

Instructor Assignable Problems

Use the following information on the relationship between two variables x and y to work Problems 1 and 2.

x	0	1	2	3	4	5
y	0	1	4	9	16	25

1. Draw a graph to show the relationship between x and y. Is the relationship positive or negative?
2. Calculate the slope of the relationship between x and y when x equals 2 and when x equals 4. How does the slope change as the value of x increases?

Use the following information on the relationship between two variables x and z to work Problems 3 and 4.

x	0	1	2	3	4	5
z	32	31	28	23	16	7

3. Is the relationship between x and z positive or negative?
4. Calculate the slope of the relationship between x and z when x equals 2 and when x equals 4. How does the slope change as the value of x increases?
5. Table 2 provides data on the price of a balloon ride, the temperature, and the number of rides a day. Draw graphs to show the relationship between
   - The price and the number of rides, when the temperature is constant.
   - The number of rides and the temperature, when the price is constant.
   - The temperature and the price, when the number of rides is constant.

TABLE 2

Price (dollars per ride)	Balloon rides (number per day)		
	50°F	70°F	90°F
5	32	50	40
10	27	40	32
15	18	32	27
20	10	27	18

Who makes the iPhone?

Apple, right? Guess again!

The iPhone is an example of how, in the pursuit of self-interest, many people and businesses around the world end up determining what, how, and for whom goods and services are produced.

2

The U.S. and Global Economies

CHAPTER CHECKLIST

When you have completed your study of this chapter, you will be able to

1. Describe what, how, and for whom goods and services are produced in the United States.
2. Describe what, how, and for whom goods and services are produced in the global economy.
3. Use the circular flow model to provide a picture of how households, firms, and governments interact in the U.S. economy and how the U.S. and other economies interact in the global economy.

2.1 WHAT, HOW, AND FOR WHOM?

Walk around a shopping mall and pay close attention to the range of goods and services that are being offered for sale. Go inside some of the shops and look at the labels to see where various items are manufactured. The next time you travel on an interstate highway, look at the large trucks and pay attention to the names and products printed on their sides and the places in which the trucks are registered. Open the Yellow Pages and flip through a few sections. Notice the huge range of goods and services that businesses are offering.

You've just done a sampling of *what* goods and services are produced and consumed in the United States today.

What Do We Produce?

We divide the vast array of goods and services produced into four large groups:

- Consumption goods and services
- Capital goods
- Government goods and services
- Export goods and services

Consumption goods and services
Goods and services that are bought by individuals and used to provide personal enjoyment and contribute to a person's quality of life.

Capital goods
Goods that are bought by businesses to increase their productive resources.

Government goods and services
Goods and services that are bought by governments.

Export goods and services
Goods and services that are produced in one country and sold in other countries.

Consumption goods and services are items that are bought by individuals and used to provide personal enjoyment and contribute to a person's quality of life. They include items such as housing, SUVs, vitamin water and ramen noodles, chocolate bars and Po' Boy sandwiches, movies, downhill skiing lessons, and doctor and dental services.

Capital goods are goods that are bought by businesses to increase their productive resources. They include items such as auto assembly lines, shopping malls, airplanes, and oil tankers.

Government goods and services are items that are bought by governments. Governments purchase missiles and weapons systems, travel services, Internet services, police protection, roads, and paper and paper clips.

Export goods and services are items that are produced in one country and sold in other countries. U.S. export goods and services include the airplanes produced by Boeing that Singapore Airlines buys, the computers produced by Dell that Europeans buy, and licenses sold by U.S. film companies to show U.S. movies in European movie theaters.

Of the four groups of goods and services that we've just defined, consumption goods and services have the largest share and a share that doesn't fluctuate much. The volume of capital goods produced fluctuates as the economy cycles from boom to recession. Goods and services bought by governments are close to a fifth of total production and export goods around one tenth.

Breaking the goods and services down into smaller categories, health services is the largest category, with 13 percent of the value of total production. Real estate services come next at 12 percent. The main component of this item is the services of rental and owner-occupied housing. Education is the next largest service, followed by retail and wholesale trades and transportation and storage.

The categories of goods production are smaller than those of services. The largest category of goods—construction—accounts for less than 5 percent of the value of total production, and the next three—utilities, food, and chemicals—each accounts for 2 percent or less.

EYE on the U.S. ECONOMY

What We Produce

In 2009, consumption goods and services accounted for 62 percent of total production, both capital goods and export goods and services accounted for 10 percent, and government goods and services for 18 percent.

Health-care and real estate services, education, retail and wholesale trades, and transportation and storage are the six largest services produced. Construction, utilities, food, and chemicals are the largest categories of goods produced. Services production greatly exceeds goods production and is growing faster.

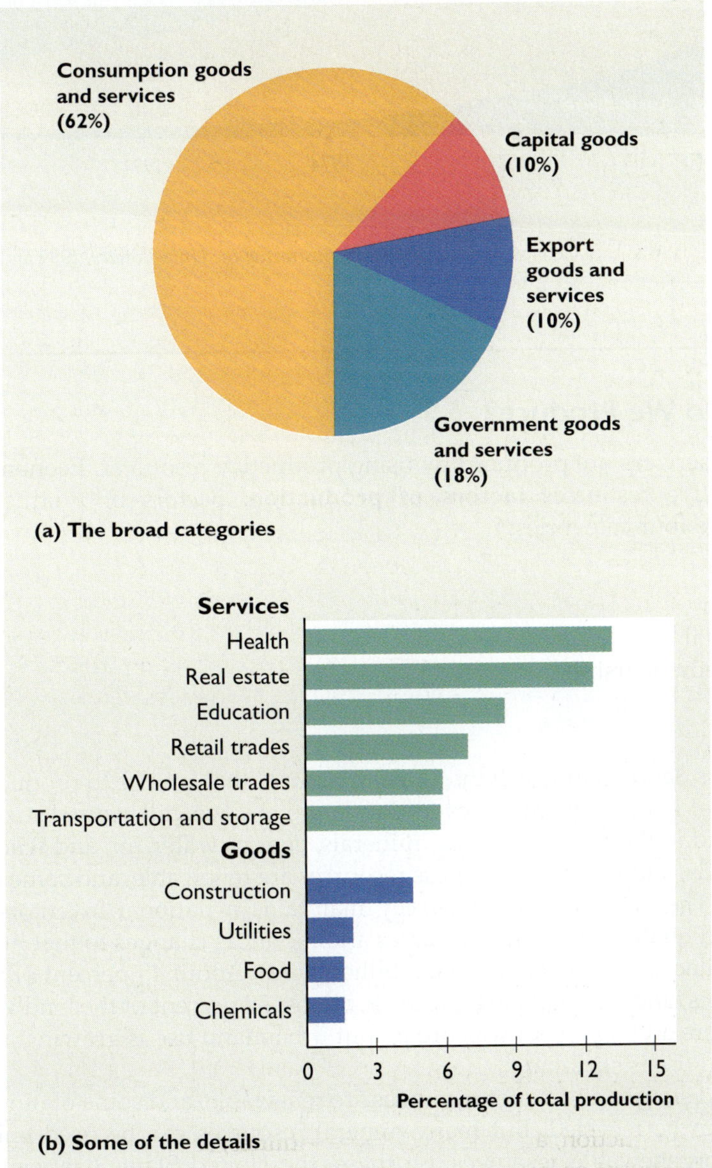

SOURCE OF DATA: Bureau of Economic Analysis.

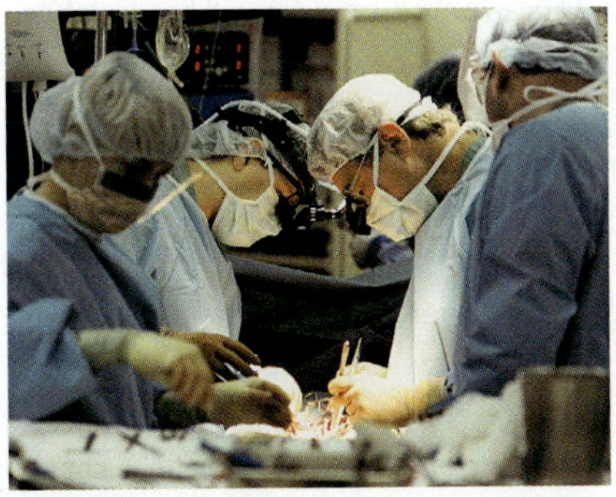

Health-care services …

education services …

retail trades …

and chemicals are among the largest categories of goods and services produced.

EYE on the PAST

Changes in What We Produce

Seventy years ago, one American in four worked on a farm. That number has shrunk to one in thirty-five. The number of people who produce goods—in mining, construction, and manufacturing—has also shrunk, from one in three to one in five. In contrast, the number of people who produce services has expanded from one in two to almost four in five. These changes in employment reflect changes in what we produce—services.

We hear a lot about globalization and American manufacturing jobs going overseas, but the expansion of service jobs and shrinking of manufacturing jobs is not new. It has been going on over the past 60 years and is likely to continue.

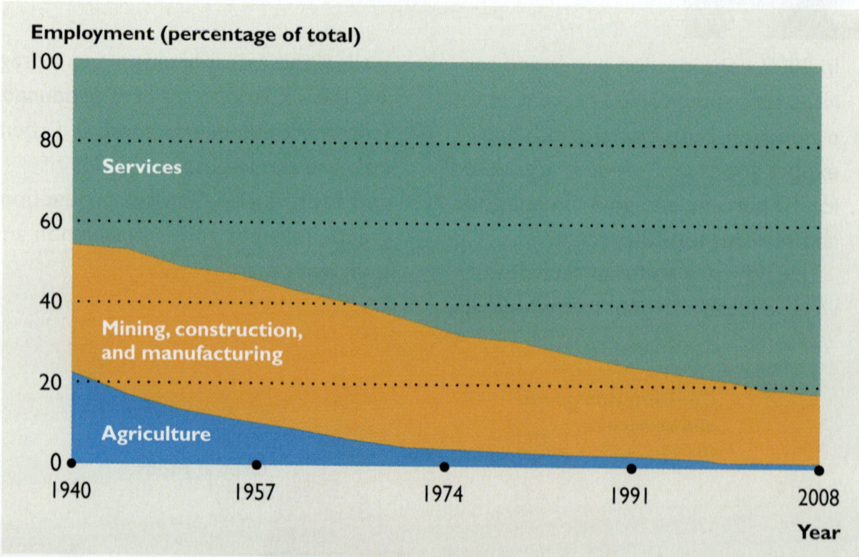

SOURCE OF DATA: U.S. Census Bureau, *Statistical Abstract of the United States*, 1999 and 2008.

How Do We Produce?

Factors of production
The productive resources that are used to produce goods and services—land, labor, capital, and entrepreneurship.

Goods and services are produced by using productive resources. Economists call the productive resources **factors of production**. Factors of production are grouped into four categories:

- Land
- Labor
- Capital
- Entrepreneurship

Land

Land
The "gifts of nature," or *natural resources*, that we use to produce goods and services.

In economics, **land** includes all the "gifts of nature" that we use to produce goods and services. Land is what, in everyday language, we call *natural resources*. It includes land in the everyday sense, minerals, energy, water, air, and wild plants, animals, birds, and fish. Some of these resources are renewable, and some are nonrenewable. The U.S. Geological Survey maintains a national inventory of the quantity and quality of natural resources and monitors changes to that inventory.

The United States covers almost 2 billion acres. About 45 percent of the land is forest, lakes, and national parks. In 2009, almost 50 percent of the land was used for agriculture and 5 percent was urban, but urban land use is growing and agricultural land use is shrinking.

Our land surface and water resources are renewable, and some of our mineral resources can be recycled. But many mineral resources can be used only once. They are nonrenewable resources. Of these, the United States has vast known reserves of coal but much smaller known reserves of oil and natural gas.

Labor

Labor is the work time and work effort that people devote to producing goods and services. Labor includes the physical and mental efforts of all the people who work on farms and construction sites and in factories, shops, and offices. The Census Bureau and Bureau of Labor Statistics measure the quantity of labor at work every month.

Labor
The work time and work effort that people devote to producing goods and services.

In the United States in April 2009, 155 million people had jobs or were available for work. Some worked full time, some worked part time, and some were unemployed but looking for an acceptable vacant job. The total amount of time worked during 2009 was about 240 billion hours.

The quantity of labor increases as the adult population increases. The quantity of labor also increases if a larger percentage of the population takes jobs. During the past 50 years, a larger proportion of women have taken paid work and this trend has increased the quantity of labor. At the same time, a slightly smaller proportion of men have taken paid work and this trend has decreased the quantity of labor.

The *quality* of labor depends on how skilled people are. A laborer who can push a hand cart but can't drive a truck is much less productive than one who can drive. An office worker who can use a computer is much more productive than one who can't. Economists use a special name for human skill: human capital. **Human capital** is the knowledge and skill that people obtain from education, on-the-job training, and work experience.

Human capital
The knowledge and skill that people obtain from education, on-the-job training, and work experience.

You are building your own human capital right now as you work on your economics course and other subjects. Your human capital will continue to grow when you get a full-time job and become better at it. Human capital improves the *quality* of labor and increases the quantity of goods and services that labor can produce.

Capital

Capital consists of the tools, instruments, machines, buildings, and other items that have been produced in the past and that businesses now use to produce goods and services. Capital includes hammers and screwdrivers, computers, auto assembly lines, office towers and warehouses, dams and power plants, airports and airplanes, shirt factories, and shopping malls.

Capital
Tools, instruments, machines, buildings, and other items that have been produced in the past and that businesses now use to produce goods and services.

Capital also includes inventories of unsold goods or of partly finished goods on a production line. And capital includes what is sometimes called *infrastructure capital*, such as highways and airports.

Capital, like human capital, makes labor more productive. A truck driver can produce vastly more transportation services than the pusher of a hand cart; the Interstate highway system enables us to produce vastly more transportation services than was possible on the old highway system that preceded it.

The Bureau of Economic Analysis in the U.S. Department of Commerce keeps track of the total value of capital in the United States and how it grows over time. Today, the value of capital in the U.S. economy is around $47 trillion.

Financial Capital Is Not Capital

In everyday language, we talk about money, stocks, and bonds as being capital. These items are *financial capital,* and they are not productive resources. They enable people to provide businesses with financial resources, but they are *not* used to produce goods and services. They are not capital.

EYE on the U.S. ECONOMY

Changes in How We Produce in the Information Economy

The information economy consists of the jobs and businesses that produce and use computers and equipment powered by computer chips. This information economy is highly visible in your daily life.

The pairs of images here illustrate two examples. In each pair, a new technology enables capital to replace labor.

The top pair of pictures illustrate the replacement of bank tellers (labor) with ATMs (capital). Although the ATM was invented almost 40 years ago, when it made its first appearance, it was located only inside banks and was not able to update customers' accounts. It is only in the last decade that ATMs have spread to corner stores and enable us to get cash and check our bank balance from almost anywhere in the world.

The bottom pair of pictures illustrate a more recent replacement of labor with capital: self-check-in. Air passengers today issue their own boarding pass, often at their own computer before leaving home. For international flights, some of these machines now even check passport details.

The number of bank teller and airport check-in clerk jobs is shrinking, but these new technologies are creating a whole range of new jobs for people who make, program, install, and repair the vast number of machines.

Entrepreneurship

Entrepreneurship
The human resource that organizes labor, land, and capital to produce goods and services.

Entrepreneurship is the human resource that organizes land, labor, and capital to produce goods and services. Entrepreneurs are creative and imaginative. They come up with new ideas about what and how to produce, make business decisions, and bear the risks that arise from these decisions. If their ideas work out, they earn a profit. If their ideas turn out to be wrong, they bear the loss.

The quantity of entrepreneurship is hard to describe or measure. During some periods, there appears to be a great deal of imaginative entrepreneurship around. People such as Sam Walton, who created Wal-Mart, one of the world's largest retailers; Bill Gates, who founded the Microsoft empire; and Mark Zuckerberg, who founded Facebook, are examples of extraordinary entrepreneurial talent. But these highly visible entrepreneurs are just the tip of an iceberg that consists of hundreds of thousands of people who run businesses, large and small.

For Whom Do We Produce?

Who gets the goods and services depends on the incomes that people earn. A large income enables a person to buy large quantities of goods and services. A small income leaves a person with a small quantity of goods and services.

People earn their incomes by selling the services of the factors of production they own. **Rent** is paid for the use of land, **wages** are paid for the services of labor, **interest** is paid for the use of capital, and entrepreneurs receive a **profit** (or incur a **loss**) for running their businesses. What are the shares of these four factor incomes in the United States? Which factor receives the largest share?

Figure 2.1(a) answers these questions. It shows that wages were 65 percent of total income in 2008 and rent, interest, and profit and were 35 percent of total income. These percentages remain remarkably constant over time. We call the distribution of income among the factors of production the **functional distribution of income**.

Figure 2.1(b) shows the **personal distribution of income**—the distribution of income among households. Some households, like that of Tiger Woods, earn many million dollars a year. These households are in the richest 20 percent who earn 51 percent of total income. Households at the other end of the scale, like those of fast-food servers, are in the poorest 20 percent who earn only 3 percent of total income. The distribution of income has been changing and becoming more unequal. The rich have become richer. But it isn't the case, on the whole, that the poor have become poorer. They just haven't become richer as fast as the rich have.

Rent
Income paid for the use of land.

Wages
Income paid for the services of labor.

Interest
Income paid for the use of capital.

Profit (or loss)
Income earned by an entrepreneur for running a business.

Functional distribution of income
The distribution of income among the factors of production.

Personal distribution of income
The distribution of income among households.

FIGURE 2.1

For Whom?

myeconlab Animation

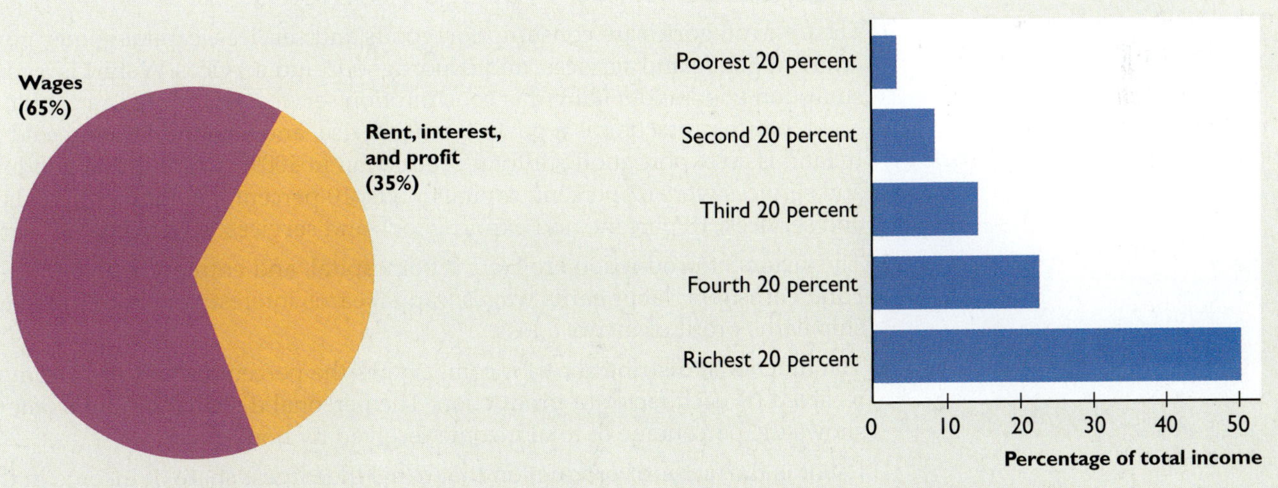

(a) Functional distribution of income

(b) Personal distribution of income

SOURCES OF DATA: Bureau of Economic Analysis, *National Income and Product Accounts*, Table 1.10 and U.S. Census Bureau, *Income, Poverty, and Health Insurance in the United States: 2008*, Current Population Reports P60-235, 2008.

In 2008, wages (the income from labor) were 65 percent of total income. Rent, interest, and profit (the income from the services of land, capital, and entrepreneurship) totaled the remaining 35 percent.

In 2008, the 20 percent of the population with the highest incomes received 51 percent of total income. The 20 percent with the lowest incomes received only 3 percent of total income.

myeconlab

Work these problems in Study Plan 2.1 to get instant feedback.

CHECKPOINT 2.1

Describe what, how, and for whom goods and services are produced in the United States.

Practice Problems

1. Name the four broad categories of goods and services that we use in economics. Provide an example of each (different from those in the chapter) and say what percentage of total production each accounted for in 2009.
2. Name the four factors of production and the incomes they earn.
3. Distinguish between the functional distribution of income and the personal distribution of income.
4. In the United States, which factor of production earned the largest share of income in 2008 and what percentage did it earn?
5. **What microloans miss**

   Muhammad Yunus (along with Grameen Bank) was awarded the Nobel Peace Prize in 2006. Yunus has said that "all people are entrepreneurs" and that microloans will pull poor people out of poverty. Only 14 percent of Americans are entrepreneurs while almost forty percent of Peruvians are.

   Source: James Surowiecki, *The New Yorker*, March 17, 2008

   With only 14 percent of Americans earning their income from entrepreneurship, from what factor of production do most Americans earn their income? What is that income called? Why do you think so many people in Peru are entrepreneurs?

Guided Solutions to Practice Problems

1. The four categories are consumption goods and services, capital goods, government goods and services, and export goods and services. A shirt is a consumption good and a haircut is consumption service. An oil rig is a capital good, police protection is a government service, and a computer chip sold to Ireland is an export good. Of total production in 2009, consumption goods and services were 62 percent; capital goods, 10 percent; government goods and services, 18 percent; and export goods and services, 10 percent.
2. The factors of production are land, labor, capital, and entrepreneurship. Land earns rent; labor earns wages; capital earns interest; and entrepreneurship earns profit or incurs a loss.
3. The functional distribution of income shows the percentage of total income received by each factor of production. The personal distribution of income shows the percentage of total income received by households.
4. Labor is the factor of production that earns the largest share of income in the United States. In 2008, labor earned 65 percent of total income.
5. Most Americans earn their income from labor and the income they earn is called a wage. Peru is a poor country in which jobs are more limited than in the United States. So to earn an income, many people are self-employed and work as small entrepreneurs.

2.2 THE GLOBAL ECONOMY

We're now going to look at *what, how,* and *for whom* goods and services get produced in the global economy. We'll begin with a brief overview of the people and countries that form the global economy.

The People

Visit the Web site of the U.S. Census Bureau and go to the population clocks to find out how many people there are today in both the United States and the entire world.

On the day these words were written, May 14, 2009, the U.S. clock recorded a population of 306,424,038. The world clock recorded a global population of 6,779,717,958. The U.S. clock ticks along showing a population increase of one person every 12 seconds. The world clock spins faster, adding 30 people in the same 12 seconds.

The Countries

The world's 6.8 billion (and rising) population lives in 175 countries, which the International Monetary Fund classifies into two broad groups of economies:

- Advanced economies
- Emerging market and developing economies

Advanced Economies

Advanced economies are the richest 29 countries (or areas). The United States, Japan, Italy, Germany, France, the United Kingdom, and Canada belong to this group. So do four new industrial Asian economies: Hong Kong, South Korea, Singapore, and Taiwan. The other advanced economies include Australia, New Zealand, and most of the rest of Western Europe. Almost 1 billion people (15 percent of the world's population) live in the advanced economies.

Emerging Market and Developing Economies

Emerging market economies are the 28 countries in Central and Eastern Europe and Asia that were, until the early 1990s, part of the Soviet Union or one of its satellites. Russia is the largest of these economies. Others include the Czech Republic, Hungary, Poland, Ukraine, and Mongolia.

Almost 500 million people live in these countries—only about half of the number in the advanced economies. But these countries are important because they are emerging (hence the name) from a system of state-owned production, central economic planning, and heavily regulated markets to a system of free enterprise and unregulated markets.

Developing economies are the 118 countries in Africa, Asia, the Middle East, Europe, and Central and South America that have not yet achieved high average incomes for their people. Average incomes in these economies vary a great deal, but in all cases, these average incomes are much lower than those in the advanced economies, and in some cases, they are extremely low. More than 5 billion people—almost four out of every five people—live in developing economies.

What in the Global Economy?

First, let's look at the big picture. Imagine that each year the global economy produces an enormous pie. In 2009, the pie was worth about $70 trillion! To give this number some meaning, if the pie were shared equally among the world's 6.8 billion people, each of us would get a slice worth a bit more than $10,300.

Where Is the Global Pie Baked?

Figure 2.2 shows us where in the world the pie is baked. The advanced economies produce 56 percent—21 percent in the United States and 35 percent in the other advanced economies. Another 8 percent comes from the emerging market economies. These economies, which produce 64 percent of the world's goods and services (by value) are home to only 21 percent of the world's population.

Most of the rest of the global pie comes from Asia. China produces 11 percent of the total and the rest of the developing Asian economies produce 10 percent. The developing countries of Africa and the Middle East produce 7 percent, and the Western Hemisphere—Mexico and South America—produces the rest.

The sizes of the slices in the global production pie are gradually changing—the U.S. share is shrinking and China's share is expanding.

Unlike the slices of an apple pie, those of the global pie have different fillings. Some slices have more oil, some more food, some more clothing, some more housing services, some more autos, and so on. Let's look at some of these different fillings starting with energy.

FIGURE 2.2

What in the Global Economy in 2008

myeconlab Animation

If we show the value of production in the world economy as a pie, the United States produces a slice that is 21 percent of the total. The other advanced economies produce 35 percent of the total.

Most of the rest of the global pie comes from Asia. China produces a slice that is 11 percent of the total, and the rest of the developing Asian economies produce 10 percent. The developing countries of Africa, the Middle East, and the Western Hemisphere produce 16 percent, and the emerging market economies produce the rest.

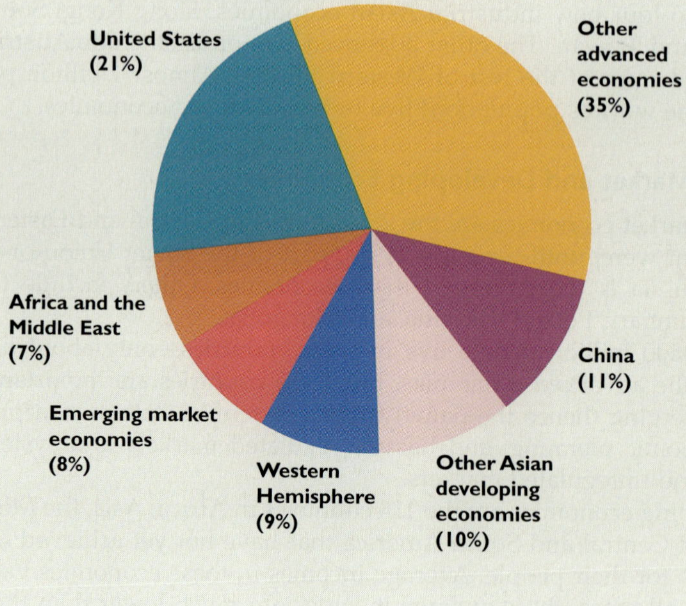

SOURCE OF DATA: International Monetary Fund, World Economic Outlook Database, April 2009.

Energy

Oil, natural gas, and coal resources are distributed unevenly across the globe and Figure 2.3 shows where these energy sources are produced. All of these resources are non-renewable and will eventually run dry. At the current rate of use, proven reserves of the world's oil will last for about 40 years, gas for about 60 years, and coal will last for 200 years. As reserves of oil, natural gas, and coal run low and the cost of accessing them rises, we will make increasing use of wind and solar power. Already, these sources provide 2 percent of the world's electricity and that percentage is growing.

Food

Food production is a small part of the U.S. and other advanced economies and a large part of the developing economies such as Brazil, China, and India. But the advanced economies produce about one third of the world's food. How come? Because *total* production is much larger in the advanced economies than in the developing economies, and a small percentage of a big number can be greater than a large percentage of a small number!

Other Goods and Services

If you were to visit a shopping mall in Canada, England, Australia, Japan, or any of the other advanced economies, you would wonder whether you had left the United States. You would see Starbucks, Burger King, Pizza Hut, Domino's Pizza, KFC, Kmart, Wal-Mart, Target, the United Colors of Benetton, Gap, Tommy

FIGURE 2.3

Energy Sources in the World Economy

myeconlab Animation

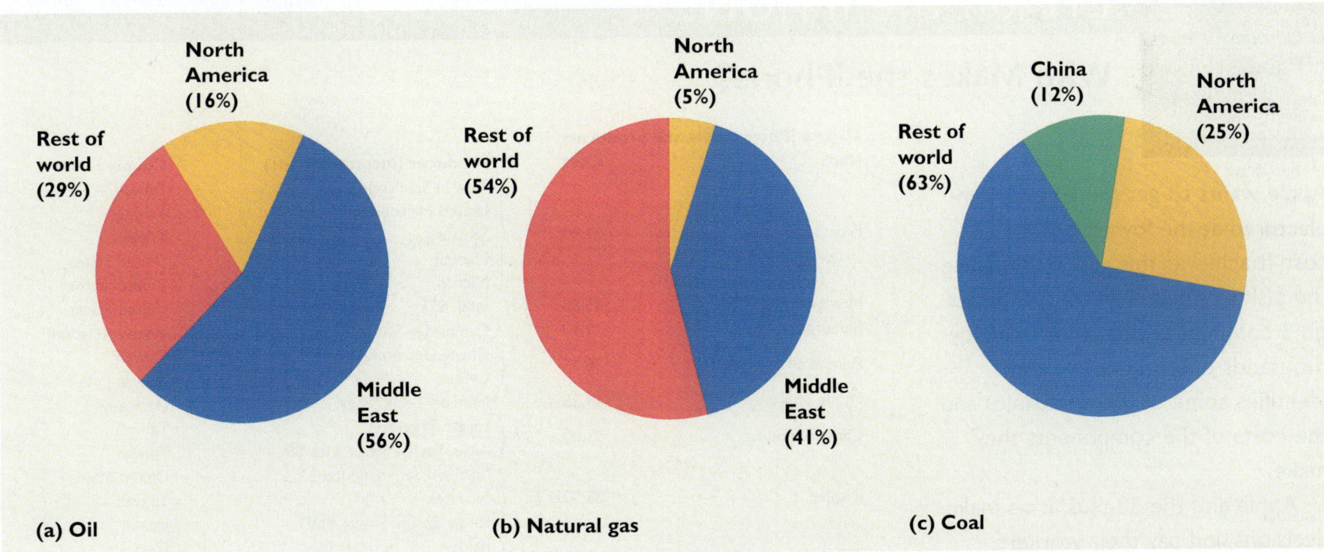

SOURCE OF DATA: Energy Information Administration.

Most of the world's proven oil reserves are in the Middle East (Saudi Arabia, Iraq, and Iran). North America has 16 percent of these reserves. The Middle East also has the largest share of natural gas reserves. North America has only 5 percent of these reserves. Coal is abundant in North America and in China.

McDonald's in Shanghai.

Hilfiger, Tie Rack, the upscale Louis Vuitton and Burberry, and a host of other familiar names. And, of course, you would see McDonald's golden arches. You would see them in any of the 119 countries in which one or more of McDonald's 30,000 restaurants are located.

The similarities among the advanced economies go beyond the view from the shopping mall. The structure of *what* is produced is similar in these economies. As percentages of the total economy, agriculture and manufacturing are a small and shrinking: services are a large and expanding.

What is produced in the developing economies contrasts sharply with that of the advanced economies. Manufacturing is the big story. Developing economies have large and growing industries producing textiles, footwear, sports gear, toys, electronic goods, furniture, steel, and even automobiles.

How in the Global Economy?

Each country or region has its own blend of land, labor, and capital. But there are some interesting common patterns and crucial differences between the advanced and developing economies that we'll now examine.

Human Capital Differences

The proportion of the population with a degree or that has completed high school is small in developing economies. And in the poorest of the developing economies, many children even miss out on basic primary education. They just don't go to school at all. On-the-job training and experience are also much less extensive in the developing economies than in the advanced economies.

EYE on the iPHONE

Who Makes the iPhone?

Apple wants to get the iPhone manufactured at the lowest possible cost. It achieves this goal by assigning the task to more than 30 companies on 3 continents who in turn employ thousands of workers. The table identifies some of the companies and the costs of the components they make.

Apple and the 30-plus firms make decisions and pay their workers, investors, and raw material suppliers to play their parts in influencing *what*, *how*, and *for whom* goods and services are produced.

4Gbyte iPhone costs and producers

Item	Cost	Producer (incomplete list)	Country
Processing chips	31.40	Taiwan Semiconductor	Taiwan
		United Microelectronics Corp	Taiwan
		Samsung	Korea
		Marvell	United States
		Micron	United States
Memory chips	45.80	Intel, SST	United States
Bluetooth	19.10	Cambridge Silicon Radio	United Kingdom
Printed circuit board	36.05	Cheng Uei, Entery	Taiwan
		Cyntec	Taiwan
Phone interface	19.25	Infineon Technology	Germany
Camera module	11.00	Largan Precision	Taiwan
		Altus-Tech, Primax, Lite On	Taiwan
Display	33.50	National Semiconductor	United States
		Novatek	Taiwan
		Sanyo Epson, Sharp, TMD	Japan
Touch screen controller	1.15	Balda	Germany
		Broadcom	United States
Battery and power management	8.60	Delta Electronics	Taiwan
Case	8.50	Catcher, Foxconn Tech	Taiwan
Assembly	15.50	Foxconn? Quanta?	Taiwan
Royalties	15.98		
Total cost	**245.83**		

Physical Capital Differences

The major feature of an advanced economy that differentiates it from a developing economy is the amount of capital available for producing goods and services. The differences begin with the basic transportation system. In the advanced economies, a well-developed highway system connects all the major cities and points of production. You can see this difference most vividly by opening a road atlas of North America and contrasting the U.S. interstate highway system with the sparse highways of Mexico. You would see a similar contrast if you flipped through a road atlas of Western Europe and Africa.

But it isn't the case that the developing economies have no highways. In fact, some of them have the newest and the best. But the new and best are usually inside and around the major cities. The smaller centers and rural areas of developing economies often have some of the worst roads in the world.

The contrast in vehicles is perhaps even greater than that in highways. You're unlikely to run across a horse-drawn wagon in an advanced economy, but in a developing economy, animal power can still be found, and trucks are often old and unreliable.

The contrasts in the transportation system are matched by those on farms and in factories. In general, the more advanced the economy, the greater are the amount and sophistication of the capital equipment used in production. But again, the contrast is not all black and white. Some factories in India, China, and other parts of Asia use the very latest technologies. Furniture manufacture is an example. To make furniture of a quality that Americans are willing to buy, firms in Asia use machines like those in the furniture factories of North Carolina.

Again, it is the extensiveness of the use of modern capital-intensive technologies that distinguishes a developing economy from an advanced economy. All the factories in the advanced economies are capital intensive compared with only some in the developing economies.

The differences in human and physical capital between advanced and developing economies have a big effect on who gets the goods and services.

Beijing has a highway system to match that of any advanced country. But away from the major cities, many of China's roads are unpaved and driving on them is slow and sometimes hazardous.

For Whom in the Global Economy?

Who gets the world's goods and services depends on the incomes that people earn. So how are incomes distributed across the world?

Personal Distribution of Income

You saw earlier (on p. 39) that in the United States, the lowest-paid 20 percent of the population receives 3 percent of total income and the highest-paid 20 percent receives 51 percent of total income. The personal distribution of income in the world economy is much more unequal. According to World Bank data, the lowest-paid 20 percent of the world's population receives 2 percent of world income, and the highest-paid 20 percent receives about 70 percent of world income.

International Distribution

Much of the greater inequality at the global level arises from differences in average incomes among countries. Figure 2.4 shows some of these differences. It shows the dollar value of what people can afford each day on average. You can see that in the United States, that number is $128 a day—an average person in the United States can buy goods and services that cost $128. This amount is around five times the world average. Canada and the United Kingdom have average incomes of around 80 percent of that of the United States. Japan, Germany, France, Italy, and the other advanced economies have average incomes around 75 percent of U.S. average income. Income levels fall off quickly as we move farther down the graph, with Africa achieving an average income of only $7 a day.

As people have lost well-paid manufacturing jobs and found lower-paid service jobs, inequality has increased in the United States and in most other advanced economies. Inequality is also increasing in the developing economies. People with skills enjoy rapidly rising incomes but the incomes of the unskilled are falling.

A Happy Paradox and a Huge Challenge

Despite the increase in inequality inside most countries, inequality across the entire world has decreased during the past 20 years. And most important, according to Xavier Sala-i-Martin, an economics professor at Columbia University, extreme poverty has declined. Professor Sala-i-Martin estimates that between 1976 and 1998, the number of people who earn $1 a day or less fell by 235 million and the number who earn $2 a day or less fell by 450 million. This happy situation arises because in China, the largest nation, incomes have increased rapidly and lifted millions from extreme poverty.

Lifting Africa from poverty is today's big challenge. In 1960, 11 percent of the world's poor lived in Africa, but in 1998, 66 percent did. Between 1976 and 1998, the number of people in Africa who earn $1 a day or less rose by 175 million, and the number who earn $2 a day or less rose by 227 million.

FIGURE 2.4

For Whom in the Global Economy in 2008

myeconlab Animation

In 2008, the average income per day in the United States was $128. It was $107 in Canada and $100 in the United Kingdom. It was $93 in both Japan and the Euro area. The number falls off rapidly to $44 in Russia, $16 in China, $8 in India, and $7 in Africa.

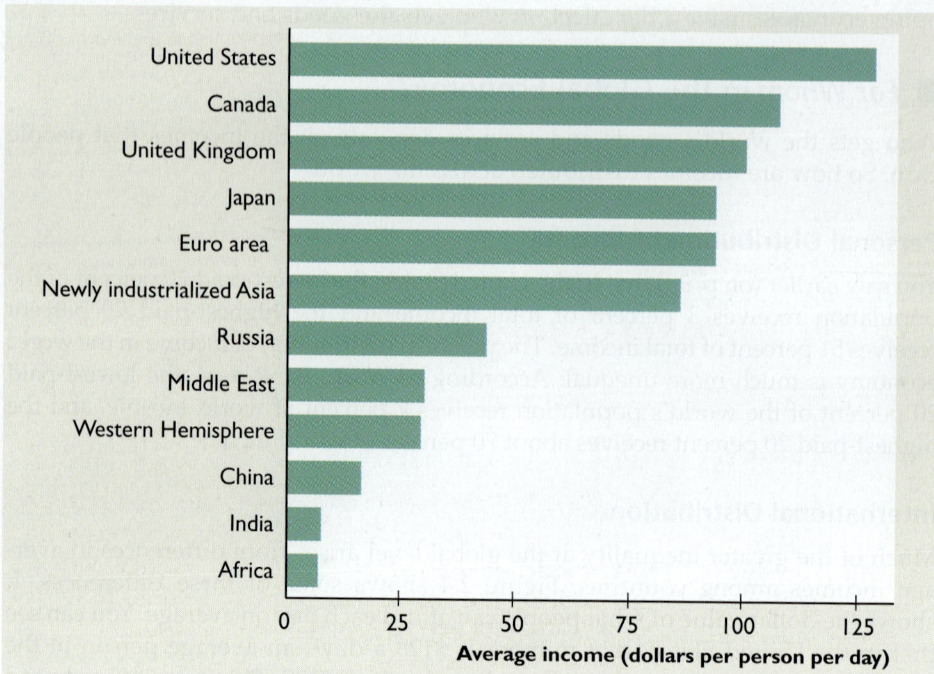

SOURCE OF DATA: International Monetary Fund, World Economic Outlook Database, April 2009.

EYE on YOUR LIFE

The U.S. and Global Economies in Your Life

You've encountered a lot of facts and trends about what, how, and for whom goods and services are produced in the U.S. economy and the global economy. How can you use this information? You can use it in two ways:

1. To inform your choice of career
2. To inform your stand on the politics of protecting U.S. jobs

Career Choices

As you think about your future career, you are now better informed about some of the key trends. You know that manufacturing is shrinking. The U.S. economy is what is sometimes called a *post-industrial economy*. Industries that provided the backbone of the economy in previous generations have fallen to barely a fifth of the economy today, and the trend continues. It is possible that by the middle of the current century, manufacturing will be as small a source of jobs as agriculture is today.

So, a job in a manufacturing business is likely to lead to some tough situations and possibly the need for several job changes over a working life.

As manufacturing shrinks, so services expand, and this expansion will continue. The provision of health care, education, communication, wholesale and retail trades, and entertainment are all likely to expand in the future and be sources of increasing employment and rising wages. A job in a service-oriented business is more likely to lead to steady advances in income.

Political Stand on Job Protection

As you think about the stand you will take on the political question of protecting U.S. jobs, you are better informed about the basic facts and trends.

When you hear that manufacturing jobs are disappearing to China, you will be able to place that news in historical perspective. You might reasonably be concerned, especially if you or a member of your family has lost a job. But you know that trying to reverse or even halt this process is flying in the face of stubborn historical trends.

In later chapters, you will learn that there are good economic reasons to be skeptical about any form of protection and placing limits on competition.

CHECKPOINT 2.2

Describe what, how, and for whom goods and services are produced in the global economy.

myeconlab

Work these problems in Study Plan 2.2 to get instant feedback.

Practice Problems

1. Describe what, how, and for whom goods and services are produced in developing economies.
2. **Success story: Rwandan coffee farmers**
   The Clinton Foundation loaned $23,000 to Misozi to support improvements to coffee washing stations and provided technical support.

   Source: The Clinton Foundation

   What was the source of the success?

Guided Solutions to Practice Problems

1. In developing countries, agriculture is the largest percentage, manufacturing is an increasing percentage, and services are important but a small percentage of total production. Most production does not use modern capital-intensive technologies, but some industries do. People who work in factories have rising income while those who work in rural industries are left behind.
2. Misozi growers improved their knowledge of coffee farming and increased their human capital and improved the operation of their washing stations.

2.3 THE CIRCULAR FLOWS

Circular flow model
A model of the economy that shows the circular flow of expenditures and incomes that result from decision makers' choices and the way those choices interact to determine what, how, and for whom goods and services are produced.

We can organize the data you've just studied using the **circular flow model**—a model of the economy that shows the circular flow of expenditures and incomes that result from decision makers' choices and the way those choices interact to determine what, how, and for whom goods and services are produced. Figure 2.5 shows the circular flow model.

Households and Firms

Households
Individuals or groups of people living together.

Firms
The institutions that organize the production of goods and services.

Households are individuals or groups of people living together. The 112 million households in the United States own the factors of production—land, labor, capital, and entrepreneurship—and choose the quantities of these resources to provide to firms. Households also choose the quantities of goods and services to buy.

Firms are the institutions that organize the production of goods and services. The 20 million firms in the United States choose the quantities of the factors of production to hire and the quantities of goods and services to produce.

Markets

Households choose the quantities of the factors of production to provide to firms, and firms choose the quantities of the services of the factors of production to hire. Firms choose the quantities of goods and services to produce, and households choose the quantities of goods and services to buy. How are these choices coordinated and made compatible? The answer is: by markets.

Market
Any arrangement that brings buyers and sellers together and enables them to get information and do business with each other.

A **market** is any arrangement that brings buyers and sellers together and enables them to get information and do business with each other. An example is the market in which oil is bought and sold—the world oil market. The world oil market is not a place. It is the network of oil producers, oil users, wholesalers, and brokers who buy and sell oil. In the world oil market, decision makers do not meet physically. They make deals by telephone, fax, and the Internet.

Goods markets
Markets in which goods and services are bought and sold.

Factor markets
Markets in which the services of factors of production are bought and sold.

Figure 2.5 identifies two types of markets: goods markets and factor markets. Goods and services are bought and sold in **goods markets**; and the services of factors of production are bought and sold in **factor markets**.

Real Flows and Money Flows

When households choose the quantities of services of land, labor, capital, and entrepreneurship to offer in factor markets, they respond to the incomes they receive—rent for land, wages for labor, interest for capital, and profit for entrepreneurship. When firms choose the quantities of factor services to hire, they respond to the rent, wages, interest, and profits they must pay to households.

Similarly, when firms choose the quantities of goods and services to produce and offer for sale in goods markets, they respond to the amounts that they receive from the expenditures that households make. And when households choose the quantities of goods and services to buy, they respond to the amounts they must pay to firms.

Figure 2.5 shows the flows that result from these choices made by households and firms. The flows shown in orange are *real flows:* the flows of the factors of production that go from households through factor markets to firms and of the goods and services that go from firms through goods markets to households. The flows in the opposite direction are *money flows:* the flows of payments made in exchange for the services of factors of production (shown in blue) and of expenditures on goods and services (shown in red).

Lying behind these real flows and money flows are millions of individual choices about what to consume and what and how to produce. These choices result in buying plans by households and selling plans by firms in goods markets. And the choices result in selling plans by households and buying plans by firms in factor markets that interact to determine the prices that people pay and the incomes they earn, and so determine for whom goods and services are produced. You'll learn in Chapter 4 how markets coordinate the buying plans and selling plans of households and firms and make them compatible.

Firms produce most of the goods and services that we consume, but governments provide some of the services that we enjoy. Governments also play a big role in modifying for whom goods and services are produced by changing the personal distribution of income. We're now going to look at the role of governments in the U.S. economy and add them to the circular flow model.

FIGURE 2.5

The Circular Flow Model

myeconlab Animation

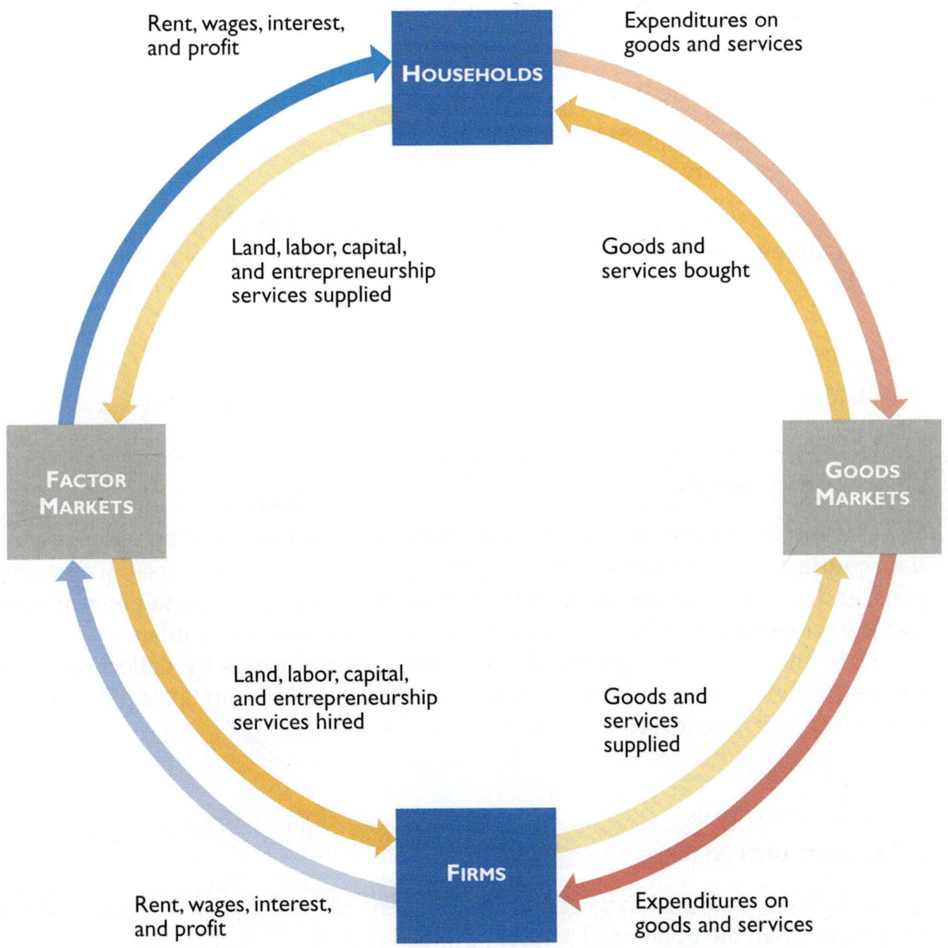

The orange flows are the services of factors of production that go from households through factor markets to firms and the goods and services that go from firms through goods markets to households. These flows are *real* flows.

The blue flow is the income earned by the factors of production, and the red flow is the expenditures on goods and services. These flows are *money* flows.

The choices that generate these real and money flows determine *what, how,* and *for whom* goods and services are produced.

Governments

More than 86,000 organizations operate as governments in the United States. Some are tiny like the Yuma, Arizona, school district and some are enormous like the U.S. federal government. We divide governments into two levels:

- Federal government
- State and local government

Federal Government

The federal government's major expenditures provide

1. Goods and services
2. Social Security and welfare payments
3. Transfers to state and local governments

The goods and services provided by the federal government include the legal system, which protects property and enforces contracts, and national defense. Social Security and welfare benefits, which include income for retired people and programs such as Medicare and Medicaid, are transfers from the federal government to households. Federal government transfers to state and local governments are payments designed to provide more equality across the states and regions.

The federal government finances its expenditures by collecting a variety of taxes. The main taxes paid to the federal government are

1. Personal income taxes
2. Corporate (business) income taxes
3. Social Security taxes

In 2008, the federal government spent $3 trillion—about 21 percent of the total value of all the goods and services produced in the United States in that year. The taxes they raised was less than this amount—the government had a deficit.

State and Local Government

The state and local governments' major expenditures are to provide

1. Goods and services
2. Welfare benefits

The goods and services provided by state and local governments include the state courts and police, schools, roads, garbage collection and disposal, water supplies, and sewage management. Welfare benefits provided by state governments include unemployment benefits and other aid to low-income families.

State and local governments finance these expenditures by collecting taxes and receiving transfers from the federal government. The main taxes paid to state and local governments are

1. Sales taxes
2. Property taxes
3. State income taxes

In 2005-06, state and local governments spent $2.1 trillion or 16 percent of the total value of all the goods and services produced in the United States.

Governments in the Circular Flow

Figure 2.6 adds governments to the circular flow model. As you study this figure, first notice that the outer circle is the same as in Figure 2.5. In addition to these flows, governments buy goods and services from firms. The red arrows that run from governments through the goods markets to firms show this expenditure.

Households and firms pay taxes to governments. The green arrows running directly from households and firms to governments show these flows. Also, governments make money payments to households and firms. The green arrows running directly from governments to households and firms show these flows. Taxes and transfers are direct transactions with governments and do not go through the goods markets and factor markets.

Not part of the circular flow and not visible in Figure 2.6, governments provide the legal framework within which all transactions occur. For example, governments operate the courts and legal system that enable contracts to be written and enforced.

FIGURE 2.6

Governments in the Circular Flow

myeconlab Animation

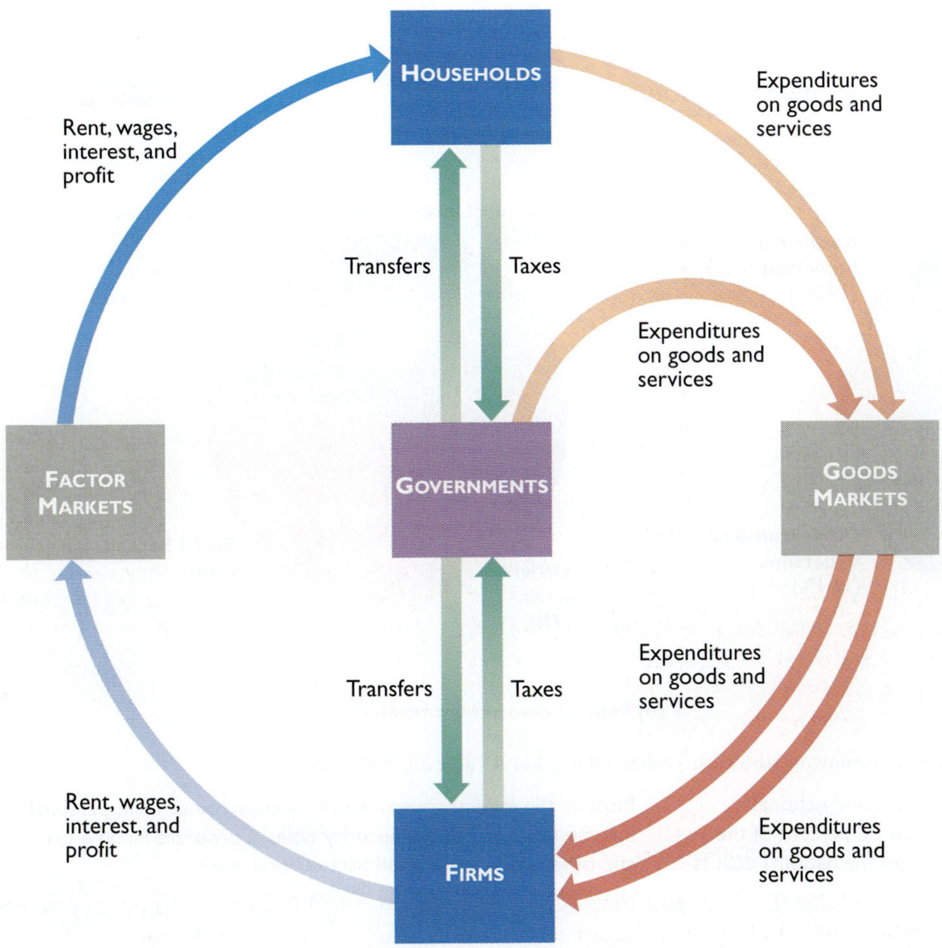

The green flows from households and firms to governments are taxes, and the green flows from governments to households and firms are money transfers.

The red flow from governments through goods markets to firms is the expenditures on goods and services by governments.

Federal Government Expenditures and Revenue

What are the main items of expenditure by the federal government on goods and services and transfers? And what are its main sources of tax revenue? Figure 2.7 answers these questions.

Three items of expenditure are similar in magnitude—and large. They are Social Security benefits, Medicare and Medicaid, and national defense and homeland security. The combined total of these items is 60 percent of the government's expenditures. Other transfers to persons, which includes unemployment benefits, are also large. The "Others" category covers a wide range of items and includes transfers to state governments, NASA's space program, and the National Science Foundation's funding of research in the universities.

National debt
The total amount that the federal government has borrowed to make expenditures that exceed tax revenue—to run a government budget deficit.

The interest payment on the national debt is another significant item. The **national debt** is the total amount that the federal government has borrowed to make expenditures that exceed tax revenue—to run a government budget deficit. The national debt is a bit like a large credit card balance, and paying the interest on the national debt is like paying the minimum required monthly payment.

Most of the tax revenue of the federal government comes from personal income taxes and Social Security taxes. Corporate income taxes and other taxes are a small part of the federal government's revenue.

FIGURE 2.7
Federal Government Expenditures and Revenue

myeconlab Animation

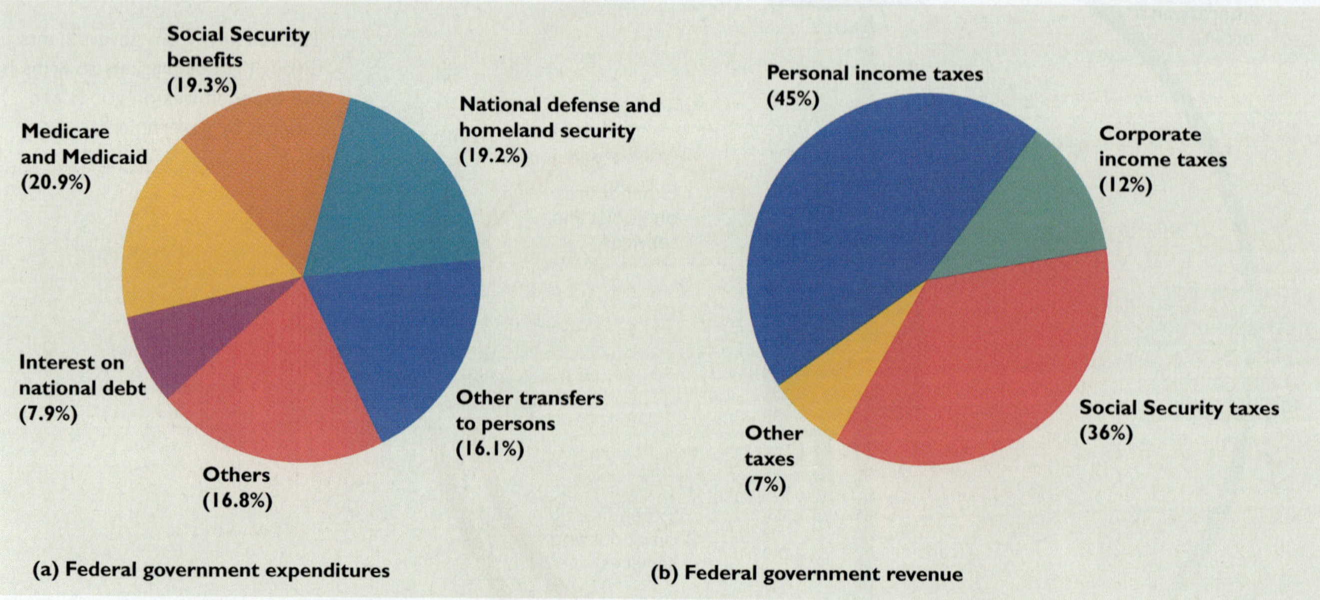

SOURCE OF DATA: Budget of the United States Government, Historical Tables, Table 2.1 and Table 3.1, 2008 data.

Social Security benefits, Medicare and Medicaid, and national defense and homeland security absorb almost 60 percent of the federal government's expenditures. Interest on the national debt is also a significant item.

Most of the federal government's revenue comes from personal income taxes and Social Security taxes. Corporate income taxes and other taxes are a small part of total revenue.

State and Local Government Expenditures and Revenue

What are the main items of expenditure by the state and local governments on goods and services and transfers? And what are the main sources of state and local government revenue? Figure 2.8 answers these questions.

You can see that education is by far the largest part of the expenditures of state and local governments. This item covers the cost of public schools, colleges, and universities. It absorbs 34 percent of total expenditures—approximately $730 billion, or $2,400 per person.

Public welfare benefits are the second largest item and they take 18 percent of total expenditures. Highways are the next largest item, and they account for 6 percent of total expenditures. The remaining 42 percent is spent on other local public goods and services such as police services, garbage collection and disposal, sewage management, and water supplies.

Sales taxes and transfers from the federal government bring in similar amounts—about 19 percent and 21 percent of total revenue, respectively. Property taxes account for 16 percent of total revenue. Individual income taxes account for 12 percent, and corporate income taxes account for 2 percent. The remaining revenue comes from other taxes such as those on gasoline, cigarettes, and beer and wine.

FIGURE 2.8

State and Local Government Expenditures and Revenue

myeconlab Animation

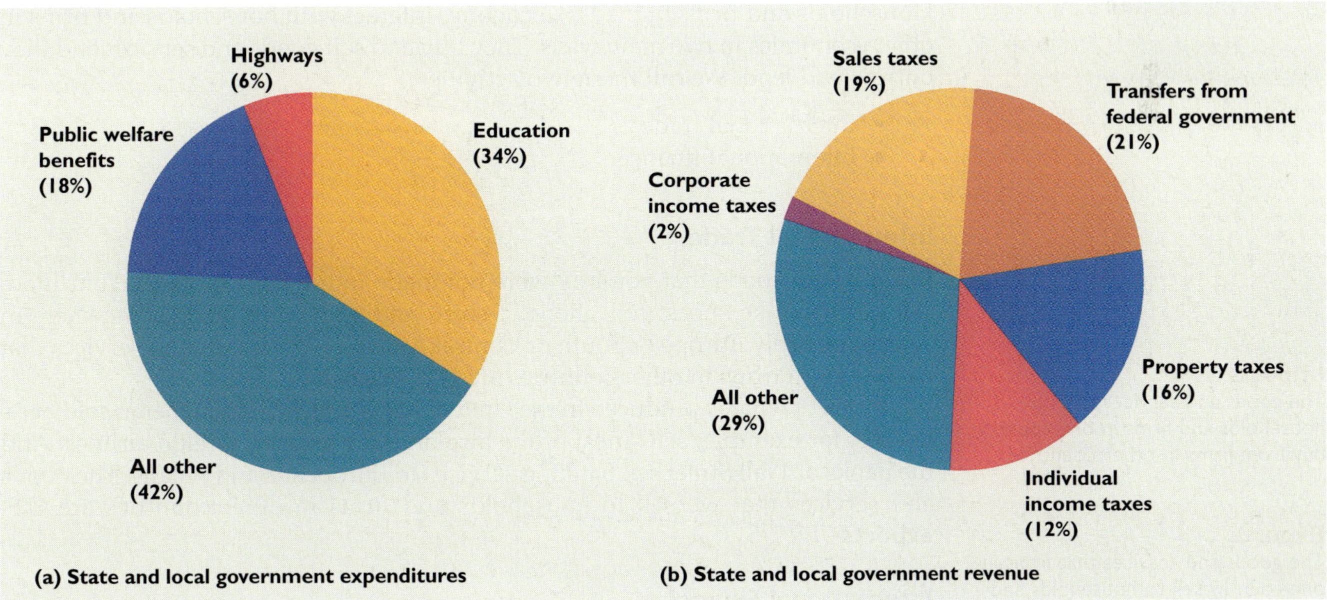

SOURCES OF DATA: *Economic Report of the President 2009*, Table B-86, 2005–2006 data..

Education, public welfare benefits, and highways are the largest slices of state and local government expenditures.

Most of the state and local government revenue comes from sales taxes, property taxes, and transfers from the federal government.

EYE on the PAST

Growing Government

One hundred years ago, the federal government spent 2 cents out of each dollar earned. Today, the federal government spends 20 cents. Government grew during the two world wars and during the 1960s and 1970s as social programs expanded.

Only during the 1980s and 1990s did big government begin to shrink in a process begun by Ronald Reagan and continued by Bill Clinton. But 9/11 saw the start of a new era of growing government.

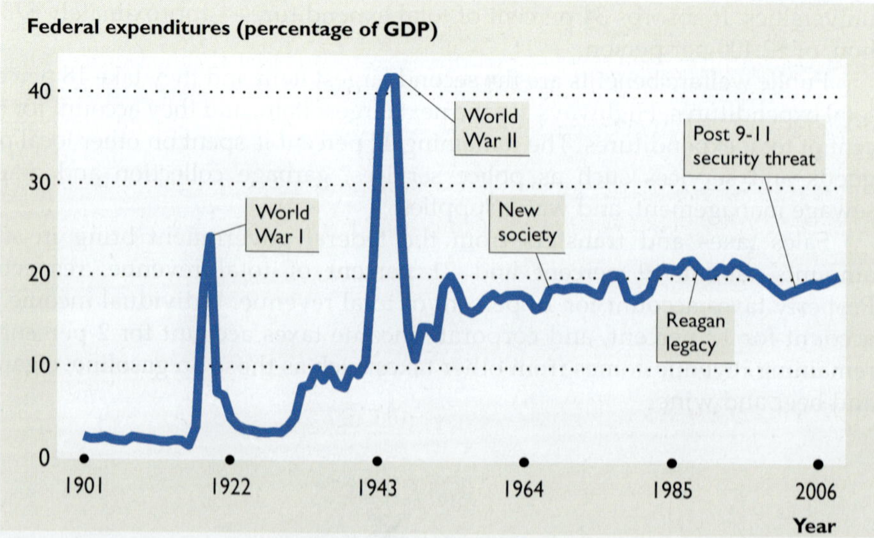

SOURCE OF DATA: Budget of the United States Government, Historical Tables, Table 1.1.

Circular Flows in the Global Economy

Households and firms in the U.S. economy interact with households and firms in other economies in two main ways: They buy and sell goods and services and they borrow and lend. We call these two activities:

- International trade
- International finance

International Trade

Many of the goods that you buy were not made in the United States. Your iPod, Wii games, Nike shoes, cell phone, T-shirt, and bike were made somewhere in Asia or possibly Europe or South or Central America. The goods and services that we buy from firms in other countries are U.S. **imports**.

Imports
The goods and services that households and firms in one country buy from firms in other countries.

Much of what is produced in the United States doesn't end up being sold here. Boeing, for example, sells most of the airplanes it makes to foreign airlines. And the banks of Wall Street sell banking services to Europeans and Asians. The goods and services that we sell to households and firms in other countries are U.S. **exports**.

Exports
The goods and services that firms in one country sell to households and firms in other countries.

International Finance

When firms or governments want to borrow, they look for the lowest interest rate available. Sometimes, that is outside the United States. Also, when the value of our imports exceeds the value of our exports, we must borrow from the rest of the world.

Firms and governments in the rest of the world behave in the same way. They look for the lowest interest rate at which to borrow and the highest at which to lend. They might borrow from or lend to Americans.

Figure 2.9 shows the flows through goods markets and financial markets in the global economy. Households and firms in the U.S. economy interact with those in the rest of the world (other economies) in goods markets and financial markets.

The red flow shows the expenditure by Americans on imports of goods and services, and the blue flow shows the expenditure by the rest of the world on U.S. exports (other countries' imports). The green flow shows U.S. lending to the rest of the world, and the orange flow shows U.S. borrowing from the rest of the world.

It is these international trade and international finance flows that tie nations together in the global economy and through which global booms and slumps are transmitted.

FIGURE 2.9

Circular Flows in the Global Economy

myeconlab Animation

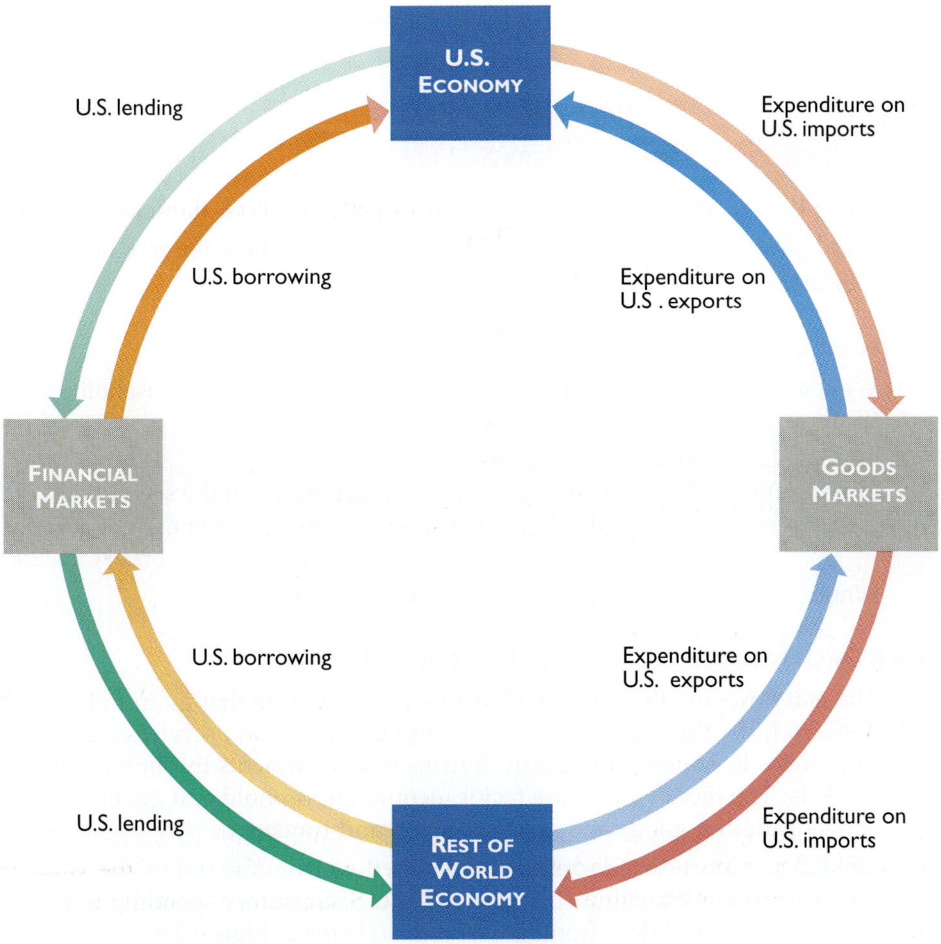

Households and firms in the U.S. economy interact with those in the rest of the world (other economies) in goods markets and financial markets.

The red flow shows the expenditure by Americans on imports of goods and services, and the blue flow show the expenditure by the rest of the world on U.S. exports (other countries' imports).

The green flow shows U.S. lending to the rest of the world, and the orange flow shows U.S. borrowing from the rest of the world.

EYE on the GLOBAL ECONOMY

The 2009 Slump in International Trade

International trade has expanded rapidly during the past 25 years. At an average growth rate of close to 7 percent a year, world trade has doubled every decade.

In 2001, a mini-recession in the United States slowed world trade growth to a crawl.

But the 2001 slowdown looks mild compared to the collapse in world trade during the 2009 global economic slump. The International Monetary Fund projects world trade shrinking in 2009 by 11 percent and zero growth in 2010.

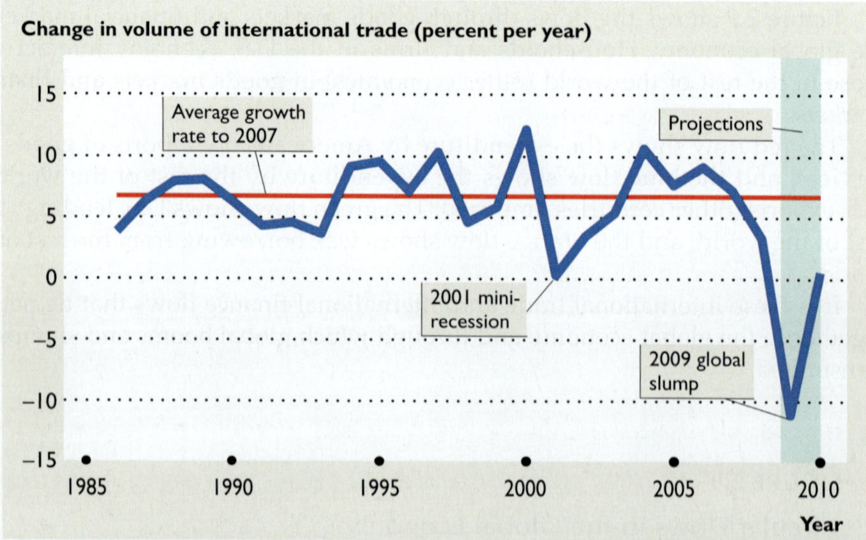

SOURCE OF DATA: International Monetary Fund, World Economic Outlook Database, April 2009.

myeconlab

Work these problems in Study Plan 2.3 to get instant feedback.

CHECKPOINT 2.3

Use the circular flow model to provide a picture of how households, firms, and governments interact in the U.S. economy and how the U.S. and other economies interact in the global economy.

Practice Problems

1. What are the real flows and money flows that run between households, firms, and governments in the circular flow model?
2. **Global slump crimps U.S. exports**

   The Commerce Department reports that export orders in the second half of 2008 fell by almost $35 billion while U.S. consumers slashed their spending.

   Source: *USA Today*, February 11, 2009

   Where, in the circular flow model, do these choices appear?

Guided Solutions to Practice Problems

1. The real flows are the services of factors of production that go from households to firms through factor markets and the goods and services that go from firms to households and from firms to governments through goods markets. The money flows are factor incomes, household and government expenditures on goods and services, taxes, and transfers.
2. The fall in exports is a decrease in the blue flow from the rest of the world to the U.S. economy in Figure 2.9. The cut in U.S. consumer spending is a decrease in the red flow from households to firms in Figure 2.6.

CHAPTER SUMMARY

Key Points

1 Describe what, how, and for whom goods and services are produced in the United States.

- Consumption goods and services represent 62 percent of total production; capital goods represent 10 percent.
- Goods and services are produced by using the four factors of production: land, labor, capital, and entrepreneurship.
- The incomes people earn (rent for land, wages for labor, interest for capital, and profit for entrepreneurship) determine who gets the goods and services produced.

2 Describe what, how, and for whom goods and services are produced in the global economy.

- Sixty-four percent of the world's production (by value) comes from the advanced industrial countries and the emerging market economies.
- Production in the advanced economies uses more capital (both machines and human), but some developing economies use the latest capital and technologies.
- The global distribution of income is more unequal than the U.S. distribution. Poverty has fallen in Asia but has increased in Africa.

3 Use the circular flow model to provide a picture of how households, firms, and governments interact in the U.S. economy and how the U.S. and other economies interact in the global economy.

- The circular flow model of the U.S. economy shows the real flows of factors of production and goods and the corresponding money flows of incomes and expenditures.
- Governments in the circular flow receive taxes, make transfers, and buy goods and services.
- The circular flow model of the global economy shows the flows of U.S. exports and imports and the international financial flows that result from lending to and borrowing from other countries.

Key Terms

myeconlab

Work these problems in Chapter 2 Study Plan to get instant feedback.

CHAPTER CHECKPOINT

Study Plan Problems and Applications

1. Explain which of the following items are not consumption goods and services:
   - A chocolate bar
   - A ski lift
   - A golf ball
2. Explain which of the following items are *not* capital goods:
   - An auto assembly line
   - A shopping mall
   - A golf ball
3. Explain which of the following items are *not* factors of production:
   - Vans used by a baker to deliver bread
   - 1,000 shares of Amazon.com stock
   - Undiscovered oil

Use the following information to work Problems 4 to 6.

Why is income inequality in America so pronounced? Consider education

Outsourcing, immigration, and the gains of the super-rich are the most common reasons for the income inequality in America. Tyler Cowen disagrees: The problem is largely the lack of education. To date, outsourcing is not yet common enough to have much effect. Immigration doesn't account for much of the change in the wages paid to unskilled workers since 1950. Advances in technology raises the incomes of highly skilled workers. Inequality will be reduced if more people undertake education.

Source: *The New York Times*, May 17, 2007

4. If outsourcing were to have a big effect on the personal distribution of income in Figure 2.1, how would the distribution have changed?
5. Immigrants to the United States include unskilled workers from Mexico and skilled workers from countries such as India and China. How would each of these types of immigrants influence the personal distribution of income?
6. Explain how more people undertaking education will change the personal distribution of income in the United States.
7. A Job Creation through Entrepreneurship Act, debated in the House of Representatives in 2009, would award grants to small business owners, some of which would be aimed at women, Native Americans, and veterans. The Act would provide $189 million in 2010 and $531 million between 2010 and 2014. Explain how you would expect this Act to influence *what*, *how*, and *for whom* goods and services are produced in the United States.
8. Indicate on a graph of the circular flow model, the real or money flow in which the following items belong:
   - You pay your tuition.
   - The University of Texas buys some Dell computers.
   - A student works at FedEx Kinko's.
   - Donald Trump rents a Manhattan building to a hotel.
   - You pay your income tax.

Instructor Assignable Problems and Applications

Your instructor can assign these problems as homework, a quiz, or a test in **MyEconLab**.

1. Buzz surrounds Apple's iPhone. Can you explain:
   - Why doesn't Apple manufacture the iPhone at its own factory in the United States?
   - Why doesn't Apple offer a cheaper version of the iPhone without a camera?
   - In view of the cost of producing an iPhone (in the table on p. 44), why do you think the price of an iPhone is so high? What other costs must be incurred to bring the iPhone to market other than the cost of manufacturing it?
2. Explain which of the following items are *not* consumption goods and services:
   - An interstate highway
   - An airplane
   - A stealth bomber
3. Explain which of the following items are *not* capital goods:
   - An interstate highway
   - An oil tanker
   - A construction worker
4. Explain which of the following items are *not* factors of production:
   - A garbage truck
   - A pack of bubble gum
   - The President of the United States
5. Explain which of the following pairs does not match:
   - Labor and wages
   - Land and rent
   - Entrepreneurship and profit
   - Capital and profit
6. Compare the scale of agricultural production in the advanced and developing economies. In which is the percentage higher? In which is the total amount produced greater?
7. Think about the trends in what and how goods and services are produced in the U.S. and global economies. Which jobs will grow fastest in the future? What will happen to the quality of labor over the next decade?
8. **China's prosperity brings income gap**

   A study by the Asian Development Bank [ADB] reports that China has the largest gap between the rich and the poor in Asia. Ifzal Ali, the ADB's chief economist, claims it is not so much that the rich are getting richer and the poor are getting poorer, but that the rich are getting richer faster than the poor.

   Source: *Financial Times*, August 9, 2007

   Explain how the personal income distribution in China can be getting more unequal even though the poorest 20 percent are getting richer.
9. In the African nation of Senegal, to enroll in school a child needs a Birth Certificate that costs $25. This price is several week's income for many families. Explain how this requirement is likely to affect the growth of human

capital in Senegal. Predict the effects of this requirement on the human capital of girls and women and explain your prediction.

10. On a graph of the circular flow model, indicate in which real or money flow the following items belong:
    - General Motors pays its workers wages.
    - IBM pays a dividend to its stockholders.
    - You buy your groceries.
    - Chrysler buys robots.
    - Southwest rents some aircraft.
    - Nike pays Tiger Woods for promoting its golf ball.

Use the following information to work Problems 11 and 12.

Poor India makes millionaires at fastest pace

India, with the world's largest population of poor people living on less than a dollar a day, also paradoxically created millionaires at the fastest pace in the world in 2007. Millionaires increased by 22.7 per cent to 123,000 (measured in dollars). In contrast, the number of Indians living on less than a dollar a day is 350 million and those living on less than $2 a day is 700 million. In other words, there are 7,000 very poor Indians for every millionaire.

Source: *The Times of India*, June 25, 2008

11. How do you think the personal distribution of income in India is changing as the number of millionaires is growing at a "blistering pace"?
12. Why might incomes of a $1 a day and $2 a day underestimate the value of the goods and services that these households actually consume?

Use the following information to work Problems 13 to 15.

According to the International Telecommunications Union the global economy has three cell phone users for every fixed line user. Two in every three cell phone users lives in a developing nation and Africa has the fastest growth rate in cell phone users. In 2000, 1 African in 50 had a cell phone. In 2008, that number was 14 in 50.

13. Describe the changes in *what* telecommunication services the global economy produces.
14. Describe the changes in *how* telecommunication services are produced in the global economy.
15. Describe the changes in *for whom* telecommunication services are produced in the global economy.
16. The entire Arctic region is believed to be rich in oil and gas reserves and the cost of extracting these resources keeps falling. On August 5, 2007, a Russian submarine visited the seabed 2.5 miles beneath the North Pole and planted its nation's flag. Canada, the United States, Russia, Norway, Iceland, and Denmark all claim to "own" seabed in the Arctic Circle. Describe the changes in *what*, *how*, and *for whom* arctic oil and gas might be extracted in the future.

Is wind power free?

South Dakota has enough wind to generate 55 percent of the nation's electricity. But what would be the cost—the opportunity cost—of that electricity?

3

The Economic Problem

CHAPTER CHECKLIST

When you have completed your study of this chapter, you will be able to

1. Explain and illustrate the concepts of scarcity, production efficiency, and tradeoff using the production possibilities frontier.
2. Calculate opportunity cost.
3. Explain what makes production possibilities expand.
4. Explain how people gain from specialization and trade.

3.1 PRODUCTION POSSIBILITIES

Every working day in mines, factories, shops, and offices and on farms and construction sites across the United States, we produce a vast array of goods and services. In the United States in 2009, 240 billion hours of labor equipped with $47 trillion worth of capital produced $14 trillion worth of goods and services.

Although our production capability is enormous, it is limited by our available resources and by technology. At any given time, we have fixed quantities of the factors of production and a fixed state of technology. Because our wants exceed our resources, we must make choices. We must rank our wants and decide which to satisfy and which to leave unsatisfied. In using our scarce resources, we make rational choices. And to make a rational choice, we must determine the costs and benefits of the alternatives.

Your first task in this chapter is to learn about an economic model of scarcity, choice, and opportunity cost—a model called the production possibilities frontier.

Production Possibilities Frontier

Production possibilities frontier
The boundary between the combinations of goods and services that can be produced and the combinations that cannot be produced, given the available factors of production and the state of technology.

The **production possibilities frontier** is the boundary between the combinations of goods and services that can be produced and the combinations that cannot be produced, given the available factors of production—land, labor, capital, and entrepreneurship—and the state of technology.

Although we produce millions of different goods and services, we can visualize the limits to production most easily if we imagine a simpler world that produces just two goods. Imagine an economy that produces only DVDs and cell phones. All the land, labor, capital, and entrepreneurship available gets used to produce these two goods.

Land can be used for movie studios and DVD factories or cell-phone factories. Labor can be trained to work as movie actors, camera and sound crews, movie producers and DVD makers or as cell-phone makers. Capital can be used for making movies, making and coating disks, and transferring images to disks, or for the equipment that makes cell phones. Entrepreneurs can put their creative talents to managing movie studios and running electronics businesses that make DVDs or to running cell-phone businesses. In every case, the more resources that are used to produce DVDs, the fewer are left to produce cell phones.

Suppose that if no factors of production are allocated to producing cell phones, the maximum number of DVDs that can be produced is 15 million a year. So one production possibility is no cell phones and 15 million DVDs. Another possibility is to allocate sufficient resources to produce 1 million cell phones a year. But these resources must be taken from DVD factories. Suppose that the economy can now produce only 14 million DVDs a year. As resources are moved from producing DVDs to producing cell phones, the economy produces more cell phones but fewer DVDs.

The table in Figure 3.1 illustrates these two combinations of cell phones and DVDs as possibilities *A* and *B*. Suppose that *C*, *D*, *E*, and *F* are other combinations of the quantities of these two goods that the economy can produce. Possibility *F* uses all the resources to produce 5 million cell phones a year and allocates no resources to producing DVDs. These six possibilities are alternative combinations of the quantities of the two goods that the economy can produce by using all of its resources, given the technology.

The graph in Figure 3.1 illustrates the production possibilities frontier, *PPF*, for cell phones and DVDs. It is a graph of the production possibilities in the table. The *x*-axis shows the production of cell phones, and the *y*-axis shows the production of DVDs. Each point on the graph labeled *A* through *F* represents the possibility in the table identified by the same letter. For example, point *B* represents the production of 1 million cell phones and 14 million DVDs. These quantities also appear in the table as possibility *B*.

The *PPF* is a valuable tool for illustrating the effects of scarcity and its consequences. The *PPF* puts three features of production possibilities in sharp focus. They are the distinctions between

- Attainable and unattainable combinations
- Efficient and inefficient production
- Tradeoffs and free lunches

FIGURE 3.1

The Production Possibilities Frontier

myeconlab Animation

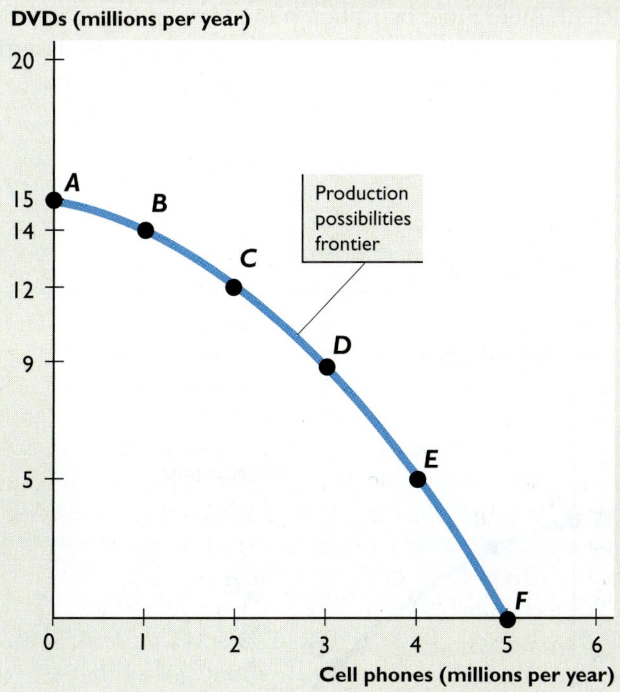

Cell phones (millions)	0	1	2	3	4	5
DVDs (millions)	15	14	12	9	5	0
Possibility	*A*	*B*	*C*	*D*	*E*	*F*

The table and the graph show the production possibilities frontier for cell phones and DVDs.

Point *A* tells us that if the economy produces no cell phones, the maximum quantity of DVDs it can produce is 15 million a year. Each point *A*, *B*, *C*, *D*, *E*, and *F* on the graph represents the possibility in the table identified by the same letter. The line passing through these points is the production possibilities frontier.

Attainable and Unattainable Combinations

Because the *PPF* shows the *limits* to production, it separates attainable combinations from unattainable ones. The economy can produce combinations of cell phones and DVDs that are smaller than those on the *PPF*, and it can produce any of the combinations *on* the *PPF*. These combinations of cell phones and DVDs are attainable. But it is impossible to produce combinations that are larger than those on the *PPF*. These combinations are unattainable.

Figure 3.2 emphasizes the attainable and unattainable combinations. Only the points on the *PPF* and inside it (in the orange area) are attainable. The combinations of cell phones and DVDs beyond the *PPF* (in the white area), such as the combination at point *G*, are unattainable. These points illustrate combinations that cannot be produced with the current resources and technology. The *PPF* tells us that the economy can produce 4 million cell phones and 5 million DVDs at point *E or* 2 million cell phones and 12 million DVDs at point *C*. But the economy cannot produce 4 million cell phones and 12 million DVDs at point *G*.

Efficient and Inefficient Production

Production efficiency
A situation in which the economy is getting all that it can from its resources and cannot produce more of one good or service without producing less of something else.

Production efficiency occurs when the economy is getting all that it can from its resources. When production is efficient it is not possible to produce more of one good or service without producing less of something else. For production to be efficient, there must be full employment—not just of labor but of all the available factors of production—and each resource must be assigned to the task that it performs comparatively better than other resources can.

FIGURE 3.2

Attainable and Unattainable Combinations

myeconlab Animation

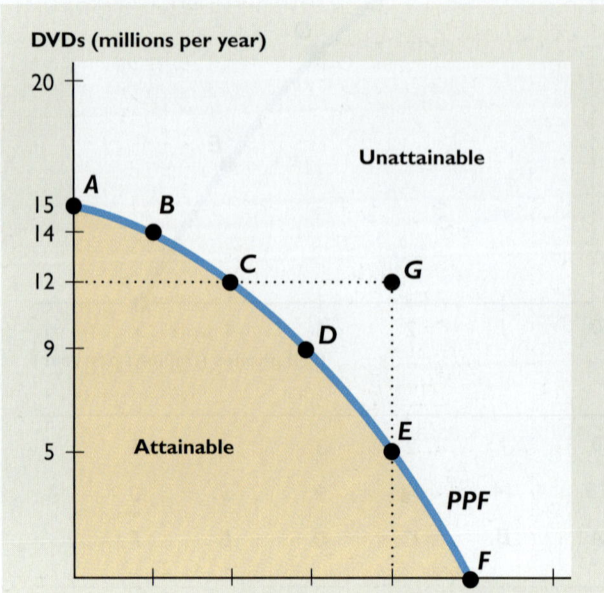

The production possibilities frontier, *PPF*, separates attainable combinations from unattainable ones. The economy can produce at any point *inside* the *PPF* (the orange area) or at any point *on* the frontier. Any point outside the production possibilities frontier, such as point *G*, is unattainable.

Figure 3.3 illustrates the distinction between efficient and inefficient production. With *inefficient* production, the economy might be producing 3 million cell phones and 5 million DVDs at point *H*. With an *efficient* use of the economy's resources, it is possible to produce at a point on the *PPF* such as point *D* or *E*. At point *D*, there are more DVDs and the same quantity of cell phones as at point *H*. And at point *E*, there are more cell phones and the same quantity of DVDs as at point *H*. At points *D* and *E*, production is efficient.

Tradeoffs and Free Lunches

A **tradeoff** is an exchange—giving up one thing to get something else. You trade off income for a better grade when you decide to cut back on the hours you spend on your weekend job and allocate the time to extra study. The Ford Motor Company faces a tradeoff when it cuts the production of trucks and uses the resources saved to produce more hybrid SUVs. The federal government faces a tradeoff when it cuts NASA's space exploration program and allocates more resources to homeland security. As a society, we face a tradeoff when we decide to cut down a forest and destroy the habitat of the spotted owl.

Tradeoff
An exchange—giving up one thing to get something else.

The production possibilities frontier illustrates the idea of a tradeoff. The *PPF* in Figure 3.3 shows how. If the economy produces at point *E* and people want to produce more DVDs, they must forgo some cell phones. In the move from point *E* to point *D*, people trade off cell phones for DVDs.

Economists often express the central idea of economics—that choices involve tradeoff—with the saying "There is no such thing as a free lunch." A *free lunch* is a gift—getting something without giving up something else. What does the

FIGURE 3.3

Efficient and Inefficient Production, Tradeoffs, and Free Lunches

myeconlab Animation

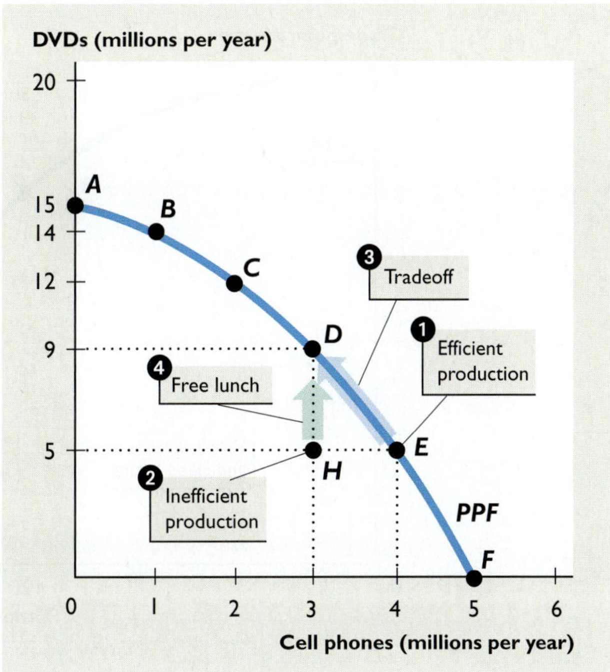

❶ When production occurs at a point on the *PPF*, such as point *E*, resources are used efficiently.

❷ When production occurs at a point inside the *PPF*, such as point *H*, resources are used inefficiently.

❸ When production is efficient—on the *PPF*—the economy faces a tradeoff. To move from point *E* to point *D* requires that some cell phones be given up for more DVDs.

❹ When production is inefficient—inside the *PPF*—there is a free lunch. To move from point *H* to point *D* does not involve a tradeoff.

famous saying mean? Suppose some resources are not being used or are not being used efficiently. Isn't it then possible to avoid a tradeoff and get a free lunch?

The answer is yes. You can see why in Figure 3.3. If production is taking place *inside* the *PPF* at point *H*, then it is possible to move to point *D* and increase the production of DVDs by using currently unused resources or by using resources in their most productive way. Nothing is forgone to increase production—there is a free lunch.

When production is efficient—at a point on the *PPF*—choosing to produce more of one good involves a tradeoff. But if production is inefficient—at a point inside the *PPF*—there is a free lunch. More of some goods and services can be produced without producing less of any others.

So "there is no such thing as a free lunch" means that when resources are used efficiently, every choice involves a tradeoff. Because economists view people as making rational choices, they expect that resources will be used efficiently. That is why they emphasize the tradeoff idea and deny the existence of free lunches. We might *sometimes* get a free lunch, but we *almost always* face a tradeoff.

EYE on YOUR LIFE

Your Production Possibilities Frontier

Two "goods" that concern you a great deal are your grade point average (GPA) and the amount of time you have available for leisure or earning an income. You face a tradeoff. To get a higher GPA you must give up leisure or income. Your forgone leisure or forgone income is the opportunity cost of a higher GPA. Similarly, to get more leisure or more income, you must accept a lower grade. A lower grade is the opportunity cost of increased leisure or increased income.

The figure illustrates a student's *PPF*. Any point on or beneath the *PPF* is attainable and any point above the *PPF* is unattainable. A student who wastes time or doesn't study efficiently ends up with a lower GPA than the highest attainable from the time spent studying. But a student who works efficiently achieves a point *on* the *PPF* and achieves production efficiency.

The student in the figure allocates the scarce 168 hours a week between studying (class and study hours) and other activities (work, leisure, and sleep hours). The student attends class and studies for 48 hours each week and works or has fun (and sleeps) for the other 120 hours. With this allocation of time, and studying efficiently, the student's GPA is 3.

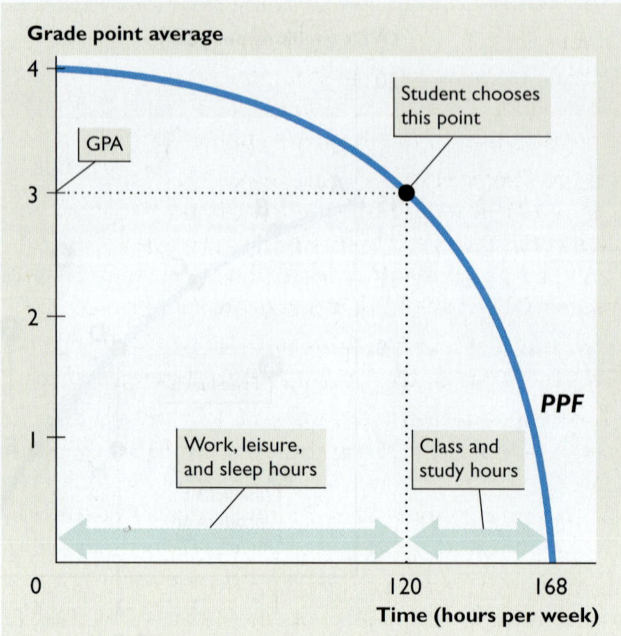

CHECKPOINT 3.1

Explain and illustrate the concepts of scarcity, production efficiency, and tradeoff using the production possibilities frontier.

MyEconLab: Work these problems in Study Plan 3.1 to get instant feedback.

Practice Problems

1. Table 1 sets out the production possibilities of a small Pacific island economy. Draw the economy's *PPF*.

Figure 1 shows an economy's production possibilities frontier and identifies some production points. Use this figure to work Problems **2** to **4**.

2. Which points are attainable? Explain why.
3. Which points are efficient and which points are inefficient? Explain why.
4. Which points illustrate a tradeoff? Explain why.
5. **Loss of honeybees is less but still a threat**
   During 2008, almost 29 percent of U.S. honeybee hives died off, less than expected, but the situation is still unsustainable. Honeybees are crucial for the pollination of many plants including almonds and pumpkins.
   Source: *USA Today*, May 20, 2009

   Farmers in the Central Valley of California grow 80 percent of the world's almonds along with other crops. In 2008, growers used 1.2 million bee hives to produce about 1 trillion pounds of almonds. Explain how a 30 percent drop in honeybees would affect the Central Valley *PPF* in 2009.

TABLE 1

Possibility	Fish (pounds)		Berries (pounds)
A	0	and	20
B	1	and	18
C	2	and	15
D	3	and	11
E	4	and	6
F	5	and	0

FIGURE 1

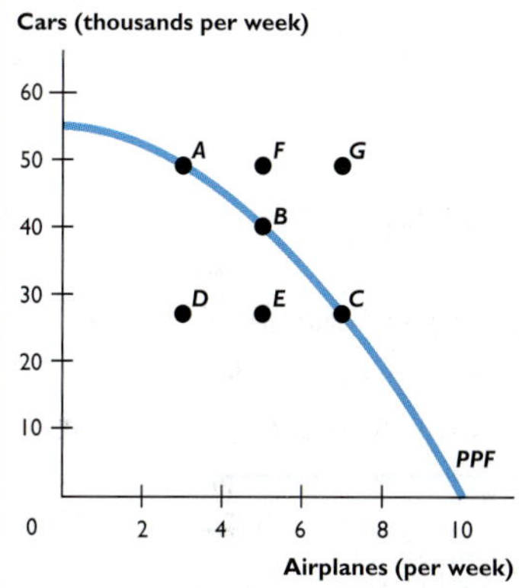

FIGURE 2

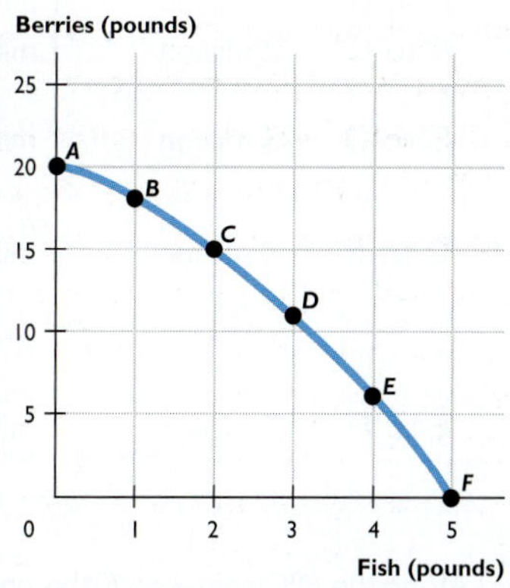

Guided Solutions to Practice Problems

1. The *PPF* is the boundary between attainable and unattainable combinations of goods. Figure 2 shows the economy's *PPF*. The graph plots each row of the table as a point with the corresponding letter.
2. Attainable points: Any point on the *PPF* is attainable and any point below (inside) the *PPF* is attainable. Any point outside the *PPF* is unattainable. In Figure 1, only points *F* and *G* are outside the *PPF*, so they are unattainable. The other points (*A*, *B*, *C*, *D*, and *E*) are attainable.
3. Efficient points: Production is efficient when it is not possible to produce more of one good without producing less of another good. To be efficient, a point must be attainable, so points *F* and *G* can't be efficient. Points inside the *PPF* can't be efficient because more goods can be produced, so *D* and *E* are not efficient. The only efficient points are those *on* the *PPF*—*A*, *B*, and *C*.

   Inefficient points: Inefficiency occurs when resources are misallocated or unemployed. Such points are *inside* the *PPF*. These points are *D* and *E*.
4. Tradeoff: Begin by recalling that a tradeoff is an exchange—giving up something to get something else. A tradeoff occurs when moving along the *PPF* from one point to another point. So moving from any point *on* the *PPF*, point *A*, *B*, or *C*, to another point *on* the *PPF* illustrates a tradeoff.
5. Honeybees are a resource used in the production of almonds. In 2008, Central Valley farmers were at a point on their *PPF*. A 30 percent drop in bees hives will reduce the quantity of almonds produced by about 30 percent. With no change in the quantity of other crops produced, the Central Valley *PPF* will shift inward.

3.2 OPPORTUNITY COST

You've seen that moving from one point to another on the *PPF* involves a tradeoff. But what are the terms of the tradeoff? *How much* of one item must be forgone to obtain an additional unit of another item—a large amount or a small amount? The answer is given by opportunity cost—the best thing you must give up to get something (see p. 11). We can use the *PPF* to calculate opportunity cost.

The Opportunity Cost of a Cell Phone

The opportunity cost of a cell phone is the number of DVDs forgone to get an additional cell phone. It is calculated as the number of DVDs forgone divided by the number of cell phones gained.

Figure 3.4 illustrates the calculation. At point *A*, the quantities produced are zero cell phones and 15 million DVDs; and at point *B*, the quantities produced are 1 million cell phones and 14 million DVDs. To gain 1 million cell phones by moving from point *A* to point *B*, 1 million DVDs are forgone, so the opportunity cost of 1 cell phone is 1 DVD.

At point *C*, the quantities produced are 2 million cell phones and 12 million DVDs. To gain 1 million cell phones by moving from point *B* to point *C*, 2 million DVDs are forgone. Now the opportunity cost of 1 cell phone is 2 DVDs.

If you repeat these calculations, moving from *C* to *D*, *D* to *E*, and *E* to *F*, you will obtain the opportunity costs shown in the table and the graph.

FIGURE 3.4

Calculating the Opportunity Cost of a Cell Phone

myeconlab Animation

Movement along *PPF*	Decrease in quantity of DVDs	Increase in quantity of cell phones	Decrease in DVDs divided by increase in cell phones
A to B	1 million	1 million	1 DVD per phone
B to C	2 million	1 million	2 DVDs per phone
C to D	3 million	1 million	3 DVDs per phone
D to E	4 million	1 million	4 DVDs per phone
E to F	5 million	1 million	5 DVDs per phone

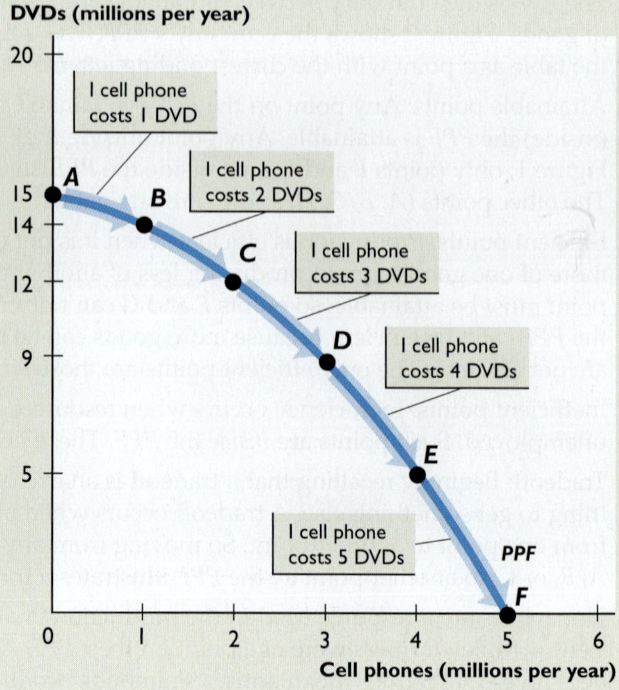

Along the *PPF* from *A* to *F*, the opportunity cost of a cell phone increases as the quantity of cell phones produced increases.

Opportunity Cost and the Slope of the *PPF*

Look at the numbers that we've just calculated for the opportunity cost of a cell phone and notice that they follow a striking pattern. The opportunity cost of a cell phone increases as the quantity of cell phones produced increases.

The magnitude of the *slope* of the *PPF* measures the opportunity cost. Because the *PPF* in Figure 3.4 is bowed outward, its slope changes and gets steeper as the quantity of cell phones produced increases.

When a small quantity of cell phones is produced—between points *A* and *B*—the *PPF* has a gentle slope and the opportunity cost of a cell phone is low. A given increase in the quantity of cell phones costs a small decrease in the quantity of DVDs. When a large quantity of cell phones is produced—between *E* and *F*—the *PPF* is steep and the opportunity cost of a cell phone is high. A given increase in the quantity of cell phones costs a large decrease in the quantity of DVDs. Figure 3.5 shows the increasing opportunity cost of a cell phone.

Opportunity Cost Is a Ratio

The opportunity cost of a cell phone is the *ratio* of DVDs forgone to cell phones gained. Similarly, the opportunity cost of a DVD is the *ratio* of cell phones forgone to DVDs gained. So the opportunity cost of a DVD is equal to the inverse of the opportunity cost of a cell phone. For example, moving along the *PPF* in Figure 3.4 from *C* to *D* the opportunity cost of a cell phone is 3 DVDs. Moving along the *PPF* in the opposite direction, from *D* to *C*, the opportunity cost of a DVD is 1/3 of a cell phone.

FIGURE 3.5

The Opportunity Cost of a Cell Phone

myeconlab Animation

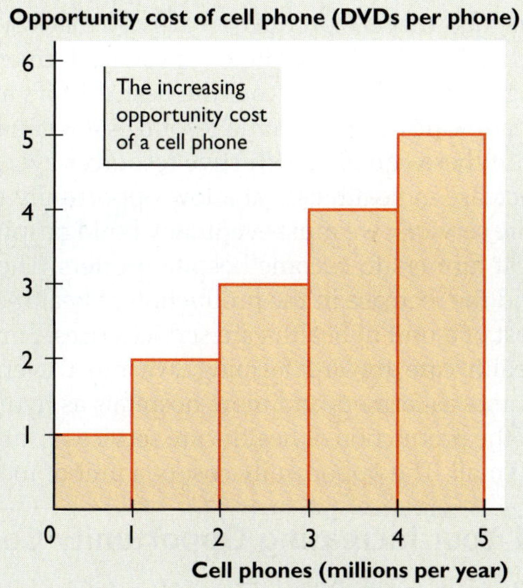

Cell phones (millions)	0 to 1	1 to 2	2 to 3	3 to 4	4 to 5
Opportunity cost (DVDs per phone)	1	2	3	4	5

Because the *PPF* in Figure 3.4 is bowed outward, the opportunity cost of a cell phone increases as the quantity of cell phones produced increases.

EYE on the ENVIRONMENT

Is Wind Power Free?

Wind power is not free. Its opportunity cost includes: (1) the cost of wind turbines, (2) the cost of transmission lines, and (3) power transmission loss.

Wind turbines can produce electricity only when there is wind, which turns out, at best, to be 40 percent of the time and, on average, about 25 percent of the time. Also some of the best wind farm locations are a long way from major population centers, so transmission lines would be long and power transmission losses large.

If we produced 55 percent of our electricity using South Dakota wind power, we would be operating inside the *PPF* at a point such as *Z*.

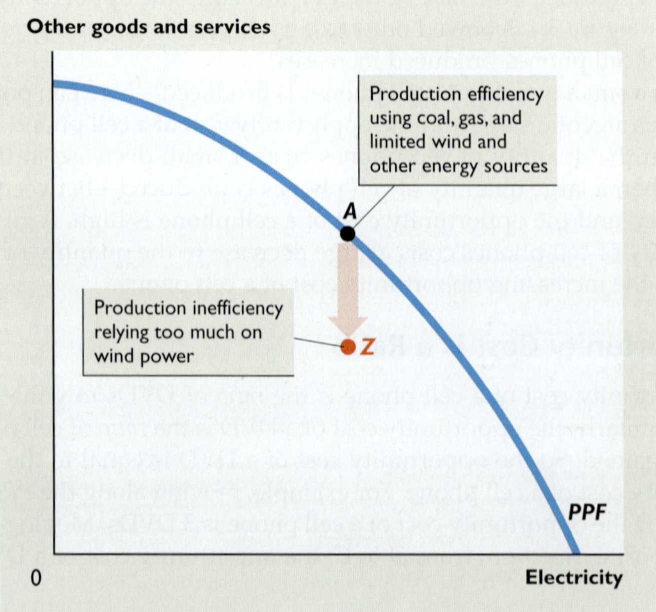

Increasing Opportunity Costs Are Everywhere

Just about every production activity that you can think of has increasing opportunity cost. We allocate the most skillful farmers and the most fertile land to producing food, and we allocate the best doctors and the least fertile land to producing health-care services. Some resources are equally productive in both activities. If we shift these equally productive resources away from farming to hospitals, we get an increase in health care at a low opportunity cost. But if we keep increasing health-care services, we must eventually build hospitals on the most fertile land and get the best farmers to become hospital porters. The production of food drops drastically and the increase in the production of health-care services is small. The opportunity cost of a unit of health-care services rises. Similarly, if we shift resources away from health care toward farming, we must eventually use more skilled doctors and nurses as farmers and more hospitals as hydroponic tomato factories. The decrease in the production of health-care services is large, but the increase in food production is small. The opportunity cost of a unit of food rises.

Your Increasing Opportunity Cost

Flip back to the *PPF* in *Eye on Your Life* on page 66 and think about its implications for your opportunity cost of a higher grade.

What is the opportunity cost of spending time with your friends in terms of the grade you might receive on your exam? What is the opportunity cost of a higher grade in terms of the activities you give up to study? Do you face increasing opportunity costs in these activities?

EYE on the U.S. ECONOMY

Guns Versus Butter

Guns versus butter is the classic economic tradeoff. "Guns" stand for defense goods and services and "butter" stands for food and more generally for all other goods and services. Recently, the U.S. economy has been producing more guns and less butter.

Figure 1 shows the fluctuations in the quantity of defense goods and services produced. (The quantity is measured by expenditure on defense using the prices in 2000 to remove the effects of price changes.) The quantity of defense goods and services produced increases in times of war and decreases in times of peace.

Figure 2 illustrates the recent changes in the production of defense goods and services using the *PPF*.

During the 1990s, the *PPF* was PPF_0. President Reagan raised the stakes in the Cold War between the United States and the (former) Soviet Union by a big expansion of military expenditure and we were at point *A*. By mid-decade, the Soviet Union had collapsed and we enjoyed a peace dividend by moving along PPF_0 to *B*.

During the next decade, production possibilities expanded from PPF_0 to PPF_1. Defense production and the production of other goods and services increased, and in 2001 we operated at point *C*. Then, in response to the attacks of September 11, 2001, defense spending increased again and by 2009 we had moved along PPF_1 to point *D*.

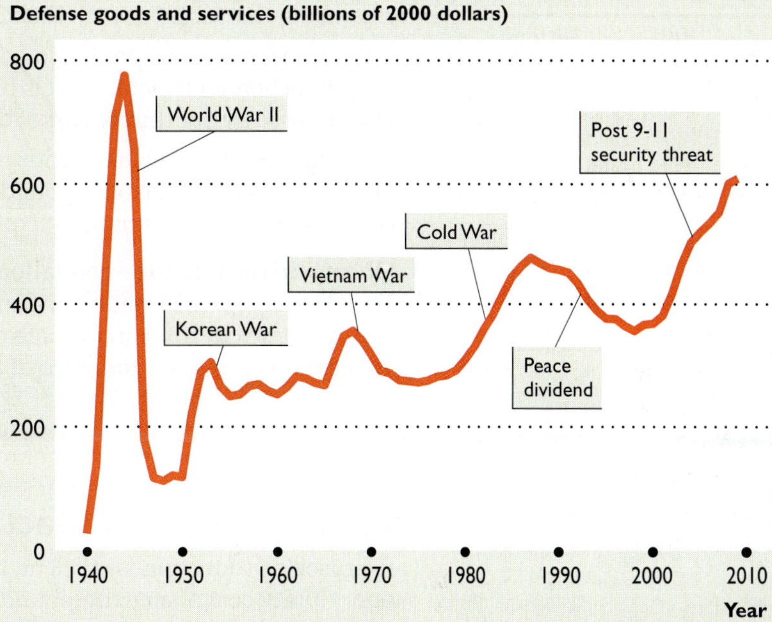

Figure 1 The quantity of defense goods produced

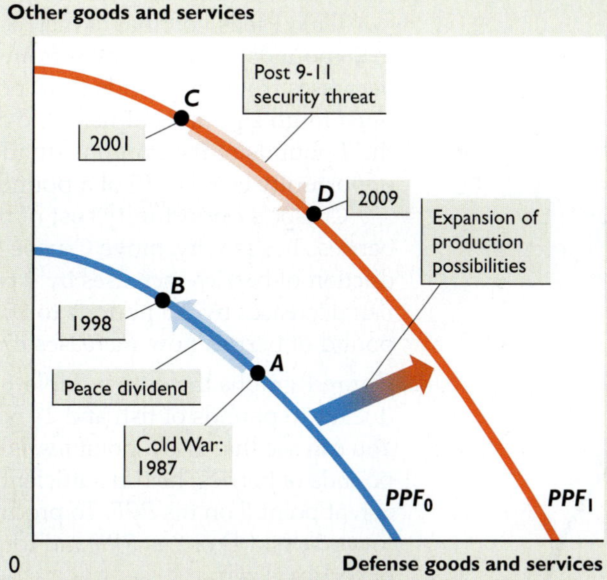

Figure 2 The guns versus butter tradeoff

myeconlab

Work these problems in Study Plan 3.2 to get instant feedback.

TABLE 1

Possibility	Fish (pounds)		Berries (pounds)
A	0	and	36
B	4.0	and	35
C	7.5	and	33
D	10.5	and	30
E	13.0	and	26
F	15.0	and	21
G	16.5	and	15
H	17.5	and	8
I	18.0	and	0

CHECKPOINT 3.2

Calculate opportunity cost.

Practice Problems

Table 1 shows Robinson Crusoe's production possibilities in summer. Use the information in this table to work Problems **1** and **2**.

1. If Crusoe increases his production of berries from 21 pounds to 26 pounds and his production is efficient, what is his opportunity cost of a pound of berries? Does Crusoe's opportunity cost of berries increase as he produces more berries?
2. If Crusoe is producing 10 pounds of fish and 21 pounds of berries, what is his opportunity cost of an extra pound of berries? And what is his opportunity cost of an extra pound of fish? Explain your answers.
3. **Obama drives up miles-per-gallon requirements**

   The Obama administration announced that emission levels of new automobiles must be cut from an average of 354 grams in 2009 to 250 grams in 2016. To meet this standard, the price of a new vehicle will rise by $1,300.

   Source: *USA Today*, May 20, 2009

   Calculate the opportunity cost of reducing the emission level by 1 gram.

Guided Solutions to Practice Problems

1. If Crusoe's production is efficient, he is producing at a point *on* his *PPF*. His opportunity cost of an extra pound of berries is the quantity of fish he must give up to get the berries and it is calculated as the decrease in the quantity of fish divided by the increase in the quantity of berries as he moves along his *PPF* in the direction of producing more berries.

   Table 1 tells you that to increase the quantity of berries from 21 pounds to 26 pounds, Crusoe moves from row *F* to row *E* and his production of fish decreases from 15 pounds to 13 pounds. To gain 5 pounds of berries, Crusoe must forgo 2 pounds of fish. The opportunity cost of 1 pound of berries is the 2 pounds of fish forgone divided by 5 pounds of berries gained. This opportunity cost is 2/5 of a pound of fish.

   Crusoe's opportunity cost of berries increases as he produces more berries. To see why, move Crusoe from row *E* to row *D* in Table 1. His production of berries increases by 4 pounds to 30 pounds and his production of fish decreases by 2.5 pounds to 10.5 pounds. His opportunity cost of 1 pound of berries now increases to 5/8 of a pound of fish.
2. Figure 1 graphs the data in Table 1 and shows Crusoe's *PPF*. If Crusoe is producing 10 pounds of fish and 21 pounds of berries, he is producing at point *Z*. You can see that *Z* is a point *inside* Crusoe's *PPF*. When Crusoe produces 21 pounds of berries, he has sufficient time available to produce 15 pounds of fish at point *F* on his *PPF*. To produce more berries, Crusoe can move from *Z* toward point *D* on his *PPF* and forgo no fish. His opportunity cost of a pound of berries is zero.
3. By spending $1,300 extra on a new car, you forgo $1,300 of other goods. With a new car, your emissions fall from 354 grams to 250 grams, a reduction of 104 grams. The opportunity cost of a 1-gram reduction in emissions is $1,300 of other goods divided by 104 grams, or $12.50 of other goods.

FIGURE 1

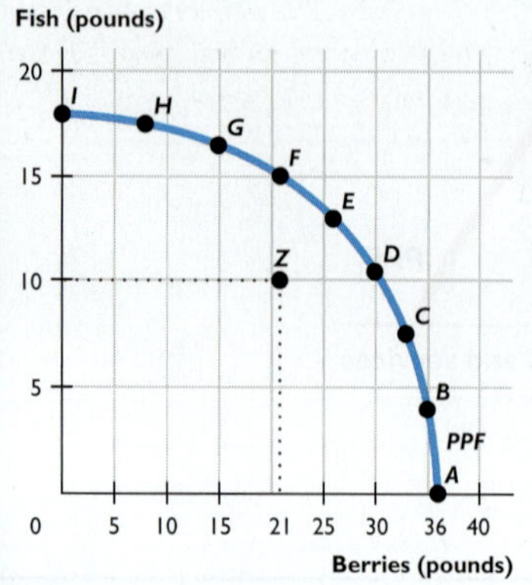

3.3 ECONOMIC GROWTH

Economic growth is the sustained expansion of production possibilities. Our economy grows when we develop better technologies for producing goods and services; improve the quality of labor by education, on-the-job training, and work experience; and acquire more machines to help us produce.

Economic growth
The sustained expansion of production possibilities.

To study economic growth, we must change the two goods and look at the production possibilities for a consumption good and a capital good. A cell phone is a consumption good and a cell-phone factory is a capital good. By using today's resources to produce cell-phone factories, the economy can expand its future production possibilities. The greater the production of new capital—number of new cell-phone factories—the faster is the expansion of production possibilities.

Figure 3.6 shows how the *PPF* can expand. If no new factories are produced (at point *L*), production possibilities do not expand and the *PPF* stays at its original position. By producing fewer cell phones and using resources to produce 2 new cell-phone factories (at point *K*), production possibilities expand and the *PPF* rotates outward to the new *PPF*.

But economic growth is *not* free. To make it happen, consumption must decrease. The move from *L* to *K* in Figure 3.6 means forgoing 2 million cell phones now. The opportunity cost of producing more cell-phone factories is producing fewer cell phones today.

Also, economic growth is no magic formula for abolishing scarcity. Economic growth shifts the *PPF* outward, but on the new *PPF* we continue to face opportunity costs. To keep producing capital, current consumption must be less than its maximum possible level.

FIGURE 3.6

Expanding Production Possibilities

myeconlab Animation

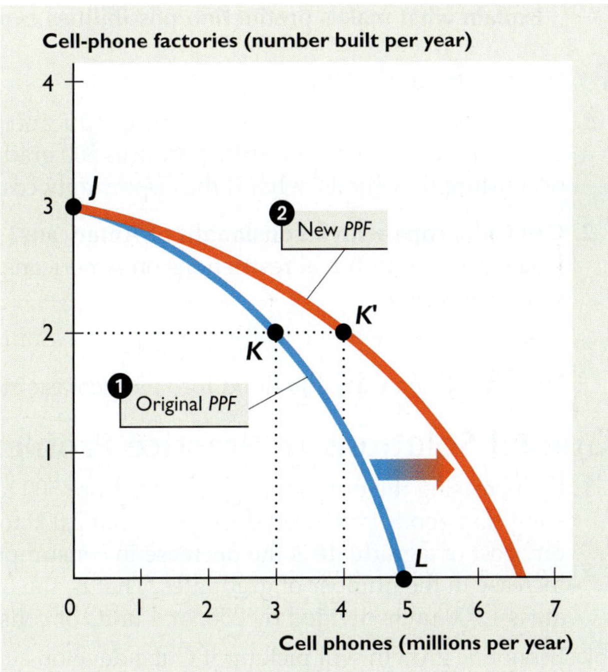

❶ If firms allocate no resources to producing cell-phone factories and produce 5 million cell-phones a year at point *L*, the *PPF* doesn't change.

❷ If firms decrease cell-phone production to 3 million a year and produce 2 cell-phone factories, at point *K*, production possibilities will expand. After a year, the *PPF* shifts outward to the new *PPF* and production can move to point *K*'.

EYE on the GLOBAL ECONOMY

Hong Kong's Rapid Economic Growth

Hong Kong's production possibilities per person were 25 percent of those of the United States in 1960. By 2009, they had grown to become 92 percent of U.S. production possibilities. Hong Kong grew faster than the United States because it allocated more of its resources to accumulating capital and less to consumption than did the United States.

In 1960, the United States and Hong Kong produced at point *A* on their respective *PPF*s. In 2009, Hong Kong was at point *B* and the United States was at point *C*.

If Hong Kong continues to produce at a point such as *B*, it will grow more rapidly than the United States and its *PPF* will eventually shift out beyond the *PPF* of the United States. But if Hong Kong produces at a point such as *D*, the pace of expansion of its *PPF* will slow.

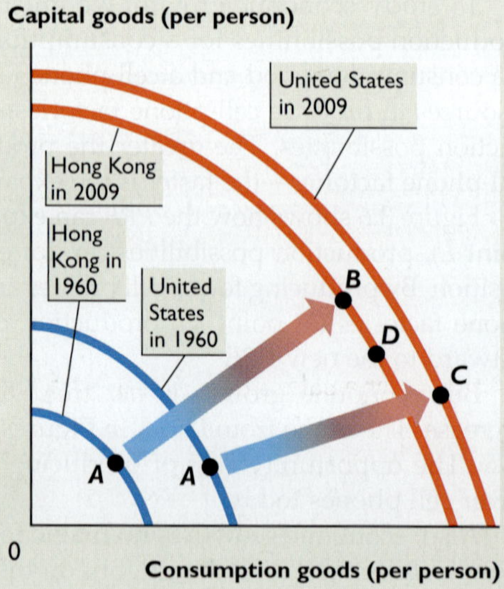

CHECKPOINT 3.3

myeconlab

Work these problems in Study Plan 3.3 to get instant feedback.

Explain what makes production possibilities expand.

Practice Problems

TABLE 1

Possibility	Education services (graduates)	Consumption goods (units)
A	1,000	0
B	750	1,000
C	500	2,000
D	0	3,000

1. Table 1 shows an economy that produces education services and consumption goods. If the economy currently produces 500 graduates a year and 2,000 units of consumption goods, what is the opportunity cost of one more graduate?
2. **Can Cuba cope with an onslaught of Americans?**
   Doing away with travel restrictions on Americans could unleash a flood of visitors to Cuba.

   Source: *USA Today*, April 14, 2009

   How can Cuba turn this flood into an increase in economic growth?

Guided Solutions to Practice Problems

1. By increasing the number of graduates from 500 to 750, the quantity of consumption goods produced decreases from 2,000 to 1,000 units. The opportunity cost of a graduate is the decrease in consumption goods divided by the increase in the number of graduates. That is, the opportunity cost of a graduate is 1,000 units divided by 250, or 4 units of consumption goods.
2. Economic growth will pick up if Cuba develops its tourist hotels and facilities. This new capital will increase its resources and shift its *PPF* outward.

3.4 SPECIALIZATION AND TRADE

A person can produce several goods or can concentrate on producing one good and then trading some of that good for those produced by others. Concentrating on the production of only one good is called *specialization.* We are going to discover how people gain by specializing in the production of the good in which they have a *comparative advantage.*

Comparative Advantage

A person has a **comparative advantage** in an activity if that person can perform the activity at a lower opportunity cost than anyone else. Let's explore the idea of comparative advantage by looking at two smoothie bars: one operated by Liz and the other operated by Joe.

Comparative advantage
The ability of a person to perform an activity or produce a good or service at a lower opportunity cost than anyone else.

Liz's Smoothie Bar

Liz produces smoothies and salads. In Liz's high-tech bar, she can turn out *either* a smoothie *or* a salad every 2 minutes. If she spends all her time making smoothies, she produces 30 an hour. If she spends all her time making salads, she also produces 30 an hour. If she splits her time equally between the two, she can produce 15 smoothies *and* 15 salads an hour. For each additional smoothie Liz produces, she must decrease her production of salads by one, and for each additional salad Liz produces, she must decrease her production of smoothies by one. So

Liz's opportunity cost of producing 1 smoothie is 1 salad,

and

Liz's opportunity cost of producing 1 salad is 1 smoothie.

Liz's customers buy smoothies and salads in equal quantities, so Liz splits her time equally between the items and produces 15 smoothies and 15 salads an hour.

TABLE 3.1 LIZ'S PRODUCTION POSSIBILITIES

Item	Minutes to produce 1	Quantity per hour
Smoothies	2	30
Salads	2	30

Joe's Smoothie Bar

Joe also produces both smoothies and salads. Joe's bar is smaller than Liz's, and he has only one blender—a slow, old machine. Even if Joe uses all his resources to produce smoothies, he can produce only 6 an hour. But Joe is pretty good in the salad department, so if he uses all his resources to make salads, he can produce 30 an hour. Joe's ability to make smoothies and salads is the same regardless of how he splits an hour between the two tasks. He can make a salad in 2 minutes or a smoothie in 10 minutes. For each additional smoothie Joe produces, he must decrease his production of salads by 5. And for each additional salad Joe produces, he must decrease his production of smoothies by 1/5 of a smoothie. So

Joe's opportunity cost of producing 1 smoothie is 5 salads,

and

Joe's opportunity cost of producing 1 salad is 1/5 of a smoothie.

Joe's customers, like Liz's, buy smoothies and salads in equal quantities. Joe spends 50 minutes of each hour making smoothies and 10 minutes of each hour making salads. With this division of his time, Joe produces 5 smoothies and 5 salads an hour.

TABLE 3.2 JOE'S PRODUCTION POSSIBILITIES

Item	Minutes to produce 1	Quantity per hour
Smoothies	10	6
Salads	2	30

Liz's Absolute Advantage

Absolute advantage
When one person is more productive than another person in several or even all activities.

You can see from the numbers that describe the two smoothie bars that Liz is three times as productive as Joe—her 15 smoothies and 15 salads an hour are three times Joe's 5 smoothies and 5 salads. Liz has an **absolute advantage**—she is more productive than Joe in producing both smoothies and salads. But Liz has a comparative advantage in only one of the activities.

Liz's Comparative Advantage

In which of the two activities does Liz have a *comparative* advantage? Recall that comparative advantage is a situation in which one person's opportunity cost of producing a good is lower than another person's opportunity cost of producing that same good. Liz has a comparative advantage in producing smoothies. Her opportunity cost of a smoothie is 1 salad, whereas Joe's opportunity cost of a smoothie is 5 salads.

Joe's Comparative Advantage

If Liz has a comparative advantage in producing smoothies, Joe must have a comparative advantage in producing salads. His opportunity cost of a salad is 1/5 of a smoothie, while Liz's opportunity cost of a salad is 1 smoothie.

Achieving Gains from Trade

Liz and Joe run into each other one evening in a singles bar. After a few minutes of getting acquainted, Liz tells Joe about her amazingly profitable smoothie business. Her only problem, she tells Joe, is that she wishes she could produce more because potential customers leave when her lines get too long.

Joe isn't sure whether to risk spoiling his chances by telling Liz about his own struggling business. But he takes the risk. When he explains to Liz that he spends 50 minutes of every hour making 5 smoothies and 10 minutes making 5 salads, Liz's eyes pop. "Have I got a deal for you!" she exclaims.

Here's the deal that Liz sketches on a paper napkin. Joe stops making smoothies and allocates all his time to producing salads. Liz stops making salads and allocates all her time to producing smoothies. That is, they both specialize in producing the good in which they have a comparative advantage—see Table 3.3(b). They then trade: Liz sells Joe 10 smoothies and Joe sells Liz 20 salads—the price of a smoothie is 2 salads—see Table 3.3(c).

After the trade, Joe has 10 salads (the 30 he produces minus the 20 he sells to Liz) and the 10 smoothies that he buys from Liz. So Joe doubles the quantities of smoothies and salads he can sell. Liz has 20 smoothies (the 30 she produces minus the 10 she sells to Joe) and the 20 salads she buys from Joe. See Table 3.3(d). From specialization and trade, each gains 5 smoothies and 5 salads—see Table 3.3(e).

Liz draws a figure (Figure 3.7) to illustrate her idea. The red *PPF* is Joe's and the blue *PPF* is Liz's. They are each producing at the points marked *A*. Liz's proposal is that they each produce at the points marked *B*. They then trade smoothies and salads at a price of 2 salads per smoothie, or 1/2 a smoothie per salad. Liz gets salads for 1/2 a smoothie each, which is less than the 1 smoothie that it costs her to produce them. Joe gets smoothies for 2 salads each, which is less than the 5 salads it costs him to produce them. Each moves to the point marked *C*, *outside* their respective *PPF*s. Because of the gains from trade, total production increases by 10 smoothies and 10 salads.

TABLE 3.3 LIZ AND JOE GAIN FROM TRADE

(a) Before Trade	Liz	Joe
Smoothies	15	5
Salads	15	5
(b) Specialization	**Liz**	**Joe**
Smoothies	30	0
Salads	0	30
(c) Trade		
Smoothies	sell 10	buy 10
Salads	buy 20	sell 20
(d) After Trade		
Smoothies	20	10
Salads	20	10
(e) Gains from Trade		
Smoothies	+5	+5
Salads	+5	+5

FIGURE 3.7

The Gains from Specialization and Trade

myeconlab Animation

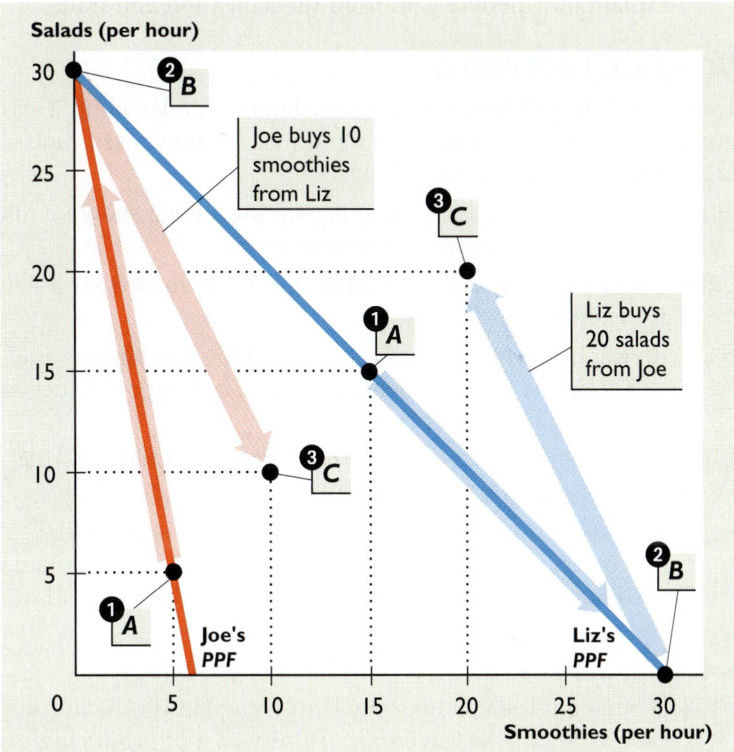

❶ Liz and Joe each produce at point *A* on their respective *PPFs*. Liz has a comparative advantage in producing smoothies, and Joe has a comparative advantage in producing salads.

❷ Joe specializes in salads and Liz specializes in smoothies, so they each produce at point *B* on their respective *PPFs*.

❸ They exchange smoothies for salads at a price of 2 salads per smoothie. Each goes to *C*—a point *outside* their individual *PPFs*. They each gain 5 salads and 5 smoothies.

EYE on YOUR LIFE

Your Comparative Advantage

What you have learned in this chapter has huge implications for the way you organize your life. It also has implications for the position that you take on the controversial issue of offshore outsourcing.

Just as an economy expands its production possibilities by accumulating capital, so also will you expand your production possibilities by accumulating human capital. That is what you're doing right now in school.

By discovering your comparative advantage, you will be able to focus on producing the items that make you as well off as possible. Think hard about what you enjoy doing and that you do comparatively better than others. That, most likely, is where your comparative advantage lies.

In today's world, it is a good idea to try to remain flexible so that you can switch jobs if you discover that your comparative advantage has changed.

Looking beyond your own self-interest, are you going to be a voice that supports or opposes offshore outsourcing?

You've learned in this chapter that regardless of whether outsourcing remains inside the United States, as it does with Liz and Joe at their smoothie bars, or is global like the outsourcing of jobs by U. S. producers to India, both parties gain from trade.

Americans pay less for goods and services and Indians earn higher incomes. But some Americans lose, at least in the short run.

myeconlab

Work these problems in Study Plan 3.4 to get instant feedback.

TABLE 1 TONY'S PRODUCTION POSSIBILITIES

Snowboards (per week)		Skis (per week)
25	and	0
20	and	10
15	and	20
10	and	30
5	and	40
0	and	50

TABLE 2 PATTY'S PRODUCTION POSSIBILITIES

Snowboards (per week)		Skis (per week)
20	and	0
10	and	5
0	and	10

CHECKPOINT 3.4

Explain how people gain from specialization and trade.

Practice Problems

Tony and Patty produce skis and snowboards. Tables 1 and 2 show their production possibilities. Each week, Tony produces 5 snowboards and 40 skis and Patty produces 10 snowboards and 5 skis.

1. Who has a comparative advantage in producing snowboards? Who has a comparative advantage in producing skis?
2. If Tony and Patty specialize and trade 1 snowboard for 1 ski, what are the gains from trade?
3. **With big boost from sugar cane, Brazil is satisfying its fuel needs**
   Brazil is almost self-sufficient in ethanol, but import duties on the Brazilian ethanol have limited its exports.

   Source: *The New York Times*, April 12, 2006

   Brazilian ethanol, which is made from sugar, costs of 83 cents per gallon. U.S. ethanol, which is made from corn, costs of $1.14 per gallon. Which country has a comparative advantage in producing ethanol? Explain why both the United States and Brazil can gain from specialization and trade.

Guided Solutions to Practice Problems

1. The person with a comparative advantage in producing snowboards is the person who has the lower opportunity cost of producing a snowboard. Tony's production possibilities show that to produce 5 more snowboards he must produce 10 fewer skis. So Tony's opportunity cost of producing a snowboard is 2 skis.

   Patty's production possibilities show that to produce 10 more snowboards, she must produce 5 fewer skis. So Patty's opportunity cost of producing a snowboard is 1/2 a ski. Patty has a comparative advantage in producing snowboards because her opportunity cost of producing a snowboard is less than Tony's. Tony has a comparative advantage in producing skis. For each ski produced, Tony must give up making 1/2 a snowboard, whereas for each ski that Patty produces, she must give up making 2 snowboards. So Tony's opportunity cost of a ski is lower than Patty's.
2. Patty has a comparative advantage in producing snowboards, so she specializes in snowboards. Tony has a comparative advantage in producing skis, so he specializes in producing skis. Patty produces 20 snowboards and Tony produces 50 skis. Before specializing, they produced 15 snowboards (Patty's 10 plus Tony's 5) and 45 skis (Tony's 40 plus Patty's 5).

   By specializing, they increase their total output by 5 snowboards and 5 skis. They can share this gain by trading 1 ski for 1 snowboard. Patty can get skis from Tony for less than it costs her to produce them. Tony can buy snowboards from Patty for less than it costs him to produce them. Both Patty and Tony achieve gains from specialization and trade.
3. The cost of producing a gallon of ethanol is less in Brazil than in the United States, so Brazil has a comparative advantage in producing ethanol. If Brazil specialized in producing ethanol and the United States specialized in producing other goods (for example, movies or food) and engaged in free trade, each country would be able to get to a point outside its own *PPF*.

CHAPTER SUMMARY

Key Points

1 Explain and illustrate the concepts of scarcity, production efficiency, and tradeoff using the production possibilities frontier.

- The production possibilities frontier, *PPF*, describes the limits to what can be produced by using all the available resources efficiently.
- Points inside and on the *PPF* are attainable. Points outside the *PPF* are unattainable.
- Production at any point on the *PPF* achieves production efficiency. Production at a point inside the *PPF* is inefficient.
- When production is efficient—on the *PPF*—people face a tradeoff. If production is at a point inside the *PPF*, there is a free lunch.

2 Calculate opportunity cost.

- Along the *PPF*, the opportunity cost of *X* (the item on the *x*-axis) is the decrease in *Y* (the item on the *y*-axis) divided by the increase in *X*.
- The opportunity cost of *Y* is the inverse of the opportunity cost of *X*.
- The opportunity cost of producing a good increases as the quantity of the good produced increases.

3 Explain what makes production possibilities expand.

- Technological change and increases in capital and human capital expand production possibilities.
- The opportunity cost of economic growth is the decrease in current consumption.

4 Explain how people gain from specialization and trade.

- A person has a comparative advantage in an activity if he or she can perform that activity at a lower opportunity cost than someone else.
- People gain by increasing the production of the item in which they have a comparative advantage and trading.

Key Terms

myeconlab

Work these problems in Chapter 3 Study Plan to get instant feedback.

TABLE 1

Corn (bushels)		Beef (pounds)
250	and	0
200	and	300
100	and	500
0	and	550

TABLE 2

Labor (hours)	Entertainment (units)		Good food (units)
0	0	or	0
10	20	or	30
20	40	or	50
30	60	or	60
40	80	or	65
50	100	or	67

FIGURE 1

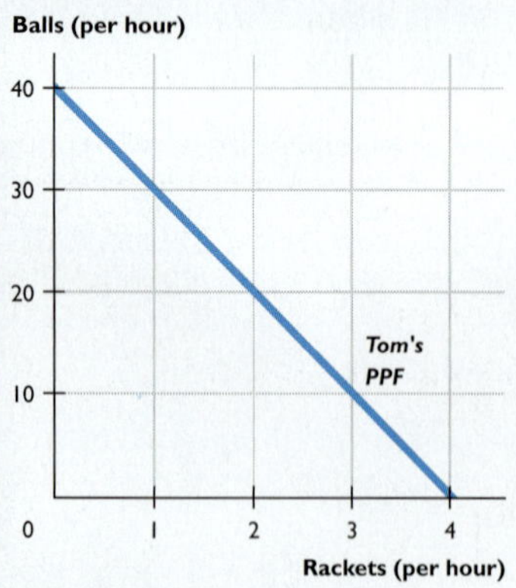

FIGURE 2

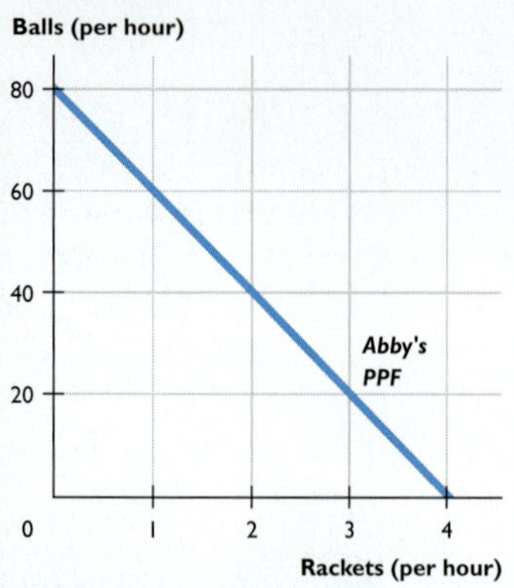

CHAPTER CHECKPOINT

Study Plan Problems and Applications

1. Table 1 shows the quantities of corn and beef that a farm can produce in a year. Draw a graph of the farm's *PPF*. Mark on the graph:
   - An inefficient combination of corn and beef—label this point *A*.
   - An unattainable combination of corn and beef—label this point *B*.
   - An efficient combination of corn and beef—label this point *C*.

Use the following information to work Problems 2 and 3.

The people of Leisure Island have 50 hours of labor a day that can be used to produce entertainment and good food. Table 2 shows the maximum quantity of *either* entertainment *or* good food that Leisure Island can produce with different quantities of labor.

2. Is an output of 50 units of entertainment and 50 units of good food attainable and efficient? With a production of 50 units of entertainment and 50 units of good food, do the people of Leisure Island face a tradeoff?
3. What is the opportunity cost of producing an additional unit of entertainment? Explain how the opportunity cost of producing a unit of entertainment changes as more entertainment is produced.

Use the following information to work Problems 4 and 5.

Malaria can be controlled

The World Health Organization's malaria chief says that it is too costly to try to fully eradicate the disease. He says that by using nets, medicine, and DDT it is possible to eliminate 90 percent of malaria cases. But to eliminate 100 percent of cases would be extremely costly.

Source: *The New York Times*, March 4, 2008

4. Make a graph of the production possibilities frontier with malaria control on the *x*-axis and other goods and services on the *y*-axis.
5. Describe how the opportunity cost of controlling malaria changes as more resources are used to reduce the number of malaria cases.
6. Explain how the following events influence U.S. production possibilities:
   - Some retail workers are re-employed building dams and wind farms.
   - More people take early retirement.
   - Drought devastates California's economy.

Use the following information to work Problems 7 and 8.

Figure 1 shows Tom's production possibilities and Figure 2 shows Abby's production possibilities. Tom uses all his resources and produces 2 rackets and 20 balls an hour. Abby uses all her resources and produces 2 rackets and 40 balls an hour.

7. What is Tom's opportunity cost of producing a racket? What is Abby's opportunity cost of a racket? Who has a comparative advantage in producing rackets? Who has a comparative advantage in producing balls?
8. If Tom and Abby specialize and trade 15 balls for 1 racket, what are the gains from trade?

Instructor Assignable Problems and Applications

Your instructor can assign these problems as homework, a quiz, or a test in **MyEconLab**.

Use the following information to work Problems **1** to **4**.

If the American Clean Energy and Security Act of 2009 becomes law, it will limit greenhouse gas emissions from electricity generation and require electricity producers to generate a minimum percentage of power using renewable fuels. Some of the rights to emit will be auctioned. The Congressional Budget Office estimates that the government will receive $846 billion from auctions and will spend $821 billion on incentive programs and compensation for higher energy prices. Electricity producers will spend $208 million a year to comply with the new rules. (Think of these dollar amounts as dollars' worth of other goods and services.)

1. Will the new law achieve production efficiency?
2. Is the $846 billion that electricity producers pay for the right to emit greenhouse gasses part of the opportunity cost of producing electricity?
3. Is the $821 billion that the government will spend on incentive programs and compensation for higher energy prices part of the opportunity cost of producing electricity?
4. Is the $208 million that electricity producers will spend to comply with the new rules part of the opportunity cost of producing electricity?
5. The people of Foodland have 40 hours of labor a day to bake pizza and bread. Table 1 shows the maximum quantity of *either* pizza *or* bread that Foodland can bake with different quantities of labor. Can Foodland produce 30 pizzas and 30 loaves of bread a day? If it can, is this output efficient, do the people of Foodland face a tradeoff, and what is the opportunity cost of producing an additional pizza?

TABLE 1

Labor (hours)	Pizzas		Bread (loaves)
0	0	or	0
10	30	or	10
20	50	or	20
30	60	or	30
40	65	or	40

Use the following information to work Problems **6** to **8**.

Cheap broadband's a winner

Inexpensive broadband access has created a new generation of television producers and the Internet is their native medium.

Source: *The New York Times*, December 2, 2007

6. How has inexpensive broadband changed the production possibilities of video entertainment and other goods and services?
7. Sketch a *PPF* for video entertainment and other goods and services before broadband.
8. Show how the arrival of inexpensive broadband has changed the *PPF*.
9. Figure 1 illustrates the *PPF* in each of the economies: Atlantis, Bikini, and Cyber. Atlantis has no economic growth, Bikini is growing slowly, and Cyber is growing rapidly. Mark on the graph three points:
   - A point that shows the situation in Atlantis—label this point *A*.
   - A point that shows the situation in Bikini—label this point *B*.
   - A point that shows the situation in Cyber—label this point *C*.

   What is the cost of the economic growth in Bikini and Cyber?

FIGURE 1

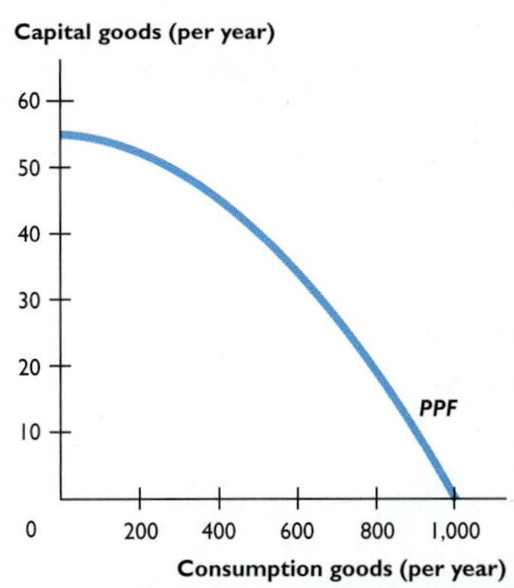

10. A farm grows wheat and fattens pigs. The opportunity cost of producing each of these goods increases as more of it is produced. If the farm adopts a new technology, which allows it to use fewer resources to fatten pigs, explain how the farm's production possibilities will change and the effect on the opportunity cost of producing a ton of wheat.

11. Table 2 shows a farm's production possibilities. If the farm uses its resources efficiently, what is the opportunity cost of an increase in beef production from 300 pounds to 500 pounds a year? Explain your answer.

TABLE 2

Corn (bushels per year)		Beef (pounds per year)
250	and	0
200	and	300
100	and	500
0	and	550

Use the following information to work Problems 12 and 13.

Viewpoint: Education and reform are vital for continued economic growth

Manoj Singh says that many Indians lack the education to participate in the expansion of the country's high tech industries. To remedy this situation, he wants India to create more world-class universities. He also believes that India's labor laws are too restrictive and discourage the movement of people and human capital between regions and industries

Source: Manoj Singh, *Financial Times*, May 15, 2007

12. How would building more universities change India's current and future production possibilities? Illustrate your answer by drawing India's current and future *PPF*s.

13. How would greater movement of people and human capital change India's production possibilities?

14. **Robust corn and soybean crops**

    Corn production in 2008 is forecast at 12.3 billion bushels, 6 percent less than the 2007 record harvest. Soybean production in 2008 is forecast at 2.97 billion bushels in 2008, an increase of 5 percent from last year.

    Source: *USDA Crop Production*, August 12, 2008

    Calculate the opportunity cost of a bushel of soybeans in terms of corn.

Use the following information to work Problems 15 and 16.

Drought affected farmers face new battle

Wheat farmers who had been struggling with a long drought now face a new battle. A South American weed called serrated tussock was spreading at a rapid rate across the bare earth of these drought-stricken wheat farms. And a major problem is that many wheat farmers cannot distinguish serrated tussock from a less harmful native tussock and are unaware of the large effect that serrated tussock can have on productivity and growing capacity.

Source: ABC News (Australia), May 18, 2009

15. Sketch Australia's production possibilities frontier with wheat on the x-axis and other goods and services on the y-axis. On your graph, show the effect of the South American weed on farmers' productivity and growing capacity.

16. Australia is a major exporter of wheat. If productivity does decrease, how will the fall in productivity influence Australia's opportunity cost of producing wheat and Australia's gains from international trade?

Why did home prices boom and bust?

In July 2006, home prices in the United States peaked at double their 1999 level. By early 2009, prices had crashed by 46 percent and were back at their 2002 levels. Why? What made home prices rise and then fall?

4

Demand and Supply

CHAPTER CHECKLIST

When you have completed your study of this chapter, you will be able to

1. Distinguish between quantity demanded and demand, and explain what determines demand.
2. Distinguish between quantity supplied and supply, and explain what determines supply.
3. Explain how demand and supply determine price and quantity in a market, and explain the effects of changes in demand and supply.

COMPETITIVE MARKETS

When you need a new pair of running shoes, want a bagel and a latte, or need to fly home for Thanksgiving, you must find a place where people sell those items or offer those services. The place where you find them is a *market*.

You learned in Chapter 2 that a market is any arrangement that brings buyers and sellers together. A market has two sides: buyers (demanders) and sellers (suppliers). There are markets for *goods* such as apples and hiking boots, for *services* such as haircuts and tennis lessons, for *resources* such as computer programmers and tractors, and for other manufactured *inputs* such as memory chips and auto parts. There are also markets for money such as Japanese yen and for financial securities such as Yahoo! stock. Only imagination limits what can be traded in markets.

Some markets are physical places where buyers and sellers meet and where an auctioneer or a broker helps to determine the prices. Examples of this type of market are the New York Stock Exchange; wholesale fish, meat, and produce markets; and used car auctions.

Some markets are virtual spaces where buyers and sellers never meet face-to-face but connect over telephone lines or the Internet. Examples include currency markets, e-commerce Web sites such as Amazon.com and bananarepublic.com, and auction sites such as eBay.

But most markets are unorganized collections of buyers and sellers. You do most of your trading in this type of market. An example is the market for basketball shoes. The buyers in this $3-billion-a-year market are the 45 million Americans who play basketball (or who want to make a fashion statement) and are looking for a new pair of shoes. The sellers are the tens of thousands of retail sports equipment and footwear stores. Each buyer can visit several different stores, and each seller knows that the buyer has a choice of stores.

Markets vary in the intensity of competition that buyers and sellers face. In this chapter, we're going to study a *competitive market* that has so many buyers and so many sellers that no single buyer or seller can influence the price.

Markets for running shoes ...

coffee and bagel ...

and airline travel.

4.1 DEMAND

First, we'll study the behavior of buyers in a competitive market. The **quantity demanded** of any good, service, or resource is the amount that people are willing and able to buy during a specified period at a specified price. For example, when spring water costs $1 a bottle, you decide to buy 2 bottles a day. The 2 bottles a day is your quantity demanded of spring water.

Quantity demanded
The amount of any good, service, or resource that people are willing and able to buy during a specified period at a specified price.

The quantity demanded is measured as an amount *per unit of time*. For example, your quantity demanded of water is 2 bottles *per day*. We could express this quantity as 14 bottles per week, or some other number per month or per year. A particular number of bottles without a time dimension has no meaning.

Many things influence buying plans, and one of them is price. We look first at the relationship between quantity demanded and price. To study this relationship, we keep all other influences on buying plans the same and we ask: How, other things remaining the same, does the quantity demanded of a good change as its price varies? The law of demand provides the answer.

The Law of Demand

The **law of demand** states

> **Other things remaining the same, if the price of a good rises, the quantity demanded of that good decreases; and if the price of a good falls, the quantity demanded of that good increases.**

So the law of demand states that when all other things remain the same, if the price of an iPhone falls, people will buy more iPhones; or if the price of a baseball ticket rises, people will buy fewer baseball tickets.

Why does the quantity demanded increase if the price falls, all other things remaining the same?

The answer is that, faced with a limited budget, people always have an incentive to find the best deals available. If the price of one item falls and the prices of all other items remain the same, the item with the lower price is a better deal than it was before, so some people buy more of this item. Suppose, for example, that the price of bottled water fell from $1 a bottle to 25 cents a bottle while the price of Gatorade remained at $1 a bottle. Wouldn't some people switch from Gatorade to water? By doing so, they save 75 cents a bottle, which they can spend on other things they previously couldn't afford.

Think about the things that you buy and ask yourself: Which of these items does *not* obey the law of demand? If the price of a new textbook were lower, other things remaining the same (including the price of a used textbook), would you buy more new textbooks? Then think about all the things that you do not now buy but would if you could afford them. How cheap would a PC have to be for you to buy *both* a desktop and a laptop? There is a price that is low enough to entice you!

Demand Schedule and Demand Curve

Demand is the relationship between the quantity demanded and the price of a good when all other influences on buying plans remain the same. The quantity demanded is *one* quantity at *one* price. *Demand* is a *list of quantities at different prices* illustrated by a demand schedule and a demand curve.

Demand
The relationship between the quantity demanded and the price of a good when all other influences on buying plans remain the same.

Demand schedule
A list of the quantities demanded at each different price when all the other influences on buying plans remain the same.

Demand curve
A graph of the relationship between the quantity demanded of a good and its price when all the other influences on buying plans remain the same.

A **demand schedule** is a list of the quantities demanded at each different price when *all the other influences on buying plans remain the same*. The table in Figure 4.1 is one person's (Tina's) demand schedule for bottled water. It tells us that if the price of water is $2.00 a bottle, Tina buys no water. Her quantity demanded is 0 bottles a day. If the price of water is $1.50 a bottle, her quantity demanded is 1 bottle a day. Tina's quantity demanded increases to 2 bottles a day at a price of $1.00 a bottle and to 3 bottles a day at a price of 50 cents a bottle.

A **demand curve** is a graph of the relationship between the quantity demanded of a good and its price when all the other influences on buying plans remain the same. The points on the demand curve labeled *A* through *D* represent the rows *A* through *D* of the demand schedule. For example, point *B* on the graph represents row *B* of the demand schedule and shows that the quantity demanded is 1 bottle a day when the price is $1.50 a bottle. Point C on the demand curve represents row C of the demand schedule and shows that the quantity demanded is 2 bottles a day when the price is $1.00 a bottle.

The downward slope of the demand curve illustrates the law of demand. Along the demand curve, when the price of the good *falls*, the quantity demanded *increases*. For example, in Figure 4.1, when the price of a bottle of water falls from $1.00 to 50 cents, the quantity demanded increases from 2 bottles a day to 3 bottles a day. Conversely, when the price *rises*, the quantity demanded *decreases*. For example, when the price rises from $1.00 to $1.50 a bottle, the quantity demanded decreases from 2 bottles a day to 1 bottle a day.

FIGURE 4.1

Demand Schedule and Demand Curve

myeconlab Animation

The table shows Tina's demand schedule that lists the quantity of water demanded at each price if all other influences on buying plans remain the same. At a price of $1.50 a bottle, the quantity demanded is 1 bottle a day.

The demand curve shows the relationship between the quantity demanded and price, other things remaining the same. The downward-sloping demand curve illustrates the law of demand. When the price falls, the quantity demanded increases; and when the price rises, the quantity demanded decreases.

	Price (dollars per bottle)	Quantity demanded (bottles per day)
A	2.00	0
B	1.50	1
C	1.00	2
D	0.50	3

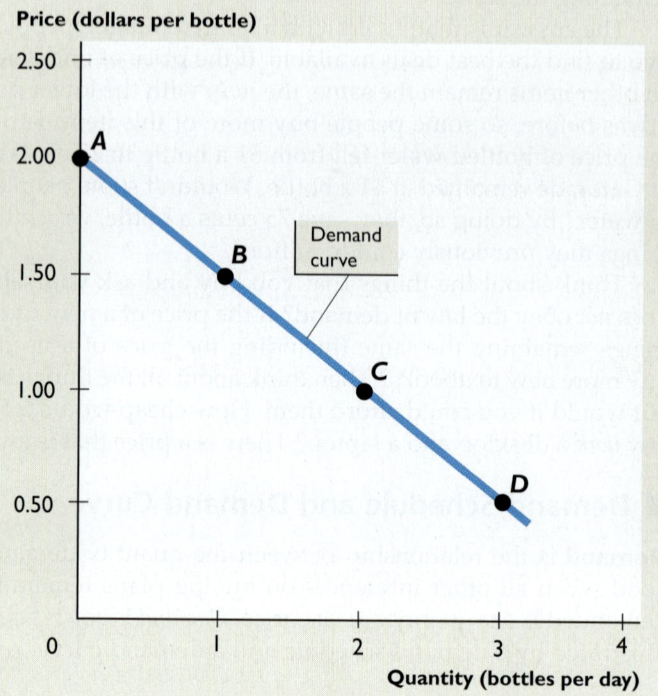

Individual Demand and Market Demand

The demand schedule and the demand curve that you've just studied are for one person. To study a market, we must determine the market demand.

Market demand is the sum of the demands of all the buyers in a market. To find the market demand, imagine a market in which there are only two buyers: Tina and Tim. The table in Figure 4.2 shows three demand schedules: Tina's, Tim's, and the market demand schedule. Tina's demand schedule is the same as before. It shows the quantity of water demanded by Tina at each different price. Tim's demand schedule tells us the quantity of water demanded by Tim at each price. To find the quantity of water demanded in the market, we sum the quantities demanded by Tina and Tim. For example, at a price of \$1.00 a bottle, the quantity demanded by Tina is 2 bottles a day, the quantity demanded by Tim is 1 bottle a day, and so the quantity demanded in the market is 3 bottles a day.

Market demand
The sum of the demands of all the buyers in the market.

Tina's demand curve in part (a) and Tim's demand curve in part (b) are graphs of the two individual demand schedules. The market demand curve in part (c) is a graph of the market demand schedule. At a given price, the quantity demanded on the market demand curve equals the horizontal sum of the quantities demanded on the individual demand curves.

FIGURE 4.2

Individual Demand and Market Demand

myeconlab Animation

Price (dollars per bottle)	Quantity demanded (bottles per day) Tina		Tim		Market
2.00	0		0		0
1.50	1		0		1
1.00	2	+	1	=	3
0.50	3		2		5

The market demand schedule is the sum of the individual demand schedules, and the market demand curve is the horizontal sum of the individual demand curves.

At a price of \$1 a bottle, the quantity demanded by Tina is 2 bottles a day and the quantity demanded by Tim is 1 bottle a day, so the total quantity demanded in the market is 3 bottles a day.

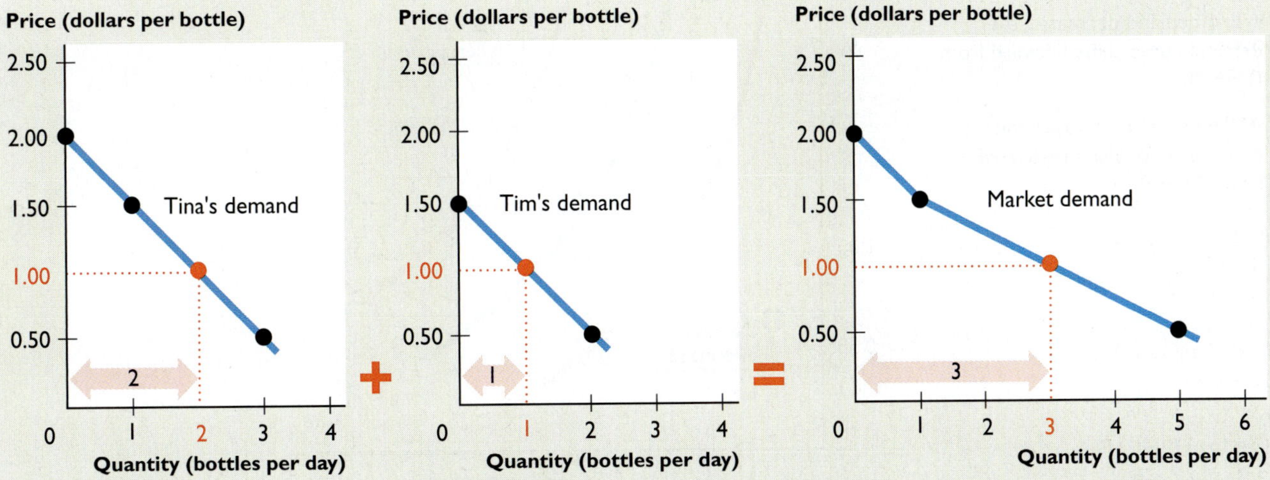

(a) Tina's demand (b) Tim's demand (c) Market demand

Changes in Demand

Change in demand
A change in the quantity that people plan to buy when any influence on buying plans other than the price of the good changes.

The demand curve shows how the quantity demanded changes when the price of the good changes but *all other influences on buying plans remain the same.* When any of these other influences on buying plans change, there is a **change in demand**, which means that there is a new demand schedule and new demand curve. *The demand curve shifts.*

Demand can either increase or decrease and Figure 4.3 illustrates the two cases. Initially, the demand curve is D_0. When demand decreases, the demand curve shifts leftward to D_1. On demand curve D_1, the quantity demanded at each price is smaller. When demand increases, the demand curve shifts rightward to D_2. On demand curve D_2, the quantity demanded at each price is greater.

The main influences on buying plans that change demand are

- Prices of related goods
- Expected future prices
- Income
- Expected future income and credit
- Number of buyers
- Preferences

Prices of Related Goods

Substitute
A good that can be consumed in place of another good.

Complement
A good that is consumed with another good.

Goods have substitutes and complements. A **substitute** for a good is another good that can be consumed in its place. Chocolate cake is a substitute for cheesecake, and bottled water is a substitute for Gatorade. A **complement** of a good is another good that is consumed with it. Wrist guards are a complement of in-line skates, and bottled water is a complement of fitness center services.

FIGURE 4.3

Changes in Demand

myeconlab Animation

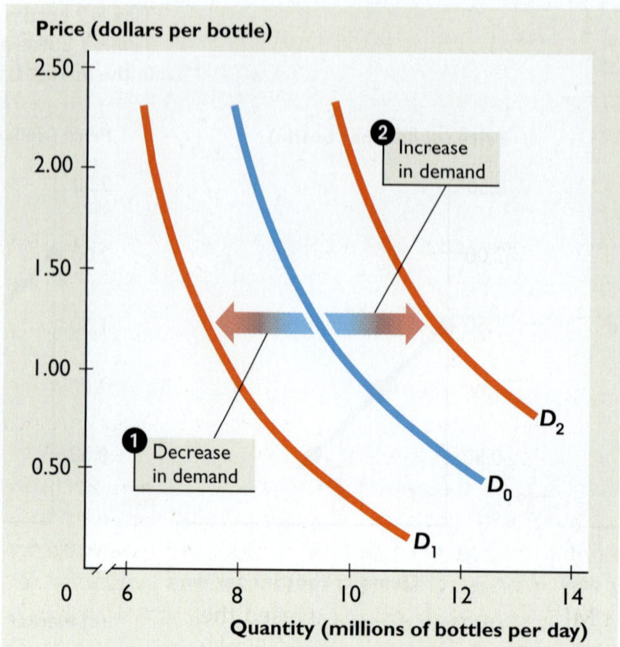

A change in any influence on buying plans, other than a change in the price of the good itself, changes demand and shifts the demand curve.

1. When demand decreases, the demand curve shifts leftward from D_0 to D_1.
2. When demand increases, the demand curve shifts rightward from D_0 to D_2.

The demand for a good and the price of one of its substitutes move in the *same direction*. The demand for a good *increases* if the price of one of its substitutes *rises* and *decreases* if the price of one of its substitutes *falls*. For example, the demand for cheesecake increases when the price of chocolate cake rises.

The demand for a good and the price of one of its complements move in *opposite directions*. The demand for a good *decreases* if the price of one of its complements *rises* and *increases* if the price of one of its complements *falls*. For example, the demand for wrist guards decreases when the price of in-line skates rises.

Expected Future Prices

A rise in the expected *future* price of a good increases the *current* demand for that good and a fall in the expected *future* price decreases *current* demand. If you expect the price of noodles to rise next week, you buy a big enough stockpile to get you through the next few weeks. Your demand for noodles today has increased. If you expect the price of noodles to fall next week, you buy none now and plan to buy next week. Your demand for noodles today has decreased.

Income

A rise in income brings an increase in demand and a fall in income brings a decrease in demand for a **normal good**. A rise in income brings a *decrease* in demand and a fall in income brings an *increase* in demand for an **inferior good.** For example, if your income increases and you decide to buy more chicken and less pasta, for you, chicken is a normal good and pasta is an inferior good.

Normal good
A good for which demand increases when income increases and demand decreases when income decreases.

Inferior good
A good for which demand decreases when income increases and demand increases when income decreases.

Expected Future Income and Credit

When income is expected to increase in the future, or when credit is easy to get and the cost of borrowing is low, the demand for some goods increases. And when income is expected to decrease in the future, or when credit is hard to get and the cost of borrowing is high, the demand for some goods decreases.

Changes in expected future income and the availability and cost of credit has the greatest effect on the demand for big ticket items such as homes and automobiles. Modest changes in expected future income or credit availability bring large swings in the demand for these items.

Number of Buyers

The greater the number of buyers in a market, the larger is demand. For example, the demand for parking spaces, movies, bottled water, or just about anything is greater in New York City than it is in Boise, Idaho.

Preferences

Tastes or *preferences*, as economists call them, influence demand. When preferences change, the demand for one item increases and the demand for another item (or items) decreases. For example, preferences have changed as people have become better informed about the health hazards of tobacco. This change in preferences has decreased the demand for cigarettes and has increased the demand for nicotine patches. Preferences also change when new goods become available. For example, the development of MP3 technology has decreased the demand for CDs and has increased the demand for Internet service and MP3 players.

Change in Quantity Demanded Versus Change in Demand

The influences on buyers' plans that you've just seen bring a *change in demand*. These are all the influences on buying plans *except for the price of the good*. To avoid confusion, when *the price of the good changes* and all other influences on buying plans remain the same, we say there has been a **change in the quantity demanded**.

Change in the quantity demanded
A change in the quantity of a good that people plan to buy that results from a change in the price of the good with all other influences on buying plans remaining the same.

The distinction between a change in demand and a change in the quantity demanded is crucial for figuring out how a market responds to the forces that hit it. Figure 4.4 illustrates and summarizes the distinction:

- If the price of bottled water *rises* when other things remain the same, the quantity demanded of bottled water *decreases* and there is a *movement up* along the demand curve D_0. If the price *falls* when other things remain the same, the quantity demanded *increases* and there is a *movement down* along the demand curve D_0.
- If some influence on buyers' plans other than the price of bottled water changes, there is a change in demand. When the demand for bottled water *decreases*, the demand curve *shifts leftward* to D_1. When the demand for bottled water *increases*, the demand curve *shifts rightward* to D_2.

When you are thinking about the influences on demand, try to get into the habit of asking: Does this influence change the quantity demanded or does it change demand? The test is: Did the price of the good change or did some other influence change? If the price changed, then quantity demanded changed. If some other influence changed and the price remained constant, then demand changed.

FIGURE 4.4

Change in Quantity Demanded Versus Change in Demand

myeconlab Animation

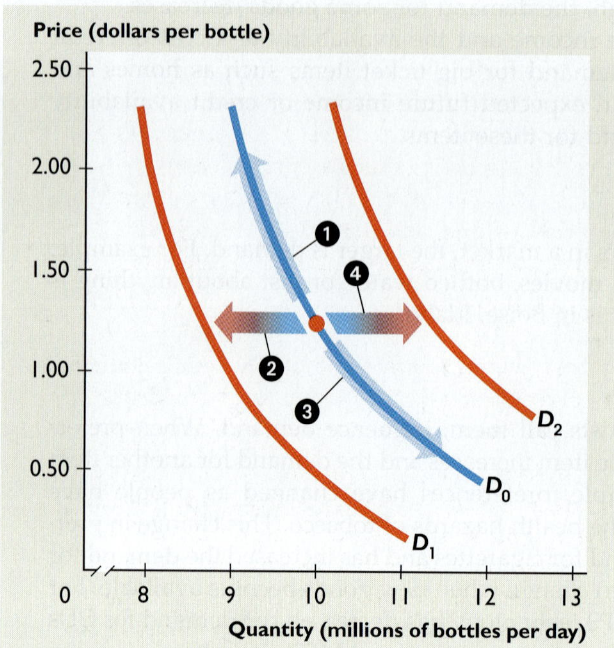

1 A decrease in the quantity demanded
If the price of a good rises, *cet. par.*, the quantity demanded decreases. There is a movement up along the demand curve D_0.

2 A decrease in demand
Demand decreases and the demand curve shifts leftward (from D_0 to D_1) if

- The price of a substitute falls or the price of a complement rises.
- The price of the good is expected to fall.
- Income decreases.*
- Expected future income or credit decreases.
- The number of buyers decreases.

3 An increase in the quantity demanded
If the price of a good falls, *cet. par.*, the quantity demanded increases. There is a movement down along the demand curve D_0.

4 An increase in demand
Demand increases and the demand curve shifts rightward (from D_0 to D_2) if

- The price of a substitute rises or the price of a complement falls.
- The price of the good is expected to rise.
- Income increases.
- Expected future income or credit increases.
- The number of buyers increases.

* Bottled water is a normal good.

CHECKPOINT 4.1

myeconlab

Work these problems in Study Plan 4.1 to get instant feedback.

Distinguish between quantity demanded and demand, and explain what determines demand.

Practice Problems

The following events occur one at a time in the market for cell phones:

- The price of a cell phone falls.
- Everyone believes that the price of a cell phone will fall next month.
- The price of a call made from a cell phone falls.
- The price of a call made from a land-line phone increases.
- The introduction of camera phones makes cell phones more popular.

Use this information to work Problems **1** to **3**.

1. Explain the effect of each event on the demand for cell phones.
2. Use a graph to illustrate the effect of each event.
3. Does any event (or events) illustrate the law of demand?
4. **Passenger numbers down**
   International Air Transport Association reported that passenger numbers fell by 11 percent last month. What will be the impact of swine flu? Recovery of passenger numbers depends on a rise in consumer confidence and a return to increased consumer spending. In response to the fall in passenger numbers, airlines cut capacity.

   The Nation, April 29, 2009

   Explain the effect of each event on the demand for air travel.

Guided Solutions to Practice Problems

1. A fall in the price of a cell phone increases the quantity of cell phones demanded but has no effect on the demand for cell phones.
   An expected fall in the price of a cell phone next month decreases the demand for cell phones today as people wait for the lower price.
   A fall in the price of a call from a cell phone increases the demand for cell phones because a cell phone call and a cell phone are complements.
   A rise in the price of a call from a land-line phone increases the demand for cell phones because a land-line phone and a cell phone are substitutes.
   With cell phones more popular, the demand for cell phones increases.
2. Figure 1 illustrates the effect of a fall in the price of a cell phone as a movement along the demand curve *D*.
   Figure 2 illustrates the effect of an increase in the demand for cell phones as the shift of the demand curve from D_0 to D_1 and a decrease in the demand for cell phones as the shift of the demand curve from D_0 to D_2.
3. A fall in the price of a cell phone (other things remaining the same), illustrates the law of demand. Figure 1 illustrates the law of demand. The other events change demand and do not illustrate the law of demand.
4. If people are worried about coming into contact with swine flu, they will cancel their travel plans. The demand for air travel will decrease. In the recovery, when consumer confidence and consumer spending increase, the demand for air travel will increase.The response of airlines to cut capacity does not influence the demand for air travel.

FIGURE 1

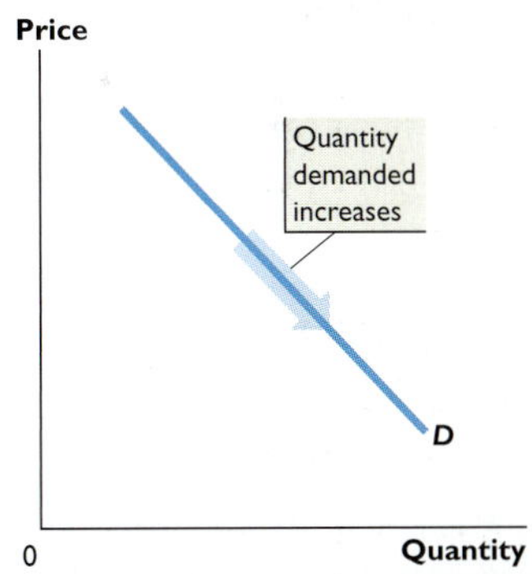

FIGURE 2

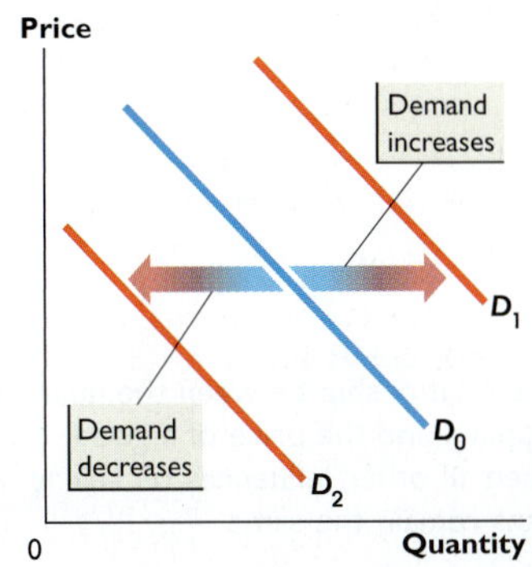

4.2 SUPPLY

A market has two sides. On one side are the buyers, or demanders, that we've just studied. On the other side of the market are the sellers, or suppliers. We now study the forces that determine suppliers' plans.

Quantity supplied
The amount of any good, service, or resource that people are willing and able to sell during a specified period at a specified price.

The **quantity supplied** of a good, service, or resource is the amount that people are willing and able to sell during a specified period at a specified price. For example, when the price of spring water is $1.50 a bottle, a spring owner decides to sell 2,000 bottles a day. The 2,000 bottles a day is the quantity supplied of spring water by this individual producer. (As in the case of demand, the quantity supplied is measured as an amount *per unit of time*.)

Many things influence selling plans, and one of them is the price. We look first at the relationship between quantity supplied of a good and its price. To study this relationship, we keep all other influences on selling plans the same, and we ask: How, other things remaining the same, does the quantity supplied of a good change as its price varies? The law of supply provides the answer.

The Law of Supply

The **law of supply** states

> **Other things remaining the same, if the price of a good rises, the quantity supplied of that good increases; and if the price of a good falls, the quantity supplied of that good decreases.**

So the law of supply states that when all other things remain the same, if the price of bottled water rises, spring owners will offer more water for sale; if the price of a flat panel TV falls, Sony Corp. will offer fewer flat panel TVs for sale.

Why, other things remaining the same, does the quantity supplied increase if the price rises and decrease if the price falls? Part of the answer lies in the principle of increasing opportunity cost (see p. 70). Because factors of production are not equally productive in all activities, as more of a good is produced, the opportunity cost of producing it increases. A higher price provides the incentive to bear the higher opportunity cost of increased production. Another part of the answer is that for a given cost, the higher price brings a larger profit, so sellers have greater incentive to increase production.

Think about the resources that you own and can offer for sale to others and ask yourself: Which of these items does *not* obey the law of supply? If the wage rate for summer jobs increased, would you have an incentive to work longer hours and bear the higher opportunity cost of forgone leisure? If the bank offered a higher interest rate on deposits, would you have an incentive to save more and bear the higher opportunity cost of forgone consumption? If the used book dealer offered a higher price for last year's textbooks, would you have an incentive to sell that handy math text and bear the higher opportunity cost of visiting the library (or finding a friend) whenever you needed the book?

Supply Schedule and Supply Curve

Supply
The relationship between the quantity supplied and the price of a good when all other influences on selling plans remain the same.

Supply is the relationship between the quantity supplied and the price of a good when all other influences on selling plans remain the same. The quantity supplied is *one* quantity at *one* price. *Supply* is a *list of quantities at different prices* illustrated by a supply schedule and a supply curve.

A **supply schedule** lists the quantities supplied at each different price when all the other influences on selling plans remain the same. The table in Figure 4.5 is one firm's (Agua's) supply schedule for bottled water. It tells us that if the price of water is 50 cents a bottle, Agua plans to sell no water. Its quantity supplied is 0 bottles a day. If the price of water is $1.00 a bottle, Agua's quantity supplied is 1,000 bottles a day. Agua's quantity supplied increases to 2,000 bottles a day at a price of $1.50 a bottle and to 3,000 bottles a day at a price of $2.00 a bottle.

Supply schedule
A list of the quantities supplied at each different price when all the other influences on selling plans remain the same.

A **supply curve** is a graph of the relationship between the quantity supplied of a good and its price when all the other influences on selling plans remain the same. The points on the supply curve labeled *A* through *D* represent the rows *A* through *D* of the supply schedule. For example, point *C* on the supply curve represents row *C* of the supply schedule and shows that the quantity supplied is 1,000 bottles a day when the price is $1.00 a bottle. Point *B* on the supply curve represents row *B* of the supply schedule and shows that the quantity supplied is 2,000 bottles a day when the price is $1.50 a bottle.

Supply curve
A graph of the relationship between the quantity supplied of a good and its price when all the other influences on selling plans remain the same.

The upward slope of the supply curve illustrates the law of supply. Along the supply curve, when the price of the good *rises*, the quantity supplied *increases*. For example, in Figure 4.5, when the price of a bottle of water rises from $1.50 to $2.00, the quantity supplied increases from 2,000 bottles a day to 3,000 bottles a day. And when the price *falls*, the quantity supplied *decreases*. For example, when the price falls from $1.50 to $1.00 a bottle, the quantity supplied decreases from 2,000 bottles a day to 1,000 bottles a day.

FIGURE 4.5

Supply Schedule and Supply Curve

myeconlab Animation

	Price (dollars per bottle)	Quantity supplied (thousands of bottles per day)
A	2.00	3
B	1.50	2
C	1.00	1
D	0.50	0

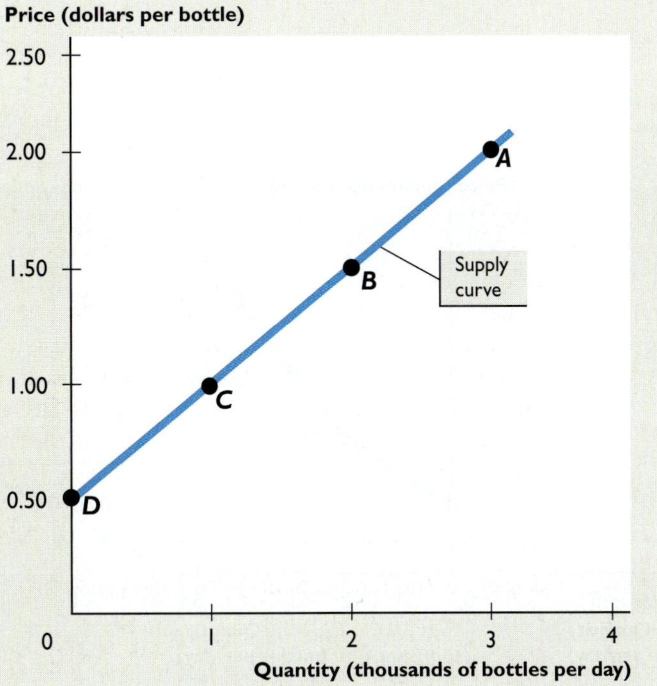

The table shows a supply schedule that lists the quantity of water supplied at each price if all other influences on selling plans remain the same. At a price of $1.50 a bottle, the quantity supplied is 2,000 bottles a day.

The supply curve shows the relationship between the quantity supplied and price, other things remaining the same. The upward-sloping supply curve illustrates the law of supply. When the price rises, the quantity supplied increases; and when the price falls, the quantity supplied decreases.

Individual Supply and Market Supply

The supply schedule and the supply curve that you've just studied are for one seller. To study a market, we must determine the market supply.

Market supply
The sum of the supplies of all the sellers in the market.

Market supply is the sum of the supplies of all the sellers in the market. To find the market supply of water, imagine a market in which there are only two sellers: Agua and Prima. The table in Figure 4.6 shows three supply schedules: Agua's, Prima's, and the market supply schedule. Agua's supply schedule is the same as before. Prima's supply schedule tells us the quantity of water that Prima plans to sell at each price. To find the quantity of water supplied in the market, we sum the quantities supplied by Agua and Prima. For example, at a price of $1.00 a bottle, the quantity supplied by Agua is 1,000 bottles a day, the quantity supplied by Prima is 2,000 bottles a day, and the quantity supplied in the market is 3,000 bottles a day.

Agua's supply curve in part (a) and Prima's supply curve in part (b) are graphs of the two individual supply schedules. The market supply curve in part (c) is a graph of the market supply schedule. At a given price, the quantity supplied on the market supply curve equals the horizontal sum of the quantities supplied on the individual supply curves.

FIGURE 4.6

Individual Supply and Market Supply

myeconlab Animation

Price (dollars per bottle)	Quantity supplied (thousands of bottles per day)		
	Agua	Prima	Market
2.00	3	4	7
1.50	2	3	5
1.00	1 +	2 =	3
0.50	0	0	0

The market supply schedule is the sum of the individual supply schedules, and the market supply curve is the horizontal sum of the individual supply curves.

At a price of $1 a bottle, the quantity supplied by Agua is 1,000 bottles a day and the quantity supplied by Prima is 2,000 bottles a day, so the total quantity supplied in the market is 3,000 bottles a day.

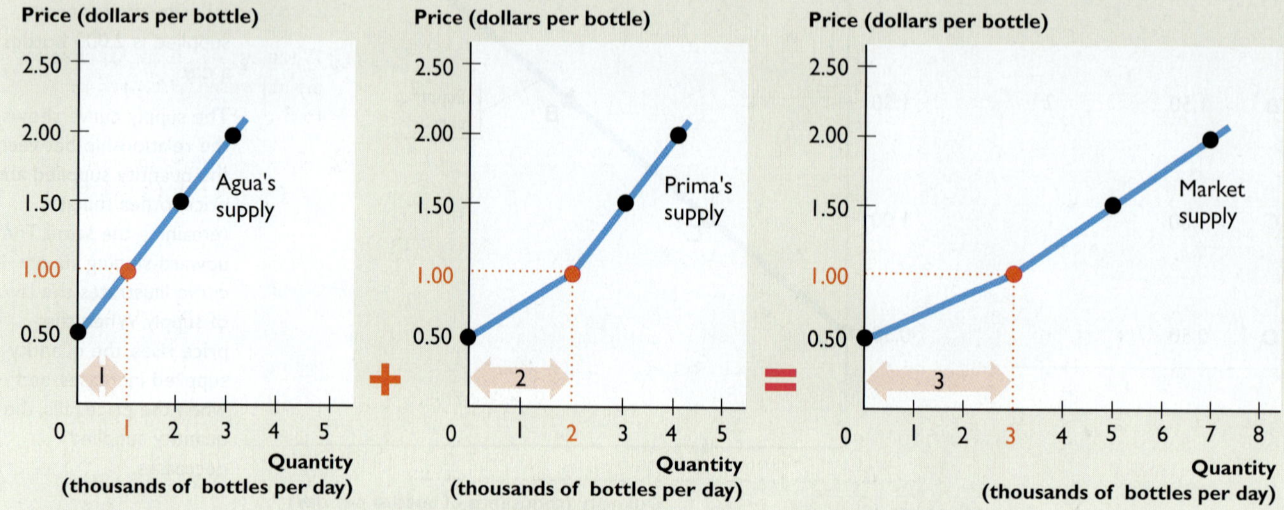

(a) Agua's supply (b) Prima's supply (c) Market supply

Changes in Supply

The supply curve shows how the quantity supplied changes when the price of the good changes but *all other influences on selling plans remain the same.* When any of these other influences on selling plans change, there is a **change in supply**, which means that there is a new supply schedule and new supply curve. *The supply curve shifts.*

Change in supply
A change in the quantity that suppliers plan to sell when any influence on selling plans other than the price of the good changes.

Supply can either increase or decrease, and Figure 4.7 illustrates the two cases. Initially, the supply curve is S_0. When supply decreases, the supply curve shifts leftward to S_1. On supply curve S_1, the quantity supplied at each price is smaller. When supply increases, the supply curve shifts rightward to S_2. On supply curve S_2, the quantity supplied at each price is greater.

The main influences on selling plans that change supply are

- Prices of related goods
- Prices of resources and other inputs
- Expected future prices
- Number of sellers
- Productivity

Prices of Related Goods

Related goods are either substitutes *in production* or complements *in production*. A **substitute in production** for a good is another good that can be produced in its place. Skinny jeans are substitutes in production for boot cut jeans in a clothing factory.

A **complement in production** of a good is another good that is produced along with it. Cream is a complement in production of skim milk in a dairy.

Substitute in production
A good that can be produced in place of another good.

Complement in production
A good that is produced along with another good.

FIGURE 4.7

Changes in Supply

myeconlab Animation

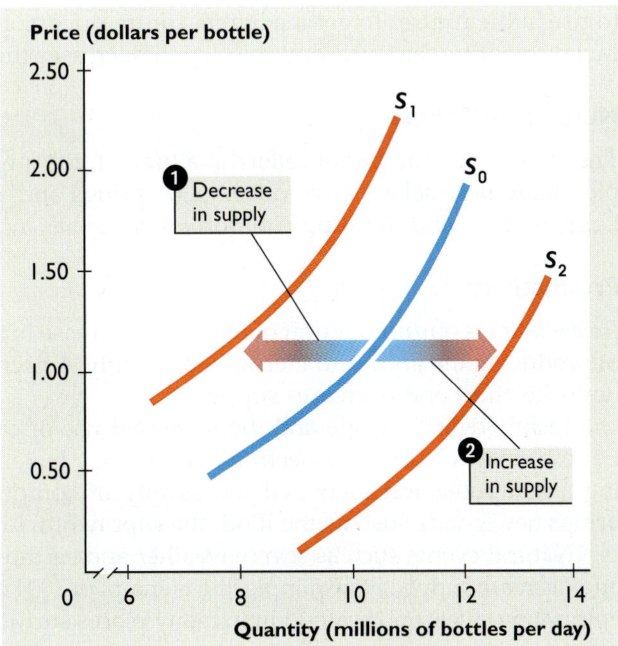

A change in any influence on selling plans other than a change in the price of the good itself changes supply and shifts the supply curve.

1. When supply decreases, the supply curve shifts leftward from S_0 to S_1.
2. When supply increases, the supply curve shifts rightward from S_0 to S_2.

A Change in the Price of a Substitute in Production The supply of a good *decreases* if the price of one of its substitutes in production *rises;* and the supply of a good *increases* if the price of one of its substitutes in production *falls*. That is, the supply of a good and the price of one of its substitutes in production move in *opposite directions*. For example, a clothing factory can produce cargo pants or button-fly jeans, so these goods are substitutes in production. When the price of button-fly jeans rises, the clothing factory switches production from cargo pants to button-fly jeans, so the supply of cargo pants decreases.

A Change in the Price of a Complement in Production The supply of a good *increases* if the price of one of its complements in production *rises;* and the supply of a good *decreases* if the price of one of its complements in production *falls*. That is, the supply of a good and the price of one of its complements in production move in the *same direction*. For example, when a dairy produces skim milk, it also produces cream, so these goods are complements in production. When the price of skim milk rises, the dairy produces more skim milk, so the supply of cream increases.

Prices of Resources and Other Inputs

Supply changes when the price of a resource or other input used to produce the good changes. The reason is that resource and input prices influence the cost of production. The more it costs to produce a good, the smaller is the quantity supplied of that good at each price (other things remaining the same). For example, if the wage rate of bottling-plant workers rises, it costs more to produce a bottle of water, so the supply of bottled water decreases.

Expected Future Prices

Expectations about future prices influence supply. For example, a severe frost that wipes out Florida's citrus crop doesn't change the production of orange juice today, but it does decrease production later in the year when the current crop would normally have been harvested. Sellers of orange juice will expect the price to rise in the future. To get the higher future price, some sellers will increase their inventory of frozen juice, and this action decreases the supply of juice today.

Number of Sellers

The greater the number of sellers in a market, the larger is the supply. For example, many new sellers have developed springs and water-bottling plants in the United States, and the supply of bottled water has increased.

Productivity

Productivity is output per unit of input. An increase in productivity lowers the cost of producing the good and increases its supply. A decrease in productivity has the opposite effect and decreases supply.

Technological change and the increased use of capital increase productivity. For example, advances in electronic technology have lowered the cost of producing a computer and increased the supply of computers. Technological change brings new goods such as the iPod, the supply of which was previously zero.

Natural events such as severe weather and earthquakes decrease productivity and decrease supply. For example, the tsunami of 2004 decreased the supply of agricultural products and seafood in in many places surrounding the Indian Ocean.

Change in Quantity Supplied Versus Change in Supply

The influences on sellers' plans you've just considered bring a *change in supply*. These are all the influences on sellers' plans *except the price of the good*. To avoid confusion, when the *price of the good changes* and all other influences on selling plans remain the same, we say there has been a **change in the quantity supplied**.

Change in the quantity supplied
A change in the quantity of a good that suppliers plan to sell that results from a change in the price of the good.

The distinction between a change in supply and a change in the quantity supplied is crucial for figuring out how a market responds to the forces that hit it. Figure 4.8 illustrates and summarizes the distinction:

- If the price of bottled water *falls* when other things remain the same, the quantity supplied of bottled water *decreases* and there is a *movement down* along the supply curve S_0. If the price *rises* when other things remain the same, the quantity supplied *increases* and there is a *movement up* along the supply curve S_0.
- If any influence on water bottlers' plans other than the price of bottled water changes, there is a change in the supply of bottled water. When the supply of bottled water *decreases*, the supply curve *shifts leftward* to S_1. When the supply of bottled water *increases*, the supply curve *shifts rightward* to S_2.

When you are thinking about the influences on supply, get into the habit of asking: Does this influence change the quantity supplied or does it change supply? The test is: Did the price change or did some other influence change? If the price of the good changed, then quantity supplied changed. If some other influence changed and the price of the good remained constant, then supply changed.

FIGURE 4.8

Change in Quantity Supplied Versus Change in Supply

myeconlab Animation

1 A decrease in the quantity supplied
If the price of a good falls, *cet. par.*, the quantity supplied decreases.
There is a movement down along the demand curve S_0.

2 A decrease in supply
Supply decreases and the supply curve shifts leftward (from S_0 to S_1) if

- The price of a substitute in production rises.
- The price of a complement in production falls.
- A resource price or other input price rises.
- The price of the good is expected to rise.
- The number of sellers decreases.
- Productivity decreases.

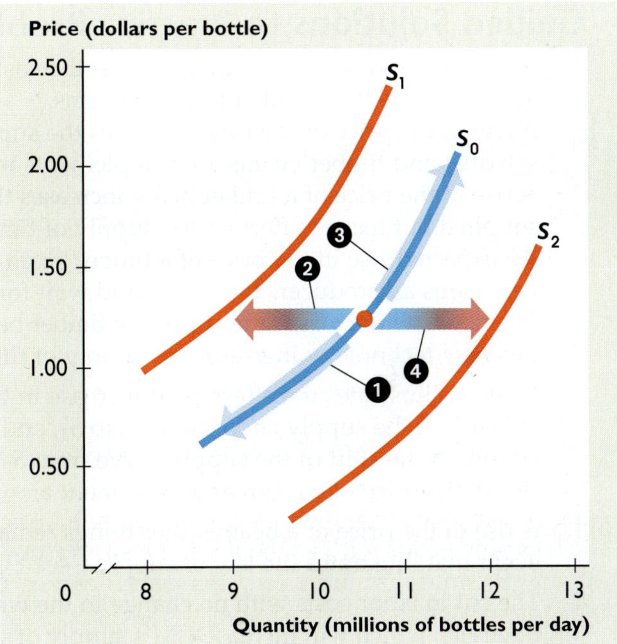

3 An increase in the quantity supplied
If the price of a good rises, *cet. par.*, the quantity supplied increases.
There is a movement up along the supply curve S_0.

4 An increase in supply
Supply increases and the supply curve shifts rightward (from S_0 to S_2) if

- The price of a substitute in production falls.
- The price of a complement in production rises.
- A resource price or other input price falls.
- The price of the good is expected to fall.
- The number of sellers increases.
- Productivity increases.

myeconlab

Work these problems in Study Plan 4.2 to get instant feedback.

CHECKPOINT 4.2

Distinguish between quantity supplied and supply, and explain what determines supply.

Practice Problems

Lumber companies make timber beams from logs. In the process of making beams, the mill produces sawdust, which is made into pressed wood. In the market for timber beams, the following events occur one at a time:

- The wage rate of sawmill workers rises.
- The price of sawdust rises.
- The price of a timber beam rises.
- The price of a timber beam is expected to rise next year.
- Environmentalists convince Congress to introduce a new law that reduces the amount of forest that can be cut for timber products.
- A new technology lowers the cost of producing timber beams.

Use this information to work Problems **1** to **3**.

1. Explain the effect of each event on the supply of timber beams.
2. Use a graph to illustrate the effect of each event.
3. Does any event (or events) illustrate the law of supply?
4. **GM, UAW reach crucial cost-cutting pact**

   General Motors has made a deal with the United Auto Workers to restructure the tasks that any worker can perform. This restructuring, with no change in the wage rate, will save GM $1 billion in labor costs a year.

   Source: *Wall Street Journal*, May 22, 2009

   Will this reduction of labor costs, with no change in the wage rate, change GM's supply of vehicles? Explain your answer.

Guided Solutions to Practice Problems

1. A rise in workers' wage rates increases the cost of producing a timber beam and decreases the supply of timber beams.
   A rise in the price of sawdust increases the supply of timber beams because sawdust and timber beams are complements in production.
   A rise in the price of a timber beam increases the quantity of timber beams supplied but has no effect on the supply of timber beams.
   An expected rise in the price of a timber beam decreases the supply of timber beams as producers hold back and wait for the higher price.
   The new law decreases the supply of timber beams.
   The new technology increases the supply of timber beams.
2. Figure 1 illustrates the effect of an increase in the supply of timber beams as the shift of the supply curve from S_0 to S_1, and it illustrates a decrease in the supply as the shift of the supply curve from S_0 to S_2. Figure 2 illustrates the rise in the price of a beam as a movement along the supply curve S.
3. A rise in the price of a beam, other things remaining the same, is the only event that illustrates the law of supply—see Figure 2.
4. The cut in labor costs with no change in the wage rate is an increase in productivity, which will increase GM's supply of vehicles.

FIGURE 1

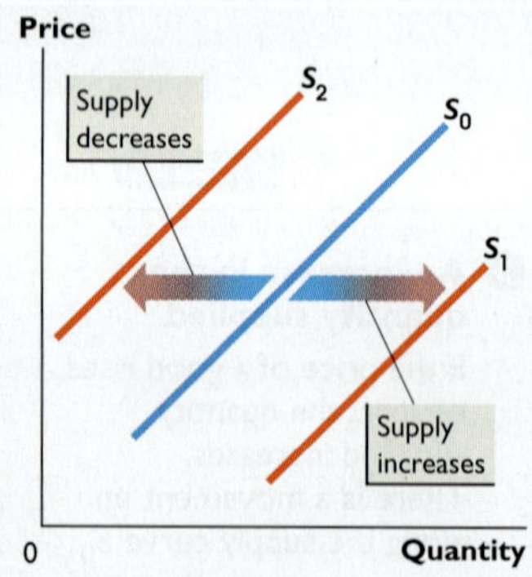

FIGURE 2

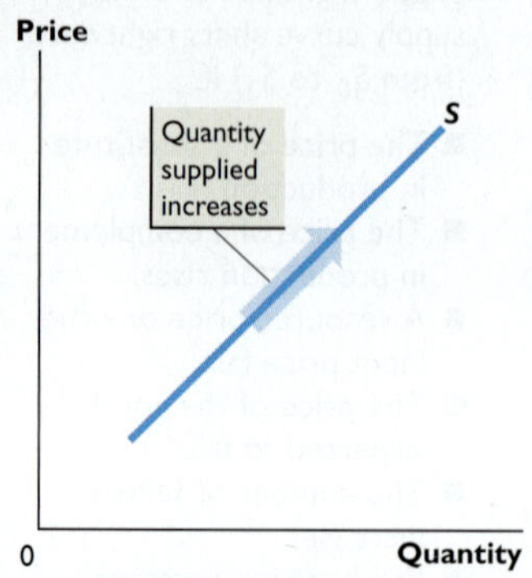

4.3 MARKET EQUILIBRIUM

In everyday language, "equilibrium" means "opposing forces are in balance." In a market, demand and supply are the opposing forces. **Market equilibrium** occurs when the quantity demanded equals the quantity supplied—when buyers' and sellers' plans are in balance. At the **equilibrium price**, the quantity demanded equals the quantity supplied. The **equilibrium quantity** is the quantity bought and sold at the equilibrium price.

In the market for bottled water in Figure 4.9, equilibrium occurs where the demand curve and the supply curve intersect. The equilibrium price is $1.00 a bottle, and the equilibrium quantity is 10 million bottles a day.

Market equilibrium
When the quantity demanded equals the quantity supplied—buyers' and sellers' plans are in balance.

Equilibrium price
The price at which the quantity demanded equals the quantity supplied.

Equilibrium quantity
The quantity bought and sold at the equilibrium price.

Price: A Market's Automatic Regulator

When equilibrium is disturbed, market forces restore it. The **law of market forces** states

When there is a surplus, the price falls; and when there is a shortage, the price rises.

A **surplus** or **excess supply** is a situation in which the quantity supplied exceeds the quantity demanded. If there is a surplus, suppliers must cut the price to sell more. Buyers are pleased to take the lower price, so the price falls. Because a surplus arises when the price is above the equilibrium price, a falling price is exactly what the market needs to restore equilibrium.

A **shortage** or **excess demand** is a situation in which the quantity demanded exceeds the quantity supplied. If there is a shortage, buyers must pay a higher price to get more. Sellers are pleased to take the higher price, so the price rises. Because a shortage arises when the price is below the equilibrium price, a rising

Surplus or excess supply
A situation in which the quantity supplied exceeds the quantity demanded.

Shortage or excess demand
A situation in which the quantity demanded exceeds the quantity supplied.

FIGURE 4.9

Equilibrium Price and Equilibrium Quantity

myeconlab Animation

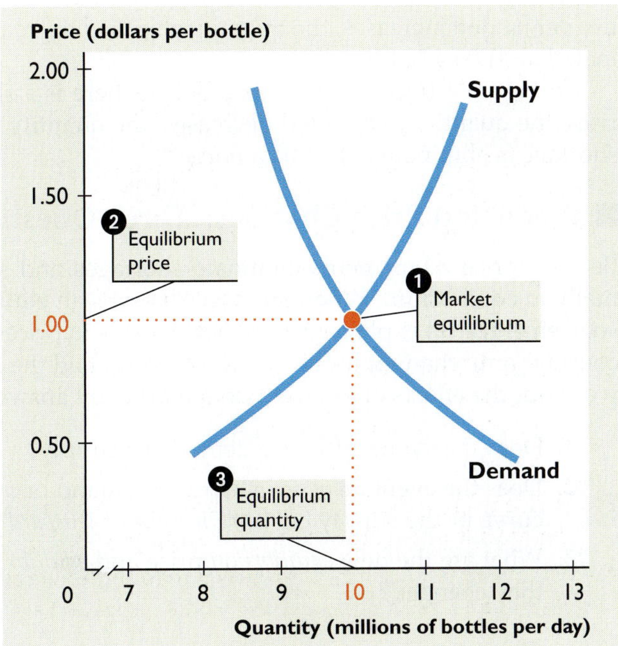

1. Market equilibrium occurs at the intersection of the demand curve and the supply curve.
2. The equilibrium price is $1.00 a bottle.
3. At the equilibrium price, the quantity demanded and the quantity supplied are 10 million bottles a day, which is the equilibrium quantity.

FIGURE 4.10

The Forces That Achieve Equilibrium

myeconlab Animation

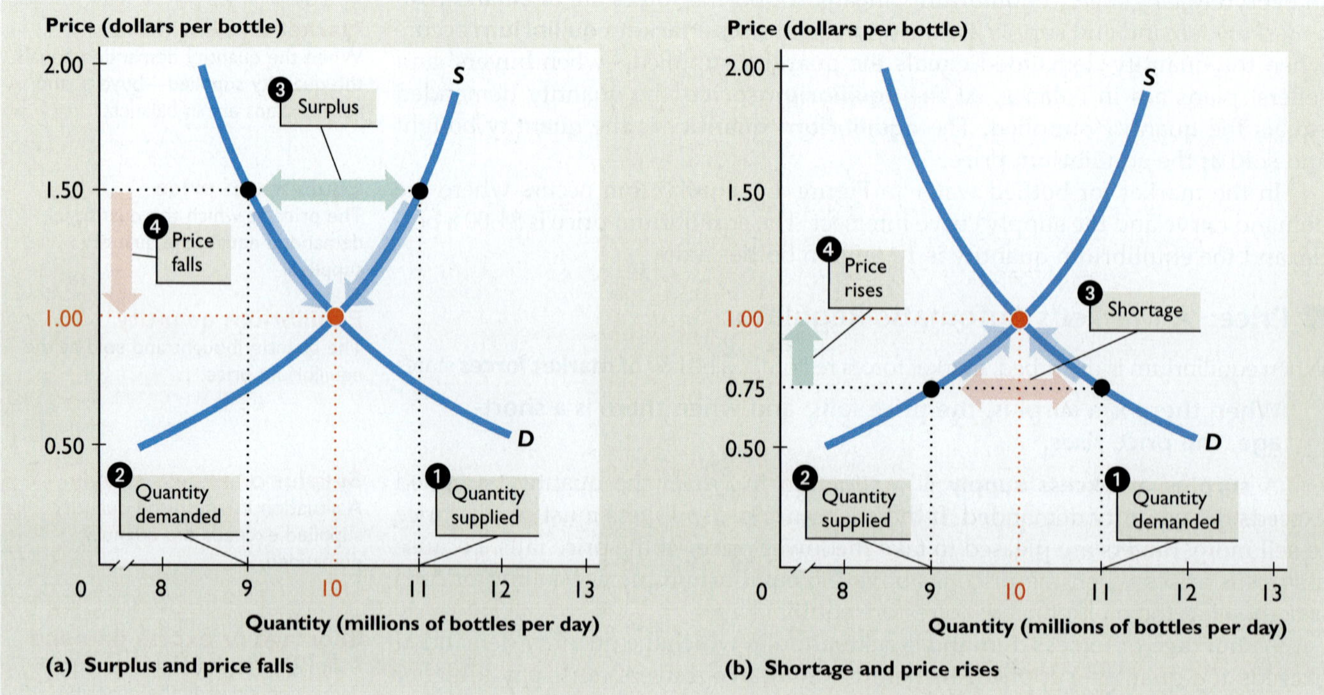

At $1.50 a bottle, ❶ the quantity supplied is 11 million bottles, ❷ the quantity demanded is 9 million bottles, ❸ the surplus is 2 million bottles, and ❹ the price falls.

At 75 cents a bottle, ❶ the quantity demanded is 11 million bottles, ❷ the quantity supplied is 9 million bottles, ❸ the shortage is 2 million bottles, and ❹ the price rises.

price is exactly what is needed to restore equilibrium.

In Figure 4.10(a), at $1.50 a bottle, there is a surplus: The price falls, the quantity demanded increases, the quantity supplied decreases, and the surplus is eliminated at $1.00 a bottle.

In Figure 4.10(b), at 75 cents a bottle, there is a shortage of water: The price rises, the quantity demanded decreases, the quantity supplied increases, and the shortage is eliminated at $1.00 a bottle.

Predicting Price Changes: Three Questions

Because price adjustments eliminate shortages and surpluses, markets are normally in equilibrium. When an event disturbs an equilibrium, a new equilibrium soon emerges. To explain and predict changes in prices and quantities, we need to consider only changes in the *equilibrium* price and the *equilibrium* quantity. We can work out the effects of an event on a market by answering three questions:

1. Does the event influence demand or supply?
2. Does the event *increase* or *decrease* demand or supply—shift the demand curve or the supply curve *rightward* or *leftward*?
3. What are the new *equilibrium* price and *equilibrium* quantity and how have they changed?

Effects of Changes in Demand

Let's practice answering the three questions by working out the effects of an event in the market for bottled water: A new study says that tap water is unsafe.

1. With tap water unsafe, the demand for bottled water changes.
2. The demand for bottled water *increases*, and the demand curve *shifts rightward*. Figure 4.11(a) shows the shift from D_0 to D_1.
3. There is now a *shortage* at \$1.00 a bottle. The *price rises* to \$1.50 a bottle, and the quantity increases to 11 million bottles.

Note that there is *no change in supply*; the rise in price brings an *increase in the quantity supplied*—a movement along the supply curve.

Let's work out what happens if the price of a zero-calorie sports drink falls.

1. The sports drink is a substitute for bottled water, so when its price changes, the demand for bottled water changes.
2. The demand for bottled water *decreases*, and the demand curve *shifts leftward*. Figure 4.11(b) shows the shift from D_0 to D_2.
3. There is now a *surplus* at \$1.00 a bottle. The price *falls* to 75 cents a bottle, and the quantity decreases to 9 million bottles.

Note again that there is *no change in supply*; the fall in price brings a *decrease in the quantity supplied*—a movement along the supply curve.

FIGURE 4.11

The Effects of a Change in Demand

myeconlab Animation

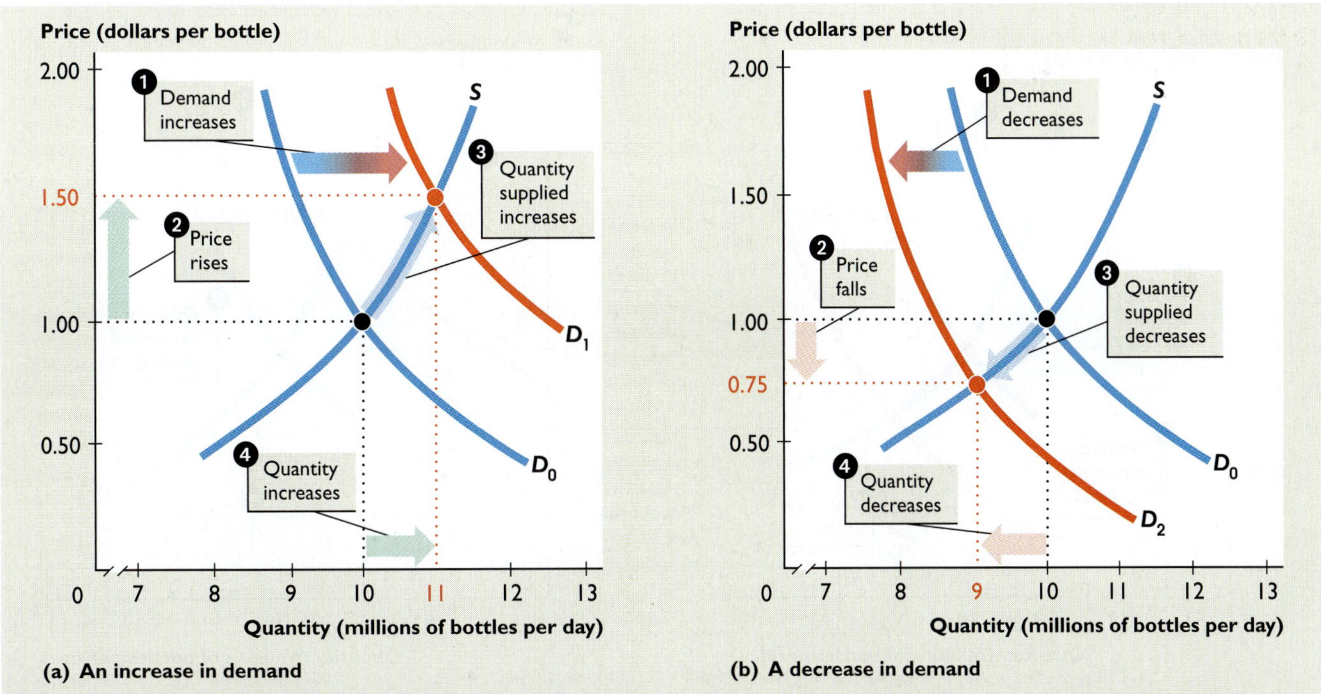

1 An increase in demand shifts the demand curve rightward to D_1 and creates a shortage. 2 The price rises, 3 the quantity supplied increases, and 4 the equilibrium quantity increases.

1 A decrease in demand shifts the demand curve leftward to D_2 and creates a surplus. 2 The price falls, 3 the quantity supplied decreases, and 4 the equilibrium quantity decreases.

Effects of Changes in Supply

You can get more practice working out the effects of another event in the market for bottled water: European water bottlers buy springs and open new plants in the United States.

1. With more suppliers of bottled water, the supply changes.
2. The supply of bottled water *increases*, and the supply curve *shifts rightward*. Figure 4.12(a) shows the shift from S_0 to S_1.
3. There is now a *surplus* at \$1.00 a bottle. The *price falls* to 75 cents a bottle, and the quantity increases to 11 million bottles.

Note that there is *no change in demand*; the fall in price brings an *increase in the quantity demanded*—a movement along the demand curve.

What happens if a drought dries up some springs?

1. The drought is a change in productivity, so the supply of water changes.
2. With fewer springs, the supply of bottled water *decreases*, and the supply curve *shifts leftward*. Figure 4.12(b) shows the shift from S_0 to S_2.
3. There is now a *shortage* at \$1.00 a bottle. The *price rises* to \$1.50 a bottle, and the quantity decreases to 9 million bottles.

Again, there is *no change in demand*; the rise in price brings a *decrease in the quantity demanded*—a movement along the demand curve.

FIGURE 4.12

The Effects of a Change in Supply

myeconlab Animation

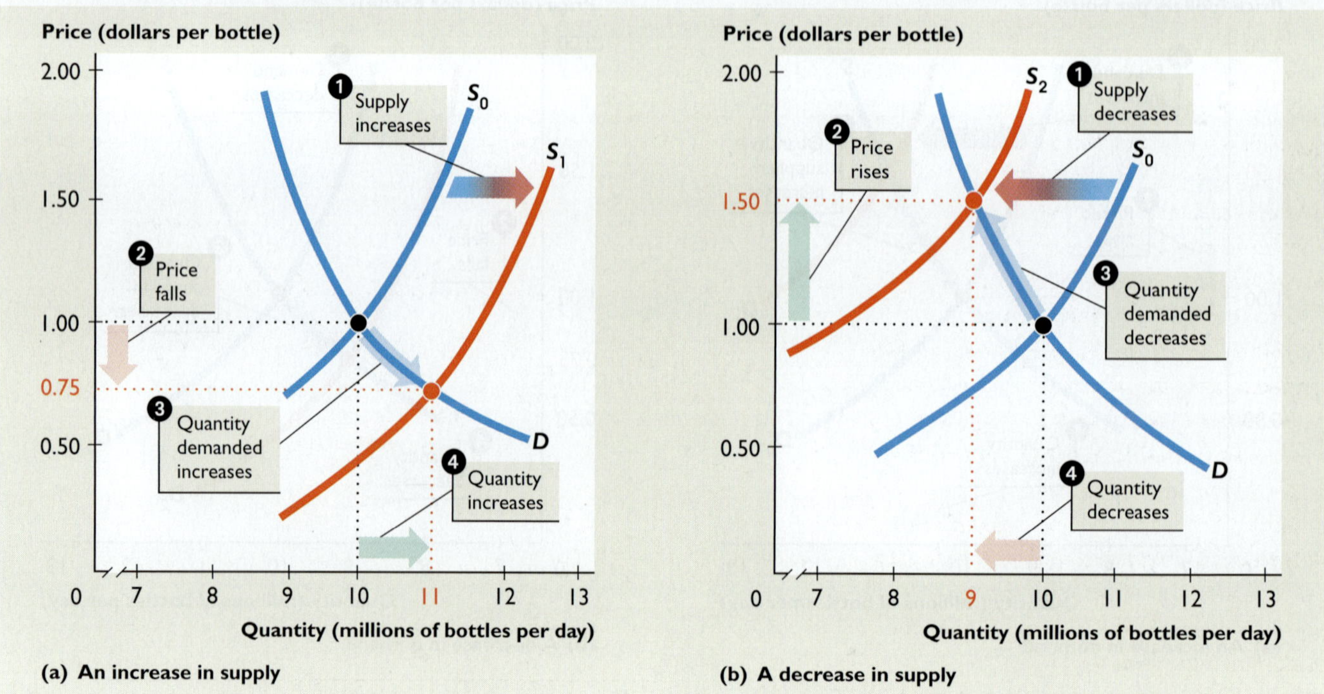

① An increase in supply shifts the supply curve rightward to S_1 and creates a surplus. ② The price falls, ③ the quantity demanded increases, and ④ the equilibrium quantity increases.

① A decrease in supply shifts the supply curve leftward to S_2 and creates a shortage. ② The price rises, ③ the quantity demanded decreases, and ④ the equilibrium quantity decreases.

EYE on the U.S. ECONOMY

The U.S. Market for Automobiles in 2008 and 2009

In 2008, the equilibrium price of an automobile was $20,000 and 16 million vehicles were bought and sold.

In 2009, millions of families decided to hold off buying a new car. Why? Layoffs had cut many people's incomes and many more feared being laid off in the near future. Also, as the value of people's homes tumbled, even those who still had a job felt poorer.

With lower incomes and lower expected future incomes, the demand for automobiles decreased from D_{08} to D_{09}.

The equilibrium price fell to $19,000 per vehicle, and the equilibrium quantity decreased to 12 million vehicles—a decrease in the quantity supplied shown by a movement along the supply curve.

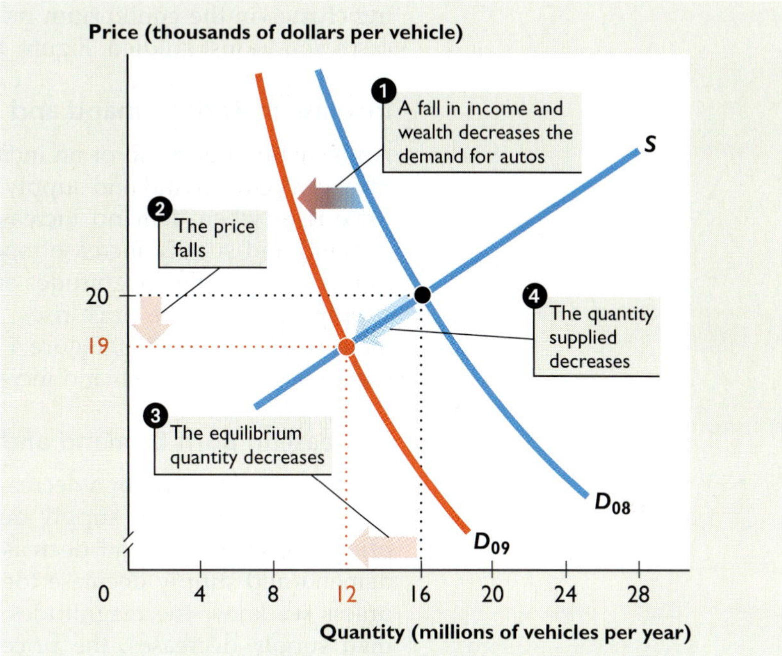

EYE on the GLOBAL ECONOMY

The Global Market for Wheat in 2008

In 2008, the price of wheat soared from $150 a ton to $240 a ton. Why? Because two events in the global wheat market decreased supply: widespread drought and a rise in the price of fertilizers.

Drought affected wheat growers in Argentina, Australia, China, Europe, and the United States, and wheat production fell.

Fertilizers—nitrogen, potassium, and potash—are used to grow wheat and the prices of fertilizers doubled.

Both of these large shocks to supply decreased the supply of wheat from S_{07} to S_{08}. The price of wheat rose to its new equilibrium price of $240 per ton. As the price rose, the quantity of wheat demanded decreased and the equilibrium quantity decreased to 780 million tons.

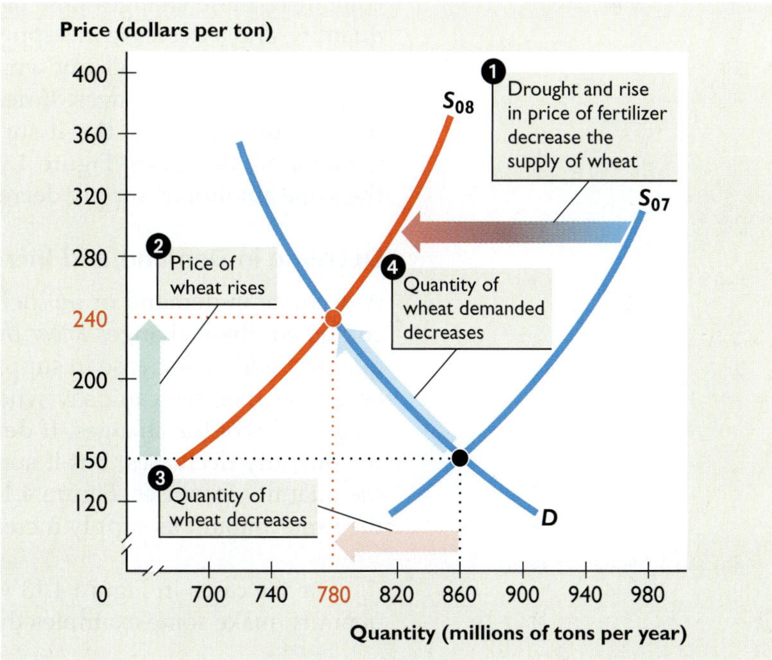

Changes in Both Demand and Supply

When events occur that change *both* demand and supply, you can find the resulting change in the equilibrium price and equilibrium quantity by combining the cases you've just studied. Figure 4.13 summarizes all the possible cases.

Increase in Both Demand and Supply

An increase in demand or an increase in supply increases the equilibrium quantity. So when demand and supply increase together, the *quantity increases*. But the price rises when demand increases and falls when supply increases. So when demand and supply increase together, we can't say what happens to the price unless we know the magnitudes of the changes. If demand increases by more than supply increases, the price rises. But if supply increases by more than demand increases, the price falls. Figure 4.13(e) shows the case when supply increases by the same amount as demand increases, so the price remains unchanged.

Decrease in Both Demand and Supply

A decrease in demand or a decrease in supply decreases the equilibrium quantity. So when demand and supply decrease together, the *quantity decreases*. But the price falls when demand decreases and rises when supply decreases. So when demand and supply decrease together, we can't say what happens to the price unless we know the magnitudes of the changes. If demand decreases by more than supply decreases, the price falls. But if supply decreases by more than demand decreases, the price rises. Figure 4.13(i) shows the case when supply decreases by the same amount as demand decreases, so the price remains unchanged.

Increase in Demand and Decrease in Supply

An increase in demand or a decrease in supply raises the equilibrium price, so combined, these changes *raise the price*. But an increase in demand increases the quantity, and a decrease in supply decreases the quantity. So when these changes occur together, we can't say what happens to the quantity unless we know the magnitudes of the changes. If demand increases by more than supply decreases, the quantity increases. But if supply decreases by more than demand increases, the quantity decreases. Figure 4.13(h) shows the case when demand increases by the same amount as supply decreases, so the quantity remains unchanged.

Decrease in Demand and Increase in Supply

A decrease in demand or an increase in supply lowers the equilibrium price, so combined, these changes *lower the price*. But a decrease in demand decreases the quantity, and an increase in supply increases the quantity. So when these changes occur together, we can't say what happens to the quantity unless we know the magnitudes of the changes. If demand decreases by more than supply increases, the quantity decreases. But if supply increases by more than demand decreases, the quantity increases. Figure 4.13(f) shows the case when demand decreases by the same amount as supply increases, so the quantity remains unchanged.

For the cases in Figure 4.13 where you "can't say" what happens to price or quantity, make some examples that go in each direction.

EYE on YOUR LIFE

Using Demand and Supply

The demand and supply model is going to be a big part of the rest of your life!

First, you will use it again and again during your economics course. The demand and supply model is one of your major tools, so having a firm grasp of it will bring an immediate payoff.

But second, and much more important, by understanding the laws of demand and supply and being aware of how prices adjust to balance these two opposing forces, you will have a much better appreciation of how your economic world works.

Every time you hear someone complaining about a price hike and blaming it on someone's greed, think about the law of market forces and how demand and supply determine that price.

As you shop for your favorite clothing, music, and food items, try to describe how supply and demand influence the prices of these goods.

FIGURE 4.13

The Effects of All the Possible Changes in Demand and Supply

myeconlab Animation

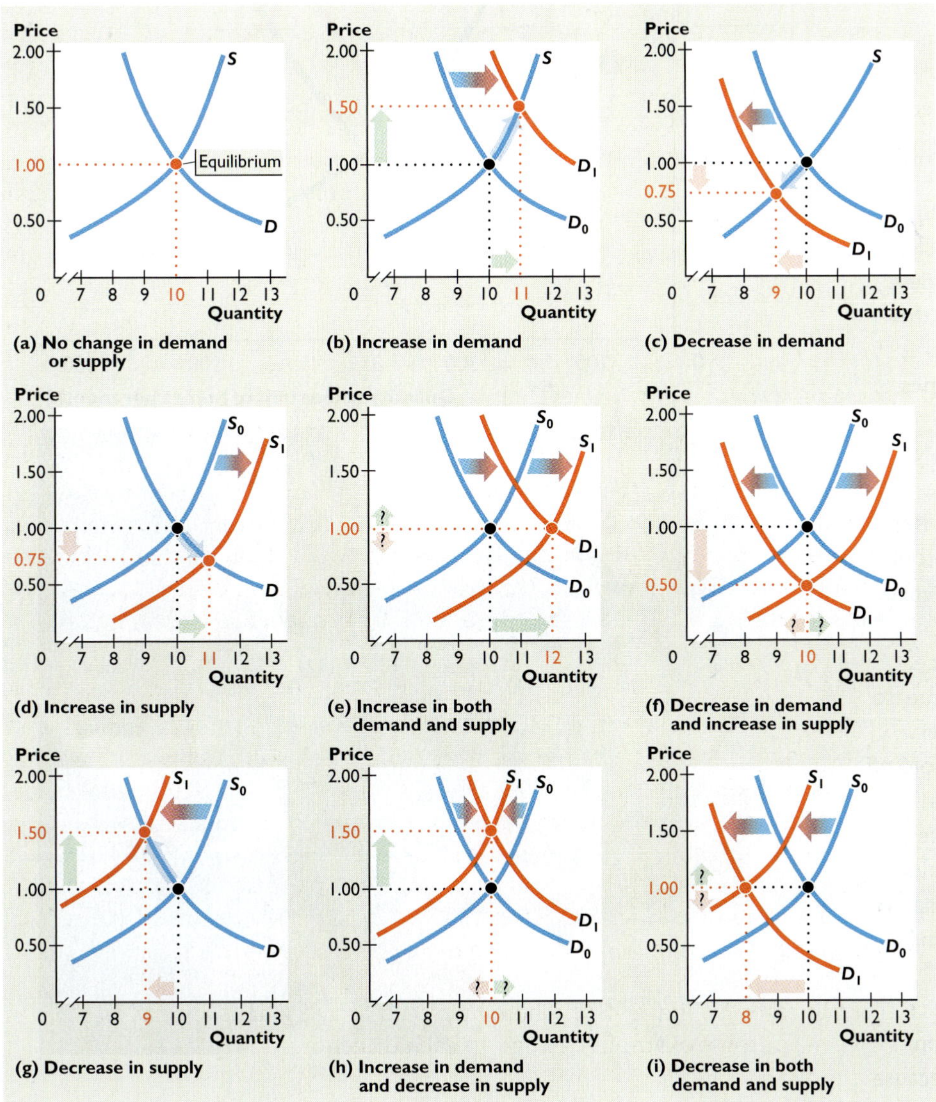

This figure shows all the possible changes in demand or supply, or both demand and supply, and their effects on the equilibrium price and equilibrium quantity.

A green arrow shows an increase in the price or quantity. A red arrow shows a decrease in the price or quantity.

A double-headed green and red arrow shows that the price might rise or fall or the quantity might increase or decrease depending on the magnitudes of the changes in demand and supply.

EYE on HOME PRICES

Why Did Home Prices Boom and Bust?

In 1999, the price of an average home was \$200,000, but home prices were rising by almost 10 percent per year. The pace of increase picked up and by 2004, home prices were rising by 15 percent per year. At the beginning of 2006, home prices stood at double their 1999 level. What caused this boom in home prices?

The Boom

Home prices rose sharply because the demand for homes increased and the supply of homes offered for sale decreased. What caused these changes in the demand for and supply of homes?

Cheap and easy loans put the dream of owning a home within the reach of millions of Americans, many of whom had modest incomes. This flow of loans increased the demand for homes at a pace that outstripped the construction of new homes. With the increase in the demand for homes outpacing the increase in supply, home prices rose.

Once home prices started to rise, the expectation of continuing price rises took hold. Expected future price rises influence both demand and supply.

With a higher expected future price, even more people want to own a home, so the demand for homes increases faster. People with a home to sell want to hold off selling today to get tomorrow's higher price, so the supply of homes decreases.

The figure above shows the effects on price of the combination of an increase in demand and a decrease in supply. Demand increased from D_{99} to D_{06}, supply decreased from S_{99} to S_{06}, and the price increased, as expected. The expectation of a higher price becomes a reality because

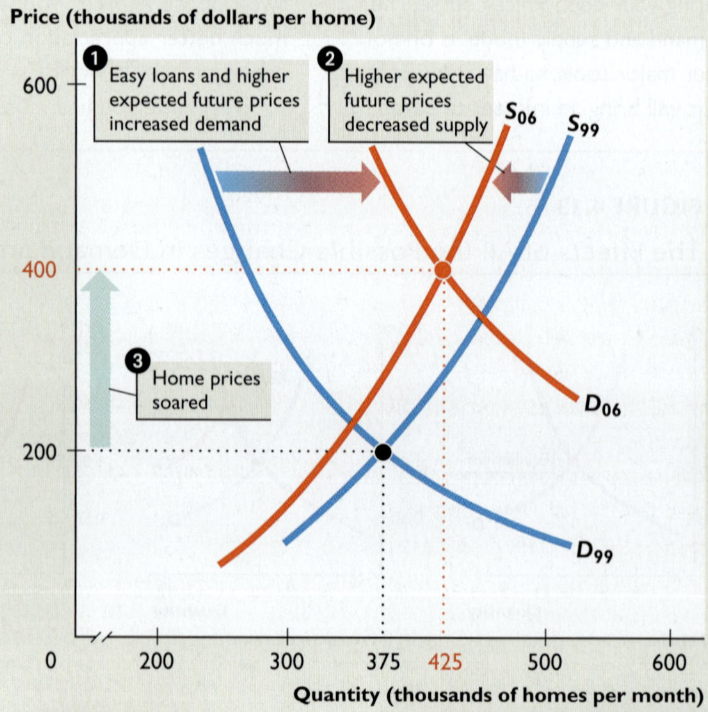

it increases demand, decreases supply, and creates what is called a *rational bubble*.

The Bust

Home prices started to fall in 2006 and the pace of decrease accelerated, and by 2009, home prices had fallen to 54 percent of their 2006 peak. What caused the fall in home prices?

Home prices fell because the demand for homes decreased and the supply of homes offered for sale increased.

The cheap and easy loans that had enabled millions of Americans to own a home dried up. Demand decreased.

Banks had made loans to many people who could afford to make loan payments only at very low interest rates. In 2006, interest rates increased and the cost of carrying a home loan became too much for many household budgets. These households stopped paying the interest on their loans. When borrowers stop paying off their loans, the banks that made the loans are in trouble. (You'll learn about the details of the problems for banks when you study money and banking in your macroeconomics course.)

The banks increased the interest rate on home loans and made loans harder to get.

As a result, the demand for homes decreased. At the same time, foreclosures increased the supply of homes for sale. The decrease in demand and increase in supply brought a falling price.

As the price continued to fall, a falling price came to be expected. The demand for homes decreased faster and the supply of homes offered for sale increased faster.

The figure below shows the effects on price of the combination of a decrease in demand and an increase in supply. Demand decreased from D_{06} to D_{09}, supply increased from S_{06} to S_{09}, and the price fell, as expected.

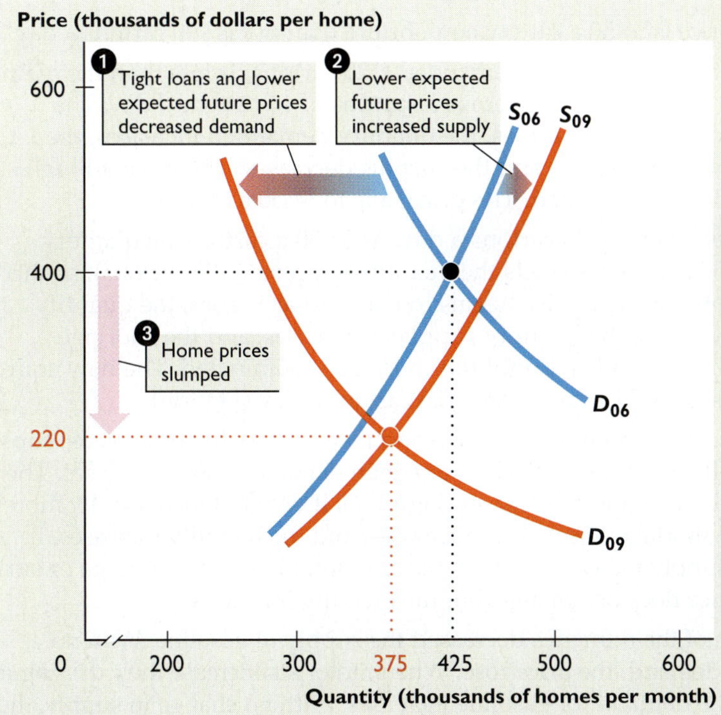

Work these problems in Study Plan 4.3 to get instant feedback.

CHECKPOINT 4.3

Explain how demand and supply determine price and quantity in a market, and explain the effects of changes in demand and supply.

Practice Problems

Use Table 1, which sets out the demand and supply schedules for milk, to work Problems **1** to **4**.

TABLE 1

Price (dollars per carton)	Quantity demanded (cartons per day)	Quantity supplied (cartons per day)
1.00	200	110
1.25	175	130
1.50	150	150
1.75	125	170
2.00	100	190

1. What is the equilibrium price and equilibrium quantity of milk?

2. Describe the situation in the milk market if the price were \$1.75 a carton and explain how the market reaches its new equilibrium.

3. A drought decreases the quantity supplied by 45 cartons a day at each price. What is the new equilibrium and how does the market adjust to it?

4. Milk becomes more popular and better feeds increase milk production. How do these events influence demand and supply? Describe how the equilibrium price and equilibrium quantity change.

5. **Summer's here. So are higher gas prices**

The price of gasoline increased 15 percent in the past three weeks, mainly because of refinery shutdowns in the United States. As motorists increase their driving in the coming months, the price is predicted to rise further.

Source: CNN Money, May 21, 2009

Explain why the price rose in the past 3 weeks and why it is expected to rise in the coming months.

Guided Solutions to Practice Problems

1. Equilibrium price is \$1.50 a carton; equilibrium quantity is 150 cartons a day.

2. At \$1.75 a carton, the quantity demanded (125 cartons) is less than the quantity supplied (170 cartons), so there is a surplus of 45 cartons a day. The price begins to fall, and as it does, the quantity demanded increases, the quantity supplied decreases, and the surplus decreases. The price will fall until the surplus is eliminated. The price falls to \$1.50 a carton.

3. The supply decreases by 45 cartons a day. At \$1.50 a carton, the quantity demanded (150 cartons) exceeds the quantity supplied (105 cartons), so there is a shortage of milk. The price begins to rise, and as it does, the quantity demanded decreases, the quantity supplied increases, and the shortage decreases. The price will rise until the shortage is eliminated. The new equilibrium occurs at \$1.75 a carton and 125 cartons a day (Figure 1).

FIGURE 1

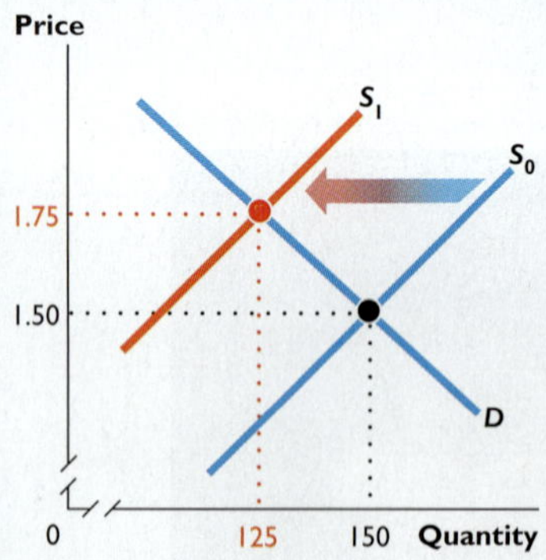

4. When milk becomes more popular, demand increases. With better feeds, supply increases. If supply increases by more than demand, a surplus arises. The price falls, and the quantity increases (Figure 2). If demand increases by more than supply, a shortage arises. The price rises, and the quantity increases. If demand and supply increase by the same amount, there is no shortage or surplus, so the price does not change, but the quantity increases.

FIGURE 2

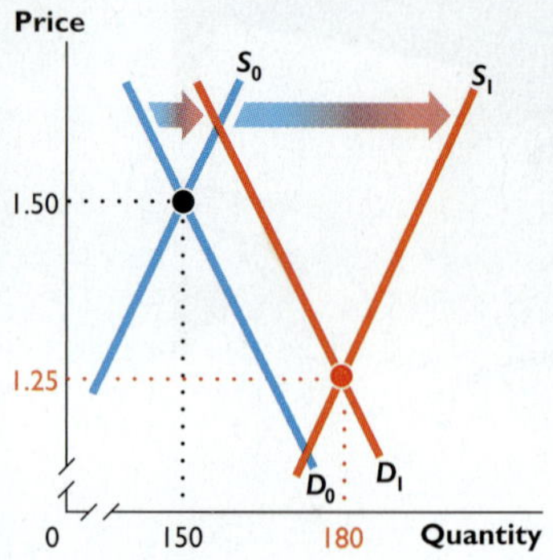

5. The shutdown of the refineries decreased the supply of gasoline. With no change in the demand, the price rose. When motorists increase their driving in the summer, the demand for gasoline increases. With no change in supply, the equilibrium price will rise further.

CHAPTER SUMMARY

Key Points

1 Distinguish between quantity demanded and demand, and explain what determines demand.

- Other things remaining the same, the quantity demanded increases as the price falls and decreases as the price rises—the law of demand.
- The demand for a good is influenced by the prices of related goods, expected future prices, income, expected future income and credit, the number of buyers, and preferences. A change in any of these influences changes the demand for the good.

2 Distinguish between quantity supplied and supply, and explain what determines supply.

- Other things remaining the same, the quantity supplied increases as the price rises and decreases as the price falls—the law of supply.
- The supply of a good is influenced by the prices of related goods, prices of resources and other inputs, expectations about future prices, the number of sellers, and productivity. A change in any of these influences changes the supply of the good.

3 Explain how demand and supply determine price and quantity in a market, and explain the effects of changes in demand and supply.

- The law of market forces brings market equilibrium—the equilibrium price and equilibrium quantity at which buyers and sellers trade.
- The price adjusts to maintain market equilibrium—to keep the quantity demanded equal to the quantity supplied. A surplus brings a fall in the price to restore market equilibrium; a shortage brings a rise in the price to restore market equilibrium.
- Market equilibrium responds to changes in demand and supply. An increase in demand increases both the price and the quantity; a decrease in demand decreases both the price and the quantity. An increase in supply increases the quantity but decreases the price; and a decrease in supply decreases the quantity but increases the price.

Key Terms

myeconlab

Work these problems in Chapter 4 Study Plan to get instant feedback.

CHAPTER CHECKPOINT

Study Plan Problems and Applications

1. Explain how each of the following events changes the demand for or supply of air travel.
   - Airfares tumble, while long-distance bus fares don't change.
   - The price of jet fuel rises.
   - Airlines reduce the number of flights each day.
   - People expect airfares to increase next summer.
   - The price of train travel falls.
   - The price of a pound of air cargo increases.

Use the laws of demand and supply to explain whether the statements in Problems 2 and 3 are true or false. In your explanation, distinguish between a change in demand and a change in the quantity demanded and between a change in supply and a change in the quantity supplied.

2. The United States does not allow oranges from Brazil (the world's largest producer of oranges) to enter the United States. If Brazilian oranges were sold in the United States, oranges and orange juice would be cheaper.
3. If the price of frozen yogurt falls, the quantity of ice cream consumed will decrease and the price of ice cream will rise.
4. Table 1 shows the demand and supply schedules for running shoes. What is the market equilibrium? If the price is $70 a pair, describe the situation in the market. Explain how market equilibrium is restored. If a rise in income increases the demand for running shoes by 100 pairs a day at each price, explain how the market adjusts to its new equilibrium.

TABLE 1

Price (dollars per pair)	Quantity demanded	Quantity supplied
	(pairs per day)	
60	1,000	400
70	900	500
80	800	600
90	700	700
100	600	800
110	500	900

5. "As more people buy fuel-efficient hybrid cars, the demand for gasoline will decrease and the price of gasoline will fall. The fall in the price of gasoline will decrease the supply of gasoline." Is this statement true? Explain.

Use the following information to work Problems 6 to 8.

Consumers eating higher food costs

The price of milk rose about 21% from July 2006 to July 2007, while the price of frozen orange juice increased 31%. At the same time, with higher gasoline prices, the demand for ethanol increased. Because ethanol is made from corn, the price of corn rose, which in turn increased the price of bread, chicken, cheese, and the fast-foods that use cheese. As people in China and India become richer, they are eating more beef and chicken and less rice and tofu—another source of higher food prices in the United States.

Source: *USA Today*, September 6, 2007

6. Explain why the demand for ethanol has influenced the price of corn.
7. Use graphs to show why the higher price of corn affects the price of milk and the price of cheese.
8. Explain why food prices in the United States will rise as people in India and China become richer and can afford to buy beef and chicken.

Instructor Assignable Problems and Applications

Your instructor can assign these problems as homework, a quiz, or a test in **MyEconLab**.

1. If home loans become harder to get and the ability of borrowers to repay is checked more thoroughly by the banks, how does
   - The demand for homes change?
   - The supply of homes change?
   - The price of homes change?

   Illustrate your answer with a graphical analysis.
2. Explain how each of the following events changes the demand for or supply of jeans:
   - A new technology reduces the time it takes to make a pair of jeans.
   - The price of the cloth (denim) used to make jeans falls.
   - The wage rate paid to garment workers increases.
   - The price of a denim skirt doubles.
   - People's incomes increase.
3. What is the effect on the equilibrium price and equilibrium quantity of orange juice if the price of apple juice decreases and the wage rate paid to orange grove workers increases?
4. What is the effect on the equilibrium in the orange juice market if orange juice becomes more popular and a cheaper robot is used to pick oranges?

Table 1 shows the demand and supply schedules for boxes of chocolates in an average week. Use this information to work Problems 5 and 6.

TABLE 1

Price (dollars per box)	Quantity demanded (boxes per week)	Quantity supplied (boxes per week)
13.00	1,600	1,200
14.00	1,500	1,300
15.00	1,400	1,400
16.00	1,300	1,500
17.00	1,200	1,600
18.00	1,100	1,700

5. If the price of chocolates is $17.00 a box, describe the situation in the market. Explain how market equilibrium is restored.
6. During Valentine's week, more people buy chocolates and chocolatiers offer their chocolates in special red boxes, which cost more to produce than the everyday box. Set out the three-step process of analysis and show on a graph the adjustment process to the new equilibrium. Describe the changes in the equilibrium price and the equilibrium quantity.
7. During 1994, Brazil experienced severe frosts, which wiped out many coffee plantations. New plantations in Brazil began to produce coffee beans in 1999. During the early 2000s, countries such as Vietnam started to produce coffee beans and Starbucks started to spring up across Europe. Use these events to explain why the price of coffee beans rose during the late 1990s, fell during the early 2000s, and rose again after 2003.
8. **Alabama food prices jump in May**

   Alabama Farmers Federation announced that food prices in May will increase. In previous unprofitable years, farmers reduced their herds with the result that in 2009 meat production will fall. Bacon is expected to rise by 32 cents a pound to $4.18 and steaks by 57 cents to $8.41 a pound.

   Source: *The Birmingham News*, May 21, 2009

   Explain why the reduction of herds will lead to a rise in meat prices today. Draw a graph to illustrate.
9. If the demand for a good decreases by 10 percent and the supply of the good decreases by 8 percent, will the price of the good rise or fall? Explain.

10. "As more people buy computers, the demand for Internet service increases and the price of Internet service decreases. The fall in the price of Internet service decreases the supply of Internet service." Is this statement true or false? Explain.

11. **Steel output set for historic drop**

    Steel producers expect to cut output by 10 percent in 2009 in response to cancelled orders from construction companies and car and household appliance producers.

    Source: *Financial Times*, December 28, 2008

    Does the cancellation of orders change the demand for steel, the quantity supplied, the supply of steel, or the quantity supplied? What happens to the equilibrium price of steel?

Use the following information to work Problems 12 to 14.

Oil soars to new record over $135

In the summer of 2008, the price of crude oil hit a record high above $135 a barrel. OPEC reported that there was no shortage of oil and that speculators had forced the price up.

Source: BBC News, May 22, 2008

12. Explain how the price of oil can rise even though there is no shortage of oil.
13. If a shortage of oil does occur, what does that imply about price adjustments and the role of price as a regulator in the market for oil?
14. If OPEC is correct, what factors might have changed demand and/or supply to cause the price to rise?
15. **Italians call for 1-day pasta strike**

    Italy's national dish is pasta. In 2007, as the world price of durum wheat rocketed, the price of durum flour rose by 20 percent. Seventy percent of pasta is durum flour. Italian consumer groups called for a one-day boycott of pasta in grocery stores, as a way of showing their unhappiness with the 20 percent increase. Be it fettuccine, linguine, or spaghetti, Italians will soon be paying up to 20 percent more for their pasta.

    Source: *The New York Times*, September 12, 2007

    Show on a graph the effect of the rise in the price of durum flour on the market price of pasta. Suppose that as a result of the one-day strike, grocery stores did not raise the price of pasta next month as predicted. Describe the situation in the market.

Use the following information to work Problems 16 and 17.

Labels seek end to 99¢ per song music download

The *Wall Street Journal* reported that five major recording companies think that music downloads at 99¢ per song are too cheap and they would like to see a price between $1.25 and $2.99 per song.

Source: *The Register*, April 9, 2004

16. What determines the price of a music download? What role does self-interest—of both the recording companies and the people who download songs—play in the market for music downloads?
17. What do you predict would happen in the market for music downloads if the major recording companies tried to hike the price to $2.99 a song?

How do we track the booms and busts of the business cycle?

How do we measure a nation's production and income and determine when a recession begins and ends?

GDP: A Measure of Total Production and Income

5

CHAPTER CHECKLIST

When you have completed your study of this chapter, you will be able to

1 Define GDP and explain why the value of production, income, and expenditure are the same for an economy.

2 Describe how economic statisticians measure GDP and distinguish between nominal GDP and real GDP.

3 Describe the uses of real GDP and explain its limitations as a measure of the standard of living.

5.1 GDP, INCOME, AND EXPENDITURE

Where is the U.S. economy heading? Will it remain weak, begin to expand more rapidly, or sink into a deeper recession?

Everyone wants to know the answers to these questions. The people who make business decisions—homebuilders, auto-producers, cell-phone service providers, airlines, oil producers, airplane makers, farmers, and retailers—want to know the answers so they can plan their production to align with demand. Governments want the answers because the amount of tax revenue that they collect depends on how much people earn and spend, which in turn depends on the state of the economy. Governments and the Federal Reserve want to know because they might be able to take actions that avoid excessive bust or boom. Ordinary citizens want the answers to plan their big decisions such as how long to remain in school and whether to rent or buy a new home.

To assess the state of the economy we measure gross domestic product, or GDP. You're about to discover that GDP measures the value of total production, total income, and total expenditure.

GDP Defined

Gross domestic product (GDP)
The market value of all the final goods and services produced within a country in a given time period.

We measure total production as **gross domestic product**, or **GDP**, which is the market value of all the final goods and services produced within a country in a given time period. This definition has four parts, which we'll examine in turn.

Value Produced

To measure total production, we must add together the production of apples and oranges, bats and balls. Just counting the items doesn't get us very far. Which is the greater total production: 100 apples and 50 oranges or 50 apples and 100 oranges?

GDP answers this question by valuing items at their *market value*—at the prices at which the items are traded in markets. If the price of an apple is 10 cents and the price of an orange is 20 cents, the market value of 100 apples plus 50 oranges is $20 and the market value of 50 apples and 100 oranges is $25. By using market prices to value production, we can add the apples and oranges together.

What Produced

Final good or service
A good or service that is produced for its final user and not as a component of another good or service.

Intermediate good or service
A good or service that is used as a component of a final good or service.

A **final good or service** is something that is produced for its final user and not as a component of another good or service. A final good or service contrasts with an **intermediate good or service**, which is used as a component of a final good or service. For example, a Ford car is a final good, but a Firestone tire that Ford buys and installs on the car is an intermediate good. But if you buy a replacement Firestone tire for your car, the tire is then a final good. The same good can be either final or intermediate depending on how it is used.

GDP does not count the value of everything that is produced. With one exception, it includes only those items that are traded in markets and does not include the value of goods and services that people produce for their own use. For example, if you buy a car wash, the value produced is included in GDP. But if you wash your own car, your production is not counted as part of GDP. The exception is the market value of homes that people own. GDP puts a rental value on these homes and pretends that the owners rent their homes to themselves.

Where Produced

Only goods and services that are produced *within a country* count as part of that country's GDP. Nike Corporation, a U.S. firm, produces sneakers in Vietnam, and the market value of those shoes is part of Vietnam's GDP, not part of U.S. GDP. Toyota, a Japanese firm, produces automobiles in Georgetown, Kentucky, and the value of this production is part of U.S. GDP, not part of Japan's GDP.

When Produced

GDP measures the value of production *during a given time period.* This time period is either a quarter of a year—called the quarterly GDP data—or a year—called the annual GDP data. The Federal Reserve and others use the quarterly GDP data to keep track of the short-term evolution of the economy, and economists use the annual GDP data to examine long-term trends.

GDP measures not only the value of total production but also total income and total expenditure. The circular flow model that you studied in Chapter 2 explains why.

Circular Flows in the U.S. Economy

Four groups buy the final goods and services produced: households, firms, governments, and the rest of the world. Four types of expenditure correspond to these groups:

- Consumption expenditure
- Investment
- Government expenditure on goods and services
- Net exports of goods and services

Consumption Expenditure

Consumption expenditure is the expenditure by households on consumption goods and services. It includes expenditures on *nondurable goods* such as orange juice and pizza, *durable goods* such as televisions and DVD players, and *services* such as rock concerts and haircuts. Consumption expenditure also includes house and apartment rents, including the rental value of owner-occupied housing.

Consumption expenditure
The expenditure by households on consumption goods and services.

Investment

Investment is the purchase of new *capital goods* (tools, instruments, machines, and buildings) and additions to inventories. Capital goods are *durable goods* produced by one firm and bought by another. Examples are PCs produced by Dell and bought by Ford Motor Company, and airplanes produced by Boeing and bought by United Airlines. Investment also includes the purchase of new homes by households.

Investment
The purchase of new *capital goods* (tools, instruments, machines, buildings) and additions to inventories.

At the end of a year, some of a firm's output might remain unsold. For example, if Ford produces 4 million cars and sells 3.9 million of them, the other 0.1 million (100,000) cars remain unsold. In this case, Ford's inventory of cars increases by 100,000. When a firm adds unsold output to inventory, we count those items as part of investment.

It is important to note that investment does *not* include the purchase of stocks and bonds. In macroeconomics, we reserve the term "investment" for the purchase of new capital goods and the additions to inventories.

Government Expenditure on Goods and Services

Government expenditure on goods and services
The expenditure by all levels of government on goods and services.

Government expenditure on goods and services is expenditure by all levels of government on goods and services. For example, the U.S. Defense Department buys missiles and other weapons systems, the State Department buys travel services, the White House buys Internet services, and state and local governments buy cruisers for law enforcement officers.

Net Exports of Goods and Services

Net exports of goods and services
The value of exports of goods and services minus the value of imports of goods and services.

Exports of goods and services
Items that firms in the United States produce and sell to the rest of the world.

Imports of goods and services
Items that households, firms, and governments in the United States buy from the rest of the world.

Net exports of goods and services is the value of exports of goods and services minus the value of imports of goods and services. **Exports of goods and services** are items that firms in the United States produce and sell to the rest of the world. **Imports of goods and services** are items that households, firms, and governments in the United States buy from the rest of the world. Imports are produced in other countries, so expenditure on imports is not included in expenditure on U.S.-produced goods and services. If exports exceed imports, net exports are positive and expenditure on U.S.-produced goods and services increases. If imports exceed exports, net exports are negative and expenditure on U.S.-produced goods and services decreases.

Total Expenditure

Total expenditure on goods and services produced in the United States is the sum of the four items that you've just examined. We call consumption expenditure C, investment I, government expenditure on goods and services G, and net exports of goods and services NX. So total expenditure, which is also the total amount received by the producers of final goods and services, is

$$\text{Total expenditure} = C + I + G + NX.$$

Income

Labor earns wages, capital earns interest, land earns rent, and entrepreneurship earns profits. Households receive these incomes. Some part of total income, called *undistributed profit*, is a combination of interest and profit that firms retain and do not pay to households. But from an economic viewpoint, undistributed profit is income paid to households and then loaned to firms.

Expenditure Equals Income

Figure 5.1 shows the circular flows of income and expenditure that we've just described. The figure is based on Figures 2.5 and 2.6 (on p. 49 and p. 51), but it includes some more details and additional flows.

We call total income Y and show it by the blue flow from firms to households. When households receive their incomes, they pay some in taxes and save some. Some households receive benefits from governments. **Net taxes** equal taxes paid minus cash benefits received and are the green flow from households to governments labeled NT. **Saving** is the amount of income that is not paid in net taxes or spent on consumption goods and services. Saving flows from households to financial markets and is the green flow labeled S. These two green flows are not expenditures on goods and services. They are just flows of money. Because households allocate all their incomes after paying net taxes to consumption and saving,

$$Y = C + S + NT.$$

Net taxes
Taxes paid minus cash benefits received from governments.

Saving
The amount of income that is not paid in net taxes or spent on consumption goods and services.

The red flows show the four expenditure flows: consumption expenditure from households to firms, government expenditure from governments to firms, and net exports from the rest of the world to firms. Investment flows from the financial markets, where firms borrow, to the firms that produce capital goods.

Because firms pay out everything they receive as incomes to the factors of production, total expenditure equals total income. That is,

$$Y = C + I + G + NX.$$

From the viewpoint of firms, the value of production is the cost of production, which equals income. From the viewpoint of purchasers of goods and services, the value of production is the cost of buying it, which equals expenditure. So

The value of production equals income equals expenditure.

The circular flow and the equality of income and expenditure provide two approaches to measuring GDP that we'll study in the next section.

FIGURE 5.1

The Circular Flow of Income and Expenditure

myeconlab Animation

The blue flow (Y) is income and the red flows (C, I, G, and NX) are expenditures on goods and services. The green flows (S and NT) are flows of money. Firms borrow in financial markets to buy goods (I) from other firms. Expenditure equals income and equals the value of production.

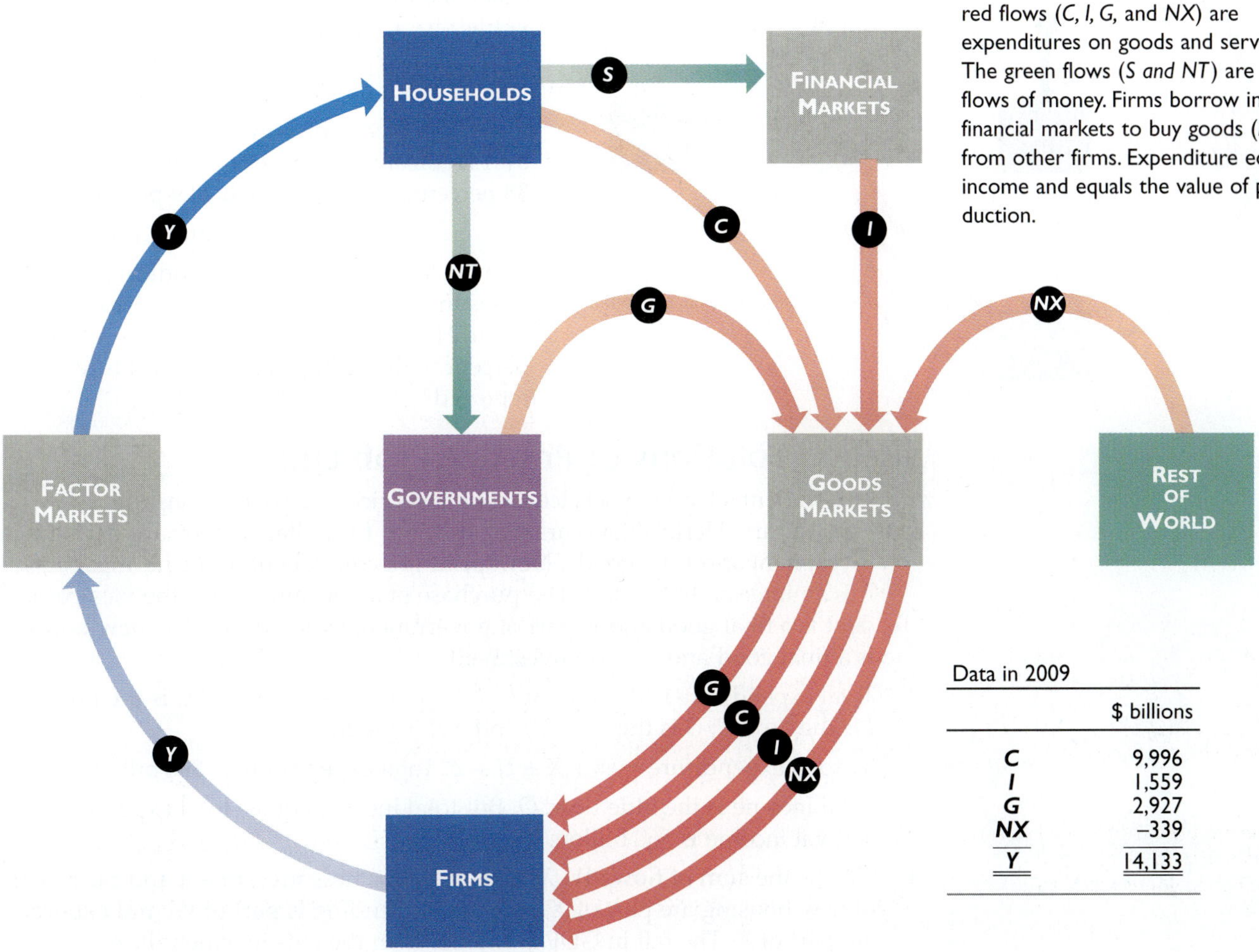

Data in 2009

	$ billions
C	9,996
I	1,559
G	2,927
NX	–339
Y	14,133

myeconlab

Work these problems in Study Plan 5.1 to get instant feedback.

CHECKPOINT 5.1

Define GDP and explain why the value of production, income, and expenditure are the same for an economy.

Practice Problems

1. Classify each of the following items as a final good or service or an intermediate good or service and identify which is a component of consumption expenditure, investment, or government expenditure on goods and services:
   - Banking services bought by a student.
   - New cars bought by Hertz, the car rental firm.
   - Newsprint bought by *USA Today* from International Paper.
   - The purchase of a new aircraft for the vice-president.
   - New house bought by the Al Gore family.

FIGURE 1

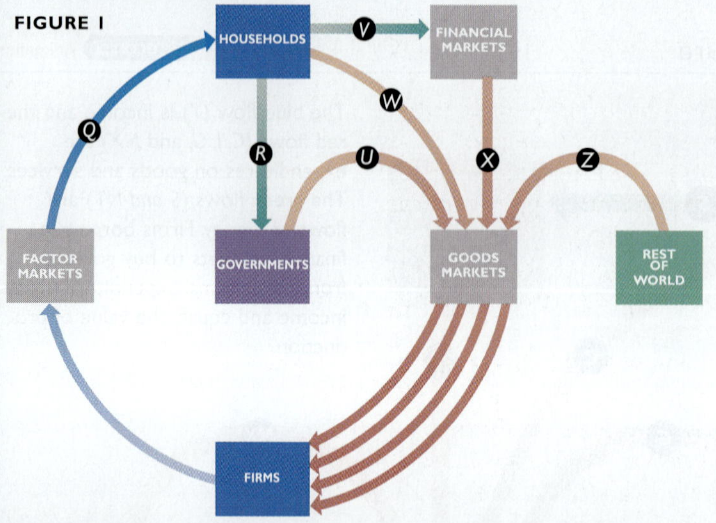

2. Figure 1 shows the flows of expenditure and income on Lotus Island. In 2008, *R* was $10 billion; *W* was $30 billion; *U* was $12 billion; *X* was $15 billion; and *Z* was $3 billion. Calculate total expenditure and total income.
3. **U.S. economy shrinks modestly**

   GDP fell at a 1 percent annual rate in the second quarter of 2009. Businesses cut investment by 8.9 percent, consumers cut spending by 1.2 percent, purchases of new houses fell 38 percent, and exports fell 29.9 percent.

   Source: Reuters, July 31, 2009

   Use the letters on Figure 1 to indicate the flows in which the items in the news clip occur. How can GDP have fallen by only 1.0 percent with the big cuts in expenditure reported?

Guided Solutions to Practice Problems

1. The student's banking service is a final service and part of consumption expenditure. Hertz's new cars are additions to capital, so they are part of investment and final goods. Newsprint is a component of the newspaper, so it is an intermediate good. The purchase of a new aircraft for the vice-president is a final good and is part of government expenditure. The new house is a final good and part of investment.
2. Total expenditure is the sum of *C*, *I*, *G*, and *NX*. In Figure 1, *C* is the flow *W*; *I* is the flow *X*; *G* is the flow *U*; and *NX* is the flow *Z*.

   So total expenditure = *W* + *X* + *U* + *Z*. Total expenditure is $60 billion.

   Total income is the blue flow, *Q*. But total income equals total expenditure, so total income is $60 billion.
3. GDP is the sum of flows *W*, *X*, *U*, and *Z*. Business investment and purchases of new housing are part of *X*, consumer spending is part of *W*, and exports are part of *Z*. The fall in GDP is smaller than the cuts in expenditures because either government expenditure increased or imports decreased.

5.2 MEASURING U.S. GDP

U.S. GDP is the market value of all the final goods and services produced within the United States during a year. In 2009, U.S. GDP was $14 trillion. The Bureau of Economic Analysis in the U.S. Department of Commerce measures GDP by using two approaches:

- Expenditure approach
- Income approach

The Expenditure Approach

The expenditure approach measures GDP by using data on consumption expenditure, investment, government expenditure on goods and services, and net exports. This approach is like attaching a meter to the circular flow diagram on all the flows running through the goods markets to firms and measuring the magnitudes of those flows. Table 5.1 shows this approach. The first column gives the terms used in the U.S. National Income and Product Accounts. The next column gives the symbols we used in the previous section.

Using the expenditure approach, GDP is the sum of consumption expenditure on goods and services (*C*), investment (*I*), government expenditure on goods and services (*G*), and net exports of goods and services (*NX*). The third column gives the expenditures in 2009. GDP measured by the expenditure approach was $14,133 billion (the data are based on the second quarter of 2009).

Net exports were negative in 2009 because imports exceeded exports. Imports were $1,831 billion and exports were $1,492 billion, so net exports—exports minus imports—were –$339 billion as shown in the table.

The fourth column in Table 5.1 shows the relative magnitudes of the expenditures. Consumption expenditure is by far the largest component of total expenditure; government expenditure is the next largest. Investment and exports are a similar size; and net export is the smallest component. In 2009, consumption expenditure was 70.7 percent, investment was 11.0 percent, government expenditure was 20.7 percent, and net exports were a negative 2.4 percent of GDP.

TABLE 5.1

GDP: The Expenditure Approach

Item	Symbol	Amount in 2009 (second quarter) (billions of dollars)	Percentage of GDP
Consumption expenditure	*C*	9,996	70.7
Investment	*I*	1,559	11.0
Government expenditure	*G*	2,927	20.7
Net exports	*NX*	–339	–2.4
GDP	*Y*	14,133	100.0

SOURCE OF DATA: U.S. Department of Commerce, Bureau of Economic Analysis.

The expenditure approach measures GDP by adding together consumption expenditure (*C*), investment (*I*), government expenditure (*G*), and net exports (*NX*).

In 2009, GDP measured by the expenditure approach was $14,133 billion.

Expenditures Not in GDP

Total expenditure (and GDP) does not include all the things that people and businesses buy. GDP is the value of *final goods and services,* so spending that is *not* on final goods and services is not part of GDP. Spending on intermediate goods and services is not part of GDP, although it is not always obvious whether an item is an intermediate good or a final good (see *Eye on the U.S. Economy* below). Also, we do not count as part of GDP spending on

- Used goods
- Financial assets

Used Goods Expenditure on used goods is not part of GDP because these goods were part of GDP in the period in which they were produced and during which time they were new goods. For example, a 2008 automobile was part of GDP in 2008. If the car is traded on the used car market in 2010, the amount paid for the car is not part of GDP in 2010.

Financial Assets When households buy financial assets such as bonds and stocks, they are making loans, not buying goods and services. The expenditure on newly produced capital goods is part of GDP, but the purchase of financial assets is not.

EYE on the U.S. ECONOMY

Is a Computer Program an Intermediate Good or a Final Good?

When American Airlines buys a new reservations software package, is that like General Motors buying tires? If it is, then software is an *intermediate good* and it is not counted as part of GDP. Airline ticket sales, like GM cars, are part of GDP, but the intermediate goods that are used to produce air transportation or cars are *not* part of GDP.

Or when American Airlines buys new software, is that like General Motors buying a new assembly-line robot? If it is, then the software is a capital good and its purchase is the purchase of a final good. In this case, the software purchase is an *investment* and it *is* counted as part of GDP.

Brent Moulton is a government economist who works in the Bureau of Economic Analysis (BEA). Moulton's job was to oversee periodic adjustments to the GDP estimates to incorporate new data and new ideas about the economy.

The biggest change made was in how the purchase of computer software by firms is classified. Before 1999, it was regarded as an *intermediate good.* But since 1999, it has been treated as an *investment.*

How big a deal is this? When the BEA recalculated the 1996 GDP, the change increased the estimate of the 1996 GDP by $115 billion. That is a lot of money. To put it in perspective, GDP in 1996 was $7,662 billion. So the adjustment was 1.5 percent of GDP.

This change is a good example of the ongoing effort by the BEA to keep the GDP measure as accurate as possible.

The Income Approach

To measure GDP using the income approach, the Bureau of Economic Analysis uses income data collected by the Internal Revenue Service and other agencies. The BEA takes the incomes that firms pay households for the services of the factors of production they hire—wages for labor services, interest for the use of capital, rent for the use of land, and profits for entrepreneurship—and sums those incomes. This approach is like attaching a meter to the circular flow diagram on all the flows running through factor markets from firms to households and measuring the magnitudes of those flows. Let's see how the income approach works.

The U.S. National Income and Product Accounts divide incomes into two big categories:

- Wage income
- Interest, rent, and profit income

Wage Income

Wage income, called *compensation of employees* in the national accounts, is the total payment for labor services. It includes net wages and salaries plus fringe benefits paid by employers such as health-care insurance, Social Security contributions, and pension fund contributions.

Interest, Rent, and Profit Income

Interest, rent, and profit income, called *net operating surplus* in the national accounts, is the total income earned by capital, land, and entrepreneurship.

Interest income is the interest that households receive on the loans they make minus the interest households pay on their own borrowing.

Rent includes payments for the use of land and other rented factors of production. It includes payments for rented housing and imputed rent for owner-occupied housing. (Imputed rent is an estimate of what homeowners would pay to rent the housing they own and use themselves. By including this item in the national accounts, we measure the total value of housing services, whether they are owned or rented.)

Profit includes the profits of corporations and the incomes of proprietors who run their own businesses. These incomes are a mixture of interest and profit.

Table 5.2 shows these two components of incomes and their relative magnitudes. The sum of wages, interest, rent, and profit is **net domestic product at factor cost.**

Net domestic product at factor cost
The sum of the wages, interest, rent, and profit.

Net domestic product at factor cost is not GDP, and we must make two further adjustments to get to GDP: one from factor cost to market prices and another from net product to gross product.

From Factor Cost to Market Price

The expenditure approach values goods and services at market prices, and the income approach values them at factor cost—the cost of the factors of production used to produce them. Indirect taxes (such as sales taxes) and subsidies (payments by government to firms) make these two values differ. Sales taxes make market prices exceed factor cost, and subsidies make factor cost exceed market prices. To convert the value at factor cost to the value at market prices, we must add indirect taxes and subtract subsidies.

TABLE 5.2

GDP: The Income Approach

The sum of all incomes equals net domestic product at factor cost. GDP equals net domestic product at factor cost plus indirect taxes less subsidies plus depreciation (capital consumption).

In 2009, GDP measured by the income approach was $13,919 billion. This amount is $214 billion less than GDP measured by the expenditure approach—a statistical discrepancy of $214 billion.

Wages are by far the largest part of total income.

Item	Amount in 2009 (second quarter) (billions of dollars)	Percentage of GDP
Wages (compensation of employees)	7,733	54.7
Interest, rent, and profit (net operating surplus)	3,358	23.8
Net domestic product at factor cost	11,091	78.5
Indirect taxes less subsidies	963	6.6
Depreciation (capital consumption)	1,865	13.2
GDP (income approach)	13,919	98.5
Statistical discrepancy	214	1.5
GDP (expenditure approach)	14,133	100.0

SOURCE OF DATA: U.S. Department of Commerce, Bureau of Economic Analysis.

From Net to Gross

Depreciation
The decrease in the value of capital that results from its use and from obsolescence.

The income approach measures *net* product and the expenditure approach measures *gross* product. The difference is **depreciation**, which is the decrease in the value of capital that results from its use and from obsolescence. Firms' profits, which are included in the income approach, are net of depreciation, so the income approach gives a *net* measure. Investment, which is included in the expenditure approach, includes the purchase of capital to replace worn out or obsolete capital, so the expenditure approach gives a *gross* measure. To get *gross* domestic product from the income approach, we must *add* depreciation to total income.

Table 5.2 summarizes these adjustments and shows that the income approach gives almost the same estimate of GDP as the expenditure approach.

Statistical Discrepancy

The expenditure approach and income approach do not deliver exactly the same estimate of GDP. If a taxi driver doesn't report all his tips, they get missed in the income approach. But they get caught by the expenditure approach when he spends his income. So the sum of expenditures might exceed the sum of incomes. But most income gets reported to the Internal Revenue Service on tax returns while many items of expenditure are not recorded and must be estimated. So the sum of incomes might exceed the sum of estimated expenditures.

Statistical discrepancy
The discrepancy between the expenditure approach and the income approach estimates of GDP, calculated as the GDP expenditure total minus the GDP income total.

The discrepancy between the expenditure approach and the income approach is called the **statistical discrepancy**, and it is calculated as the GDP expenditure total minus the GDP income total.

The two measures of GDP provide a check on the accuracy of the numbers. If the two are wildly different, we will want to know what mistakes we've made. Have we omitted some item? Have we counted something twice? The fact that the two estimates are close gives some confidence that they are reasonably accurate. But the expenditure total is regarded as the more reliable estimate of GDP, so the discrepancy is added to or subtracted from income to reconcile the two estimates.

GDP and Related Measures of Production and Income

Although GDP is the main measure of total production, you will sometimes encounter another: gross *national* product or GNP.

Gross National Product

A country's **gross national product**, or **GNP**, is the market value of all the final goods and services produced anywhere in the world in a given time period by the factors of production supplied by the residents of that country. For example, Nike's income from the capital that it supplies to its Vietnam shoe factory is part of U.S. GNP but not part of U.S. GDP. It is part of Vietnam's GDP. Similarly, Toyota's income on the capital it supplies to its Kentucky auto plant is part of U.S. GDP but not part of U.S. GNP. It is part of Japan's GNP.

Gross national product (GNP)
The market value of all the final goods and services produced anywhere in the world in a given time period by the factors of production supplied by the residents of the country.

GNP equals GDP plus net factor income received from or paid to other countries. The difference between U.S. GDP and GNP is small. But in an oil-rich Middle Eastern country such as Bahrain, where a large amount of capital is owned by foreigners, GNP is much smaller than GDP; and in a poor country such as Bangladesh, whose people work abroad and send income home, GNP is much larger than GDP.

Disposable Personal Income

You've seen that consumption expenditure is the largest component of aggregate expenditure. The main influence on consumption expenditure is **disposable personal income**, which is the income received by households minus personal income taxes paid. Because disposable personal income plays an important role in influencing spending, the national accounts measure this item along with a number of intermediate totals that you can see in Figure 5.2. This figure shows how disposable personal income is calculated and how it relates to GDP and GNP.

Disposable personal income
Income received by households minus personal income taxes paid.

FIGURE 5.2

GDP and Related Product and Income Measures

myeconlab Animation

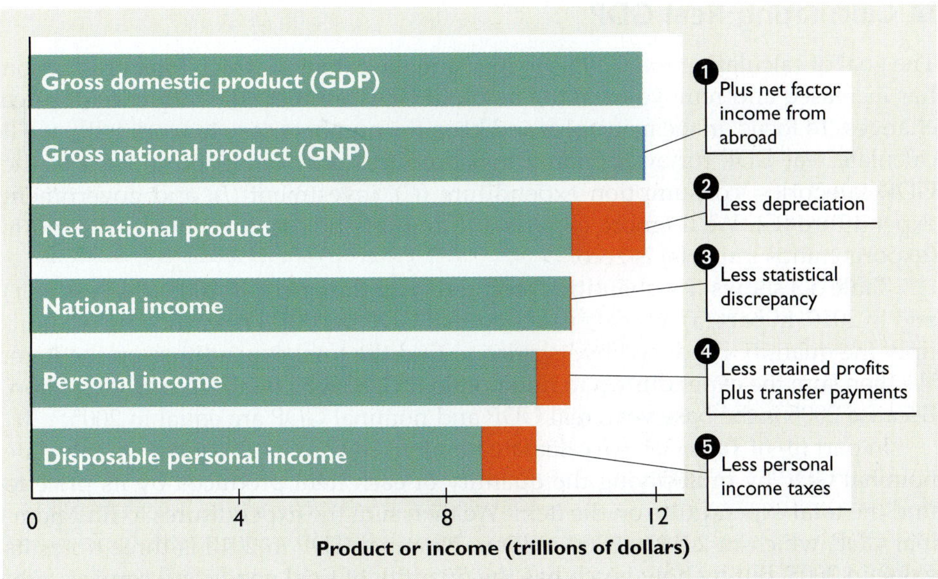

SOURCE OF DATA: U.S. Department of Commerce, Bureau of Economic Analysis.

The green bars show six related product and income measures and the relationship among them.

1. Add net factor income from abroad to GDP to get GNP.
2. Subtract depreciation from GNP to get net national product.
3. Subtract the statistical discrepancy between the expenditure and income measures (almost invisible in the figure because it is tiny) to get national income.
4. Subtract profits retained by firms and add transfer payments by governments to get personal income.
5. Finally, subtract personal income taxes to get disposable personal income.

Real GDP and Nominal GDP

You've seen that GDP measures total expenditure on final goods and services in a given period. Suppose that we want to compare GDP in two periods, say 2005 and 2009. In 2005, GDP was $12,638 billion and by 2009, it was $14,133 billion—11.8 percent higher than in 2005. What does this 11.8 percent increase mean?

The answer is a combination of two things:

- We produced more goods and services.
- We paid higher prices for our goods and services.

Producing more goods and services contributes to an improvement in our standard of living. Paying higher prices means that our *cost of living* has increased but our standard of living has not. So it matters a great deal why GDP has increased. If the 11.8 percent increase is accounted for mainly by higher prices, our standard of living hasn't changed much. But if the 11.8 percent increase is accounted for mainly by the production of more goods and services, our standard of living might have increased a lot.

You're now going to see how economists at the Bureau of Economic Analysis isolate the effects on GDP of an increase in production. Their first step is to distinguish between two GDP concepts: real GDP and nominal GDP.

Real GDP
The value of the final goods and services produced in a given year expressed in terms of the prices in a *base year.*

Nominal GDP
The value of final goods and services produced in a given year expressed in terms of the prices of that same year.

Real GDP is the value of final goods and services produced in a given year expressed in terms of the prices in a *reference base year.* The *reference base year* is the year we choose against which to compare all other years. In the United States today, the *reference base year* is 2005.

Real GDP contrasts with **nominal GDP**, which is the value of the final goods and services produced in a given year expressed in terms of the prices of that same year. Nominal GDP is just a more precise name for GDP.

The method used to calculate real GDP has changed in recent years and is now a bit technical, but the essence of the calculation hasn't changed. Here, we describe the essence of the calculation. An appendix to this chapter describes the technical details of the method used by the Bureau of Economic Analysis.

Calculating Real GDP

The goal of calculating *real GDP* is to measure the extent to which total production has increased and remove from the nominal GDP numbers the influence of price changes. To focus on the principles and keep the numbers easy to work with, we'll calculate real GDP for an economy that produces only one good in each of the GDP categories: consumption expenditure (*C*), investment (*I*), and government expenditure (*G*). We'll ignore exports and imports by assuming that net exports (exports minus imports) is zero.

Table 5.3 shows the quantities produced and the prices in 2005 (the *base year*) and in 2010. In part (a), we calculate nominal GDP in 2005. For each item, we multiply the quantity produced by its price to find the total expenditure on the item. We then sum the expenditures to find nominal GDP, which in 2005 is $100 million. Because 2005 is the base year, real GDP and nominal GDP are equal in 2005.

In part (b) of Table 5.3, we calculate nominal GDP in 2010. Again, we calculate nominal GDP by multiplying the quantity of each item produced by its price to find the total expenditure on the item. We then sum the expenditures to find nominal GDP, which in 2010 is $300 million. Nominal GDP in 2010 is three times its value in 2005. But by how much has the quantity of final goods and services produced increased? That's what real GDP will tell us.

TABLE 5.3

Calculating Nominal GDP and Real GDP in 2005 and 2010

	Item	Quantity (millions of units)	Price (dollars per unit)	Expenditure (millions of dollars)
(a) In 2005				
C	T-shirts	10	5	50
I	Computer chips	3	10	30
G	Security services	1	20	20
Y	**Real GDP and Nominal GDP in 2005**			**100**
(b) In 2010				
C	T-shirts	4	5	20
I	Computer chips	2	20	40
G	Security services	6	40	240
Y	**Nominal GDP in 2010**			**300**
(c) Quantities of 2010 valued at prices of 2005				
C	T-shirts	4	5	20
I	Computer chips	2	10	20
G	Security services	6	20	120
Y	**Real GDP in 2010**			**160**

The base year is 2005, so real GDP and nominal GDP are equal in that year.

Between 2005 and 2010, the production of security services (*G*) increased, but the production of T-shirts (*C*) and computer chips (*I*) decreased. In the same period, the price of a T-shirt remained constant, but the other two prices doubled.

Nominal GDP increased from $100 million in 2005 in part (a) to $300 million in 2010 in part (b).

Real GDP in part (c), which is calculated by using the quantities of 2010 in part (b) and the prices of 2005 in part (a), increased from $100 million in 2005 to $160 million in 2010, a 60 percent increase.

In part (c) of Table 5.3, we calculate real GDP in 2010. You can see that the quantity of each good and service produced in part (c) is the same as that in part (b). They are the quantities of 2010. You can also see that the prices in part (c) are the same as those in part (a). They are the prices of the base year—2005.

For each item, we now multiply the quantity produced in 2010 by its price in 2005 to find what the total expenditure would have been in 2010 if prices had remained the same as they were in 2005. We then sum these expenditures to find real GDP in 2010, which is $160 million.

Nominal GDP in 2010 is three times its value in 2005, but real GDP in 2010 is only 1.6 times its 2005 value—a 60 percent increase in *real* GDP.

Using the Real GDP Numbers

In the example that we've just worked through, we found the value of real GDP in 2010 based on the prices of 2005. This number alone enables us to compare production in two years only. By repeating the calculation that we have done for 2010 using the data for each year between 2005 and 2010, we can calculate the *annual* percentage change of real GDP—the annual growth rate of real GDP. This is the most common use of the real GDP numbers. Also, by calculating real GDP every three months—known as *quarterly real GDP*—the Bureau of Economic Analysis is able to provide valuable information that is used to interpret the current state of the economy. This information is used to guide both government macroeconomic policy and business production and investment decisions.

myeconlab

Work these problems in Study Plan 5.2 to get instant feedback.

CHECKPOINT 5.2

Describe how economic statisticians measure GDP and distinguish between nominal GDP and real GDP.

Practice Problems

Table 1 shows some of the items in the U.S. National Income and Product Accounts in 2005. Use Table 1 to work Problems **1** to **3**.

1. Use the expenditure approach to calculate U.S. GDP in 2005.
2. What was U.S. GDP as measured by the income approach in 2005? By how much did gross product and net product differ in 2005?
3. Calculate U.S. GNP and U.S. national income in 2005.
4. Table 2 shows some data for an economy. If the base year is 2006, calculate the economy's nominal GDP and real GDP in 2008.
5. **As consumers reduce their spending, inventories are rising**
   The Commerce Department reported that sales of nondurable goods fell 0.6 percent, while sales of durable goods decreased 1.5 percent in August. Inventories of durable goods increased 1.4 percent.
   Source: Reuters, October 9, 2008

   Which component of GDP changed when (i) sales of nondurable goods fell, (ii) sales of durable goods decreased, and (iii) inventories of durable goods increased? Provide an example of each item of expenditure.

TABLE 1

Item	Amount (trillions of dollars)
Consumption expenditure	8.7
Government expenditure	2.3
Indirect taxes less subsidies	0.8
Depreciation	1.5
Net factor income from abroad	0.1
Investment	2.0
Net exports	–0.7
Statistical discrepancy	0

TABLE 2

(a) In 2006:

Item	Quantity	Price
Apples	60	$0.50
Oranges	80	$0.25

(b) In 2008:

Item	Quantity	Price
Apples	160	$1.00
Oranges	220	$2.00

Guided Solutions to Practice Problems

1. GDP was $12.3 trillion. The expenditure approach sums the expenditure on final goods and services. That is, GDP $= C + I + G + NX$.
   In 2005, U.S. GDP = ($8.7 + $2.0 + $2.3 − $0.7) trillion = $12.3 trillion.
2. GDP as measured by the income approach was $12.3 trillion.
   GDP (expenditure approach) = GDP (income approach) + Statistical discrepancy. The statistical discrepancy is zero, so GDP is $12.3 trillion.
   Gross product minus net product is depreciation, which was $1.5 trillion.
3. GNP = GDP + Net factor income from abroad.
   In 2005, GNP = $12.3 trillion + $0.1 trillion, which was $12.4 trillion.
   National income = GNP − Depreciation − Statistical discrepancy.
   The statistical discrepancy is zero, so in 2005,
   National income = $12.4 trillion − $1.5 trillion = $10.9 trillion.
4. Nominal GDP in 2008 equals (160 apples × $1) + (220 oranges × $2) = $600.
   Real GDP in 2008 at 2006 prices is equals (160 apples × $0.50 per apple) + (220 oranges × $0.25 per orange) = $135.
5. Sales of nondurable goods such as strawberries are bought by households and are part of consumption expenditure, *C*. Sales of durable goods such as iPhones that are bought by households are part of consumption expenditure, *C*, and sales of durable goods such as tower cranes bought by firms are part of investment, *I*. An inventory of durable goods, such as the auto parts at a Ford plant, is part of investment, *I*.

5.3 THE USES AND LIMITATIONS OF REAL GDP

We use estimates of real GDP for three main purposes:

- To compare the standard of living over time
- To track the course of the business cycle
- To compare the standard of living among countries

The Standard of Living Over Time

A nation's **standard of living** is measured by the value of goods and services that its people enjoy, *on average*. Income per person determines what people can afford to buy and real GDP is a measure of real income. So **real GDP per person**—real GDP divided by the population—is a commonly used measure for comparing the standard of living over time.

Standard of living
The level of consumption of goods and services that people enjoy, *on average*.

Real GDP per person
Real GDP divided by the population.

Real GDP per person tells us the value of goods and services that the average person can enjoy. By using *real* GDP, we remove any influence that rising prices and a rising cost of living might have had on our comparison.

A handy way of comparing real GDP per person over time is to express it as a ratio of its value in some reference year. Table 5.4 provides the numbers for the United States that compare 2009 with 50 years earlier, 1959. In 1959, real GDP per person was $15,540 and in 2009 it was $42,106, or 2.7 times its 1959 level. To the extent that real GDP per person measures the standard of living, people were 2.7 times as well off in 2009 as their grandparents had been in 1959.

TABLE 5.4 REAL GDP PER PERSON IN 1959 AND 2009

Year	1959	2009
Real GDP (billions)	$2,763	$12,893
Population (millions)	177.8	306.2
Real GDP per person	$15,540	$42,106

Figure 5.3 shows the entire 50 years of real GDP per person from 1959 to 2009 and displays two features of our changing standard of living:

1. The growth of potential GDP per person
2. Fluctuations of real GDP per person around potential GDP

Potential GDP is the level of real GDP when all the economy's factors of production—labor, capital, land, and entrepreneurial ability—are fully employed. When some factors of production are *unemployed*, real GDP is *below* potential GDP. And when some factors of production are *over-employed* and working harder and for longer hours than can be maintained in the long run, real GDP *exceeds* potential GDP.

Potential GDP
The value of real GDP when all the economy's factors of production—labor, capital, land, and entrepreneurial ability—are fully employed.

You've seen that real GDP per person in 2009 was 2.7 times that of 1959. But in 2009, some labor and other factors of production were unemployed and the economy was producing less than potential GDP. To measure the trend in the standard of living, we must remove the influence of short-term fluctuations and focus on the path of potential GDP.

The growth rate of potential GDP fluctuates less than real GDP. During the 1960s, potential GDP per person grew at an average rate of 2.8 percent a year, but since 1970, its growth rate has slowed to 2 percent a year. This growth slowdown means that potential GDP is lower today (and lower by a large amount) than it would have been if the 1960s growth rate could have been maintained. If potential GDP had kept growing at the 1960s pace, potential GDP per person in 2009 would have been $20,000 more than it actually was. The cumulatively lost income from the growth slowdown of the 1970s is a staggering $284,500 per person. Understanding the reasons for the growth slowdown is one of the major tasks of macroeconomists.

FIGURE 5.3

Real GDP and Potential GDP Per Person in the United States: 1959–2009

myeconlab Animation

Real GDP grows and fluctuates around the growth path of potential GDP. Potential GDP per person grew at an annual rate of 2.8 percent during the 1960s and slowed to 2.0 percent after 1970.

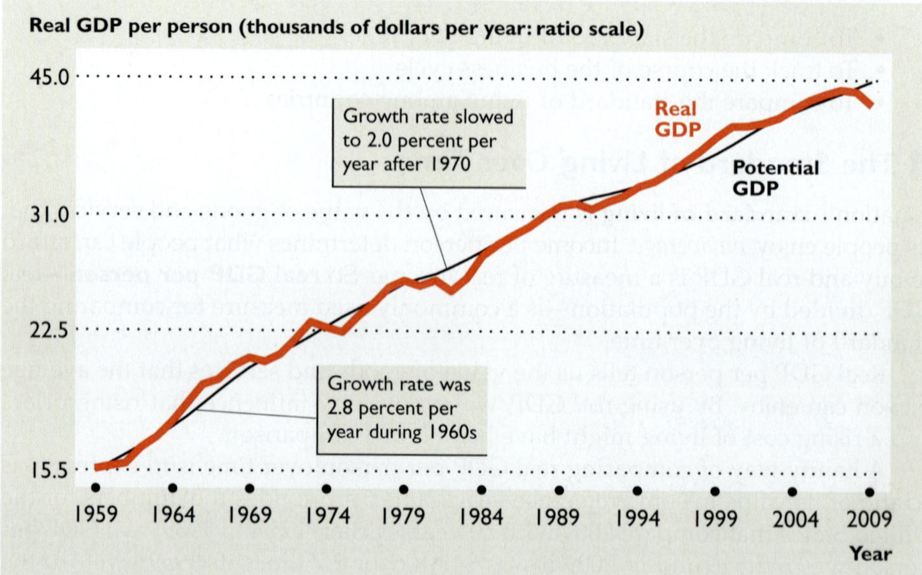

SOURCES OF DATA: Bureau of Economic Analysis and the Congressional Budget Office.

Tracking the Course of the Business Cycle

Business cycle
A periodic but irregular up-and-down movement of total production and other measures of economic activity.

We call the fluctuations in the pace of economic activity the business cycle. A **business cycle** is a periodic but irregular up-and-down movement of total production and other measures of economic activity such as employment and income. The business cycle isn't a regular, predictable, and repeating cycle like the phases of the moon. The timing and the intensity of the business cycle vary a lot, but every cycle has two phases:

1. Expansion
2. Recession

and two turning points:

1. Peak
2. Trough

Figure 5.4 shows these features of the most recent U.S. business cycle using real GDP as the measure of economic activity. An *expansion* is a period during which real GDP increases. In the early stage of an expansion, real GDP returns to potential GDP and as the expansion progresses, potential GDP grows and real GDP eventually exceeds potential GDP.

Recession
A period during which real GDP decreases for at least two successive quarters; or defined by the NBER as "a period of significant decline in total output, income, employment, and trade, usually lasting from six months to a year, and marked by contractions in many sectors of the economy."

A common definition of **recession** is a period during which real GDP decreases—its growth rate is negative—for at least two successive quarters. The National Bureau of Economic Research (NBER), which dates the U.S. business cycle phases and turning points, defines a recession more broadly as "a period of significant decline in total output, income, employment, and trade, usually lasting from

FIGURE 5.4

The Most Recent U.S. Business Cycle

myeconlab Animation

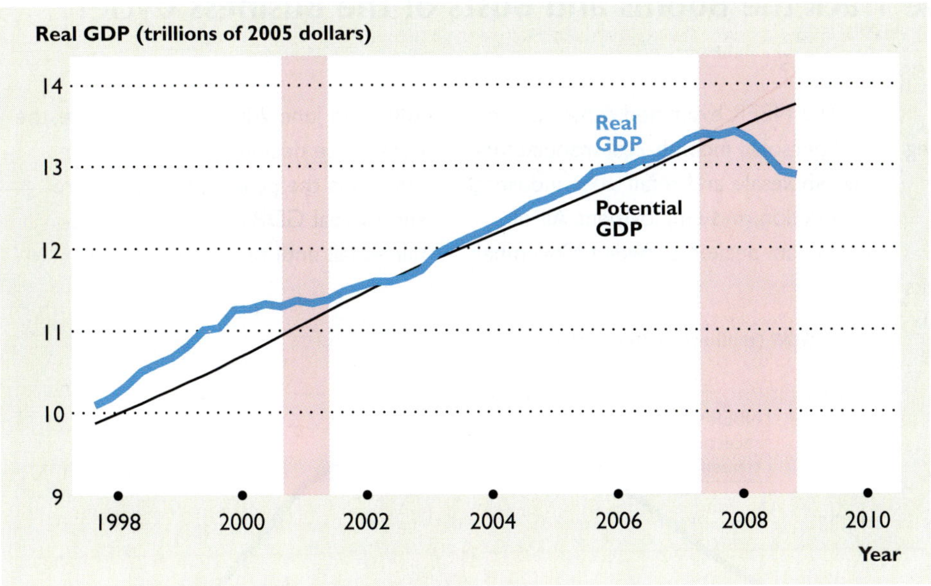

SOURCES OF DATA: Bureau of Economic Analysis the Congressional Budget Office, and the National Bureau of Economic Research.

The most recent business cycle peak was in December 2007 and the trough had not been reached by mid-2009. The most recent complete cycle had its peak in March 2001 and its trough in November 2001, but the recession was extremely shallow.

six months to a year, and marked by contractions in many sectors of the economy." This definition means that sometimes, the NBER declares a recession even though real GDP has not decreased for two successive quarters. The recession in 2001 was such a recession. An expansion ends and a recession begins at a business cycle peak. A peak is the highest level of real GDP that has been attained up to that time. A recession ends at a trough when real GDP reaches a temporary low point and from which the next expansion begins.

The shaded bars in Figure 5.4 highlight the 2001 and 2008–2009 recessions. The recession of 2001 was so mild that real GDP didn't fall. But the recession of 2008-2009 was so severe that it lowered real GDP per person back to its level at the end of 2005.

The period that began in 1991 following a severe recession and that ended with the global financial crisis of 2008 was so free from serious downturns in real GDP and other indicators of economic activity that it was called the *Great Moderation*, a name that contrasts it with the Great Depression. Some starry-eyed optimists even began to declare that the business cycle was dead. This long period of expansion also turned the attention of macroeconomists away from the business cycle and toward a focus on economic growth and the possibility of achieving faster growth.

But the 2008–2009 recession puts the business cycle back on the agenda. Economists were criticized for not predicting it, and old divisions among economists that many thought were healed erupted in the pages of *The Economist* and *The New York Times* and online on a host of blogs.

We'll be examining the causes of recession and the alternative views among economists in greater detail as you progress through the rest of your study of macroeconomics.

EYE on the BUSINESS CYCLE

How Do We Track the Booms and Busts of the Business Cycle?

The National Bureau of Economic Research (NBER) Business Cycle Dating Committee determines the dates of U.S. business cycle turning points.

To identify the date of a business cycle peak, the NBER committee looks at data on industrial production, total employment, real GDP, and wholesale and retail sales.

The NBER committee met in November 2008 to determine when the economy went into recession.

The committee reported that the two most reliable measures of aggregate domestic production are real GDP measured using the expenditure approach and the income approach.

Because of a statistical discrepancy, these two estimates of aggregate production differ and for a few quarters in 2007 and 2008 they told conflicting stories. As the committee noted: These estimates did "not speak clearly about the date of a peak in activity."

The NBER examined other data on real personal income, real manufacturing, wholesale and retail sales, industrial production, and employment. All of these data peaked between November 2007 and June 2008 and on balance, the committee decided that November 2007 was the peak. But as the figure shows, real GDP didn't begin a sustained fall until two quarters later.

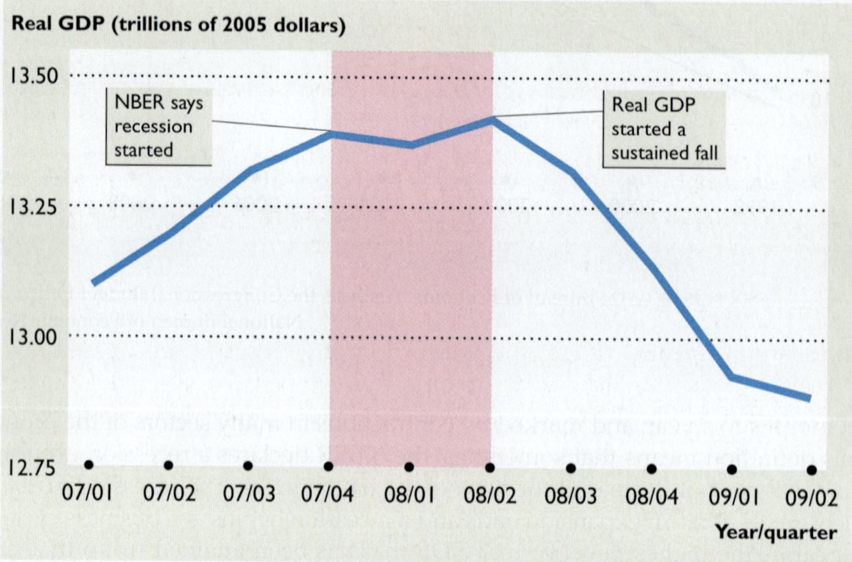

SOURCES OF DATA: Bureau of Economic Analysis and the National Bureau of Economic Research.

Let's now leave comparisons of the standard of living over time and business cycles and briefly see how we compare the standard of living among countries.

■ The Standard of Living Among Countries

To use real GDP per person to compare the standard of living among countries, we must convert the numbers for other countries into U.S. dollars. To calculate real GDP, we must also use a common set of prices—called *purchasing power parity prices*—for all countries. The International Monetary Fund performs these calculations and if you turn back to Figure 2.4 on p. 46 you can see some comparisons based on these data. They tell, for example, that an average American has a standard of living almost 8 times that of an average person in China.

Real GDP provides an easy way of comparing living standards. But real GDP doesn't include *all* the goods and services produced. Also, real GDP has nothing to say about factors other than the goods and services that affect the standard of living. Let's explore these limitations of real GDP.

Goods and Services Omitted from GDP

GDP measures the value of goods and services that are bought in markets. GDP excludes

- Household production
- Underground production
- Leisure time
- Environment quality

Household Production

Household production is the production of goods and services (mainly services) in the home. Examples of this production are preparing meals, changing a light bulb, cutting grass, washing a car, and helping a student with homework. Because we don't buy these services in markets, they are not counted as part of GDP. The result is that GDP *underestimates* the value of the production.

Household production
The production of goods and services in the home.

Many items that were traditionally produced at home are now bought in the market. For example, more families now eat in fast-food restaurants—one of the fastest-growing industries in the United States—and use day-care services. These trends mean that food preparation and child-care services that were once part of household production are now measured as part of GDP. So real GDP grows more rapidly than does real GDP plus home production.

Underground Production

Underground production is the production of goods and services hidden from the view of government because people want to avoid taxes and regulations or their actions are illegal. Because underground production is unreported, it is omitted from GDP.

Underground production
The production of goods and services hidden from the view of government.

Examples of underground production are the distribution of illegal drugs, farm work that uses illegal workers who are paid less than the minimum wage, and jobs that are done for cash to avoid paying income taxes. This last category might be quite large and includes tips earned by cab drivers, hairdressers, and hotel and restaurant workers.

Edgar L. Feige, an economist at the University of Wisconsin, estimates that U.S. underground production was about 16 percent of GDP during the early 1990s. Underground production in many countries is estimated to be larger than that in the United States and in most developing countries, much larger.

Leisure Time

Leisure time is an economic good that is not valued as part of GDP. Yet the marginal hour of leisure time must be at least as valuable to us as the wage we earn for working. If it were not, we would work instead. Over the years, leisure time has steadily increased as the workweek gets shorter, more people take early retirement, and the number of vacation days increases. These improvements in our standard of living are not measured in real GDP.

Environment Quality

Pollution is an economic *bad* (the opposite of a *good*). The more we pollute our environment, other things remaining the same, the lower is our standard of living. This lowering of our standard of living is not measured by real GDP.

Other Influences on the Standard of Living

The quantity of goods and services consumed is a major influence on the standard of living. But other influences are

- Health and life expectancy
- Political freedom and social justice

Health and Life Expectancy

Good health and a long life—the hopes of everyone—do not show up directly in real GDP. A higher real GDP enables us to spend more on medical research, health care, a good diet, and exercise equipment. As real GDP has increased, our life expectancy has lengthened. But we face new health and life expectancy problems every year. Diseases, such as AIDS, and drug abuse are taking young lives at a rate that causes serious concern. When we take these negative influences into account, real GDP growth might overstate the improvements in the standard of living.

Political Freedom and Social Justice

A country might have a very large real GDP per person but have limited political freedom and social justice. For example, a small elite might enjoy political liberty and extreme wealth while the majority of people have limited freedom and live in poverty. Such an economy would generally be regarded as having a lower standard of living than one that had the same amount of real GDP but in which everyone enjoyed political freedom.

EYE on YOUR LIFE

Making GDP Personal

As you read a newspaper or business magazine, watch a TV news show, or browse a news Web site, you often come across reports about GDP.

What do these reports mean for you? Where in the National Income and Product Accounts do *your* transactions appear? How can you use information about GDP in your life?

Your Contribution to GDP

Your own economic transactions show up in the National Income and Product Accounts on both the expenditure side and the income side—as part of the expenditure approach and part of the income approach to measuring GDP.

Most of your expenditure is part of Consumption Expenditure. If you were to buy a new home, that item would appear as part of Investment. Because much of what you buy is produced in another country, expenditure on these goods shows up as part of Imports.

If you have a job, your income appears in Compensation of Employees.

Because the GDP measure of the value of production includes only market transactions, some of your own production of goods and services is most likely not counted in GDP.

What are the nonmarket goods and services that you produce? How would you go about valuing them?

Making Sense of the Numbers

To use the GDP numbers in a news report, you must first check whether the reporter is referring to *nominal* GDP or *real* GDP.

Using U.S. real GDP per person, check how your income compares with the average income in the United States. When you see GDP numbers for other countries, compare your income with that of a person in France, or Canada, or China.

EYE on the GLOBAL ECONOMY

Which Country Has the Highest Standard of Living?

You've seen that as a measure of the standard of living, GDP has limitations. To compare the standard of living across countries, we must consider factors additional to GDP.

GDP measures only the market value of all the final goods and services produced and bought in markets. GDP omits some goods and services (those produced in the home and in the hidden economy). It omits the value of leisure time, of good health and long life expectancy, as well as of political freedom and social justice. It also omits the damage (negative value) that pollution does to the environment.

These limitations of GDP as a measure of the standard of living apply in every country. So to make international comparisons of the standard of living, we must look at real GDP and other indicators. Nonetheless, real GDP per person is a major component of international comparisons.

Many alternatives to GDP have been proposed. One, called Green GDP, subtracts from GDP an estimate of the cost of greenhouse gas emissions and other negative influences on the environment. Another measure, called the Happy Planet Index, or HPI, goes further and subtracts from GDP an estimate of the cost of depleting nonrenewable resources.

Neither the Green GDP nor the HPI are reliable measures because they rely on guesses about the costs of pollution and resource depletion that are subjective and unreliable.

Taking an approach that focuses on the quality of life factors, the United Nations (UN) has constructed a Human Development Index, or HDI, which combines real GDP, life expectancy and health, and education.

The figure shows the relationship between the HDI and GDP in 2007. (In the figure, each dot represents a country.) These two measures of the standard of living tell a similar but not identical story.

The United States has the highest GDP per person but only the 7th highest HDI. Why does the United States not have a higher HDI?

The UN says that the people who live in the 6 countries with higher HDIs live longer, have access to universal health care, and have better schools than do people in the United States. The HDI emphasized equality of access to these services.

The HDI doesn't include political freedoms and social justice. If it did, the United States would score highly on that component of the index.

The bottom line is that we don't know which country has the highest standard of living. We do know that GDP per person alone does not provide the complete answer.

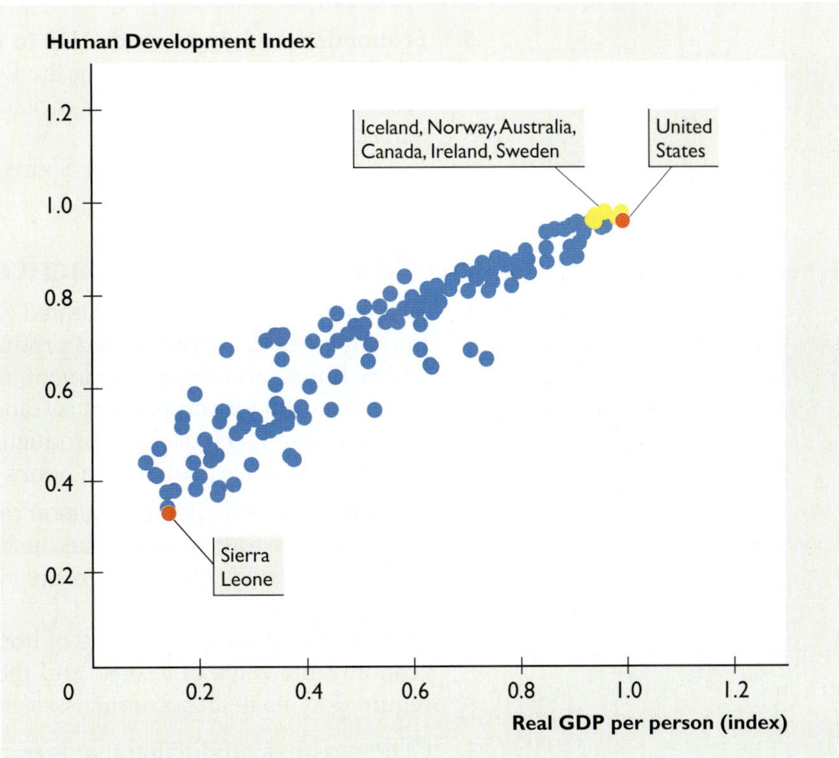

SOURCE OF DATA: *United Nations Human Development Report*, 2007, http://hdr.undp.org/.

myeconlab

Work these problems in Study Plan 5.3 to get instant feedback.

CHECKPOINT 5.3

Describe the uses of real GDP and explain its limitations as a measure of the standard of living.

Practice Problems

The United Nations Human Development Report gives the following data for real GDP per person in 2002: China, $4,580; Russia, $8,230; Canada, $29,480; United States, $35,750. Other information suggests that household production is similar in Canada and the United States and smaller in these two countries than in the other two. The underground economy is largest in Russia and China and a similar proportion of these economies. Canadians and Americans enjoy more leisure hours than do the Chinese and Russians. Canada and the United States spend significantly more to protect the environment, so air, water, and land pollution levels are lower in these countries than in China and Russia. Use this information and ignore any other influences to work Problems **1** and **2**.

1. In which pair (or pairs) of these four countries is it easiest to compare the standard of living? In which pair (or pairs) of these four countries is it most difficult to compare the standard of living? Why?
2. Do the differences in real GDP per person correctly rank the standard of living in these four countries? What additional information would we need to be able to make an accurate assessment of the relative standard of living in these four countries?
3. **Economists look to expand GDP to include the quality of life**
   Robert Kennedy, when seeking the Democratic presidential nomination 40 years ago, remarked that GDP measures everything except that which makes life worthwhile.

   Source: *The New York Times*, September 1, 2008

   Which items did Robert Kennedy probably think were missing?

Guided Solutions to Practice Problems

1. Two pairs—Canada and the United States, and China and Russia—are easy to compare because household production, the underground economy, leisure hours, and the environment are similar in the countries in each pair. The most difficult comparison is Canada and the United States with either China or Russia. Household production and the underground economy narrow the differences but leisure hours and the environment widen them.
2. Differences in real GDP per person probably correctly rank the standard of living in these four countries because where the gap is small (Canada and the United States), other factors are similar, and where other factors differ, the gaps are huge.
   More information on the value of household production, the underground economy, the value of leisure, and the value of environmental differences is required to make an accurate assessment of relative living standards.
3. GDP measures production that is traded in markets. GDP does not include household production, leisure time, health and life expectancy, political freedom, and social justice. These items are probably the ones that Kennedy believed were missing from GDP as a measure of the quality of life.

CHAPTER SUMMARY

Key Points

1 Define GDP and explain why the value of production, income, and expenditure are the same for an economy.

- GDP is the market value of all final goods and services produced within a country in a given time period.
- We can value goods and services either by what they cost to produce (incomes) or by what people are willing to pay (expenditures).
- The value of production equals income equals expenditure.

2 Describe how economic statisticians measure GDP and distinguish between nominal GDP and real GDP.

- BEA measures GDP by summing expenditures and by summing incomes. With no errors of measurement the two totals are the same, but in practice, a small statistical discrepancy arises.
- A country's GNP is similar to its GDP, but GNP is the value of production by factors of production supplied by the residents of a country.
- Nominal GDP is the value of production using the prices of the current year and the quantities produced in the current year.
- Real GDP is the value of production using the prices of a base year and the quantities produced in the current year.

3 Describe the uses of real GDP and explain its limitations as a measure of the standard of living.

- We use real GDP per person to compare the standard of living over time.
- We use real GDP to determine when the economy has reached a business cycle peak or trough.
- We use real GDP per person expressed in purchasing power parity dollars to compare the standard of living among counties.
- Real GDP omits some goods and services and ignores some factors that influence the standard of living.
- The Human Development Index takes some other factors into account.

Key Terms

Business cycle, 128
Consumption expenditure, 115
Depreciation, 122
Disposable personal income, 123
Exports of goods and services, 116
Final good or service, 114
Government expenditure on goods and services, 116
Gross domestic product (GDP), 114
Gross national product (GNP), 123
Household production, 131
Imports of goods and services, 116
Intermediate good or service, 114
Investment, 115
Net domestic product at factor cost, 121
Net exports of goods and services, 116
Net taxes, 116
Nominal GDP, 124
Potential GDP, 127
Real GDP, 124
Real GDP per person, 127
Recession, 128
Saving, 116
Standard of living, 127
Statistical discrepancy, 122
Underground production, 131

myeconlab

Work these problems in Chapter 5 Study Plan to get instant feedback.

CHAPTER CHECKPOINT

Study Plan Problems and Applications

1. Figure 1 shows the flows of income and expenditure in an economy. In 2009, U was $2 trillion, V was $1.5 trillion, W was $7 trillion, X was $1.5 trillion, and Z was zero. Calculate total income, net taxes, and GDP.

FIGURE 1

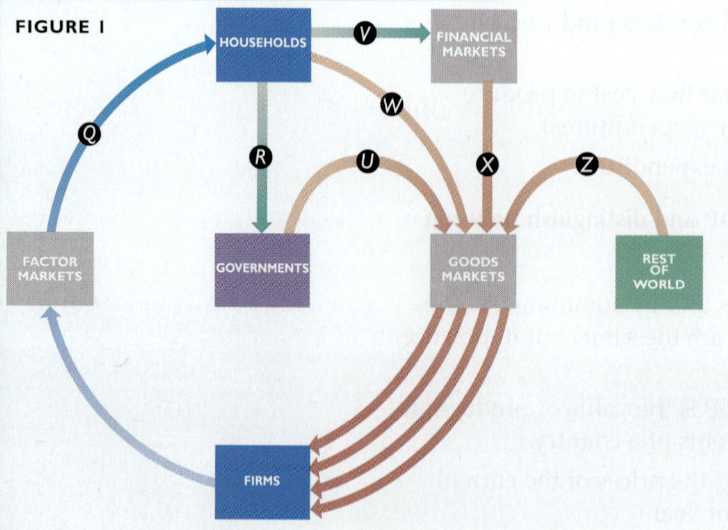

Use the following information to work Problems 2 and 3.

The national accounts of Parchment Paradise are kept on (you guessed it) parchment. A fire destroys the statistics office. The accounts are now incomplete but they contain the following data:

- GDP (income approach) $2,900
- Consumption expenditure $2,000
- Indirect taxes less subsidies $100
- Interest, rental, and profit $500
- Investment $800
- Government expenditure $400
- Wages $2,000
- Net factor income from abroad $50
- Net exports –$200

2. Calculate GDP (expenditure approach) and depreciation.
3. Calculate net domestic product at factor cost, the statistical discrepancy, and GNP.

Use the following information to work Problems 4 to 6.

An economy produces only fun and food. Table 1 shows the prices and the quantities of fun and food produced in 2009 and 2010. The base year is 2009.

TABLE 1

(a) In 2009:

Item	Quantity	Price
Fun	40	$2
Food	60	$3

(b) In 2010:

Item	Quantity	Price
Fun	35	$3
Food	65	$2

4. Calculate nominal GDP in 2009 and 2010.
5. Calculate the percentage increase in production in 2010.
6. If potential GDP was $270 in 2009 and it grew by 1 percent in 2010, in which phase of the business cycle is the economy? Explain.

Use the following information to work Problems 6 to 8.

Higher prices pushed up consumer spending for June

The Commerce Department reported that retail sales increased 0.8 percent in June. But net exports were down 0.3 percent in the second quarter of 2009 and inventories held by business fell by 1.1 percent in June, while sales at all levels of production were up 0.9 percent.

Source: Commerce Department, August 13, 2009

7. Which component of GDP changed because retail sales increased? Which component of GDP changed because inventories held by businesses rose?
8. Explain the effect of the fall in net exports on GDP.
9. Does the statement that sales at all levels of production were up 0.9 percent mean that GDP increased by 0.9 percent? Explain your answer.

Instructor Assignable Problems and Applications

Your instructor can assign these problems as homework, a quiz, or a test in **MyEconLab**.

1. In 2008, the population of China was 1.3 billion and real GDP (in purchasing power parity prices) was $4.4 trillion. In the same year, the population of India was 1.2 billion and real GDP (in purchasing power parity prices) was $1.2 trillion. In 2005, the most recent year for which we have the data, China's HDI was 0.777 and India's was 0.619.

   Based on this information, which country has the higher standard of living? What features of the information provided lead you to your conclusion?

2. Classify each of the following items as a final good or service or an intermediate good or service and identify which is a component of consumption expenditure, investment, or government expenditure on goods and services:
   - Banking services bought by Wal-Mart.
   - Security system bought by the White House.
   - Coffee beans bought by Starbucks.
   - New coffee grinders bought by Starbucks
   - Starbuck's grande mocha frappuccino bought by a student.
   - New battle ship bought by the U.S. navy.

Use the following data on the economy of Iberia to work Problems 3 and 4.
- Net taxes $18 billion
- Government expenditure on goods and services $20 billion
- Household saving $15 billion
- Consumption expenditure $67 billion
- Investment $21 billion
- Exports of goods and services $30 billion

3. Calculate Iberia's GDP.
4. Calculate Iberia's imports of goods and services.

Use Table 1, which shows an economy's total production and the prices of the final goods it produced in 2009 and 2010, to work Problems 5 to 7.

5. Calculate nominal GDP in 2009 and 2010.
6. The base year is 2009. Calculate real GDP in 2009 and 2010 .
7. Calculate the percentage increase in production in 2010.

TABLE 1

(a) In 2009:

Item	Quantity	Price
Fish	100	$2
Berries	50	$6

(b) In 2010:

Item	Quantity	Price
Fish	75	$5
Berries	65	$10

Use the following information to work Problems 8 and 9.

New-home sales jump as prices fall sharply

Sales of new homes rose 11.0 percent in June, their largest monthly gain in nearly eight year, a sign that the housing market is bottoming as buyers take advantage of lower prices. Sales of previously owned homes also rose for another month.

Source: *The New York Times*, July 27, 2009

8. Where do new-home sales appear in the U.S. National Income and Product Accounts and the circular flow of expenditure and income ? How does a rise in new home sales affect real GDP? Explain your answer.
9. Where do sales of previously owned homes appear in the U.S. National Income and Product Accounts and the circular flow of expenditure and income? How does a rise in sales of previously owned homes affect real GDP? Explain your answer.

FIGURE 1

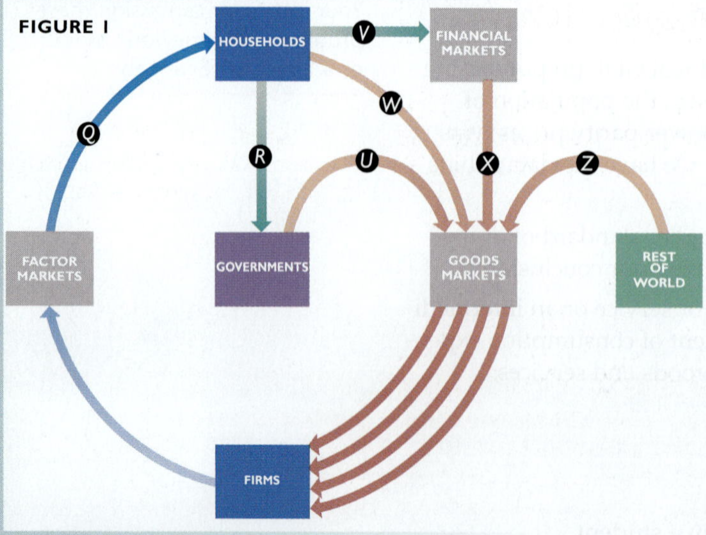

10. Figure 1 shows the flows of income and expenditure in an economy. In 2007, Q was \$1,000 billion, U was \$250 billion, W was \$650 billion, R was \$250 billion, and Z was \$50 billion. Calculate investment and saving.
11. Figure 1 shows the flows of income and expenditure in an economy. In 2008, X was \$2 trillion, R was \$3 trillion, Z was –\$1 trillion, Q was \$10 trillion, and U was \$4 trillion. Calculate saving and consumption expenditure.

Use the following information to work Problems 12 and 13.

Mitsubishi Heavy Industries makes the wings of the new Boeing 787 Dreamliner in Japan. Toyota assembles cars for the U.S. market in Kentucky.

12. Explain where these activities appear in the National Income and Product Accounts of the United States.
13. Explain where these activities appear in the National Income and Product Accounts of Japan.

TABLE 2

Item	Amount (billions of dollars)
Consumption expenditure	885
Wages	815
Government expenditure	350
Interest, rent, and profit	400
Indirect taxes less subsidies	165
Depreciation	200
Investment	300
Net exports	35

Use Table 2, which shows some of the items in Canada's National Income and Product Accounts in 2008, to work Problems 14 to 16.

14. Use the expenditure approach to calculate Canada's GDP in 2008.
15. Calculate Canada's net domestic product at factor cost in 2008.
16. What was Canada's GDP as measured by the income approach in 2008? Calculate the statistical discrepancy.
17. **A bit more bounce in the global economy**

    The global economy is in the early stages of an upturn that will deliver more GDP growth than is expected but less than is needed. The latest economic news points to sustained above-trend global growth.

    Source: J.P. Morgan Global Data Watch, September, 2009

    Does this news mean that the 2008–2009 recession had ended by September 2009? Does recession end only when real GDP returns to potential GDP?
18. The United Nation's HDI is based on GDP per person, life expectancy at birth, and indicators of the quality and quantity of education. Why does the United States not have the highest HDI? What items might be included in an expanded HDI to create a better standard of living index?
19. **Garage sales booming as recession grinds on**

    The Commerce Department report showed total retail sales across the country fell 0.1% in July, although garage sales springing up across the country are proving popular with buyers. Cathy, an unemployed nurse said that she uses the money she makes from her garage sales to pay bills.

    Source: Reuters, August 14, 2009

    Where do the items in the news clip appear in the U.S. National Income and Product Accounts and the circular flow of expenditure and income?

APPENDIX: MEASURING REAL GDP

This appendix explains the principles used by the Bureau of Economic Analysis (BEA) to calculate real GDP using a measure called **chained-dollar real GDP**. We begin by explaining the problem that arises from using the prices of the base year (the method on pp. 520–521) and how the problem can be overcome.

Chained-dollar real GDP
The measure of real GDP calculated by the Bureau of Economic Analysis.

The Problem With Base-Year Prices

When we calculated real GDP on pp. 520–521, we found that real GDP in 2010 was 60 percent greater than it was in 2005. But instead of using the prices of 2005 as the constant prices, we could have used the prices of 2010. In this case, we would have valued the quantities produced in 2005 at the prices of 2010. By comparing the values of real GDP in 2005 and 2010 at the constant prices of 2010, we get a different number for the percentage increase in production. If you use the numbers in Table 5.3 on p. 521 to value 2005 production at 2010 prices, you will get a real GDP in 2005 of $150 million (2010 dollars). Real GDP in 2010 at 2010 prices is $300 million. So by using the prices of 2010, production doubled—a 100 percent increase—from 2005 to 2010. Did production in fact increase by 60 percent or 100 percent?

The problem arises because to calculate real GDP, we weight the quantity of each item produced by its price. If all prices change by the same percentage, then the *relative* weight on each good or service doesn't change and the percentage change in real GDP from the first year to the second is the same regardless of which year's prices we use. But if prices change by different percentages, then the *relative* weight on each good or service *does* change and the percentage change in real GDP from the first year to the second depends on which prices we use. So which year's prices should we use: those of the first year or those of the second?

The answer given by the BEA method is to use the prices of both years. If we calculate the percentage change in real GDP twice, once using the prices of the first year and again using the prices of the second year, and then take the average of those two percentage changes, we get a unique measure of the change in real GDP and one that gives equal importance to the *relative* prices of both years.

To illustrate the calculation of the BEA measure of real GDP, we'll work through an example. The method has three steps:

- Value production in the prices of adjacent years.
- Find the average of two percentage changes.
- Link (chain) to the base year.

Value Production in the Prices of Adjacent Years

The first step is to value production in *adjacent* years at the prices of both years. We'll make these calculations for 2010, and its preceding year, 2009.

Table A5.1 shows the quantities produced and prices in the two years. Part (a) shows the nominal GDP calculation for 2009—the quantities produced in 2009 valued at the prices of 2009. Nominal GDP in 2009 is $145 million. Part (b) shows the nominal GDP calculation for 2010—the quantities produced in 2010 valued at the prices of 2010. Nominal GDP in 2010 is $172 million. Part (c) shows the value of the quantities produced in 2010 at the prices of 2009. This total is $160 million. Finally, part (d) shows the value of the quantities produced in 2009 at the prices of 2010. This total is $158 million.

TABLE A5.1

Real GDP Calculation Step 1: Value Production in Adjacent Years at Prices of Both Years

Step I is to value the production of adjacent years at the prices of both years.

Here, we value the production of 2009 and 2010 at the prices of both 2009 and 2010.

The value of 2009 production at 2009 prices, in part (a), is nominal GDP in 2009.

The value of 2010 production at 2010 prices, in part (b), is nominal GDP in 2010.

Part (c) calculates the value of 2010 production at 2009 prices, and part (d) calculates the value of 2009 production at 2010 prices.

We use these numbers in Step 2.

	Item	Quantity (millions of units)	Price (dollars per unit)	Expenditure (millions of dollars)
(a) In 2009				
C	T-shirts	3	5	15
I	Computer chips	3	10	30
G	Security services	5	20	100
Y	Nominal GDP in 2009			145
(b) In 2010				
C	T-shirts	4	4	16
I	Computer chips	2	12	24
G	Security services	6	22	132
Y	Nominal GDP in 2010			172
(c) Quantities of 2010 valued at prices of 2009				
C	T-shirts	4	5	20
I	Computer chips	2	10	20
G	Security services	6	20	120
Y	2010 production at 2009 prices			160
(d) Quantities of 2009 valued at prices of 2010				
C	T-shirts	3	4	12
I	Computer chips	3	12	36
G	Security services	5	22	110
Y	2009 production at 2010 prices			158

Find the Average of Two Percentage Changes

The second step is to find the percentage change in the value of production based on the prices in the two adjacent years. Table A5.2 summarizes these calculations.

Valued at the prices of 2009, production increased from $145 million in 2009 to $160 million in 2010, an increase of 10.3 percent. Valued at the prices of 2010, production increased from $158 million in 2009 to $172 million in 2010, an increase of 8.9 percent. The average of these two percentage changes in the value of production is 9.6. That is, $(10.3 + 8.9) \div 2 = 9.6$.

By applying this percentage change to real GDP, we can find the value of real GDP in 2010. Because real GDP in 2009 is in 2009 dollars, real GDP in 2010 is also in 2009 dollars. GDP in 2009 is $145 million, so a 9.6 percent increase is $14 million. Real GDP in 2010, expressed in 2009 dollars, is $145 million plus $14 million, which equals $159 million.

Although the real GDP of $159 million is expressed in 2009 dollars, the calculation uses the average of the *relative prices* of the final goods and services that make up GDP in 2009 and 2010.

Table A5.2

Real GDP Calculation Step 2: Find Average of Two Percentage Changes

Value of Production in Adjacent Years		Millions of dollars
2009 production at 2009 prices		145
2010 production at 2009 prices		160
Percentage change in production at 2009 prices	10.3	
2009 production at 2010 prices		158
2010 production at 2010 prices		172
Percentage change in production at 2010 prices	8.9	
Average of two percentage changes in production	9.6	

Using the numbers calculated in Step 1, we find the percentage change in production from 2009 to 2010 valued at 2009 prices, which is 10.3 percent.

We also find the percentage change in production from 2009 to 2010 valued at 2010 prices, which is 8.9 percent.

We then find the average of these two percentage changes, which is 9.6 percent.

Link (Chain) to the Base Year

The final step repeats the calculation that we've just described to obtain the real GDP growth rate each year. In the base year, which currently is 2005, real GDP equals nominal GDP. By applying the calculated growth rates to each successive year, we obtain *chained-dollar real GDP* in 2005 dollars.

Figure A5.1 shows an example. In the base year, 2005, real GDP equals nominal GDP, which is $66 million. The table shows the growth rates for each year between 2000 and 2010, the final one of which is the 9.6 percent that we calculated in Table A5.2 above.

Starting with real GDP in the base year, we apply the calculated percentage changes to find real GDP in other years. For example, in 2006, the growth rate was 8.2 percent, so real GDP in 2006 is 8.2 percent higher than $66 million and is $72 million. In 2005, the growth rate was 7.1 percent, so $66 million is 7.1 percent higher than real GDP in 2004, which is $62 million. Repeating the calculations, by 2009, real GDP was $83 million. In 2010, real GDP grew by 9.6 percent of $83 million, which is $8 million, so real GDP in 2010 was $91 million.

FIGURE A5.1

Real GDP Calculation Step 3: Link (Chain) to the Base Year

myeconlab Animation

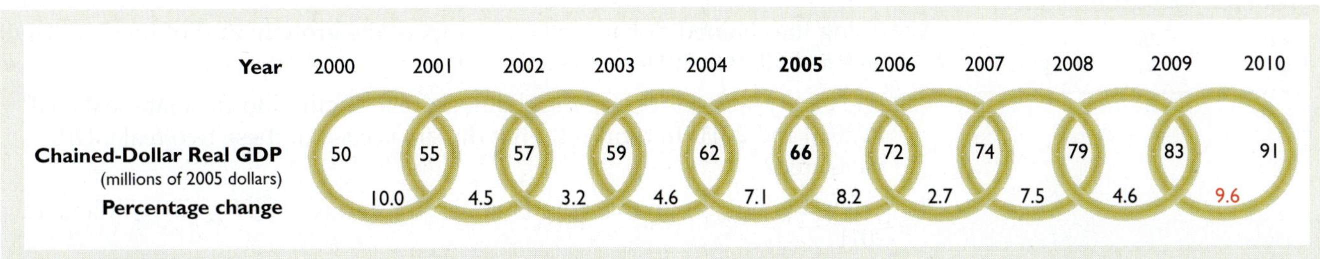

The percentage change in real GDP from one year to the next is calculated for every pair of years and then linked to the base year. Suppose that real GDP was $66 million in the base year, 2005. By applying the percentage change between each pair of years, we find chained-dollar real GDP for each year, expressed in terms of the value of the dollar in the base year. Here, the percentages for 2001 through to 2009 are assumed. By 2010, the chained-dollar real GDP has increased to $91 million in 2005 dollars.

myeconlab

Work these problems in Chapter 5 Study Plan to get instant feedback.

TABLE 1

(a) In 2010:

Item	Quantity	Price
Bananas	100	$10
Coconuts	50	$12

(b) In 2011:

Item	Quantity	Price
Bananas	110	$15
Coconuts	60	$10

APPENDIX CHECKPOINT

Study Plan Problems

An island economy produces only bananas and coconuts. Table 1 gives the quantities produced and prices in 2010 and in 2011.

1. Calculate nominal GDP in 2010 and nominal GDP in 2011.
2. Calculate the value of 2011 production in 2010 prices and the percentage increase in production when valued at 2010 prices.
3. Calculate the value of 2010 production in 2011 prices and the percentage increase in production when valued at 2011 prices.
4. The base year is 2010. Use the chained-dollar method to calculate real GDP in 2010 and 2011. In terms of what dollars is each of these two real GDPs measured?
5. Using the chained-dollar method, compare the growth rates of nominal GDP and real GDP in 2011.
6. The base year is 2011. Use the chained-dollar method to calculate real GDP in 2010 and 2011. In terms of what dollars is each of these two real GDPs measured?
7. Compare the growth rates of nominal GDP and real GDP in 2011 dollars in 2011.

Your instructor can assign these problems as homework, a quiz, or a test in **MyEconLab**.

TABLE 2

(a) In 2010:

Item	Quantity	Price
Food	100	$2
Fun	50	$6

(b) In 2011:

Item	Quantity	Price
Food	75	$5
Fun	65	$10

Instructor Assignable Problems

An economy produces only food and fun. Table 2 shows the quantities produced and prices in 2010 and 2011.

1. Calculate nominal GDP in 2010 and nominal GDP in 2011.
2. Calculate the value of 2011 production in 2010 prices and the percentage increase in production when valued at 2010 prices.
3. Calculate the value of 2010 production in 2011 prices and the percentage increase in production when valued at 2011 prices.
4. Using the chained-dollar method, calculate real GDP in 2010 and 2011 if the base year is 2011. In terms of what dollars is each of these two real GDPs measured?
5. Using the chained-dollar method, compare the growth rates of nominal GDP and real GDP in 2011.
6. The base year is 2010. Use the chained-dollar method to calculate real GDP in 2010 and 2011. In terms of what dollars is each of these two real GDPs measured?
7. Compare the growth rates of nominal GDP and real GDP in 2010 dollars in 2011.

How long does it take to find a new job?

Does it take longer in a recession than at full employment? And who is most likely to be looking for a job?

6

Jobs and Unemployment

CHAPTER CHECKLIST

When you have completed your study of this chapter, you will be able to

1. Define the unemployment rate and other labor market indicators.
2. Describe the trends and fluctuations in the indicators of labor market performance in the United States.
3. Describe the sources of unemployment, define full employment, and explain the link between unemployment and real GDP.

6.1 LABOR MARKET INDICATORS

Every month, 1,600 field interviewers and supervisors working on a joint project between the Bureau of Labor Statistics (or BLS) and the Bureau of the Census survey 60,000 households and ask a series of questions about the age and labor market status of its members. This survey is called the *Current Population Survey*. Let's look at the types of data collected by this survey.

Current Population Survey

Working-age population
The total number of people aged 16 years and over who are not in jail, hospital, or some other form of institutional care or in the U.S. Armed Forces.

Labor force
The number of people employed plus the number unemployed.

Figure 6.1 shows the categories into which the BLS divides the population. It also shows the relationships among the categories. The first category divides the population into two groups: the working-age population and others. The **working-age population** is the total number of people aged 16 years and over who are not in jail, hospital, or some other form of institutional care or in the U.S. Armed Forces. In June 2009, the estimated population of the United States was 306.8 million. In June 2009, the working-age population was 235.7 million; and 71.1 million people were under 16 years of age, in the military, or living in institutions.

The second category divides the working-age population into two groups: those in the labor force and those not in the labor force. The **labor force** is the number of people employed plus the number unemployed. In June 2009, the U.S. labor force was 154.9 million and 80.8 million people were not in the labor force. Most of those not in the labor force were in school full time or had retired from work.

The third category divides the labor force into two groups: the employed and the unemployed. In June 2009 in the United States, 140.2 million people were employed and 14.7 million people were unemployed.

Population Survey Criteria

The survey counts as *employed* all persons who, during the week before the survey, either

1. Worked at least 1 hour as paid employees or worked 15 hours or more as unpaid workers in their family business or
2. Were not working but had jobs or businesses from which they were temporarily absent.

The survey counts as *unemployed* all persons who, during the week before the survey,

1. Had no employment,
2. Were available for work,

and either

1. Had made specific efforts to find employment during the previous four weeks or
2. Were waiting to be recalled to a job from which they had been laid off.

People in the working-age population who by the above criteria are neither employed nor unemployed are classified as not in the labor force.

To be counted as unemployed, a person must not only want a job but also have tried to find one.

FIGURE 6.1

Population Labor Force Categories

myeconlab Animation

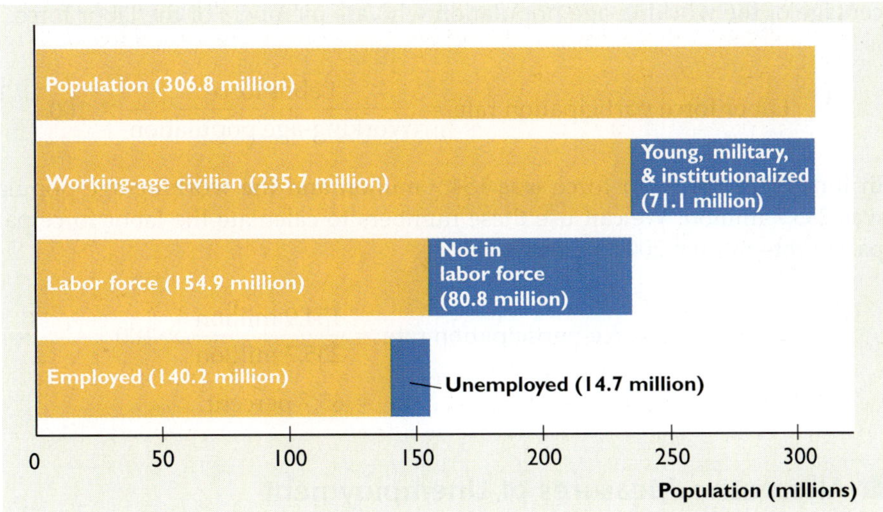

SOURCE OF DATA: Bureau of Labor Statistics.

The U.S. population is divided into the working-age population and the young, military, and institutionalized. The working-age population is divided into the labor force and those not in the labor force. The labor force is divided into the employed and the unemployed. The figure shows the data for June 2009.

Two Main Labor Market Indicators

Using the numbers from the Current Population Survey, the BLS calculates several indicators of the state of the labor market. The two main labor market indicators are

- The unemployment rate
- The labor force participation rate

The Unemployment Rate

The amount of unemployment is an indicator of the extent to which people who want jobs can't find them. It tells us the amount of slack in the labor market. The **unemployment rate** is the percentage of the people in the labor force who are unemployed. That is,

Unemployment rate
The percentage of the people in the labor force who are unemployed.

$$\text{Unemployment rate} = \frac{\text{Number of people unemployed}}{\text{Labor force}} \times 100.$$

In June 2009, the number of people unemployed was 14.7 million and the labor force was 154.9 million. We can use these numbers to calculate the unemployment rate in June 2009, which is

$$\text{Unemployment rate} = \frac{14.7 \text{ million}}{154.9 \text{ million}} \times 100$$
$$= 9.5 \text{ percent.}$$

The Labor Force Participation Rate

Labor force participation rate
The percentage of the working-age population who are members of the labor force.

The number of people in the labor force is an indicator of the willingness of people of working age to take jobs. The **labor force participation rate** is the percentage of the working-age population who are members of the labor force. That is,

$$\text{Labor force participation rate} = \frac{\text{Labor force}}{\text{Working-age population}} \times 100.$$

In June 2009, the labor force was 154.9 million and the working-age population was 235.7 million. We can use these numbers to calculate the labor force participation rate in June 2009, which is

$$\text{Labor force participation rate} = \frac{154.9 \text{ million}}{235.7 \text{ million}} \times 100$$
$$= 65.7 \text{ percent.}$$

Alternative Measures of Unemployment

The unemployment rate based on the official definition of unemployment omits some types of underutilization of labor. The omissions are

- Marginally attached workers
- Part-time workers

Marginally Attached Workers

Marginally attached worker
A person who does not have a job, is available and willing to work, has not made specific efforts to find a job within the previous four weeks, but has looked for work sometime in the recent past.

Discouraged worker
A marginally attached worker who has not made specific efforts to find a job within the past four weeks because previous unsuccessful attempts to find a job were discouraging.

Some people who think of themselves as being in the labor force and unemployed are not counted in the official labor force numbers. They are marginally attached workers. A **marginally attached worker** is a person who does not have a job, is available and willing to work, has not made specific efforts to find a job within the previous four weeks, but has looked for work sometime in the recent past. A **discouraged worker** is a marginally attached worker who has not made specific efforts to find a job within the previous four weeks because previous unsuccessful attempts were discouraging. Other marginally attached workers differ from discouraged workers only in their reasons for not having looked for a job during the previous four weeks. For example, Martin doesn't have a job and is available for work, but he hasn't looked for work in the past four weeks because he was busy cleaning up his home after a flood. He is a marginally attached worker but not a discouraged worker. Lena, Martin's wife, doesn't have a job and is available for work, but she hasn't looked for work in the past four weeks because she's been looking for six months and not managed to get a single job offer. She is a discouraged worker.

Neither the unemployment rate nor the labor force participation rate includes marginally attached workers. In June 2009, 860,000 people were discouraged workers. If we add them to both the number unemployed and the labor force, the unemployment rate becomes 10 percent—only slightly higher than the standard definition of the unemployment rate. Also in June 2009, 1,256,000 people were other marginally attached workers. If we add them and the discouraged workers to both the number unemployed and the labor force, the unemployment rate becomes 10.8 percent—1.3 percentage points to the standard definition.

EYE on the U.S. ECONOMY

The Current Population Survey

The Bureau of Labor Statistics and the Bureau of the Census go to great lengths to collect accurate labor force data. They constantly train and retrain around 1,600 field interviewers and supervisors. Each month, each field interviewer contacts 37 households and asks basic demographic questions about everyone living at the address and detailed labor force questions about those aged 16 or over.

Once a household has been selected for the survey, it is questioned for four consecutive months and then again for the same four months a year later. Each month, the addresses that have been in the panel eight times are removed and 6,250 new addresses are added. The rotation and overlap of households provide very reliable information about month-to-month and year-to-year changes in the labor market.

The first time that a household is in the panel, an interviewer, armed with a laptop computer, visits it. If the household has a telephone, most of the subsequent interviews are conducted by phone, many of them from one of the three telephone interviewing centers in Hagerstown, Maryland; Jeffersonville, Indiana; and Tucson, Arizona.

For more information about the Current Population Survey, visit http://www.bls.gov/cps/cps_faq.htm.

Part-Time Workers

The Current Population Survey measures the number of full-time workers and part-time workers. **Full-time workers** are those who usually work 35 hours or more a week. **Part-time workers** are those who usually work less than 35 hours a week. Part-time workers are divided into two groups: part time for economic reasons and part time for noneconomic reasons.

People who work **part time for economic reasons** (also called *involuntary part-time workers)* are people who work 1 to 34 hours but are looking for full-time work. These people are unable to find full-time work because of unfavorable business conditions or seasonal decreases in the availability of full-time work.

People who work part time for noneconomic reasons do not want full-time work and are not available for such work. This group includes people with health problems, family or personal responsibilities, or education commitments that limit their availability for work.

The Bureau of Labor Statistics uses the data on full-time and part-time status to measure the slack in the labor market that results from people being underemployed—employed but not able to find as much employment as they would like.

In June 2009, when employment was 140.2 million, full-time employment was 112.9 million and part-time employment was 27.3 million. An estimated 10.7 million people worked part time for economic reasons. When this number along with marginally attached workers is added to both the number unemployed and the labor force, the unemployment rate becomes 16.5 percent.

Full-time workers
People who usually work 35 hours or more a week.

Part-time workers
People who usually work less than 35 hours a week.

Part time for economic reasons
People who work 1 to 34 hours per week but are looking for full-time work and cannot find it because of unfavorable business conditions.

myeconlab

Work these problems in Study Plan 6.1 to get instant feedback.

CHECKPOINT 6.1

Define the unemployment rate and other labor market indicators.

Practice Problems

The BLS reported that in July 2009, the labor force was 154.5 million, employment was 140.0 million, and the working-age population was 235.9 million. Use this information to work Problems **1** and **2**.

1. Calculate the unemployment rate and the labor force participation rate.
2. The BLS also reported that 24 percent of all employment in July 2009 was part time and that 9.1 million people worked part time for economic reasons. How many people worked part time for noneconomic reasons?
3. The Bureau of Labor Statistics reported that in July 2009, the labor force in Michigan was 4,864 thousand and employment was 4,134 thousand. Calculate the unemployment rate in Michigan in July 2009.
4. **Hawaiian Airlines hires 100 workers, plans to add 170 more**
   Hawaiian Airlines will hire more workers as it expands its fleet. The new hirings are a welcome sign for Hawaii's economy, which lost jobs during the year to May 2009 as the state's unemployment rate rose from 4% to 7%.

   Source: *USA Today*, August 18, 2009

   The labor force was 602,000 in May 2009 and 622,600 in May 2008. Calculate the change in the number unemployed between May 2008 and May 2009.

Guided Solutions to Practice Problems

1. The unemployment rate is 9.4 percent. The labor force is the sum of the number employed plus the number unemployed. So the number unemployed equals the labor force minus the number employed, which equals 154.5 million minus 140.0 million, or 14.5 million. The unemployment rate is the number unemployed as a percentage of the labor force. The unemployment rate = (14.5 million ÷ 154.5 million) × 100, or 9.4 percent. The labor force participation rate is 65.5 percent. The labor force participation rate is the percentage of the working-age population who are in the labor force. Labor force participation rate = (154.5 ÷ 235.9) × 100, or 65.5 percent.
2. 24.5 million people worked part time for noneconomic reasons. Employment was 140 million. Part-time employment was 24 percent of 140 million, which equals 33.6 million. Given that 9.1 million worked part time for economic reasons, 33.6 million minus 9.1 million, or 24.5 million worked part time for noneconomic reasons.
3. The unemployment rate is 15 percent. The number unemployed equals the labor force minus the number employed. Unemployment equals 4,864 thousand minus 4,134 thousand, which equals 730 thousand. The unemployment rate = (730 thousand ÷ 4,864 thousand) × 100, or 15 percent.
4. The change in the number unemployed was 17,260.
   Unemployment rate = (Unemployment ÷ Labor force) × 100. Rearranging this equation gives: Unemployment = (unemployment rate × labor force) ÷ 100. In May 2008, unemployment was (4 × 622,600) ÷ 100, or 24,880. In May 2009, unemployment was (7 × 602,000) ÷ 100, or 42,140. The number unemployed increased by 42,140 minus 24,880, which equals 17,260.

6.2 LABOR MARKET TRENDS AND FLUCTUATIONS

What do we learn about the U.S. labor market from changes in the unemployment rate, the labor force participation rate, and the alternative measures of unemployment? Let's explore the trends and fluctuations in these indicators.

Unemployment Rate

Figure 6.2 shows the U.S. unemployment rate over the 80 years from 1929 to 2009. Over these years, the average U.S. unemployment rate was 5.7 percent. The rate was below this long-term average during the 1940s through the 1960s and during the 2000s. It was above the long-term average during the 1970s to the mid 1990s.

During the 1960s, the unemployment rate gradually fell to 3.5 percent. These years saw a rapid rate of job creation, partly from the demands placed on the economy by the growth of defense production during the Vietnam War and partly from an expansion of consumer spending encouraged by an expansion of social programs. Another burst of rapid job creation driven by the "new economy"—the high-technology sector driven by the expansion of the Internet—lowered the unemployment rate from 1995 through most of the 2000s to below average.

The most striking event visible in Figure 6.2 is the **Great Depression,** a period of high unemployment, low incomes, and extreme economic hardship that lasted from 1929 to 1939. By 1933, the worst of the Great Depression years, real GDP had fallen by a huge 30 percent and as the figure shows, one in four of the people who wanted jobs couldn't find them. The horrors of the Great Depression led to the New Deal and shaped political attitudes that persist today.

Great Depression
A period of high unemployment, low incomes, and extreme economic hardship that lasted from 1929 to 1939.

During the recessions of 1973–1975, 1981–1982, 1990–1991, and 2008–2009, the

FIGURE 6.2

The U.S. Unemployment Rate: 1929–2009

myeconlab Animation

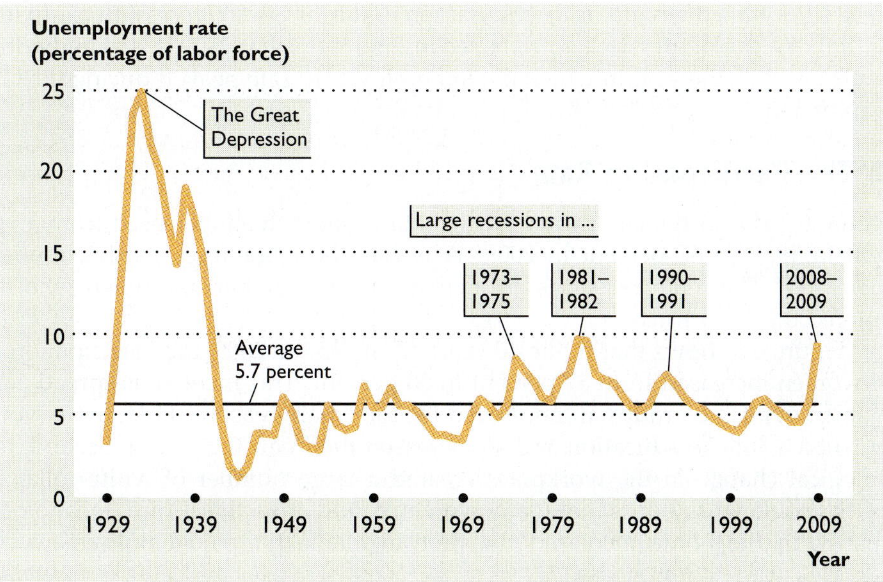

SOURCE OF DATA: Bureau of Labor Statistics.

The average unemployment rate from 1929 to 2009 was 5.7 percent. The unemployment rate increases in recessions and decreases in expansions. Unemployment was at its lowest during the expansions of the 1960s and the 1990s and at its highest during the Great Depression and the recessions of 1981–1982 and 2008–2009.

EYE on the GLOBAL ECONOMY

Unemployment Around the World

Before the 2008–2009 recession, the U.S. unemployment rate fell in the middle of the range experienced by other countries. The highest unemployment rates have been in Europe, Canada, and the United Kingdom and the lowest unemployment rates have been in Japan and the newly industrializing countries of Asia.

Differences in unemployment rates were much greater during the 1980s and 1990s than in the 2000s.

All of the countries with higher average unemployment rates than the United States also have higher unemployment benefits and more regulated labor markets.

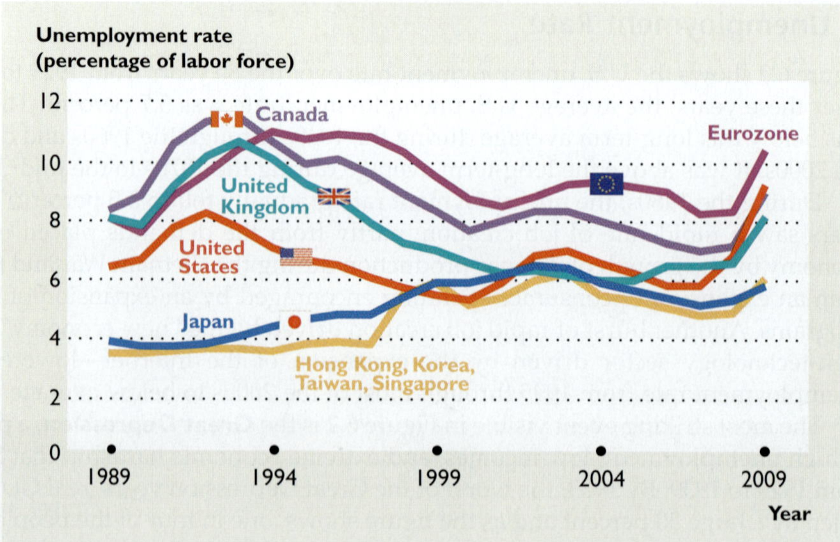

SOURCE OF DATA: International Monetary Fund, *World Economic Outlook*, April 2009.

unemployment rate increased. During the post-War years, the unemployment rate peaked in November–December 1982 when 10.8 percent of the labor force were unemployed. By mid-2009, with the economy still in recession, the unemployment rate stood at 9.5 percent, but it was expected to rise above the 1982 peak level during 2010. While the popular representation of the 2008–2009 recession compares it with the Great Depression, you can see in Figure 6.2 that 2009 is strikingly different from 1933, the year in which the unemployment rate peaked during the Great Depression.

■ The Participation Rate

Figure 6.3 shows the labor force participation rate, which increased from 59 percent in 1959 to 67 percent in 2009. Why has the labor force participation rate increased? The main reason is an increase in the number of women who have entered the labor force.

Figure 6.3 shows that in the 40 years from 1959 to 2009, the participation rate of women increased from 37 percent to 60 percent. This increase is spread across women of all age groups and occurred for four main reasons. First, more women pursued a college education and so increased their earning power. Second, technological change in the workplace created a large number of white-collar jobs with flexible work hours that many women found attractive. Third, technological change in the home increased the time available for paid employment. And

FIGURE 6.3

The Changing Face of the Labor Market: 1959–2009

myeconlab Animation

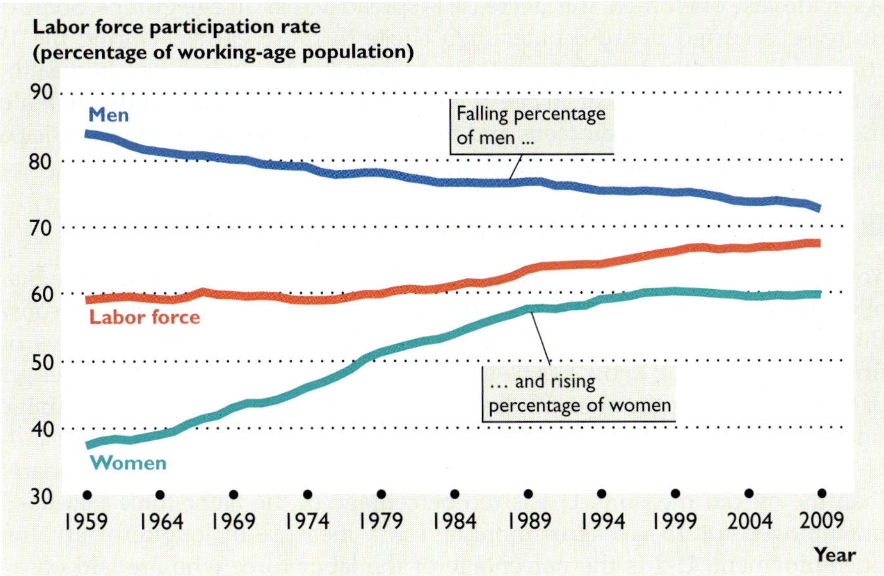

During the past 50 years, the labor force participation rate has increased. The labor force participation rate of men has decreased, and that of women has increased.

SOURCE OF DATA: Bureau of Labor Statistics.

EYE on the GLOBAL ECONOMY

Women in the Labor Force

The labor force participation rate of women has increased in most advanced nations. But the participation rate of women in the labor force varies a great deal around the world. The figure compares seven other countries with the United States.

Cultural factors play a role in determining national differences in women's work choices. But economic factors such as the percentage of women with a college degree will ultimately dominate cultural influences and bring a convergence.

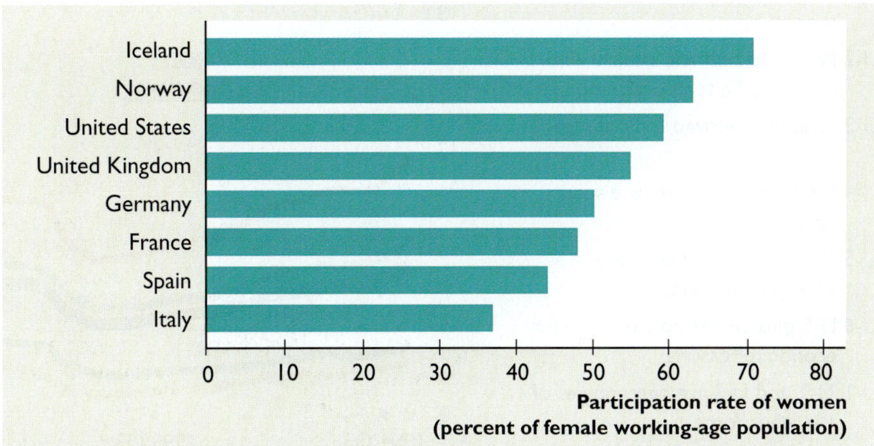

SOURCE OF DATA: OECD.

fourth, families looked increasingly to a second income to balance tight budgets.

Figure 6.3 also shows another remarkable trend in the U.S. labor force: The participation rate of men *decreased* from 84 percent in 1959 to 72 percent in 2009. As in the case of women, this decrease is spread across all age groups. Some of the decrease occurred because older men chose to retire earlier. During the 1990s, some of this earlier retirement was made possible by an increase in wealth. But some arose from job loss at an age at which finding a new job is difficult. For other men, mainly those in their teens and twenties, decreased labor force participation occurred because more chose to remain in full-time education.

Alternative Measures of Unemployment

You've seen that the official measure of unemployment does not include marginally attached workers and people who work part time for economic reasons. The Bureau of Labor Statistics (BLS) now provides three broader measures of the unemployment rate, known as U-4, U-5, and U-6, that include these wider groups of the jobless. The official unemployment rate (based on the standard definition of unemployment) is called U-3 and as these names imply, there is also a U-1 and U-2 measure. The U-1 and U-2 measures of the unemployment rate are narrower than the official measure. U-1 is the percentage of the labor force that has been unemployed for 15 weeks or more and is a measure of long-term involuntary unemployment. U-2 is the percentage of the labor force who are laid off and is another measure of involuntary unemployment.

Figure 6.4 shows the history of these six measures of unemployment since 1994 (the year in which the BLS started to measure them). The relative magnitudes of the six measures are explained by what they include—the broader the measure,

FIGURE 6.4

Alternative Measures of Unemployment: 1994–2009

myeconlab Animation

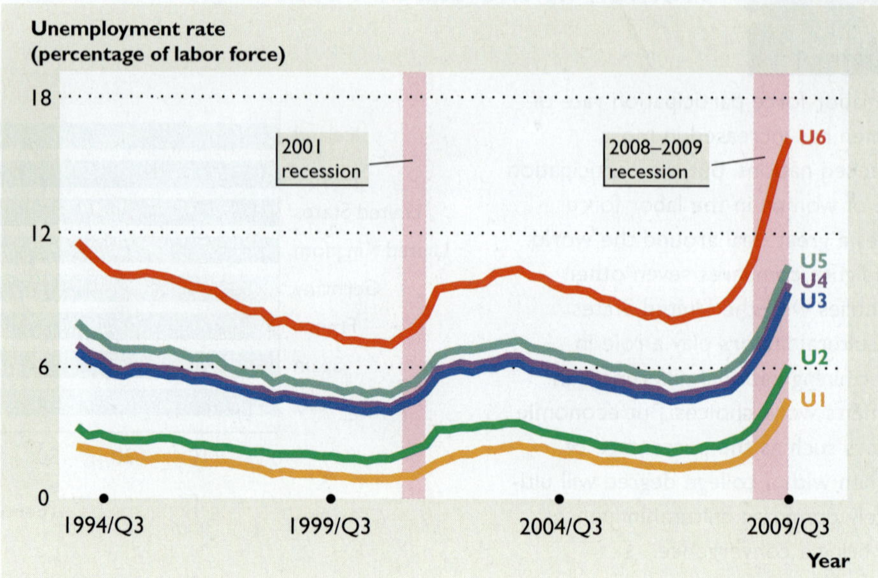

The alternative measures of unemployment are:

U-1 People unemployed 15 weeks or longer

U-2 People laid off and others who completed a temporary job

U-3 Total unemployed (official measure)

U-4 Total unemployed plus discouraged workers

U-5 U-4 plus other marginally attached workers

U-6 U-5 plus employed part time for economic reasons

U-1, U-2, and U-3 are percentages of the labor force.

U-4, U-5, and U-6 are percentages of the labor force plus the unemployed in the added category.

SOURCE OF DATA: Bureau of Labor Statistics.

the higher the average. The six measures follow similar but not identical tracks, rising during the recessions and falling in the expansions between the recessions. But during the 2001 recession, U-1 barely changed while during the 2008–2009 recession, it more than doubled in less than a year.

A Closer Look at Part-Time Employment

The broadest measure of the unemployment rate, U-6, includes people who work part time for economic reasons. Let's take a closer look at part-time employment.

A part-time job is attractive to many workers because it enables them to balance family and other commitments with work. Part-time jobs are attractive to employers because they don't have to pay benefits to part-time workers and are less constrained by government regulations. People who choose part-time jobs are part time for noneconomic reasons. People who take a part-time job because they can't find a full-time job are part time for economic reasons. The BLS measures these two groups and Figure 6.5 shows the data since 1979 (but with a change in the definitions in 1994).

The number of people who work part time for noneconomic reasons is double the number who work part time for economic reasons. Also, the percentage of the labor force who are part time for noneconomic reasons is remarkably steady at an average of 13 percent (old definition) and 14 percent (new definition) of the labor force, and that percentage barely fluctuates with the business cycle.

The percentage of the labor force who work part-time for economic reasons experiences large swings. In the 1981–1982 recession, it climbed to 6.2 percent and in the 2008–2009 recession, it climbed to 6.4 percent.

FIGURE 6.5

Part-Time Workers: 1979–2009

myeconlab Animation

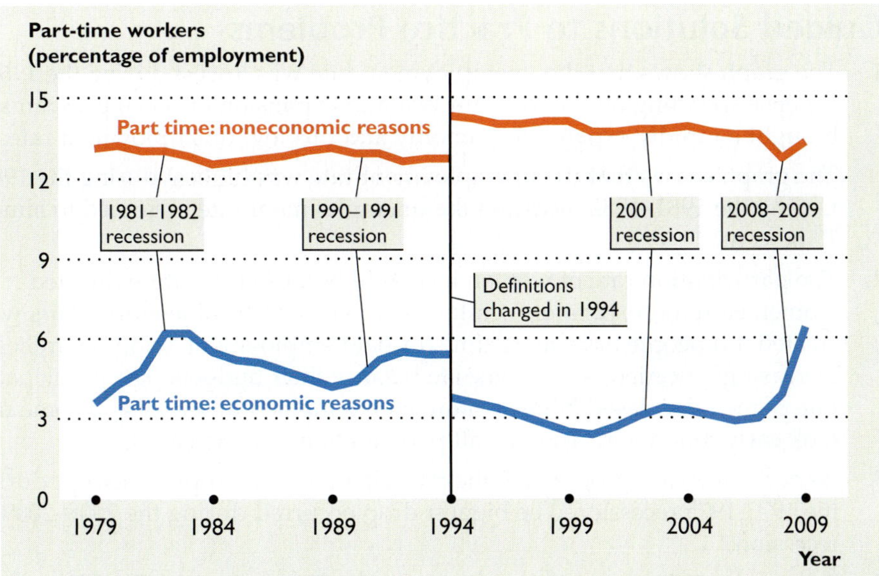

SOURCE OF DATA: Bureau of Labor Statistics.

The annual average percentage of all employed workers who are part time for noneconomic reasons is a steady 13 percent (old definition) and 14 percent (new definition) and this percentage barely fluctuates with the business cycle.

But the percentage of all employed workers who are part time for economic reasons fluctuates with the business cycle. It increases in a recession and decreases in an expansion.

myeconlab

Work these problems in Study Plan 6.2 to get instant feedback.

CHECKPOINT 6.2

Describe the trends and fluctuations in the indicators of labor market performance in the United States.

Practice Problems

FIGURE 1

1. Figure 1 shows the unemployment rate in the United States from 1960 to 2010. In which decade—the 1960s, 1970s, 1980s, 1990s, or 2000s—was the average unemployment rate the lowest and what brought low unemployment in that decade? In which decade was the average unemployment rate the highest and what brought high unemployment in that decade?
2. Describe the trends in the participation rates of men and women and of all workers.

Use the following information to work Problems **3** and **4**.

For young people, a jobless summer

July, the peak for youth summer jobs, saw the youth unemployment rate hit 18.5% in July 2009, the highest level since the BLS started recording youth labor statistics in 1948. The participation rate of young people was 51.4%, another historic low for the month of July.

Source: *The Wall Street Journal*, August 27, 2009

In addition, Table 1 sets out data for the youth participation rate and unemployment rate during four major recent U.S. recessions.

TABLE 1

Recession years	Participation rate (percent in July)	Unemployment rate (percent in July)
1973	71.9	11.1
1974	73.2	12.4
1975	73.0	16.3
1981	75.3	16.2
1982	74.7	18.6
1990	75.1	10.9
1991	73.6	13.7
2008	65.1	14.0
2009	63.0	18.5

3. Compare the changes in the labor force participation rate during the recessions in Table 1. During which recession did the labor force participation rate drop the most?
4. Compare the changes in the unemployment rate during the recessions in Table 1. During which recession did the unemployment rate rise the most?

Guided Solutions to Practice Problems

1. The graph shows that the unemployment rate was lowest during the 1960s. Defense spending on the Vietnam War and expansion of social programs brought a rapidly expanding economy and this low unemployment rate.

   The graph shows that the unemployment rate was highest during the 1980s. During the 1981–1982 recession the unemployment rate increased to almost 10 percent.
2. The participation rate of women increased because (1) better-educated women earn more, (2) more white-collar jobs with flexible work hours were created, (3) people have more time for paid employment, and (4) families increasingly needed two incomes to balance their budgets. The participation rate of men decreased because more men remained in school and some men took early retirement. The overall participation rate increased.
3. As each recession progressed, the participation rate dropped, except during the 1973-1975 recession. The biggest drop occurred during the 2008–2009 recession.
4. As each recession progressed, the unemployment rate rose. The biggest rise occurred during the 1973–1975 recession when youth unemployment in July rose from 11.1 percent to 16.3 percent—a 5.2 percentage point rise.

6.3 UNEMPLOYMENT AND FULL EMPLOYMENT

Why do people become unemployed, how long do they remain unemployed, and who is at greatest risk of becoming unemployed? What is full employment? How does the unemployment rate compare with real GDP as an indicator of the state of the economy? We begin to answer these questions by looking at the sources of unemployment.

Sources of Unemployment

The labor market is constantly churning. New jobs are created, and old ones are destroyed; and some people move into the labor force, and some move out of it. Around 5 million people start a new job every month and a similar but normally slightly smaller number lose or leave their job every month. This churning creates unemployment. People become unemployed if they are

1. Job losers
2. Job leavers
3. Entrants or reentrants

Job Losers

A *job loser* is someone who is gets a pink slip or is laid off from a job, either permanently or temporarily. People lose their jobs for many reasons. Some people are just not a good match for the job they're doing. Firms fail, or a new technology destroys some types of jobs. Offshore outsourcing also takes some jobs—but fewer than 2 million a year are lost for this reason (less than a half of a month's job turnover).

A job loser has two choices: Either look for another job or withdraw from the labor force. A job loser who decides to look for a new job remains in the labor force and becomes unemployed. A job loser who decides to withdraw from the labor force is classified as "not in the labor force." Most job losers decide to look for a new job, and some of them take a long time to find one.

Some job losers take a long time to find a new job.

Job Leavers

A *job leaver* is someone who voluntarily quits a job. Most people who leave their jobs do so for one of two reasons: Either they've found a better job or they've decided to withdraw from the labor force. Neither of these types of job leavers becomes unemployed. But a few people quit their jobs because they want to spend time looking for a better one. These job leavers become unemployed.

Entrants and Reentrants

An *entrant* is someone who has just left school and is looking for a job. Some entrants get a job right away and are never unemployed. But many entrants spend time searching for their first job, and during this period, they are unemployed.

A *reentrant* is someone who has previously had a job, has then quit and left the labor force, and has now decided to look for a job again. Some reentrants are people who have been out of the labor force rearing children, but most are discouraged workers—people who gave up searching for jobs because they were not able to find suitable ones and who have now decided to look again.

FIGURE 6.6

Unemployment by Reasons: 1979–2009

myeconlab Animation

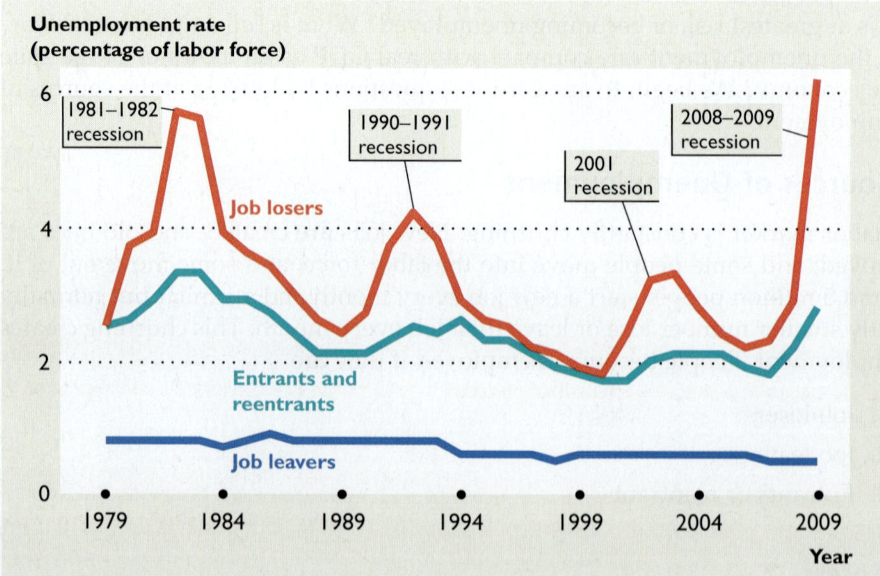

Everyone who is unemployed is a job loser, a job leaver, or an entrant or reentrant into the labor force.

Job losers are the biggest group, and their number fluctuates most.

Entrants and reentrants are the second biggest group. Their number also fluctuates.

Job leavers are the smallest group and their number fluctuates least.

SOURCE OF DATA: Bureau of Labor Statistics.

Figure 6.6 shows the magnitudes of the three sources of unemployment. Most unemployed people are job losers, and their number fluctuates most. The number of entrants and reentrants is also large and fluctuates. Job leavers are the smallest and most stable source of unemployment.

People who end a period of unemployment are either

1. Hires and recalls or
2. Withdrawals

Hires and Recalls

A *hire* is someone who has been unemployed and has started a new job. A *recall* is someone who has been temporarily laid off and has started work again. Firms are constantly hiring and recalling workers, so there are always people moving from unemployment to employment.

Withdrawals

A *withdrawal* is someone who has been unemployed and has decided to stop looking for a job. Most of these people are *marginally attached workers.* They will reenter the labor force later when job prospects improve.

Types of Unemployment

Unemployment is classified into four types:

- Frictional
- Structural
- Seasonal
- Cyclical

Frictional Unemployment

Frictional unemployment is the unemployment that arises from normal labor turnover—from people entering and leaving the labor force, from quitting jobs to find better ones, and from the ongoing creation and destruction of jobs. Frictional unemployment is a permanent and healthy phenomenon in a dynamic, growing economy.

Frictional unemployment
The unemployment that arises from normal labor turnover—from people entering and leaving the labor force, from quitting jobs to find better ones, and from the ongoing creation and destruction of jobs.

A new graduate interviews for a job.

Businesses don't usually hire the first person who applies for a job, and unemployed people don't always take the first job that comes their way. Instead, both firms and workers spend time searching out what they believe will be the best attainable match. By this search process, people can match their own skills and interests with the available jobs and find a satisfying job and income. While these unemployed people are searching, they are frictionally unemployed.

The amount of frictional unemployment changes slowly, and it depends on the rate at which people enter and reenter the labor force and on the rate at which jobs are created and destroyed. During the 1970s, the amount of frictional unemployment increased because of the postwar baby boom that began during the 1940s. By the late 1970s, the baby boom created a bulge in the number of people leaving school. As these people entered the labor force, the amount of frictional unemployment increased. Frictional unemployment remained high until the information-age expansion of the mid-1990s. Since 1994, frictional unemployment has decreased.

The amount of frictional unemployment is also influenced by unemployment compensation. The greater the number of unemployed people eligible for benefits and the more generous those benefits, the longer is the average time taken in job search and the greater is the amount of frictional unemployment. Unemployment benefits in Canada and Western Europe exceed those in the United States, and these economies have higher average unemployment rates.

Structural Unemployment

Structural unemployment is the unemployment that arises when changes in technology or international competition change the skills needed to perform jobs or change the locations of jobs. Structural unemployment usually lasts longer than frictional unemployment because workers must retrain and possibly relocate to find a job. For example, when a telephone exchange in Gary, Indiana, is automated, some jobs in that city are destroyed. Meanwhile, new jobs for life-insurance salespeople and retail clerks are created in Chicago, Indianapolis, and other cities. The former telephone operators remain unemployed for several months until they move, retrain, and get one of these jobs. Structural unemployment is painful, especially for older workers for whom the best available option might be to retire early but with a lower income than they had expected.

Structural unemployment
The unemployment that arises when changes in technology or international competition change the skills needed to perform jobs or change the locations of jobs.

A job lost to computer technology.

Sometimes, the amount of structural unemployment is small. At other times, it is large, and at such times, structural unemployment can become a serious long-term problem. It was especially large during the late 1970s and early 1980s. During those years, oil price hikes and an increasingly competitive international environment destroyed jobs in traditional U.S. industries, such as auto and steel making, and created jobs in new industries, such as information processing, electronics, and bioengineering. Structural unemployment was also present during the early 1990s as many businesses and governments downsized.

Seasonal Unemployment

Seasonal unemployment
The unemployment that arises because of seasonal patterns.

Seasonal unemployment is the unemployment that arises because of seasonal weather patterns. Seasonal unemployment increases during the winter months and decreases during the spring and summer. A fruit picker who is laid off after the fall harvest and who gets rehired the following summer experiences seasonal unemployment. A construction worker who gets laid off during the winter and who gets rehired in the spring also experiences seasonal unemployment.

Cyclical Unemployment

Cyclical unemployment
The fluctuating unemployment over the business cycle that increases during a recession and decreases during an expansion.

Cyclical unemployment is the fluctuating unemployment over the business cycle. Cyclical unemployment increases during a recession and decreases during an expansion. An autoworker who is laid off because the economy is in a recession and who gets rehired some months later when the expansion begins has experienced cyclical unemployment.

The causes of cyclical unemployment are complex and are explained in Chapters 13 and 14.

You've seen that there is always *some* unemployment—someone looking for a job or laid off and waiting to be recalled. Yet one of the goals of economic policy is to achieve full employment. What do we mean by *full employment?*

EYE on THE UNEMPLOYED

How Long Does it Take to Find a New Job?

Some people are unemployed for a week or two and others for a year or more. Short unemployment spells are not a major problem, especially if they end by finding a job that is better than the previous one. But long spells of unemployment impose a large personal cost to the unemployed, lead to a loss of human capital, and lead to underproduction and waste.

The average duration of unemployment varies over the business cycle. In a recession, when the unemployment rate exceeds the natural rate, the average duration increases, and during an expansion, when the unemployment rate is below the natural rate, the average duration decreases.

The table opposite compares three years—2000, when the economy was expanding strongly and the unemployment rate was below the natural rate at 4 percent, 2006, when the economy was at full employment and the unemployment rate was 4.8 percent, and 2009, when the economy was in a deep recession and the unemployment rate was above the natural rate at almost 10 percent.

The average unemployment spell lasted for 6 weeks in the boom year 2000, 25 weeks in the recession year 2009, and for 17 weeks at full employment in 2006.

In 2000, 77 percent of the unemployed found jobs in 14 weeks or less and only 11 percent took 27 weeks or more. But in 2009, only 48 percent of the unemployed found jobs in 14 weeks or less and 29 percent took 27 weeks or more. And at full employment, 68 percent found jobs in 14 weeks or less and 18 percent took 27 weeks or longer.

These data tell us that not only does the number of people unemployed vary over the business cycle but also the severity with which it impacts the unemployed.

Unemployment does not affect all demographic groups in the same way and some of the differences are large. The figure opposite shows some averages for 2000–2009. During this ten-

Full Employment

There can be a lot of unemployment at full employment, and the term "full employment" is an example of a technical economic term that does not correspond with everyday language. **Full employment** occurs when there is no cyclical unemployment or, equivalently, when all the unemployment is frictional, structural, or seasonal. The divergence of the unemployment rate from full employment is cyclical unemployment. The unemployment rate when the economy is at full employment is called the **natural unemployment rate**. The term "natural unemployment rate" is another example of a technical economic term that does not correspond with everyday language.

Full employment
When there is no cyclical unemployment or, equivalently, when *all* the unemployment is frictional, structural, or seasonal.

Natural unemployment rate
The unemployment rate when the economy is at full employment.

Why do economists call a situation with a lot of unemployment one of full employment? And why is the unemployment rate at full employment called the "natural" unemployment rate? The reason is that the natural state of the economy is one of change in its players, structure, and direction. For example, in 2007, around 3 million people retired and more than 3 million new workers entered the labor force. Thousands of businesses (including new startups) expanded and created jobs while thousands of others downsized or failed and destroyed jobs. This process of change creates frictions and dislocations that are unavoidable—that are natural. And they create unemployment.

year period, black teenagers had the highest unemployment rates, which averaged 30 percent. White people aged 20 years and over had the lowest unemployment rates, which averaged 4 percent. Women had slightly lower unemployment rates than men.

Why are teenage unemployment rates so high? There are two reasons.

First, young people are still discovering what they are good at and trying different lines of work, so they leave their jobs more frequently than older workers do.

Second, because teenagers have little job experience, firms often hire them on a short-term or trial basis, so the rate of job loss is higher for teenagers than for older workers.

UNEMPLOYMENT DURATION

Duration	2000	2006	2009
Average duration (weeks)	6	17	25
Percentages unemployed for			
14 weeks or less	77	68	48
15 to 26 weeks	12	14	23
27 weeks or more	11	18	29

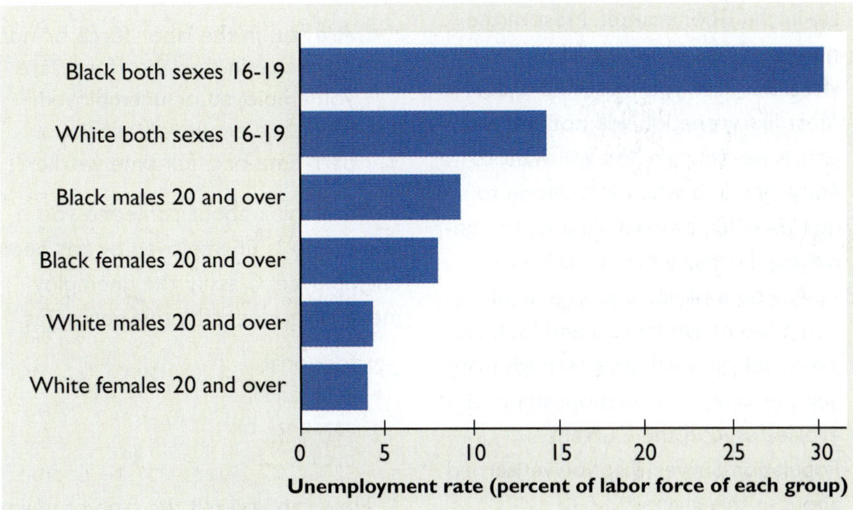

SOURCE OF DATA FOR TABLE AND FIGURE: Bureau of Labor Statistics.

Unemployment and Real GDP

Cyclical unemployment is the fluctuating unemployment over the business cycle—unemployment that increases during a recession and decreases during an expansion. At full employment, there is *no* cyclical unemployment. At a business cycle trough, cyclical unemployment is *positive* and at a business cycle peak, cyclical unemployment is *negative*.

Figure 6.7(a) shows the unemployment rate in the United States between 1977 and 2009. It also shows the natural unemployment rate and cyclical unemployment. The natural unemployment rate in this figure was estimated by the Congressional Budget Office (CBO).

In Figure 6.7(a), you can see that during most of the 1980s, the early 1990s, early 2000s, and in 2008–2009, unemployment was above the natural unemployment rate, so cyclical unemployment was positive (shaded red). You can also see that during the late 1980s and from 1997 to 2001 unemployment was below the natural unemployment rate, so cyclical unemployment was negative (shaded blue).

Potential GDP
The value of real GDP when all the economy's factors of production—labor, capital, land, and entrepreneurial ability—are employed.

Output gap
Real GDP minus potential GDP expressed as a percentage of potential GDP.

As the unemployment rate fluctuates around the natural unemployment rate, real GDP fluctuates around potential GDP. **Potential GDP** is the value of real GDP when all the economy's factors of production—labor, capital, land, and entrepreneurial ability—are employed. Real GDP equals potential GDP when the economy is at full employment. Real GDP minus potential GDP expressed as a percentage of potential GDP is called the **output gap**.

Figure 6.7(b) shows the *U.S. output gap* from 1977 to 2009. You can see that as

EYE on YOUR LIFE

Your Labor Market Status and Activity

You are going to spend a lot of your life in the labor market. Most of the time, you'll be supplying labor services. But first, you must find a job. Most likely, one job will not last your entire working life. You will want to find a new job when you decide to quit or when changing economic conditions destroy your current job.

As you look for a job, get a job, quit a job or get laid off and look for a new job, you will pass through many and possibly all of the population categories used in the Current Population Survey that you've learned about in this chapter.

Think about your current labor market status while you are studying economics.

- Are you in the labor force or not?
- If you are in the labor force, are you employed or unemployed?
- If you are employed, are you a part-time or a full-time worker?

Now think about someone you know who is unemployed or has been unemployed. Classify the unemployment experienced by this person as

- frictional,
- structural,
- seasonal, or
- cyclical.

How can you tell the type of unemployment experienced by this person?

The labor market conditions that you face today or when you graduate and look for a job depend partly on general national economic conditions—on whether the economy is in recession or booming.

Labor market conditions also depend on where you live. Visit the Bureau of Labor Statistics' Web site at www.bls.gov/sae/sm_mrs.htm.

There you can find information on employment and unemployment for your state and metropolitan area or county. By comparing the labor market conditions in your own region with those in other areas, you can figure out where it might be easier to find work.

FIGURE 6.7

The Relationship Between Unemployment and the Output Gap

myeconlab Animation

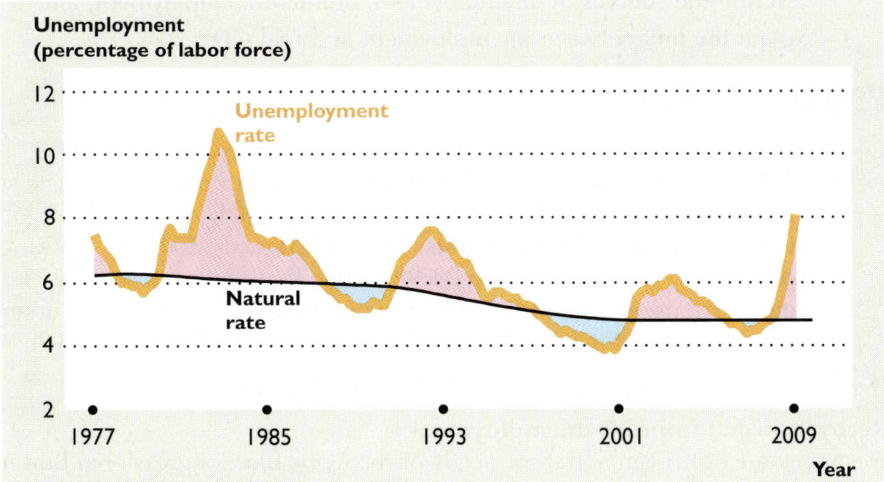

(a) Cyclical and natural unemployment

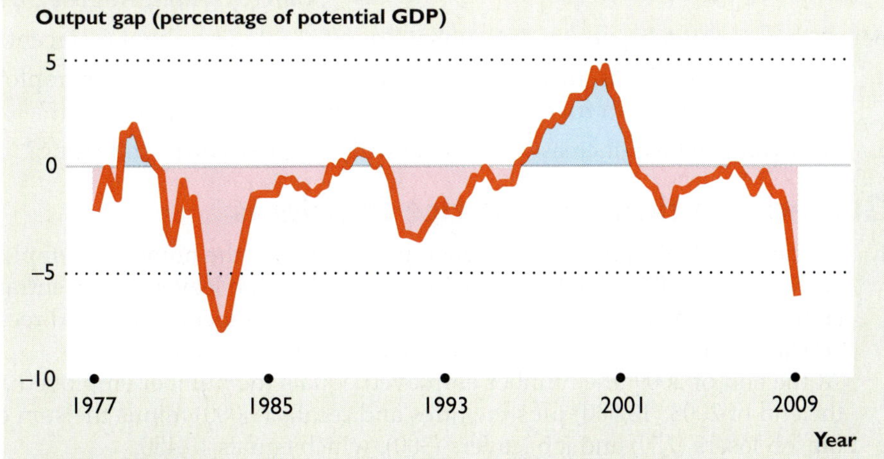

(b) The output gap

As the unemployment rate fluctuates around the natural unemployment rate in part (a), the output gap—real GDP minus potential GDP expressed as a percentage of potential GDP—fluctuates in part (b).

When the unemployment rate exceeds the natural unemployment rate, real GDP is below potential GDP and the output gap is negative (red shaded areas in both parts).

When the unemployment rate is below the natural unemployment rate, real GDP is above potential GDP and the output gap is positive (blue shaded areas in both parts).

SOURCES OF DATA: Bureau of Economic Analysis, Bureau of Labor Statistics, and Congressional Budget Office.

the unemployment rate fluctuates around the natural unemployment rate, the output gap also fluctuates. When the unemployment rate is above the natural unemployment rate, in part (a), the output gap is negative (real GDP is below potential GDP), in part (b); when the unemployment rate is below the natural unemployment rate, the output gap is positive (real GDP is above potential GDP); and when the unemployment rate equals the natural unemployment rate, the output gap is zero (real GDP equals potential GDP).

You can also see in Figure 6.7 that the unemployment rate is a lagging indicator of the business cycle. Long after a recession is over, the unemployment rate is still rising. You can expect the unemployment rate to rise through 2010.

You will learn what determines potential GDP in Chapter 8, and what brings the fluctuating output gap and cyclical unemployment in Chapters 13 and 14.

myeconlab

Work these problems in Study Plan 6.3 to get instant feedback.

CHECKPOINT 6.3

Describe the sources of unemployment, define full employment, and explain the link between unemployment and real GDP.

Practice Problems

1. A labor force survey records the following data for December 31, 2008: employed, 13,500; unemployed, 1,500; not in the labor force, 7,500. The survey also recorded during 2009: hires and recalls, 1,000; job losers, 750; job leavers 300; entrants, 150; reentrants, 450; withdrawals, 500. The working-age population increased during 2009 by 100. If all the job losers, job leavers, entrants, and reentrants became unemployed, calculate the unemployment rate and the labor force participation rate in December 2009.

Use the following information to work Problems **2** and **3**.

Recovery won't improve unemployment

Despite some optimism about the seeds of recovery, the Congressional Budget Office (CBO) sees joblessness rising. The CBO sees unemployment peaking at 10.4% next year from an average of 9.3% this year, before it falls to 9.1% in 2011.

Source: *Fortune*, August 25, 2009

Before the recession began, the U.S. unemployment rate was about 6 percent.

2. As a recession begins, firms quickly make layoffs. Is this rise in unemployment mostly a rise in frictional, structural, or cyclical unemployment?
3. How can real GDP increase (recovery) with unemployment still rising?

Guided Solutions to Practice Problems

1. At the end of 2009, the number unemployed equals the number unemployed at the end of 2008 (1,500) plus the job losers (750), job leavers (300), entrants (150), and reentrants (450) minus the sum of the number of hires and recalls (1,000) and withdrawals (500), which equals 1,650.
   At the end of 2009, the number employed equals the number employed at the end of 2008 (13,500) plus the hires and recalls (1,000) minus the sum of the job losers (750) and job leavers (300), which equals 13,450.
   The labor force is the sum of the number unemployed and employed, which equals 15,100. The unemployment rate is 10.9 percent.
   The labor force participation rate is the percentage of the working-age population who are in the labor force. The working-age population at the end of 2008 is the sum of number employed (13,500), number unemployed (1,500), and the number not in the labor force (7,500), which equals 22,500. The working-age population increased during 2009 by 100, so at the end of 2009, the working-age population was 22,600. The labor force participation rate is $(15,100 \div 22,600) \times 100 = 66.8$ percent.
2. When a recession starts, firms are quick to layoff workers. Most of the rise in unemployment is cyclical—related to the state of the economy. The unemployment rate rises quickly as the number of layoffs increases.
3. The unemployment rate is a lagging indicator of the business cycle. When the recovery begins, firms start hiring. Unemployed workers get jobs, but re-entry into the labor force increases as marginally attached workers start to look for jobs. In the early stages of a recovery, the number of entrants and re-entrants exceeds the number of hires and the number unemployed increases.

CHAPTER SUMMARY

Key Points

1 Define the unemployment rate and other labor market indicators.

- The unemployment rate is the number of people unemployed as a percentage of the labor force, and the labor force is the sum of the number of people employed and the number unemployed.
- The labor force participation rate is the labor force as a percentage of the working-age population.

2 Describe the trends and fluctuations in the indicators of labor market performance in the United States.

- The unemployment rate fluctuates with the business cycle, increasing in recessions and decreasing in expansions.
- The labor force participation rate of women has increased, and the labor force participation rate of men has decreased.

3 Describe the sources of unemployment, define full employment, and explain the link between unemployment and real GDP.

- Unemployment arises from the process of job creation and job destruction and from the movement of people into and out of the labor force.
- Unemployment can be frictional, structural, seasonal, or cyclical.
- Full employment occurs when there is no cyclical unemployment and at full employment, the unemployment rate equals the natural unemployment rate.
- Potential GDP is the real GDP produced when the economy is at full employment.
- As the unemployment rate fluctuates around the natural unemployment rate, real GDP fluctuates around potential GDP and the output gap fluctuates between negative and positive values.

Key Terms

myeconlab

Work these problems in Chapter 6 Study Plan to get instant feedback.

CHAPTER CHECKPOINT

Study Plan Problems and Applications

Use the following information gathered by a BLS labor market survey of four households to work Problems 1 and 2.

- Household 1: Candy worked 20 hours last week setting up her Internet shopping business. The rest of the week, she completed application forms and attended two job interviews. Husband Jerry worked 40 hours at his job at GM. Daughter Meg, a student, worked 10 hours at her weekend job at Starbucks.
- Household 2: Joey, a full-time bank clerk, was on vacation. Wife, Serena, who wants a full-time job, worked 10 hours as a part-time checkout clerk.
- Household 3: Ari had no work last week but was going to be recalled to his regular job in two weeks. Partner Kosta, after months of searching for a job and not being able to find one, has stopped looking and will go back to school.
- Household 4: Mimi and Henry are retired. Son Hank is a professional artist, who painted for 12 hours last week and sold one picture.

1. Classify each of the 10 people into the labor market category used by the BLS. Who are part-time workers and who are full-time workers? Of the part-time workers, who works part time for economic reasons?
2. Calculate the unemployment rate and the labor force participation rate, and compare these rates with those in the United States in 2009.
3. Give two examples of people who work part time for economic reasons and two examples of people who work part time for noneconomic reasons.
4. What are the labor market flows that create unemployment and that end a spell of unemployment? Of these flows, which fluctuate most and account for fluctuations in the unemployment rate?
5. Distinguish among the four types of unemployment: frictional, structural, seasonal and cyclical. Provide an example of each type of unemployment in the United States today.
6. Describe the relationship between the unemployment rate and the natural unemployment rate as the output gap fluctuates between being positive and being negative.

Use the following information to work Problems 7 and 8.

July unemployment dips in 17 states, rises in 26

The Labor Department said that the largest job gains occurred in New York, which added 62,100 jobs, while Minnesota added 10,300 jobs, its first gains in almost a year. Vermont added 900 jobs but its unemployment rate fell from 7.3% to 6.8%—the biggest drop of all states.

Source: The Associated Press, August 21, 2009

7. Explain how, other things remaining the same, the increase of 62,100 jobs in New York and of 10,300 in Minnesota changed the number of people employed, the labor force, and the unemployment rate.
8. Explain why when Vermont added only 900 jobs, its unemployment fell by more than any other state.

Instructor Assignable Problems and Applications

Your instructor can assign these problems as homework, a quiz, or a test in **MyEconLab**.

1. In the United States,
   - Compare the duration of unemployment in 2009 with that in 2000 and explain whether the difference was most likely the result of frictions, structural change, or the business cycle.
   - Why are teenage unemployment rates much higher than those for older workers?
   - How do the unemployment rates of women compare with those of men? Suggest a reason for the difference using the concept of marginally attached workers.
2. The Bureau of Labor Statistics reported that in the second quarter of 2008 the working-age population was 233,410,000, the labor force was 154,294,000, and employment was 146,089,000. Calculate for that quarter the labor force participation rate and the unemployment rate.
3. In March 2007, the U.S. unemployment rate was 4.4 percent. In August 2008, the unemployment rate was 6.1 percent. Predict what happened between March 2007 and August 2008 to the numbers of (i) job losers and job leavers and (ii) entrants and reentrants into the labor force.
4. In July 2009, in the economy of Sandy Island, 10,000 people were employed and 1,000 were unemployed. During August 2009, 80 people lost their jobs and didn't look for new ones, 20 people quit their jobs and retired, 150 people were hired or recalled, 50 people withdrew from the labor force, and 40 people entered or reentered the labor force to look for work. Calculate the change in the unemployment rate from July 2009 to August 2009.
5. The BLS survey reported the following data in a community of 320 people: 200 worked at least 1 hour as paid employees; 20 did not work but were temporarily absent from their jobs; 40 had no employment; 10 were available for work and last week they had looked for work; and 6 were available for work and were waiting to be recalled to their previous job. Calculate the unemployment rate and the labor force participation rate.
6. Describe the trends and fluctuations in the unemployment rate in the United States from 1949 through 2009. In which periods was the unemployment rate above average and in which periods was it below average?
7. Describe the trends and fluctuations in the labor force participation rate in the United States from 1967 through 2009, and contrast and explain the different trends for women and men.

Use the following information to work Problems 8 and 9.

Nation's economic pain deepens

The unemployment rate jumped to 5.5% in May 2008 from 5% in April 2008. This jump was the biggest one-month jump in unemployment since February 1986, and the 5.5% rate is the highest level seen since October 2004.

Source: CNN, June 6, 2008

8. Compare the unemployment rate in May 2008 with the unemployment rate during the past three recessions.
9. Why might the unemployment rate tend to actually underestimate the unemployment problem, especially during a recession?

10. The BLS survey reported the following data in a community of 100 people:
    - Total number of persons: 100
    - Worked at least 1 hour as paid employees or worked 15 hours or more as unpaid workers in their family business: 50
    - Were not working but had jobs or businesses from which they were temporarily absent: 20
    - Had no employment: 10
    - Were available for work and had made specific efforts to find employment some time during the previous 4 weeks: 15
    - Were available for work and were waiting to be recalled to a job from which they had been laid off: 5

    Calculate the unemployment rate and the labor force participation rate.
11. "Economics is supposed to be about scarcity. But if some labor is always unemployed, how can there be scarcity? All we need to do to produce more goods and services is employ the unemployed people." Do you agree or disagree with this statement? Why? Explain why scarcity and unemployment are not incompatible.

Use the following information to work Problems 12 and 13.

Michigan unemployment tops 15%

The U.S. Department of Labor reported that Michigan's unemployment rate in June 2009 rose to 15.2%, becoming the first state in 25 years to suffer an unemployment rate exceeding 15%. Michigan has been battered by the collapse of the auto industry and the housing crisis and has had the highest unemployment rate in the nation for the past 12 months.

Source: CNNMoney, July 17, 2009

12. Why is the reality of the unemployment problem in Michigan actually worse than the unemployment rate statistic of 15.2 percent?
13. Is this higher unemployment rate in Michigan frictional, structural, or cyclical? Explain.
14. Visit the Bureau of Labor Statistics Web site and find the following labor market data for the United States in the most recent month and for the same month one year ago: the labor force, the number employed, the number unemployed, and the working-age population. Calculate the unemployment rate and the labor force participation rate for the two months and describe the change in the labor market over the past year.

How do we measure the changing value of money?

Transformers: Revenge of the Fallen earned $400 million at the box office. *Gone with the Wind* (made in 1939) earned $200 million. Which movie really had the larger box office revenues?

7

The CPI and the Cost of Living

CHAPTER CHECKLIST

When you have completed your study of this chapter, you will be able to

1. Explain what the Consumer Price Index (CPI) is and how it is calculated.
2. Explain the limitations of the CPI and describe other measures of the price level.
3. Adjust money values for inflation and calculate real wage rates and real interest rates.

7.1 THE CONSUMER PRICE INDEX

Consumer Price Index
A measure of the average of the prices paid by urban consumers for a fixed market basket of consumption goods and services.

The **Consumer Price Index** (CPI) is a measure of the average of the prices paid by urban consumers for a fixed market basket of consumption goods and services. The Bureau of Labor Statistics (BLS) calculates the CPI every month, and we can use these numbers to compare what the fixed market basket costs this month with what it cost in some previous month or other period.

Reading the CPI Numbers

Reference base period
A period for which the CPI is defined to equal 100. Currently, the reference base period is 1982–1984.

The CPI is defined to equal 100 for a period called the **reference base period**. Currently, the reference base period is 1982–1984. That is, the CPI equals 100 on the average over the 36 months from January 1982 through December 1984.

In June 2009, the CPI was 214.5. This number tells us that the average of the prices paid by urban consumers for a fixed market basket of consumption goods and services was 114.5 percent higher in June 2009 than it was on the average during 1982–1984.

In May 2009, the CPI was 212.9. Comparing the June CPI with the May CPI tells us that the average of the prices paid by urban consumers for a fixed market basket of consumption goods and services *increased* by 1.6 of a percentage point in June 2009.

Constructing the CPI

Constructing the CPI is a huge operation that costs millions of dollars and involves three stages:

- Selecting the CPI market basket
- Conducting the monthly price survey
- Calculating the CPI

The CPI Market Basket

The first stage in constructing the CPI is to determine the *CPI market basket.* This "basket" contains the goods and services represented in the index and the relative importance, or weight, attached to each of them. The idea is to make the weight of the items in the CPI basket the same as in the budget of an average urban household. For example, if the average household spends 2 percent of its income on public transportation, then the CPI places a weight of 2 percent on the prices of bus, subway, and other transit system rides.

Although the CPI is calculated every month, the CPI market basket isn't updated every month. The information used to determine the CPI market basket comes from a survey, called the *Consumer Expenditure Survey*, that discovers what people actually buy. This survey is an ongoing activity, and the CPI market basket in 2009 was based on a survey conducted during 2005 and 2006. More than 30,000 individuals and families contributed information. Some of them were interviewed every three months, and others kept detailed diaries for two weeks in which they listed absolutely everything they bought. (Before 1999, the Consumer Expenditure Survey was conducted much less frequently.)

The reference base period for the CPI has been fixed at 1982–1984 for more than 20 years and doesn't change when a new Consumer Expenditure Survey is used to update the market basket.

Figure 7.1 shows the CPI market basket at the end of 2008. The basket contains around 80,000 goods and services arranged in the eight large groups shown in the figure. The most important item in a household's budget is housing, which accounts for 43.4 percent of total expenditure. Food and beverage comes next at 15.8 percent. Third in relative importance is transportation at 15.3 percent. These three groups account for almost three quarters of the average household budget. Medical care, recreation, and education and communication take about 6 percent each, and apparel (clothing and footwear) takes 3.7 percent. Another 3.4 percent is spent on other goods and services.

The BLS breaks down each of these categories into smaller ones. For example, education and communication breaks down into textbooks and supplies, tuition, telephone services, and personal computer services.

As you look at these numbers, remember that they apply to the average household. Each individual household is spread around the average. Think about your own expenditure and compare it with the average.

The Monthly Price Survey

Each month, BLS employees check the prices of the 80,000 goods and services in the CPI market basket in 30 metropolitan areas. Because the CPI aims to measure price changes, it is important that the prices recorded each month refer to exactly the same items. For example, suppose the price of a box of jelly beans has increased but a box now contains more beans. Has the price of a jelly bean increased? The BLS employee must record the details of changes in quality, size, weight, or packaging so that price changes can be isolated from other changes.

Once the raw price data are in hand, the next task is to calculate the CPI.

FIGURE 7.1

The CPI Market Basket

myeconlab Animation

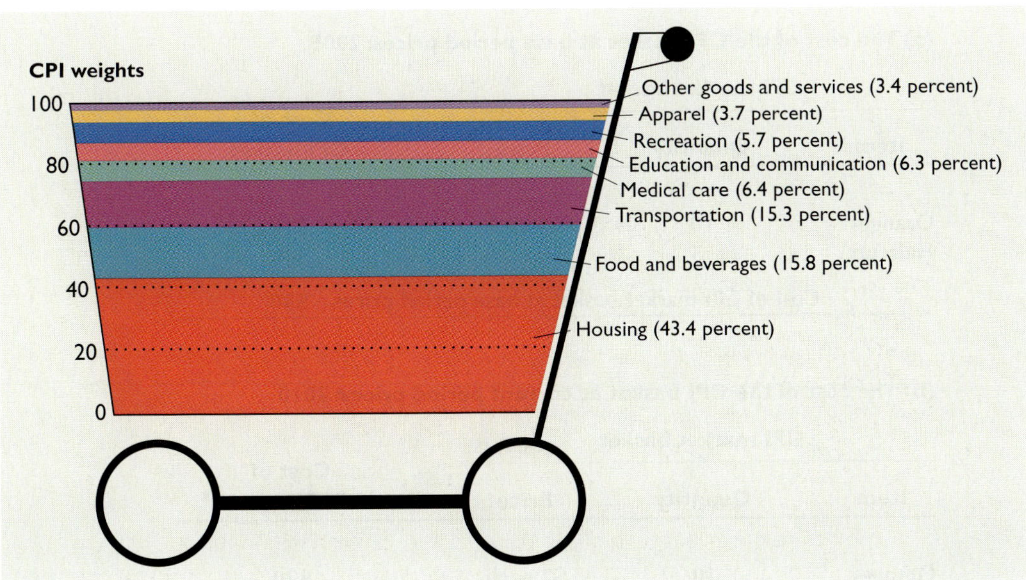

SOURCE OF DATA: Bureau of Labor Statistics.

This shopping cart is filled with the items that an average household buys. Housing (43.4 percent), food and beverages (15.8 percent), and transportation (15.3 percent) take almost 75 percent of household income.

Calculating the CPI

The CPI calculation has three steps:

- Find the cost of the CPI market basket at base period prices.
- Find the cost of the CPI market basket at current period prices.
- Calculate the CPI for the base period and the current period.

We'll work through these three steps for a simple example. Suppose the CPI market basket contains only two goods and services: oranges and haircuts. We'll construct an annual CPI rather than a monthly CPI with the reference base period 2005 and the current period 2010.

Table 7.1 shows the quantities in the CPI market basket and the prices in the base period and the current period. Part (a) contains the data for the base period. In that period, consumers bought 10 oranges at $1 each and 5 haircuts at $8 each. To find the cost of the CPI market basket in the base period prices, multiply the quantities in the CPI market basket by the base period prices. The cost of oranges is $10 (10 at $1 each), and the cost of haircuts is $40 (5 at $8 each). So total expenditure in the base period on the CPI market basket is $50 ($10 + $40).

Part (b) contains the price data for the current period. The price of an orange increased from $1 to $2, which is a 100 percent increase ($1 ÷ $1 × 100 = 100 percent). The price of a haircut increased from $8 to $10, which is a 25 percent increase ($2 ÷ $8 × 100 = 25 percent).

The CPI provides a way of averaging these price increases by comparing the cost of the basket rather than the price of each item. To find the cost of the CPI market basket in the current period, 2010, multiply the quantities in the basket by their 2010 prices. The cost of oranges is $20 (10 at $2 each), and the cost of haircuts is $50 (5 at $10 each). So total expenditure on the fixed CPI market basket at current period prices is $70 ($20 + $50).

TABLE 7.1

The Consumer Price Index: A Simplified CPI Calculation

(a) The cost of the CPI basket at base period prices: 2005

CPI market basket			
Item	**Quantity**	**Price**	**Cost of CPI basket**
Oranges	10	$1 each	$10
Haircuts	5	$8 each	$40
Cost of CPI market basket at base period prices			$50

(b) The cost of the CPI basket at current period prices: 2010

CPI market basket			
Item	**Quantity**	**Price**	**Cost of CPI basket**
Oranges	10	$2 each	$20
Haircuts	5	$10 each	$50
Cost of CPI market basket at current period prices			$70

You've now taken the first two steps toward calculating the CPI. The third step uses the numbers you've just calculated to find the CPI for 2005 and 2010. The formula for the CPI is

$$\text{CPI} = \frac{\text{Cost of CPI basket at current period prices}}{\text{Cost of CPI basket at base period prices}} \times 100.$$

In Table 7.1, you established that in 2005, the cost of the CPI market basket was \$50 and in 2010, it was \$70. If we use these numbers in the CPI formula, we can find the CPI for 2005 and 2010. The base period is 2005, so

$$\text{CPI in 2005} = \frac{\$50}{\$50} \times 100 = 100.$$

$$\text{CPI in 2010} = \frac{\$70}{\$50} \times 100 = 140.$$

The principles that you've applied in this simplified CPI calculation apply to the more complex calculations performed every month by the BLS.

Figure 7.2(a) shows the CPI in the United States during the 30 years between 1979 and 2009. The CPI increased every year during this period until 2009 when it fell slightly. During the late 1970s and in 1980, the CPI was increasing rapidly, but since the early 1980s, the rate of increase has slowed.

Measuring Inflation and Deflation

A major purpose of the CPI is to measure *changes* in the cost of living and in the value of money. To measure these changes, we calculate the **inflation rate**, which is the percentage change in the price level from one year to the next. To calculate the inflation rate, we use the formula

Inflation rate
The percentage change in the price level from one year to the next.

$$\text{Inflation rate} = \frac{(\text{CPI in current year} - \text{CPI in previous year})}{\text{CPI in previous year}} \times 100.$$

Suppose that the current year is 2010 and the CPI for 2010 is 140. And suppose that in the previous year, 2009, the CPI was 120. Then in 2010,

$$\text{Inflation rate} = \frac{(140 - 120)}{120} \times 100 = 16.7 \text{ percent}.$$

If the inflation rate is *negative*, the price level is *falling* and we have **deflation**. The United States has rarely experienced deflation but 2009 was one of those rare years. You can check the latest data by visiting the BLS Web site. In June 2009, the CPI was 214.5, and in June 2008, it was 217.0. So during the year to June 2009,

Deflation
A situation in which the price level is *falling* and the inflation rate is *negative*.

$$\text{Inflation rate} = \frac{(214.5 - 217.0)}{217.0} \times 100 = -1.2 \text{ percent}.$$

Figure 7.2(b) shows the inflation rate in the United States between 1979 and 2009. The change in the price level in part (a) and the inflation rate in part (b) are related. When the price *level* rises rapidly, the inflation rate is high; when the price level rises slowly, the inflation rate is low; and when the price level is falling, the inflation rate is negative.

EYE on the PAST

700 Years of Inflation and Deflation

These extraordinary data show that inflation became a persistent problem only after 1900. During the preceding 600 years, inflation was almost unknown. Inflation increased slightly during the sixteenth century after Europeans discovered gold in America. But this inflation barely reached 2 percent a year—less than we have today—and eventually subsided. The Industrial Revolution saw a temporary burst of inflation followed by a period of deflation.

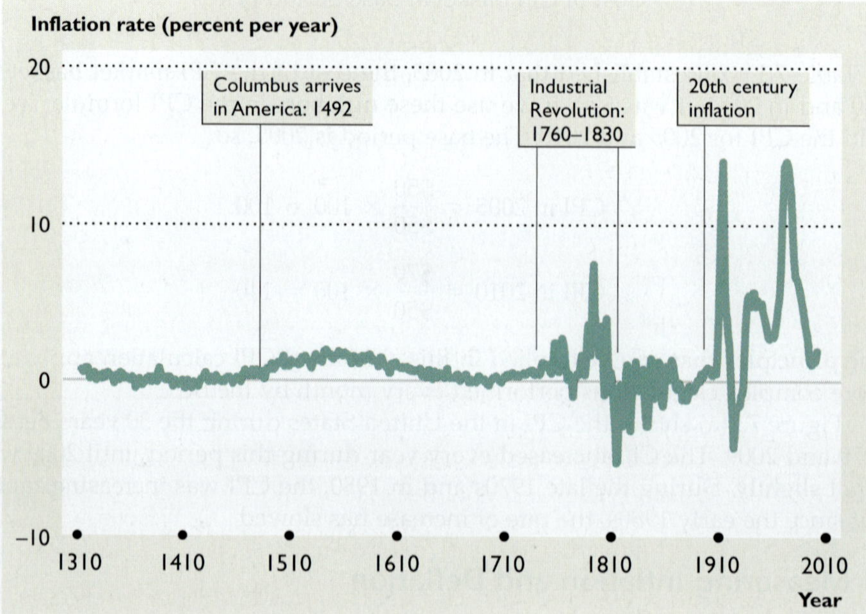

SOURCES OF DATA: E.H. Phelps Brown and Sheila V. Hopkins, *Economica*, 1955, and Robert Sahr, http://oregonstate.edu/dept/pol_sci/fac/sahr/sahr.htm.

FIGURE 7.2

The CPI and the Inflation Rate: 1979–2009

myeconlab Animation

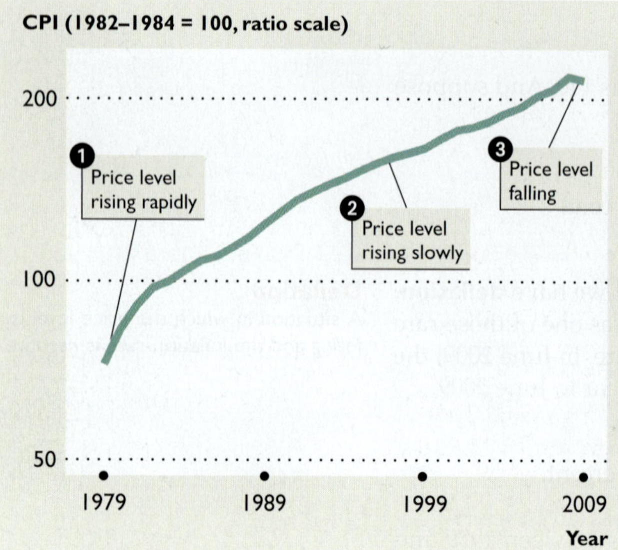

(a) CPI: 1979–2009

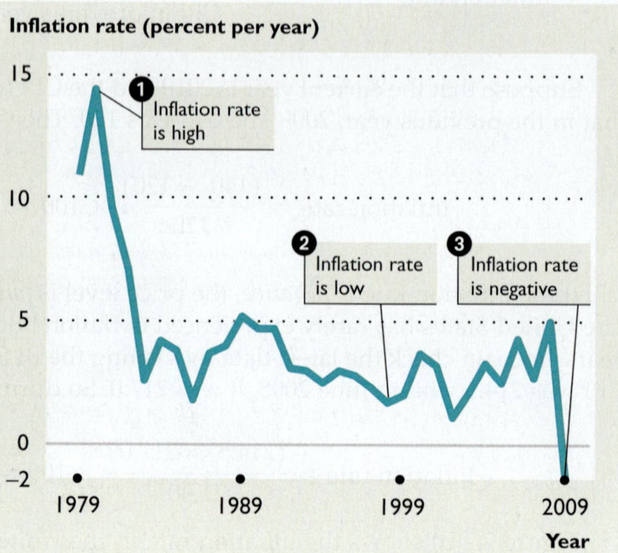

(b) CPI inflation rate: 1979–2009

SOURCE OF DATA: Bureau of Labor Statistics.

❶ The price *level* (in part a) was rising rapidly in 1980 and the inflation rate (in part b) was high. ❷ The price level was rising slowly during the 1990s and 2000s and the inflation rate was low. ❸ In 2009, the price level fell and the inflation rate was negative.

CHECKPOINT 7.1

Explain what the Consumer Price Index (CPI) is and how it is calculated.

myeconlab

Work these problems in Study Plan 7.1 to get instant feedback.

Practice Problems

A Consumer Expenditure Survey in Sparta shows that people buy only juice and cloth. In 2008, the year of the Consumer Expenditure Survey and also the reference base year, the average household spent \$40 on juice and \$25 on cloth. Table 1 sets out the prices of juice and cloth in 2008 and 2010. Use this information to work Problems **1** and **2**.

TABLE 1 PRICES

	2008	2010
Juice	\$4 a bottle	\$4 a bottle
Cloth	\$5 a yard	\$6 a yard

1. Calculate the CPI market basket and the percentage of household budget spent on juice in the reference base year.
2. Calculate the CPI in 2010 and the inflation rate between 2008 and 2010.
3. Table 2 shows the CPI in Russia. Calculate the inflation rates in 2006 and 2007. Did the price level rise in 2007? Did the inflation rate increase in 2007?

TABLE 2

Year	CPI
2005	200
2006	219
2007	237

4. **Consumer prices rise less than expected in May**
   The CPI in May 2009 was 212.9, 0.1% higher than the April CPI. The gasoline price rose 9.6% in May 2009, but gasoline was still cheaper than in May 2008 when it exceeded \$4 a gallon. Because of the lower gas price, the CPI fell by 1.3% in the year to May 2009, the steepest drop since 1950.
   Source: *USA Today*, June 17, 2009

   Use the information in the news clip to distinguish between the price level and the inflation rate. Explain why the reason suggested for the fall in the CPI can't be entirely correct.

Guided Solutions to Practice Problems

1. The CPI market basket is the quantities bought during the Consumer Expenditure Survey year, 2008. Households spent \$40 on juice at \$4 a bottle, so the quantity of juice bought was 10 bottles. Households spent \$25 on cloth at \$5 a yard, so the quantity of cloth bought was 5 yards. The CPI market basket is made up of 10 bottles of juice and 5 yards of cloth.
   In the reference base year, the average household spent \$40 on juice and \$25 on cloth, so the household budget was \$65. Expenditure on juice was 61.5 percent of the household budget: (\$40 ÷ \$65) × 100 = 61.5 percent.

2. To calculate the CPI in 2010, find the cost of the CPI market basket in 2008 and 2010. In 2008, the CPI basket costs \$65 (\$40 for juice + \$25 for cloth). In 2010, the CPI market basket costs \$70 (10 bottles of juice at \$4 a bottle + 5 yards of cloth at \$6 a yard). The CPI in 2010 is (\$70 ÷ \$65) × 100 = 107.7.

   The inflation rate is [(107.7 − 100) ÷ 100] × 100 = 7.7 percent.

3. The inflation rate in 2006 is [(219 − 200) ÷ 200] × 100 = 9.5 percent. The inflation rate in 2007 is [(237 − 219) ÷ 219] × 100 = 8.2 percent. In 2007, the price level increased, but the inflation rate decreased.

4. The CPI is the price level. The percentage change in the CPI is the inflation rate. Gasoline is one component of the transportation item in the CPI basket. The entire transportation item is only 15.3 percent of the CPI basket, so gasoline represents a small part of the CPI basket. For the CPI to have fallen in the year to May 2009, many other prices must also have fallen. The fall in gas prices is not the only or even the main reason why the CPI fell.

7.2 THE CPI AND OTHER PRICE LEVEL MEASURES

Cost of living index
A measure of the change in the amount of money that people need to spend to achieve a given standard of living.

The purpose of the CPI is to measure the cost of living or what amounts to the same thing, the *value of money*. The CPI is sometimes called a **cost of living index**—a measure of the change in the amount of money that people need to spend to achieve a given standard of living. The CPI is not a perfect measure of the cost of living (value of money) for two broad reasons.

First, the CPI does not try to measure all the changes in the cost of living. For example, the cost of living rises in a severe winter as people buy more natural gas and electricity to heat their homes. A rise in the prices of these items increases the CPI. The increased quantities of natural gas and electricity bought don't change the CPI because the CPI market basket is fixed. So part of this increase in spending—the increase in the cost of maintaining a given standard of living—doesn't show up as an increase in the CPI.

Second, even those components of the cost of living that are measured by the CPI are not always measured accurately. The result is that the CPI is possibly a biased measure of changes in the cost of living.

Let's look at some of the sources of bias in the CPI and the ways the BLS tries to overcome them.

Sources of Bias in the CPI

The potential sources of bias in the CPI are

- New goods bias
- Quality change bias
- Commodity substitution bias
- Outlet substitution bias

New Goods Bias

Every year, some new goods become available and some old goods disappear. Make a short list of items that you take for granted today that were not available 10 or 20 years ago. This list includes cell phones, iPods, laptop computers, and flat-panel, large-screen television sets. A list of items no longer available or rarely bought includes audiocassette players, vinyl records, photographic film, and typewriters.

When we want to compare the price level in 2009 with that in 1999, 1989, or 1979, we must do so by comparing the prices of different baskets of goods. We can't compare the same baskets because today's basket wasn't available 20 years ago and the basket of 20 years ago isn't available today.

To make comparisons, the BLS tries to measure the price of the service performed by yesterday's goods and today's goods. It tries to compare, for example, the price of listening to recorded music, regardless of the technology that delivers that service. But the comparison is hard to make. Today's iPod delivers an improved quality of sound and level of convenience compared to yesterday's Walkman and Discman.

How much of the new product represents an increase in consumption and how much represents a higher price? The BLS does its best to answer this question, but there is no sure way of making the necessary adjustment. It is believed that the arrival of new goods puts an upward bias into the CPI and its measure of the inflation rate.

To measure the CPI, the BLS must compare the price of today's iPod with that of the 1970s Walkman and 1980s Discman.

Quality Change Bias

Cars, cell phones, laptops, and many other items get better every year. For example, central locking, airbags, and antilock braking systems all add to the quality of a car. But they also add to the cost. Is the improvement in quality greater than the increase in cost? Or do car prices rise by more than can be accounted for by quality improvements? To the extent that a price rise is a payment for improved quality, it is not inflation. Again, the BLS does the best job it can to estimate the effects of quality improvements on price changes. But the CPI probably counts too much of any price rise as inflation and so overstates inflation.

To compare the price of today's cars with those of earlier years, the BLS must value the improvements in features and quality.

Commodity Substitution Bias

Changes in relative prices lead consumers to change the items they buy. People cut back on items that become relatively more costly and increase their consumption of items that become relatively less costly. For example, suppose the price of carrots rises while the price of broccoli remains constant. Now that carrots are more costly relative to broccoli, you might decide to buy more broccoli and fewer carrots. Suppose that you switch from carrots to broccoli, spend the same amount on vegetables as before, and get the same enjoyment as before. Your cost of vegetables has not changed. The CPI says that the price of vegetables has increased because it ignores your substitution between goods in the CPI market basket.

When consumers substitute lower priced broccoli for higher priced carrots, the CPI overstates the rise in the price of vegetables.

Outlet Substitution Bias

When confronted with higher prices, people use discount stores more frequently and convenience stores less frequently. This phenomenon is called *outlet substitution.* Suppose, for example, that gas prices rise by 10¢ a gallon. Instead of buying from your nearby gas station for \$4.579 a gallon, you now drive farther to a gas station that charges \$4.479 a gallon. Your cost of gas has increased because you must factor in the cost of your time and the gas that you use driving several blocks down the road. But your cost has not increased by as much as the 10¢ a gallon increase in the pump price. However, the CPI says that the price of gas has increased by 10¢ a gallon because the CPI does not measure outlet substitution.

The growth of online shopping in recent years has provided an alternative to discount stores that makes outlet substitution even easier and potentially makes this source of bias more serious.

As consumers shop around for the lowest prices, outlet substitution occurs and the CPI overstates the rise in prices actually paid.

The Magnitude of the Bias

You have reviewed the sources of bias in the CPI. But how big is the bias? When this question was tackled in 1996 by a Congressional Advisory Commission chaired by Michael Boskin, an economics professor at Stanford University, the answer was that the CPI overstated inflation by 1.1 percentage points a year. That is, if the CPI reports that inflation is 3.1 percent a year, most likely inflation is actually 2 percent a year.

In the period since the Boskin Commission reported, the BLS has taken steps to reduce the CPI bias. The more frequent Consumer Expenditure Survey that we described earlier in this chapter is one of these steps. Beyond that, the BLS uses ever more sophisticated models and methods to try to eliminate the sources of bias and make the CPI as accurate as possible.

Two Consequences of the CPI Bias

Avoiding bias in the CPI is important for two main reasons. Bias leads to

- Distortion of private contracts
- Increases in government outlays and decreases in taxes

Distortion of Private Contracts

Many wage contracts contain a cost of living adjustment. For example, the United Auto Workers Union (UAW) and Ford Motor Company might agree on a wage rate of $30 an hour initially that increases over three years at the same rate as the cost of living increases. The idea is that both the union and the employer want a contract in "real" terms. As the cost of living rises, the firm wants to pay the workers the number of dollars per hour that buys a given market basket of goods and services. And the firm is happy to pay the higher wage because it can sell its output for a higher price.

Suppose that over the three years of a UAW and Ford contract, the CPI increases by 5 percent each year. The wage rate paid by Ford will increase to $31.50 in the second year and $33.08 in the third year.

But suppose that the CPI is biased and the true price increase is 3 percent a year. The workers' cost of living increases by this amount, so in the second year, $30.90 rather than $31.50 is the intended wage. In the third year, a wage rate of $31.83 and not $33.08 compensates for the higher cost of living. So in the second year, the workers gain 60¢ an hour, or $21 for a 35-hour workweek. And in the third year, they gain $1.25 an hour, or $43.75 for a 35-hour workweek.

The workers' gain is Ford's loss. With a work force of a few thousand, the loss amounts to several thousand dollars a week and a few million dollars over the life of a 3-year wage contract.

If the CPI bias was common knowledge and large, the CPI would not be used without some adjustment in contracts. Unions and employers would seek agreement on the extent of the bias and make an appropriate adjustment to their contract. But for a small bias, the cost of negotiating a more complicated agreement might be too large.

Increases in Government Outlays and Decreases in Taxes

Because rising prices decrease the buying power of the dollar, the CPI is used to adjust the incomes of the 49 million Social Security beneficiaries, 27 million food stamp recipients, and 4 million retired former military personnel and federal civil servants (and their surviving spouses). The CPI is also used to adjust the budget for 3 million school lunches.

Close to a third of federal government outlays are linked directly to the CPI. If the CPI has a 1.1 percentage point bias, all of these expenditures increase by more than required to compensate for the fall in the buying power of the dollar and, although a bias of 1.1 percent a year seems small, accumulated over a decade, it adds up to almost a trillion dollars of additional government outlays.

The CPI is also used to adjust the income levels at which higher tax rates apply. The tax rates on large incomes are higher than those on small incomes so, as incomes rise, if these adjustments were not made, the burden of taxes would rise relentlessly. To the extent that the CPI is biased upward, the tax adjustments over-compensate for rising prices and decrease the amount paid in taxes.

Alternative Measures of the Price Level and Inflation Rate

Several alternative measures of the price level and inflation rate are available. One based on wholesale prices and another based on producers' prices are similar to the CPI, both in the way they are constructed and their potential for bias. But three other price indexes that we'll briefly describe here are less biased. These indexes are the

- GDP price index
- Personal consumption expenditures (PCE) price index
- PCE price index excluding food and energy

GDP Price Index

The **GDP price index** (also called the *GDP deflator*) is an average of the current prices of all the goods and services included in GDP expressed as a percentage of base-year prices. Two key differences between the GDP price index and the CPI result in different estimates of the price level and inflation rate.

GDP price index
An average of the current prices of all the goods and services included in GDP expressed as a percentage of base-year prices.

First, the GDP price index uses the prices of all the goods and services in GDP—consumption, investment, government purchases, and exports—while the CPI uses prices of consumption goods and services only. For example, the GDP price index includes the prices of paper mills bought by 3M to make Post-it® Notes, nuclear submarines bought by the Defense Department, and Boeing 747s bought by British Airways.

Second, the GDP price index weights each item using information about current quantities. In contrast, the CPI weights each item using information from a *past* Consumer Expenditure Survey. But because of the breadth of the items that the GDP price index includes, it is not an alternative to the CPI as a measure of the cost of living.

Personal Consumption Expenditures (PCE) Price Index

The **Personal Consumption Expenditures price index** (or **PCE price index**) is an average of the current prices of the goods and services included in the consumption expenditure component of GDP expressed as a percentage of base-year prices. The PCE price index has the same advantages as the GDP price index—it uses current information on quantities and to some degree overcomes the sources of bias in the CPI. It also has an advantage shared by the CPI of focusing on consumption expenditure and therefore being a possible measure of the cost of living.

PCE price index
An average of the current prices of the goods and services included in the consumption expenditure component of GDP expressed as a percentage of base-year prices.

A weakness of the PCE price index is that it is based on data that become known after the lapse of several months. So the CPI provides more current information about the inflation rate than what the PCE price index provides.

PCE Price Index Excluding Food and Energy

Food and energy prices fluctuate much more than other prices and their changes can obscure the underlying trends in prices. By excluding these highly variable items, the underlying price level and inflation trends can be seen more clearly. The percentage change in the PCE price index excluding food and energy is called the **core inflation rate**.

Core inflation rate
The annual percentage increase in the PCE price index excluding the prices of food and energy.

Figure 7.3(a) shows the three consumer price inflation rates measured by the CPI, the PCE price index, and PCE price index excluding food and energy. These measures move up and down in similar ways, but the CPI measure exceeds the

PCE price index measures. The average difference between the CPI and PCE measures is about a half a percentage point. The core inflation rate has exactly the same average as the PCE inflation rate but fluctuates less. You can see why this measure provides a better indication of the inflation trend than the index that includes food and energy prices.

Figure 7.3(b) shows the three price *levels*. The two measures based on the PCE price index are very similar but the CPI measure rises above the other two and the gap widens to 40 percentage points over the 30 years shown here.

This higher CPI is a reflection of its bias and a confirmation that the PCE price index, which is based on current period actual expenditures, avoids most of the sources of bias in the CPI.

FIGURE 7.3

Three Measures of Consumer Prices

myeconlab Animation

The three measures of the inflation rate in part (a) fluctuate together, but the CPI inflation rate is higher than the PCE price index inflation rate or the core inflation rate. The core inflation rate fluctuates less than the other two measures.
In part (b), the CPI rises above the two PCE measures of the price level reflecting the bias in the CPI.

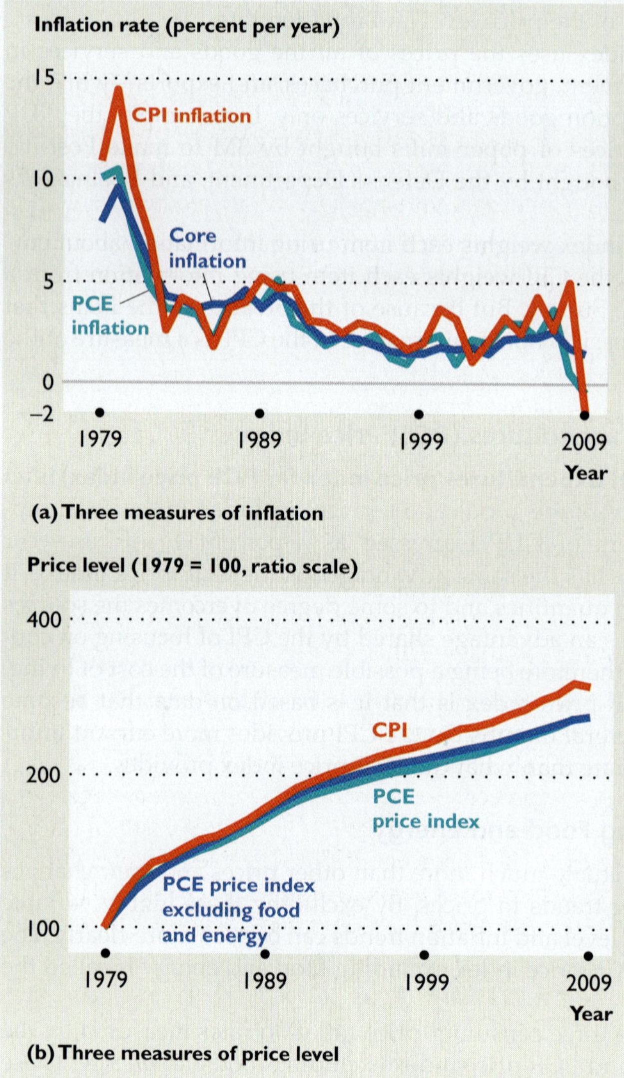

SOURCES OF DATA: Bureau of Labor Statistics and Bureau of Economic Analysis.

CHECKPOINT 7.2

Explain the limitations of the CPI and describe other measures of the price level.

myeconlab

Work these problems in Study Plan 7.2 to get instant feedback.

Practice Problems

Economists in the Statistics Bureau decide to check the CPI substitution bias. To do so, they conduct a Consumer Expenditure Survey in both 2008 and 2009. Table 1 shows the results of the survey. It shows the items that consumers buy and their prices. The Statistics Bureau fixes the reference base year as 2008. Use this information to work Problems **1** to **3**.

TABLE 1

	2008		2009	
Item	**Quantity**	**Price**	**Quantity**	**Price**
Broccoli	10	$3.00	15	$3.00
Carrots	15	$2.00	10	$4.00

1. Calculate the CPI in 2009 if the CPI basket contains the 2008 quantities.
2. Calculate the CPI in 2009 if the CPI basket contains the 2009 quantities.
3. Is there any substitution bias in the CPI that uses the 2008 basket? Explain.
4. **News release**
   Personal consumption expenditures (PCE) increased from $9,978.2 billion in May to $10,019.6 billion in June, an increase of 0.4%. Real personal consumption expenditures decreased from $9,185.5 billion in May to $9,173.5 billion in June, a decrease of 0.1%.
   Source: Bureau of Economic Analysis, August 4, 2009

   Calculate the PCE price index in May 2009 and June 2009. How can real personal consumption expenditures decrease when personal consumption expenditures increases?

Guided Solutions to Practice Problems

1. Table 2 shows the calculation of the CPI in 2009 when the CPI basket is made of the 2008 quantities. The cost of the 2008 basket at 2008 prices is $60, and the cost of the 2008 basket at 2009 prices is $90. So the CPI in 2009 using the 2008 basket is ($90 ÷ $60) × 100 = 150.

TABLE 2

Item	**2008 basket at 2008 prices**	**2008 basket at 2009 prices**
Broccoli	$30	$30
Carrots	$30	$60
Total	$60	$90

2. Table 3 shows the calculation of the CPI in 2009 when the CPI basket is made of the 2009 quantities. The cost of the 2009 basket at 2008 prices is $65, and the cost of the 2009 basket at 2009 prices is $85. So the CPI in 2009 using the 2009 basket is ($85 ÷ $65) × 100 = 131.

TABLE 3

Item	**2009 basket at 2008 prices**	**2009 basket at 2009 prices**
Broccoli	$45	$45
Carrots	$20	$40
Total	$65	$85

3. The CPI that uses the 2008 basket displays some bias. With the price of broccoli constant and the price of carrots rising, consumers buy fewer carrots and more broccoli and they spend $85 on vegetables. But they would have spent $90 if they had not substituted broccoli for some carrots. The cost of vegetables does not rise by 50 percent as shown by the CPI. Because of substitution, the cost of vegetables rises by only 42 percent ($85 is 42 percent greater than $60). Using the 2009 basket, the price of vegetables increases by only 31 percent ($85 compared with $65). The CPI is biased upward because it ignores the substitutions that people make when prices change.
4. The PCE price index = (Nominal PCE ÷ Real PCE) × 100. In May 2009, the PCE price index equaled (9,978.2 billion ÷ $9,185.5 billion) × 100, or 108.63. In June 2009, the PCE price index equaled ($10,019.6 billion ÷ $9,173.5 billion) × 100 or 109.7. The PCE price index rose by 0.55 percent, which exceeded the 0.4 percent increase in nominal PCE, so real PCE fell by 0.13 percent.

Which postage stamp has the higher real price: the 2¢ stamp of 1909 or the 44¢ stamp of 2009?

7.3 NOMINAL AND REAL VALUES

In 2009, it cost 44 cents to mail a first-class letter. One hundred years earlier, in 1909, that same letter would have cost 2 cents to mail. Does it *really* cost you 22 times the amount that it cost your great-great-grandmother to mail a letter?

You know that it does not. You know that a dollar today buys less than what a dollar bought in 1909, so the cost of a stamp has not really increased to 22 times its 1909 level. But has it increased at all? Did it really cost you any more to mail a letter in 2009 than it cost your great-great-grandmother in 1909?

The CPI can be used to answer questions like these. In fact, that is one of the main reasons for constructing a price index. Let's see how we can compare the price of a stamp in 1909 and the price of a stamp in 2009.

Dollars and Cents at Different Dates

To compare dollar amounts at different dates, we need to know the CPI at those dates. Currently, the CPI has a base of 100 for 1982–1984. That is, the average of the CPI in 1982, 1983, and 1984 is 100. (The numbers for the three years are 96.4, 99.6, and 103.9, respectively. Calculate the average of these numbers and check that it is indeed 100.)

In 2009, the CPI was 214.5, and in 1909, it was 9.6. By using these two numbers, we can calculate the relative value of the dollar in 1909 and 2009. To do so, we divide the 2009 CPI by the 1909 CPI. That ratio is 214.5 ÷ 9.6 = 22.3. That is, prices on average were 22.3 times higher in 2009 than in 1909.

We can use this ratio to convert the price of a 2-cent stamp in 1909 into its 2009 equivalent. The formula for this calculation is

$$\text{Price of stamp in 2009 dollars} = \text{Price of stamp in 1909 dollars} \times \frac{\text{CPI in 2009}}{\text{CPI in 1909}}$$

$$= 2 \text{ cents} \times \frac{214.5}{9.6} = 44.69 \text{ cents.}$$

So your great-great-grandmother paid a bit more than you pay! It really cost her almost a cent more to mail that first-class letter as it cost you in 2009. She paid the equivalent of 44.69 cents in 2009 money, and you paid 44 cents.

We've just converted the 1909 price of a stamp to its 2009 equivalent. We can do a similar calculation the other way around—converting the 2009 price to its 1909 equivalent. The formula for this alternative calculation is

$$\text{Price of stamp in 1909 dollars} = \text{Price of stamp in 2009 dollars} \times \frac{\text{CPI in 1909}}{\text{CPI in 2009}}$$

$$= 44 \text{ cents} \times \frac{9.6}{214.5} = 1.97 \text{ cents.}$$

The interpretation of this number is that you pay the *equivalent* of 1.97 cents in 1909 dollars. Your *real* price of a stamp is 1.97 cents expressed in 1909 dollars.

The calculations that we've just done are examples of converting a *nominal* value into a *real* value. A nominal value is one that is expressed in current dollars. A real value is one that is expressed in the dollars of a given year. We're now going to see how we convert nominal macroeconomic variables into real variables using a similar method.

Nominal and Real Values in Macroeconomics

Macroeconomics makes a big issue of the distinction between nominal and real values. Three nominal and real variables occupy a central position in macroeconomics. They are

- Nominal GDP and real GDP
- The nominal wage rate and the real wage rate
- The nominal interest rate and the real interest rate

We begin our examination of real and nominal variables in macroeconomics by reviewing what you've already learned about the distinction between nominal GDP and real GDP and interpreting that distinction in a new way.

Nominal GDP and Real GDP

When we calculated the 1909 value of a 44 cent 2009 postage stamp, we multiplied the 2009 price by the ratio of the CPI in 1909 to the CPI in 2009. By this calculation, we found the "real" value of a 2009 stamp in 1909 dollars.

But when we calculated the real GDP of 2010 in 2005 dollars in Chapter 5 (pp. 520–521 and 535–537), we didn't multiply nominal GDP in 2010 by the ratio of a price index in the two years. Instead, we expressed the values of the goods and services produced in 2010 in terms of the prices that prevailed in 2005. We calculated real GDP directly.

But we can *interpret* real GDP in 2010 as nominal GDP in 2010 multiplied by the ratio of the GDP price index in 2005 to the GDP price index in 2010. The GDP price

EYE on the U.S. ECONOMY

Deflating the GDP Balloon

Nominal GDP increased every year between 1980 and 2008. Part of the increase reflects increased production, and part of it reflects rising prices.

You can think of GDP as a balloon that is blown up by growing production and rising prices. In the figure, the GDP price index or *GDP deflator* lets the inflation air—the contribution of rising prices—out of the nominal GDP balloon so that we can see what has happened to real GDP.

The small red balloon for 1980 shows real GDP in that year. The green balloon shows nominal GDP in 2008. The red balloon for 2008 shows real GDP for that year.

To see real GDP in 2008, we use the GDP price index to deflate nominal GDP. With the inflation air removed, we can see by how much real GDP grew from 1980 to 2008.

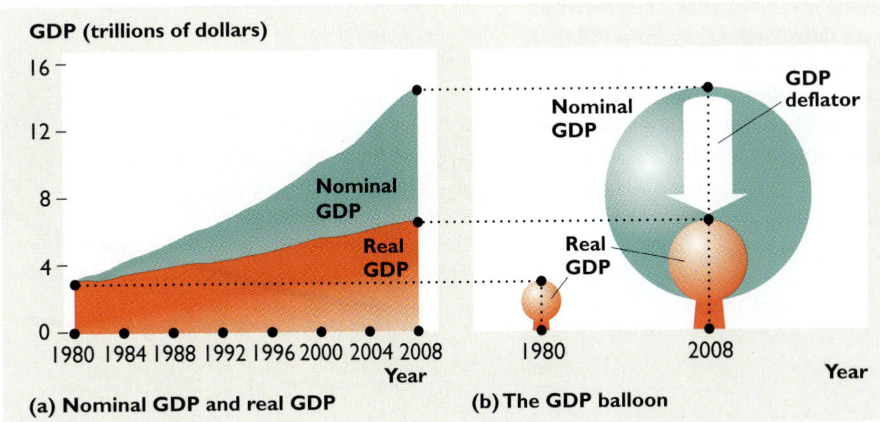

(a) Nominal GDP and real GDP

(b) The GDP balloon

SOURCE OF DATA: Bureau of Economic Analysis.

index in 2005 (the base year) is defined to be 100, so we can interpret real GDP in any year as nominal GDP divided by the GDP price index in that year multiplied by 100. We don't calculate real GDP this way, but we can interpret it this way.

The GDP price index, or the CPI, or some other price index might be used to convert a nominal variable to a real variable.

Nominal Wage Rate and Real Wage Rate

Nominal wage rate
The average hourly wage rate measured in *current* dollars.

Real wage rate
The average hourly wage rate measured in the dollars of a given reference base year.

The price of labor services is the wage rate—the income that an hour of labor earns. In macroeconomics, we are interested in economy-wide performance, so we focus on the *average* hourly wage rate. The **nominal wage rate** is the average hourly wage rate measured in *current* dollars. The **real wage rate** is the average hourly wage rate measured in the dollars of a given reference base year.

To calculate the real wage rate relevant to a consumer, we divide the nominal wage rate by the CPI and multiply by 100. That is,

$$\text{Real wage rate in 2008} = \frac{\text{Nominal wage rate in 2008}}{\text{CPI in 2008}} \times 100.$$

In 2008, the nominal wage rate (average hourly wage rate) of production workers was \$18.00 and the CPI was 215.3, so

$$\text{Real wage rate in 2008} = \frac{\$18.00}{215.3} \times 100 = \$8.36.$$

Because we measure the real wage rate in constant base-period dollars, a change in the real wage rate measures the change in the quantity of goods and ser-

FIGURE 7.4

Nominal and Real Wage Rates: 1984–2008

myeconlab Animation

The nominal wage rate has increased every year since 1984. The real wage rate decreased slightly from 1984 through the mid-1990s, after which it increased slightly again. Over the entire 24-year period, the real wage rate remained steady.

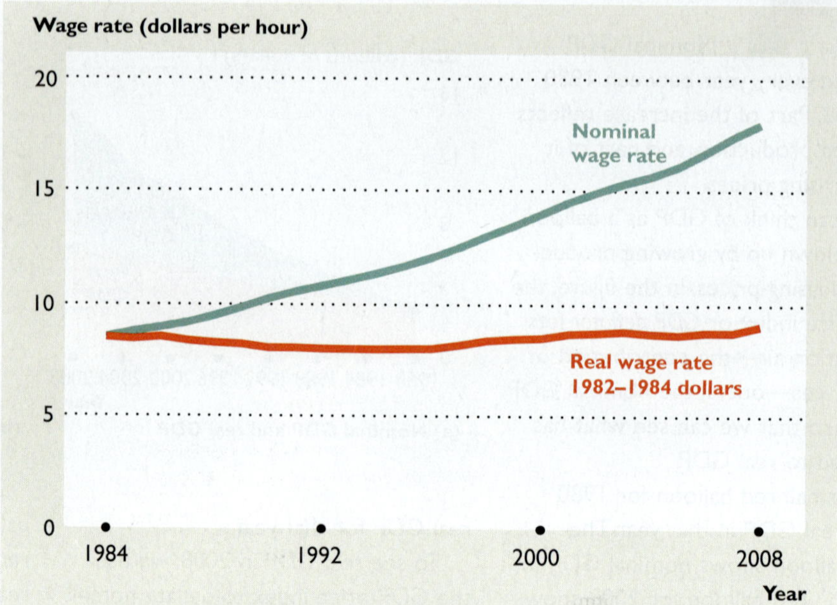

SOURCE OF DATA: *Economic Report of the President*, 2009.

vices that an hour's work can buy. In contrast, a change in the nominal wage rate measures a combination of a change in the quantity of goods and services that an hour's work can buy and a change in the price level. So the real wage rate removes the effects of inflation from the changes in the nominal wage rate.

The real wage rate is a significant economic variable because it measures the real reward for labor, which is a major determinant of the standard of living. The real wage rate is also significant because it measures the real cost of labor services, which influences the quantity of labor that firms are willing to hire.

Figure 7.4 shows what has happened to the nominal wage rate and the real wage rate in the United States between 1984 and 2008. The nominal wage rate is the average hourly earnings of production workers. This measure is just one of several different measures of average hourly earnings that we might have used.

The nominal wage rate increased from $8.48 an hour in 1984 to $18.00 an hour in 2008, but the real wage rate barely changed. In 1982–1984 dollars (the CPI base period dollars), the real wage rate in 2008 was only $8.36 an hour in 1982–1984 dollars.

The real wage rate barely changed as the nominal wage rate increased because the nominal wage rate grew at a rate almost equal to the inflation rate. When the effects of inflation are removed from the nominal wage rate, we can see what is happening to the buying power of the average wage rate.

You can also see that the real wage rate has fluctuated a little. It decreased slightly until the mid-1990s, after which it increased slightly.

EYE on the PAST

The Nominal and Real Wage Rates of Presidents of the United States

Who earned more, Barack Obama in 2008, or George Washington in 1789? George Washington's pay was $25,000 (on the green line) but in 2005 dollars it was $521,000 (on the red line). Barack Obama was paid $400,000 in 2009.

But presidential accommodations are more comfortable today, and presidential travel arrangements are a breeze compared to earlier times. So adding in the perks of the job, Barack Obama doesn't get such a raw deal.

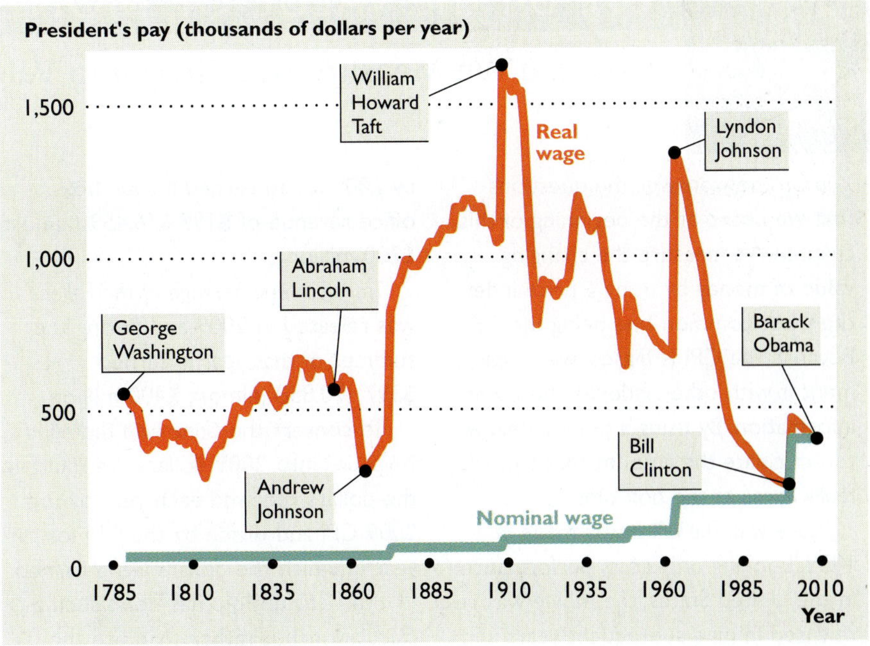

SOURCE OF DATA: Robert Sahr, Oregon State University, http://www.orst.edu/dept/pol_sci/sci/fac/sahr/sahr.htm.

Nominal Interest Rate and Real Interest Rate

You've just seen that we can calculate real values from nominal values by deflating them using the CPI. And you've seen that to make this calculation, we *divide* the nominal value by a price index. Converting a nominal interest rate to a real interest rate is a bit different. To see why, we'll start with their definitions.

Nominal interest rate
The dollar amount of interest expressed as a percentage of the amount loaned.

Real interest rate
The goods and services forgone in interest expressed as a percentage of the amount loaned and calculated as the nominal interest rate minus the inflation rate.

A **nominal interest rate** is the dollar amount of interest expressed as a percentage of the amount loaned. For example, suppose that you have $1,000 in a bank deposit—a loan by you to a bank—on which you receive interest of $50 a year. The nominal interest rate is $50 as a percentage of $1,000, which is 5 percent a year.

A **real interest rate** is the goods and services forgone in interest expressed as a percentage of the amount loaned. Continuing with the above example, at the end of one year your bank deposit has increased to $1,050—the original $1,000 plus the $50 interest. Suppose that prices have increased by 3 percent, so now you need $1,030 to buy what $1,000 would have bought a year earlier. How much interest have you *really* received? The answer is $20, or a real interest rate of 2 percent a year.

To convert a nominal interest rate to a real interest rate, we *subtract* the *inflation rate*. That is,

$$\text{Real interest rate} = \text{Nominal interest rate} - \text{Inflation rate.}$$

Plug your numbers into this formula. Your nominal interest rate is 5 percent a year, and the inflation rate is 3 percent a year. Your real interest rate is 5 percent minus 3 percent, which equals 2 percent a year.

Figure 7.5 shows the nominal and the real interest rates in the United States between 1968 and 2008. When the inflation rate is high, the gap between the real interest rate and nominal interest rate is large. Sometimes, the real interest rate is negative (as it was in the mid-1970s) and the lender pays the borrower!

EYE on the VALUE OF MONEY

How Do We Measure the Changing Value of Money?

You can now answer the questions that we posed at the beginning of this chapter. We measure the changing value of money by using a price index, the most common one being the CPI. Because the CPI is biased, we supplement it with other indexes and other information. By using a price index, we can calculate the amount that a movie *really* earns at the box office.

Gone with the Wind was made in 1939. Looking only at its performance in the United States, the movie was re-released in nine subsequent years and by 2009 it had earned a total box office revenue of $198,676,459 (almost $200 million).

Transformers: Revenge of the Fallen was released in 2009 and during the summer of that year it earned $397,470,858 (almost $400 million).

To convert the *Gone with the Wind* revenues into 2009 dollars, we multiply the dollars received each year by the 2009 CPI and divide by the CPI for the year in which the dollars were earned.

Box-Office Mojo has done such a calculation, but rather than use the CPI, it uses the average prices of movie tickets (www.boxofficemojo.com).

According to Box-Office Mojo, valuing the tickets for *Gone with the Wind* at 2009 movie-ticket prices, it has earned $1,450,680,400, or $1,451 million, about 3.6 times *Transformers'* revenue.

Because Box-Office Mojo uses average ticket prices, the real variable that it compares is the number of tickets sold. The average ticket price in 2009 was $7.18, so 202 million have seen *Gone with the Wind* and 55 million have seen *Transformers: Revenge of the Fallen*.

FIGURE 7.5

Nominal and Real Interest Rates: 1968–2008

myeconlab Animation

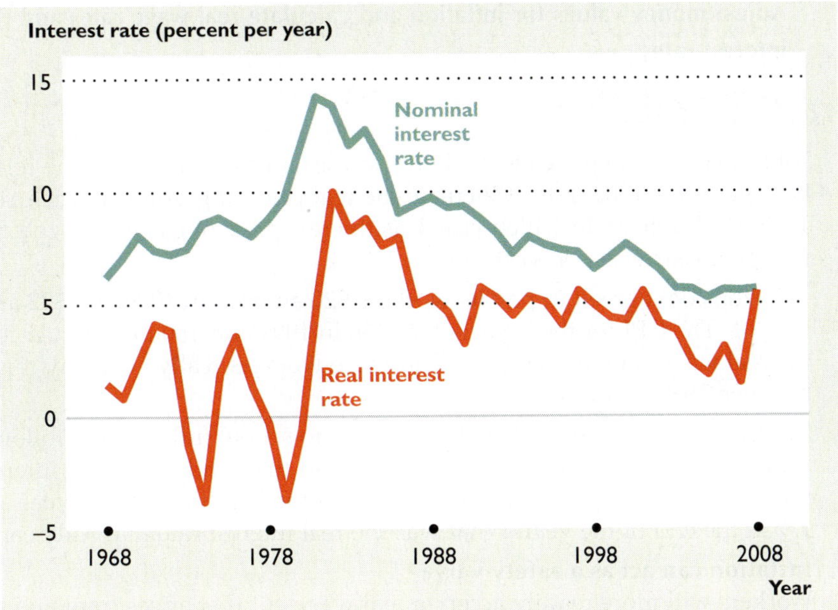

The real interest rate equals the nominal interest rate minus the inflation rate. The vertical gap between the nominal interest rate and the real interest rate is the inflation rate. The real interest rate is usually positive, but during the 1970s, it became negative.

SOURCE OF DATA: *Economic Report of the President*, 2009.

EYE on YOUR LIFE

A Student's CPI

The CPI measures the percentage change in the average prices paid for the basket of goods and services bought by a typical urban household.

A student is not a typical household. How have the prices of a student's basket of goods and services changed? The answer is by a lot more than those of an average household.

Suppose that a student spends 25 percent of her income on rent, 25 percent on tuition, 25 percent on books and study supplies, 10 percent on food, 10 percent on transportation, and 5 percent on clothing.

We can use these weights and the data collected by the BLS on individual price categories to find the student's CPI and the inflation rate that it implies.

The graph shows this student's inflation rate compared to that of the official CPI. Between 2001 and 2009, a student's CPI rose 23 percent above the official CPI. Rent, textbooks, and tuition are the main items whose prices rose faster than average.

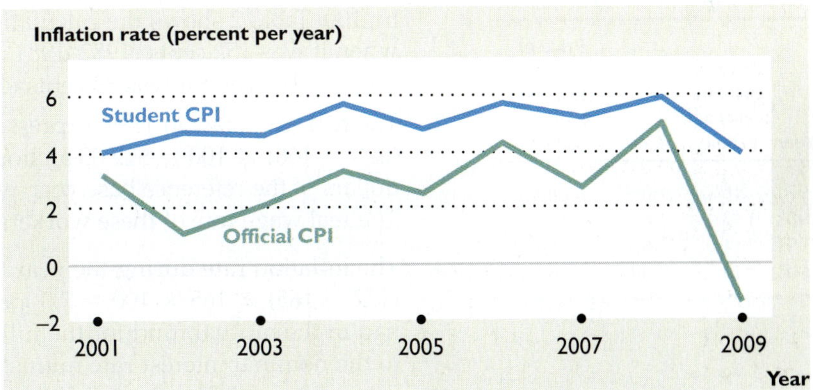

SOURCE OF DATA: Bureau of Labor Statistics.

myeconlab

Work these problems in Study Plan 7.3 to get instant feedback.

CHECKPOINT 7.3

Adjust money values for inflation and calculate real wage rates and real interest rates.

Practice Problems

TABLE 1

Year	Price of gasoline (cents per gallon)	CPI
1971	36	40.5
1981	138	90.9
1991	114	136.2
2001	146	176.6

1. Table 1 shows the price of gasoline and the CPI for four years. The reference base period is 1982–1984. Calculate the real price of gasoline in each year in 1982–1984 dollars. In which year was the real price of gasoline highest and in which year was it lowest?
2. Amazon.com agreed to pay its workers \$20 an hour in 1999 and \$22 an hour in 2001. The CPI for these years was 166 in 1999 and 180 in 2001. Calculate the real wage rate in each year. Did these workers really get a pay raise between 1999 and 2001?
3. Sally worked all year so that she could go to school full time the following year. She put her savings into a mutual fund that paid a nominal interest rate of 7 percent a year. The CPI was 165 at the beginning of the year and 177 at the end of the year. What was the real interest rate that Sally earned?
4. **Inflation can act as a safety valve**

   Workers will more readily accept a real wage cut that arises from an increase in the consumer prices than a cut in their nominal wage rate.

   Source: FT.com, May 28. 2009

   Explain why inflation influences a worker's real wage rate. Why might this observation be true?

Guided Solutions to Practice Problems

TABLE 2

Year	Price of gasoline (cents per gallon)	CPI	Price of gasoline (1982–1984 cents per gallon)
1971	36	40.5	89
1981	138	90.9	152
1991	114	136.2	84
2001	146	176.6	83

1. To calculate the real price, divide the nominal price by the CPI and multiply by 100. Table 2 shows the calculations. The real price was highest in 1981, when it was 152 cents (1982–1984 cents) per gallon. The real price was lowest in 2001, when it was 83 cents (1982–1984 cents) per gallon.
2. The real wage rate in 1999, expressed in dollars of the reference base year, was (\$20 ÷ 166) × 100 = \$12.05 an hour. The real wage rate in 2001, expressed in dollars of the reference base year, was (\$22 ÷ 180) × 100 = \$12.22 an hour. The real wage rate of these workers increased between 1999 and 2001.
3. The inflation rate during the year that Sally worked was equal to (177 − 165) ÷ 165 × 100 = 7.3 percent. On the savings that Sally had in the mutual fund for the full year, she earned a real interest rate equal to the nominal interest rate minus the inflation rate, which is 7.0 − 7.3 = −0.3 percent. Sally's real interest rate was negative. (If Sally had just kept her savings in cash, her nominal interest rate would have been zero, and her real interest rate would have been −7.3 percent. She would have been worse off.)
4. The real wage rate in 2009 = (Nominal wage rate ÷ CPI in 2009) × 100. Inflation occurs when the CPI increases. If inflation during 2009 is 3 percent, then the CPI at the end of 2009 is 3 percent higher than at the start of 2009, and the real wage rate has fallen by 3 percent during 2009. Inflation gradually lowers the real wage rate over the year, while a cut in the nominal wage rate lowers the real wage rate at a point in time.

CHAPTER SUMMARY

Key Points

1 Explain what the Consumer Price Index (CPI) is and how it is calculated.

- The Consumer Price Index (CPI) is a measure of the average of the prices of the goods and services that an average urban household buys.
- The CPI is calculated by dividing the cost of the CPI market basket in the current period by its cost in the base period and then multiplying by 100.

2 Explain the limitations of the CPI and describe other measures of the price level.

- The CPI does not include all the items that contribute to the cost of living.
- The CPI cannot provide an accurate measure of price changes because of new goods, quality improvements, and substitutions that consumers make when relative prices change.
- Other measures of the price level include the GDP price index, the PCE price index, and the PCE price index excluding food and energy.
- Both the GDP price index and the PCE price index use current information on quantities and to some degree overcome the sources of bias in the CPI.
- The PCE price index excluding food and energy is used to calculate the core inflation rate, which shows the inflation trend.

3 Adjust money values for inflation and calculate real wage rates and real interest rates.

- To adjust a money value (also called a nominal value) for inflation, we express the value in terms of the dollars of a given year.
- To convert a dollar value of year *B* to the dollars of year *A*, multiply the value in year *B* by the price level in year *A* and divide by the price level in year *B*.
- The real wage rate equals the nominal wage rate divided by the CPI and multiplied by 100.
- The real interest rate equals the nominal interest rate minus the inflation rate.

Key Terms

Consumer Price Index, 168
Core inflation rate, 177
Cost of living index, 174
Deflation, 171
GDP price index, 177
Inflation rate, 171
Nominal interest rate, 184
Nominal wage rate, 182
PCE price index, 177
Real interest rate, 184
Real wage rate, 182
Reference base period, 168

myeconlab

Work these problems in Chapter 7 Study Plan to get instant feedback.

CHAPTER CHECKPOINT

Study Plan Problems and Applications

1. Looking at some travel magazines, you read that the CPI in Turkey in 2008 was 434 and in Russia, it was 224. You do some further investigating and discover that the reference base period in Turkey is 2000 and in Russia it is 2001. The CPI in Russia in 2000 was 82. Calculate the percentage rise in the CPI in Turkey and in Russia from 2000 to 2008.
2. In Brazil, the reference base period for the CPI is 2000. By 2005, prices had risen by 51 percent since the base period. The inflation rate in Brazil in 2006 was 10 percent, and in 2007, the inflation rate was 9 percent. Calculate the CPI in Brazil in 2006 and 2007. Brazil's CPI in 2008 was 173. Did Brazil's inflation rate increase or decrease in 2008?
3. Tables 1 and 2 show the quantities of the goods that Suzie bought and the prices she paid during two consecutive weeks. Suzie's CPI market basket contains the goods she bought in Week 1. Calculate the cost of Suzie's CPI market basket in Week 1 and in Week 2. What percentage of the CPI market basket is gasoline? Calculate the value of Suzie's CPI in Week 2 and her inflation rate in Week 2.

TABLE 1 DATA FOR WEEK 1

Item	Quantity	Price (per unit)
Coffee	11 cups	$3.25
DVDs	1	$25.00
Gasoline	15 gallons	$2.50

TABLE 2 DATA FOR WEEK 2

Item	Quantity	Price (per unit)
Coffee	11 cups	$3.25
DVDs	3	$12.50
Gasoline	5 gallons	$3.00
Concert	1 ticket	$95.00

Use the following information to work Problems **4** and **5**.

The GDP price index in the United States in 2000 was about 90, and real GDP in 2000 was $11 trillion (2005 dollars). The GDP price index in the United States in 2008 was about 108, and real GDP in 2008 was $13.3 trillion (2005 dollars).

4. Calculate nominal GDP in 2000 and in 2008 and the percentage increase in nominal GDP between 2000 and 2008.
5. What was the percentage increase in production between 2000 and 2008, and by what percentage did the cost of living rise between 2000 and 2008?
6. Table 3 shows the prices that Terry paid for some of his expenditures in June and July 2009. Explain and discuss why these prices might have led to commodity substitution or outlet substitution.

TABLE 3

Item	Price in June	Price in July
	(dollars per unit)	
Steak	4.11	4.01
Bread	3.25	3.12
Bacon	3.62	3.64
Milk	2.62	2.62
Tomatoes	1.60	1.62
Apples	1.18	1.19
Bananas	0.62	0.66
Chicken	1.28	1.26
Lettuce	1.64	1.68

7. In 2008, Annie, an 80-year-old, is telling her granddaughter Susie about the good old days. Annie says that in 1938, you could buy a nice house for $15,000 and a jacket for $5. Susie says that today such a house costs $220,000 and such a jacket costs $70. The CPI in 1938 was 14.1 and in 2008 it was 215.3. Which house and which jacket have the lower prices?

Use the following information to work Problems **8** and **9**.

U.S. July CPI down 0.1%

The CPI was down 0.1% in July in line with expectations. Housing prices fell 0.2%, while transportation prices rose 0.2% and apparel prices rose 0.6%.

Source: BLS, August 14, 2009

8. What percentage change in the CPI is accounted for by the changes in housing, transportation, and apparel in July 2009?
9. Given the changes in the prices of housing, transportation, and apparel, by what percentage did the prices of the other items in the CPI basket change?

Instructor Assignable Problems and Applications

Your instructor can assign these problems as homework, a quiz, or a test in **MyEconLab**.

1. Made in 1982, *E.T.: The Extra-Terrestrial* earned $435 million at the box office. Made in 1997, *Titanic* earned $601 million. Using BLS data for the CPI in 1982 and 1997, determine which movie had the greater *real* box office revenues.
2. Pete is a student who spends 10 percent of his expenditure on books and supplies, 30 percent on tuition, 30 percent on rent, 10 percent on food and drink, 10 percent on transportation, and the rest on clothing. The price index for each item was 100 in 2000. Table 1 shows the prices in 2009. What is Pete's CPI in 2009? [Hint: The contribution of each item to the CPI is its price weighted by its share of total expenditure.] Did Pete experience a higher or lower inflation rate between 2000 and 2009 than the student whose CPI is shown on p. 581?

TABLE 1

Item	Price in 2009
Books and supplies	172.6
Tuition	169.0
Rent	159.0
Food and drink	129.8
Transportation	115.4
Clothing	92.9

3. The people on Coral Island buy only juice and cloth. The CPI market basket contains the quantities bought in 2009. The average household spent $60 on juice and $30 on cloth in 2009 when the price of juice was $2 a bottle and the price of cloth was $5 a yard. In the current year, 2010, juice is $4 a bottle and cloth is $6 a yard. Calculate the CPI and the inflation rate in 2010.
4. Tables 2 and 3 show the quantities of the goods that Harry bought and the prices he paid during two consecutive weeks. Harry's CPI market basket contains the goods he bought in Week 1. Calculate Harry's CPI in Week 2. What was his inflation rate in Week 2?

TABLE 2 DATA FOR WEEK 1

Item	Quantity	Price (per unit)
Coffee	5 cups	$3.00
iTunes songs	5	$1.00
Gasoline	10 gallons	$2.00

TABLE 3 DATA FOR WEEK 2

Item	Quantity	Price (per unit)
Coffee	4 cups	$3.25
iTunes songs	10	$1.00
Gasoline	10 gallons	$3.00

Use the following information to work Problems 5 and 6.

The base year is 2005. Real GDP in 2005 was $10 trillion (2005 dollars). The GDP price index in 2009 was 112, and real GDP in 2009 was $11 trillion (2005 dollars).

5. Calculate nominal GDP in 2005 and in 2009 and the percentage increase in nominal GDP from 2005 to 2009.
6. What was the percentage increase in production from 2005 to 2009, and by what percentage did the cost of living rise from 2005 to 2009?

Use the following information to work Problems 7 and 8.

Money market funds are yielding almost nothing

Last month, the interest rate on a money fund averaged 0.08% a year and on 5-year CDs it was 2.6% a year. The inflation rate was 0.1% a year.

Source: *USA Today*, August 12, 2009

7. Calculate the real interest rates on each of these financial assets.
8. To maintain these real interest rates in the coming months, how will the nominal rates change if the inflation rate increases to 0.2 percent a year?
9. In Sahara, the CPI market basket contains 80 bottles of water, 20 units of food, and 10 units of housing. In Arctica, the CPI market basket contains 80 units of housing, 20 units of food, and no bottled water. The prices in these two countries are the same. In the base year, water is $1 a unit, food is $5 a unit, and housing is $10 a unit. In the current year, water is $2 a unit, food is $6 a unit, and housing is $11 a unit. In the current year, calculate the CPI and the inflation rate in each country. Which country's CPI is rising faster?

10. In 1988, the average wage rate was \$9.45 an hour and in 2008 the average wage rate was \$18.00 an hour. The CPI in 1988 was 118.3 and in 2008 it was 215.3. Which real wage rate is higher?

11. Table 3 sets out the CPI for the United States and for four regions of the United States in May 2008 and 2009. In which region was the price level highest in May 2009? In which regions did consumer prices fall by more than the U.S. average? In which region was the fall in consumer prices the smallest?

TABLE 3 CPI IN MAY

Region	2008	2009
Midwest	207	203
Northeast	230	228
West	221	218
South	210	207
United States	217	214

12. If the interest rate is 19 percent a year in Argentina and 0.01 percent a year in Japan, and the inflation rate is 39 percent a year in Argentina and −0.9 percent a year in Japan, which country has the higher real interest rate?

13. Table 4 shows the prices of the major components of the U.S. CPI market basket in August 2007 and August 2008. In August 2007, the CPI was 207.9 and in August 2008, it was 219.1. Compared to the CPI market basket, which components experienced a higher price increase and which experienced a lower price increase?

TABLE 4 PRICES IN AUGUST

Item	2007	2008
Food	203.9	216.4
Apparel	114.4	116.4
Housing	211.1	219.1
Transport	184.5	206.7
Medical care	353.0	364.5
Education	120.3	124.7
Other goods	333.3	347.0

14. In 1982–1984 dollars, the real average hourly wage rate in 2006 was \$8.24 and in 2007, it was \$8.32. In 2006, the CPI was 201.6 and in 2007, the CPI was 207.3. Calculate the nominal wage rates in 2006 and 2007.

Use the following information to work Problems 15 and 16.

Imagine that you are given \$1,000 to spend and told that you must spend it all buying items from a Sears' catalog. But you do have a choice of catalog. You may select from the 1903 catalog or from Sears.com today. You will pay the prices quoted in the catalog that you choose.

15. Why might you lean toward choosing the 1903 catalog? Why might you lean toward choosing Sears.com?

16. Which catalog will you choose and why? Refer to any biases in the CPI that might be relevant to your choice.

17. Bureau of Economic Analysis data show that for the period 1929 through 2008 the average annual increase in the GDP price index is 3.0 percent. The Bureau of Labor Statistics data show that for the period 1929 through 2008, the average annual increase in the CPI is 3.2 percent. Although the difference of 0.2 percentage points is small, maintained over the 79 year period, the CPI rose by 17 percent more than the GDP price index. How would you explain the difference in these two inflation measures?

18. Bureau of Economic Analysis data show that with base year 2005 = 100, the GDP price index was 109.7 in the second quarter of 2009. In that same quarter, the PCE price index was 108.8. Given the further information that the prices of capital goods (investment) and foreign traded goods (exports and imports) increased at a slower pace than the prices of consumption goods and services, how would you explain the difference in the GDP price index and PCE price index measures of inflation?

Why do Americans earn more and produce more than Europeans?

Compared to the average European, the average American works longer hours, produces more, earns more, and faces a labor market with less unemployment. Why?

Potential GDP and the Natural Unemployment Rate

8

CHAPTER CHECKLIST

When you have completed your study of this chapter, you will be able to

1. Explain what determines potential GDP.
2. Explain what determines the natural unemployment rate.

MACROECONOMIC APPROACHES AND PATHWAYS

In the three previous chapters, you learned how economists define and measure real GDP, employment and unemployment, the price level, and the inflation rate—the key variables that *describe* macroeconomic performance. Your task in this chapter and those that follow is to learn the *macroeconomic theory* that *explains* macroeconomic performance and provides the basis for *policies* that might improve it.

The macroeconomic theory that we present is today's consensus view on how the economy works. But it isn't the view of all macroeconomists. Today's consensus is a merger of three earlier schools of thought that have sharply contrasting views about the causes of recessions and the best policies for dealing with them. Some economists continue to identify with these schools of thought, and the severity of the 2008–2009 global recession intensified debate and gave economists of all shades of opinion a platform from which to present their views.

We begin with an overview of the three schools of thought from which today's consensus has emerged.

The Three Main Schools of Thought

The three main schools of macroeconomic thought are:

- Classical macroeconomics
- Keynesian macroeconomics
- Monetarist macroeconomics

Classical Macroeconomics

Classical macroeconomics
The view that the market economy works well, that aggregate fluctuations are a natural consequence of an expanding economy, and that government intervention cannot improve the efficiency of the market economy.

According to **classical macroeconomics**, markets work well and deliver the best available macroeconomic performance. Aggregate fluctuations are a natural consequence of an expanding economy with rising living standards, and government intervention can only hinder the ability of the market to allocate resources efficiently. The first classical macroeconomists included Adam Smith, David Ricardo, and John Stuart Mill, all of whom worked in the 18th and 19th centuries. Modern day classical economists include the 2004 Nobel Laureates Edward C. Prescott of the University of Arizona and Finn E. Kydland of Carnegie-Mellon University and the University of California at Santa Barbara.

Classical macroeconomics fell into disrepute during the Great Depression of the 1930s, a time when many people believed that *capitalism*, the political system of private ownership, free markets, and democratic political institutions, could not survive and began to advocate *socialism*, a political system based on state ownership of capital and central economic planning.

Classical macroeconomics predicted that the Great Depression would eventually end but offered no method for ending it more quickly.

Keynesian Macroeconomics

Keynesian macroeconomics
The view that the market economy is inherently unstable and needs active government intervention to achieve full employment and sustained economic growth.

According to **Keynesian macroeconomics**, the market economy is inherently unstable and requires active government intervention to achieve full employment and sustained economic growth. One person, John Maynard Keynes, and his book *The General Theory of Employment, Interest, and Money*, published in 1936, began this school of thought. Keynes' theory was that depression and high unemployment occur when households don't spend enough on consumption goods and services and businesses don't spend enough investing in new capital. That is, too little *private* spending is the cause of depression (and recession). To counter the problem of too little private spending, *government* spending must rise.

This Keynesian view picked up many followers and by the 1950s it was the mainstream, but it lost popularity during the inflationary 1970s when it seemed ever more remote from the problems of that decade. The global recession of 2008–2009 and the fear of another great depression revived interest in Keynesian ideas and brought a new wave of attacks on classical macroeconomics with Nobel Laureate Paul Krugman leading the charge in the columns of the *New York Times*.

Monetarist Macroeconomics

According to **monetarist macroeconomics**, the *classical* view of the world is broadly correct but in addition to fluctuations that arise from the normal functioning of an expanding economy, fluctuations in the quantity of money also bring the business cycle. A slowdown in the growth rate of money brings recession and a large decrease in the quantity of money brought the Great Depression.

Monetarist macroeconomics
The view that the market economy works well, that aggregate fluctuations are a natural consequence of an expanding economy, but that fluctuations in the quantity of money also bring the business cycle.

Milton Friedman, intellectual leader of the Chicago School of economists during the 1960s and 1970s, was the most prominent monetarist. The view that monetary contractions are the sole source of recessions and depressions is held by few economists today. But the view that the quantity of money plays a role in economic fluctuations is accepted by all economists and is part of today's consensus.

Today's Consensus

Each of the earlier schools provides insights and ingredients that survive in today's consensus. *Classical* macroeconomics provides the story of the economy at or close to full employment. But the classical approach doesn't explain how the economy performs in the face of a major slump in spending.

Keynesian macroeconomics takes up the story in a recession or depression. When spending is cut and the demand for most goods and services and the demand for labor all decrease, prices and wage rates don't fall but the quantity of goods and services sold and the quantity of labor employed do fall and the economy goes into recession. In a recession, an increase in spending by governments, or a tax cut that leaves people with more of their earnings to spend, can help to restore full employment.

Monetarist macroeconomics elaborates the Keynesian story by emphasizing that a contraction in the quantity of money brings higher interest rates and borrowing costs, which are a major source of cuts in spending that bring recession. Increasing the quantity of money and lowering the interest rate in a recession can help to restore full employment. And keeping the quantity of money growing steadily in line with the expansion of the economy's production possibilities can help to keep inflation in check and can also help to moderate the severity of a recession.

Another component of today's consensus is the view that the *long-term* problem of economic growth is more important than the *short-term* problem of recessions. Take a look at *Eye on the U.S. Economy,* on p. 194, and you will see why. Even a small slowdown in economic growth brings a huge cost in terms of a permanently lower level of income per person. This cost is much larger than that arising from the income lost during recessions. But the costs of recessions are serious because they are concentrated on those who are unemployed.

The Road Ahead

This book bases your tour of macroeconomics on the new consensus. We begin in this chapter and the two that follow by explaining what determines potential GDP and the pace at which it grows. We then study money and explain what brings inflation. Finally, we explain how real and monetary forces interact to bring about the business cycle. We also explain the policy tools available to governments and central banks to improve macroeconomic performance.

EYE on the U.S. ECONOMY

The Lucas Wedge and the Okun Gap

During the 1960s, U.S. real GDP per person grew at a rate of 2.9 percent a year. The black line in part (a) shows the path that would have been followed if this growth rate had been maintained. After 1970, growth slowed to 2.0 percent per year and the red line shows the path that potential GDP followed. University of Chicago economist Robert E. Lucas, Jr. pointed out the large output loss that resulted from this growth slowdown. Part (a) shows this loss as the **Lucas wedge**, which is equivalent to a staggering $284,500 per person or more than 6 years' income.

Real GDP fluctuates around potential GDP and when the output gap is negative, output is lost. Brookings Institution economist Arthur B. Okun drew attention to this loss. Part (b) shows this loss as the **Okun gap**, which is equivalent to $12,850 per person or about 3 months' income.

Smoothing the business cycle and eliminating the Okun gap has a big payoff. But finding ways of restoring real GDP growth to its 1960s rate has a vastly bigger payoff.

SOURCES OF DATA: Bureau of Economic Analysis and the Congressional Budget Office.

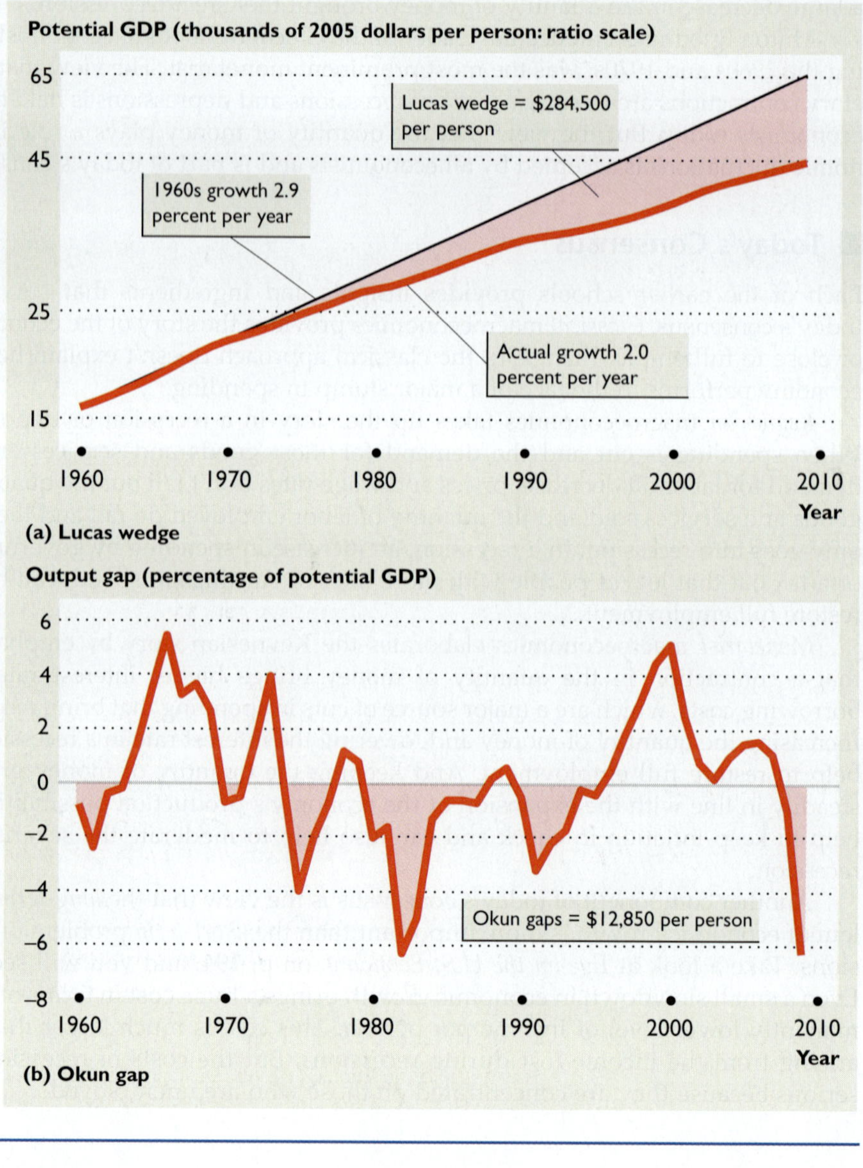

(a) Lucas wedge

(b) Okun gap

8.1 POTENTIAL GDP

Potential GDP is the value of real GDP when all the economy's factors of production—labor, capital, land, and entrepreneurial ability—are fully employed. It is vital to understand the forces that determine potential GDP for three reasons. First, when the economy is *at* full employment, real GDP equals potential GDP; so actual real GDP is determined by the same factors that determine potential GDP. Second, real GDP can exceed potential GDP only temporarily as it approaches and then recedes from a business cycle peak. So potential GDP is the *sustainable* upper limit of production. Third, real GDP fluctuates around potential GDP, which means that on the average over the business cycle, real GDP equals potential GDP.

Potential GDP
The value of real GDP when all the economy's factors of production—labor, capital, land, and entrepreneurial ability—are fully employed.

We produce the goods and services that make up real GDP by using the *factors of production:* labor and human capital, physical capital, land (and natural resources), and entrepreneurship. At any given time, the quantities of capital, land, and entrepreneurship and the state of technology are fixed. But the quantity of labor is not fixed. It depends on the choices that people make about the allocation of time between work and leisure. So with fixed quantities of capital, land, and entrepreneurship and fixed technology, real GDP depends on the quantity of labor employed. To describe this relationship between real GDP and the quantity of labor employed, we use a relationship that is similar to the production possibilities frontier, which is called the production function.

EYE on the GLOBAL ECONOMY

Potential GDP in the United States and European Union

In 2008, potential GDP per person in the United States was $44,000. In 11 major European economies, it was only $32,000—a gap of 38 percent. (Both numbers are measured in 2005 U.S. dollars.) Part (a) of the figure shows this large difference.

In the United States in 2008, the real wage rate was $34 an hour and in Europe, it was $29 an hour—a 17 percent gap.

How can the average American produce 38 percent more than the average European but earn in wages only 17 percent more?

The answer is that Americans work more than Europeans and in two ways.

First, 48 out of every 100 Americans have jobs compared with 46 out of every 100 Europeans.

Second, Europeans work shorter hours than Americans—30.5 hours a week compared to the 34 hours that an average American works—a 12 percent difference shown in part (c).

Europeans achieve their shorter work hours by taking longer vacations and having more sick days than Americans.

This chapter will enable you to understand the deeper sources of these differences in production and work.

Sources of data: Bureau of Economic Analysis, Bureau of Labor Statistics, and International Monetary Fund.

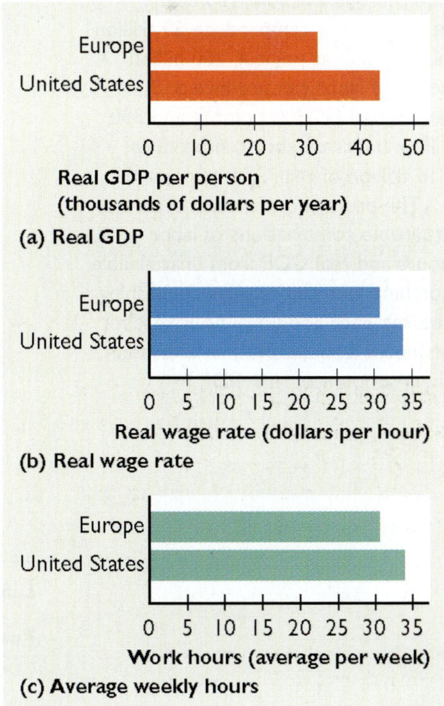

The Production Function

Production function
A relationship that shows the maximum quantity of real GDP that can be produced as the quantity of labor employed changes and all other influences on production remain the same.

The **production function** is a relationship that shows the maximum quantity of real GDP that can be produced as the quantity of labor employed changes and all other influences on production remain the same. Figure 8.1 shows a production function, which is the curve labeled *PF*.

In Figure 8.1, 100 billion labor hours can produce a real GDP of $9 trillion (at point *A*); 200 billion hours can produce a real GDP of $13 trillion (at point *B*); and 300 billion hours can produce a real GDP of $16 trillion (at point *C*).

The production function shares a feature of the *production possibilities frontier* that you studied in Chapter 3 (p. 62). Like the *PPF*, the production function is a boundary between the attainable and the unattainable. It is possible to produce at any point along the production function and beneath it in the shaded area. But it is not possible to produce at points above the production function. Those points are unattainable.

Diminishing returns
The tendency for each additional hour of labor employed to produce a successively smaller additional amount of real GDP.

The production function displays **diminishing returns**—each additional hour of labor employed produces a successively smaller additional amount of real GDP. The first 100 billion hours of labor produces $9 trillion of real GDP. The second 100 billion hours of labor increases real GDP to $13 trillion and so produces only an

FIGURE 8.1

The Production Function

myeconlab Animation

The production function shows the maximum quantity of real GDP that can be produced as the quantity of labor employed changes and all other influences on production remain the same. In this example, 100 billion hours of labor can produce $9 trillion of real GDP at point *A*, 200 billion hours of labor can produce $13 trillion of real GDP at point *B*, and 300 billion hours of labor can produce $16 trillion of real GDP at point *C*.

The production function separates attainable combinations of labor hours and real GDP from unattainable combinations and displays diminishing returns: Each additional hour of labor produces a successively smaller additional amount of real GDP.

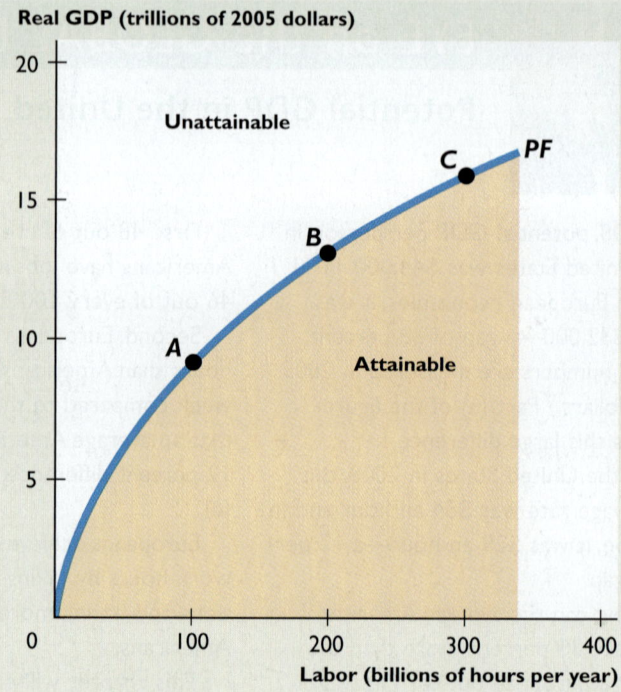

Labor (billions of hours per year)	100	200	300
Real GDP (trillions of 2005 dollars)	9	13	16
	A	B	C

additional $4 trillion of real GDP. The third 100 billion hours of labor increases real GDP to $16 trillion and so produces only an additional $3 trillion of real GDP.

Diminishing returns arise because the quantity of capital (and other factors of production) is fixed. As more labor is hired, the additional output produced decreases because the extra workers have less capital with which to work. For example, a forest service has three chain saws and an axe and hires three workers to clear roads and trails of fallen trees and debris during the spring thaw. Hiring a fourth worker will contribute less to the amount cleared than the amount that the third worker added, and hiring a fifth worker will add even less.

Because real GDP depends on the quantity of labor employed, potential GDP depends on the production function and the quantity of labor employed. To find potential GDP, we must understand what determines the quantity of labor employed.

The Labor Market

You've already studied the tool that we use to determine the quantity of labor employed: demand and supply. In macroeconomics, we apply the concepts of demand, supply, and market equilibrium to the economy-wide labor market.

The quantity of labor employed depends on firms' decisions about how much labor to hire (the demand for labor). It also depends on households' decisions about how to allocate time between employment and other activities (the supply of labor). And it depends on how the labor market coordinates the decisions of firms and households (labor market equilibrium). So we will study

- The demand for labor
- The supply of labor
- Labor market equilibrium

The Demand for Labor

The **quantity of labor demanded** is the total labor hours that all the firms in the economy plan to hire during a given time period at a given real wage rate. The **demand for labor** is the relationship between the quantity of labor demanded and the real wage rate when all other influences on firms' hiring plans remain the same. The lower the real wage rate, the greater is the quantity of labor demanded.

Quantity of labor demanded
The total labor hours that all the firms in the economy plan to hire during a given time period at a given real wage rate.

Demand for labor
The relationship between the quantity of labor demanded and the real wage rate when all other influences on firms' hiring plans remain the same.

The real wage rate is the *nominal wage rate* (the dollars per hour that people earn on average) divided by the price level (see Chapter 7, p. 182). We express the real wage rate in constant dollars—today in 2005 dollars. Think of the real wage rate as the quantity of real GDP that an hour of labor earns.

The lower the real wage rate, the greater is the quantity of labor that firms find it profitable to hire. The real wage rate influences the quantity of labor demanded because what matters to firms is not the number of dollars they pay for an hour of labor (the nominal wage rate) but how much output they must sell to earn those dollars. So firms compare the extra output that an hour of labor can produce with the real wage rate.

If an additional hour of labor produces at least as much additional output as the real wage rate, a firm hires that labor. At a small quantity of labor, an extra hour of labor produces more output than the real wage rate. But each additional hour of labor produces less additional output than the previous hour. As a firm hires more labor, eventually the extra output from an extra hour of labor equals the real wage rate. This equality determines the quantity of labor demanded at the real wage rate.

The Demand for Labor in a Soda Factory You might understand the demand for labor better by thinking about a single firm rather than the economy as a whole. Suppose that the money wage rate is $15 an hour and that the price of a bottle of soda is $1.50. For the soda factory, the real wage rate is a number of bottles of soda. To find the soda factory's real wage rate, divide the money wage rate by the price of its output—$15 an hour ÷ $1.50 a bottle. The real wage rate is 10 bottles of soda an hour. It costs the soda factory 10 bottles of soda to hire an hour of labor. As long as the soda factory can hire labor that produces more than 10 additional bottles of soda an hour, it is profitable to hire more labor. Only when the extra output produced by an extra hour of labor falls to 10 bottles an hour has the factory reached the profit-maximizing quantity of labor.

Labor Demand Schedule and Labor Demand Curve We can represent the demand for labor as either a demand schedule or a demand curve. The table in Figure 8.2 shows part of a demand for labor schedule. It tells us the quantity of labor demanded at three different real wage rates. For example, if the real wage rate is $40 an hour (row *B*), the quantity of labor demanded is 200 billion hours a year. If the real wage rate rises to $65 an hour (row *A*), the quantity of labor demanded decreases to 100 billion hours a year. And if the real wage rate falls to $20 an hour (row *C*), the quantity of labor demanded increases to 300 billion hours a year.

Figure 8.2 shows the demand for labor curve. Points *A*, *B*, and *C* on the demand curve correspond to rows *A*, *B*, and *C* of the demand schedule.

FIGURE 8.2

The Demand for Labor

myeconlab Animation

Firms are willing to hire labor only if the labor produces more than its real wage rate. So the lower the real wage rate, the more labor firms can profitably hire and the greater is the quantity of labor demanded.

At a real wage rate of $40 an hour, the quantity of labor demanded is 200 billion hours at point *B*.

❶ If the real wage rate rises to $65 an hour, the quantity of labor demanded decreases to 100 billion hours at point *A*.

❷ If the real wage rate falls to $20 an hour, the quantity of labor demanded increases to 300 billion hours at point *C*.

	Real wage rate (2005 dollars per hour)	Quantity of labor demanded (billions of hours per year)
A	65	100
B	40	200
C	20	300

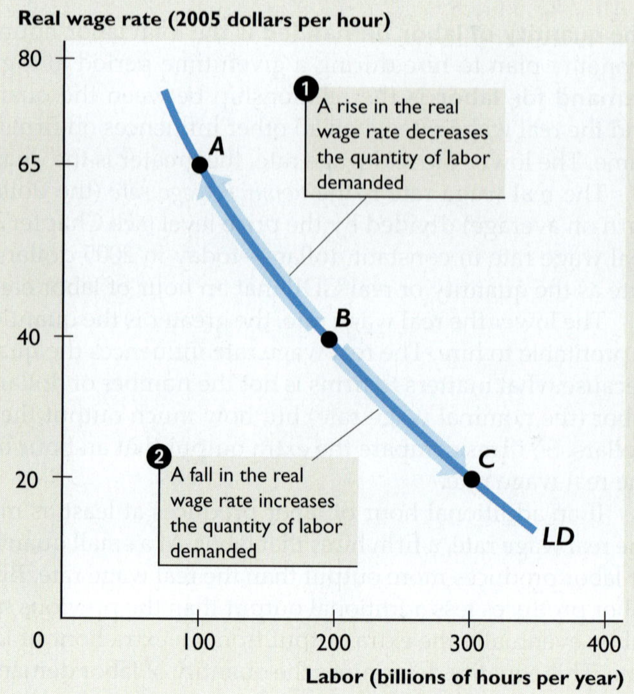

The Supply of Labor

The **quantity of labor supplied** is the number of labor hours that all the households in the economy plan to work during a given time period at a given real wage rate. The **supply of labor** is the relationship between the quantity of labor supplied and the real wage rate when all other influences on work plans remain the same.

Quantity of labor supplied
The number of labor hours that all the households in the economy plan to work during a given time period at a given real wage rate.

Supply of labor
The relationship between the quantity of labor supplied and the real wage rate when all other influences on work plans remain the same.

We can represent the supply of labor as either a supply schedule or a supply curve. The table in Figure 8.3 shows a supply of labor schedule. It tells us the quantity of labor supplied at three different real wage rates. For example, if the real wage rate is $40 an hour (row *B*), the quantity of labor supplied is 200 billion hours a year. If the real wage rate falls to $20 an hour (row *A*), the quantity of labor supplied decreases to 100 billion hours a year. And if the real wage rate rises to $60 an hour (row *C*), the quantity of labor supplied increases to 300 billion hours a year.

Figure 8.3 shows the supply of labor curve. It corresponds to the supply schedule, and the points *A*, *B*, and *C* on the supply curve correspond to the rows *A*, *B*, and *C* of the supply schedule.

The real wage rate influences the quantity of labor supplied because what matters to people is not the number of dollars they earn but what those dollars will buy.

The quantity of labor supplied increases as the real wage rate increases for two reasons:

- Hours per person increase.
- Labor force participation increases.

FIGURE 8.3

The Supply of Labor

myeconlab Animation

	Real wage rate (2005 dollars per hour)	Quantity of labor supplied (billions of hours per year)
C	60	300
B	40	200
A	20	100

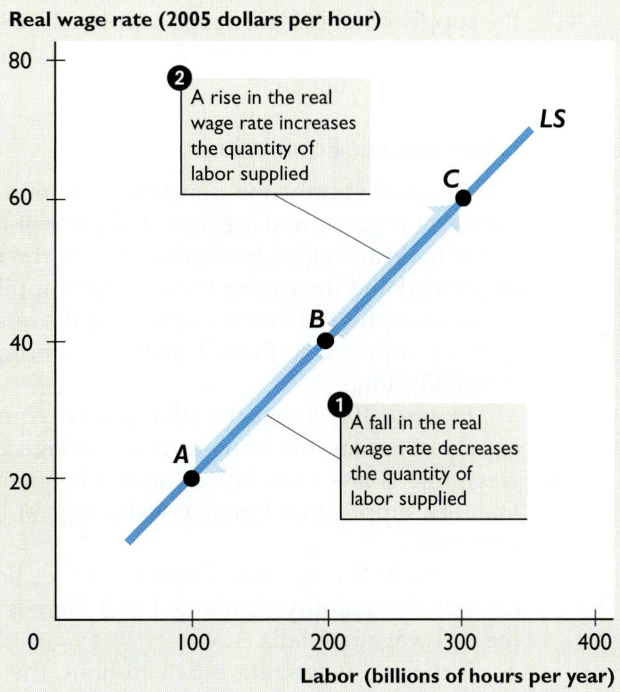

Households are willing to supply labor only if the real wage rate is high enough to attract them from other activities. The higher the real wage rate, the greater is the quantity of labor supplied.

At a real wage rate of $40 an hour, the quantity of labor supplied is 200 billion hours at point *B*.

❶ If the real wage rate falls to $20 an hour, the quantity of labor supplied decreases to 100 billion hours at point *A*.

❷ If the real wage rate rises to $60 an hour, the quantity of labor supplied increases to 300 billion hours at point *C*.

Hours per Person The real wage rate is the opportunity cost of taking leisure and not working. As the opportunity cost of taking leisure rises, other things remaining the same, households choose to work more. But other things don't remain the same. A higher real wage rate brings a higher income, which increases the demand for leisure and encourages less work.

So a rise in the real wage rate has two opposing effects. But for most households, the opportunity cost effect is stronger than the income effect, so a rise in the real wage rate brings an increase in the quantity of labor supplied.

Labor Force Participation Most people have productive opportunities outside the labor force and choose to work only if the real wage rate exceeds the value of other productive activities. For example, a parent might spend time caring for her or his child. The alternative is day care. The parent will choose to work only if he or she can earn enough per hour to pay the cost of day care and have enough left to make the work effort worthwhile. The higher the real wage rate, the more likely it is that a parent will choose to work and so the greater is the labor force participation rate.

Other Influences on Labor Supply Decisions Many factors other than the real wage rate influence labor supply decisions and influence the position of the labor supply curve. Income taxes and unemployment benefits are two of these factors.

The work-leisure decision depends on the *after-tax* wage rate—the wage rate actually received by the household. So, for a given wage rate, the income tax decreases the after-tax wage rate and the quantity of labor supplied decreases. The result is a decrease in the supply of labor. (The income tax rate doesn't change the demand for labor because for the employer, the cost of labor is the before-tax wage rate.)

Unemployment benefits lower the cost of searching for a job and encourage unemployed workers to take longer to find the best job available. The result is a decrease in the supply of labor.

Higher income tax rates and more generous unemployment benefits decrease the supply of labor—the labor supply curve lies farther to the left.

Let's now see how the labor market determines employment, the real wage rate, and potential GDP.

Labor Market Equilibrium

The forces of supply and demand operate in labor markets just as they do in the markets for goods and services. The price of labor services is the real wage rate. A rise in the real wage rate eliminates a shortage of labor by decreasing the quantity demanded and increasing the quantity supplied. A fall in the real wage rate eliminates a surplus of labor by increasing the quantity demanded and decreasing the quantity supplied. If there is neither a shortage nor a surplus, the labor market is in equilibrium.

Figure 8.4(a) shows the labor market equilibrium. The demand curve and the supply curve are the same as those in Figures 8.2 and 8.3. In part (a), if the real wage rate is less than \$40 an hour, the quantity of labor demanded exceeds the quantity supplied and there is a shortage of labor. In this situation, the real wage rate rises.

If the real wage rate exceeds \$40 an hour, the quantity of labor supplied exceeds the quantity demanded and there is a surplus of labor. In this situation, the real wage rate falls.

If the real wage rate is \$40 an hour, the quantity of labor demanded equals the quantity supplied and there is neither a shortage nor a surplus of labor. In this

FIGURE 8.4

Labor Market Equilibrium and Potential GDP

myeconlab Animation

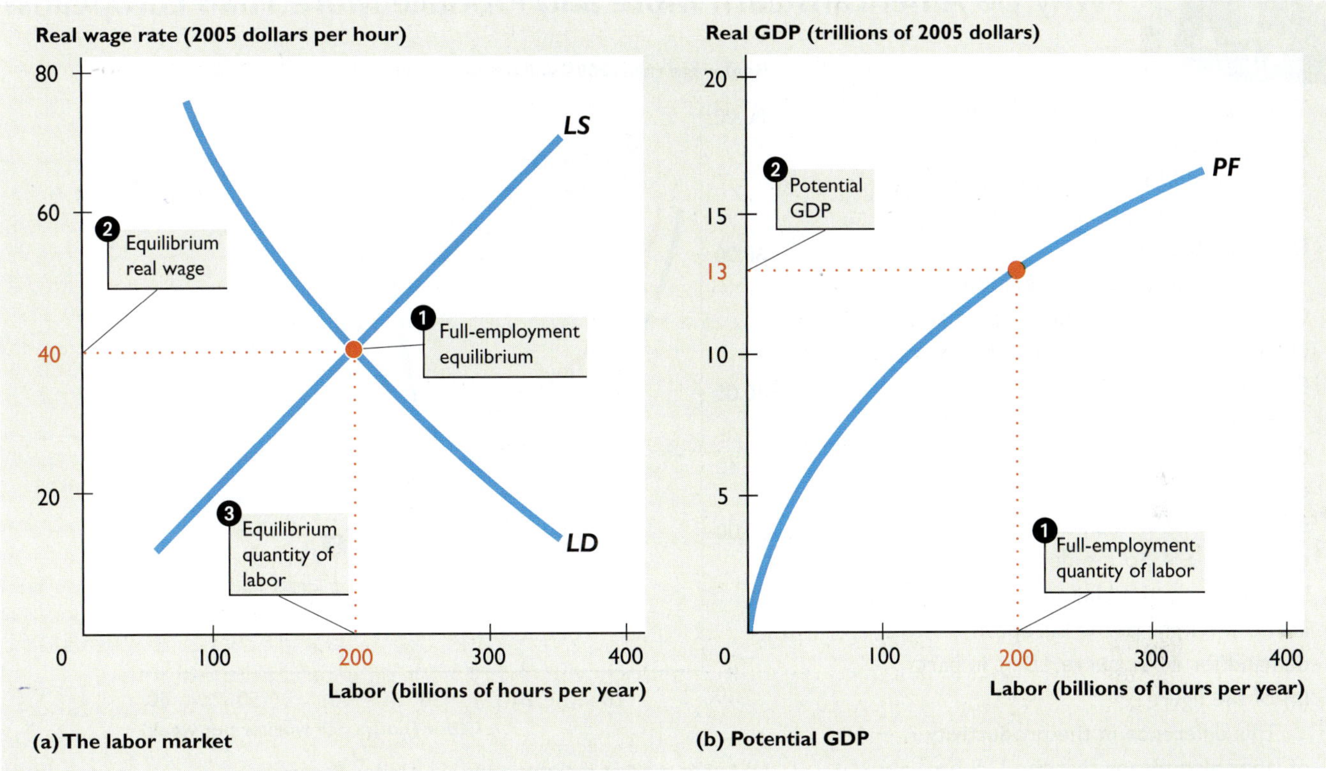

❶ Full employment occurs when the quantity of labor demanded equals the quantity of labor supplied. ❷ The equilibrium real wage rate is \$40 an hour, and ❸ the equilibrium quantity of labor employed is 200 billion hours a year.

Potential GDP is the real GDP produced on the production function by the full-employment quantity of labor. ❶ The full-employment quantity of labor, 200 billion hours a year, produces a ❷ potential GDP of \$13 trillion.

situation, the labor market is in equilibrium and the real wage rate remains constant. The equilibrium quantity of labor is 200 billion hours a year. When the equilibrium quantity of labor is employed, the economy is at full employment. So the full-employment quantity of labor is 200 billion hours a year.

Full Employment and Potential GDP

When the labor market is in equilibrium, the economy is at full employment and real GDP equals potential GDP.

You've seen that the quantity of real GDP depends on the quantity of labor employed. The production function tells us how much real GDP a given amount of employment can produce. Now that we've determined the full-employment quantity of labor, we can find potential GDP.

Figure 8.4(b) shows the relationship between labor market equilibrium and potential GDP. The equilibrium quantity of labor employed in Figure 8.4(a) is 200 billion hours. The production function in Figure 8.4(b) tells us that 200 billion hours of labor produces \$13 trillion of real GDP. This quantity of real GDP is potential GDP.

EYE on U.S. POTENTIAL GDP

Why Do Americans Earn More and Produce More Than Europeans?

The quantity of capital per worker is greater in the United States than in Europe, and U.S. technology, on the average, is more productive than European technology.

These differences between the United States and Europe mean that U.S. labor is more productive than European labor.

Because U.S. labor is more productive than European labor, U.S. employers are willing to pay more for a given quantity of labor than European employers are. So the demand for labor curve in the United States, LD_{US}, lies to the right of the European demand for labor curve, LD_{EU}, in part (a) of the figure.

This difference in the productivity of labor also means that the U.S. production function, PF_{US}, lies above the European production function, PF_{EU}, in part (b) of the figure.

Higher income taxes and unemployment benefits in Europe mean that to induce a person to take a job, a firm in Europe must offer a higher wage rate than a firm in the United States has to offer. So the European labor supply curve, LS_{EU}, lies to the left of the U.S. labor supply curve, LS_{US}.

Equilibrium employment is higher in the United States than in Europe—Americans work longer hours—and equilibrium real wage rate is higher in the United States than in Europe.

Potential GDP is higher in the United States than in Europe for two reasons: U.S. workers are more productive per hour of work and they work longer hours than Europeans.

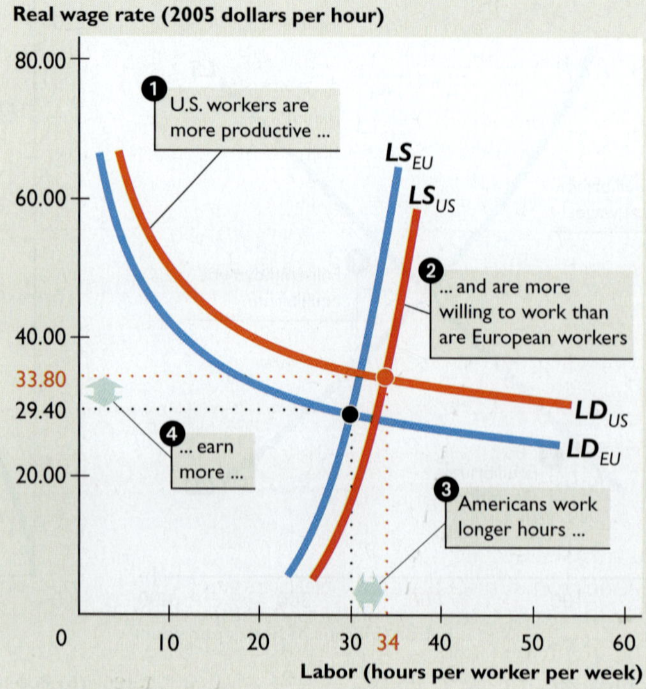

(a) Labor market in Europe and the United States

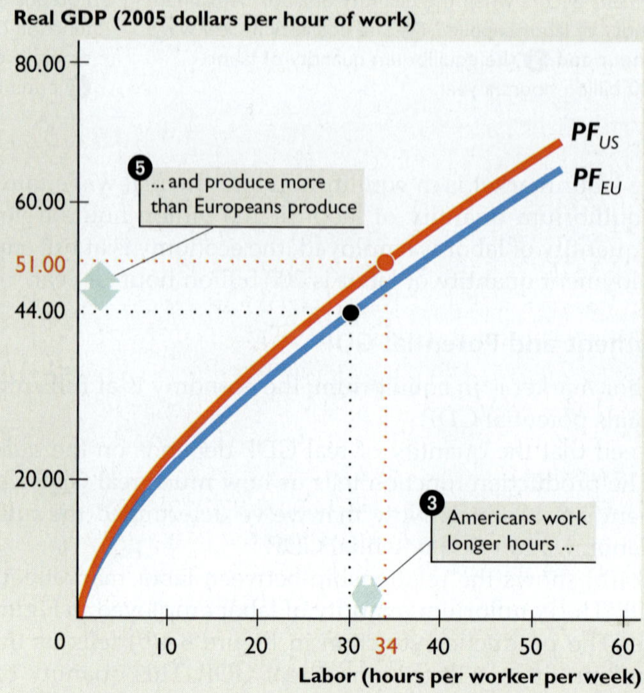

(b) Production function in Europe and the United States

CHECKPOINT 8.1

Explain what determines potential GDP.

myeconlab

Work these problems in Study Plan 8.1 to get instant feedback.

Practice Problems

1. Table 1 describes an economy's production function and demand for labor.

TABLE 1

Quantity of labor demanded (billions of hours per year)	0	1	2	3	4
Real GDP (billions of 2005 dollars)	0	40	70	90	100
Real wage rate (2005 dollars per hour)	50	40	30	20	10

Table 2 describes the supply of labor in this economy.

TABLE 2

Quantity of labor supplied (billions of hours per year)	0	1	2	3	4
Real wage rate (2005 dollars per hour)	10	20	30	40	50

Use the data in Tables 1 and 2 to make graphs of the labor market and production function. What are the equilibrium, real wage rate, and employment? What is potential GDP?

2. **Chevron signs $73b gas deal**
Gorgon, Chevron's huge liquefied natural gas project, is finally going forward. The company, along with Exxon Mobil and Shell will produce natural gas off the northwest coast of Australia. Gorgon and surrounding fields hold an estimated 40 trillion cubic feet of natural gas, the equivalent of 6.7 billion barrels of oil. Gorgon is located for easy shipment to growing markets in China and India and at its peak will employ 10,000 workers.
Source: Radio Australia, September 10, 2009

Explain how this huge project will influence Australia's potential GDP and U.S. potential GDP.

Guided Solutions to Practice Problems

1. The demand for labor is a graph of the first and last row of Table 1 and the supply of labor is a graph of the data in Table 2 (Figure 1). The production function is a graph of the first two rows of Table 1 (Figure 2).

Labor market equilibrium occurs when the real wage rate is $30 an hour and 2 billion hours of labor are employed (Figure 1). Potential GDP is the real GDP produced by the equilibrium quantity of labor (2 billion hours in Figure 1). Potential GDP is $70 billion (Figure 2).

2. Australia's potential GDP will increase, but U.S. potential GDP will not change. Accessing these new resources will shift Australia's production function upward. With no change in employment, real GDP would increase. But the project will increase the demand for labor, increase the full-employment quantity of labor, and increase potential GDP. Even though this project is undertaken by U.S. firms, the production takes place in Australia. Neither the U.S. production function nor the U.S. demand for labor changes, so the project has no effect on U.S. potential GDP.

FIGURE 1

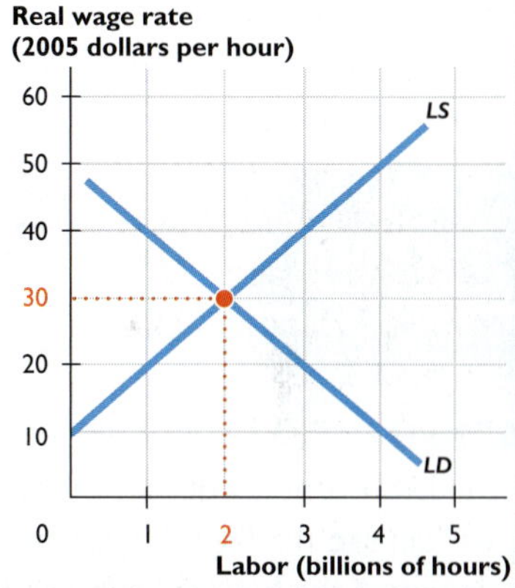

FIGURE 2

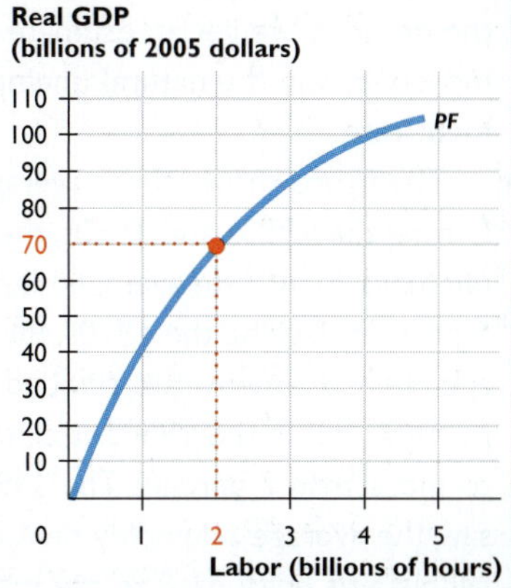

8.2 THE NATURAL UNEMPLOYMENT RATE

So far, we've focused on the forces that determine the real wage rate, the quantity of labor employed, and real GDP at full employment. We're now going to bring unemployment into the picture.

You learned in Chapter 6 how unemployment is measured. You also learned how people become unemployed by losing or leaving their jobs and by entering or reentering the labor force. And you learned how we classify unemployment as frictional, structural, seasonal, or cyclical. Finally, you learned that when the economy is at full employment, all the unemployment is frictional, structural, or seasonal, and the unemployment rate is called the *natural unemployment rate.*

Measuring, describing, and classifying unemployment tell us a lot about it. But these activities do not *explain* the amount of unemployment that exists or why its rate changes over time and varies across economies.

Many forces interact to determine the unemployment rate. Understanding these forces is a challenging task. Economists approach this task in two steps. The first step is to understand what determines the natural unemployment rate—the unemployment rate when the economy is at full employment. The second step is to understand what makes unemployment fluctuate around the natural unemployment rate. In this chapter, we take the first of these steps. We take the second step in Chapters 13–15 when we study economic fluctuations.

EYE on the PAST

Average Unemployment Rates over Six Decades

If we look back at the U.S. economy decade by decade, we can see through the ups and downs of the business cycle and focus on the broad trends. By looking at the average unemployment rates across the decades, we get an estimate of movements in the natural unemployment rate.

The figure shows these averages. During the 1950s and 1960s, the unemployment rate averaged less than 5 percent. During the 1970s, the average unemployment rate climbed to 6 percent, and in the 1980s, it climbed to more than 7 percent. The 1990s saw the average unemployment rate fall but not quite back to the rate of the 1950s and 1960s.

You will be a member of the labor force of the 2010s. The average unemployment rate of the second decade of the 2000s will have a big effect on your job market success.

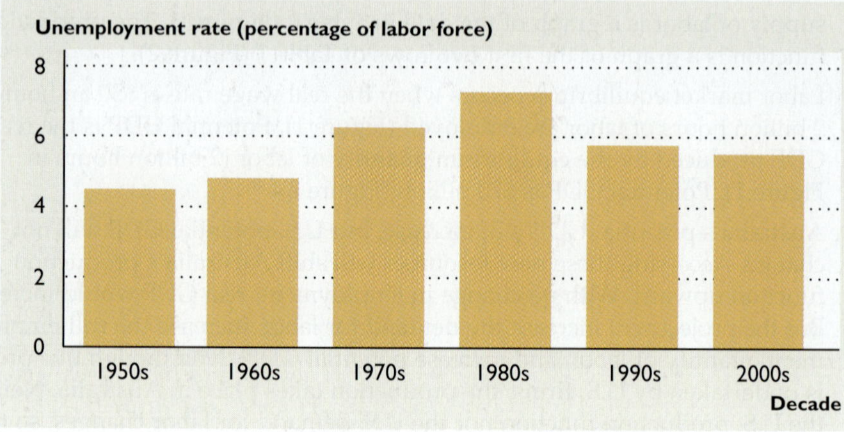

SOURCE OF DATA: Bureau of Labor Statistics.

To understand the amount of frictional and structural unemployment that exists at the natural unemployment rate, economists focus on two fundamental causes of unemployment that cut across the frictional-structural classification. These two fundamental causes of unemployment are

- Job search
- Job rationing

Job Search

Job search The activity of looking for an acceptable vacant job.

Job search is the activity of looking for an acceptable vacant job. Because the labor market is in a constant state of change, there are always some people who have not yet found suitable jobs and who are actively searching. The failure of businesses destroys jobs. The expansion of businesses and the startup of new businesses create jobs. As people pass through different stages of life, some enter or reenter the labor market, others leave their jobs to look for better ones, and others retire. This constant churning in the labor market means that there are always some people looking for jobs, and these people are part of the unemployed.

The amount of job search depends on a number of factors that change over time. The main ones are

- Demographic change
- Unemployment benefits
- Structural change

Demographic Change

An increase in the proportion of the population that is of working age brings an increase in the entry rate into the labor force and an increase in the unemployment rate. This factor was important in the U.S. labor market during the 1970s. The bulge in the birth rate that occurred in the late 1940s and early 1950s increased the proportion of new entrants into the labor force during the 1970s and brought an increase in the unemployment rate.

As the birth rate declined, the bulge moved into higher age groups and the proportion of new entrants declined during the 1990s. During this period, the unemployment rate decreased.

Another source of demographic change has been an increase in the number of households with two incomes. When unemployment comes to one of these workers, it is possible, with income still flowing in, to take longer to find a new job. This factor might have increased frictional unemployment.

Unemployment Benefits

The opportunity cost of job search influences the length of time that an unemployed person spends searching for a job. With no unemployment benefits, the opportunity cost of job search is high, and a person is likely to accept a job that is found quickly. With generous unemployment benefits, the opportunity cost of job search is low, and a person is likely to spend a considerable time searching for the ideal job.

Generous unemployment benefits are a large part of the story of high unemployment rates in Europe and some other countries such as Canada—see *Eye on the Global Economy* on p. 602.

EYE on the GLOBAL ECONOMY

Unemployment Benefits and the Natural Unemployment Rate

Europe has higher unemployment benefits than the United States but are higher benefits the source of Europe's higher natural unemployment rate?

To isolate the effects of unemployment benefits, we need to keep other things the same. Canada provides an experiment in which other things are very similar to the United States.

The natural unemployment rate in Canada equalled that in the United States until 1980 but then it increased. Why? The key change in the 1980s was an increase in Canadian unemployment benefits. Close to 100 percent of Canada's unemployed receive generous benefits compared to 38 percent in the United States.

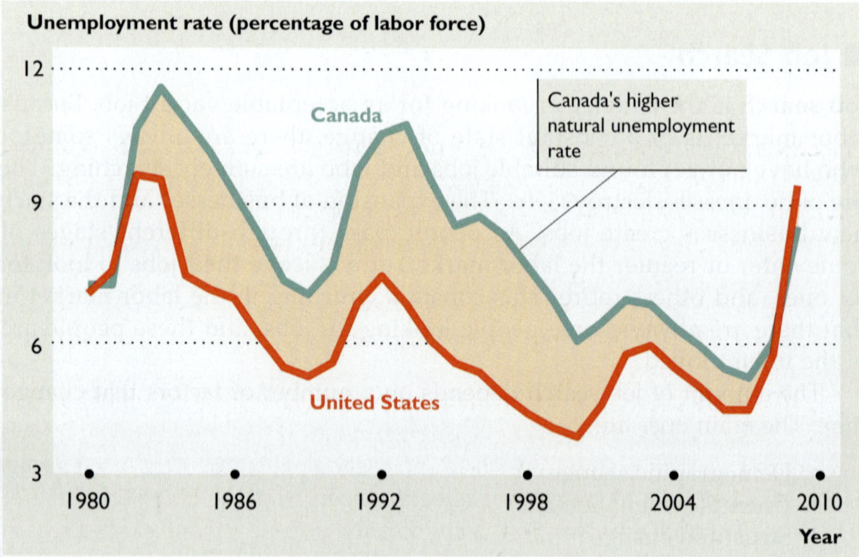

SOURCES OF DATA: Bureau of Labor Statistics and Statistics Canada.

Unemployment benefits appear to have a large effect on the natural unemployment rate. The gap narrowed after 2000 as cyclical unemployment rose less in Canada than in the United States during the last two recessions.

Structural Change

Technological change influences unemployment. Sometimes it brings a structural slump, a condition in which some industries and even regions contract while other industries and regions flourish. When these events occur, labor turnover is high, job search increases, and the natural unemployment rate rises.

At other times, technological change brings a structural boom. It creates new jobs that are a good match for the people who are losing their jobs. When these events occur, labor turnover might be high, but job search decreases because new jobs are found quickly, and the natural unemployment rate falls. The Internet economy of the 1990s is an example of a structural boom. Lots of new jobs were created in every major population center, and these jobs were a good match for the skills available, so the natural unemployment rate decreased.

■ Job Rationing

Job rationing
A situation that arises when the real wage rate is above the full-employment equilibrium level.

Job rationing occurs when the real wage rate is above the full-employment equilibrium level. You have learned that markets allocate scarce resources by adjusting the market price to bring buying plans and selling plans into balance. You can think of the market as *rationing* scarce resources. In the labor market, the real wage rate rations employment and therefore rations jobs. Changes in the real wage rate keep the number of people seeking work and the number of jobs available in balance. But the real wage rate is not the only possible instrument for rationing jobs.

In some industries, the real wage rate is set above the full-employment equilibrium level, which brings a surplus of labor. In these labor markets, jobs are rationed by some other means.

The real wage rate might be set above the full-employment equilibrium level for three reasons:

- Efficiency wage
- Minimum wage
- Union wage

Efficiency Wage

An **efficiency wage** is a real wage rate that is set above the full-employment equilibrium wage rate to induce a greater work effort. The idea is that if a firm pays only the going market average wage, employees have no incentive to work hard because they know that even if they are fired for slacking off, they can find a job with another firm at a similar wage rate. But if a firm pays *more* than the going market average wage, employees have an incentive to work hard because they know that if they are fired, they *cannot* expect to find a job with another firm at a similar wage rate.

Efficiency wage
A real wage rate that is set above the full-employment equilibrium wage rate to induce greater work effort.

Further, by paying an efficiency wage, a firm can attract the most productive workers. Also, its workers are less likely to quit their jobs, so the firm faces a lower rate of labor turnover and lower training costs. Finally, the firm's recruiting costs are lower because it always faces a steady stream of available new workers.

Paying an efficiency wage is costly, so only those firms that can't directly monitor the work effort of their employees use this device. For example, truck drivers and plant maintenance workers might receive efficiency wages. If enough firms pay an efficiency wage, the average real wage rate will exceed the full-employment equilibrium level.

The Minimum Wage

A **minimum wage law** is a government regulation that makes hiring labor for less than a specified wage illegal. If the minimum wage is set below the equilibrium wage, the minimum wage has no effect. The minimum wage law and market forces are not in conflict. But if a minimum wage is set above the equilibrium wage, the minimum wage is in conflict with market forces and unemployment arises.

Minimum wage law
A government regulation that makes hiring labor for less than a specified wage illegal.

The current federal minimum wage is $7.25 an hour, and the minimum wage has a major effect in the markets for low-skilled labor. Because skill grows with work experience, teenage labor is particularly affected by the minimum wage.

Union Wage

A **union wage** is a wage rate that results from collective bargaining between a labor union and a firm. Because a union represents a group of workers, it can usually achieve a wage rate that exceeds the level that would prevail in a competitive labor market.

Union wage
A wage rate that results from collective bargaining between a labor union and a firm.

For the United States, it is estimated that, on the average, union wage rates are 30 percent higher than nonunion wage rates. But this estimate probably overstates the true effects of labor unions on the wage rate. In some industries, union wages are higher than nonunion wages because union members do jobs that require greater skill than nonunion jobs. In these cases, even without a union, those workers would earn a higher wage.

One way to calculate the effects of unions is to examine the wages of union and nonunion workers who do nearly identical work. For workers with similar skill levels, the union-nonunion wage difference is between 10 and 25 percent. For example, pilots who are members of the Air Line Pilots Association earn about 25 percent more than nonunion pilots with the same level of skill.

Labor unions are much more influential in Europe than in the United States. In Europe, unions not only achieve wage rates above those of a competitive market but also have broad political influence on labor market conditions.

Job Rationing and Unemployment

Whether because of efficiency wages, a minimum wage law, or the actions of labor unions, if the real wage rate is above the full-employment equilibrium level, the natural unemployment rate increases. The above-equilibrium real wage rate decreases the quantity of labor demanded and increases the quantity of labor supplied.

Figure 8.5 illustrates job rationing and the frictional and structural unemployment it creates. The full-employment equilibrium real wage rate is $40 an hour, and the equilibrium quantity of labor is 200 billion hours a year. The existence of efficiency wages, the minimum wage, and union wages raises the economy's average real wage rate to $50 an hour. At this wage rate, the quantity of labor demanded decreases to 150 billion hours and the quantity of labor supplied increases to 250 billion hours. Firms ration jobs and choose the workers to hire on the basis of criteria such as education and previous job experience. The labor market is like a game of musical chairs in which a large number of chairs have been removed. So the quantity of labor supplied persistently exceeds the quantity demanded, and additional unemployment arises from job rationing.

FIGURE 8.5

Job Rationing Increases the Natural Unemployment Rate

myeconlab Animation

The full-employment equilibrium real wage rate is $40 an hour. Efficiency wages, the minimum wage, and union wages put the average real wage rate above the full-employment equilibrium level—at $50 an hour.

1. The quantity of labor demanded decreases to 150 billion hours.
2. The quantity of labor supplied increases to 250 billion hours.
3. A surplus of labor arises and increases the natural unemployment rate.

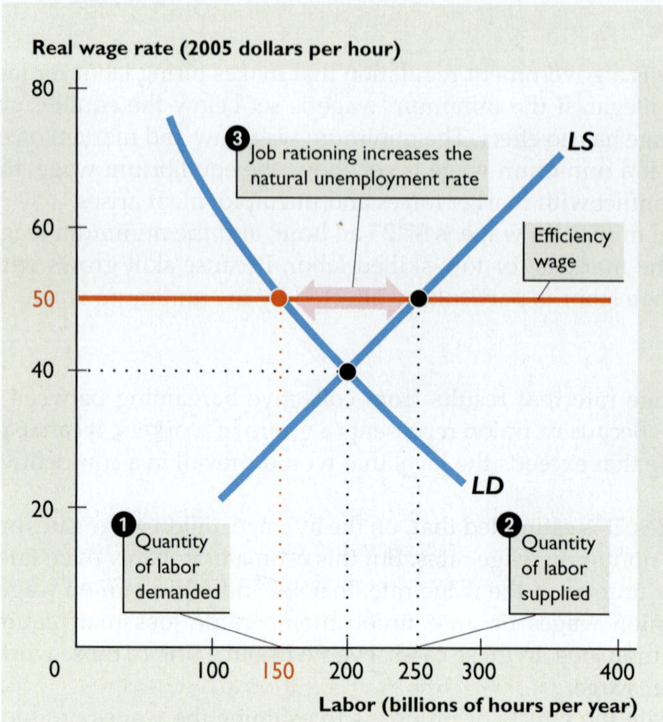

EYE on the U.S. ECONOMY

The Federal Minimum Wage

The Fair Labor Standards Act of 1938 set the federal minimum wage in the United States at 25¢ an hour. Over the years, the minimum wage has increased, and in 2009 it was $7.25 an hour. Although the minimum wage has increased, it hasn't kept up with the rising cost of living.

The figure shows the real minimum wage rate in 2005 dollars. You can see that during the late 1960s, the minimum wage in 2005 dollars was $7.50 an hour. It decreased during the 1970s and 1980s and has fluctuated around an average of about $6 an hour since the mid-1980s.

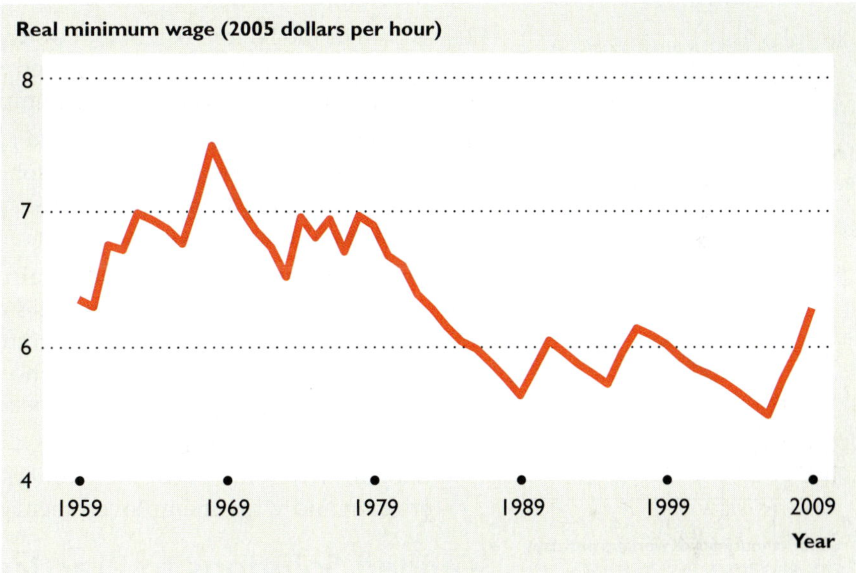

SOURCE OF DATA: Bureau of Labor Statistics.

EYE on YOUR LIFE

Natural Unemployment

You will encounter natural unemployment at many points in your life.

If you now have a job, you probably went through a spell of natural unemployment as you searched for it.

When you graduate and look for a full-time job, you will most likely spend some more time searching for the best match for your skills and location preferences.

In today's world of rapid technological change, most of us must retool and change our jobs at least once and for many of us, more than once.

You might know an older worker who has recently lost a job and is going through the agony of figuring out what to do next.

Although natural unemployment can be painful for people who experience it, from a social perspective, it is productive. It enables scarce labor resources to be *re*-allocated to their most valuable uses.

myeconlab

Work these problems in Study Plan 8.2 to get instant feedback.

CHECKPOINT 8.2

Explain what determines the natural unemployment rate.

Practice Problems

During the past 50 years, Singapore has seen huge changes: rapid population growth and the introduction of newer and newer technologies. Singapore has modest unemployment benefits, no minimum wage, and weak labor unions. Use this information to work Problems **1** and **2**.

1. Does Singapore's unemployment arise mainly from job search or job rationing?
2. Which of the factors listed above suggest that Singapore has a higher natural unemployment rate than the United States and which suggest that Singapore has a lower natural unemployment rate?
3. Figure 1 illustrates the labor market in an economy in which at full employment, 1,000 people a day job search. What is the full-employment equilibrium real wage rate and the quantity of labor employed? Calculate the natural unemployment rate.
4. **The minimum wage increases again**
   A minimum wage increase provides a silver lining for part-time workers, as employers choose to promote more from within the firm than from outside. Low-skilled and youth workers who are employed gain, but for unemployed teenage workers, job prospects look grim.
   Source: laborlawcenter.com
   Explain why some part-time workers, low-skilled workers, and youth workers gain and why unemployed teenagers find it hard to get jobs.

FIGURE 1

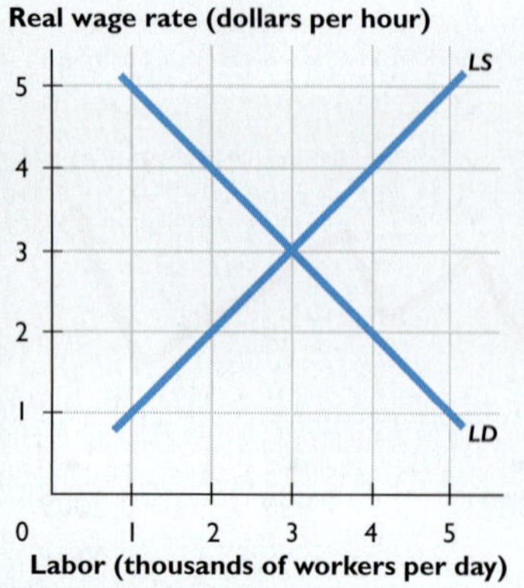

Guided Solutions to Practice Problems

1. Singapore's unemployment arises mainly from job search. Of the sources of job rationing (efficiency wages, minimum wages, and union wages) only efficiency wages applies.
2. The factors that point toward a higher natural unemployment rate in Singapore are rapid population growth and the introduction of new technologies, both of which increase the amount of job search.

   The factors that point toward a lower natural unemployment rate in Singapore than in the United States are modest unemployment benefits, which limit the amount of job search, and the absence of a minimum wage and weak labor unions, which limit the amount of job rationing.
3. At full employment, the equilibrium real wage rate and the quantity of labor employed are determined by the demand for labor and the supply of labor. At full employment, the real wage rate is \$3 an hour and 3,000 workers are employed. Unemployment is 1,000, so the labor force is 4,000, and the natural unemployment rate equals (1,000 ÷ 4,000) × 100, or 25 percent.
4. When the minimum wage rate is raised, firms retain those workers who produce at least as much output in an hour as the minimum wage rate. The job experience will help part-time and low-skilled employees retain their jobs, but teenagers with no experience will find it hard to get jobs.

CHAPTER SUMMARY

Key Points

1 Explain what determines potential GDP.

- Potential GDP is the quantity of real GDP that the full-employment quantity of labor produces.
- The production function describes the relationship between real GDP and the quantity of labor employed when all other influences on production remain the same. As the quantity of labor increases, real GDP increases.
- The quantity of labor demanded increases as the real wage rate falls, other things remaining the same.
- The quantity of labor supplied increases as the real wage rate rises, other things remaining the same.
- At full-employment equilibrium, the real wage rate makes the quantity of labor demanded equal the quantity of labor supplied.

2 Explain what determines the natural unemployment rate.

- The unemployment rate at full employment is the natural unemployment rate.
- Unemployment is always present because of job search and job rationing.
- Job search is influenced by demographic change, unemployment benefits, and structural change.
- Job rationing arises from an efficiency wage, the minimum wage, and a union wage.

Key Terms

Classical macroeconomics, 192
Demand for labor, 197
Diminishing returns, 196
Efficiency wage, 207
Job rationing, 206
Job search, 205
Keynesian macroeconomics, 192
Minimum wage law, 207
Monetarist macroeconomics, 193
Potential GDP, 195
Production function, 196
Quantity of labor demanded, 197
Quantity of labor supplied, 199
Supply of labor, 199
Union wage, 207

myeconlab

Work these problems in Chapter 8 Study Plan to get instant feedback.

CHAPTER CHECKPOINT

Study Plan Problems and Applications

Use the following list of events that occur one at a time in the United States to work Problems 1 to 4.

- Dell introduces a new supercomputer that everyone can afford.
- A major hurricane hits Florida.
- More high school graduates go to college.
- The CPI rises.
- An economic slump in the rest of the world decreases U.S. exports.

1. Sort the items into four groups: those that change the production function, those that change the demand for labor, those that change the supply of labor, and those that do not change the production function, the demand for labor, or the supply of labor. Say in which direction any changes occur.
2. Which of the events increase the equilibrium quantity of labor and which decrease it?
3. Which of the events raise the real wage rate and which lower it?
4. Which of the events increase potential GDP and which decrease it?

Use the information set out in Table 1 and Table 2 about the economy of Athabasca to work Problems 5 and 6.

TABLE 1 PRODUCTION FUNCTION

Labor hours (millions)	Real GDP (millions of 2005 dollars)
0	0
1	10
2	19
3	27
4	34
5	40

TABLE 2 LABOR MARKET

Real wage rate (dollars per hour)	Quantity of labor demanded (millions of hours per year)	Quantity of labor supplied (millions of hours per year)
10	1	5
9	2	4
8	3	3
7	4	2
6	5	1

5. Calculate the quantity of labor employed, the real wage rate, and potential GDP.
6. If the labor force participation increases, explain how employment, the real wage rate, and potential GDP change.
7. Two island economies, Cocoa Island and Plantation Island, are identical in every respect except one. A survey tells us that at full employment, people on Cocoa Island spend 1,000 hours a day on job search, while the people on Plantation Island spend 2,000 hours a day on job search. Which economy has the greater level of potential GDP? Which has the higher real wage rate? And which has the higher natural unemployment rate?
8. If the United States cracks down on illegal immigrants and returns millions of workers to their home countries, explain what happens to U.S. employment, U.S. real wage rate, and U.S. potential GDP.

   In the countries to which the immigrants return, explain what happens to employment, the real wage rate, and potential GDP.
9. **Job openings and labor turnover: July 2009**

   Job openings were 2.4 million, down from 3.9 million in July 2008; hires were 4.1 million, down from 4.7 million in July 2008; and job losers were 4.3 million, down from 4.8 million in July 2008.

   Bureau of Labor Statistics, September 10, 2009

   Compare U.S. labor turnover (hires minus job losers) in July 2009 with that in July 2008. Is the U.S. labor market moving toward full employment? Is real GDP increasing or decreasing? Is U.S. potential GDP increasing or decreasing?

Instructor Assignable Problems and Applications

Your instructor can assign these problems as homework, a quiz, or a test in **MyEconLab**.

Use the following information to work Problems 1 and 2.

In Korea, real GDP per hour of labor is $22, the real wage rate is $15 per hour, and people work an average of 46 hours per week.

1. Draw a graph of the demand for and supply of labor in Korea and the United States. Mark a point at the equilibrium quantity of labor per person per week and the real wage rate in each economy. Explain the difference in the two labor markets.
2. Draw a graph of the production functions in Korea and the United States. Mark a point on each production function that shows potential GDP per hour of work in each economy. Explain the difference in the two production functions.

Use the following list of events that occur one at a time in the United States to work Problems 3 to 6.

- An oil embargo in the Middle East cuts supplies of oil to the United States.
- The New York Yankees win the World Series.
- U.S. labor unions negotiate wage hikes that affect all workers.
- A huge scientific breakthrough doubles the output that an additional hour of U.S. labor can produce.
- Migration to the United States increases the working-age population.

3. Sort the items into four groups: those that change the production function, those that change the demand for labor, those that change the supply of labor, and those that do not change the production function, the demand for labor, or the supply of labor. Say in which direction each change occurs.
4. Which of the events increase the equilibrium quantity of labor and which decrease the equilibrium quantity of labor?
5. Which of the events raise the real wage rate and which of the events lower the real wage rate?
6. Which of the events increase potential GDP and which decrease potential GDP?

Use the following information to work Problems 7 and 8.

Obama vows to speed hurricane Katrina recovery effort

On the fourth anniversary of Hurricane Katrina, President Obama pledged to speed up the recovery effort along the Gulf Coast. Over a thousand people lost their lives, more than a million people were displaced, and whole neighborhoods were left in ruins.

Source: *The New York Times*, September 10, 2009

7. Explain the effect of hurricane Katrina on employment along the Gulf Coast. Did the state of Louisiana move along its production function or did its production function shift? How did Louisiana's potential GDP change?
8. Explain how a speedup of the recovery effort will affect U.S. employment and potential GDP.

TABLE 1 PRODUCTION FUNCTION

Labor hours (per day)	Real GDP (2005 dollars per year)
0	0
10	100
20	180
30	240
40	280

TABLE 2 LABOR MARKET

Real wage rate (dollars per hour)	Quantity of labor demanded	Quantity of labor supplied
	(hours per day)	
1.00	10	50
0.80	20	40
0.60	30	30
0.40	40	20

Use the information set out in Table 1 and Table 2 about the economy of Nautica to work Problems 9 and 10.

9. What is the quantity of labor employed, potential GDP, the real wage rate, and total labor income?
10. Suppose that the government introduces a minimum wage of $0.80 an hour. What is the real wage rate, the quantity of labor employed, potential GDP, and unemployment? Does the unemployment arise from job search or job rationing? Is the unemployment cyclical? Explain.
11. If the minimum wage were abolished, what do you predict would happen to the equilibrium real wage rate, the full-employment quantity of labor, and potential GDP?
12. How do you think the natural unemployment rate and potential GDP would change if the United States adopted the level of unemployment benefits that Canada has? Refer to *Eye on the Global Economy* on p. 206 for information on the comparison between Canada and the United States.
13. The figure in *Eye on U.S. Potential GDP* on p. 202 compares the United States and Europe. Speculate by looking 40 years ahead. Do you think the comparison of the United States and Europe in the 2050s will be similar or different in some significant ways? Provide reasons for your speculation.

Use the following information to work Problems 14 and 15.

Tsunami 2004 social cost yet to come

Relief experts estimated it could take up to a decade for some places to fully recover, and reconstruction will cost about $9 billion. The Indonesian government estimated total damage from the tsunami at $4.5 billion to $5 billion. The people hardest-hit were mainly fishermen, farmers, and people running small businesses.

Source: CNN, December 19, 2005

14. Explain the effect of the tsunami on employment in Indonesia in 2005. At the time of the Tsunami did Indonesia move along its production function or did its production function shift? How did Indonesia's potential GDP change?
15. According to the CNN news article, people hardest-hit by the tsunami were mainly fishermen, farmers, and people running small businesses. Explain how this information changes Indonesia's employment and potential GDP.

Why are some nations rich and others poor?

Why are incomes rising rapidly in China, moderately in the United States, and slowly or not at all in some African countries?

9

Economic Growth

CHAPTER CHECKLIST

When you have completed your study of this chapter, you will be able to

1 Define and calculate the economic growth rate, and explain the implications of sustained growth.

2 Identify the main sources of economic growth.

3 Review the theories of economic growth that explain why growth rates vary over time and across countries.

4 Describe policies that might speed economic growth.

9.1 THE BASICS OF ECONOMIC GROWTH

Economic growth is a sustained expansion of production possibilities. Maintained over decades, rapid economic growth can transform a poor nation into a rich one. Such has been the experience of Hong Kong, South Korea, Taiwan, and some other Asian economies. Slow economic growth or the absence of growth can condemn a nation to devastating poverty. Such has been the fate of Sierra Leone, Somalia, Zambia, and much of the rest of Africa.

Economic growth is different from the rise in incomes that occurs during the recovery from a recession. Economic growth is a sustained trend, not a temporary cyclical expansion.

Calculating Growth Rates

Economic growth rate
The annual percentage change of real GDP.

We express the **economic growth rate** as the annual percentage change of real GDP. To calculate this growth rate, we use the formula:

$$\text{Growth rate of real GDP} = \frac{\begin{matrix}\text{Real GDP} \\ \text{in current year}\end{matrix} - \begin{matrix}\text{Real GDP} \\ \text{in previous year}\end{matrix}}{\text{Real GDP in previous year}} \times 100.$$

For example, if real GDP in the current year is \$8.4 trillion and if real GDP in the previous year was \$8.0 trillion, then

$$\text{Growth rate of real GDP} = \frac{\$8.4 \text{ trillion} - \$8.0 \text{ trillion}}{\$8.0 \text{ trillion}} \times 100 = 5 \text{ percent}.$$

The growth rate of real GDP tells us how rapidly the total economy is expanding. This measure is useful for telling us about potential changes in the balance of economic power among nations, but it does not tell us about changes in the standard of living.

Real GDP per person
Real GDP divided by the population.

The standard of living depends on **real GDP per person** (also called *per capita real GDP*), which is real GDP divided by the population. So the contribution of real GDP growth to the change in the *standard of living* depends on the growth rate of real GDP per person. We use the above formula to calculate this growth rate, replacing real GDP with real GDP per person.

Suppose, for example, that in the current year, when real GDP is \$8.4 trillion, the population is 202 million. Then real GDP per person in the current year is \$8.4 trillion divided by 202 million, which equals \$41,584. And suppose that in the previous year, when real GDP was \$8.0 trillion, the population was 200 million. Then real GDP per person in that year was \$8.0 trillion divided by 200 million, which equals \$40,000.

Use these two values of real GDP per person with the growth formula to calculate the growth rate of real GDP per person. That is,

$$\text{Growth rate of real GDP per person} = \frac{\$41{,}584 - \$40{,}000}{\$40{,}000} \times 100 = 4 \text{ percent}.$$

We can also calculate the growth rate of real GDP per person by using the formula:

$$\text{Growth rate of real GDP per person} = \text{Growth rate of real GDP} - \text{Growth rate of population.}$$

In the example you've just worked through, the growth rate of real GDP is 5 percent. The population changes from 200 million to 202 million, so

$$\text{Growth rate of population} = \frac{202 \text{ million} - 200 \text{ million}}{200 \text{ million}} \times 100 = 1 \text{ percent}$$

and

$$\text{Growth rate of real GDP per person} = 5 \text{ percent} - 1 \text{ percent} = 4 \text{ percent.}$$

This formula makes it clear that real GDP per person grows only if real GDP grows faster than the population grows. If the growth rate of the population exceeds the growth of real GDP, then real GDP per person falls.

The Magic of Sustained Growth

Sustained growth of real GDP per person can transform a poor society into a wealthy one. The reason is that economic growth is like compound interest. Suppose that you put $100 in the bank and earn 5 percent a year interest on it. After one year, you have $105. If you leave that money in the bank for another year, you earn 5 percent interest on the original $100 and on the $5 interest that you earned last year. You are now earning interest on interest! The next year, things get even better. Then you earn 5 percent on the original $100 and on the interest earned in the first year and the second year. Your money in the bank is *growing* at a rate of 5 percent a year. Before too many years have passed, you'll have $200 in the bank. But after *how many* years?

The answer is provided by a powerful and general formula known as the **Rule of 70,** which states that the number of years it takes for the level of any variable to double is approximately 70 divided by the annual percentage growth rate of the variable. Using the Rule of 70, you can now calculate how many years it takes your $100 to become $200. It is 70 divided by 5, which is 14 years.

Rule of 70
The number of years it takes for the level of any variable to double is approximately 70 divided by the annual percentage growth rate of the variable.

The Rule of 70 applies to any variable, so it applies to real GDP per person. Table 9.1 shows the doubling time for a selection of other growth rates. You can see that real GDP per person doubles in 70 years (70 divided by 1)—an average human life span—if the growth rate is 1 percent a year. It doubles in 35 years if the growth rate is 2 percent a year and in just 10 years if the growth rate is 7 percent a year.

TABLE 9.1 GROWTH RATES

Growth rate (percent per year)	Years for level to double
1	70
2	35
3	23
4	18
5	14
6	12
7	10
8	9
9	8
10	7

We can use the Rule of 70 to answer other questions about economic growth. For example, in 2000, U.S. real GDP per person was approximately 8 times that of China. China's recent growth rate of real GDP per person was 7 percent a year. If this growth rate were maintained, how long would it take China's real GDP per person to reach that of the United States in 2000? The answer, provided by the Rule of 70, is 30 years. China's real GDP per person doubles in 10 (70 divided by 7) years. It doubles again to 4 times its current level in another 10 years, and it doubles yet again to 8 times its current level in another 10 years. So after 30 years of growth at 7 percent a year, China's real GDP per person is 8 times its current level and equals that of the United States in 2000.

EYE on the PAST

How Fast Has Real GDP per Person Grown?

Professor Michael Kremer of Harvard University and Professor J. Bradford DeLong of the University of California, Berkeley, have constructed an extraordinary picture of real GDP in the global economy going back one million years. According to their numbers, human societies lived for a million years with no economic growth.

The top figure shows the numbers using the value of the dollar in 2005 as the measuring rod. Real GDP per person averaged $150 a year from 1,000,000 BC until 1620! It rose to $190 when Aristotle and Plato were teaching in Athens, around 500 BC, but slipped back over the next thousand years to $140 as the Roman Empire collapsed around 400 AD. When the Black Death gripped Europe in the 1340s, incomes fell to a 1 million-year low and even when the Pilgrim Fathers began to arrive in America in the 1620s, incomes were still the same as those of Ancient Greece!

Then, beginning around 1750, first in England and then in Europe and the United States, an astonishing change known as the Industrial Revolution occurred. Real GDP per person began to increase, apparently without limit. By 1850, real GDP per person was twice its 1650 level. By 1950, it was more than five times its 1850 level, and by 2000, it was four times its 1950 level.

The lower figure gives you a close-up view of U.S. real GDP per person over the past 100 years. In 2009, real GDP per person was almost eight times its level in 1909. It has grown by 2 percent a year, but the growth rate has been uneven: Almost no growth in the 1930s and the fastest growth in the 1940s. Measured decade by decade, growth has slowed since the 1960s.

The growth rate between 1999 and 2009 is lower than that in any decade except the 1930s. But the reason is not that potential GDP growth slowed. Rather, it is because 2009 was a year of deep recession. If we measure the growth rate of potential GDP, the 2000s had a higher growth rate than the 1990s.

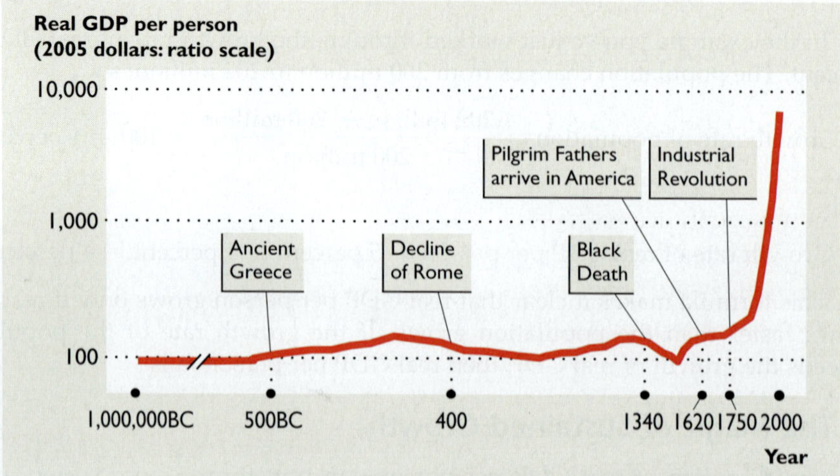

SOURCE OF DATA: J. Bradford DeLong, *"Estimating World GDP, One Million B.C.—Present."*

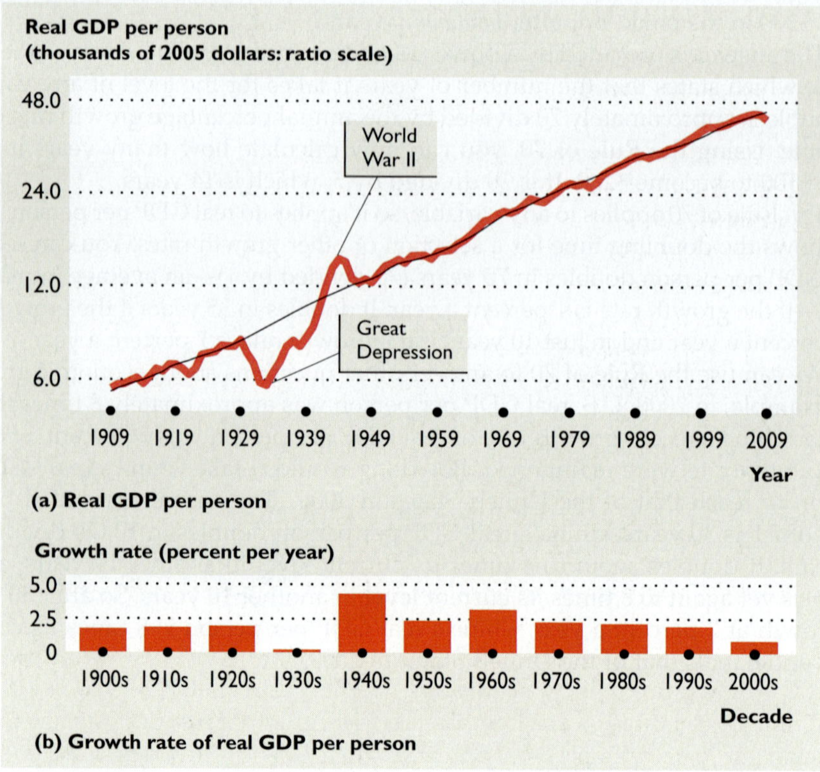

SOURCES OF DATA: Bureau of Economic Analysis and the Bureau of Labor Statistics.

CHECKPOINT 9.1

Define and calculate the economic growth rate, and explain the implications of sustained growth.

myeconlab

Work these problems in Study Plan 9.1 to get instant feedback.

Practice Problems

1. Mexico's real GDP was 1,448 billion pesos in 1998 and 1,501 billion pesos in 1999. Mexico's population growth rate in 1999 was 1.8 percent. Calculate Mexico's economic growth rate in 1999 and the growth rate of real GDP per person in Mexico in 1999.
2. Calculate the approximate number of years it will take for real GDP per person to double if an economy maintains an economic growth rate of 12 percent a year and a population growth rate of 2 percent a year.
3. Calculate the change in the number of years it will take for real GDP per person in India to double if real GDP per person increases from 8 percent a year to 10 percent a year.
4. **China's economy picks up speed**
   China's trend growth rate of real GDP per person was 2.2 percent per year before 1980 and 8.7 percent per year after 1980. In the 12 months to August 2009, China's output increased by 11.3 percent.
   Source: *World Economic Outlook* and FT.com, September 14, 2009

   Distinguish between a rise in China's economic growth rate and a temporary cyclical expansion. How long, at the current growth rate, will it take for China to double its real GDP per person?

Guided Solutions to Practice Problems

1. Mexico's economic growth rate in 1999 was 3.7 percent. The economic growth rate equals the percentage change in real GDP: [(Real GDP in 1999 − Real GDP in 1998) ÷ Real GDP in 1998] × 100. When we substitute the numbers, Mexico's economic growth rate equals [(1,501 billion − 1,448 billion) ÷ 1,448 billion] × 100, which is 3.7 percent. The growth rate of real GDP per person was 1.9 percent. Growth rate of real GDP per person equals the growth rate of real GDP minus the population growth rate, which equals 3.7 percent minus 1.8 percent, or 1.9 percent.
2. It will take 7 years for real GDP per person to double. The growth rate of real GDP per person equals the economic growth rate minus the population growth rate. Real GDP per person grows at 12 percent minus 2 percent, which is 10 percent a year. The Rule of 70 tells us that the level of a variable that grows at 10 percent a year will double in 70 ÷ 10 years, or 7 years, if the growth rates are maintained.
3. Two years. The Rule of 70 tells us that a variable that grows at 8 percent a year will double in 70 ÷ 8 years, which is approximately 9 years. By increasing its growth rate to 10 percent a year, the variable will double in 7 years.
4. Because the pace of growth was maintained over decades, the increase from 2.2 percent a year before 1980 to 8.7 percent a year after 1980 is a rise in China's economic growth rate. The 11.3 percent increase in 2009 is a temporary cyclical expansion. At the current trend growth rate of 8.7 percent a year, China's real GDP per person will double in 8 years (70 ÷ 8.7).

9.2 THE SOURCES OF ECONOMIC GROWTH

Real GDP grows when the quantities of the factors of production grow or when persistent advances in technology make them increasingly productive. To understand what determines the growth rate of real GDP, we must understand what determines the growth rates of the factors of production and the rate of increase in their productivity. You're going to see how saving and investment determine the growth rate of physical capital and how the growth of physical capital and human capital and advances in technology interact to determine the economic growth rate.

We are interested in real GDP growth because it contributes to improvements in our standard of living. But our standard of living improves only if we produce more goods and services with each hour of labor. So our main concern is to understand the forces that make our labor more productive. For this reason, we begin by dividing all the influences on real GDP growth into those that increase

- Quantity of labor
- Labor productivity

■ Quantity of Labor

The quantity of labor is the total number of labor hours available and equals the labor force multiplied by average hours per worker. Average hours worked have *decreased* and average leisure hours have increased. But the labor force has grown at a fast enough pace to more than offset the decrease in average work hours and has brought a sustained increase in the quantity of labor.

The labor force depends on the population and the *labor force participation rate.* You saw in Chapter 6 (pp. 150–151) that the participation rate has increased over the past few decades. But the labor force participation rate has an upper limit, and most of the growth in the quantity of labor comes from population growth. Population growth is the *only* source of growth in the quantity of labor that can be sustained over long periods.

Population growth brings economic growth, but it does not bring growth in real GDP per person unless labor becomes more productive.

■ Labor Productivity

Labor productivity
The quantity of real GDP produced by one hour of labor.

The quantity of real GDP produced by one hour of labor is called **labor productivity.** It is calculated by using the formula:

$$\text{Labor productivity} = \frac{\text{Real GDP}}{\text{Aggregate hours}}.$$

For example, if real GDP is \$8,000 billion and if aggregate hours are 200 billion, then we can calculate labor productivity as

$$\text{Labor productivity} = \frac{\$8{,}000 \text{ billion}}{200 \text{ billion hours}} = \$40 \text{ per hour}.$$

You can turn this formula around and see that

$$\text{Real GDP} = \text{Aggregate hours} \times \text{Labor productivity}.$$

When labor productivity grows, real GDP per person grows. So the growth in labor productivity is the basis of the rising standard of living. The growth of labor productivity depends on three things:

- Saving and investment in physical capital
- Expansion of human capital
- Discovery of new technologies

These three sources of growth in labor productivity interact and are the primary sources of the extraordinary growth in productivity during the past 200 years. Let's look at each in turn.

Saving and Investment in Physical Capital

Saving and investment in physical capital increase the amount of capital per worker and increase labor productivity. Labor productivity took a dramatic upturn when the amount of capital per worker increased during the Industrial Revolution. Production processes that use hand tools can create beautiful objects, but production methods that use large amounts of capital per worker, such as auto plant assembly lines, enable workers to be much more productive. The accumulation of capital on farms and building sites, in textile factories, iron foundries and steel mills, coal mines, chemical plants, and auto plants, and at banks and insurance companies has added incredibly to the productivity of our labor.

A strong and experienced farm worker of 1830, using a scythe, could harvest 3 acres of wheat a day. A farm worker of 1831, using a mechanical reaper, could harvest 15 acres a day. And a farm worker of today, using a combine harvester, can harvest and thresh 100 acres a day.

The next time you see a movie set in the old West, look carefully at how little capital there is. Try to imagine how productive you would be in such circumstances compared with your productivity today.

Expansion of Human Capital

Human capital—the accumulated skill and knowledge of people—comes from two sources:

1. Education and training
2. Job experience

A hundred years ago, most people attended school for around eight years. A hundred years before that, most people had no formal education at all. Today, 90 percent of Americans complete high school and more than 60 percent go to college or university. Our ability to read, write, and communicate effectively contributes enormously to our productivity.

While formal education is productive, school is not the only place where people acquire human capital. We also learn from on-the-job experience—from *learning by doing.* One carefully studied example illustrates the importance of learning by doing. Between 1941 and 1944 (during World War II), U.S. shipyards produced 2,500 Liberty Ships—cargo ships built to a standardized design. In 1941, it took 1.2 million person-hours to build a ship. By 1942, it took 600,000, and by 1943, it took only 500,000. Not much change occurred in the physical capital employed during these years, but an enormous amount of human capital was accumulated. Thousands of workers and managers learned from experience and more than doubled their productivity in two years.

Production using 1950s technology.

Production using 2000s technology.

The expansion of human capital is the most fundamental source of economic growth because it directly increases labor productivity and is the source of the discovery of new technologies.

Discovery of New Technologies

The growth of physical capital and the expansion of human capital have made large contributions to economic growth, but the discovery and application of new technologies have made an even greater contribution.

The development of writing, one of the most basic human skills, was the source of some of the earliest productivity gains. The ability to keep written records made it possible to reap ever-larger gains from specialization and trade. Imagine how hard it would be to do any kind of business if all the accounts, invoices, and agreements existed only in people's memories.

Later, the development of mathematics laid the foundation for the eventual extension of knowledge in physics, chemistry, and biology. This base of scientific knowledge was the foundation for the technological advances of the Industrial Revolution 200 years ago and of today's Information Revolution.

Since the Industrial Revolution, technological change has become a part of everyday life. Firms routinely conduct research to develop technologies that are more productive, and partnerships between business and the universities are commonplace in fields such as biotechnology and electronics.

To reap the benefits of technological change, capital must increase. Some of the most powerful and far-reaching technologies are embodied in human capital—for example, language, writing, and mathematics. But most technologies are embodied in physical capital. For example, to reap the benefits of the internal combustion engine, millions of horse-drawn carriages had to be replaced by automobiles and trucks; more recently, to reap the benefits of computerized word processing, millions of typewriters had to be replaced by PCs and printers.

■ Sources of Growth: A Summary

Figure 9.1 summarizes the sources of economic growth. Your next task is to learn how these sources combine and how we identify the separate contributions of capital growth and the other influences on labor productivity.

FIGURE 9.1

The Sources of Economic Growth

myeconlab Animation

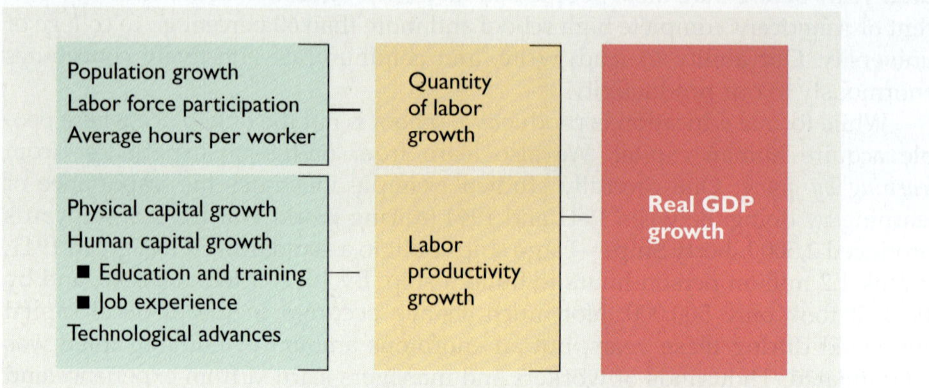

Real GDP depends on the quantity of labor and labor productivity. The quantity of labor depends on the population, labor force participation rate, and average hours per worker. Labor productivity depends on the amount of physical capital and human capital and the state of technology. Growth in quantity of labor and growth in labor productivity bring real GDP growth.

EYE on the U.S. ECONOMY

U.S. Labor Productivity Growth Since 1960

The top figure shows labor productivity growth (red line) and its changing trends (black line). Rapid growth during the 1960s was followed by slower growth after 1969 and even slower growth after 1974. It is this productivity slowdown that brought the enormous Lucas wedge described in Chapter 8, p. 194.

Why does labor productivity growth fluctuate? The bottom figure provides a summary of the answer. Using a method developed by MIT economist Robert Solow, we've separated the contribution of capital accumulation from those of human capital growth and technological change.

You can see that the 1960s were years of rapid human capital growth and technological change. Spillover effects from World War II, plastics, and the transistor were some of the key sources of this rapid growth.

The contribution of human capital growth and technological change slowed during the 1970s for several reasons.

First, oil price hikes in 1973–1974 and 1979–1980 diverted technological change toward saving energy rather than increasing labor productivity. (For example, airplanes became more fuel efficient, but they didn't operate with smaller crews.)

Second, taxes and government regulation increased during the late 1960s and 1970s, so incentives were weakened.

Third, rapid inflation distorted saving and investment decisions and shortened the horizon over which firms made their borrowing and lending plans.

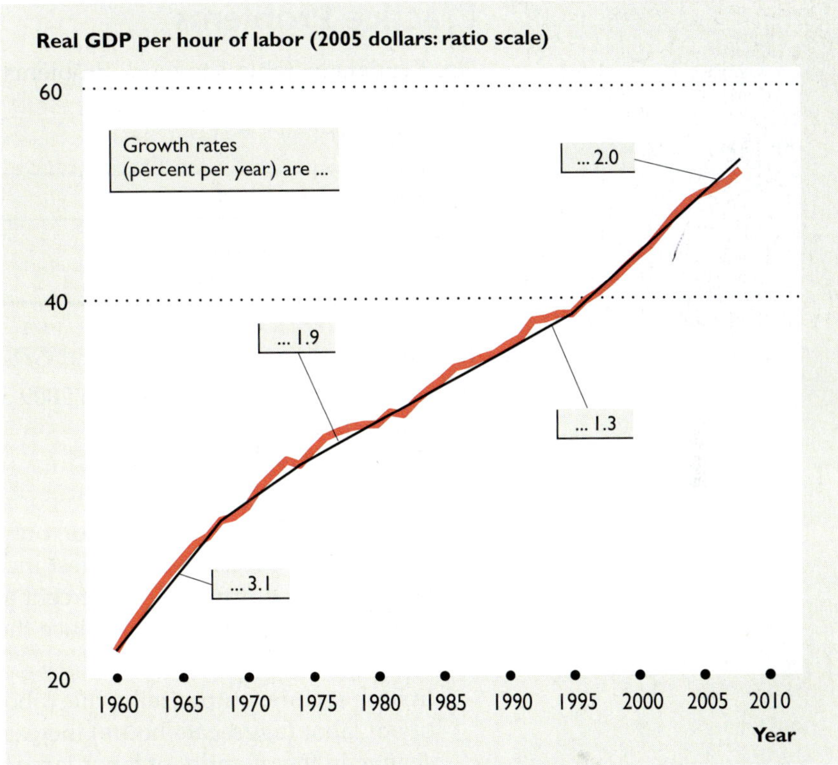

SOURCES OF DATA: Bureau of Economic Analysis and the Bureau of Labor Statistics.

The contribution of human capital growth and technological change remained low until the 1990s, when computer and information technology kicked in to bring faster labor productivity growth again. But the technological advances of the 1990s and 2000s did not bring labor productivity gains to match those that occurred during the 1960s.

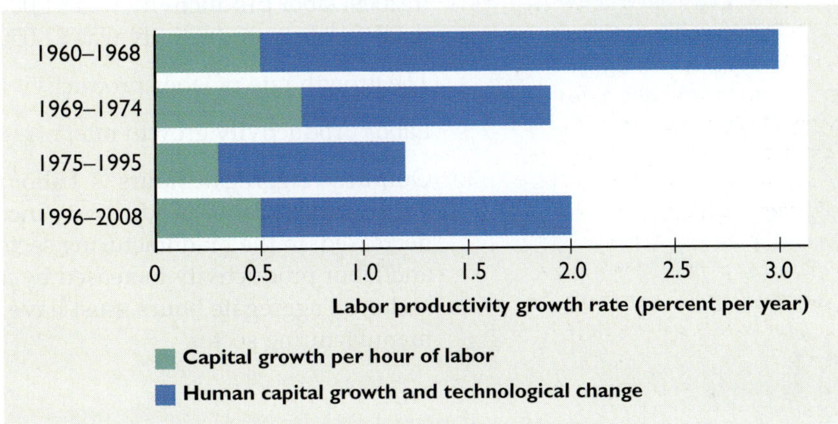

SOURCES OF DATA: Bureau of Economic Analysis and the Bureau of Labor Statistics.

myeconlab

Work these problems in Study Plan 9.2 to get instant feedback.

CHECKPOINT 9.2

Identify the main sources of economic growth.

Practice Problems

Use the data in Table 1 to work Problems **1** and **2**.

TABLE 1

Item	2009	2010
Aggregate labor hours (billions)	25.0	25.6
Real GDP (billions of 2005 dollars)	1,000	1,050

1. Calculate the growth rate of real GDP in 2010.
2. Calculate labor productivity in 2009 and 2010, and the growth rate of labor productivity in 2010.
3. **Labor productivity on the rise**
   The Bureau of Labor Statistics reported the following data for the year to June 2009: In the nonfarm sector, output fell 5.5 percent as labor productivity increased 1.9 percent—the largest increase since 2003—but in the manufacturing sector, output fell 9.8 percent as labor productivity increased by 4.9 percent—the largest increase since the first quarter of 2005.

   Source: bls.gov/news.release

   In both sectors, output fell while labor productivity increased. Did the quantity of labor (aggregate hours) increase or decrease? In which sector was the change in the quantity of labor larger?

Guided Solutions to Practice Problems

1. The growth rate of real GDP in 2010 was 5 percent.
   Growth rate = ($1,050 − $1,000) ÷ $1,000) × 100 = 5 percent.
2. Labor productivity is $40.00 an hour in 2009 and $41.05 an hour in 2010.

   Labor productivity equals real GDP divided by total labor hours.
   In 2009, labor productivity was $1,000 ÷ 25 = $40.00 an hour of labor.
   In 2010, labor productivity was $1,050 ÷ 25.6 = $41.05 an hour of labor.

   The growth rate of labor productivity in 2010 was 3.75 percent.

   Labor productivity growth rate = (41.05 − 40.00) ÷ 40.00 × 100 = 3.75 percent.
3. Output = Aggregate hours × Labor productivity. In each sector, output decreased and labor productivity increased, so aggregate hours must have decreased. In the manufacturing sector, output fell by a larger percentage and labor productivity increased by a larger percentage than in the nonfarm sector, so aggregate hours must have fallen by a larger percentage in the manufacturing sector.

9.3 THEORIES OF ECONOMIC GROWTH

You've seen that real GDP grows when the quantity of labor grows and when labor productivity grows. You've also seen that labor productivity grows when saving and investment increase physical capital, when education and on-the-job training expand human capital, and when research leads to the discovery of new technologies.

But what is cause and what is effect? Do growth of the quantity of labor, saving and investment, the expansion of human capital, and the discovery of new technologies *cause* economic growth? Or does just one of these factors cause real GDP to grow, the others being side effects of real GDP growth? We're now going to study the interactions among the sources of economic growth by reviewing the theories of growth.

Economists have been trying to understand why and how poor countries become rich and rich countries become richer since the time of Adam Smith in the eighteenth century. Three main theories that have been proposed are

- Classical growth theory
- Neoclassical growth theory
- New growth theory

Classical Growth Theory

Classical growth theory predicts that the clash between an exploding population and limited resources will eventually bring economic growth to an end. According to classical growth theory, labor productivity growth is temporary. When labor productivity rises and lifts real GDP per person above the subsistence level, which is the minimum real income needed to maintain life, a population explosion occurs. Eventually, the population grows so large that labor productivity falls and returns real GDP per person back to the subsistence level.

Classical growth theory
The theory that the clash between an exploding population and limited resources will eventually bring economic growth to an end.

Adam Smith, Thomas Robert Malthus, and David Ricardo, the leading economists of the late eighteenth and early nineteenth centuries, proposed this theory, but the view is most closely associated with Malthus and is sometimes called the **Malthusian theory.** It is also sometimes called the Doomsday theory.

Malthusian theory
Another name for classical growth theory—named for Thomas Robert Malthus.

Many people today are Malthusians. They say that if today's global population of 6.7 billion explodes to 11 billion by 2200, we will run out of resources and return to a primitive standard of living. We must act, say the Malthusians, to contain the population growth. This dismal implication led to economics being called the dismal science.

Illustrating the Classical Growth Theory

Figure 9.2 illustrates the classical growth theory using the model of the full-employment economy that you met in Chapter 8 (pp. 200–201). Part (a) shows the labor market, and part (b) shows the production function.

In part (a), the current wage is \$35 an hour, at the intersection of the demand for labor curve, *LD*, and the supply of labor curve, LS_0, and 200 billion hours of labor are employed. In part (b), the production function, *PF*, shows that with 200 billion hours of labor employed, real GDP is \$10 trillion.

The subsistence real wage rate is \$25 an hour. Because the real wage rate exceeds the subsistence wage rate, the population increases. The increase in the

FIGURE 9.2

The Effects of an Increase in Population

myeconlab Animation

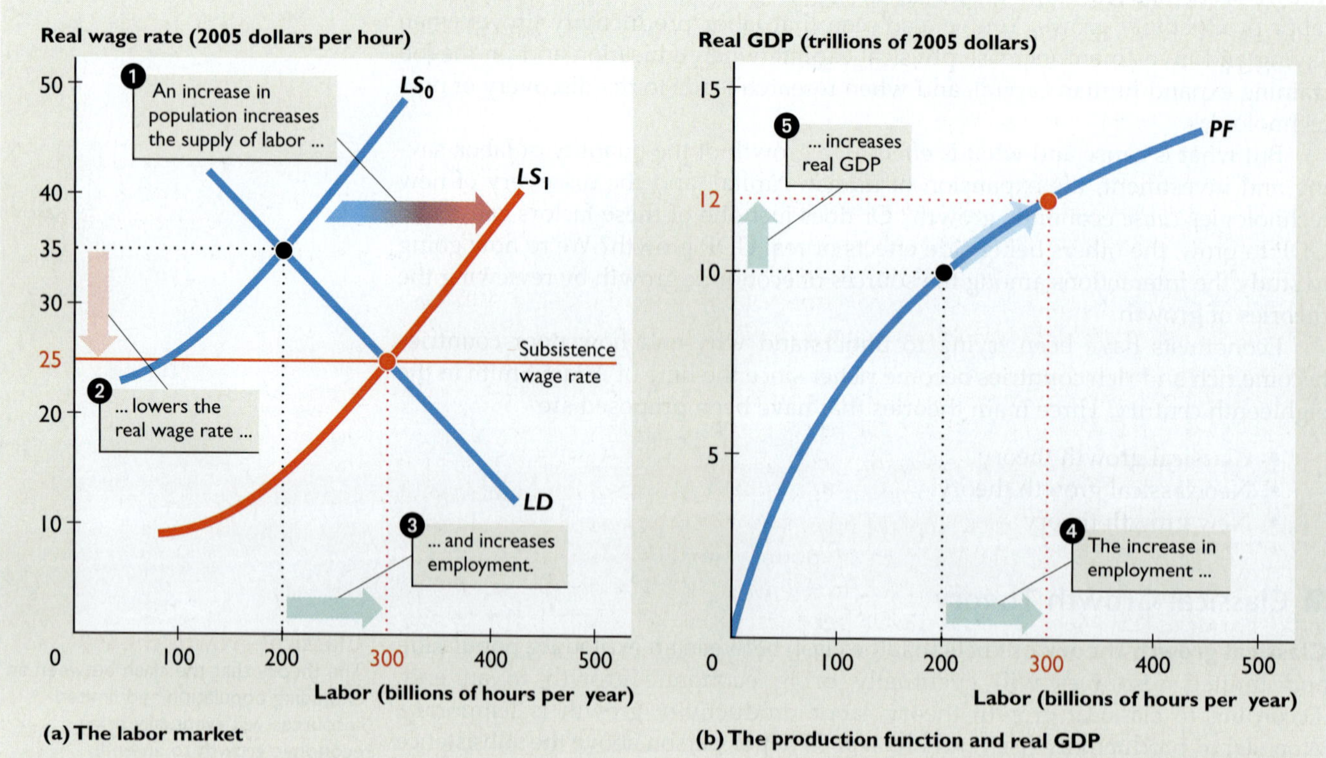

The subsistence real wage rate is \$25 an hour. Initially, with demand for labor curve *LD*, and supply of labor curve LS_0, the equilibrium real wage rate is \$35 an hour and is above the subsistence wage rate.

❶ Because the real wage rate is above its subsistence level, the population increases and the labor supply curve shifts rightward. The population and the labor supply keep increasing until the real wage rate has fallen to the subsistence real wage rate.

❷ When the supply of labor has increased to LS_1, the real wage rate has fallen to the subsistence level. ❸ Labor hours have increased and ❹ the increased labor hours bring ❺ an increase in real GDP.

population increases the supply of labor and shifts the labor supply curve rightward. The population and labor supply keep increasing as long as the real wage rate exceeds the subsistence level. So the labor supply curve keeps shifting rightward until it reaches LS_1 and the real wage rate has fallen to \$25 an hour.

In the new equilibrium, the quantity of labor employed is 300 billion hours a year and real GDP is \$12 trillion.

You can see that the increase in population increases employment and real GDP and lowers the real wage rate. The increase in population also decreases labor productivity.

You can calculate labor productivity by dividing real GDP by total labor hours. Initially, with real GDP at \$10 trillion and labor hours at 200 billion, labor productivity was \$50. With the increase in population, real GDP is \$12 trillion and labor hours are 300 billion, so labor productivity is \$40.

Diminishing returns—the tendency for each additional hour of labor employed to produce a successively smaller additional amount of output—is the source of the decrease in labor productivity (see Chapter 8, p. 196).

So if for some reason the real wage rate exceeds the subsistence real wage rate, according to the classical theory, population growth brings a fall in the real wage rate and a fall in labor productivity (and real GDP per person).

Neoclassical Growth Theory

Neoclassical growth theory (developed by Robert Solow of MIT during the 1950s) predicts that real GDP per person will increase as long as technology keeps advancing. Real GDP will grow at a rate equal to the population growth rate plus the labor productivity growth rate induced by technological change and the expansion of human capital. Neoclassical growth theory asserts that population growth and the pace of technological change determine, but are not themselves influenced by, the growth rate of real GDP.

Neoclassical growth theory
The theory that real GDP per person will increase as long as technology keeps advancing.

To understand neoclassical growth theory, let's go back to the mid-1950s when Robert Solow put forth his idea. Real GDP per person is growing, but slowly. Then the transistor revolutionizes an emerging electronics industry. New plastics revolutionize the manufacture of household appliances. An Interstate highway system is being built. Jet airliners start to replace piston engine airplanes and speed transportation. And Elvis changes the face of popular music. These technological advances bring new profit opportunities. Investment and saving increase, so capital per hour of labor increases. Real GDP per person grows rapidly driven by this technological change. According to neoclassical theory, this technological change is just a lucky accident.

New Growth Theory

New growth theory predicts that our unlimited wants will lead us to ever greater productivity and perpetual economic growth. According to new growth theory, real GDP per person grows because of the choices people make in the pursuit of profit. Paul Romer of Stanford University developed this theory during the 1980s, building on ideas developed by Joseph Schumpeter during the 1930s and 1940s.

New growth theory
The theory that our unlimited wants will lead us to ever greater productivity and perpetual economic growth.

Choices and Innovation

The new growth theory emphasizes three facts about market economies:

- Human capital expands because of choices.
- Discoveries result from choices.
- Discoveries bring profit, and competition destroys profit.

Human Capital Expansion and Choices People decide how long to remain in school, what to study, and how hard to study. And when they graduate from school, people make more choices about job training and on-the-job learning. All these choices govern the speed at which human capital expands.

Discoveries and Choices When people discover a new product or technique, they consider themselves lucky. They are right, but chance does not determine the pace at which new discoveries are made—and at which technology advances. It depends on how many people are looking for a new technology and how intensively they are looking.

Discoveries and Profits Profit is the spur to technological change. The forces of competition squeeze profits, so to increase profit, people constantly seek either lower-cost methods of production or new and better products for which people are willing to pay a higher price. Inventors can maintain a profit for several years by taking out a patent or copyright, but eventually, a new discovery is copied, and profits disappear.

Two other facts play a key role in the new growth theory:

- Many people can use discoveries at the same time.
- Physical activities can be replicated.

Discoveries Used by All Once a profitable new discovery has been made, everyone can use it. For example, when Marc Andreeson created Mosaic, the Web browser that led to the creation of Netscape Navigator and Microsoft's Internet Explorer, everyone who was interested in navigating the Internet had access to a new and more efficient tool. One person's use of a Web browser does not prevent others from using it. This fact means that as the benefits of a new discovery spread, free resources become available. These resources are free because nothing is given up when an additional person uses them. They have a zero opportunity cost.

Replicating Activities Production activities can be replicated. For example, there might be 2, 3, or 53 identical firms making fiber-optic cable by using an identical assembly line and production technique. If one firm increases its capital and output, that *firm* experiences diminishing returns. But the economy can increase its capital and output by adding another identical fiber cable factory, and the *economy* does not experience diminishing returns.

The assumption that capital does not experience diminishing returns is the central novel proposition of the new growth theory. The implication of this simple and appealing idea is astonishing. As capital accumulates, labor productivity grows indefinitely as long as people devote resources to expanding human capital and introducing new technologies.

Illustrating the Effects of Labor Productivity Growth

Figure 9.3 shows the effects of an increase in labor productivity that results from an increase in capital or an advance in technology. Part (a) shows the production function, which initially is PF_0. Part (b) shows the labor market. Initially, the demand for labor curve is LD_0, and the supply of labor curve is LS. The real wage rate is $15 an hour, and full employment is 200 billion hours a year. With 200 billion hours of labor employed, real GDP is $5 trillion in part (a).

Now an increase in physical capital or human capital or an advance in technology increases labor productivity. In Figure 9.3(a), the increase in labor productivity shifts the production function upward to PF_1. In Figure 9.3(b), the demand for labor increases and the demand curve shifts rightward to LD_1. At the original real wage rate of $15 an hour, there is now a shortage of labor, so the real wage rate rises. In this example, the real wage rate keeps rising until it reaches $25 an hour. At $25 an hour, the quantity of labor demanded equals the quantity of labor supplied and full employment increases to 300 billion hours a year.

Figure 9.3(a) shows the effects on real GDP of the increase in employment combined with the new production function. As full employment increases from 200 billion hours to 300 billion hours, real GDP increases from $5 trillion to $12

FIGURE 9.3

The Effects of an Increase in Labor Productivity

myeconlab Animation

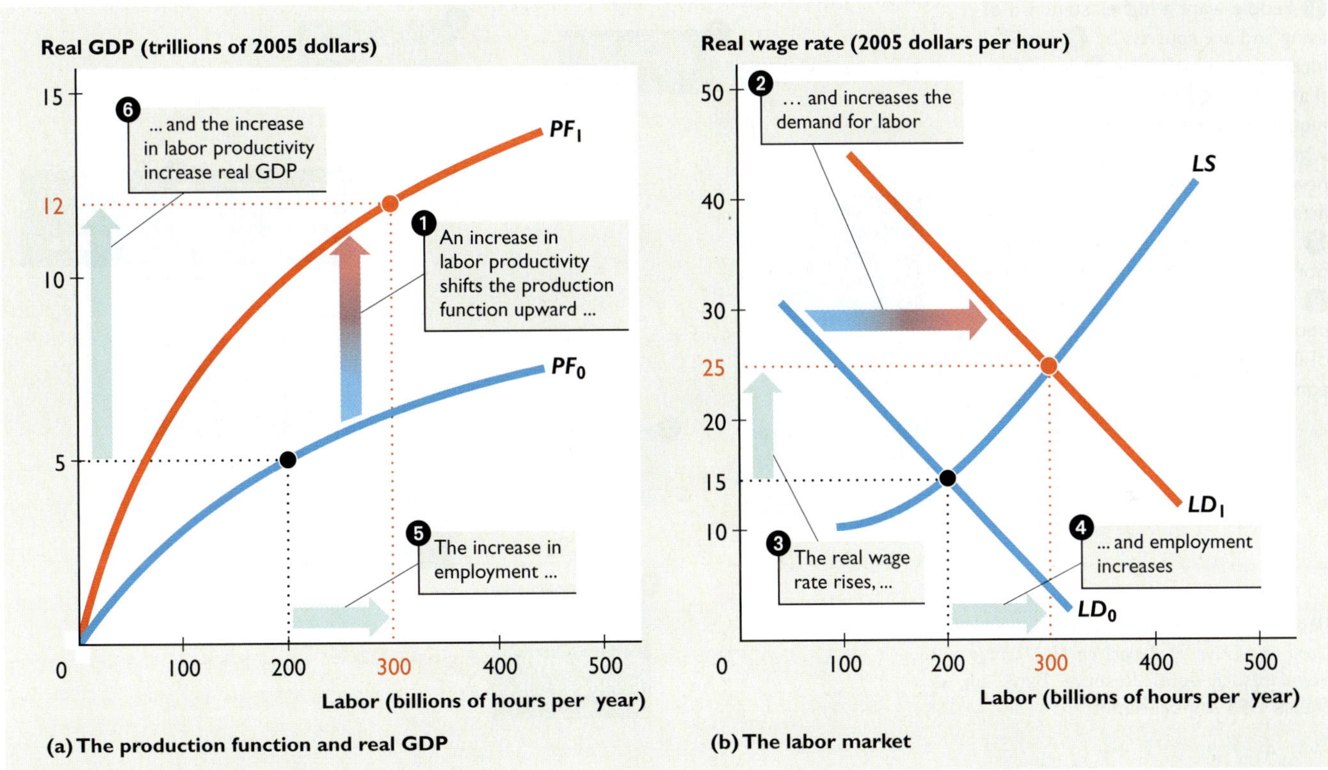

1 An increase in labor productivity shifts the production function upward from PF_0 to PF_1 in part (a) and 2 increases the demand for labor—shifts the demand for labor curve rightward from LD_0 to LD_1—in part (b).

3 The real wage rate rises and 4 the quantity of labor employed increases in part (b).

5 The increase in employment and 6 the increase in labor productivity increase real GDP in part (a).

trillion. Labor productivity also increases. You can see this increase by dividing real GDP by total labor hours. Initially, with real GDP at $5 trillion and labor hours at 200 billion, labor productivity was $25. With the increase in capital or the advance in technology, real GDP is $12 trillion and labor hours are 300 billion, so labor productivity is $40.

We've just studied the effects of a one-shot increase in labor productivity, but the forces that bring it about are ongoing.

Perpetual Motion

Economic growth is like the perpetual motion machine in Figure 9.4. Growth is driven by insatiable wants that lead us to pursue profit and innovate. New and better products result from this process; new firms start up, and old firms go out of business. As firms start up and die, jobs are created and destroyed. New and better jobs lead to more leisure and more consumption. But our insatiable wants are still there, so the process continues—wants, profit incentives, innovation, and new products. The economic growth rate depends on the ability and the incentive to innovate.

FIGURE 9.4

A Perpetual Motion Machine

myeconlab Animation

❶ People want a higher standard of living and are spurred by ❷ profit incentives to make the ❸ innovations that lead to ❹ new and better techniques and new and better products, which in turn lead to ❺ the birth of new firms and the death of some old firms, ❻ new and better jobs, and ❼ more leisure and more consumption goods and services. The result is ❽ a higher standard of living. But people want a yet higher standard of living, and the growth process continues.

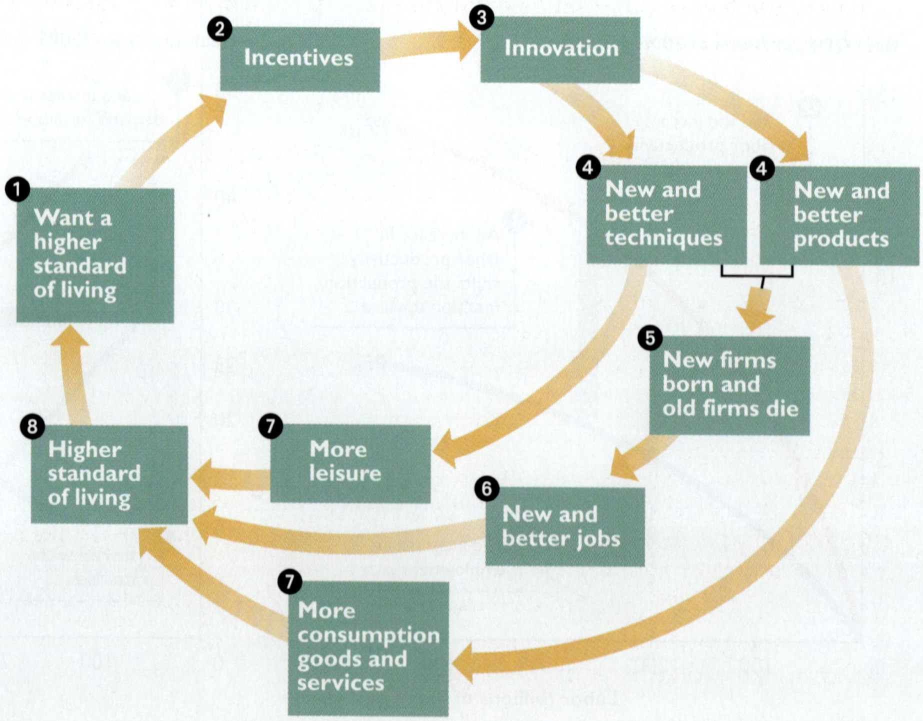

Based on a similar figure in *These Are the Good Old Days: A Report on U.S. Living Standards*, Federal Reserve Bank of Dallas 1993 Annual Report.

EYE on YOUR LIFE

How You Influence and Are Influenced by Economic Growth

Many of the choices that you make affect your personal economic growth rate—the pace of expansion of your own standard of living. And these same choices, in combination with similar choices made by millions of other people, have a profound effect on the economic growth of the nation and the world.

The most important of these choices right now is your choice to increase your human capital. By being in school, you have decided to make your human capital expand.

You will continue to expand your human capital long after you finish school as your earning power rises with on-the-job experience. You might even decide to return to school at a later stage in your life.

A choice that will become increasingly important later in your life is to accumulate a retirement fund. This choice provides not only a source of income for you when you eventually retire but also financial resources that firms can use to finance the expansion of physical capital.

Not only do your choices influence economic growth; economic growth also has a big influence on you—on how you earn your income and on the standard of living that your income makes possible.

Because of economic growth, the jobs available today are more interesting and less dangerous and strenuous than those of 100 years ago; and jobs are hugely better paid. But for many of us, economic growth means that we must accept change and be ready to learn new skills and get new jobs.

CHECKPOINT 9.3

Review the theories of economic growth that explain why growth rates vary over time and across countries.

myeconlab

Work these problems in Study Plan 9.3 to get instant feedback.

Practice Problems

1. What does classical growth theory say will eventually end economic growth?
2. What does neoclassical growth theory say about the source of persistent growth in real GDP per person?
3. What does neoclassical growth theory say is the process that will bring the growth of real GDP per person to a stop?
4. What is the driving force of economic growth according to new growth theory?
5. **The productivity watch**
   Former Federal Reserve chairman Alan Greenspan attributes the growth of labor productivity to IT investments that boosted labor productivity, which boosted company profits, which led to more IT investments, and so on, leading to a nirvana of high growth.

   Source: *Fortune* Magazine, September 4, 2006

   Which of the growth theories that you've studied in this chapter best corresponds to the explanation given by Mr. Greenspan?

Guided Solutions to Practice Problems

1. Classical growth theory predicts that when the real wage rate exceeds the subsistence real wage rate, the population grows. With an increasing population, the supply of labor increases, the real wage rate falls and is pulled back toward subsistence level. Real GDP increases, but real GDP per person decreases.
2. Neoclassical growth theory says that technological advance is the source of persistent growth in real GDP per person.
3. If technology stops advancing, real GDP growth slows because capital accumulation brings diminishing returns. With real GDP growth slowing, saving and investment fall and the growth rate of capital decreases to the population growth rate. Real GDP per person stops growing.
4. The driving force of economic growth according to new growth theory is a persistent incentive to innovate and an absence of diminishing returns.
5. Mr. Greenspan is describing the new growth theory. According to this theory, the endless pursuit of profit leads to innovations (IT innovations in the period described here) that increase labor productivity, shift the production function upward, increase the demand for labor, raise the real wage rate, and increase profit. The perpetual pursuit of profit will bring persistent economic growth.

9.4 ACHIEVING FASTER GROWTH

Why did it take more than a million years of human life before economic growth began? Why are some countries even today still barely growing? Why don't all societies save and invest in new capital, expand human capital, and discover and apply new technologies on a scale that brings rapid economic growth? What actions can governments take to encourage growth?

Preconditions for Economic Growth

The main reason economic growth is either absent or slow is that some societies lack the incentive system that encourages growth-producing activities. One of the fundamental preconditions for creating the incentives that lead to economic growth is economic freedom.

Economic Freedom

Economic freedom
A condition in which people are able to make personal choices, their private property is protected by the rule of law, and they are free to buy and sell in markets.

Economic freedom is present when people are able to make personal choices, their private property is protected by the rule of law, and they are free to buy and sell in markets. The rule of law, an efficient legal system, and the ability to enforce contracts are essential foundations for creating economic freedom. Impediments to economic freedom are corruption in the courts and government bureaucracy; barriers to trade, such as import bans; high tax rates; stringent regulations on business, such as health, safety, and environmental regulation; restrictions on banks; labor market regulations that limit a firm's ability to hire and lay off workers; and illegal markets, such as those that violate intellectual property rights.

No unique political system is necessary to deliver economic freedom. Democratic systems do a good job, but the rule of law, not democracy, is the key requirement for creating economic freedom. Nondemocratic political systems that respect the rule of law can also work well. Hong Kong is the best example of a place with little democracy but a lot of economic freedom—and a lot of economic growth. No country with a high level of economic freedom is economically poor, but many countries with low levels of economic freedom stagnate.

Property Rights

Property rights
The social arrangements that govern the protection of private property.

Economic freedom requires the protection of private property—the factors of production and goods that people own. The social arrangements that govern the protection of private property are called **property rights.** They include the rights to physical property (land, buildings, and capital equipment), to financial property (claims by one person against another), and to intellectual property (such as inventions). Clearly established and enforced property rights provide people with the incentive to work and save. If someone attempts to steal their property, a legal system will protect them. Such property rights also assure people that government itself will not confiscate their income or savings.

Markets

Economic freedom also requires free markets. Buyers and sellers get information and do business with each other in *markets.* Market prices send signals to buyers and sellers that create incentives to increase or decrease the quantities demanded and supplied. Markets enable people to trade and to save and invest. But markets cannot operate without property rights.

Property rights and markets create incentives for people to specialize and trade, to save and invest, to expand their human capital, and to discover and apply new technologies. Early human societies based on hunting and gathering did not experience economic growth because they lacked property rights and markets. Economic growth began when societies evolved the institutions that create incentives. But the presence of an incentive system and the institutions that create it do not guarantee that economic growth will occur. They permit economic growth but do not make it inevitable.

Growth begins when the appropriate incentive system exists because people can specialize in the activities at which they have a comparative advantage and trade with each other. You saw in Chapter 3 how everyone gains from such activity. By specializing and trading, everyone can acquire goods and services at the lowest possible cost. Consequently, people can obtain a greater volume of goods and services from their labor.

As an economy moves from one with little specialization to one that reaps the gains from specialization and trade, its production and consumption grow. Real GDP per person increases, and the standard of living rises.

But for growth to be persistent, people must face incentives that encourage them to pursue the three activities that generate *ongoing* economic growth: saving and investment, expansion of human capital, and the discovery and application of new technologies.

Policies to Achieve Faster Growth

To achieve faster economic growth, we must increase the growth rate of capital per hour of labor, increase the growth rate of human capital, or increase the pace of technological advance. The main actions that governments can take to achieve these objectives are

- Create incentive mechanisms.
- Encourage saving.
- Encourage research and development.
- Encourage international trade.
- Improve the quality of education.

Create Incentive Mechanisms

Economic growth occurs when the incentives to save, invest, and innovate are strong enough. These incentives require property rights enforced by a well-functioning legal system. Property rights and a legal system are the key ingredients that are missing in many societies. For example, they are absent throughout much of Africa. The first priority for growth policy is to establish these institutions so that incentives to save, invest, and innovate exist. Russia is a leading example of a country that is striving to take this step toward establishing the conditions in which economic growth can occur.

Encourage Saving

Saving finances investment, which brings capital accumulation. So encouraging saving can increase the growth of capital and stimulate economic growth. The East Asian economies have the highest saving rates and the highest growth rates. Some African economies have the lowest saving rates and the lowest growth rates.

Tax incentives can increase saving. Individual Retirement Accounts (IRAs) are an example of a tax incentive to save. Economists claim that a tax on consumption rather than on income provides the best incentive to save.

Encourage Research and Development

Everyone can use the fruits of basic research and development efforts. For example, all biotechnology firms can use advances in gene-splicing technology. Because basic inventions can be copied, the inventor's profit is limited and so the market allocates too few resources to this activity.

Governments can direct public funds toward financing basic research, but this solution is not foolproof. It requires a mechanism for allocating public funds to their highest-valued use. The National Science Foundation is one possibly efficient channel for allocating public funds to universities and public research facilities to finance and encourage basic research. Government programs such as national defense and space exploration also lead to innovations that have wide use. Laptop computers and nonstick coatings are two prominent examples of innovations that came from the U.S. space program.

Encourage International Trade

Free international trade stimulates economic growth by extracting all the available gains from specialization and trade. The fastest-growing nations today are those with the fastest-growing exports and imports. The creation of the North American Free Trade Agreement and the integration of the economies of Europe through the formation of the European Union are examples of successful actions that governments have taken to stimulate economic growth through trade.

Improve the Quality of Education

The free market would produce too little education because it brings social benefits beyond the benefits to the people who receive the education. By funding basic education and by ensuring high standards in skills such as language, mathematics, and science, governments can contribute enormously to a nation's growth potential. Education can also be expanded and improved by using tax incentives to encourage improved private provision. Singapore's Information Technology in Education program is one of the best examples of a successful attempt to stimulate growth through education.

How Much Difference Can Policy Make?

It is easy to make a list of policy actions that could increase a nation's economic growth rate. It is hard to convert that list into acceptable actions that make a big difference.

Societies are the way they are because they balance the interests of one group against the interests of another group. Change brings gains for some and losses for others, so change is slow. And even when change occurs, if the economic growth rate can be increased by even as much as half a percentage point, it takes many years for the full benefits to accrue.

A well-intentioned government cannot dial up a big increase in the economic growth rate, but it can pursue policies that will nudge the economic growth rate upward. Over time, the benefits from these policies will be large.

EYE on CONVERGENCE AND GAPS

Why Are Some Nations Rich and Others Poor?

Political stability, property rights protected by the rule of law, limited government intervention in markets: These are key features of the economies that enjoy high incomes and they are the features missing in those that remain poor.

Most of the rich nations have experienced sustained economic growth over many decades. Europe's Big 4 economies (France, Germany, Italy, and the United Kingdom) have been enjoying economic growth for 200 years. The United States started to grow rapidly 150 years ago and overtook Europe in the early 20th century. In the past 50 years, the gaps between these countries haven't changed much. (See part (a) of the figure.)

In a transition from Communism to a market economy, Central Europe is growing faster than the United States.

Economic growth in Africa and Central and South America has been persistently slow and the gap between the United States and these regions has widened.

Real GDP per person in East Asian economies, in part (b), has converged toward that in the United States. These economies are like fast trains running on the same track at similar speeds with roughly constant gaps between them. Hong Kong and Singapore are the lead trains and run about 15 years in front of Taiwan, 20 years in front of South Korea, and almost 40 years in front of China.

Between 1960 and 2008, Hong Kong and Singapore transformed themselves from poor developing economies to take their places among the world's richest economies.

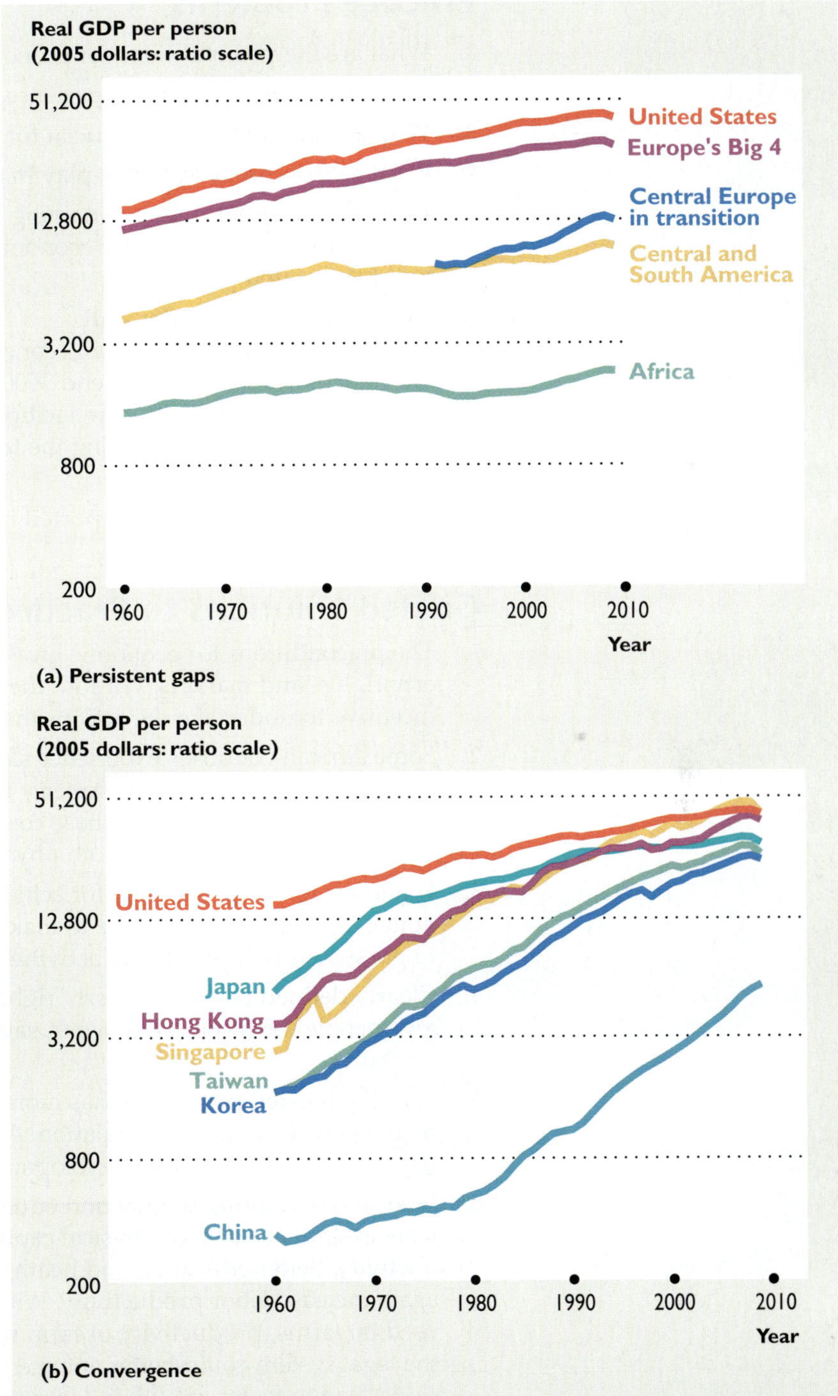

SOURCES OF DATA: Alan Heston, Robert Summers, and Bettina Aten, Penn World Table Version 6.2, Center for International Comparisons at the University of Pennsylvania, September 2006 and International Monetary Fund, *World Economic Outlook Database*.

myeconlab

Work these problems in Study Plan 9.4 to get instant feedback.

CHECKPOINT 9.4

Describe policies that might speed economic growth.

Practice Problems

1. What are the preconditions for economic growth?
2. Why does much of Africa experience slow economic growth?
3. Why is economic freedom crucial for achieving economic growth?
4. What role do property rights play in encouraging economic growth?
5. Explain why, other things remaining the same, a country with a well-educated population has a faster economic growth rate than a country that has a poorly educated population.
6. **India's economy hits the wall**

   Just six months ago, the Indian economy was growing rapidly; now growth has halted. India needs to spend $500 billion upgrading its infrastructure and education and health-care facilities. Agriculture remains unproductive; and reforms, like strengthening the legal system, have been ignored.

   Source: *BusinessWeek*, July 1, 2008

   Explain how the measures reported in the news clip could lead to faster economic growth in India.

Guided Solutions to Practice Problems

1. The preconditions for economic growth are economic freedom, private property rights, and markets. Without these preconditions, people have little incentive to undertake the actions that lead to economic growth.
2. Some African countries experience slow economic growth because they lack economic freedom, private property rights are not enforced, and markets do not function well. People in these countries have little incentive to specialize and trade or to accumulate both physical and human capital.
3. Economic freedom is crucial for achieving economic growth because economic freedom allows people to make choices and gives them the incentives to pursue growth-producing activities.
4. Clearly defined private property rights and a legal system to enforce them give people the incentive to work, save, invest, and accumulate human capital.
5. A well-educated population has more skills and greater labor productivity than a poorly educated population. A well-educated population can contribute to the research and development that create new technology.
6. Investment in infrastructure and education and heath-care facilities would increase India's stock of physical capital, which would increase labor productivity. Better education and heath care would increase human capital and again increase labor productivity. With better technology and more capital used on farms, productivity of farm workers would increase. Strengthening the legal system could better enforce property rights. Each of these measures could lead to faster growth in labor productivity and faster growth in real GDP per person in India.

CHAPTER SUMMARY

Key Points

1 Define and calculate the economic growth rate, and explain the implications of sustained growth.

- Economic growth is the sustained expansion of production possibilities. The annual percentage change in real GDP measures the economic growth rate.
- Real GDP per person must grow if the standard of living is to rise.
- Sustained economic growth transforms poor nations into rich ones.
- The Rule of 70 tells us the number of years in which real GDP doubles—70 divided by the percentage growth rate of real GDP.

2 Identify the main sources of economic growth.

- Real GDP grows when aggregate hours and labor productivity grow.
- Real GDP per person grows when labor productivity grows.
- Saving, investment in physical capital, expansion of human capital, and technological advances bring labor productivity growth.

3 Review the theories of economic growth that explain why growth rates vary over time and across countries.

- Classical growth theory predicts that economic growth will end because a population explosion will lower real GDP per person to its subsistence level.
- Neoclassical theory predicts that economic growth will persist at a rate that is determined by the pace of technological change.
- New growth theory predicts that capital accumulation, human capital growth, and technological change respond to incentives and can bring persistent growth in labor productivity.

4 Describe policies that might speed economic growth.

- Economic growth requires an incentive system created by economic freedom, property rights, and markets.
- It might be possible to achieve faster growth by encouraging saving, subsidizing research and education, and encouraging international trade.

Key Terms

myeconlab

Work these problems in Chapter 9 Study Plan to get instant feedback.

CHAPTER CHECKPOINT

Study Plan Problems and Applications

1. Explain why sustained growth of real GDP per person can transform a poor country into a wealthy one.
2. In 2005 and 2006, India's real GDP grew by 9.2 percent a year and its population grew by 1.6 percent a year. If these growth rates are sustained, in what years would
   - Real GDP be twice what it was in 2006?
   - Real GDP per person be twice what it was in 2006?
3. Describe how U.S. real GDP per person has changed over the last 100 years.
4. Explain the link between labor hours, labor productivity, and real GDP.
5. Explain how saving and investment and advances in technology change labor productivity. Use a graph to illustrate your answer.

Use Table 1 and Table 2 to work Problems 6 to 9. Table 1 describes an economy's labor market in 2009 and Table 2 describes its production function in 2009.

TABLE 1 LABOR MARKET

Real wage rate (2005 dollars per hour)	Labor hours supplied	Labor hours demanded
80	45	5
70	40	10
60	35	15
50	30	20
40	25	25
30	20	30
20	15	35
10	10	40

TABLE 2 PRODUCTION FUNCTION

Labor (hours)	Real GDP (2005 dollars)
5	425
10	800
15	1,125
20	1,400
25	1,625
30	1,800
35	1,925
40	2,000

6. What are the equilibrium real wage rate, the quantity of labor employed in 2009, labor productivity, and potential GDP in 2009?
7. In 2010, the population increases and labor hours supplied increase by 10 at each real wage rate. What are the equilibrium real wage rate, labor productivity, and potential GDP in 2010?
8. In 2010, the population increases and labor hours supplied increase by 10 at each real wage rate. Does the standard of living in this economy increase in 2010? Explain why or why not.
9. If the subsistence real wage rate is $20 an hour, what will happen to the economy's population according to the classical growth theory?

Use the following information to work Problems 10 and 11.

China's economy to grow 8% annually from 2006 to 2010

The Chinese economy is expected to grow at a rate of 8 percent a year during the period of the 11th Five-Year Plan (2006–10). If China does maintain this growth rate, then China will achieve this goal of quadrupling its GDP from 2000 to 2020 ahead of schedule. Zhang Xiaoji, a senior researcher at the State Council Development Research Centre, reported that by the end of 2010, China's GDP will be equal to US $2.3 trillion or US $1,700 per person (2000 dollars) and by 2020, China's GDP will be equal to US $4.7 trillion, or US $3,200 per person.

Source: *China Daily*, March 21, 2005

10. If China continues to grow at 8 percent a year, how many years will it take for GDP to quadruple? In what year will China meet its goal?
11. What is the population growth rate assumed in the calculations of GDP per person from 2010 to 2020?

Instructor Assignable Problems and Applications

Your instructor can assign these problems as homework, a quiz, or a test in **MyEconLab**.

1. Distinguish between a low and high income and a low and high economic growth rate. What are the key features of an economy that are present when incomes are high or fast growing and absent when incomes are low and stagnating or growing slowly? Provide an example of an economy with a low income and slow growth rate, a low income and rapid growth rate, and a high income with sustained growth over many decades.

Use the following information to work Problems 2 and 3. China's growth rate of real GDP in 2005 and 2006 was 10.5 percent a year and its population growth rate was 0.5 percent a year .

2. If these growth rates continue, in what year would real GDP be twice what it was in 2006?
3. If these growth rates continue, in what year would real GDP per person be twice what it was in 2006?
4. Explain how an increase in physical capital and an increase in human capital change labor productivity. Use a graph to illustrate your answer.

Use Table 1 and Table 2 to work Problems 5 to 7. Table 1 describes an economy's labor market in 2009, and Table 2 describes its production function in 2009.

5. What are the equilibrium real wage rate, employment, and real GDP in 2009?
6. What are labor productivity and potential GDP in 2009?
7. Suppose that labor productivity increases in 2010. What effect does the increased labor productivity have on the demand for labor, the supply of labor, potential GDP, and real GDP per person?

TABLE 1 LABOR MARKET

Real wage rate (2005 dollars per hour)	Labor hours supplied	Labor hours demanded
80	55	15
70	50	20
60	45	25
50	40	30
40	35	35
30	30	40
20	25	45
10	20	50

TABLE 2 PRODUCTION FUNCTION

Labor (hours)	Real GDP (2005 dollars)
15	1,425
20	1,800
25	2,125
30	2,400
35	2,625
40	2,800
45	2,925
50	3,000

Use the following information to work Problems 8 to 10.

India's growth could be even better, says OECD

India's already impressive economic growth could improve even more if it further opened its markets and relaxed government controls, according to the Organization for Economic Co-operation and Development (OECD).

The OECD said that while the current growth that has averaged 8.5 percent a year over the past four years was sustainable, a rate of 10 percent was possible if greater reforms were introduced. The OECD suggests that ongoing economic liberalization, which India began in 1991, could help the country double its real GDP per person in 10 years. The OECD said it would have taken India 55 years to double real GDP per person if it had stayed on the growth path experienced in the 30 years following independence in 1947.

Source: *The Independent*, October 10, 2007

8. What was the average growth rate achieved by India in the 30 years after 1947?
9. By raising the real GDP growth rate from 8.5 percent a year to 10 percent a year and maintaining a constant population growth rate, how many years earlier will real GDP per person be doubled?
10. Suggest some government controls that if removed might spur India's growth rate to a sustained 10 percent a year.

Use the following information to work Problems 11 to 13.

Make way for India—the next China

China grows at around 9 percent a year, but its one-child policy will start to reduce the size of China's working-age population within the next 10 years. India, by contrast, will have an increasing working-age population for another generation at least.

Source: *The Independent*, March 1, 2006

11. Given the expected population changes, do you think China or India will have the greater economic growth rate? Why?
12. Would China's growth rate remain at 9 percent a year without the restriction on its population growth rate?
13. India's population growth rate is 1.6 percent a year while China's population growth rate is 0.6 percent a year. If India keeps its economic growth rate at 8 percent a year, and China keeps its economic growth rate at 9 percent a year, in what year will real GDP per person double in each country?

Use the following information to work Problems 14 and 15.

Optimistic about globalization

Mark Carney, governor of the Bank of Canada, is optimistic that while the adjustment to the global financial crisis will be difficult, flexible labor markets will make it possible for workers to retrain and find more productive jobs.

Source: *Toronto Star*, February 9, 2008

14. Explain which growth theory most closely describes the arguments made in this news clip.
15. Explain the suggestions that can help an economy achieve faster economic growth.
16. What can governments in Africa do to encourage economic growth and raise their standard of living?
17. Why do you think the standard of living in Asian economies has increased in the last decade by so much more than the increase in the standard of living in the United States?
18. What are the ingredients of economic freedom and how does each ingredient make economic growth more likely? Provide examples of nations that do not enjoy political freedom and that have a low economic growth rate and examples of nations that do enjoy political freedom and have a high economic growth rate. Are there any notable examples that contradict the view that economic freedom and economic growth go together?
19. Why might high taxes hold back economic growth? Would you recommend any changes in the U.S. tax laws to encourage faster growth? How would the changes that you recommend work?
20. An increasing number of Chinese citizens who are educated in the United States are returning to China to work. How do you think this development might influence economic growth in China? Do you think the Chinese government would be wise to adopt policies that encourage more Chinese students to return to China when they have completed their studies?

What created the global financial crisis?

Why did borrowing and lending almost disappear in the depth of the crisis?

10

Finance, Saving, and Investment

CHAPTER CHECKLIST

When you have completed your study of this chapter, you will be able to

1 Describe the financial markets and the key financial institutions.

2 Explain how borrowing and lending decisions are made and how these decisions interact in the market for loanable funds.

3 Explain how a government budget surplus or deficit influences the real interest rate, investment, and saving.

10.1 FINANCIAL INSTITUTIONS AND MARKETS

Financial institutions and markets provide the channels through which saving flows to finance the investment in capital that makes our economy grow. The health of these institutions and markets spreads to affect the performance of every other market—of the labor market and the markets for goods and services.

When financial institutions are in good health and financial markets are working well, a high level of investment brings a rapidly growing economy and rising living standards. When financial institutions get sick and financial markets dry up, a low level of investment slows economic growth and sometimes puts the economy in recession with falling living standards.

Some Finance Definitions

Finance, money, and capital are three terms that we use in our everyday lives almost interchangeably. Yet these terms have distinctly different meanings in the study of financial markets. Let's examine their differences.

Finance and Money

Finance is the lending and borrowing that moves funds from savers to spenders. *Money* is the object (or objects) that people use to make payments. You might say "I'm going to borrow some money to buy a car." Your borrowing and someone else's lending is a financial transaction—*finance*. You pay for the new car using *money*. By distinguishing between finance and money and studying them separately, we can better understand their roles and effects on the economy. For the rest of this chapter, we study finance and in Chapters 11 and 12, we study money.

Capital: Physical and Financial

Capital or physical capital
The tools, instruments, machines, buildings, and other items that have been produced in the past and that are used to produce goods and services.

Capital—also called **physical capital**—is the tools, instruments, machines, buildings, and other items that have been produced in the past and that are used to produce goods and services. Inventories of raw materials, semifinished goods, and components are part of physical capital. *Financial capital* is the funds used to buy physical capital. You're going to see how decisions about investment and saving, along with borrowing and lending, influence the quantity of physical capital.

Investment, Capital, Wealth, and Saving

Gross investment
The total amount spent on new capital goods.

Net investment
The change in the quantity of capital—equals gross investment minus depreciation.

Wealth
The value of all the things that people own.

Investment (Chapter 5, p. 115) increases the quantity of capital and *depreciation* (Chapter 5, p. 122) decreases it. The total amount spent on new capital is called **gross investment**. The change in the quantity of capital is called **net investment**. Net investment equals gross investment minus depreciation. Figure 10.1 illustrates these concepts. Tom's end-of-year capital of $40,000 equals his initial capital of $30,000 plus net investment of $10,000; and net investment equals gross investment of $30,000 minus depreciation of $20,000.

Wealth is the value of all the things that people own. What people own is related to what they earn, but it is not the same thing. People earn an income, which is the amount they receive during a given time period from supplying the services of the resources they own. *Saving* (Chapter 5, p. 116), the amount of income that is not paid in taxes or spent on consumption, adds to wealth. Wealth also increases when the market value of assets rises—called *capital gains*.

FIGURE 10.1

Capital and Investment

myeconlab Animation

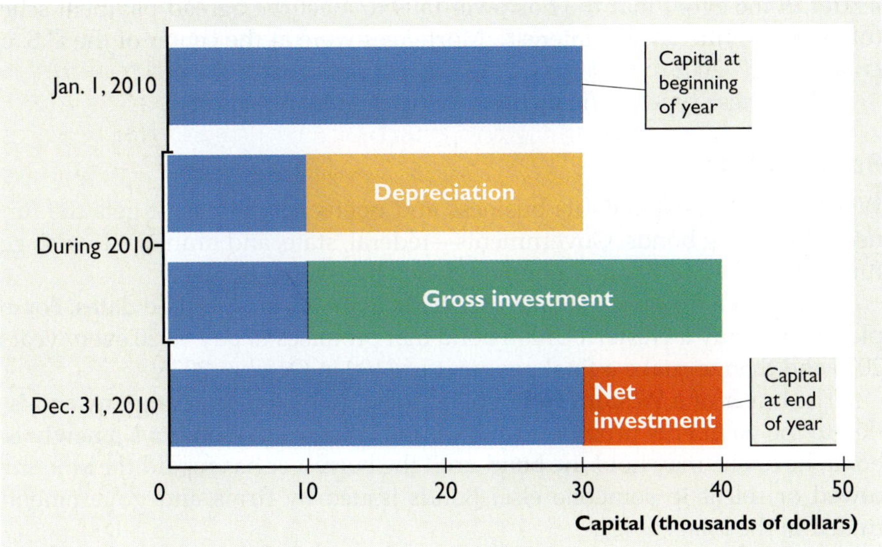

On January 1, 2010, Tom's DVD Burning, Inc. had DVD-recording machines valued at $30,000. During 2010, the value of Tom's machines fell by $20,000—depreciation—and he spent $30,000 on new machines—gross investment. Tom's net investment was $10,000, so at the end of 2010, Tom had capital valued at $40,000.

If at the end of the school year, you have $250 in the bank and textbooks worth $300 and that's all that you own, your wealth is $550. If during the summer, you earn $5,000 (after-tax income) and spend $1,000 on consumption, your bank account increases to $4,250 and your wealth becomes $4,550. Your wealth has increased by $4,000, which equals your saving—your income of $5,000 minus your consumption expenditure of $1,000.

National wealth and national saving work like this personal example. The wealth of a nation at the end of a year equals its wealth at the start of the year plus its saving during the year, which equals income minus consumption expenditure.

To make real GDP grow, saving and wealth must be transformed into investment and capital. This transformation takes place in the markets for financial capital and through the activities of financial institutions that we now describe.

Markets for Financial Capital

Saving is the source of the funds that are used to finance investment, and these funds are supplied and demanded in three types of financial markets:

- Loan markets
- Bond markets
- Stock markets

Loan Markets

Businesses often want short-term loans to buy inventories or to extend credit to their customers. Sometimes they get these funds in the form of a loan from a bank. Households often want funds to purchase big-ticket items, such as automobiles or household furnishings and appliances. They get these funds as bank loans, often in the form of outstanding credit card balances.

Households also get funds to buy new homes. (Expenditure on new homes is counted as part of investment.) These funds are usually obtained as a loan that is secured by a *mortgage*—a legal contract that gives ownership of a home to the lender in the event that the borrower fails to meet the agreed payment schedule (of loan repayments and interest). Mortgages were at the center of the U.S. credit crisis of 2007–2008.

All of these types of financing take place in loan markets.

Bond Markets

When Wal-Mart expands its business and opens new stores, it gets the funds it needs by selling bonds. Governments—federal, state, and municipal—also get the funds they need to finance a budget deficit by issuing bonds.

Bond
A promise to pay specified sums of money on specified dates.

A **bond** is a promise to make specified payments on specified dates. For example, you can buy a Western Union bond that promises to pay $6.20 every year until 2035 and then to make a final payment of $100 in October 2036.

The buyer of a Western Union bond makes a loan to the company and is entitled to the payments promised by the bond. When a person buys a newly issued bond, he or she may hold the bond until the borrower has repaid the amount borrowed or sell it to someone else. Bonds issued by firms and governments are traded in the *bond market*.

The term of a bond might be long (decades) or short (just a month or two). Firms often issue very short-term bonds as a way of getting paid for their sales before the buyer is able to pay. For example, when GM sells $100 million of railway locomotives to Union Pacific, GM wants to be paid when the items are shipped. But Union Pacific doesn't want to pay until the locomotives are earning an income. In this situation, Union Pacific might promise to pay GM $101 million three months in the future. A bank would be willing to buy this promise for (say) $100 million. GM gets $100 million immediately and the bank gets $101 million in three months when Union Pacific honors its promise. The U.S. Treasury issues promises of this type, called *Treasury bills*.

Another type of bond is a *mortgage-backed security*, which entitles its holder to the income from a package of mortgages. Mortgage lenders create mortgage-backed securities. They make mortgage loans to home buyers and then create securities that they sell to obtain more funds to make more mortgage loans. The holder of a mortgage-backed security is entitled to receive payments that derive from the payments received by the mortgage lender from the homebuyer–borrower.

Mortgage-backed securities were at the center of the storm in the financial markets in 2007–2008.

Stock Markets

Stock
A certificate of ownership and claim to the profits that a firm makes.

When Boeing wants to raise funds to expand its airplane building business, it issues stock. A **stock** is a certificate of ownership and claim to a firm's profits. Boeing has issued about 900 million shares of its stock. If you owned 900 Boeing shares, you would own one millionth of Boeing and be entitled to receive one millionth of its profits.

A *stock market* is a financial market in which shares in corporations' stocks are traded. The New York Stock Exchange, the London Stock Exchange (in England), the Frankfurt Stock Exchange (in Germany), and the Tokyo Stock Exchange are all examples of stock markets.

Financial Institutions

Financial markets are highly competitive because of the role played by financial institutions in those markets. A **financial institution** is a firm that operates on both sides of the markets for financial capital: It borrows in one market and lends in another. The key financial institutions are

Financial institution
A firm that operates on both sides of the markets for financial capital: It borrows in one market and lends in another.

- Investment banks
- Commercial banks
- Government-sponsored mortgage lenders
- Pension funds
- Insurance companies

Investment Banks

Investment banks are firms that help other financial institutions and governments raise funds by issuing and selling bonds and stocks, as well as providing advice on transactions such as mergers and acquisitions. Until the late 1980s, the United States maintained a sharp separation between investment banking and commercial banking—a separation that was imposed by the Glass-Steagall Act of 1933. Until 2008, four big Wall Street firms, Goldman Sachs, Lehman Brothers, Merrill Lynch, and Morgan Stanley provided investment banking services. But in the financial meltdown of 2008, Lehman disappeared and Merrill Lynch was taken over by the Bank of America, a commercial bank.

Commercial Banks

The bank that you use for your own banking services and that issues your credit card is a commercial bank. We'll explain their role in Chapter 11 where we study the role of money in our economy.

Government-Sponsored Mortgage Lenders

Two large financial institutions, the Federal National Mortgage Association, or Fannie Mae, and the Federal Home Loan Mortgage Corporation, or Freddie Mac, are government-sponsored enterprises that buy mortgages from banks, package them into *mortgage-backed securities*, and sell them. In September 2008, Fannie Mae and Freddie Mac owned or guaranteed $6 trillion worth of mortgages (half of the U.S. total of $12 trillion) and were taken over by the federal government.

Pension Funds

Pension funds are financial institutions that use the pension contributions of firms and workers to buy bonds and stocks. The mortgage-backed securities of Fannie Mae and Freddie Mac are among the assets of pension funds. Some pension funds are very large and play an active role in the firms whose stock they hold.

Insurance Companies

Insurance companies enter into agreements with households and firms to provide compensation in the event of accident, theft, fire, ill-health, and a host of other misfortunes. Some companies, for example, provide insurance that pays out if a firm fails and cannot meet its bond obligations; and some insure other insurers in a complex network of reinsurance.

Insurance companies receive premiums from their customers, make payments against claims, and use the funds they have received but not paid out as claims to buy bonds and stocks on which they earn interest.

In normal times, insurance companies have a steady flow of funds coming in from premiums and interest on the financial assets they hold and a steady, but smaller, flow of funds paying claims. Their profit is the gap between the two flows. But in unusual times, when large and widespread losses are being incurred, insurance companies can run into difficulty in meeting their obligations. Such a situation arose in 2008 for one of the biggest insurers, AIG, and the firm was taken into public ownership.

Insolvency and Illiquidity

Net worth
The total market value of what a financial institution has lent minus the market value of what it has borrowed.

A financial institution's **net worth** is the total market value of what it has lent minus the market value of what it has borrowed. If net worth is positive, the institution is *solvent* and can remain in business. But if net worth is negative, the institution is *insolvent* and must stop trading. The owners of an insolvent financial institution—usually its stockholders—bear the loss when the assets are sold and debts paid.

A financial institution both borrows and lends, so it is exposed to the risk that its net worth might become negative. To limit that risk, institutions are regulated and a minimum amount of their lending must be backed by their net worth.

Sometimes, a financial institution is solvent but illiquid. A firm is *illiquid* if it has made long-term loans with borrowed funds and is faced with a sudden demand to repay more of what it has borrowed than its available cash. In normal times, a financial institution that is illiquid can borrow from another institution. But if all financial institutions are short of cash, the market for loans among financial institutions dries up.

Insolvency and illiquidity were at the core of the financial meltdown of 2007–2008.

Interest Rates and Asset Prices

Stocks, bonds, short-term securities, and loans are collectively called *financial assets*. The *interest rate* on a financial asset is a percentage of the price of the asset.

Because the interest rate is a percentage of the price of an asset, if the asset price rises, other things remaining the same, the interest rate falls. And conversely, if the asset price falls, other things remaining the same, the interest rate rises.

To see this *inverse relationship* between an asset price and interest rate, look at the example of a Microsoft share. In September 2009, the price of a Microsoft share was \$25 and each share entitled its owner to 50 cents of Microsoft profit. The interest rate on a Microsoft share as a percentage was

$$\text{Interest rate} = (\$0.50 \div \$25) \times 100 = 2 \text{ percent.}$$

If the price of a Microsoft share increased to \$50 and each share still entitled its owner to 50 cents of Microsoft profit, the interest rate on a Microsoft share as a percentage would become

$$\text{Interest rate} = (\$0.50 \div \$50) \times 100 = 1 \text{ percent.}$$

This relationship means that an asset price and interest rate are determined simultaneously—one implies the other. In the next part of this chapter, we learn how asset prices and interest rates are determined in the financial markets.

CHECKPOINT 10.1

Describe the financial markets and the key financial institutions.

myeconlab

Work these problems in Study Plan 10.1 to get instant feedback.

Practice Problems

1. Michael is an Internet service provider. On December 31, 2009, he bought an existing business with servers and a building worth $400,000. During 2010, he bought new servers for $500,000. The market value of his older servers fell by $100,000. What was Michael's gross investment, depreciation, and net investment during 2010? What is Michael's capital at the end of 2010?
2. Lori is a student who teaches golf on the weekend and in a year earns $20,000 after paying her taxes. At the beginning of 2009, Lori owned $1,000 worth of books, DVDs, and golf clubs and she had $5,000 in a savings account at the bank. During 2009, the interest on her savings account was $300 and she spent a total of $15,300 on consumption goods and services. There was no change in the market value of her books, DVDs, and golf clubs. How much did Lori save in 2009? What was her wealth at the end of 2009?
3. **G-20 leaders look to shake off lingering economic troubles**

   The G-20 aims to take stock of the economic recovery. One achievement in Pittsburgh could be a deal to require that financial institutions hold more capital.

   Source: *USA Today*, September 24, 2009

   What are the financial institutions that the G-20 might require to hold more capital? What exactly is the "capital" referred to in the news clip? How might the requirement to hold more capital make financial institutions safer?

Guided Solutions to Practice Problems

1. Michael's gross investment during 2010 was $500,000—the market value of the new servers he bought.

   Michael's depreciation during 2010 was $100,000—the fall in the market value of his older servers.

   Michael's net investment during 2010 was $400,000. Net investment equals gross investment minus depreciation, which is ($500,000 − $100,000).

   At the end of 2010, Michael's capital was $800,000. The capital grew during 2010 by the amount of net investment, so at the end of 2010 capital was $400,000 + $400,000, which equals $800,000.
2. Lori saved $5,000. Saving equals income (after tax) minus the amount spent. That is, Lori's saving equaled $20,300 minus $15,300, or $5,000.

   Lori's wealth at the end of 2009 was $11,000—the sum of her wealth at the start of 2009 ($6,000) plus her saving during 2009 ($5,000).
3. The institutions are banks and insurance companies. "Capital" in the news clip is the institutions' own funds. By using more of its own funds and less borrowed funds, a financial institution decreases its risk of insolvency.

10.2 THE MARKET FOR LOANABLE FUNDS

Market for loanable funds
The aggregate of all the individual financial markets.

In macroeconomics, we group all the individual financial markets into a single market for loanable funds. The **market for loanable funds** is the aggregate of the markets for loans, bonds, and stocks. In the market for loanable funds, there is just one average interest rate that we refer to as *the* interest rate.

Thinking about financial markets as a single market for loanable funds makes sense because the individual markets are highly interconnected with many common influences that move the interest rates on individual assets up and down together.

Flows in the Market for Loanable Funds

The circular flow model (see Chapter 5, pp. 116–117) provides the accounting framework that describes the flows in the market for loanable funds.

Loanable funds are used for three purposes:

1. Business investment
2. Government budget deficit
3. International investment or lending

And loanable funds come from three sources:

1. Private saving
2. Government budget surplus
3. International borrowing

Firms often use *retained earnings*—profits not distributed to stockholders—to finance business investment. These earnings belong to the firm's stockholders and are borrowed from the stockholders rather than being paid to them as dividends. To keep the accounts in the clearest possible way, we think of these retained earnings as being both a use and a source of loanable funds. They are part of business investment on the uses side and part of private saving on the sources side.

We measure all the flows of loanable funds in real terms—in constant 2005 dollars.

You're now going to see how these real flows and the real interest rate are determined in the market for loanable funds by studying

- The demand for loanable funds
- The supply of loanable funds
- Equilibrium in the market for loanable funds

The Demand for Loanable Funds

The *quantity of loanable funds demanded* is the total quantity of funds demanded to finance investment, the government budget deficit, and international investment or lending during a given period. Investment is the major item and the focus of our explanation of the forces that influence the demand side of the market for loanable funds. The other two items—the government budget deficit and international investment and lending—can be thought of as amounts to be added to investment. (We study the effects of the government budget later in this chapter on pp. 258–262 and international borrowing and lending in Chapter 19.)

What determines investment and the demand for loanable funds? How does Amazon.com decide how much to borrow to build some new warehouses? Many details influence such a decision, but we can summarize them in two factors:

1. The real interest rate
2. Expected profit

The real interest rate is the opportunity cost of the funds used to finance the purchase of capital, and firms compare the real interest rate with the rate of profit they expect to earn on their new capital. Firms invest only when they expect to earn a rate of profit that exceeds the real interest rate. Fewer projects are profitable at a high real interest rate than at a low real interest rate, so:

Other things remaining the same, the higher the real interest rate, the smaller is the quantity of loanable funds demanded; and the lower the real interest rate, the greater is the quantity of loanable funds demanded.

Demand for Loanable Funds Curve

The **demand for loanable funds** is the relationship between the quantity of loanable funds demanded and the real interest rate when all other influences on borrowing plans remain the same. Figure 10.2 illustrates the demand for loanable funds as a schedule and as a curve.

Demand for loanable funds
The relationship between the quantity of loanable funds demanded and the real interest rate when all other influences on borrowing plans remain the same.

FIGURE 10.2

The Demand for Loanable Funds

myeconlab Animation

	Real interest rate (percent per year)	Loanable funds demanded (trillions of 2005 dollars)
A	10	1.0
B	8	1.5
C	6	2.0
D	4	2.5
E	2	3.0

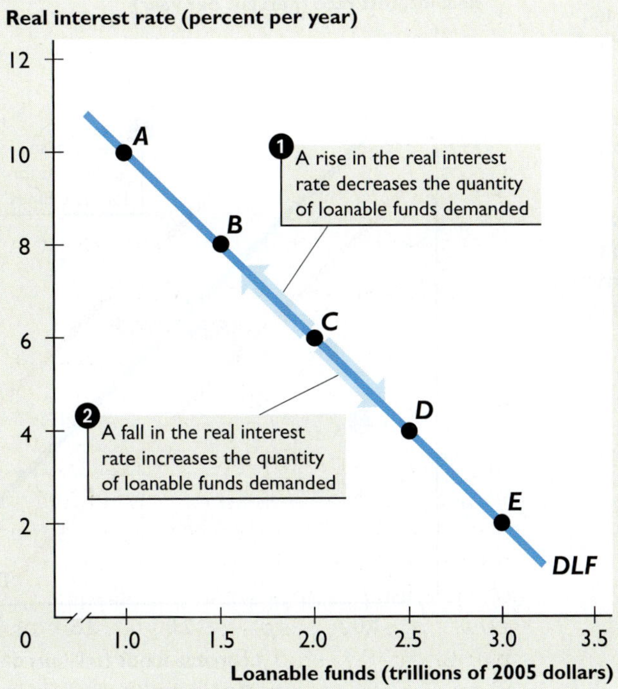

The table shows the quantity of loanable funds demanded at five real interest rates. The graph shows the demand for loanable funds curve, *DLF*. Points *A* through *E* correspond to the rows of the table.

1. If the real interest rate rises, the quantity of loanable funds demanded decreases.
2. If the real interest rate falls, the quantity of loanable funds demanded increases.

To understand the demand for loanable funds, think about Amazon.com's decision to borrow $100 million to build some new warehouses. Suppose that Amazon expects to get a return of $5 million a year from this investment before paying interest costs. If the interest rate is less than 5 percent a year, Amazon expects to make a profit, so it builds the warehouses. If the interest rate is more than 5 percent a year, Amazon expects to incur a loss, so it doesn't build the warehouses. The quantity of loanable funds demanded is greater, the lower is the interest rate.

Changes in the Demand for Loanable Funds

When the expected profit changes, the demand for loanable funds changes. Other things remaining the same, the greater the expected profit from new capital, the greater is the amount of investment and the greater is the demand for loanable funds.

The expected profit rises during a business cycle expansion and falls during a recession; rises when technological change creates profitable new products; rises as a growing population brings increased demand; and fluctuates with contagious swings of optimism and pessimism, called "animal spirits" by Keynes and "irrational exuberance" by Alan Greenspan.

Figure 10.3 shows how the demand for loanable funds curve shifts when the expected profit changes. With average profit expectations, the demand for loanable funds is DLF_0. A rise in expected profit shifts the demand curve rightward to DLF_1 and a fall in expected profit shifts the demand curve leftward to DLF_2.

FIGURE 10.3

Changes in the Demand for Loanable Funds

myeconlab Animation

A change in expected profit changes the demand for loanable funds and shifts the demand for loanable funds curve.

❶ An increase in expected profit increases the demand for loanable funds and shifts the demand curve rightward to DLF_1.

❷ A decrease in expected profit decreases the demand for loanable funds and shifts the demand curve leftward to DLF_2.

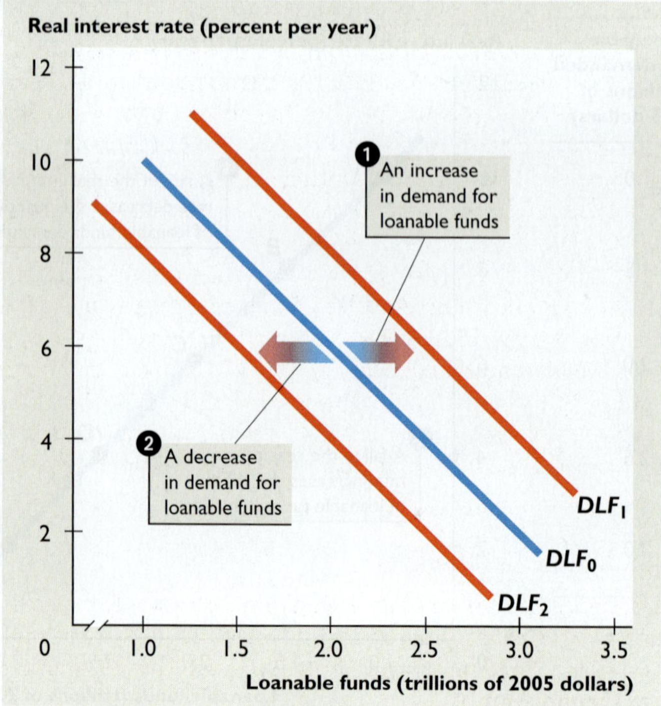

The Supply of Loanable Funds

The *quantity of loanable funds supplied* is the total funds available from private saving, the government budget surplus, and international borrowing during a given period. Saving is the main source of supply of loanable funds. A government budget surplus and international borrowing are other sources.

Saving and the supply of loanable funds are determined by decisions by people like you. Suppose that you've graduated and landed a great job that pays you \$50,000 a year. How do you decide how much of your income to spend on consumption goods and how much to save and supply in the market for loanable funds? Your decision will be influenced by many factors, but chief among them are

1. The real interest rate
2. Disposable income
3. Wealth
4. Expected future income
5. Default risk

We begin by focusing on the real interest rate.

Other things remaining the same, the higher the real interest rate, the greater is the quantity of loanable funds supplied; and the lower the real interest rate, the smaller is the quantity of loanable funds supplied.

The Supply of Loanable Funds Curve

The **supply of loanable funds** is the relationship between the quantity of loanable funds supplied and the real interest rate when all other influences on lending plans remain the same. Figure 10.4 illustrates the supply of loanable funds.

Supply of loanable funds
The relationship between the quantity of loanable funds supplied and the real interest rate when all other influences on lending plans remain the same.

The key reason the supply of loanable funds curve slopes upward is that the real interest rate is the *opportunity cost* of consumption expenditure. A dollar spent is a dollar not saved, so the interest that could have been earned on that saving is forgone. Forgone interest is the opportunity cost of consumption regardless of whether a person is a lender or a borrower. For a lender, saving less means receiving less interest. For a borrower, saving less means paying less off a loan (or increasing a loan) and paying more interest.

By thinking about student loans, you can see why the real interest rate influences saving and the supply of loanable funds. If the real interest rate on student loans jumped to 20 percent a year, graduates would save more (buying cheaper food and finding lower-rent accommodations) to pay off their loans as quickly as possible and avoid, as much as possible, paying the higher interest cost of their loan. If the real interest rate on student loans fell to 1 percent a year, graduates would save less and take longer to pay off their loans because the interest burden was easier to bear.

Changes in the Supply of Loanable Funds

A change in any influence on saving, other than the real interest rate, changes the supply of loanable funds. The other three factors listed above—disposable income, wealth, expected future income, and default risk—are the main things that change the supply of loanable funds.

FIGURE 10.4

The Supply of Loanable Funds

myeconlab Animation

The table shows the quantity of loanable funds supplied at five real interest rates. The graph shows the supply of loanable funds curve, *SLF*. Points *A* through *E* correspond to the rows of the table.

1 If the real interest rate rises, the quantity of loanable funds supplied increases.

2 If the real interest rate falls, the quantity of loanable funds supplied decreases.

	Real interest rate (percent per year)	Loanable funds supplied (trillions of 2005 dollars)
A	10	3.0
B	8	2.5
C	6	2.0
D	4	1.5
E	2	1.0

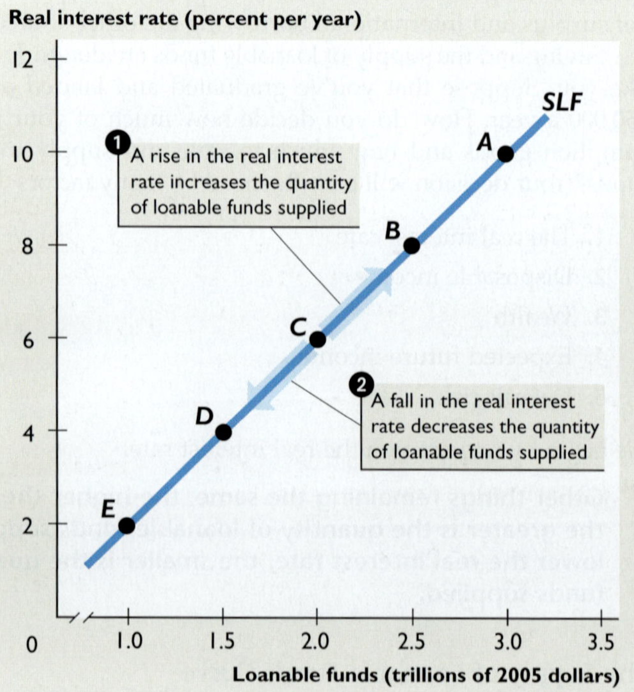

Disposable Income A household's *disposable income* is the income earned minus net taxes. The greater a household's disposable income, other things remaining the same, the greater is its saving. For example, a student whose disposable income is $10,000 a year spends the entire $10,000 and saves nothing. An economics graduate whose disposable income is $50,000 a year spends $40,000 and saves $10,000.

Wealth A household's wealth is what it owns. The greater a household's wealth, other things remaining the same, the less it will save.

Patty is a department store executive who has $15,000 in the bank and no debts: She decides to spend $5,000 on a vacation and save nothing this year. Tony, another department store executive, has nothing in the bank and owes $10,000 on his credit card: He decides to cut consumption and start saving.

Expected Future Income The higher a household's expected future income, other things remaining the same, the smaller is its saving today: If two households have the same current disposable income, the household with the larger expected future disposable income will spend a larger portion of its current disposable income on consumption goods and services and so save less today.

Look at Patty and Tony again. Patty has just been promoted and will receive a $10,000 pay raise next year. Tony has just been told that he will be laid off at the end of the year. On receiving this news, Patty buys a new car—increases her consumption expenditure and cuts her saving—and Tony sells his car and takes the bus—decreases his consumption expenditure and increases his saving.

Most young households expect to have a higher future income for some years and then to have a lower income during retirement. Because of this pattern of income over the life cycle, young people save a small amount, middle-aged people save a lot, and retired people gradually spend their accumulated savings.

Default Risk Default risk is the risk that a loan will not be repaid, or not repaid in full. The greater that risk, the higher is the interest rate needed to induce a person to lend and the smaller is the supply of loanable funds. In normal times, default risk is low but in times of financial crisis when asset prices tumble, default can become widespread as financial institutions become *illiquid* or *insolvent*.

Shifts of the Supply of Loanable Funds Curve

When any of the four influences we've just described changes, the supply of loanable funds changes and the supply curve shifts. An increase in disposable income, or a decrease in wealth, expected future income, or default risk increases the supply of loanable funds.

Figure 10.5 shows how the supply of loanable funds curve shifts. Initially, the supply of loanable funds is SLF_0. Then disposable income increases or wealth, expected future income, or default risk decreases. The supply of loanable funds curve shifts rightward from SLF_0 to SLF_1. Changes in these factors in the opposite direction shift the supply curve leftward from SLF_0 to SLF_2.

FIGURE 10.5

Changes in the Supply of Loanable Funds

myeconlab Animation

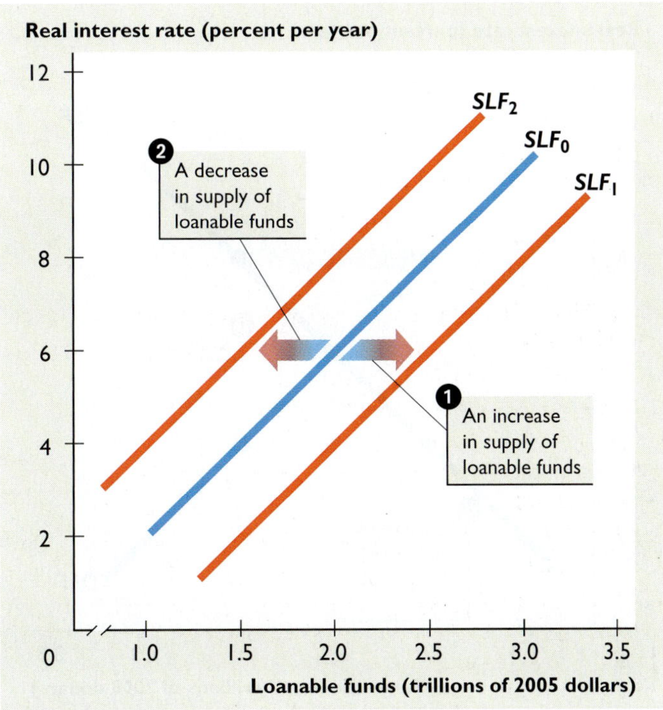

❶ An increase in disposable income or a decrease in wealth, expected future income, or default risk increases the supply of loanable funds and shifts the supply of loanable funds curve rightward from SLF_0 to SLF_1.

❷ A decrease in disposable income or an increase in wealth, expected future income, or default risk decreases the supply of loanable funds and shifts the supply of loanable funds curve leftward from SLF_0 to SLF_2.

Equilibrium in the Market for Loanable Funds

You've seen that, other things remaining the same, the quantities of loanable funds demanded and supplied depend on the real interest rate. The higher the real interest rate, the greater is the amount of saving and the larger is the quantity of loanable funds supplied. But the higher the real interest rate, the smaller is the amount of investment and the smaller is the quantity of loanable funds demanded. There is one interest rate at which the quantities of loanable funds demanded and supplied are equal, and that interest rate is the equilibrium real interest rate.

Figure 10.6 shows how the demand for and supply of loanable funds determine the real interest rate. The *DLF* curve is the demand curve and the *SLF* curve is the supply curve. When the real interest rate exceeds 6 percent a year, the quantity of loanable funds supplied exceeds the quantity demanded. Borrowers have an easy time finding the funds they want, but lenders are unable to lend all the funds they have available. The real interest rate falls and continues to fall until the quantity of funds supplied equals the quantity of funds demanded.

Alternatively, when the interest rate is less than 6 percent a year, the quantity of loanable funds supplied is less than the quantity demanded. Borrowers can't find the funds they want, but lenders are able to lend all the funds they have available. So the real interest rate rises and continues to rise until the quantity of funds supplied equals the quantity demanded.

Regardless of whether there is a surplus or a shortage of loanable funds, the real interest rate changes and is pulled toward an equilibrium level. In Figure 10.6,

FIGURE 10.6

Equilibrium in the Market for Loanable Funds

myeconlab Animation

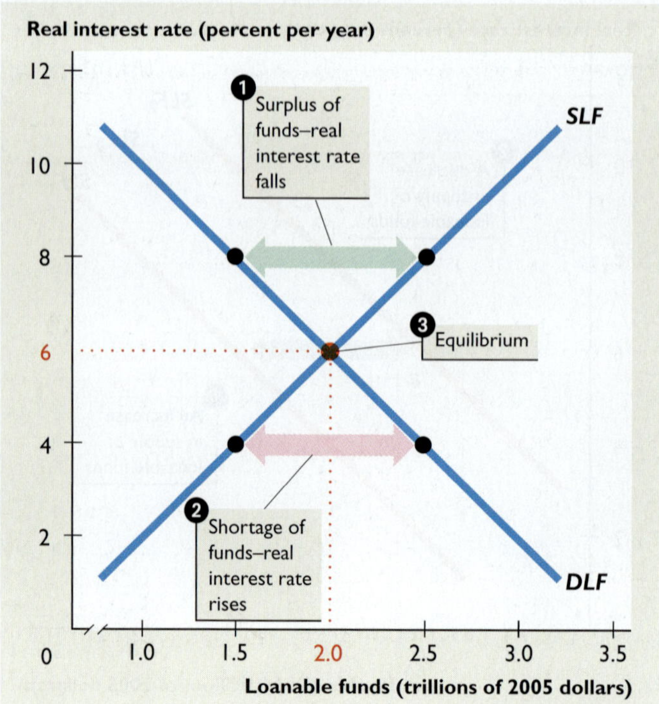

1. If the real interest rate is 8 percent a year, the quantity of loanable funds demanded is less than the quantity supplied. There is a surplus of funds, and the real interest rate falls.
2. If the real interest rate is 4 percent a year, the quantity of loanable funds demanded exceeds the quantity supplied. There is a shortage of funds, and the real interest rate rises.
3. When the real interest rate is 6 percent a year, the quantity of loanable funds demanded equals the quantity supplied. There is neither a shortage nor a surplus of funds, and the real interest rate is at its equilibrium level.

the equilibrium real interest rate is 6 percent a year. At this interest rate, there is neither a surplus nor a shortage of funds. Borrowers can get the funds they want, and lenders can lend all the funds they have available. The plans of borrowers (investors) and lenders (savers) are consistent with each other.

Changes in Demand and Supply

Fluctuations in either the demand for loanable funds or the supply of loanable funds bring fluctuations in the real interest rate and in the equilibrium quantity of funds lent and borrowed. Here we'll illustrate the effects of an increase in each.

An increase in expected profit increases the demand for loanable funds. With no change in supply, there is a shortage of funds and the interest rate rises until the equilibrium is restored. In Figure 10.7(a), the increase in the demand for loanable funds shifts the demand for loanable funds curve rightward from DLF_0 to DLF_1. At a real interest rate of 6 percent a year, there is a shortage of funds. The real interest rate rises to 8 percent a year, and the equilibrium quantity of funds increases.

If one of the influences on saving plans changes and increases saving, the supply of loanable funds increases. With no change in demand, there is a surplus of funds and the interest rate falls until the equilibrium is restored. In Figure 10.7(b), the increase in the supply of loanable funds shifts the supply of loanable funds curve rightward from SLF_0 to SLF_1. At a real interest rate of 6 percent a year, there is a surplus of funds. The real interest rate falls to 4 percent a year, and the equilibrium quantity of funds increases.

Over time, both demand and supply in the market for loanable funds fluctuate and the real interest rate rises and falls. Both the supply of loanable funds and the demand for loanable funds tend to increase over time. On the average, they increase at a similar pace, so although demand and supply trend upward, the real interest rate has no trend. It fluctuates around a constant average level.

FIGURE 10.7

Changes in Demand and Supply in the Market for Loanable Funds

myeconlab Animation

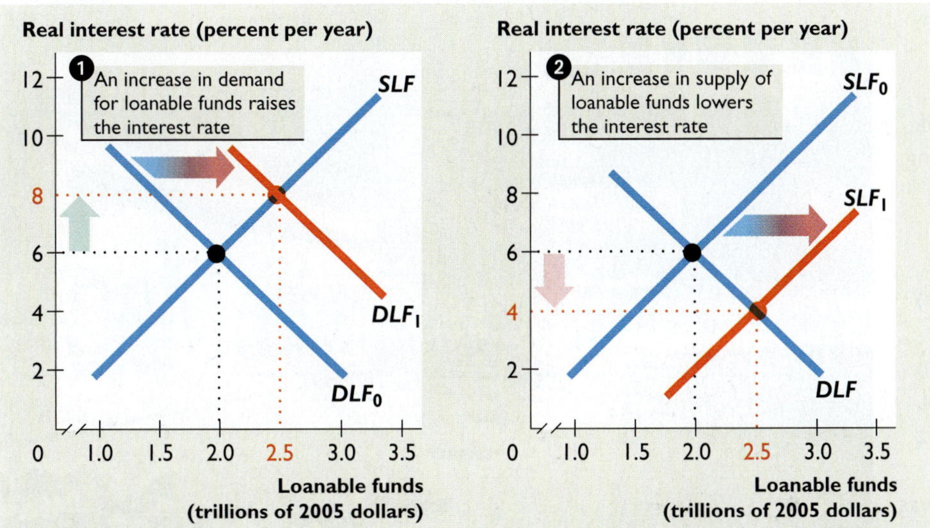

(a) An increase in investment

(b) An increase in saving

1. If the demand for loanable funds increases and the supply of loanable funds remains the same, the real interest rate rises and the equilibrium quantity of funds increases.

2. If the supply of loanable funds increases and the demand for loanable funds remains the same, the real interest rate falls and the equilibrium quantity of funds increases.

EYE on FINANCIAL CRISIS

What Created the Global Financial Crisis?

Events in the market for loanable funds, on both the supply side and demand side, created the global financial crisis.

An increase in default risk decreased supply; and the disappearance of some major Wall Street institutions and lowered profit expectations decreased demand.

Bear Stearns was absorbed by JP Morgan with help from the Federal Reserve; Lehman Brothers' assets were taken over by Barclays; Fannie Mae and Freddie Mac went into government oversight with U.S. taxpayer guarantees; Merrill Lynch became part of the Bank of America; AIG received an $85 billion lifeline from the Federal Reserve and sold off parcels of its business to financial institutions around the world; Wachovia was taken over by Wells Fargo and Washington Mutual by JP Morgan Chase.

But what caused the increase in default risk and the failure of so many financial institutions?

Between 2002 and 2005, interest rates were low. There were plenty of willing borrowers and plenty of willing lenders. Fuelled by easy loans, home prices rose rapidly. Lenders bundled their loans into mortgage-backed securities and sold them to eager buyers around the world.

Then, in 2006, interest rates began to rise and home prices began to fall. People defaulted on mortgages; banks took losses and some became insolvent. A downward spiral of lending was under way.

CHECKPOINT 10.2

myeconlab

Work these problems in Study Plan 10.2 to get instant feedback.

Explain how borrowing and lending decisions are made and how these decisions interact in the market for loanable funds.

Practice Problems

First Call, Inc. is a cellular phone company. It plans to build an assembly plant that costs $10 million if the real interest rate is 6 percent a year. If the real interest rate is 5 percent a year, First Call will build a larger plant that costs $12 million. And if the real interest rate is 7 percent a year, First Call will build a smaller plant that costs $8 million. Use this information to work Problems **1** and **2**.

1. Draw a graph of First Call's demand for loanable funds curve.
2. First Call expects its profit from the sale of cellular phones to double next year. If other things remain the same, explain how this increase in expected profit influences First Call's demand for loanable funds.
3. Draw graphs that illustrate how an increase in the supply of loanable funds and a decrease in the demand for loanable funds can lower the real interest rate and leave the equilibrium quantity of loanable funds unchanged.
4. **Poof! How home loans transform**
   Banks make a profit by transforming home loans into mortgage-backed securities and trading them on financial loans markets. Banks then use this profit to issue more home loans. During the credit crisis, the market for mortgage-backed securities issued by banks almost stopped functioning.
   Source: *The New York Times*, September 18, 2009

   Explain why the market for mortgage-backed securities almost stopped functioning during the credit crisis of 2007–2008.

Guided Solutions to Practice Problems

1. The demand for loanable funds curve is the downward-sloping curve DLF_0 and passes through the points highlighted in Figure 1.
2. An increase in the expected profit increases investment today, which increases the quantity of loanable funds demanded at each real interest rate. The demand for loanable funds curve shifts rightward to DLF_1 (Figure 1).
3. The increase in the supply of loanable funds shifts the supply curve rightward. The decrease in the demand for loanable funds shifts the demand curve leftward. The real interest rate falls. If the shifts are of the same magnitude, the equilibrium quantity of funds remains unchanged (Figure 2). If the shift of the supply curve is greater (less) than that of the demand curve, then the equilibrium quantity of funds increases (decreases).
4. The banks that create and sell mortgage-backed securities demand loanable funds and the banks that buy these securities supply loanable funds. When home prices started to fall and home owners defaulted, banks made fewer home loans and the demand for mortgage-backed securities decreased. These securities also became riskier, so the supply of loanable funds to buy them dried up.

FIGURE 1

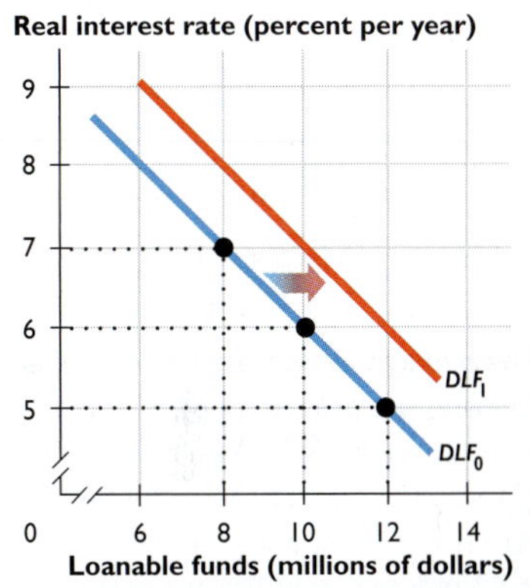

FIGURE 2

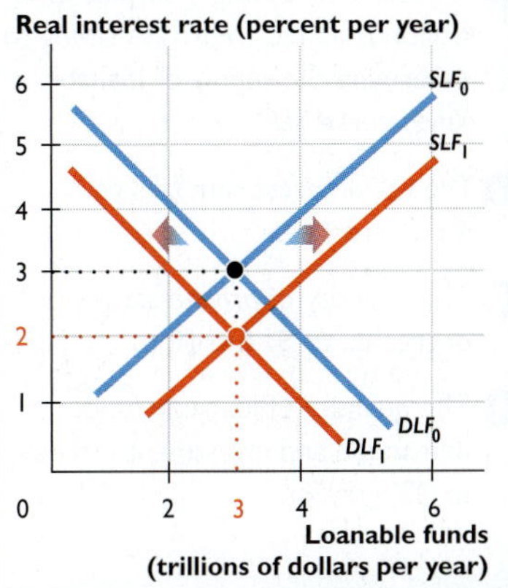

10.3 GOVERNMENT IN LOANABLE FUNDS MARKET

The government enters the market for loanable funds when it has a budget surplus or budget deficit. So actions that change the government's budget balance influence the market for loanable funds and the real interest rate. A change in the real interest rate influences both saving and investment. To complete our study of the forces that determine the quantity of investment and the real interest rate, we investigate the role played by the government's budget balance.

A Government Budget Surplus

A government budget surplus increases the supply of loanable funds. The real interest rate falls, which decreases private saving and decreases the quantity of private funds supplied. The lower real interest rate increases the quantity of loanable funds demanded and increases investment.

Figure 10.8 shows these effects of a government budget surplus. The private supply of loanable funds curve is *PSLF*. The supply of loanable funds curve, *SLF*, shows the sum of the private supply and the government budget surplus. Here, the government budget surplus is $1 trillion, so at each real interest rate the *SLF* curve lies $1 trillion to the right of the *PSLF* curve. That is, the horizontal distance between the *PSLF* curve and the *SLF* curve is the government budget surplus.

FIGURE 10.8

Government Budget Surplus

myeconlab Animation

The demand for loanable funds curve is *DLF*, and the private supply of loanable funds curve is *PSLF*. With a balanced government budget, the real interest rate is 6 percent a year and investment is $2 trillion a year. Private saving and investment are $2 trillion a year.

1. A government budget surplus of $1 trillion is added to private saving to determine the supply of loanable funds curve *SLF*.
2. The real interest rate falls to 4 percent a year.
3. The quantity of private saving decreases to $1.5 trillion.
4. The quantity of loanable funds demanded and investment increase to $2.5 trillion.

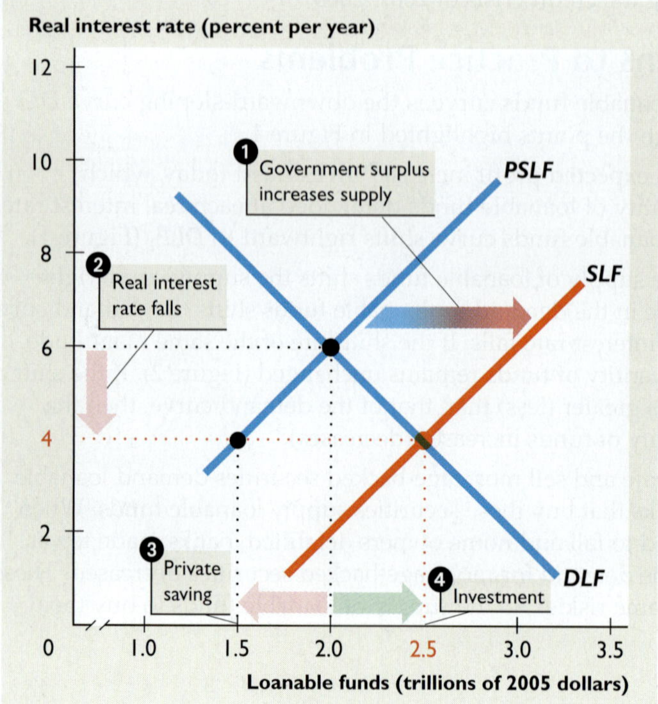

With no government budget surplus, the real interest rate is 6 percent a year, the quantity of loanable funds is $2 trillion a year and investment is $2 trillion a year. But with the government budget surplus of $1 trillion a year, the equilibrium real interest rate falls to 4 percent a year and the quantity of loanable funds increases to $2.5 trillion a year.

The fall in the real interest rate decreases private saving to $1.5 trillion, but investment increases to $2.5 trillion, which is financed by private saving and the government budget surplus (government saving).

A Government Budget Deficit

A government budget deficit increases the demand for loanable funds. The real interest rate rises, which increases private saving and increases the quantity of private funds supplied. But the higher real interest rate decreases investment and the quantity of loanable funds demanded by firms to finance investment.

Figure 10.9 shows these effects of a government budget deficit. The private demand for loanable funds curve is *PDLF.* The demand for loanable funds curve, *DLF*, shows the sum of the private demand and the government budget deficit. Here, the government budget deficit is $1 trillion, so at each real interest rate the *DLF* curve lies $1 trillion to the right of the *PDLF* curve. That is, the horizontal distance between the *PDLF* curve and the *DLF* curve equals the government budget deficit.

With no government budget deficit, the real interest rate is 6 percent a year, the quantity of loanable funds is $2 trillion a year and investment is $2 trillion a

FIGURE 10.9

Government Budget Deficit

myeconlab Animation

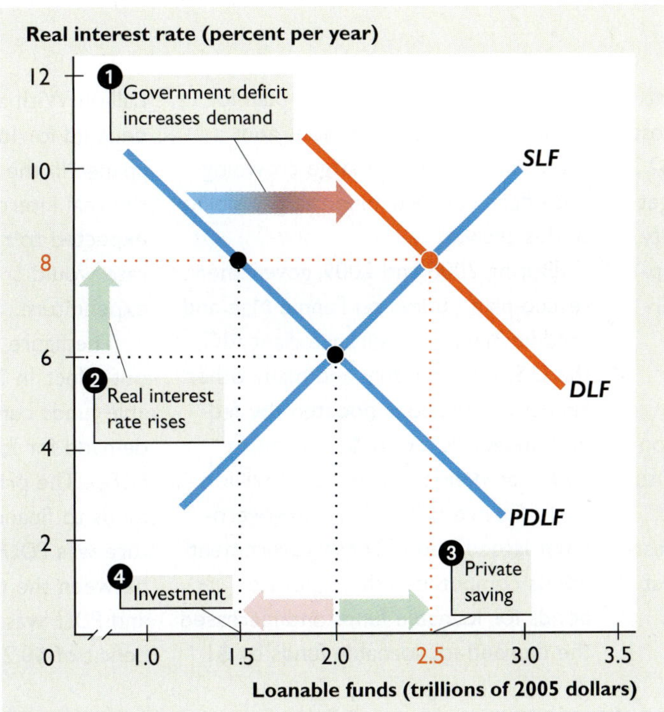

The supply of loanable funds curve is *SLF* and the private demand for loanable funds curve is *PDLF*. With a balanced government budget, the real interest rate is 6 percent a year and the quantity of loanable funds is $2 trillion a year. Private saving and investment are $2 trillion a year.

1. A government budget deficit of $1 trillion is added to the private demand for funds to determine the demand for loanable funds curve *DLF.*
2. The real interest rate rises to 8 percent a year.
3. The quantity of private fund supplied and the quantity of loanable funds increase to $2.5 trillion.
4. Investment decreases to $1.5 trillion. Investment is crowded out.

year. But with the government budget deficit of $1 trillion, the real interest rate rises from 6 percent a year to 8 percent a year and the quantity of loanable funds increases from $2 trillion to $2.5 trillion.

The rise in the real interest rate increases private saving to $2.5 trillion, but investment decreases to $1.5 trillion. The tendency for a government budget deficit to raise the real interest rate and decrease investment is called the **crowding-out effect**. Investment does not decrease by the full amount of the government budget deficit because private saving increases. In this example, private saving increases by $0.5 trillion to $2.5 trillion.

Crowding-out effect
The tendency for a government budget deficit to raise the real interest rate and decrease investment.

The Ricardo-Barro Effect

First suggested by the English economist David Ricardo in the eighteenth century and refined by Robert J. Barro of Harvard University during the 1980s, the Ricardo-Barro effect holds that the effects we've just shown are wrong and that the government budget deficit has no effect on the real interest rate or investment. Barro says that rational taxpayers can see that a deficit today means that future taxes will be higher and future disposable incomes will be smaller. With smaller expected future disposable incomes, saving increases. The increase in saving increases the supply of loanable funds—shifts the *SLF* curve rightward—by an amount equal to the government budget deficit. The supply of loanable fund might increase and lessen the influence of the government budget deficit on the real interest rate and investment, but most economists regard the full Ricardo-Barro effect as unlikely.

EYE on the U.S. ECONOMY

Did the Rescue Plan Crowd Out Investment?

In mid-2007, on the eve of the onset of the global financial crisis, U.S. investment expenditure was running at $2.2 trillion. The government had a budget deficit of $0.2 trillion, so the quantity of loanable funds demanded and supplied was $2.4 trillion. The real interest rate at that time was 3 percent per year.

By mid-2009, U.S. investment expenditure had fallen to $1.5 trillion and the real interest rate had risen to 4.5 percent per year.

What caused the collapse of investment and the rise in the real interest rate?

One possible answer is that the federal government's rescue plan for troubled financial institutions and other firms created a large crowding-out effect. Let's examine the plausibility of this answer.

During 2008 and 2009, government rescue-plan outlays on Fannie Mae and Freddie Mac, the insurance giant AIG, the U.S. auto industry, and many other financial institutions boosted the federal budget deficit by $1 trillion. In 2009, the deficit reached $1.2 trillion.

To finance this deficit, the government issued bonds. These government bonds competed with corporate bonds for loanable funds and increased the demand for loanable funds by $1 trillion. With an increase in the demand for loanable funds and no change in the supply of loanable funds, the real interest rate would be expected to rise. The higher interest rate would crowd out investment expenditure.

The figure illustrates this crowding-out effect. In 2007, the supply of loanable funds curve was *SLF* and the demand for loanable funds curve was DLF_{07}. The private demand for loanable funds to finance investment expenditure was *PDLF*, and the horizontal gap between the two demand curves DLF_{07} and *PDLF* was the government budget deficit of $0.2 trillion.

EYE on YOUR LIFE

Your Participation in the Loanable Funds Market

Think about the amount of saving that you do. How much of your disposable income do you save? Is it a positive amount or a negative amount?

If you save a positive amount, what do you do with your savings? Do you put them in a bank, in the stock market, in bonds, or just keep money at home? What is the interest rate you earn on your savings?

If you save a negative amount, just what does that mean? It means that you have a deficit (like a government deficit). You're spending more than your disposable income. In this case, how do you finance your deficit? Do you get a student loan? Do you run up an outstanding credit card balance? How much do you pay to finance your negative saving (your *dissaving*)?

How do you think your saving will change when you graduate and get a better-paying job?

Also think about the amount of investment that you do. You are investing in your human capital by being in school. What is this investment costing you? How are you financing this investment?

When you graduate and start a well-paying job, you will need to decide whether to buy an apartment or a house or to rent your home.

How would you make a decision whether to buy or rent a home? Would it be smart to borrow $300,000 to finance the purchase of a home? How would the interest rate influence your decision?

These examples show just some of the many decisions and transactions you will make in the market for loanable funds—the link between your saving and your investment.

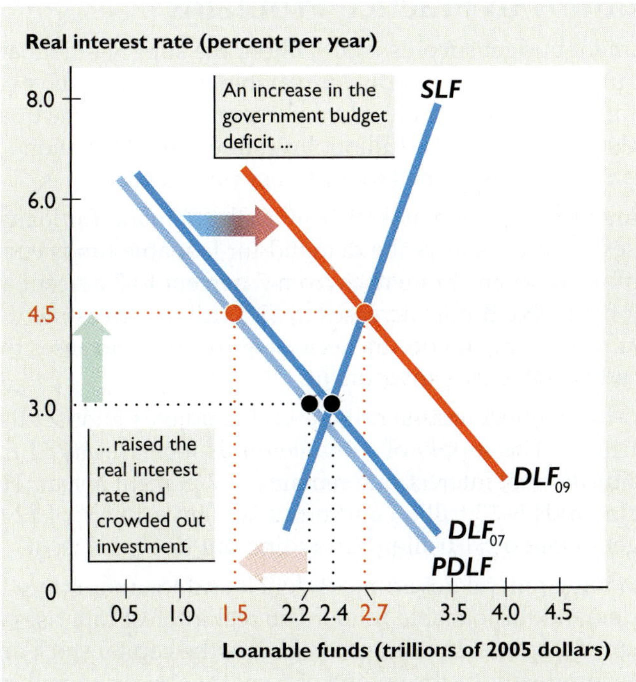

The rescue-plan expenditures increased the demand for loanable funds and shifted the demand curve rightward to DLF_{09}.

The increase in the demand for loanable funds raised the equilibrium interest rate to 4.5 percent per year and the higher interest rate brought a decrease in the quantity of loanable funds demanded to finance a smaller volume of investment expenditure.

Although the higher real interest rate crowded out some investment, without the rescue package, depressed profit expectations might have lowered investment even more.

SOURCES OF DATA: Bureau of Economic Analysis and Federal Reserve. The interest rate is the average of the Aaa and Baa corporate bond rates adjusted for inflation measured by the GDP price index.

myeconlab

Work these problems in Study Plan 10.3 to get instant feedback.

CHECKPOINT 10.3

Explain how a government budget surplus or deficit influences the real interest rate, investment, and saving.

Practice Problems

Table 1 shows the demand for loanable funds schedule and the supply of loanable funds schedule when the government budget is balanced. Use Table 1 to work Problems **1** to **3**.

1. If the government budget surplus is $1 trillion, what are the real interest rate, the quantity of investment, and the quantity of private saving? Is there any crowding out in this situation?
2. If the government budget deficit is $1 trillion, what are the real interest rate, the quantity of investment, and the quantity of private saving? Is there any crowding out in this situation?
3. If the government budget deficit is $1 trillion and the Ricardo-Barro effect occurs, what are the real interest rate and the quantity of investment?
4. **Federal deficit surges to $1.38 trillion through August**
   House Republican Leader John Boehner of Ohio asks: When will the White House tackle these jaw-dropping deficits that pile more and more debt on future generations while it massively increases federal spending?
   Source: *USA Today*, September 11, 2009

   Explain what effect the ballooning federal deficit and mounting debt have on U.S. economic growth.

TABLE 1

Real interest rate (percent per year)	Loanable funds demanded (trillions of 2005 dollars per year)	Loanable funds supplied (trillions of 2005 dollars per year)
4	3.5	0.5
5	3.0	1.0
6	2.5	1.5
7	2.0	2.0
8	1.5	2.5
9	1.0	3.0
10	0.5	3.5

FIGURE 1

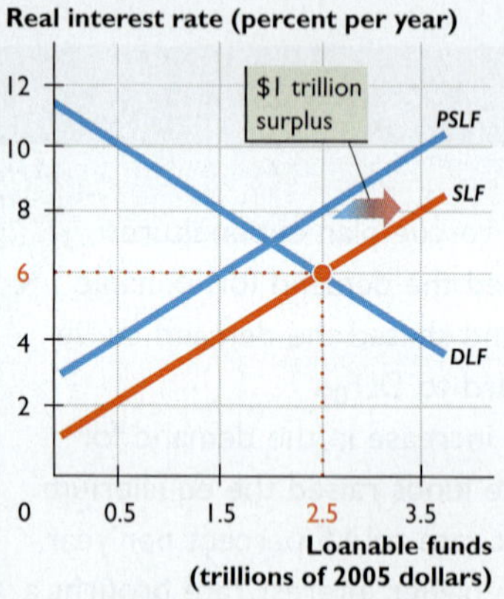

FIGURE 2

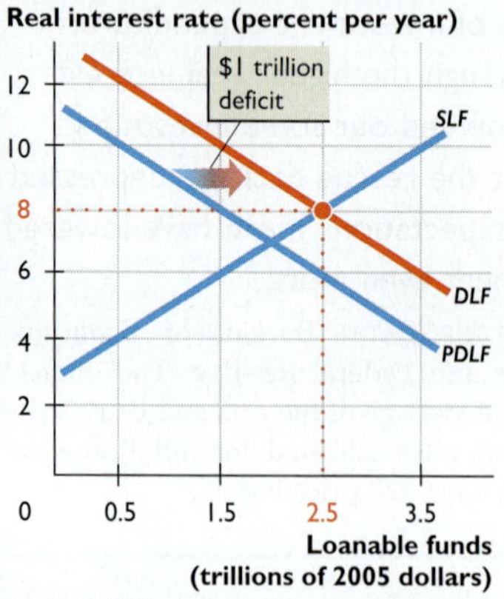

Guided Solutions to Practice Problems

1. If the government budget surplus is $1 trillion, the supply of loanable funds increases. Figure 1 shows the supply of loanable funds *SLF*. The equilibrium real interest rate falls from 7 percent to 6 percent a year and the quantity of loanable funds increases to $2.5 trillion. Investment is $2.5 trillion and private saving is $1.5 trillion. Crowding out does not occur.
2. If the government budget deficit is $1 trillion, the demand for loanable funds increases. Figure 2 shows the demand for loanable funds curve *DLF*. The equilibrium real interest rate rises from 7 percent to 8 percent a year and the quantity of loanable funds increases to $2.5 trillion. Investment decreases to $1.5 trillion. Crowding out occurs because the deficit increases the real interest rate, which decreases investment.
3. If the Ricardo-Barro effect occurs, private saving adjusts to offset the budget deficit of $1 trillion. The supply of loanable funds increases by $1 trillion and the equilibrium real interest rate remains at 7 percent a year. The quantity of loanable funds is $3 trillion and it finances investment of $2 trillion and the budget deficit of $1 trillion. Crowding out does not occur.
4. Both the ballooning federal government deficit and the mounting debt increase the demand for loanable funds. The real interest rate rises and private investment decreases. Investment increases the capital stock and increases labor productivity, the engine of growth. The rising real interest rate will slow the growth of the capital stock and slow the growth of labor productivity and economic growth.

CHAPTER SUMMARY

Key Points

1 Describe the financial markets and the key financial institutions.

- Firms use financial capital to buy and operate physical capital.
- Gross investment is the total amount spent on physical capital in a given period. Net investment equals gross investment minus depreciation.
- Wealth is the value of what people own; saving is the amount of disposable income that is not spent, and it adds to wealth.
- The market for financial capital is a market made up of the markets for loans, bonds, and stocks.

2 Explain how borrowing and lending decisions are made and how these decisions interact in the market for loanable funds.

- Other things remaining the same, the lower the real interest rate or the higher the expected profit rate, the greater is the quantity of loanable funds demanded.
- The demand for loanable funds changes when the expected profit rate changes.
- Other things remaining the same, the higher the real interest rate, the greater is the quantity of loanable funds supplied.
- The supply of loanable funds changes when disposable income, wealth, expected future income, or default risk changes.
- Equilibrium in the loanable funds market determines the real interest rate.
- At the equilibrium real interest rate, the quantity of loanable funds demanded equals the quantity of loanable funds supplied.

3 Explain how a government budget surplus or deficit influences the real interest rate, investment, and saving.

- A government budget surplus increases the supply of loanable funds and a government budget deficit increases the demand for loanable funds.
- With no change in private saving, an increase in the government budget deficit raises the real interest rate and crowds out investment.
- A government budget deficit might increase private saving because it decreases expected future disposable income.

Key Terms

Bond, 244
Capital or physical capital, 242
Crowding-out effect, 260
Demand for loanable funds, 249
Financial institution, 245
Gross investment, 242
Market for loanable funds, 248
Net investment, 242
Net worth, 246
Stock, 244
Supply of loanable funds, 251
Wealth, 242

myeconlab

Work these problems in Chapter 10 Study Plan to get instant feedback.

CHAPTER CHECKPOINT

Study Problems and Applications

1. On January 1, 2009, Terry's Towing Service owned 4 tow trucks valued at $300,000. During 2009, Terry's bought 2 new trucks for a total of $180,000. At the end of 2009, the market value of all of the firm's trucks was $400,000. What was Terry's gross investment? Calculate Terry's depreciation and net investment.

Use the following information to work Problems 2 and 3.

The Bureau of Economic Analysis reported that the U.S. capital stock was $31.4 trillion at the end of 2006, $32.2 trillion at the end of 2007, and $32.7 trillion at the end of 2008. Depreciation in 2007 was $1.4 trillion, and gross investment during 2008 was $2.0 trillion (all in 2005 dollars).

2. Calculate U.S. net investment and gross investment during 2007.
3. Calculate U.S. depreciation and net investment during 2008.
4. Mike takes a summer job washing cars. During the summer, he earns an after-tax income of $3,000 and he spends $1,000 on goods and services. What was Mike's saving during the summer and the change, if any, in his wealth?
5. What is the market for financial capital? What is financial capital? Explain why, when the real interest rate rises, the demand for loanable funds does not change but the quantity of funds demanded decreases.
6. With an increase in global tension during 2005 and 2006, many governments increased defense spending, which decreased government budget surpluses. Show, on a graph, the effects of a decrease in government budget surpluses if there is no Ricardo-Barro effect. Explain how the effects differ if there is a partial Ricardo-Barro effect.
7. **Riding the digital express**

   The first undersea fiber-optic cable, Seacom, reached the east African coast in July 2009. This "Digital Express" is the most important infrastructure investment in east Africa since the construction of the Uganda Railway in 1903. The $700m project will reduce business costs, create an e-commerce sector, and open up the region to foreign investment. Its impact will be unparalleled in contemporary African economic history.

   Source: BBCNews, September 15, 2009

   Draw a graph of the loanable funds market. Suppose that firms decide to invest in east Africa and they borrow the required funds in the loanable funds market. How will this borrowing change the real interest rate and the quantity of saving?
8. **G-20 leaders look to shake off lingering economic troubles**

   For the world economy to emerge stronger from the global financial crisis, experts say that savings by the United States, investment by Japan, and consumption by China will all have to increase.

   Source: *USA Today*, September 23, 2009

   Explain how the experts' advice will affect the market for loanable funds in the United States, in Japan, and in China.

Instructor Assignable Problems and Applications

Your instructor can assign these problems as homework, a quiz, or a test in **MyEconLab**.

1. Explain why the supply of loanable funds and the demand for loanable funds decreased during the global financial crisis of 2007–2008. Draw a graph of the loanable funds market before the crisis and use your graph to illustrate the source and effects of the crisis on saving, investment, and the real interest rate.
2. On January 1, 2009, Sophie's Internet Cafe owned 10 computer terminals valued at $8,000. During 2009, Sophie's bought 5 new computer terminals at a cost of $1,000 each, and at the end of the year, the market value of all of Sophie's computer terminals was $11,000. What was Sophie's gross investment, depreciation, and net investment?
3. The numbers in the second column of Table 1 are the Federal Reserve's estimates of personal wealth at the end of each year. The numbers in the third column are the Bureau of Economic Analysis's estimates of personal saving each year. In which years did the change in wealth exceed saving? In which years did saving exceed the change in wealth? Given the definitions of saving and wealth, how can the change in wealth differ from saving?

TABLE 1

Year	Wealth (billions of dollars)	Saving (billions of dollars)
2005	58,823	128
2006	63,335	235
2007	63,911	179
2008	52,917	286

4. Cindy takes a summer job painting houses. During the summer, she earns an after-tax income of $8,000 and she spends $2,000 on living expenses. What was Cindy's saving during the summer and the change, if any, in her wealth?
5. The stock market boom of 2002–2007 increased wealth by trillions of dollars. Explain the effect of this increase in wealth on the equilibrium real interest rate, investment, and saving.

Use the following information and the loanable funds market to work Problems 6 to 8.

IMF says it battled crisis well

The International Monetary Fund (IMF) reported that it acted effectively in combating the global recession, especially in Eastern Europe. Since September 2008, the IMF made $163 billion available to developing countries. While the IMF urged the United States, Western European countries, and China to run deficits to stimulate their economies, the IMF required countries in Eastern Europe with large deficits to cut spending and not increase spending.

The Wall Street Journal, September 29, 2009

6. Explain how an increase in government expenditure will change the government's budget balance and the loanable funds market.
7. Why do you think the IMF required countries with large deficits, like those in Eastern Europe, to cut spending rather than increase it?
8. The Center for Economic and Policy Research in Washington, D.C., claims that the IMF didn't allow developing countries that were looking for loans to expand their deficits sufficiently. Would these developing countries have weathered the global recession better if they had obtained larger loans from the IMF?

During the late 1990s, governments had budget deficits, which in the early 2000s began to turn into surpluses. Use this information to work Problems **9** and **10**.

9. Show, on a graph, the effects of a switch from a government budget deficit to a government budget surplus if there is no Ricardo-Barro effect.

10. What are the effects of a switch from a government budget deficit to a government budget surplus if there is a partial Ricardo-Barro effect?

The U.S. saving rate increased from –0.2 percent in 2006 to 4.8 percent in 2007 and 8.7 percent in 2008. Use this information to work Problems **11** and **12**.

11. How can the saving rate be negative? Why might a negative saving rate be something to worry about? How might U.S. saving be increased?

12. Explain why the U.S. saving rate might have increased and its effect on the supply of loanable funds.

Use the following information to work Problems **13** and **14**.

India's economy hits the wall

At the start of 2008, India had an annual growth of 9%, huge consumer demand, and increasing foreign investment. But by July 2008, India had 11.4% inflation, large government deficits, and rising interest rates. Economic growth is expected to fall to 7% by the end of 2008. A Goldman Sachs report suggests that India needs to lower the government's deficit, raise educational achievement, control inflation, and liberalize its financial markets.

Source: *Business Week*, July 1, 2008

13. If the Indian government reduces its deficit and returns to a balanced budget, how will the demand or supply of loanable funds in India change?

14. With economic growth forecasted to slow, future incomes are expected to fall. If other things remain the same, how will the demand or supply of loanable funds in India change?

Use the following information to work Problems **15** and **16**.

Greenspan's conundrum spells confusion for us all

In January 2005, the interest rate on bonds was 4% a year and it was expected to rise to 5% a year by the end of 2005. As the rate rose to 4.3% during February, most commentators focused, not on why the interest rate rose, but on it was so low before. Explanations of this "conundrum" included that unusual buying and expectations for an economic slowdown were keeping the interest rate low.

Source: *Financial Times*, February 26, 2005

15. Explain how "unusual buying" might lead to a low real interest rate.

16. Explain how "expectations for an economic slowdown" might lead to a lower real interest rate.

17. After Lehman, U.S. firms adjust to new face of credit

The cost of capital for corporations remains higher than in the boom years before the crisis hit, even as official U.S. interest rates are near zero.

Source: Reuters, September 11, 2009

Explain why the cost of capital for corporations is higher than near zero.

How does the Fed create money?

How did the Fed regulate the quantity of money in the 2008 financial crisis?

11

The Monetary System

CHAPTER CHECKLIST

When you have completed your study of this chapter, you will be able to

1. Define money and describe its functions.
2. Describe the functions of banks.
3. Describe the functions of the Federal Reserve System (the Fed).
4. Explain how banks create money and how the Fed controls the quantity of money.

11.1 WHAT IS MONEY?

Money, like fire and the wheel, has been around for a very long time. An incredible array of items has served as money. North American Indians used wampum (beads made from shells), Fijians used whales' teeth, and early American colonists used tobacco. Cakes of salt served as money in Ethiopia and Tibet. What do wampum, whales' teeth, tobacco, and salt have in common? Why are they examples of money? Today, when we want to buy something, we use coins or notes (dollar bills), write a check, send an e-check, present a credit or debit card, or use a "smart card." Are all these things that we use today money? To answer these questions, we need a definition of money.

Definition of Money

Money
Any commodity or token that is generally accepted as a *means of payment.*

Money is any commodity or token that is generally accepted as a *means of payment.* This definition has three parts that we'll examine in turn.

A Commodity or Token

Money is always something that can be recognized and that can be divided up into small parts. So money might be an actual commodity, such as a bar of silver or gold. But it might also be a token, such as a quarter or a $10 bill. Money might also be a virtual token, such as an electronic record in a bank's database (more about this type of money later).

Generally Accepted

Money is *generally* accepted, which means that it can be used to buy *anything and everything*. Some tokens can be used to buy some things but not others. For example, a bus pass is accepted as payment for a bus ride, but you can't use your bus pass to buy toothpaste. So a bus pass is not money. In contrast, you can use a $5 bill to buy either a bus ride or toothpaste—or anything else that costs $5 or less. So a $5 bill is money.

Means of Payment

Means of payment
A method of settling a debt.

A **means of payment** is a method of settling a debt. When a payment has been made, the deal is complete. Suppose that Gus buys a car from his friend Ann. Gus doesn't have enough money to pay for the car right now, but he will have enough three months from now, when he gets paid. Ann agrees that Gus may pay for the car in three months' time. Gus buys the car with a loan from Ann and then pays off the loan. The loan isn't money. Money is what Gus uses to pay off the loan.

So what wampum, whales' teeth, tobacco, and salt have in common is that they have served as a generally accepted means of payment, and that is why they are examples of money.

The Functions of Money

Money performs three vital functions. It serves as a

- Medium of exchange
- Unit of account
- Store of value

Medium of Exchange

A **medium of exchange** is an object that is generally accepted in return for goods and services. Money is a medium of exchange. Without money, you would have to exchange goods and services directly for other goods and services—an exchange called **barter**. Barter requires a *double coincidence of wants.* For example, if you want a soda and have only a paperback novel to offer in exchange for it, you must find someone who is selling soda and who also wants your paperback novel. Money guarantees that there is a double coincidence of wants because people with something to sell will always accept money in exchange for it. Money acts as a lubricant that smoothes the mechanism of exchange. Money enables you to specialize in the activity in which you have a comparative advantage (see Chapter 3, pp. 75–77) instead of searching for a double coincidence of wants.

Medium of exchange
An object that is generally accepted in return for goods and services.

Barter
The direct exchange of goods and services for other goods and services, which requires a double coincidence of wants.

Unit of Account

A **unit of account** is an agreed-upon measure for stating the prices of goods and services. To get the most out of your budget, you have to figure out whether going to a rock concert is worth its opportunity cost. But that cost is not dollars and cents. It is the number of movies, cappuccinos, ice-cream cones, or sticks of gum that you must give up to attend the concert. It's easy to do such calculations when all these goods have prices in terms of dollars and cents (see Table 11.1). If a rock concert costs $64 and a movie costs $8, you know right away that going to the concert costs you 8 movies. If a cappuccino costs $4, going to the concert costs 16 cappuccinos. You need only one calculation to figure out the opportunity cost of any pair of goods and services. For example, the opportunity cost of the rock concert is 128 sticks of gum ($64 ÷ 50¢ = 128 sticks of gum).

Now imagine how troublesome it would be if the rock concert ticket agent posted its price as 8 movies, and if the movie theater posted its price as 2 cappuccinos, and if the coffee shop posted the price of a cappuccino as 2 ice-cream cones, and if the ice-cream shop posted its price as 4 sticks of gum! Now how much running around and calculating do you have to do to figure out how much that rock concert is going to cost you in terms of the movies, cappuccino, ice cream, or sticks of gum that you must give up to attend it? You get the answer for movies right away from the sign posted by the ticket agent. For all the other goods, you're going to have to visit many different places to establish the price of each commodity in terms of another and then calculate prices in units that are relevant for your own decision. Cover up the column labeled "price in money units" in Table 11.1 and see how hard it is to figure out the number of sticks of gum it costs to attend a rock concert. It's enough to make a person swear off rock! How much simpler it is using dollars and cents.

Unit of account
An agreed-upon measure for stating the prices of goods and services.

TABLE 11.1 A UNIT OF ACCOUNT SIMPLIFIES PRICE COMPARISONS

Good	Price in money units	Price in units of another good
Rock concert	$64.00	8 movies
Movie	$8.00	2 cappuccinos
Cappuccino	$4.00	2 ice-cream cones
Ice-cream cone	$2.00	4 sticks of gum
Stick of gum	$0.50	

Store of Value

Any commodity or token that can be held and exchanged later for goods and services is called a **store of value**. Money acts as a store of value. If it did not, it would not be accepted in exchange for goods and services. The more stable the value of a commodity or token, the better it can act as a store of value and the more useful it is as money. No store of value is completely stable. The value of a physical object, such as a house, a car, or a work of art, fluctuates over time. The value of the commodities and tokens that we use as money also fluctuates, and when there is inflation, money persistently falls in value.

Store of value
Any commodity or token that can be held and exchanged later for goods and services.

Money Today

Fiat money
Objects that are money because the law decrees or orders them to be money.

Money in the world today is called **fiat money**. *Fiat* is a Latin word that means decree or order. Fiat money is money because the law decrees it to be so. The objects used as money have value only because of their legal status as money.

Today's fiat money consists of

- Currency
- Deposits at banks and other financial institutions

Currency

Currency
Notes (dollar bills) and coins.

The notes (dollar bills) and coins that we use in the United States today are known as **currency**. The government declares notes to be money with the words printed on every dollar bill, "This note is legal tender for all debts, public and private."

Deposits

Deposits at banks, credit unions, savings banks, and savings and loan associations are also money. Deposits are money because they can be used to make payments. You don't need to go to the bank to get currency to make a payment. You can write a check or use your debit card to tell your bank to move some money from your account to someone else's.

Currency Inside the Banks Is Not Money

Although currency and bank deposits are money, currency *inside the banks* is *not money*. The reason is while currency is inside a bank, it isn't available as a means of payment. When you get some cash from the ATM, you convert your bank deposit into currency. You change the form of your money, but there is no change in the quantity of money that you own. Your bank deposit decreases, and your currency holding increases.

If we counted both bank deposits and currency inside the banks as money, when you get cash at the ATM, the quantity of money would appear to decrease—your currency would increase, but both bank deposits and currency inside the banks would decrease.

You can see that counting both bank deposits and currency inside the banks as money would be double counting.

Official Measures of Money: M1 and M2

M1
Currency, traveler's checks, and checkable deposits owned by individuals and businesses.

M2
M1 plus savings deposits and small time deposits, money market funds, and other deposits.

Figure 11.1 shows the items that make up two official measures of money. **M1** consists of currency, traveler's checks, and checkable deposits owned by individuals and businesses. **M2** consists of M1 plus savings deposits and time deposits (less than $100,000), money market funds, and other deposits. Time deposits are deposits that can be withdrawn only after a fixed term. Money market funds are deposits that are invested in short-term securities.

Are M1 and M2 Means of Payment?

The test of whether something is money is whether it is a generally accepted means of payment. Currency passes the test. Checkable deposits also pass the test because they can be transferred from one person to another by using a debit card or writing a check. So all the components of M1 serve as means of payment.

FIGURE 11.1

Two Measures of Money: September 2009

myeconlab Animation

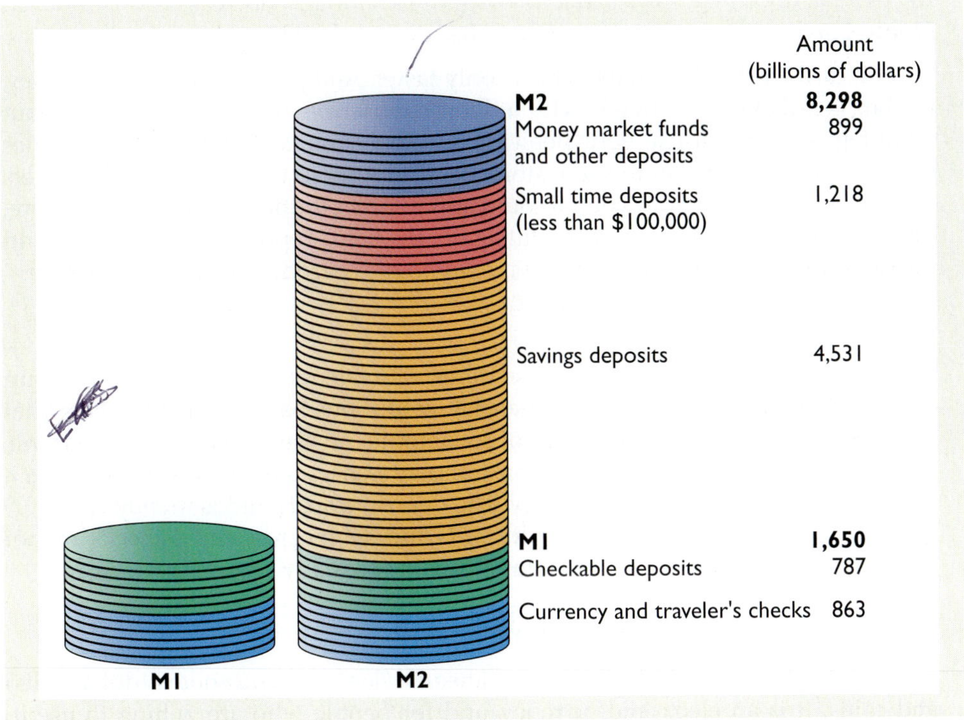

SOURCE OF DATA: Federal Reserve.

M1 Currency held by individuals and businesses and traveler's checks plus checkable deposits owned by individuals and businesses.

M2 M1 plus savings deposits plus small time deposits plus money market funds and other deposits.

Some of the savings deposits in M2 are also instantly convertible into a means of payment. You can use the ATM to get currency to pay for your groceries or gas. But other savings deposits, time deposits, and money market funds are not instantly convertible and are *not* a means of payment.

Checks, Credit Cards, Debit Cards, and E-Checks

In defining money and describing the things that serve as money today, we have not included checks, credit cards and debit cards, or e-checks. Aren't these things that we use when we buy something also money?

Checks

A check is not money. It is an instruction to a bank to make a payment. The easiest way to see why a check is not money is to think about how the quantity of money you own changes if you write a check. You don't suddenly have more money because you've written a check to pay a bill. Your money is your bank deposit, not the value of the checks you've written.

Credit Cards

A credit card is not money. It is a special type of ID card that gets you an instant loan. Suppose that you use your credit card to buy a textbook. You sign or enter your PIN and leave the store with your book. The book may be in your possession, but you've not yet paid for it. You've taken a loan from the bank that issued your credit card. Your credit card issuer pays the bookstore and you eventually get your credit card bill, which you pay using money.

Debit Cards

A debit card works like a paper check, only faster. And just as a check isn't money, neither is a debit card. To see why a debit card works like a check, think about what happens if you use your debit card to buy your textbook. When the sales clerk swipes your card in the bookstore, the computer in the bookstore's bank gets a message: Take $100 from your account and put it in the account of the bookstore. The transaction is done in a flash. But again, the bank deposits are the money and the debit card is the tool that causes money to move from you to the bookstore.

E-Checks

An *electronic check* (or *e-check*) is an electronic equivalent of a paper check. A group of more than 90 banks and other financial institutions have formed the Financial Services Technology Consortium to collaborate on developing the electronic check. Bank of Internet USA offers an Internet e-check system via e-mail. Like a paper check, an e-check is not money. The deposit transferred is money.

You now know that checks, credit cards and debit cards, and e-checks are not money, but one new information-age money is gradually emerging—e-cash.

An Embryonic New Money: E-Cash

Electronic cash (or *e-cash*) is an electronic equivalent of paper notes (dollar bills) and coins. It is an electronic currency, and for people who are willing to use it, e-cash works like other forms of money. But for e-cash to become a widely used form of money, it must evolve some of the characteristics of physical currency.

People use physical currency because it is portable, recognizable, transferable, untraceable, and anonymous and can be used to make change. The designers of e-cash aim to reproduce all of these features of notes and coins. Today's e-cash is portable, untraceable, and anonymous, but it has not yet reached the level of recognition that makes it universally accepted as a means of payment. E-cash doesn't yet meet the definition of money.

Like notes and coins, e-cash can be used in shops. It can also be used over the Internet. To use e-cash in a shop, the buyer uses a smart card that stores some e-cash and the shop uses a smart card reader. When a transaction is made, e-cash is transferred from the smart card directly to the shop's bank account. Users of smart cards receive their e-cash by withdrawing it from a bank account by using a special ATM or a special cell phone.

Several versions of e-cash in U.S. dollars, euros, and other currencies are available on the Internet. The most popular and widely used e-cash system is PayPal, which is owned by eBay. Transactions using PayPal can be conducted in more than 50 countries between any pair of people, as long as each of them has an e-mail address.

A handy advantage of e-cash over paper notes arises when you lose your wallet. If it is stuffed with dollar bills, you're out of luck. If it contains e-cash recorded on your smart card, your bank can cancel the e-cash stored on the card and issue you replacement e-cash.

Although e-cash is not yet widely accepted, it is likely that its use will grow and that it will gradually replace physical forms of currency.

CHECKPOINT 11.1

myeconlab

Work these problems in Study Plan 11.1 to get instant feedback.

Define money and describe its functions.

Practice Problems

1. In the United States today, which of the following items are money?
   - Your Visa card
   - The quarters inside public phones
   - U.S. dollar bills in your wallet
   - The check that you have just written to pay for your rent
   - The loan you took out last August to pay for your school fees
2. In June 2009, currency held by individuals and businesses was $853 billion; traveler's checks were $5 billion; checkable deposits owned by individuals and businesses were $792 billion; savings deposits were $4,472 billion; small time deposits were $1281 billion; and money market funds and other deposits were $967 billion. Calculate M1 and M2 in June 2009.
3. In June 2008, M1 was $1,394 billion; M2 was $7,681 billion; checkable deposits owned by individuals and businesses were $619 billion; time deposits were $1,209 billion; and money market funds and other deposits were $1,057 billion. Calculate currency and traveler's checks held by individuals and businesses and calculate savings deposits.
4. **One more thing cell phones could do: Replace wallets**

   In the next few years, you'll be able to pull out your cell phone and wave it over a scanner to make a payment. The convenience of whipping out your phone as a payment mechanism is driving the transition.

   Source: *USA Today*, November 21, 2007

   As people use their cell phones to make payments, will currency disappear? How will the components of M1 change? Will debit cards disappear?

Guided Solutions to Practice Problems

1. Money is defined as a means of payment. Only the quarters inside public phones and U.S. dollar bills in your wallet are money.
2. M1 is $1,650 billion. M1 is the sum of currency held by individuals and businesses ($853 billion), traveler's checks ($5 billion), and checkable deposits owned by individuals and businesses ($792 billion).

   M2 is $8,370 billion. M2 is the sum of M1 ($1,650 billion), savings deposits ($4,472 billion), small time deposits ($1,281 billion), and money market funds and other deposits ($967 billion).
3. Currency and traveler's checks held by individuals and businesses is $775 billion. Currency and traveler's checks equals M1 ($1,394 billion) minus checkable deposits owned by individuals and businesses ($619 billion).

   Saving deposits are $4,021 billion. Saving deposits equals M2 ($7,681 billion) minus M1 ($1,394 billion) minus time deposits ($1,209 billion) minus money market funds and other deposits ($1,057 billion).
4. Most people will probably carry less currency, but it won't disappear because currency is used in the underground economy. Most of M1 will be checkable deposits. Cell phones and debit cards will be perfect substitutes, so debit cards will probably disappear.

11.2 THE BANKING SYSTEM

Banking system
The Federal Reserve and the banks and other institutions that accept deposits and provide the services that enable people and businesses to make and receive payments.

The **banking system** consists of the Federal Reserve and the banks and other institutions that accept deposits and that provide the services that enable people and businesses to make and receive payments. Sitting at the top of the system (see Figure 11.2), the Federal Reserve (or Fed) sets the rules and regulates and influences the activities of the banks and other institutions. Three types of financial institutions accept the deposits that are part of the nation's money:

- Commercial banks
- Thrift institutions
- Money market funds

Here, we describe the functions of these institutions, and in the next section, we describe the structure and functions of the Fed.

Commercial Banks

Commercial bank
A firm that is chartered by the Comptroller of the Currency in the U.S. Treasury (or by a state agency) to accept deposits and make loans.

A **commercial bank** is a firm that is chartered by the Comptroller of the Currency in the U.S. Treasury (or by a state agency) to accept deposits and make loans. In 2009, about 7,250 commercial banks operated in the United States, down from 13,000 a few years ago. The number of banks has shrunk because in 1997 the rules under which banks operate were changed, permitting them to open branches in every state. A wave of mergers followed this change of rules. Also, more than 130 banks failed during the financial crisis of 2008–2009.

Bank Deposits

A commercial bank accepts three broad types of deposits: checkable deposits, savings deposits, and time deposits. A bank pays a low interest rate (sometimes zero) on checkable deposits, and it pays the highest interest rate on time deposits.

FIGURE 11.2
The Institutions of the Banking System

myeconlab Animation

The Federal Reserve regulates and influences the activities of the commercial banks, thrift institutions, and money market funds, whose deposits make up the nation's money.

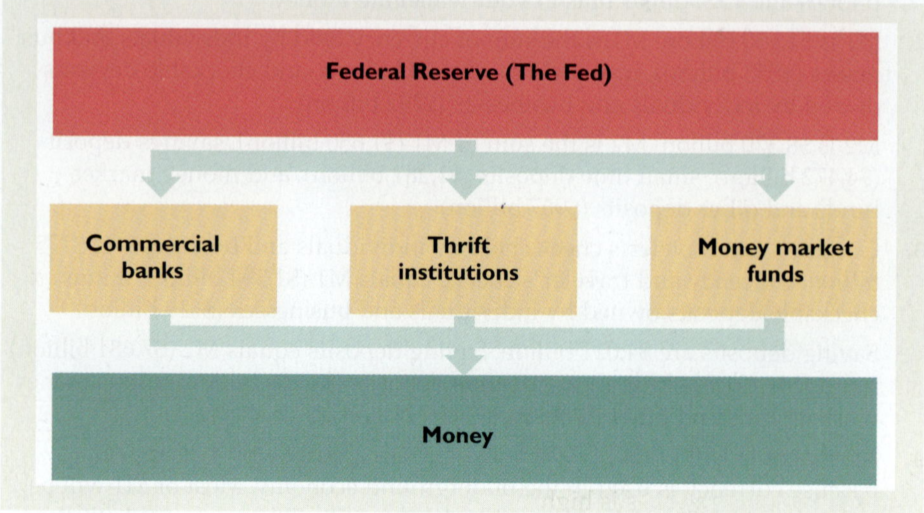

EYE on the PAST

The "Invention" of Banking

It is the sixteenth century somewhere in Europe: Because gold is valuable and easy to steal, goldsmiths have well-guarded safes in which people "deposit" their gold. The goldsmiths issue gold receipts entitling owners to reclaim their "deposits" on demand.

Isabella, who has a receipt for 100 ounces of gold deposited with Samuel Goldsmith, buys some land from Henry. She can pay for the land in one of two ways: She can visit Samuel, collect her gold, and hand the gold to Henry. Or she can give Henry her gold receipt, which enables Henry to claim the 100 ounces of gold.

It is a simpler and safer transaction to use the receipt. When Henry wants to buy something, he too can pass the receipt on to someone else.

So Samuel Goldsmith's gold receipt is circulating as a means of payment. It is money!

Because the receipts circulate while the gold remains in his safe, Samuel realizes that he can lend gold receipts and charge interest for doing so. Samuel writes receipts for gold that he doesn't own, but has on deposit, and lends these receipts. Samuel is one of the first bankers.

Profit and Risk: A Balancing Act

Commercial banks try to maximize their stockholders' wealth by lending for long terms at high interest rates and borrowing from depositors and others. But lending is risky. Risky loans sometimes don't get repaid and the prices of risky securities sometimes fall. In either of these events, a bank incurs a loss that could even wipe out the stockholders' wealth. Also, when depositors see their bank incurring losses, mass withdrawals—called a run on the bank—might create a crisis. So a bank must perform a balancing act. It must be careful in the way it uses the depositors' funds and balance security for depositors and stockholders against high but risky returns. To trade off between risk and profit a bank divides its assets into four parts: reserves, liquid assets, securities, and loans.

Reserves

A bank's **reserves** consist of currency in its vaults plus the balance on its reserve account at a Federal Reserve Bank.

Reserves
The currency in the bank's vaults plus the balance on its reserve account at a Federal Reserve Bank.

The currency in a bank's vaults is a reserve to meet its depositors' withdrawals. Your bank must replenish currency in its ATM every time you and your friends have raided it for cash for a midnight pizza.

A commercial bank's deposit at a Federal Reserve Bank is similar to your own bank deposit. The bank uses its reserve account at the Fed to receive and make payments to other banks and to obtain currency. The Fed requires banks to hold a minimum percentage of deposits as reserves, called the **required reserve ratio**. Banks *desired* reserves might exceed the required reserves, especially when the cost of borrowing reserves is high.

Required reserve ratio
The minimum percentage of deposits that the Fed requires banks and other financial institutions to hold in reserves.

Liquid Assets

Federal funds rate
The interest rate on interbank loans (loans made in the federal funds market).

Banks' *liquid assets* are short-term Treasury Bills and overnight loans to other banks. The interest rates on liquid assets are low but these are low-risk assets. The interest rate on interbank loans, called the **federal funds rate**, is the central target of the Fed's monetary policy actions.

Securities and Loans

Securities are bonds issued by the U.S. government and by other organizations. Some bonds have low interest rates and are safe. Some bonds have high interest rates and are risky. Mortgage-backed securities are examples of risky securities.

Loans are the provision of funds to businesses and individuals. Loans earn the bank a high interest rate, but they are risky and, even when not very risky, cannot be called in before the agreed date. Banks earn the highest interest rate on unpaid credit card balances, which are loans to credit card holders.

Bank Deposits, Other Borrowing, and Assets: The Relative Magnitudes

Figure 11.3 shows the relative magnitudes of the banks' assets, deposits, and other borrowing in 2009. After performing their profit-versus-risk balancing acts, the banks kept 8 percent of total assets in reserves, placed 10 percent in liquid assets, 20 percent in securities, and 62 percent in loans. Checkable deposits (part of M1) were 6 percent of total assets. Another 43 percent of assets were savings deposits and small time deposits (part of M2).

In the financial crisis of 2008 and 2009, the percentage of total assets held in reserves was unusually large and the percentage in loans and securities was unusually small—see *Eye on the U.S. Economy* on the next page.

FIGURE 11.3

Commercial Banks' Assets, Deposits, Other Borrowing, and Net Worth

myeconlab Animation

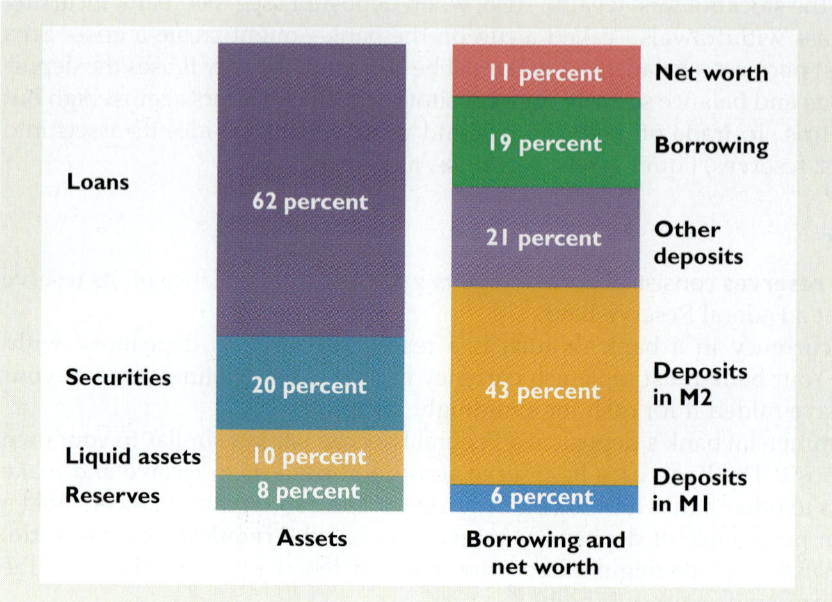

In 2009, commercial bank loans were 62 percent of total assets, securities were 20 percent, liquid assets were 10 percent, and reserves were 8 percent. Reserves were unusually large in 2009.

The banks obtained the funds allocated to these assets from checkable deposits in M1, which were 6 percent of total assets; savings deposits and small time deposits in M2 were 43 percent; other deposits were 21 percent; other borrowing was 19 percent; and bank stockholders' net worth was 11 percent.

Source of data: Federal Reserve.

EYE on the U.S. ECONOMY

Commercial Banks Under Stress in the Financial Crisis

In normal times, bank reserves are less than 1 percent of total assets and liquid assets are less than 4 percent. Loans are 68 percent and securities 28 percent. July 2007 was such a normal time (the orange bars).

During the financial crisis that started in 2007 and intensified in September 2008, the banks took big hits as the value of their securities and loans fell.

Faced with a riskier world, the banks increased their liquid assets and reserves. In September 2009 (the blue bars), liquid assets were almost 10 percent of total assets and reserves were 8 percent.

The balancing act tipped away from risk-taking and toward security.

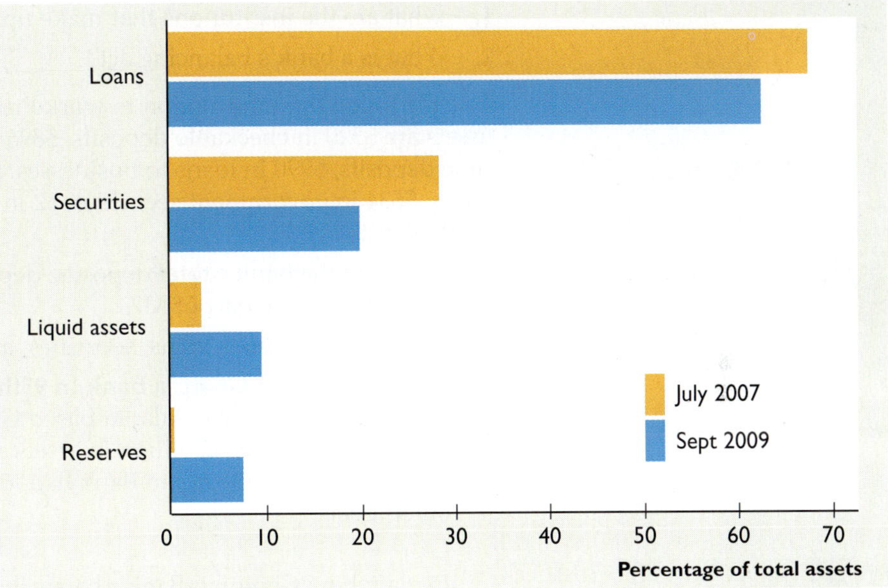

SOURCE OF DATA: Federal Reserve.

Thrift Institutions

The three types of thrift institutions are savings and loan associations, savings banks, and credit unions. A *savings and loan association (S&L)* is a financial institution that accepts checkable deposits and savings deposits and that makes personal, commercial, and home-purchase loans. A *savings bank* is a financial institution that accepts savings deposits and makes mostly consumer and home-purchase loans. The depositors own some savings banks (called mutual savings banks). A *credit union* is a financial institution owned by a social or economic group, such as a firm's employees, that accepts savings deposits and makes mostly consumer loans.

Like commercial banks, the thrift institutions hold reserves and must meet minimum reserve ratios set by the Fed.

Money Market Funds

A *money market fund* is a financial institution that obtains funds by selling shares and uses these funds to buy assets such as U.S. Treasury bills. Money market fund shares act like bank deposits. Shareholders can write checks on their money market fund accounts, but there are restrictions on most of these accounts. For example, the minimum deposit accepted might be $2,500 and the smallest check a depositor is permitted to write might be $500.

myeconlab

Work these problems in Study Plan 11.2 to get instant feedback.

CHECKPOINT 11.2

Describe the functions of banks.

Practice Problems

1. What are the institutions that make up the banking system?
2. What is a bank's balancing act?

Use the following information to work Problems **3** and **4**. A bank's deposits and assets are $320 in checkable deposits, $896 in savings deposits, $840 in small time deposits, $990 in loans to businesses, $400 in outstanding credit card balances, $634 in government securities, $2 in currency, and $30 in its reserve account at the Fed.

3. Calculate the bank's total deposits, deposits that are part of M1, and deposits that are part of M2.
4. Calculate the bank's loans, securities, and reserves.
5. **Regulators close Georgia bank in 95th failure for the year**
   Regulators shut down Atlanta-based Georgian Bank. On July 24, 2009, Georgian Bank has $2 billion in assets and $2 billion in deposits. By 29 September, 2009, Georgian Bank had lost about $2 billion in home loans and other assets.

   Source: *USA Today*, September 30, 2009

   Explain how Georgian Bank's balancing act failed.

Guided Solutions to Practice Problems

1. The institutions that make up the banking system are the Fed, commercial banks, thrift institutions, and money market funds.
2. A bank makes a profit by borrowing from depositors at a low interest rate and lending at a higher interest rate. The bank must hold enough reserves to meet depositors' withdrawals. The bank's balancing act is to balance the risk of loans (profits for stockholders) against the security for depositors.
3. Total deposits are $320 + $896 + $840 = $2,056.
   Deposits that are part of M1 are checkable deposits, $320.
   Deposits that are part of M2 include all deposits, $2,056.
4. Loans are $990 + $400 = $1,390.
   Securities are $634.
   Reserves are $30 + $2 = $32.
5. In July, Georgian Bank's $2 billion of assets (home loans and securities) balanced its deposits of $2 billion. The bank expected to make a profit on its assets that exceeded the interest it paid to depositors. The financial crisis increased the risk on all financial assets. The bank was now holding assets that were more risky than it had planned to hold. As people defaulted on their home loans and the value of securities fell, the value of Georgian Bank's assets crashed to about minus $2 billion. With fewer assets than deposits, regulators had no choice other than close the bank and sell its assets and deposits. The bank failed to balance risk against profit.

11.3 THE FEDERAL RESERVE SYSTEM

The **Federal Reserve System (the Fed)** is the central bank of the United States. A **central bank** is a public authority that provides banking services to banks and governments and regulates financial institutions and markets. A central bank does not provide banking services to businesses and individual citizens. Its only customers are banks such as Bank of America and Citibank and the U.S. government. The Fed is organized into 12 Federal Reserve districts shown in Figure 11.4.

The Fed's main task is to regulate the interest rate and quantity of money to achieve low and predictable inflation and sustained economic expansion.

Federal Reserve System (the Fed)
The central bank of the United States.

Central bank
A public authority that provides banking services to banks and governments and regulates financial institutions and markets.

The Structure of the Federal Reserve

The key elements in the structure of the Federal Reserve are

- The Chairman of the Board of Governors
- The Board of Governors
- The regional Federal Reserve Banks
- The Federal Open Market Committee

The Chairman of the Board of Governors

The Chairman of the Board of Governors is the Fed's chief executive, public face, and center of power and responsibility. When things go right, the Chairman gets the credit; when they go wrong, he gets the blame. Ben S. Bernanke, a former Princeton University economics professor, is the Fed's current Chairman.

Fed Chairman Ben S. Bernanke

FIGURE 11.4

The Federal Reserve Districts

myeconlab Animation

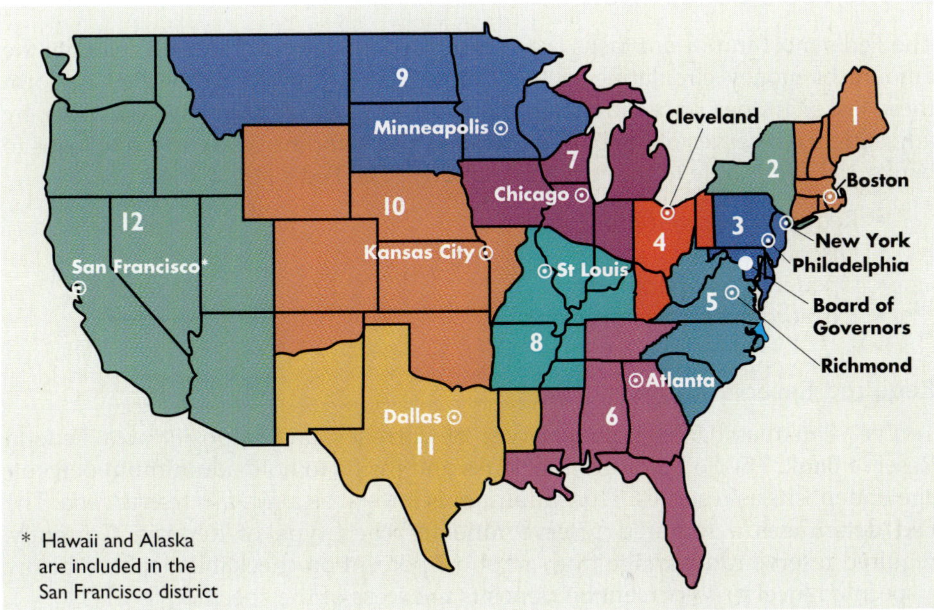

SOURCE: *Federal Reserve Bulletin.*

The nation is divided into 12 Federal Reserve districts, each having a Federal Reserve Bank. (Some of the larger districts also have branch banks.) The Board of Governors of the Federal Reserve System is located in Washington, D.C.

The Board of Governors

The Board of Governors has seven members (including the Chairman), who are appointed by the President of the United States and confirmed by the Senate, each for a 14-year term. The terms are staggered so that one seat on the board becomes vacant every two years. The President appoints one of the board members as Chairman for a term of four years, which is renewable.

The Regional Federal Reserve Banks

There are 12 regional Federal Reserve Banks, one for each of the 12 Federal Reserve districts shown in Figure 11.4. Each regional Federal Reserve Bank has nine directors, three of whom are appointed by the Board of Governors and six of whom are elected by the commercial banks in the Federal Reserve district. The directors of each regional Federal Reserve Bank appoint that Bank's president, and the Board of Governors approves this appointment.

The Federal Reserve Bank of New York (known as the New York Fed) occupies a special place because it implements some of the Fed's most important policy decisions.

The Federal Open Market Committee

Federal Open Market Committee
The Fed's main policy-making committee.

The **Federal Open Market Committee** (FOMC) is the Fed's main policy-making committee. The FOMC consists of the following twelve members:

- The Chairman and the other six members of the Board of Governors
- The president of the Federal Reserve Bank of New York
- Four presidents of the other regional Federal Reserve Banks (on a yearly rotating basis)

The FOMC meets approximately every six weeks to review the state of the economy and to decide the actions to be carried out by the New York Fed.

The Fed's Policy Tools

The Fed's most important tasks are to influence the interest rate and regulate the amount of money circulating in the United States. How does the Fed perform these tasks? It does so by adjusting the reserves of the banking system. Also, by adjusting the reserves of the banking system and standing ready to make loans to banks, the Fed is able to prevent bank failures. The Fed's policy tools are:

- Required reserve ratios
- Discount rate
- Open market operations
- Extraordinary crisis measures

Required Reserve Ratios

You've seen that banks hold reserves of currency and deposits at a Federal Reserve Bank. The Fed requires the banks and thrifts to hold a minimum percentage of deposits as reserves. This minimum is known as a *required reserve ratio.* The Fed determines a required reserve ratio for each type of deposit. Currently, required reserve ratios range from zero to 3 percent on checkable deposits below a specified level to 10 percent on deposits in excess of the specified level.

Discount Rate

The **discount rate** is the interest rate at which the Fed stands ready to lend reserves to commercial banks. A change in the discount rate begins with a proposal to the FOMC by at least one of the 12 Federal Reserve Banks. If the FOMC agrees that a change is required, it proposes the change to the Board of Governors for its approval.

Discount rate
The interest rate at which the Fed stands ready to lend reserves to commercial banks.

Open Market Operations

An **open market operation** is the purchase or sale of government securities—U.S. Treasury bills and bonds—by the Federal Reserve in the open market. When the Fed conducts an open market operation, it makes a transaction with a bank or some other business but it does not transact with the federal government. The New York Fed conducts the Fed's open market operations.

Open market operation
The purchase or sale of government securities—U.S. Treasury bills and bonds—by the New York Fed in the open market.

Extraordinary Crisis Measures

Before the financial crisis of 2008, the three tools that we've just described were regarded as sufficient for all situations. But following the collapse of Lehman Brothers, a major Wall Street investment bank, in September 2008, the Fed (working closely with the U.S. Treasury Department) took a number of major policy moves that created new policy tools. These new tools can be grouped under two broad headings:

- Quantitative easing
- Credit easing

Quantitative Easing When the Fed creates bank reserves by conducting a large-scale open market purchase at a low or possibly zero federal funds rate, the action is called *quantitative easing*. This action differs from a normal open market purchase in its scale and purpose, and it might require the Fed to buy any of a number of private securities rather than government securities.

Credit Easing When the Fed buys private securities or makes loans to financial institutions to stimulate their lending, the action is called *credit easing*.

How the Fed's Policy Tools Work

The Fed's normal policy tools work by changing either the demand for or the supply of the monetary base, which in turn changes the interest rate. The **monetary base** is the sum of coins, Federal Reserve notes, and banks' reserves at the Fed.

Monetary base
The sum of coins, Federal Reserve notes, and banks' reserves at the Fed.

By increasing the required reserve ratio, the Fed can force the banks to hold a larger quantity of monetary base. By raising the discount rate, the Fed can make it more costly for the banks to borrow reserves—borrow monetary base. And by selling securities in the open market, the Fed can decrease the monetary base. All of these actions lead to a rise in the interest rate.

Similarly, by decreasing the required reserve ratio, the Fed can permit the banks to hold a smaller quantity of monetary base. By lowering the discount rate, the Fed can make it less costly for the banks to borrow monetary base. And by buying securities in the open market, the Fed can increase the monetary base. All of these actions lead to a decrease in the interest rate.

Open market operations are the Fed's main tool and in the next section you will learn in more detail how they work.

myeconlab

Work these problems in Study Plan 11.3 to get instant feedback.

CHECKPOINT 11.3

Describe the functions of the Federal Reserve System (the Fed).

Practice Problems

1. What is the Fed and what is the FOMC?
2. Who is the Fed's chief executive, and what are the Fed's main policy tools?
3. What is the monetary base?
4. Suppose that at the end of December 2009, the monetary base in the United States was $700 billion, Federal Reserve notes were $650 billion, and banks' reserves at the Fed were $20 billion. Calculate the quantity of coins.
5. **Risky assets: Counting to a trillion**

   Prior to the September 15, 2008, collapse of Lehman Brothers, which marked the start of the credit crisis, the Fed held less than $1 trillion in assets, most of which were in safe U.S. government securities. By mid-December, 2008, the Fed's balance sheet had more than doubled to over $2.3 trillion. Much of the increase was in mortgage-backed securities. The massive expansion began when the Fed rolled out its lending program—sending banks cash in exchange for risky assets.

   Source: CNNMoney, September 29, 2009

   What are the Fed's policy tools and which policy tool did the Fed use to increase its assets to $2.3 trillion in 2008?

Guided Solutions to Practice Problems

1. The Federal Reserve (Fed) is the central bank in the United States. The central bank in the United States is a public authority that provides banking services to banks and the U.S. government and that regulates the quantity of money and the banking system. The FOMC is the Federal Open Market Committee. The FOMC is the Fed's main policy-making committee.
2. The Fed's chief executive is the Chairman of the Board of Governors, currently Ben Bernanke. The Fed's main policy tools are required reserve ratios, the discount rate, and open market operations.
3. The monetary base is the sum of coins, Federal Reserve notes (dollar bills), and banks' reserves at the Fed.
4. To calculate the quantity of coins, we use the definition of the monetary base: coins plus Federal Reserve notes plus banks' reserves at the Fed.

   Quantity of coins = Monetary base − Federal Reserve notes − Banks' reserves at the Fed.

   So at the end of December 2009,

   Quantity of coins = $700 billion − $650 billion − $20 billion = $30 billion.
5. The Fed's policy tools are the required reserve ratio, discount rate, open market operations, and extraordinary crisis measures. The Fed used an extraordinary crisis measure called credit easing—the Fed's lending program took banks' own risky assets to increase their reserve deposits at the Fed.

11.4 REGULATING THE QUANTITY OF MONEY

Banks create money, but this doesn't mean that they have smoke-filled back rooms in which counterfeiters are busily working. Remember, most money is deposits, not currency. What banks create is deposits, and they do so by making loans.

Creating Deposits by Making Loans

The easiest way to see that banks create deposits is to think about what happens when Andy, who has a Visa card issued by Citibank, uses his card to buy a tank of gas from Chevron. When Andy signs the card sales slip, he takes a loan from Citibank and obligates himself to repay the loan at a later date. At the end of the business day, a Chevron clerk takes a pile of signed credit card sales slips, including Andy's, to Chevron's bank. For now, let's assume that Chevron also banks at Citibank. The bank immediately credits Chevron's account with the value of the slips (minus the bank's commission).

You can see that these transactions have created a bank deposit and a loan. Andy has increased the size of his loan (his credit card balance), and Chevron has increased the size of its bank deposit. And because deposits are money, Citibank has created money.

If, as we've just assumed, Andy and Chevron use the same bank, no further transactions take place. But the outcome is essentially the same when two banks are involved. If Chevron's bank is the Bank of America, then Citibank uses its reserves to pay the Bank of America. Citibank has an increase in loans and a decrease in reserves; the Bank of America has an increase in reserves and an increase in deposits. The banking system as a whole has an increase in loans, an increase in deposits, and no change in reserves.

EYE on YOUR LIFE

Money and Your Role in Its Creation

Imagine a world without money in which you must barter for everything you buy. What kinds of items would you have available for these trades? Would you keep some stocks of items that you know lots of people are willing to accept? Would you really be bartering, or would you be using a commodity as money? How much longer would it take you to conduct all the transactions of a normal day?

Now think about your own holdings of money today. How much money do you have in your pocket or wallet? How much do you have in the bank? How does the money you hold change over the course of a month?

Of the money you're holding, which items are part of M1 and which are part of M2? Are all the items in M2 means of payment?

Now think about the role that *you* play in creating money. Every time you charge something to your credit card, you help the bank that issued it to create money. The increase in your credit card balance is a loan from the bank to you. The bank pays the seller right away. So the seller's bank deposit and your outstanding balance increase together. Money is created.

You contribute to the currency drain that limits the ability of your bank to create money when you visit the ATM and get some cash to pay for your late-night pizza.

Of course, your transactions are a tiny part of the total. But together, you and a few million other students like you play a big role in the money creation process.

If Andy had swiped his card at an automatic payment pump, all these transactions would have occurred at the time he filled his tank, and the quantity of money would have increased by the amount of his purchase (minus the bank's commission for conducting the transactions).

Three factors limit the quantity of deposits that the banking system can create:

- The monetary base
- Desired reserves
- Desired currency holding

The Monetary Base

You've seen that the monetary base is the sum of coins, Federal Reserve notes, and banks' deposits at the Fed. The size of the monetary base limits the total quantity of money that the banking system can create because banks have a desired level of reserves and households and firms have a desired level of currency holding and both of these desired holdings of the monetary base depend on the quantity of money.

Desired Reserves

A bank's *desired* reserves are the reserves that the bank chooses to hold. The *desired reserve ratio* is the ratio of reserves to deposits that a bank wants to hold. This ratio exceeds the *required reserve ratio* by an amount that the banks determine to be prudent on the basis of their daily business requirements.

A bank's *actual reserve ratio* changes when its customers make a deposit or a withdrawal. If a bank's customer makes a deposit, reserves and deposits increase by the same amount, so the bank's reserve ratio increases. Similarly, if a bank's customer makes a withdrawal, reserves and deposits decrease by the same amount, so the bank's reserve ratio decreases.

Excess reserves
A bank's actual reserves minus its desired reserves.

A bank's **excess reserves** are its actual reserves minus its desired reserves. When the banking system as a whole has excess reserves, banks can create money by making new loans. When the banking system as a whole is short of reserves, banks must destroy money by decreasing the quantity of loans.

Desired Currency Holding

We hold our money in the form of currency and bank deposits. The proportion of money held as currency isn't constant but at any given time, people have a definite view as to how much they want to hold in each form of money.

Because households and firms want to hold some proportion of their money in the form of currency, when the total quantity of bank deposits increases, so does the quantity of currency that they want to hold.

Because desired currency holding increases when deposits increase, currency leaves the banks when loans are made and deposits increase. We call the leakage of currency from the banking system the *currency drain*. And we call the ratio of currency to deposits the *currency drain ratio*.

The greater the currency drain ratio, the smaller is the quantity of deposits and money that the banking system can create from a given amount of monetary base. The reason is that as currency drains from the banks, they are left with a smaller level of reserves (and smaller excess reserves) so they make fewer loans.

How Open Market Operations Change the Monetary Base

When the Fed buys securities in an open market operation, it pays for them with newly created bank reserves and money. With more reserves in the banking system, the supply of interbank loans increases, the demand for interbank loans decreases, and the federal funds rate—the interest rate in the interbank loans market—falls.

Similarly, when the Fed sells securities in an open market operation, buyers pay for the securities with bank reserves and money. With smaller reserves in the banking system, the supply of interbank loans decreases, the demand for interbank loans increases, and the federal funds rate rises. The Fed sets a target for the federal funds rate and conducts open market operations on the scale needed to hit its target.

A change in the federal funds rate is only the first stage in an adjustment process that follows an open market operation. If banks' reserves increase, the banks can increase their lending and create even more money. If banks' reserves decrease, the banks must decrease their lending, which decreases the quantity of money. We'll study the effects of open market operations in some detail, beginning with an open market purchase.

The Fed Buys Securities

Suppose the Fed buys $100 million of U.S. government securities in the open market. There are two cases to consider, depending on who sells the securities. A bank might sell some of its securities, or a person or business that is not a commercial bank—the general public—might sell. The outcome is essentially the same in the two cases. To convince you of this fact, we'll study the two cases, starting with the simpler case in which a commercial bank sells securities. (The seller will be someone who thinks the Fed is offering a good price for securities and it is profitable to make the sale.)

FOMC meeting.

A Commercial Bank Sells When the Fed buys $100 million of securities from the Manhattan Commercial Bank, two things happen:

1. The Manhattan Commercial Bank has $100 million less in securities, and the Fed has $100 million more in securities.
2. To pay for the securities, the Fed increases the Manhattan Commercial Bank's reserve account at the New York Fed by $100 million.

Figure 11.5 shows the effects of these actions on the balance sheets of the Fed and the Manhattan Commercial Bank. Ownership of the securities passes from the commercial bank to the Fed, so the bank's securities decrease by $100 million and the Fed's securities increase by $100 million, as shown by the red-to-blue arrow running from the Manhattan Commercial Bank to the Fed.

The Fed increases the Manhattan Commercial Bank's reserves by $100 million, as shown by the green arrow running from the Fed to the Manhattan Commercial Bank. This action increases the reserves of the banking system.

The commercial bank's total assets remain constant, but their composition changes. Its holdings of government securities decrease by $100 million, and its reserves increase by $100 million. The bank can use these additional reserves to make loans. When the bank makes loans, it creates deposits and the quantity of money increases.

We've just seen that when the Fed buys government securities from a bank, the bank's reserves increase. What happens if the Fed buys government securities from the public—say, from AIG, an insurance company?

FIGURE 11.5

The Fed Buys Securities from a Commercial Bank

myeconlab Animation

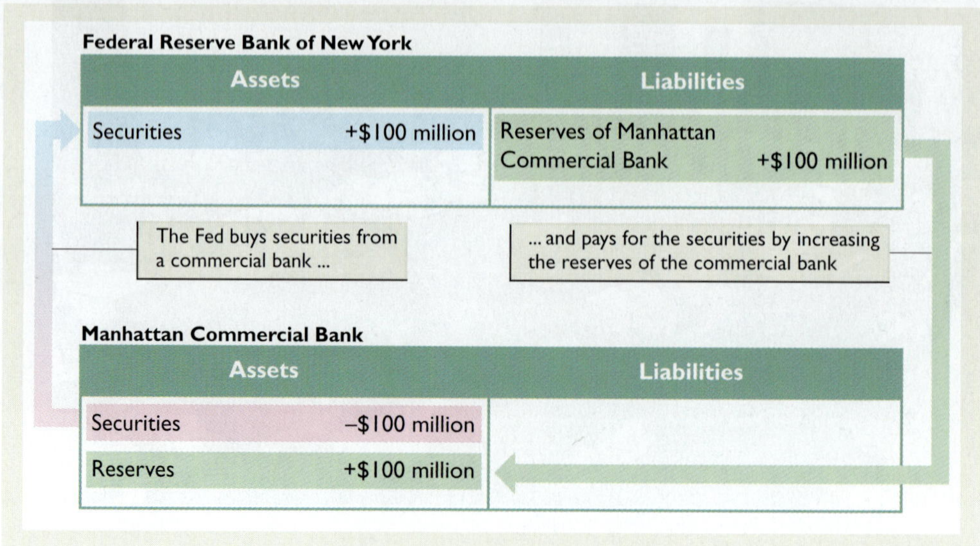

The Nonbank Public Sells When the Fed buys $100 million of securities from AIG, three things happen:

1. AIG has $100 million less in securities, and the Fed has $100 million more in securities.
2. The Fed pays for the securities with a check for $100 million drawn on itself, which AIG deposits in its account at the Manhattan Commercial Bank.
3. The Manhattan Commercial Bank collects payment of this check from the Fed, and the Manhattan Commercial Bank's reserves increase by $100 million.

Figure 11.6 shows the effects of these actions on the balance sheets of the Fed, AIG, and the Manhattan Commercial Bank. Ownership of the securities passes from AIG to the Fed, so AIG's securities decrease by $100 million and the Fed's securities increase by $100 million (red-to-blue arrow). The Fed pays for the securities with a check payable to AIG, which AIG deposits in the Manhattan Commercial Bank. This payment increases Manhattan's reserves by $100 million (green arrow). It also increases AIG's deposit at the Manhattan Commercial Bank by $100 million (blue arrow). This action increases the reserves of the banking system.

FIGURE 11.6

The Fed Buys Securities from the Public

myeconlab Animation

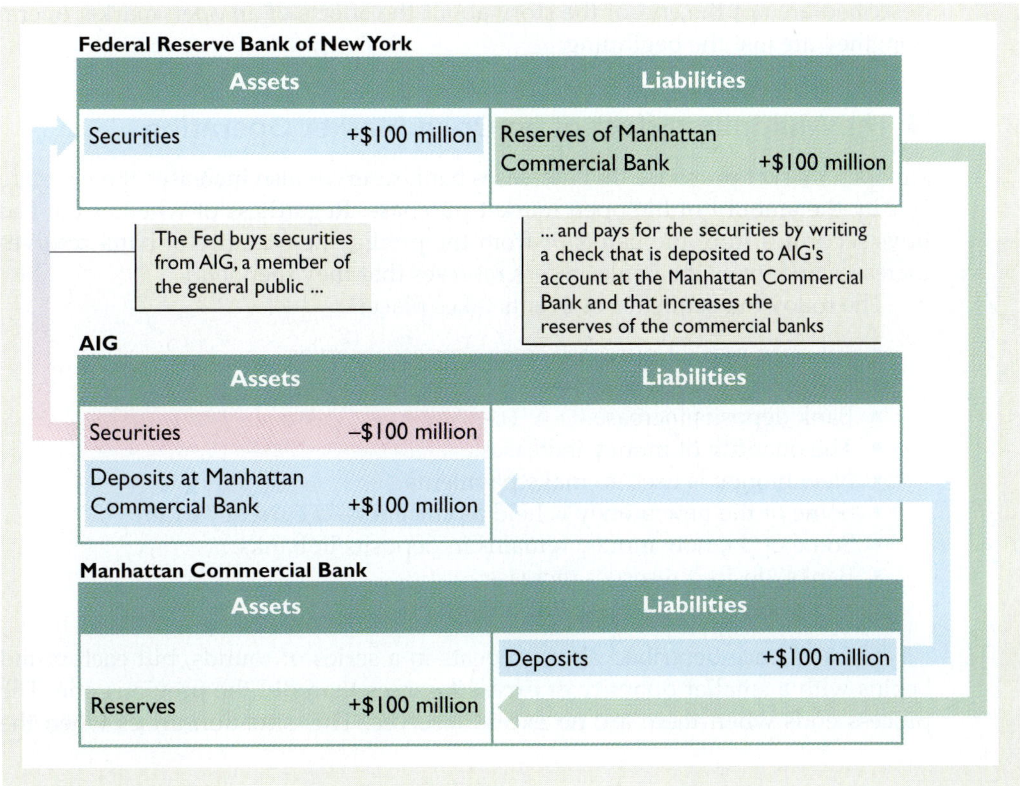

AIG has the same total assets as before, but their composition has changed. It now has more money and fewer securities. The Manhattan Commercial Bank's reserves increase, and so do its deposits—both by $100 million. Because bank reserves and deposits have increased by the same amount, the bank has excess reserves, which it can use to make loans. When it makes loans, the quantity of money increases.

We've worked through what happens when the Fed buys government securities from either a bank or the public. When the Fed sells securities, the transactions that we've just traced operate in reverse.

The Fed Sells Securities

If the Fed sells $100 million of U.S. government securities in the open market, most likely a person or business other than a bank buys them. (A bank would buy them only if it had excess reserves and couldn't find a better use for its funds.)

When the Fed sells $100 million of securities to AIG, three things happen:

1. AIG has $100 million more in securities, and the Fed has $100 million less in securities.
2. AIG pays for the securities with a check for $100 million drawn on its deposit account at the Manhattan Commercial Bank.
3. The Fed collects payment of this check from the Manhattan Commercial Bank by decreasing its reserves by $100 million.

These actions decrease the reserves of the banking system. The Manhattan Commercial Bank is now short of reserves and must borrow in the federal funds market to meet its desired reserve ratio.

The changes in the balance sheets of the Fed and the banks that we've just described are not the end of the story about the effects of an open market operation; they are just the beginning.

The Multiplier Effect of an Open Market Operation

An open market purchase that increases bank reserves also increases the *monetary base* by the amount of the open market purchase. Regardless of whether the Fed buys securities from the banks or from the public, the quantity of bank reserves increases and gives the banks excess reserves that they then lend.

The following sequence of events takes place:

- An open market purchase creates excess reserves.
- Banks lend excess reserves.
- Bank deposits increase.
- The quantity of money increases.
- New money is used to make payments.
- Some of the new money is held as currency—a currency drain.
- Some of the new money remains in deposits in banks.
- Banks' desired reserves increase.
- Excess reserves decrease but remain positive.

The sequence described above repeats in a series of rounds, but each round begins with a smaller quantity of excess reserves than did the previous one. The process ends when there are no excess reserves. This situation arises when the increase in the monetary base resulting from the open market operation is willingly held—when the increase in desired reserves plus the increase in desired currency holding equals the increase in the monetary base. Figure 11.7 illustrates and summarizes the sequence of events in one round of the multiplier process.

An open market *sale* works similarly to an open market *purchase*, but the sale *decreases* the monetary base and sets off a multiplier process similar to that described in Figure 11.7. At the end of the process the quantity of money has decreased by an amount that lowers desired reserves and desired currency holding by an amount equal to the decrease in the monetary base resulting from the open market sale. (Make your own version of Figure 11.7 to trace the multiplier process when the Fed *sells* and the banks or public *buys* securities.)

The magnitude of the change in the quantity of money brought about by an open market operation is determined by the money multiplier that we now explain.

The Money Multiplier

The **money multiplier** is the number by which a change in the monetary base is multiplied to find the resulting change in the quantity of money. It is also the ratio of the change in the quantity of money to the change in the monetary base.

The magnitude of the money multiplier depends on the desired reserve ratio and the currency drain ratio. Call the desired reserve ratio *R* and call the currency drain ratio (the ratio of currency to deposits) *C*.

Money multiplier
The number by which a change in the monetary base is multiplied to find the resulting change in the quantity of money.

FIGURE 11.7

A Round in the Multiplier Process Following an Open Market Operation

myeconlab Animation

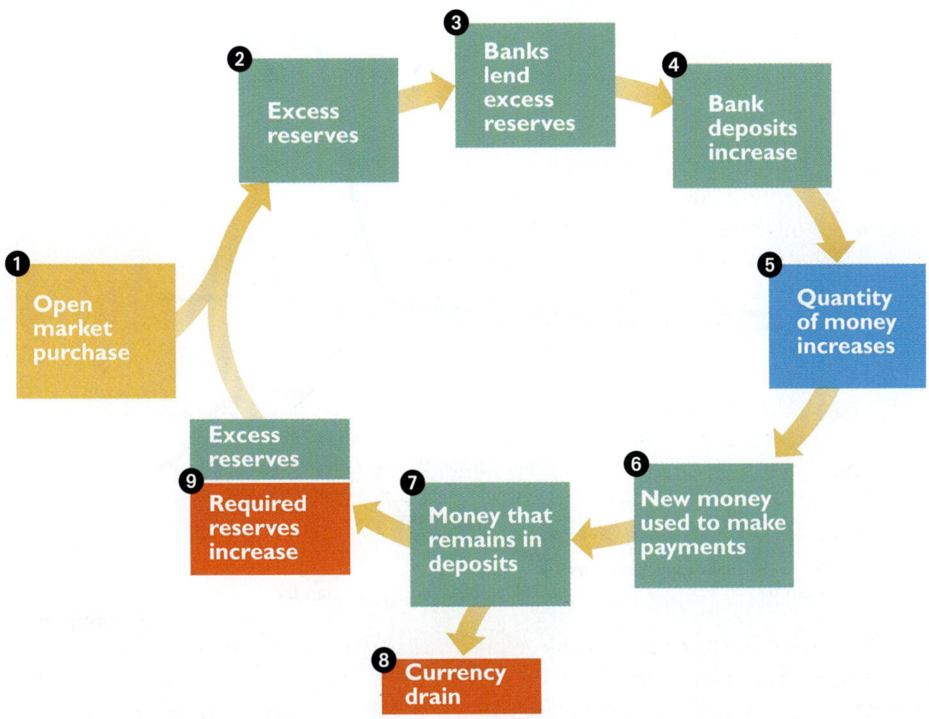

1 An open market purchase increases bank reserves and
2 creates excess reserves.

3 Banks lend the excess reserves,
4 new deposits are created, and
5 the quantity of money increases.

6 New money is used to make payments.

7 Households and firms receiving payments keep some on deposit in banks and 8 some in the form of currency—a currency drain.

The increase in bank deposits increases banks' reserves but also
9 increases banks' desired reserves.

Desired reserves increase by less than actual reserves, so the banks still have some excess reserves, but less than before. The process repeats until excess reserves have been eliminated.

To see how the desired reserve ratio and the currency drain ratio determine the size of the money multiplier, begin with the two facts that

$$\text{Desired reserves} = R \times \text{Deposits} \quad \text{and} \quad \text{Currency} = C \times \text{Deposits}.$$

The monetary base, *MB*, is the sum of reserves and currency, so

$$MB = (R + C) \times \text{Deposits}.$$

The quantity of money, *M*, is the sum of deposits and currency, so

$$M = \text{Deposits} + \text{Currency} = (1 + C) \times \text{Deposits}.$$

Now divide the quantity of money, *M*, by the monetary base, *MB*, using the fact that $M = (1 + C) \times \text{Deposits}$ and $MB = (R + C) \times \text{Deposits}$ to get

$$\frac{M}{MB} = \frac{(1 + C)}{(R + C)}.$$

EYE on CREATING MONEY

How Did the Fed Regulate the Quantity of Money in the 2008 Financial Crisis?

During the Great Depression, many banks failed, bank deposits were destroyed, and the quantity of money crashed by 25 percent. Most economists believe that it was these events that turned an ordinary recession in 1929 into a deep and decade-long depression.

Fed Chairman Ben Bernanke is one of the economists who has studied this tragic episode in U.S. economic history, and he had no intention of witnessing a similar event on his watch.

Figure 1 shows what the Fed did to pump reserves into the banking system. The Fed doubled the monetary base during the months following the collapse of Lehman Brothers in September 15, 2008, and reserves remained at this level into 2009.

This extraordinary increase in the monetary base did not bring a similar increase in the quantity of

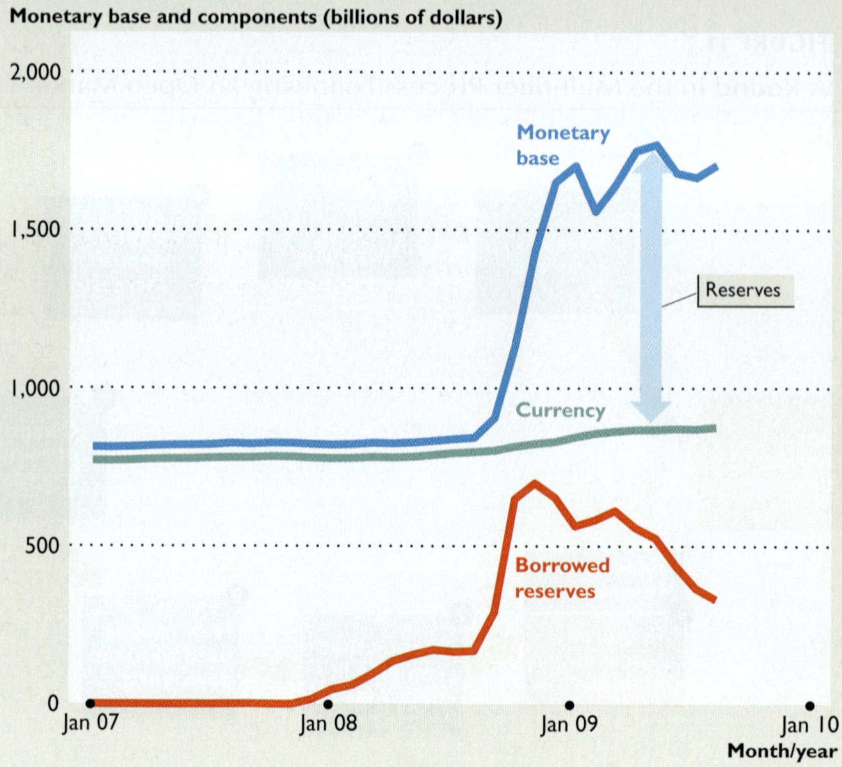

Figure 1 The Monetary Base

Now multiply both sides of the above equation by MB to get

$$M = \frac{(1 + C)}{(R + C)} \times MB.$$

The quantity of money *changes* by the *change* in the monetary base multiplied by $(1 + C)/(R + C)$.

If the desired reserve ratio is 10 percent and the currency drain ratio is 50 percent, $R = 0.1$ and $C = 0.5$, so the money multiplier is $1.5/0.6 = 2.5$.

The larger the desired reserve ratio and the larger the currency drain ratio, the smaller is the money multiplier.

The desired reserve ratio and the currency drain ratio that determine the magnitude of the money multiplier are not constant, so neither is the money multiplier constant. You can see in *Eye on Money Creation* below that the desired reserve ratio and money multiplier changed dramatically in 2008.

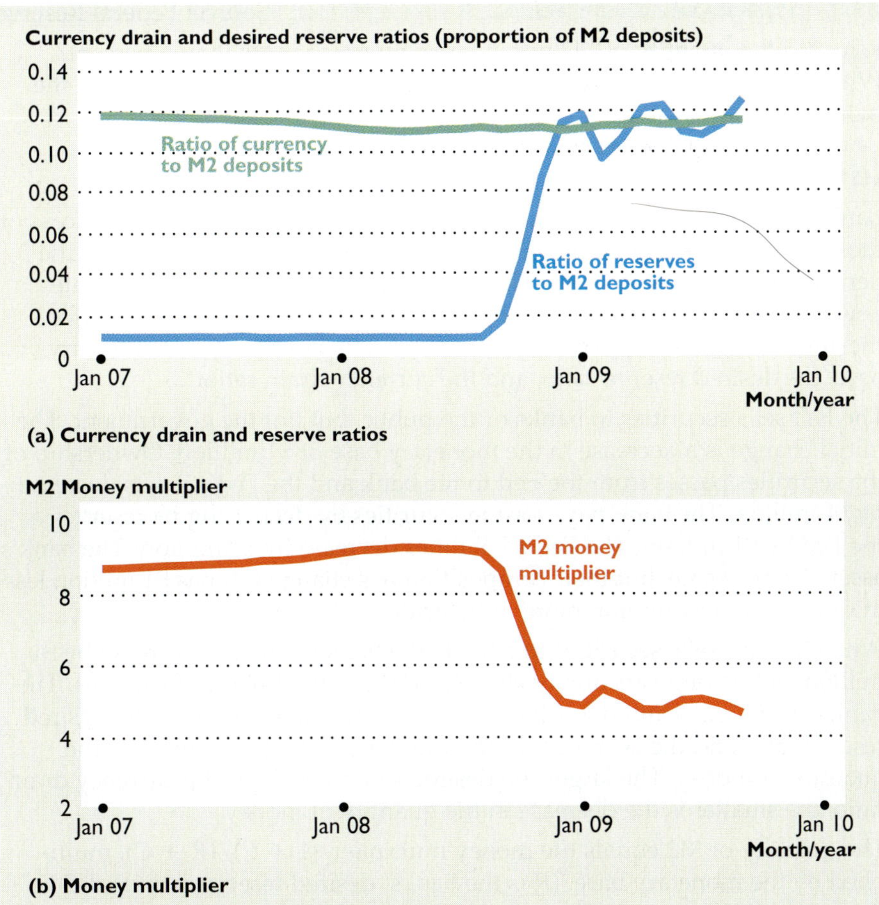

Figure 2 The Changing Money Multiplier

money. Figure 2 shows the reason.

In 2008, the banks' desired reserve ratio, in part (a), increased tenfold from its normal level of 0.012 (1.2 percent) to 0.12 (12 percent). This increase brought a crash in the money multiplier, in part (b), from its normal value of 9 to an unusually low value of 5.

The surge in the desired reserve ratio is the sole reason for the collapse in the money multiplier. You can see, in part (a), that the other influence on the multiplier, the currency drain ratio, barely changed.

The failure of Lehman Brothers signalled to the banks that they faced an unusually high level of risk and this was the main source of the increase in the desired reserve ratio. As the risk faced by banks returns to normal, the desired reserve ratio will fall, and when this happens the Fed will need to decrease the monetary base or face an explosion in the quantity of money.

SOURCES OF DATA: Federal Reserve and Bureau of Economic Analysis.

myeconlab

Work these problems in Study Plan 11.4 to get instant feedback.

CHECKPOINT 11.4

Explain how banks create money and how the Fed controls the quantity of money.

Practice Problems

1. How do banks create new deposits by making loans, and what factors limit the amount of deposits and loans that they can create?
2. If the Fed makes an open market sale of $1 million of securities, who can buy the securities from the Fed? What initial changes occur in the economy if the Fed sells to a bank?
3. If the Fed makes an open market sale of $1 million of securities, what is the process by which the quantity of money changes? What factors determine the change in the quantity of money?
4. **Fed doubles monetary base**
   During the fourth quarter of 2008, the Fed doubled the monetary base but the quantity of money (M2) increased by only 5 percent.

   Source: Federal Reserve

   Why did the quantity of M2 not increase by much more than 5 percent? What would have happened to the quantity of M2 if the Fed had kept the monetary base constant?

Guided Solutions to Practice Problems

1. Banks can make loans when they have excess reserves—reserves in excess of those desired. When a bank makes a loan, it creates a new deposit for the person who receives the loan. The bank uses its excess reserves to create new deposits. The amount of loans that the bank can make, and therefore the amount of new deposits that it can create, is limited by the monetary base, the desired reserve ratio, and the currency drain ratio.
2. The Fed sells securities to banks or the public, but not the government. The initial change is a decrease in the monetary base of $1 million. Ownership of the securities passes from the Fed to the bank and the Fed's assets decrease by $1 million. The bank pays for the securities by decreasing its reserves at the Fed by $1 million. The Fed's liabilities decrease by $1 million. The bank's assets are the same, but their composition has changed. It has $1 million less in reserves and $1 million more in securities.
3. When the Fed sells securities to a bank, the bank's reserves decrease by $1 million, but its deposits do not change, so the bank is short of reserves. The bank calls in loans and deposits decrease by the same amount. The desired reserve ratio and the currency drain ratio determine the decrease in the quantity of money. The larger the desired reserve ratio or the currency drain ratio, the smaller is the decrease in the quantity of money.
4. The quantity of M2 equals the money multiplier, $(1 + C)/(R + C)$, multiplied by the monetary base. (R is the banks' desired reserve ratio and C is the currency drain ratio). The quantity of M2 didn't increase by more because the banks increased their desired reserve ratio, R, which decreased the money multiplier. If the Fed had not increased the monetary base, the quantity of M2 would have decreased because the money multiplier decreased.

CHAPTER SUMMARY

Key Points

1 Define money and describe its functions.

- Money is anything that serves as a generally accepted means of payment.
- Money functions as a medium of exchange, unit of account, and store of value.
- M1 consists of currency, travelers' checks, and checkable deposits. M2 consists of M1 plus savings deposits, small time deposits, and money market funds.

2 Describe the functions of banks.

- The deposits of commercial banks and thrift institutions are money.
- Banks borrow short term and lend long term and make a profit on the spread between the interest rates that they pay and receive.

3 Describe the functions of the Federal Reserve System (the Fed).

- The Federal Reserve is the central bank of the United States.
- The Fed influences the economy by setting the required reserve ratio for banks, by setting the discount rate, by open market operations, and by taking extraordinary quantitative easing and credit easing measures in a financial crisis.

4 Explain how banks create money and how the Fed controls the quantity of money.

- Banks create money by making loans.
- The maximum quantity of deposits the banks can create is limited by the monetary base, the banks' desired reserves, and desired currency holding.
- When the Fed buys securities in an open market operation, it creates bank reserves. When the Fed sells securities in an open market operation, it destroys bank reserves.
- An open market operation has a multiplier effect on the quantity of money.

Key Terms

myeconlab

Work these problems in Chapter 11 Study Plan to get instant feedback.

CHAPTER CHECKPOINT

Study Plan Problems and Applications

1. What is money? Would you classify any of the following items as money?
   - Store coupons for cat food
   - A $100 Amazon.com gift certificate
   - Frequent Flier Miles
   - Credit available on your Visa card
   - The dollar coins that a coin collector owns
2. What are the three functions that money performs? Which of the following items perform some but not all of these functions, and which perform all of these functions? Which of the items are money?
   - A checking account at the Bank of America
   - A dime
   - A debit card
3. Monica transfers $10,000 from her savings account at the Bank of Alaska to her money market fund. What is the immediate change in M1 and M2?
4. Terry takes $100 from his checking account and deposits the $100 in his savings account. What is the immediate change in M1 and M2?
5. Suppose that banks had deposits of $500 billion, a desired reserve ratio of 4 percent and no excess reserves. The banks had $15 billion in notes and coins. Calculate the banks' reserves at the central bank.
6. The Fed buys $2 million of securities from AIG. If the desired reserve ratio is 0.1 and there is no currency drain, calculate the bank's excess reserves as soon as the open market purchase is made, the maximum amount of loans that the banking system can make, and the maximum amount of new money that the banking system can create.

Use the following information to work Problems 7 and 8.

If the desired reserve ratio is 5 percent, the currency drain ratio is 20 percent of deposits, and the central bank makes an open market purchase of $1 million of securities, calculate the change in

7. The monetary base and the change in its components.
8. The quantity of money, and how much of the new money is currency and how much is bank deposits.

Use the following information to work Problems 9 and 10.

South Korea: Bank reserves raised

To rein in spending, the Bank of Korea raised the required reserve ratio to 7 percent from 5 percent—the first raise in almost 17 years. With higher required reserves, banks will have to cut the amount of loans they make.

Source: *The New York Times*, November 24, 2006

9. Explain why the higher required reserve ratio means that banks will have to cut the amount of loans they can make.
10. Assuming that the currency drain is zero and that the desired reserve ratio equals the required reserve ratio, calculate the change in the money multiplier that results from the increase in Korea's required reserve ratio.

Instructor Assignable Problems and Applications

Your instructor can assign these problems as homework, a quiz, or a test in **MyEconLab**.

1. When the Fed increased the monetary base in 2008, which component of the monetary base increased most: banks' reserves or currency? What happened to the reserves that banks borrowed from the Fed?
2. What happened to the money multiplier in 2008? What would the money multiplier have been if the currency drain ratio had not changed? What would the money multiplier have been if the banks' desired reserve ratio had not changed?
3. What are the three functions that money performs? Which of the following items perform some but not all of these functions and which of the items are money?
   - An antique clock
   - An S&L savings deposit
   - Your credit card
   - The coins in the Fed's museum
   - Government securities
4. Naomi buys $1,000 worth of American Express travelers' checks and charges the purchase to her American Express card. What is the immediate change in M1 and M2?
5. What can the Fed do to increase the quantity of money and keep the monetary base constant? Explain why the Fed would or would not
   - Change the currency drain ratio.
   - Change the required reserve ratio.
   - Change the discount rate.
   - Conduct an open market operation.

Use Table 1, which shows a bank's balance sheet, to work Problems 6 and 7. The desired reserve ratio on all deposits is 5 percent and there is no currency drain.

TABLE 1

Assets		Liabilities	
(millions of dollars)			
Reserves at the Fed	25	Checkable deposits	90
Cash in vault	15	Savings deposits	110
Securities	60		
Loans	100		

6. Calculate the bank's excess reserves. If the bank uses all of these excess reserves to make a loan, what is the quantity of the loan and the quantity of total deposits after the bank has made the loan?
7. If there is no currency drain, what is the quantity of loans and the quantity of total deposits when the bank has no excess reserves?

Use the following information to work Problems 8 and 9.

China tightens bank credit again

For the second time in the month and fourth in a year, the People's Bank of China raised the required reserve ratio on big banks to 11 percent of deposits on May 15, 2007, up from 10.5 percent.

Source: *The New York Times*, April 30, 2007

8. Compare the required reserve ratio in China on May 15, 2007 and the required reserve ratio on checkable deposits in the United States today.
9. If the currency drain ratio in China and the United States is 1 percent of deposits, compare the money multipliers in the two countries.

Use the following information to work Problems **10** and **11**.

A bank has $500 million in checkable deposits, $600 million in savings deposits, $400 million in small time deposits, $950 million in loans to businesses, $500 million in government securities, $20 million in currency, and $30 million in its reserve account at the Fed.

10. Calculate the bank's total deposits, deposits that are part of M1, and deposits that are part of M2.

11. Calculate the bank's loans, securities, and reserves.

12. If the Fed wants to decrease the quantity of money, what type of open market operation might it undertake? Explain the process by which the quantity of money decreases.

Use the following information to work Problems **13** and **14**.

An early goldsmith banker earned a profit (sometimes a large profit) simply by writing notes to certify that a person had deposited a certain amount of gold in his vault. By writing more notes than the amount of gold held, the goldsmith could lend the notes and charge interest on them.

13. Did the goldsmith bankers make money out of thin air in a form of legal theft? Should the goldsmith bankers have been regulated to ensure that the amount of gold in their vaults equaled the value of the notes they created?

14. What were the main benefits from the activities of the goldsmith bankers?

15. If the central bank makes an open market purchase of $1 million of securities, what is the process by which the quantity of money changes? What factors determine the change in the quantity of money?

16. In an economy, the currency drain is 10 percent of deposits and the desired reserve ratio is 1 percent of deposits. If the central bank buys $100,000 of securities on the open market, calculate the money multiplier.

TABLE 2

Assets (millions of dollars)		Liabilities	
Reserves at the Fed	20	Checkable deposits	80
Cash in vault	5	Savings deposits	120
Securities	75		
Loans	100		

Table 2 shows a bank's balance sheet. The bank has no excess reserves and there is no currency drain. Use the following information to work Problems **17** and **18**.

17. Calculate the bank's desired reserve ratio.

18. Calculate the new money that this bank can create if it sells $5 million of securities to the central bank in an open market operation.

19. Fed starts buying government debt

The Fed announced that it would buy up to $300 billion in Treasury securities over the next six months from big government "primary" securities dealers, such as Barclays Capital, Banc of America Securities, and Citigroup Global Markets.

Source: *USA Today*, March 24, 2009

What type of a transaction is the Fed's purchase of government securities from securities dealers? With no other actions, will these transactions change the quantity of money? If so, will they increase or decrease the quantity of money?

What causes inflation?

Does inflation, deflation, or a stable price level lie in our future?

12

Money, Interest, and Inflation

CHAPTER CHECKLIST

When you have completed your study of this chapter, you will be able to

1 Explain what determines the demand for money and how the demand for money and the supply of money determine the *nominal* interest rate.

2 Explain how in the long run, the quantity of money determines the price level and money growth brings inflation.

3 Identify the costs of inflation and the benefits of a stable value of money.

WHERE WE ARE AND WHERE WE'RE HEADING

Before we explore the effects of money on the interest rate and the inflation rate, let's take stock of what we've learned and preview where we are heading.

The Real Economy

Real factors that are independent of the price level determine potential GDP and the natural unemployment rate (Chapter 8). The demand for labor and supply of labor determine the quantity of labor employed and the real wage rate at full employment. The full-employment equilibrium quantity of labor and the production function determine potential GDP. At full employment, real GDP equals potential GDP and the unemployment rate equals the natural unemployment rate.

Investment and saving along with population growth, human capital growth, and technological change determine the growth rate of real GDP (Chapter 9).

Investment and saving plans influence the demand for and supply of loanable funds, which in turn determine the real interest rate and the equilibrium amount of investment and saving (Chapter 10).

The Money Economy

Money consists of currency and bank deposits. Banks create deposits by making loans, and the Fed influences the quantity of money through its open market operations, which determine the monetary base and the federal funds rate—the interest rate on interbank loans.

The effects of the Fed's actions and of changes in the quantity of money are complex. In the current chapter, we focus on the immediate effects and on the long-run or ultimate effects of the Fed's actions.

The immediate effects are on the short-term nominal interest rate. If the Fed increases (or decreases) the quantity of money, the short-term nominal interest rate falls (or rises).

The long-run effects of the Fed's actions are on the price level and the inflation rate. In the long run, the loanable funds market determines the real interest rate and the Fed's actions determine only the price level and the inflation rate. If the Fed increases (or decreases) the quantity of money, the price level rises (or falls). And if the Fed speeds up (or slows down) the rate at which the quantity of money grows, the inflation rate increases (or decreases).

Real and Money Interactions and Policy

When the Fed changes the short-term nominal interest rate, other changes ripple through the economy. Expenditure plans change and real GDP, employment, unemployment, and the price level (and inflation rate) all change. In the long run, the real effects fade, leaving changes in only the price level and inflation rate. We lay the foundation for studying the ripple effects of the Fed's actions in Chapters 13–15. These chapters explain how the real and monetary factors interact and describe the short-run constraint on the Fed's choices.

Chapters 16 and 17 build on the foundation of all the preceding chapters. Chapter 16 explains how the government uses fiscal policy to sustain economic growth and stabilize output and employment. Chapter 17 explains how the Fed uses monetary policy to achieve those same goals and to control inflation.

12.1 MONEY AND THE INTEREST RATE

To understand the Fed's influence on the interest rate, we study the demand for money, the supply of money, and the forces that bring equilibrium in the market for money. We'll begin with the demand for money.

The Demand for Money

The amount of money that households and firms choose to hold is the **quantity of money demanded**. What determines the quantity of money demanded? The answer is the "price" of money. But what is that "price"?

Quantity of money demanded
The amount of money that households and firms choose to hold.

Two possible answers, both correct, are the value of money and the opportunity cost of holding money. The value of money is the quantity of goods and services that a dollar will buy, which is related to the *price level*. We'll explore this "price" of money when we study the long-run effects of money in the next part of this chapter. The opportunity cost of holding money is the goods and services forgone by holding money rather than some other asset.

To determine the quantity of money to hold, households and firms compare the benefit from holding money to its opportunity cost. They choose to hold the quantity that balances the benefit of holding an *additional* dollar of money against its opportunity cost. What are the benefit and opportunity cost of holding money?

Benefit of Holding Money

You've seen that money is the means of payment (Chapter 11, p. 268). The more money you hold, the easier it is for you to make payments. By holding enough money you can settle your bills at the end of each month without having to spend time and effort raising a loan or selling some other financial asset.

The marginal benefit of holding money is the change in total benefit that results from holding one more dollar as money. The marginal benefit of holding money diminishes as the quantity of money held increases. If you hold only a few dollars in money, then holding a few more dollars brings large benefits—you can buy a coffee or take a bus ride. If you hold enough money to make your normal weekly payments, then holding more dollars brings only a small benefit because you're not very likely to want to spend those extra dollars. Holding even more money brings only a small additional benefit. You barely notice the difference in the benefit of having $1,000 versus $1,001 in your bank account.

To get the most out of your assets, you hold money only up to the point at which its marginal benefit equals its opportunity cost.

Opportunity Cost of Holding Money

The opportunity cost of holding money is the interest rate forgone on an alternative asset. If you can earn 8 percent a year on a mutual fund account, then holding an additional $100 in money costs you $8 a year. Your opportunity cost of holding $100 in money is the goods and services worth $8 that you must forgo.

A fundamental principle of economics is that if the opportunity cost of something increases, people seek substitutes for it. Money is no exception. Other assets such as a mutual fund account are substitutes for money. The higher the opportunity cost of holding money—the higher the interest income forgone by not holding other assets—the smaller is the quantity of money demanded.

Opportunity Cost: *Nominal* Interest Is a *Real* Cost

The opportunity cost of holding money is the nominal interest rate. In Chapter 7, (p. 184), you learned the distinction between the *nominal* interest rate and the *real* interest rate and that

Nominal interest rate = Real interest rate + Inflation rate.

We can use this equation to find the real interest rate for a given nominal interest rate and inflation rate. For example, if the nominal interest rate on a mutual fund account is 8 percent a year and the inflation rate is 2 percent a year, the real interest rate is 6 percent a year. Why isn't the real interest rate of 6 percent a year the opportunity cost of holding money? That is, why isn't the opportunity cost of holding $100 in money only $6 worth of goods and services forgone?

The answer is that if you hold $100 in money rather than in a mutual fund, your buying power decreases by $8, not by $6. With inflation running at 2 percent a year, on each $100 that you hold as money and that earns no interest, you lose $2 worth of buying power a year. On each $100 that you put into your mutual fund account, you gain $6 worth of buying power a year. So if you hold money rather than a mutual fund, you lose the buying power of $6 plus $2, or $8—equivalent to the nominal interest rate on the mutual fund, not the real interest rate.

Because the opportunity cost of holding money is the nominal interest rate on an alternative asset,

Other things remaining the same, the higher the nominal interest rate, the smaller is the quantity of money demanded.

This relationship describes the decision made by an individual or a firm about how much money to hold. It also describes money-holding decisions for the economy—the sum of the decisions of every individual and firm.

We summarize the influence of the nominal interest rate on money-holding decisions in a demand for money schedule and curve.

The Demand for Money Schedule and Curve

Demand for money
The relationship between the quantity of money demanded and the nominal interest rate, when all other influences on the amount of money that people wish to hold remain the same.

The **demand for money** is the relationship between the quantity of money demanded and the nominal interest rate, when all other influences on the amount of money that people wish to hold remain the same. We illustrate the demand for money with a demand for money schedule and a demand for money curve, such as those in Figure 12.1. If the interest rate is 5 percent a year, the quantity of money demanded is $1 trillion. The quantity of money demanded decreases to $0.98 trillion if the interest rate rises to 6 percent a year and increases to $1.02 trillion if the interest rate falls to 4 percent a year.

The demand for money curve is *MD*. When the interest rate rises, everything else remaining the same, the opportunity cost of holding money rises and the quantity of money demanded decreases—there is a movement up along the demand for money curve. When the interest rate falls, the opportunity cost of holding money falls and the quantity of money demanded increases—there is a movement down along the demand for money curve.

FIGURE 12.1

The Demand for Money

myeconlab Animation

	Nominal interest rate (percent per year)	Quantity of money demanded (trillions of dollars)
A	6	0.98
B	5	1.00
C	4	1.02

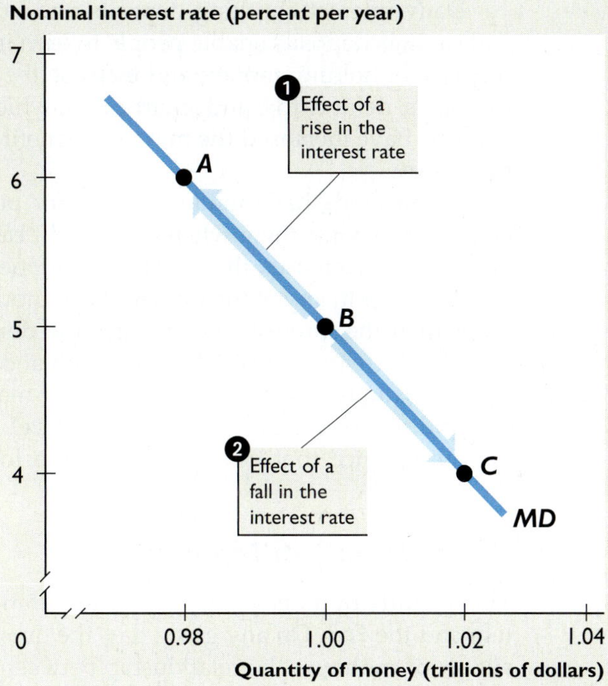

The demand for money schedule is graphed as the demand for money curve, *MD*. Rows *A*, *B*, and *C* in the table correspond to points *A*, *B*, and *C* on the curve. The nominal interest rate is the opportunity cost of holding money.

Other things remaining the same, ❶ an increase in the nominal interest rate decreases the quantity of money demanded, and ❷ a decrease in the nominal interest rate increases the quantity of money demanded.

Changes in the Demand for Money

A change in the nominal interest rate brings a change in the quantity of money demanded and a movement along the demand for money curve. A change in any other influence on money holding changes the demand for money. The three main influences on the demand for money are

- The price level
- Real GDP
- Financial technology

The Price Level

The demand for money is proportional to the price level—an x percent rise in the price level brings an x percent increase in the quantity of money demanded at each nominal interest rate. The reason is that we hold money to make payments: If the price level changes, the quantity of dollars that we need to make payments changes in the same proportion.

Real GDP

The demand for money increases as real GDP increases. The reason is that when real GDP increases, expenditures and incomes increase. To make the increased expenditures and income payments, households and firms must hold larger average amounts of money.

Financial Technology

Changes in financial technology change the demand for money. Most changes in financial technology come from advances in computing and record keeping. Some advances increase the quantity of money demanded, and some decrease it.

Daily interest checking deposits and automatic transfers between checking and savings deposits enable people to earn interest on money, lower the opportunity cost of holding money, and increase the demand for money. Automatic teller machines, debit cards, and smart cards, which have made money easier to obtain and use, have increased the marginal benefit of money and increased the demand for money.

Credit cards have made it easier for people to buy goods and services on credit and pay for them when their credit card account becomes due. This development has decreased the demand for money.

A change in any of the influences on money holdings that we've just reviewed other than the interest rate changes the demand for money. A rise in the price level, an increase in real GDP, or an advance in financial technology that lowers the opportunity cost of holding money or makes money more useful increases the demand for money. A fall in the price level, a decrease in real GDP, or a technological advance that creates a substitute for money decreases the demand for money.

The Supply of Money

Supply of money
The relationship between the quantity of money supplied and the nominal interest rate.

The quantity of money supplied is determined by the actions of the banking system and the Fed. On any given day, the quantity of money supplied is fixed. The **supply of money** is the relationship between the quantity of money supplied and the nominal interest rate. In Figure 12.2, the quantity of money supplied is $1 trillion regardless of the nominal interest rate, so the supply of money curve is the vertical line *MS*.

The Nominal Interest Rate

People hold some of their financial wealth as money and some in the form of other financial assets. You have seen that the amount of wealth that people hold as money depends on the nominal interest rate that they can earn on other financial assets. Demand and supply determine the nominal interest rate. We can study the forces of demand and supply in either the market for financial assets or the market for money. Because the Fed influences the quantity of money, we focus on the market for money.

On a given day, the price level, real GDP, and the state of financial technology are fixed. Because these influences on the demand for money are fixed, the demand for money curve is given.

The interest rate is the only influence on the quantity of money demanded that is free to fluctuate. Every day, the interest rate adjusts to make the quantity of money demanded equal the quantity of money supplied—to achieve money market equilibrium.

In Figure 12.2, the demand for money curve is *MD*. The equilibrium interest rate is 5 percent a year. At any interest rate above 5 percent a year, the quantity of money demanded is less than the quantity of money supplied. At any interest rate below 5 percent a year, the quantity of money demanded exceeds the quantity of money supplied.

FIGURE 12.2

Money Market Equilibrium

myeconlab Animation

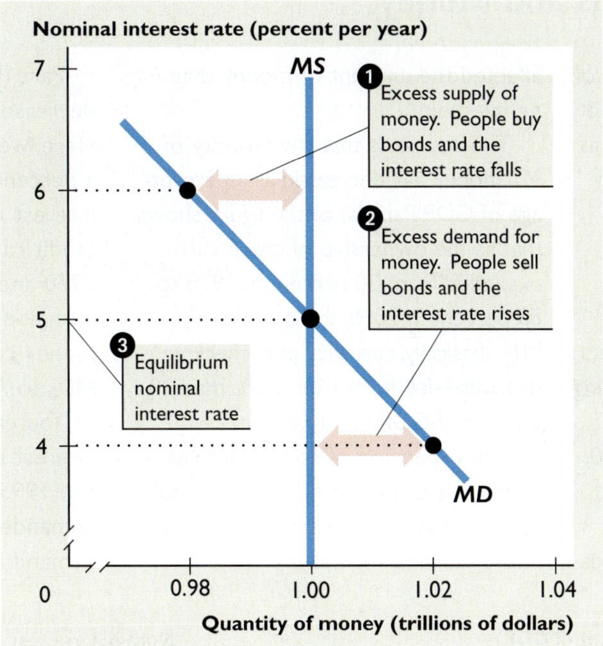

The supply of money curve is *MS*, and the demand for money curve is *MD*.

1. If the interest rate is 6 percent a year, the quantity of money held exceeds the quantity demanded. People buy bonds, the price of a bond rises, and the interest rate falls.
2. If the interest rate is 4 percent a year, the quantity of money held falls short of the quantity demanded. People sell bonds, the price of a bond falls, and the interest rate rises.
3. If the interest rate is 5 percent a year, the quantity of money held equals the quantity demanded. The money market is in equilibrium.

The Interest Rate and Bond Price Move in Opposite Directions When the government issues a bond, it specifies the dollar amount of interest that it will pay each year on the bond. Suppose that the government issues a bond that pays $100 of interest a year. The interest *rate* that you receive on this bond depends on the price that you pay for it. If the price is $1,000, the interest rate is 10 percent a year—$100 is 10 percent of $1,000.

If the price of the bond *falls* to $500, the interest rate *rises* to 20 percent a year. The reason is that you still receive an interest payment of $100, but this amount is 20 percent of the $500 price of the bond. If the price of the bond *rises* to $2,000, the interest rate *falls* to 5 percent a year. Again, you still receive an interest payment of $100, but this amount is 5 percent of the $2,000 price of the bond.

Interest Rate Adjustment If the interest rate is above its equilibrium level, people would like to hold less money than they are actually holding. They try to get rid of some money by buying other financial assets such as bonds. The demand for financial assets increases, the prices of these assets rise, and the interest rate falls. The interest rate keeps falling until the quantity of money that people want to hold increases to equal the quantity of money supplied.

Conversely, when the interest rate is below its equilibrium level, people are holding less money than they would like to hold. They try to get more money by selling other financial assets. The demand for these financial assets decreases, the prices of these assets fall, and the interest rate rises. The interest rate keeps rising until the quantity of money that people want to hold decreases to equal the quantity of money supplied.

EYE on the U.S. ECONOMY

Credit Cards and Money

Today, 80 percent of U.S. households own a credit card, and most of us use a credit card account as a substitute for money. When we buy goods or services, we use our credit card. When the monthly bill arrives, most of us pay off some of the outstanding balance but not all of it. In 2008, 57 percent of credit card holders had an outstanding balance after making their most recent payment, and the average card balance exceeded $5,000.

But back in 1970, only 20 percent of U.S. households had a credit card.

How has the spread of credit cards affected the amount of money that people hold?

The answer is that the quantity of M1 money has decreased as a percentage of GDP. Part (a) of the figure shows that as the ownership of credit cards expanded from 20 percent in 1970 to 80 percent in 2008, the quantity of M1—basically, currency plus checking deposits—fell from a bit more than 20 percent of GDP to 11 percent.

The expansion of credit card ownership is a change in financial technology that has led to a steady decrease in the demand for money.

Part (b) of the figure shows the decrease in the demand for money. Here, we graph the quantity of M1 as a percentage of GDP against the interest rate. You can see that as credit card use increased between 1970 and 2008, the demand for money decreased and the demand for money curve shifted leftward from MD_0 to MD_1 to MD_2.

You can also see that when the interest rate decreased between 1981 and 1993, the quantity of money demanded increased along the demand for money curve MD_1.

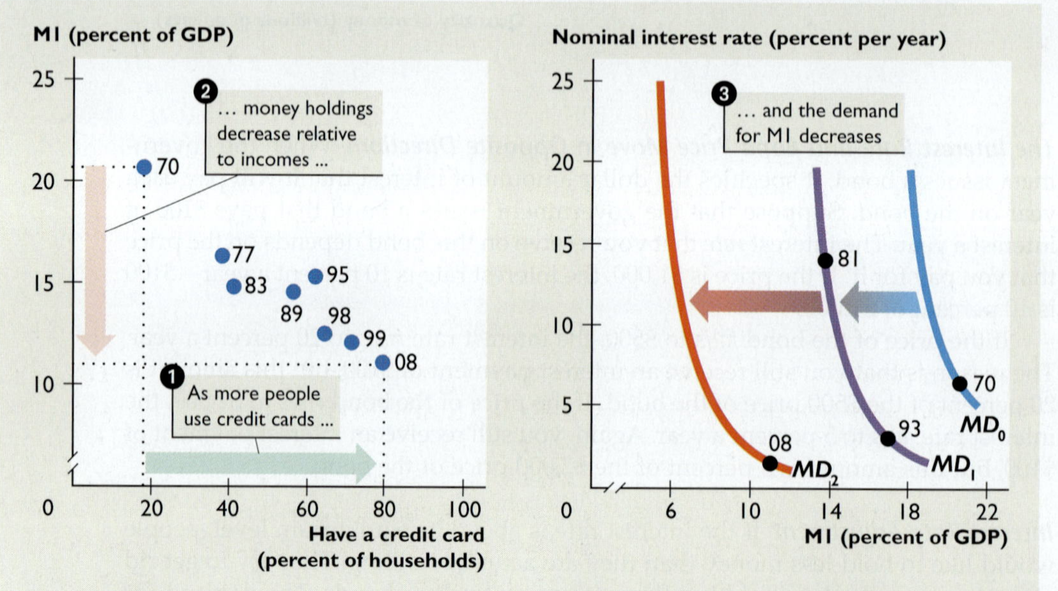

(a) Changes in the use of credit cards and money

(b) Changes in the demand for M1

SOURCE OF DATA: Federal Reserve.

Changing the Interest Rate

To change the interest rate, the Fed changes the quantity of money. Figure 12.3 illustrates two changes. The demand for money curve is *MD*. If the Fed increases the quantity of money to $1.02 trillion, the supply of money curve shifts rightward from MS_0 to MS_1 and the interest rate falls to 4 percent a year. If the Fed decreases the quantity of money to $0.98 trillion, the supply of money curve shifts leftward from MS_0 to MS_2 and the interest rate rises to 6 percent a year.

FIGURE 12.3

Interest Rate Changes

myeconlab Animation

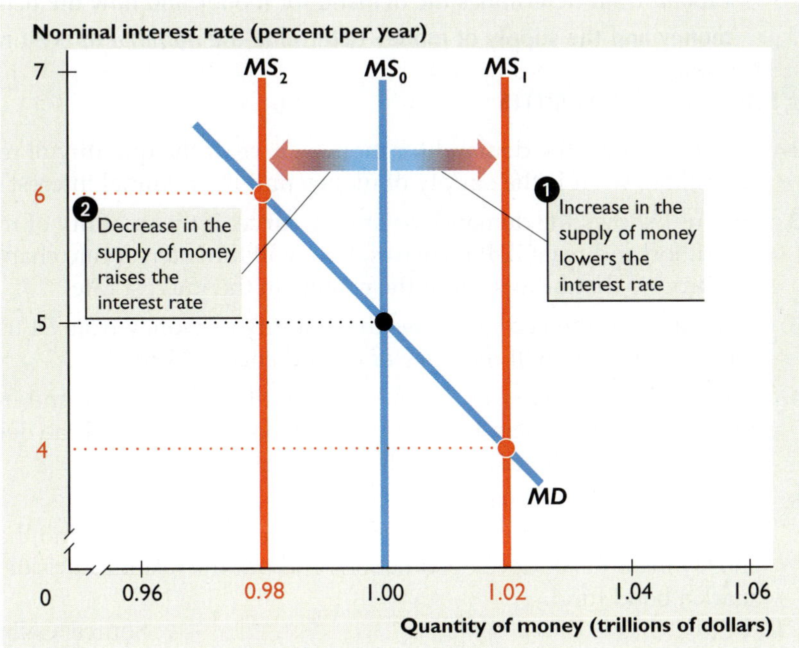

The demand for money is *MD*, and initially, the supply of money is MS_0. The interest rate is 5 percent a year.

❶ If the Fed increases the quantity of money and the supply of money curve shifts rightward to MS_1, the interest rate falls to 4 percent a year.

❷ If the Fed decreases the quantity of money and the supply of money curve shifts leftward to MS_2, the interest rate rises to 6 percent a year.

EYE on YOUR LIFE

Money Holding and Fed Watching

How much currency (cash) do you have in your wallet, on average? How much money do you keep in your bank account on average?

Why don't you hold a larger average bank balance by paying off a smaller part of your credit card balance than you can afford to pay?

Wouldn't it be better to keep a bit more money in the bank?

Almost certainly, that would not be a smart idea. Why? Because the opportunity cost of holding that money would be too high.

If you have an outstanding credit card balance, the interest rate on that balance is the opportunity cost of holding money.

By paying off as much of your credit card balance as you can afford, you avoid a high interest rate on the outstanding balance.

Your demand for money is sensitive to this opportunity cost.

Do you watch the Fed? Probably not, but you can learn to become an effective Fed watcher. In the process, you will become much better informed about the state of the U.S. economy and the state of the economy in your region.

To become a Fed watcher, try to get into the habit of visiting the Fed's Web site at www.federalreserve.gov.

Look specifically at the Beige Book, in which you can learn what is happening in your region. Also, keep an eye on the FOMC calendar for the dates of interest rate announcements. On these dates, check the media for opinions on what the Fed's interest rate decision will be. After the decision is made, check the Fed's explanation as to why it made its decision.

myeconlab

Work these problems in Study Plan 12.1 to get instant feedback.

FIGURE 1

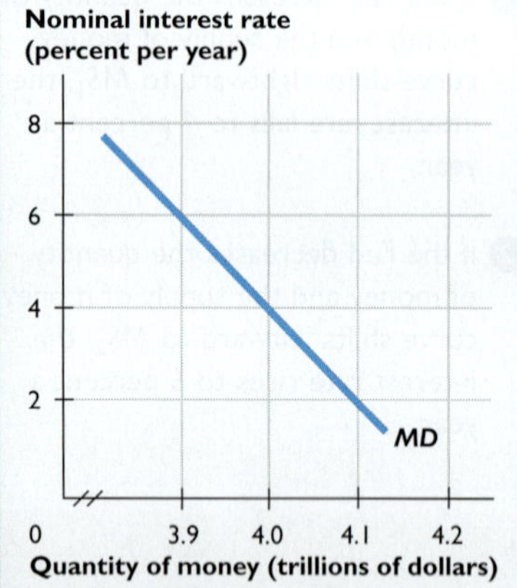

FIGURE 2

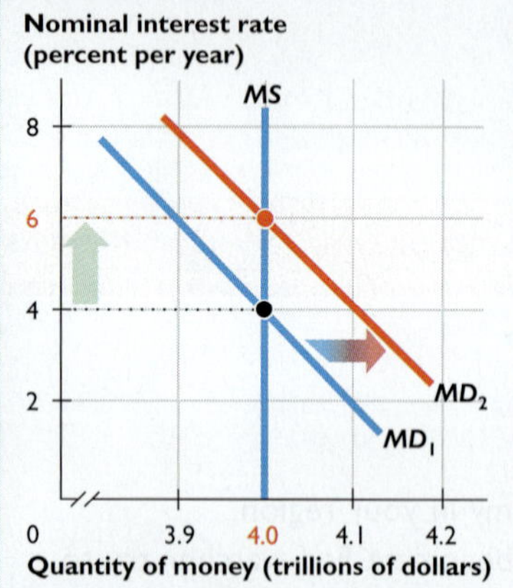

FIGURE 3

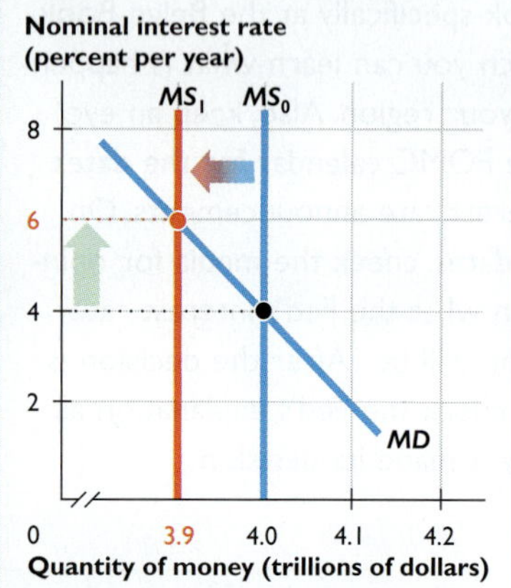

CHECKPOINT 12.1

Explain what determines the demand for money and how the demand for money and the supply of money determine the *nominal* interest rate.

Practice Problems

1. Figure 1 shows the demand for money curve. If the quantity of money is \$4 trillion, what is the supply of money and the nominal interest rate?
2. Figure 1 shows the demand for money curve. If the quantity of money is \$4 trillion and real GDP increases, how will the interest rate change? Explain the process that brings about the change in the interest rate.
3. In Figure 1, if the Fed decreases the quantity of money from \$4 trillion to \$3.9 trillion, how will the price of a bond change? Why?
4. If banks introduce a user fee on every credit card purchase and increase the interest rate on outstanding credit card balances, how will the demand for money and the nominal interest rate change?
5. **What to do with \$50,000 now**

   A good strategy: Put about two-thirds of the money into a fund that invests mostly in bonds of developed nations and put the rest into a riskier emerging-market bond fund.

   Source: CNNMoney.com

   What is the opportunity cost of holding money? If lots of people followed this advice and put their money into bonds, explain what will happen to the demand for money, the price of bonds, and the interest rate on bonds.

Guided Solutions to Practice Problems

1. The supply of money is the curve *MS*. The interest rate is 4 percent a year, at the intersection of MD_1 and *MS* (Figure 2).
2. The demand for money increases, and the demand for money curve shifts from MD_1 to MD_2 (Figure 2). At an interest rate of 4 percent a year, people want to hold more money, so they sell bonds. The price of a bond falls, and the interest rate rises.
3. At an interest rate of 4 percent a year, people would like to hold \$4 trillion. With only \$3.9 trillion of money available, they sell bonds in an attempt to get more money. The price of a bond falls, and the interest rate rises. The price will continue to fall and the interest rate will continue to rise until the quantity of money that people want to hold equals the \$3.9 trillion available. The new equilibrium nominal interest rate is 6 percent a year (Figure 3).
4. With a fee on each transaction, people will use credit cards less frequently. With a higher interest rate on outstanding balances, the opportunity cost of holding money increases. The demand for money will increase and with no change in the supply of money, the nominal interest rate will rise.
5. The opportunity cost of cash is the highest interest rate forgone by not holding bonds of a similar risk. As lots of people decide to buy bonds, the demand for money decreases. The demand for bonds increases and with no change in the supply of bonds the price of a bond rises and the interest rate on bonds falls.

12.2 MONEY, THE PRICE LEVEL, AND INFLATION

A change in the nominal interest rate is the initial effect of a change in the quantity of money, but it is not the ultimate or long-run effect. When the interest rate changes, borrowing and lending and investment and consumption spending also change, which in turn change production and prices—change real GDP and the price level.

The details of this adjustment process are complex, and we explore them in the next two chapters. But the place where the process comes to rest—the *long-run* outcome—is easier to describe. It is crucial to understand the long-run outcome because that is where the economy is heading. We're now going to examine the long-run equilibrium in the money market.

The Money Market in the Long Run

The *long run* refers to the economy at full employment when real GDP equals potential GDP (Chapter 8, p. 195). Over the business cycle, real GDP fluctuates around potential GDP. But averaging over an expansion and recession and a peak and trough, real GDP equals potential GDP. That is, real GDP equals potential GDP *on average*. So another way to think about the *long run* is as a description of the economy *on average* over the business cycle.

The Long-Run Demand for Money

In the long run, equilibrium in the market for loanable funds determines the real interest rate (Chapter 10, pp. 248–255). The nominal interest rate that influences money holding plans equals the real interest rate plus the inflation rate. For now, we'll consider an economy that has no inflation, so the real interest rate equals the nominal interest rate. (We'll consider inflation later in this chapter.)

With the interest rate determined by real forces in the long run, what is the variable that adjusts to make the quantity of money that people plan to hold equal the quantity of money supplied? The answer is the "price" of money. The law of demand applies to money just as it does to any other object. The lower the "price" of money, the greater is the quantity of money that people are willing to hold. What is the "price" of money? It is the *value* of money.

The Value of Money

The *value of money* is the quantity of goods and services that a unit of money will buy. It is the inverse of the *price level, P,* which equals the GDP price index divided by 100. That is,

$$\text{Value of money} = 1/P.$$

To see why, suppose that you have \$100 in your wallet. If you spend that money, you can buy goods and services valued at \$100. Now suppose that the price level rises by 10 percent. After the price rise, the quantity of goods and services that \$100 can buy has fallen. Your \$100 can now buy only \$100 ÷ 1.1 or \$91 of goods and services. Yesterday's \$100 is worth \$91 today. The price level has risen and the value of money has fallen and each percentage change is the same. The higher the value of money, the smaller is the quantity of money that people plan to hold. If it seems strange that a higher value of money makes people want to hold less money, think about how much money you would plan to hold if the price of a restaurant meal was 20 cents and the price of movie ticket was 10 cents. You would be happy to hold (say) $1 on average. But if the price of a meal is $20 and the price of a movie ticket is $10, you would want to hold $100 on average. The price level is lower and the value of money higher in the first case than in the second; and the amount of money you would plan to hold is lower in the first case than in the second.

Money Market Equilibrium in the Long Run

In the long run, money market equilibrium determines the value of money. If the quantity of money supplied exceeds the long-run quantity demanded, people go out and spend their surplus money. The quantity of goods and services available is fixed equal to potential GDP, so the extra spending forces prices upward. As the price level rises, the value of money falls.

If the quantity of money supplied is less than the long-run quantity demanded, people lower their spending to build up the quantity of money they hold. The shortage of money translates into a surplus of goods and services, so the spending cut-back forces prices downward. The price level falls and the value of money rises. When the quantity of money supplied equals the long-run quantity demanded, the price level and the value of money are at their equilibrium levels.

Figure 12.4 illustrates long-run money market equilibrium. The long-run demand for money curve is *LRMD*. Its position depends on potential GDP and the equilibrium interest rate. The supply of money is *MS*. Equilibrium occurs when the value of money is 1.

FIGURE 12.4

Long-Run Money Market Equilibrium

myeconlab Animation

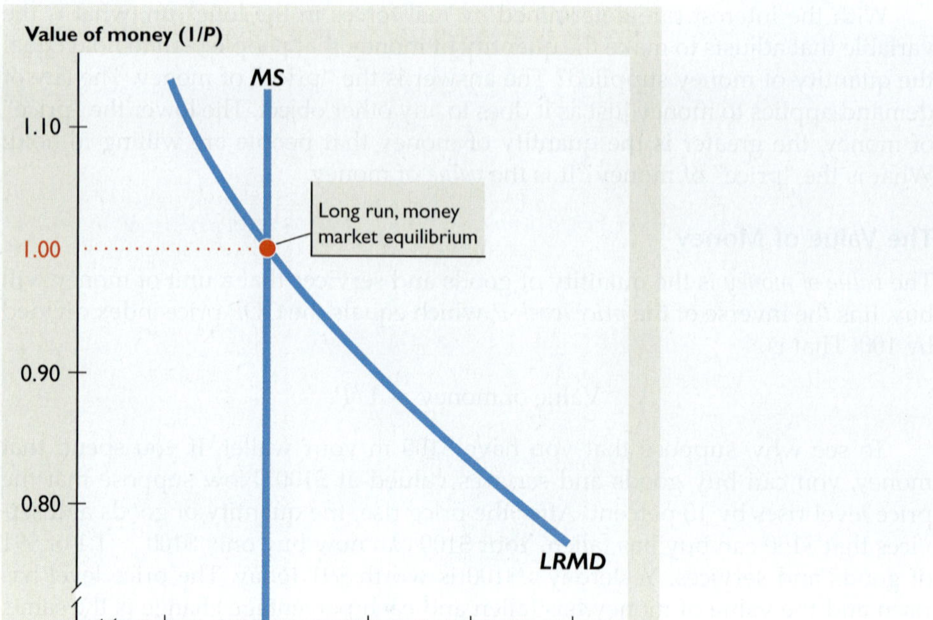

The long-run demand for money is determined by potential GDP and the equilibrium interest rate.

The *LRMD* curve shows how the quantity of money that households and firms plan to hold, in the long run, depends on the value of money (or 1/*P*, the inverse of the price level).

The *MS* curve shows the quantity of money supplied, which is $1 trillion.

The price level adjusts to make the value of money equal 1 and achieve long-run money market equilibrium.

A Change in the Quantity of Money

Suppose that starting from a long-run equilibrium, the Fed increases the quantity of money by 10 percent. In the short run, the greater quantity of money lowers the nominal interest rate. With a lower interest rate, people and businesses borrow more and spend more. But with real GDP equal to potential GDP, there are no more goods and services to buy, so when people go out and spend, prices start to rise. Eventually, a new long-run equilibrium is reached at which the price level has increased in proportion to the increase in the quantity of money. Because the quantity of money increased by 10 percent, the price level has also risen by 10 percent from 1.0 to 1.1.

Figure 12.5 illustrates this outcome. Initially, the supply of money is MS_0 and the quantity of money is \$1 trillion. The Fed increases the supply of money to MS_1 and the quantity of money is now \$1.1 trillion—a 10 percent increase. There is now a surplus of money and people go out and spend it. The increased spending on the same unchanged quantity of goods and services raises the price level and lowers the value of money. Eventually, the price level has increased by 10 percent from 1.0 to 1.1 and the value of money has decreased by 10 percent from 1.00 to 0.91.

You've just seen a key proposition about the quantity of money and the price level.

In the long run and other things remaining the same, a given percentage change in the quantity of money brings an equal percentage change in the price level.

FIGURE 12.5

The Long-Run Effect of a Change in the Quantity of Money

myeconlab Animation

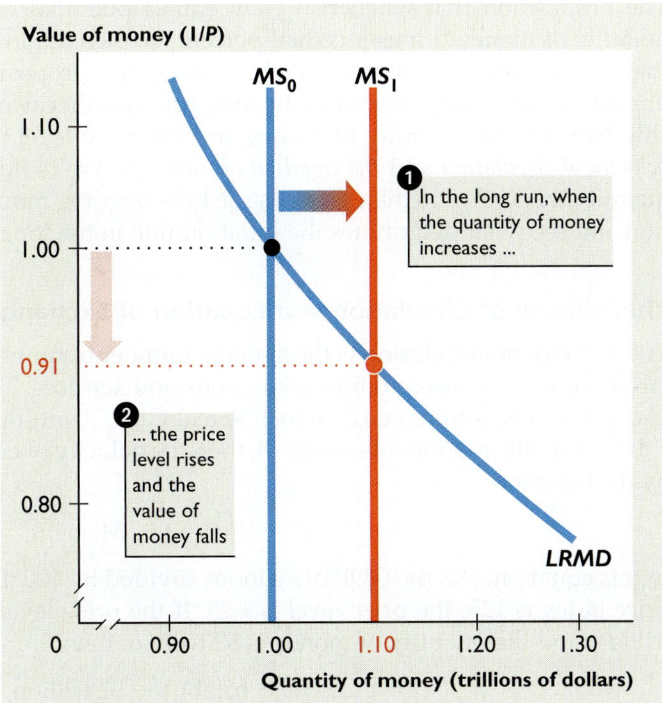

1. The Fed increases the supply of money from MS_0 to MS_1 and the quantity of money increases from \$1 trillion to \$1.1 trillion, a 10 percent increase.
2. The price level rises by 10 percent and the value of money falls by 10 percent to restore long-run money market equilibrium.

The Price Level in a Baby-Sitting Club

It is hard to visualize a long-run equilibrium and even harder to visualize and compare two long-run equilibrium situations like those that we've just described. An example of a simpler situation might help.

In an isolated neighborhood, there are no teenagers but lots of young children, and parents can't find any babysitters. So they form a club and sit for each other. The deal is that each time a parent sits for someone else, he or she receives a token that can be used to buy one babysitting session from another member of the club. The organizer notices that the club is inactive. Every member has a few unspent tokens, but they spend them infrequently. To make the club more active, the organizer decides to issue every member one token for each token that is currently held, so the supply of tokens doubles.

With more tokens to spend, parents start to plan more evenings out. Suddenly, the phones are ringing as parents seek babysitters. Every member of the club wants a sitter, but there are no more sitters than before. After making a few calls and finding no sitters available, anxious parents who really do need a sitter start to offer a higher price: two tokens per session. That does the trick. At the higher price, the quantity of baby-sitting services demanded decreases and the quantity supplied increases. Equilibrium is restored. Nothing real has changed, but the quantity of tokens and the price level have doubled.

Think of the equilibrium quantity of baby-sitting services as potential GDP, the quantity of tokens as the quantity of money, and the price of a baby-sitting session as the price level. You can then see how a given percentage change in the quantity of money at full employment brings an equal percentage change in the price level.

The Quantity Theory of Money

Quantity theory of money
The proposition that when real GDP equals potential GDP, an increase in the quantity of money brings an equal percentage increase in the price level.

The proposition that when real GDP equals potential GDP, an increase in the quantity of money brings an equal percentage increase in the price level is called the **quantity theory of money**. We've derived this proposition by looking at equilibrium in the money market in the long run. Another way of seeing the relationship between the quantity of money and the price level uses the concepts of *the velocity of circulation* and *the equation of exchange*. We're now going to explore the quantity theory. We're then going to see how ongoing money growth brings inflation and see what determines the inflation rate in the long run.

The Velocity of Circulation and Equation of Exchange

Velocity of circulation
The average number of times in a year that each dollar of money gets used to buy final goods and services.

The **velocity of circulation** is the average number of times in a year that each dollar of money gets used to buy final goods and services. The value of final goods and services is nominal GDP, which is real GDP, *Y*, multiplied by the price level, *P*. If we call the quantity of money *M*, then the velocity of circulation is determined by the equation:

$$V = (P \times Y) \div M.$$

In this equation, *P* is the GDP price index divided by 100. For example, if the GDP price index is 125, the price level is 1.25. If the price level is 1.25, real GDP is \$8 trillion, and the quantity of money is \$2 trillion, then the velocity of circulation is

$$V = (1.25 \times \$8 \text{ trillion}) \div \$2 \text{ trillion, or}$$

$$V = 5.$$

That is, with \$2 trillion of money, each dollar gets used an average of 5 times, so \$2 trillion × 5 equals \$10 trillion of goods and services bought.

The **equation of exchange** states that the quantity of money, M, multiplied by the velocity of circulation, V, equals the price level P, multiplied by real GDP, Y. That is,

Equation of exchange
An equation that states that the quantity of money multiplied by the velocity of circulation equals the price level multiplied by real GDP.

$$M \times V = P \times Y.$$

The equation of exchange is *always* true because it is implied by the definition of the velocity of circulation. That is, if you multiply both sides of the equation on page 310 that defines the velocity of circulation by M, you get the equation of exchange.

Using the above numbers—a price level of 1.25, real GDP of \$8 trillion, the quantity of money of \$2 trillion, and the velocity of circulation of 5—you can see that

$$M \times V = \$2 \text{ trillion} \times 5 = \$10 \text{ trillion},$$

and

$$P \times Y = 1.25 \times \$8 \text{ trillion} = \$10 \text{ trillion}.$$

So,

$$M \times V = P \times Y = \$10 \text{ trillion}.$$

The Quantity Theory Prediction

We can rearrange the equation of exchange to isolate the price level on the left side. To do so, divide both sides of the equation of exchange by real GDP to obtain

$$P = M \times V \div Y.$$

On the left side is the price level, and on the right side are all the things that influence the price level. But this equation is still just an implication of the definition of the velocity of circulation. To turn the equation into a theory of what determines the price level, we use two other facts: (1) At full employment, real GDP equals potential GDP, which is determined only by real factors and not by the quantity of money; and (2) the velocity of circulation is relatively stable and does not change when the quantity of money changes.

So with V and Y constant, if M increases P must increase, and the percentage increase in P must equal the percentage increase in M.

We can use the above numbers to illustrate this prediction. Real GDP is \$8 trillion, the quantity of money is \$2 trillion, and the velocity of circulation is 5. Put these values into the equation:

$$P = M \times V \div Y$$

to obtain

$$P = \$2 \text{ trillion} \times 5 \div \$8 \text{ trillion} = 1.25.$$

Now increase the quantity of money from \$2 trillion to \$2.4 trillion. The percentage increase in the quantity of money is

$$(\$2.4 \text{ trillion} - \$2 \text{ trillion}) \div \$2 \text{ trillion} \times 100 = 20 \text{ percent}.$$

Now find the new price level. It is

$$P = \$2.4 \text{ trillion} \times 5 \div \$8 \text{ trillion} = 1.50.$$

The price level rises from 1.25 to 1.50. The percentage increase in the price level is

$$(1.50 - 1.25) \div 1.25 \times 100 = 20 \text{ percent.}$$

When the economy is at full employment (real GDP equals potential GDP) and the velocity of circulation is stable, the price level and the quantity of money increase by the same 20 percent.

Inflation and the Quantity Theory of Money

The equation of exchange tells us about the price *level,* the quantity of money, the level of real GDP, and the level of the velocity of circulation. We can turn the equation into one that tells us about *rates of change* or *growth rates* of these variables. We want to make this conversion because we want to know what determines the inflation rate—the rate of change of the price level.

In rates of change or growth rates,

$$\text{Money growth} + \text{Velocity growth} = \text{Inflation rate} + \text{Real GDP growth,}$$

which means that

$$\text{Inflation rate} = \text{Money Growth} + \text{Velocity growth} - \text{Real GDP growth.}$$

Constant Inflation

Figure 12.6 illustrates three cases in which the inflation rate is constant—at zero, at a low or moderate rate, and at a high or rapid rate. In each case, the velocity growth rate is 1 percent a year and the real GDP growth rate is 3 percent a year. The money growth rate is the only thing that is different across the three cases, and it is this difference that brings the different inflation rates.

If the quantity of money grows at 2 percent a year, there is no inflation. That is,

$$\text{Inflation rate} = 2 \text{ percent} + 1 \text{ percent} - 3 \text{ percent} = 0 \text{ percent a year.}$$

With the quantity of money growing at 4 percent a year, the inflation rate is 2 percent a year. That is,

$$\text{Inflation rate} = 4 \text{ percent} + 1 \text{ percent} - 3 \text{ percent} = 2 \text{ percent a year.}$$

And with the quantity of money growing at 10 percent a year, the inflation rate is 8 percent a year. That is,

$$\text{Inflation rate} = 10 \text{ percent} + 1 \text{ percent} - 3 \text{ percent} = 8 \text{ percent a year.}$$

A Change in the Inflation Rate

We've looked at three different inflation rates—zero, moderate, and rapid—with given growth rates of real GDP and velocity of circulation. We're now going to see what happens when the growth rate of money *changes*. We'll start with an increase in the money growth rate.

FIGURE 12.6

Money Growth and Inflation

myeconlab Animation

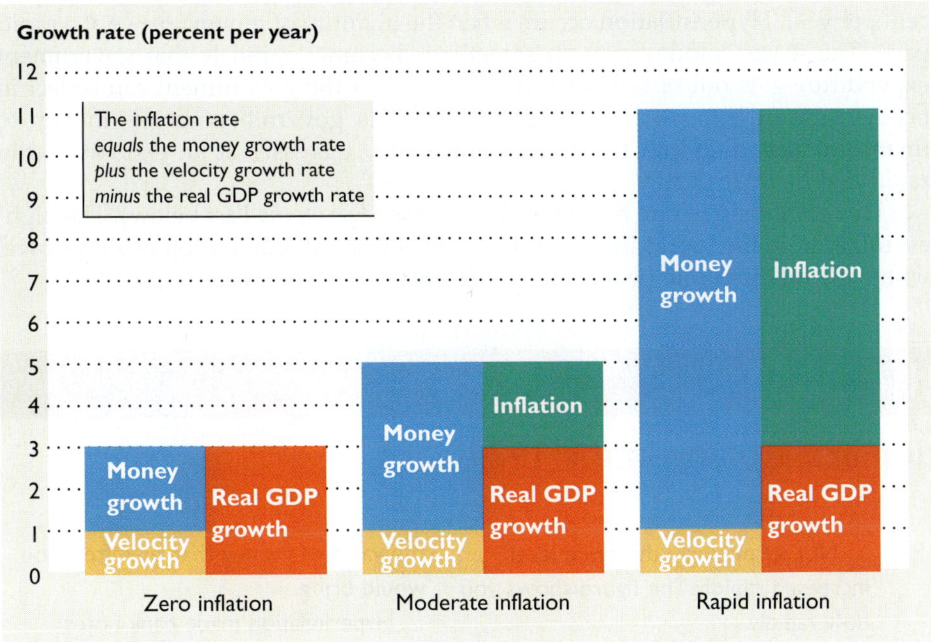

The velocity of circulation grows at 1 percent a year (the orange block), and real GDP grows at 3 percent a year (the red block). The inflation rate (green block) is determined by money growth (blue block).

If the quantity of money grows at 2 percent a year, the inflation rate is zero.

If the quantity of money grows at 4 percent a year, the inflation rate is a moderate 2 percent a year.

But if the quantity of money grows at 10 percent a year, the inflation rate is a rapid 8 percent a year.

Increase in Money Growth Rate When the money growth rate increases, the inflation rate increases slowly and there is a temporary (short-run) increase in the real GDP growth rate. The velocity of circulation increases as the inflation rate speeds up but this increase does not persist. Once the velocity has increased in response to a higher inflation rate, it remains constant at its new level. (You can see in *Eye on the Cause of Inflation* on p. 315 that velocity growth has been zero for most of the past 40 years. It increased during the 1990s but decreased again during the 2000s.)

A faster inflation reduces potential GDP and slows real GDP growth (for reasons that we explore in the final section of this chapter) but for low inflation rates, these effects are small and are dominated by the main direct effect of money growth on the inflation rate. Eventually, real GDP growth slows to that of potential GDP, velocity growth returns to its long-run rate, and the inflation rate changes by the full amount of the change in the money growth rate.

Decrease in Money Growth Rate When the money growth rate decreases, the effects that we've just described work in the opposite direction.

You can see in *Eye on the Cause of Inflation* (p. 315) that changes in the growth rate of real GDP and changes in velocity growth have been small in comparison to the changes in the growth rate of money and the inflation rate. So,

In the long run and other things remaining the same, a change in the *growth rate* of the quantity of money brings an equal change in the inflation rate.

The relationship between the money growth rate and the inflation rate is at its clearest when inflation is rapid in *hyperinflation*.

Hyperinflation

Hyperinflation
Inflation at a rate that exceeds 50 percent *a month* (which translates to 12,875 percent per year).

When the inflation rate exceeds 50 percent *a month,* it is called **hyperinflation**. An inflation rate of 50 percent per month translates to an inflation rate of 12,875 percent per year. Hyperinflation occurs when the quantity of money grows at a rapid pace. The reason money growth sometimes becomes rapid is that government expenditure gets out of control and exceeds what the government can collect in tax revenue or borrow. In such a situation, the government prints money to finance its spending and the quantity of money increases at an extraordinarily rapid and increasing rate.

Hyperinflation is rare but not unknown (see *Eye on the Past* below). The highest inflation in the world in recent times was in the African nation of Zimbabwe, where the inflation rate peaked at 231,150,888.87 percent a year in July 2008.

EYE on the PAST

Hyperinflation in Germany in the 1920s

An international treaty signed in 1919 required Germany to pay large amounts as compensation for war damage to other countries in Europe. To meet its obligations, Germany started to print money. The quantity of money increased by 24 percent in 1921, by 220 percent in 1922, and by 43 *billion* percent in 1923!

Not surprisingly, the price level increased rapidly. The figure shows you how rapidly.

In November 1923 when the hyperinflation reached its peak, the price level was more than doubling every day. Wages were paid twice a day, and people spent their morning's wages at lunchtime to avoid the loss in the value of money that the afternoon would bring.

Hyperinflation made bank notes more valuable as fire kindling than as money. The sight of people burning Reichmarks (the name of Germany's money at that time) was a common one, as the photo shows.

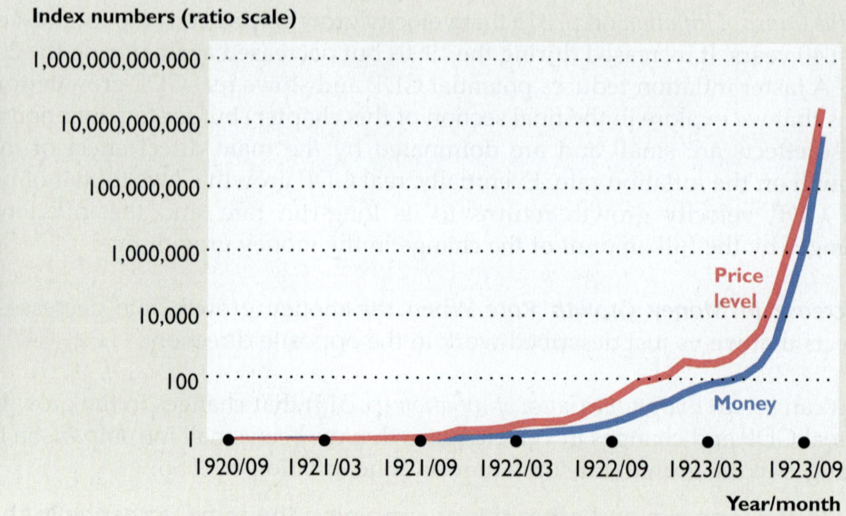

SOURCE OF DATA: Phillip Cagan, "The Monetary Dynamics of Hyperinflation," in Milton Friedman (editor), *Studies in the Quantity Theory of Money*, University of Chicago Press, 1956.

EYE on the CAUSE of INFLATION

Does Inflation, Deflation, or a Stable Price Level Lie in Our Future?

According to the quantity theory of money, whether we face a future with inflation, deflation, or a stable price level depends entirely on the rate at which the Fed permits the quantity of money to grow.

But is the quantity theory correct? Does it explain our past inflation with enough accuracy to be a guide to future inflation?

The quantity theory does not predict the year-to-year changes in the inflation rate. The quantity theory does an especially bad job of explaining 2008 and 2009 because in those years, the velocity of circulation tumbled.

But on average, over a number of years, the quantity theory is a remarkably accurate predictor of the inflation rate. The figure shows that the quantity theory explains our past decade-average inflation rates.

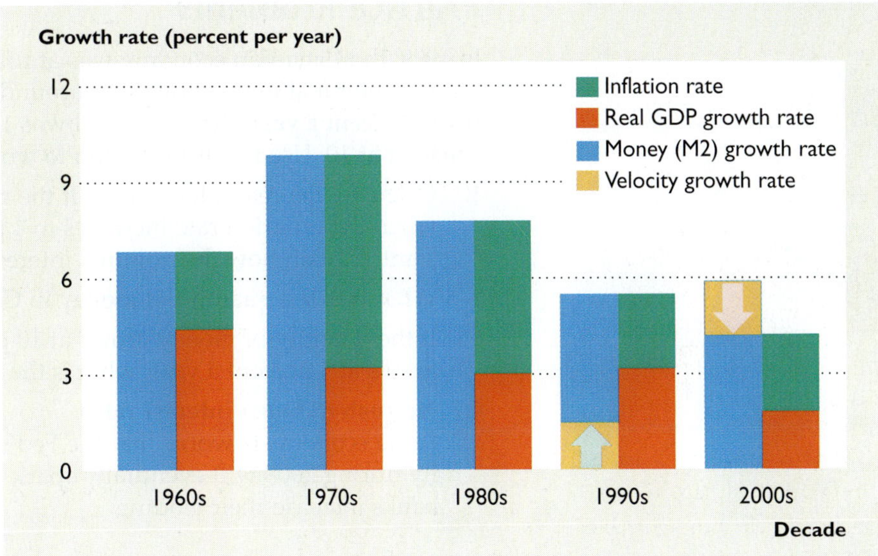

SOURCE OF DATA: Federal Reserve and Bureau of Economic Analysis.

During the 1960s, 1970s, and 1980s, the velocity of circulation (of M2) was constant. The growth rate of real GDP slowed from the fast-expanding 1960s to a more moderate pace during the 1970s and 1980s. The growth rate of the quantity of M2 increased in the 1970s and slowed in the 1980s and the inflation rate moved in line with the changed money growth rate, exactly as predicted by the quantity theory of money.

During the 1990s the M2 growth slowed again but the velocity of circulation increased. With the real GDP growth rate unchanged, the inflation rate slowed.

The 2000s saw the M2 growth rate increase but the velocity of circulation shrank at a similar rate to that at which it had grown during the 1990s. Real GDP growth and inflation remained close to their levels in the previous decade.

Aside from the small changes in velocity growth during the 1990s and 2000s, which cancelled each other out, all the decade-by-decade variation in the inflation rate has resulted from changes in the growth rate of the quantity of money.

To predict our future decade-average inflation rates, we must predict the future growth rate of money.

The Fed is able to influence the inflation rate and the money growth rate and absent any pressures that the Fed finds impossible to resist, we can expect that the Fed will do a good job of keeping inflation in check. That doesn't mean zero inflation. It means an inflation rate running at around 2 percent per year.

Will the Fed face irresistible pressure to create money too rapidly or too slowly? It is unlikely that pressure will force the Fed to shrink the quantity of money and generate deflation.

But there could be pressure in the opposite direction. Inflation is a tax. If the Fed creates money by buying government bonds, the government gets revenue just like it gets tax revenue.

With a large and long-lasting federal budget deficit, Congress might be tempted to lean on the Fed to keep interest rates down. If Congress were successful in such a move, the result would be money creation at too rapid a pace and an outbreak of inflation.

myeconlab

Work these problems in Study Plan 12.2 to get instant feedback.

CHECKPOINT 12.2

Explain how in the long run, the quantity of money determines the price level and money growth brings inflation.

Practice Problems

In 1999, the Canadian economy was at full employment. Real GDP was $886 billion, the nominal interest rate was around 6 percent per year, the inflation rate was 2 percent a year, the price level was 1.1, and the velocity of circulation was constant at 10. Use this information to work Problems **1** and **2**.

1. Calculate the real interest rate. If the real interest rate remains unchanged when the inflation rate increases to 4 percent a year and then remains constant, explain how the nominal interest rate changes in the long run.
2. What was the quantity of money in Canada?
3. If the quantity of money grows at 10 percent a year and potential GDP grows at 3 percent a year, what is the inflation rate in the long run?
4. **No rush to boost interest rates**

   Some economists worry that the Fed's policy of generating so much liquidity during 2008 will eventually spark inflation as the economy improves and banks increase their lending.

   Source: *USA Today*, October 8, 2009

   Explain why some economists are worried about inflation taking hold.

Guided Solutions to Practice Problems

1. The real interest rate equals the nominal interest rate minus the inflation rate. That is, the real interest rate equals 6 percent a year minus 2 percent a year, which equals 4 percent a year.

   The nominal interest rate rises from 6 percent a year to 8 percent a year.
2. The quantity of money was $97.5 billion.

   Velocity of circulation (V) = Nominal GDP ($P \times Y$) ÷ Quantity of money (M).
   Rewrite this equation as: $M = (P \times Y) \div V$.
   $(P \times Y) = 1.1 \times \$886$ billion, or $975 billion, so $M = \$975$ billion $\div$ 10, or $97.5 billion.
3. With velocity constant, velocity growth is zero. So the inflation rate in the long run equals the money growth rate minus the real GDP growth rate, which is 10 percent a year minus 3 percent a year, or 7 percent a year.
4. In the short run, an increase in liquidity is an increase in the quantity of money. With a given demand for money, an increase in the quantity of money lowers the interest rate in the short run. With no change in the interest rate, as the economy recovers from the recession of 2008–2009 and banks increase their lending, the quantity of money demanded will increase and there will be pressure on the interest rate to rise. Some economists worry that to keep the interest rate constant in an attempt not to hinder the recovery, the Fed will increase the quantity of money. In the long run, as the quantity of money increases the value of money falls. A falling value of money is a rising price level—inflation.

12.3 THE COST OF INFLATION

Inflation decreases potential GDP, slows economic growth, and consumes leisure time. These outcomes occur for four reasons that we classify as the four costs of inflation:

- Tax costs
- Shoe-leather costs
- Confusion costs
- Uncertainty costs

Tax Costs

We've seen that inflation occurs when the quantity of money grows more rapidly than real GDP. But why would we ever want to make this happen? Why don't we keep the quantity of money growing at the same pace as real GDP grows? One part of the answer is that the government gets revenue from inflation.

Inflation Is a Tax

A government can pay its expenses with newly created money. But the things a government buys with this money aren't free. They are paid for by people and businesses in proportion to the amount of money they hold—by a tax on money holding that we call the inflation tax.

When the government spends newly created money, the quantity of money increases and, as predicted by the quantity theory, the price level rises. The inflation rate equals the growth rate of the quantity of money (other things remaining the same).

To see how the inflation tax gets paid, suppose that the Coca-Cola Company is holding \$110,000 in money. The annual inflation rate is 10 percent, and the price level rises from 1.0 to 1.1. At the end of the year, Coca-Cola's money will buy only \$100,000 of goods and services (\$110,000 ÷ 1.1 = \$100,000). The firm has lost \$10,000—it has "paid" a \$10,000 inflation tax.

Governments in today's world don't create new money by printing it. Money gets created when the central bank buys government bonds. In the United States, the Fed doesn't buy bonds directly from the government: it buys them in open market operations. When the Fed buys bonds, the monetary base increases and through the money multiplier, the quantity of money increases. The Fed pays its profits to the government, so the government ends up paying no interest on its bonds held by the Fed. By this process, the government prints money.

Inflation, Saving, and Investment

The income tax on interest income drives a wedge between the before-tax interest rate paid by borrowers and the after-tax interest rate received by lenders. A rise in the income tax rate increases the before-tax interest rate and decreases the after-tax interest rate; and the rise in the before-tax interest rate decreases borrowing and investment; and the fall in the after-tax interest rate decreases lending and saving.

An increase in the inflation rate increases the true tax rate on interest income, and strengthens the effect that we have just described. To see why, let's consider an example.

Suppose that the real interest rate is 4 percent a year and the income tax rate is 50 percent. With no inflation, the nominal interest rate is also 4 percent a year and the real after-tax interest rate is 2 percent a year (50 percent of 4 percent).

Now suppose the inflation rate rises to 4 percent a year, so the nominal interest rate rises to 8 percent a year. The after-tax nominal interest rate rises to 4 percent a year (50 percent of 8 percent). Subtract the 4 percent inflation rate from this amount, and you see that the after-tax real interest rate is zero! The true income tax rate has increased to 100 percent.

The fall in the after-tax real interest rate weakens the incentive to lend and save and the rise in the before-tax interest rate weakens the incentive to borrow and invest. With a fall in saving and investment, the rates of capital accumulation and real GDP growth slow down.

Shoe-Leather Costs

The "shoe-leather costs" of inflation are costs that arise from an increase in the velocity of circulation of money and an increase in the amount of running around that people do to try to avoid incurring losses from the falling value of money.

When money loses value at a rapid anticipated rate, it does not function well as a store of value and people try to avoid holding it. They spend their incomes as soon as they receive them, and firms pay out incomes—wages and dividends—as soon as they receive revenue from their sales. The velocity of circulation increases.

During the 1990s when inflation in Brazil was around 80 percent a year, people would end a taxi ride at the ATM closest to their destination, get some cash, pay the driver, and finish their journey on foot. The driver would deposit the cash in his bank account before looking for the next customer.

During the 1920s when inflation in Germany exceeded 50 percent a month—hyperinflation—wages were paid and spent twice in a single day!

Imagine the inconvenience of spending most of your time figuring out how to keep your money holdings close to zero.

One way of keeping money holdings low is to find other means of payment such as tokens, commodities, or even barter. All of these are less efficient than money as a means of payment. For example, in Israel during the 1980s, when inflation reached 1,000 percent a year, the U.S. dollar started to replace the increasingly worthless shekel. Consequently, people had to keep track of the exchange rate between the shekel and the dollar hour by hour and had to engage in many additional and costly transactions in the foreign exchange market.

Confusion Costs

We make economic decisions by comparing marginal cost and marginal benefit. Marginal cost is a real cost—an opportunity forgone. Marginal benefit is a real benefit—a willingness to forgo an opportunity. Although costs and benefits are real, we use money as our unit of account and standard of value to calculate them. Money is our measuring rod of value. Borrowers and lenders, workers and employers, all make agreements in terms of money. Inflation makes the value of money change, so it changes the units on our measuring rod.

Does it matter that our units of value keep changing? Some economists think it matters a lot. Others think it matters only a little.

Economists who think it matters a lot point to the obvious benefits of stable units of measurement in other areas of life. For example, suppose that we had not invented an accurate time-keeping technology and clocks and watches gained 5 to

15 minutes a day. Imagine the hassle you would have arriving at class on time or catching the start of the ball game. For another example, suppose that a tailor used an elastic tape measure. You would end up with a jacket that was either too tight or too loose, depending on how tightly the tape was stretched.

For a third example, recall the crash of the Mars Climate Orbiter.

> "Mars Climate Orbiter . . . failed to achieve Mars orbit because of a navigation error. . . . Spacecraft operating data needed for navigation were provided . . . in English units rather than the specified metric units. This was the direct cause of the failure." (Mars Program Independent Assessment Team Summary Report, March 14, 2000)

If rocket scientists can't make correct calculations that use just two units of measurement, what chance do ordinary people and business decision makers have of making correct calculations that involve money when its value keeps changing?

These examples of confusion and error that can arise from units of measurement don't automatically mean that a changing value of money is a big problem. But they raise the possibility that it might be.

Uncertainty Costs

A high inflation rate brings increased uncertainty about the long-term inflation rate. Will inflation remain high for a long time or will price stability be restored? This increased uncertainty makes long-term planning difficult and gives people a shorter-term focus. Investment falls, and so the economic growth rate slows.

But this increased uncertainty also misallocates resources. Instead of concentrating on the activities at which they have a comparative advantage, people find it more profitable to search for ways of avoiding the losses that inflation inflicts. As a result, inventive talent that might otherwise work on productive innovations works on finding ways of profiting from the inflation instead.

Uncertainty about inflation makes the economy behave a bit like a casino in which some people gain and some lose and no one can predict where the gains and losses will fall. Gains and losses occur because of unpredictable changes in the value of money. In a period of rapid, unpredictable inflation, resources get diverted from productive activities to forecasting inflation. It becomes more profitable to forecast the inflation rate correctly than to invent a new product. Doctors, lawyers, accountants, farmers—just about everyone—can make themselves better off, not by specializing in the profession for which they have been trained but by spending more of their time dabbling as amateur economists and inflation forecasters and managing their investment portfolios.

From a social perspective, this diversion of talent resulting from uncertainty about inflation is like throwing scarce resources onto the garbage heap. This waste of resources is a cost of inflation.

How Big Is the Cost of Inflation?

The cost of inflation depends on its rate and its predictability. The higher the inflation rate, the greater is the cost. And the more unpredictable the inflation rate, the greater is the cost. Peter Howitt of Brown University, building on work by Robert Barro of Harvard University, has estimated that if inflation is lowered from 3 percent a year to zero, the growth rate of real GDP will rise by between 0.06 and 0.09 percentage points a year. These numbers might seem small, but they are growth rates. After 30 years, real GDP would be 2.3 percent higher and the accumulated value of all the additional future output would be worth 85 percent of current GDP, or $11.7 trillion!

In hyperinflation, the costs are much greater. Hyperinflation is rare, but there have been some spectacular examples of it. Several European countries experienced hyperinflation during the 1920s after World War I and again during the 1940s after World War II. In these examples the costs of inflation were enormous.

Hyperinflation is more than just a historical curiosity. It has occurred in the recent past. In 1994, the African nation of Zaire had a hyperinflation that peaked at a monthly inflation rate of 76 percent. Also in 1994, Brazil almost reached the hyperinflation stratosphere with a monthly inflation rate of 40 percent. A cup of coffee that cost 15 cruzeiros in 1980 cost 22 billion cruzeiros in 1994. In 1989 to 1994, Russia experienced a near hyperinflation.

The most spectacular recent hyperinflation was in Zimbabwe, which peaked at 231,150,888.87 percent per year. At that point, the monetary system collapsed, the Zimbabwe dollar was taken out of circulation and replaced by the U.S. dollar, and economic life was at a near standstill.

myeconlab

Work these problems in Study Plan 12.3 to get instant feedback.

CHECKPOINT 12.3

Identify the costs of inflation and the benefits of a stable value of money.

Practice Problems

1. Ben has $1,000 in his savings account and the bank pays an interest rate of 5 percent a year. The inflation rate is 3 percent a year. The government taxes the interest that Ben earns on his deposit at 20 percent. Calculate the after-tax nominal interest rate and the after-tax real interest rate that Ben earns.

2. **Inflation-adjusted savings bonds hit 0% rate for first time**

   Inflation-adjusted savings bonds purchased from May through October 2009 will earn 0% for the first six months. The fixed interest rate on these bonds is 0.1% and over the previous 6 months, inflation fell at an annual rate of 5.56%. The minimum interest rate on savings bonds is set at 0%.

   Source: *USA Today*, May 5, 2009

   Are these savings bonds a better deal than cash under the mattress?

Guided Solutions to Practice Problems

1. Ben's interest income equals 5 percent of $1,000, which is $50. The government takes $10 of his $50 of interest in tax, so the interest income Ben earns after tax is $40. The after-tax nominal interest rate is ($40 ÷ $1,000) × 100, which equals 4 percent a year.

   The after-tax real interest rate equals the after-tax nominal interest rate minus the inflation rate. The after-tax nominal interest rate is 4 percent a year. So the after-tax real interest rate equals 4 percent a year minus the inflation rate of 3 percent a year, which is 1 percent a year.

2. At 0 percent interest rate, these bonds are just as good a deal as cash under the mattress, but if inflation starts to rise as the economy recovers from recession, the nominal interest rate will exceed 0.1 percent but the real interest rate will be certain and equal 0.1 percent a year—a better deal than cash.

CHAPTER SUMMARY

Key Points

1 **Explain what determines the demand for money and how the demand for money and the supply of money determine the *nominal* interest rate.**

- The demand for money is the relationship between the quantity of money demanded and the nominal interest rate, other things remaining the same—the higher the nominal interest rate, other things remaining the same, the smaller is the quantity of money demanded.
- Increases in real GDP increase the demand for money. Some advances in financial technology increase the demand for money, and some advances decrease it.
- Each day, the price level, real GDP, and financial technology are given and money market equilibrium determines the nominal interest rate.
- To lower the interest rate, the Fed increases the supply of money. To raise the interest rate, the Fed decreases the supply of money.

2 **Explain how in the long run, the quantity of money determines the price level and money growth brings inflation.**

- In the long run, real GDP equals potential GDP and the real interest rate is the level that makes the quantity of loanable funds demanded equal the quantity of loanable funds supplied in the global financial market.
- The nominal interest rate in the long run equals the equilibrium real interest rate plus the inflation rate.
- Money market equilibrium in the long run determines the price level.
- An increase in the quantity of money, other things remaining the same, increases the price level by the same percentage.
- The inflation rate in the long run equals the growth rate of the quantity of money minus the growth rate of potential GDP.
- The equation of exchange and the velocity of circulation provide an alternative way of viewing the relationship between the quantity of money and the price level (and money growth and inflation).

3 **Identify the costs of inflation and the benefits of a stable value of money.**

- Inflation has four costs: tax costs, shoe-leather costs, confusion costs, and uncertainty costs.
- The higher the inflation rate, the greater are these four costs.

Key Terms

myeconlab

Work these problems in Chapter 12 Study Plan to get instant feedback.

CHAPTER CHECKPOINT

Study Plan Problems and Applications

1. Draw a graph to illustrate the demand for money curve. On the graph show the effect of an increase in real GDP and the effect of an increase in the number of families that have a credit card.
2. The Fed decreases the quantity of money. Explain the effects of this action in the short run on the quantity of money demanded and the nominal interest rate.
3. The Fed conducts an open market purchase of securities. [Hint: Check back with Chapter 11 if you need a reminder about the effects of an open market operation.] Explain the effects of this action on the nominal interest rate in the short run and the value of money in the long run.

In 2000, the United States was at full employment. The quantity of money was growing at 8.3 percent a year, the nominal interest rate was 9.5 percent a year, real GDP grew at 5 percent a year, and the inflation rate was 3.1 percent a year. Use this information to work Problems **4** and **5**.

4. Calculate the real interest rate.
5. Was the velocity of circulation constant? [Hint: Use the quantity theory of money.] If velocity of circulation was not constant, how did it change and why might it have changed?
6. Suppose that the government passes a new law that sets a limit on the interest rate that credit card companies can charge on overdue balances. As a result, the nominal interest rate charged by credit card companies falls from 15 percent a year to 7 percent a year. If the average income tax rate is 30 percent, explain how the after-tax real interest rate on overdue credit card balances changes.
7. If the quantity of money is $3 trillion, real GDP is $10 trillion, the price level is 0.9, the real interest rate is 2 percent a year, and the nominal interest rate is 7 percent a year, calculate the velocity of circulation, the value of $M \times V$, and nominal GDP.
8. If the velocity of circulation is growing at 1 percent a year, the real interest rate is 2 percent a year, the nominal interest rate is 7 percent a year, and the growth rate of real GDP is 3 percent a year, calculate the inflation rate, the growth rate of money, and the growth rate of nominal GDP.

Zimbabwe inflation eases

Zimbabwe's inflation rate in July 2009 was reported at 1 percent a month. Last year, Zimbabwe's annual inflation rate was more than 231,000,000%, a kilo of tomatoes cost 61 billion Zimbabwe dollars, and the shelves in stores were almost empty. Now the Zimbabwean dollar has disappeared, the U.S. dollar is king, and the shelves and aisles of stores are full. Although no annual inflation rate is reported, the indication is that Zimbabwe is recovering from hyperinflation.

Source: BBCNews, September 16, 2009

9. What is hyperinflation? Compare inflation in Zimbabwe in 2008 with that in Germany in 1923. Why did Germany print money in 1923 and create hyperinflation? Why is Zimbabwe printing less money today?

Instructor Assignable Problems and Applications

Your instructor can assign these problems as homework, a quiz, or a test in **MyEconLab**.

1. Explain what causes inflation. Why is it easier to predict the decade-average inflation rate than the inflation rate in a single year?
2. If the Fed doubled the quantity of money and nothing else changed, what would happen to the price level in the short run and the long run? What would happen to the inflation rate?
3. Suppose that banks launch an aggressive marketing campaign to get everyone to use debit cards for every conceivable transaction. They offer prizes to new debit card holders and introduce a charge on using a credit card. How would the demand for money and the nominal interest rate change?
4. The Fed conducts an open market sale of securities. Explain the effects of this action in the short run on the nominal interest rate and in the long run on the value of money and the price level.
5. Draw a graph of the money market to illustrate equilibrium in the short run. If the growth rate of the quantity of money increases, explain what happens to the real interest rate and the nominal interest rate in the short run.
6. What is the quantity theory of money? Define the velocity of circulation and explain how it is measured.
7. If the velocity of circulation is constant, real GDP is growing at 3 percent a year, the real interest rate is 2 percent a year, and the nominal interest rate is 7 percent a year, calculate the inflation rate, the growth rate of money, and the growth rate of nominal GDP.

Use the following information to work Problems **8** to **11**.

The Fed's $2.2 trillion fire hose

The Fed threw a lot of money at the financial crisis in 2008 to unfreeze credit markets and encourage economic activity. As part of its effort to keep the interest rate low, the Fed purchased government bonds worth $300 billion between March and September 2009. The Fed now holds about $770 billion in government securities, nearly double its pre-crisis total. Before the crisis, the Fed held mainly government securities, which it used to control the quantity of money in the economy. Now government securities make up just 35% of the Fed's balance sheet.

Source: CNN Money, October 9, 2009

8. If government securities make up just 35 percent of the Fed's assets, calculate the Fed's total assets. What effect did the Fed's purchase of $300 billion of government bonds have on the Fed's total liabilities?
9. If the Fed purchased the government securities on the open market, explain why the purchase of $300 billion of government securities would influence the interest rate.
10. As the Fed purchased $300 billion of government securities, did the price of government securities fall or rise? Explain your answer.
11. Explain how the Fed uses its government securities to control the nominal interest rate.

12. Show on a graph of the money market the effect in the long run of an increase in the quantity of money on the value of money.
13. Sara has $200 in currency and $2,000 in a bank account on which the bank pays no interest. The inflation rate is 2 percent a year. Calculate the amount of inflation tax that Sara pays in a year.

Use the following information to work Problems 14 to 16.

When will U.S. interest rates rise?

The Federal Reserve Chairman Ben Bernanke said Thursday that while interest rates will stay low for some time, interest rates will rise as the recovery picks up, in order to fight off the threat of inflation.

Source: CNNMoney, October 9, 2009

14. Explain why Ben Bernanke says "interest rates will stay low" for some time.
15. Explain why, other things remaining the same, interest rates will rise as the economy recovers from recession.
16. Explain why when the economy starts to recover from recession and interest rates are low, there is a "threat of inflation."
17. If the economy is at full employment and the Fed increases the growth rate of the quantity of money, explain what happens to the inflation rate in the long run if velocity of circulation is constant and real GDP grows at 3 percent a year.
18. Explain why businesses paid workers twice a day during the hyperinflation in Germany after World War I and why workers spent their incomes as soon as they were paid.
19. With the spread of credit cards, debit cards, and e-cash, people will want to hold less and less money. Eventually, no one will want to hold any money and inflation will not occur. Critically evaluate this view.
20. The Federal Reserve could easily eliminate inflation by making the quantity of money grow at a rate equal to the growth rate of real GDP minus the growth rate of the velocity of circulation. Do you think the Fed should pursue this objective? Explain why or why not.
21. The Federal Reserve could hold the interest rate constant by making the quantity of money adjust to match the quantity of money demanded at the chosen interest rate. What effect will such a policy have on the inflation rate and the price of bonds as the economy recovers from recession? Explain your answer.
22. Do you think the Federal Reserve could simultaneously pursue a fixed interest rate and a money growth rate equal to the growth rate of real GDP minus the growth rate of the velocity of circulation? Explain why or why not.
23. Explain how the spread of ATMs and the increased use of debit cards have influenced the demand for money.

What causes the business cycle?

Why did the U.S. economy go into recession in 2008?

13

Aggregate Supply and Aggregate Demand

CHAPTER CHECKLIST

When you have completed your study of this chapter, you will be able to

1 Define and explain the influences on aggregate supply.

2 Define and explain the influences on aggregate demand.

3 Explain how fluctuations in aggregate demand and aggregate supply create the business cycle.

13.1 AGGREGATE SUPPLY

The purpose of the aggregate supply–aggregate demand model is to explain how real GDP and the price level are determined. The model uses similar ideas to those that you encountered in Chapter 4 where you learned how the quantity and price in a competitive market are determined. But the *aggregate* supply–*aggregate* demand model (*AS-AD* model) isn't just an application of the competitive market model. Some differences arise because the *AS-AD* model is a model of an imaginary market for the total of all the final goods and services that make up real GDP. The quantity in this "market" is real GDP and the price is the price level measured by the GDP price index.

The *quantity of real GDP supplied* is the total amount of final goods and services that firms in the United States plan to produce and it depends on the quantities of

- Labor employed
- Capital, human capital, and the state of technology
- Land and natural resources
- Entrepreneurial talent

You saw in Chapter 8 that at full employment, real GDP equals *potential GDP.* The quantities of land, capital and human capital, the state of technology, and the amount of entrepreneurial talent are fixed. Labor market equilibrium determines the quantity of labor employed, which is equal to the quantity of labor demanded and the quantity of labor supplied at the equilibrium real wage rate.

Over the business cycle, real GDP fluctuates around potential GDP because the quantity of labor employed fluctuates around its full employment level. The aggregate supply–aggregate demand model explains these fluctuations.

We begin on the supply side with the basics of aggregate supply.

Aggregate Supply Basics

Aggregate supply
The relationship between the quantity of real GDP supplied and the price level when all other influences on production plans remain the same.

Aggregate supply is the relationship between the quantity of real GDP supplied and the price level when all other influences on production plans remain the same. This relationship can be described as follows:

Other things remaining the same, the higher the price level, the greater is the quantity of real GDP supplied, and the lower the price level, the smaller is the quantity of real GDP supplied.

Figure 13.1 illustrates aggregate supply as an aggregate supply schedule and aggregate supply curve. The aggregate supply schedule lists the quantities of real GDP supplied at each price level, and the upward-sloping *AS* curve graphs these points.

The figure also shows potential GDP: $13 trillion in the figure. When the price level is 110, the quantity of real GDP supplied is $13 trillion, which equals potential GDP (at point *C* on the *AS* curve).

Along the aggregate supply curve, the price level is the only influence on production plans that changes. A rise in the price level brings an increase in the quantity of real GDP supplied and a movement up along the aggregate supply curve; a fall in the price level brings a decrease in the quantity of real GDP supplied and a movement down along the aggregate supply curve.

FIGURE 13.1

Aggregate Supply Schedule and Aggregate Supply Curve

myeconlab Animation

	Price level (GDP price index, 2005 = 100)	Quantity of real GDP supplied (trillions of 2005 dollars)
E	120	14.0
D	115	13.5
C	110	13.0
B	105	12.5
A	100	12.0

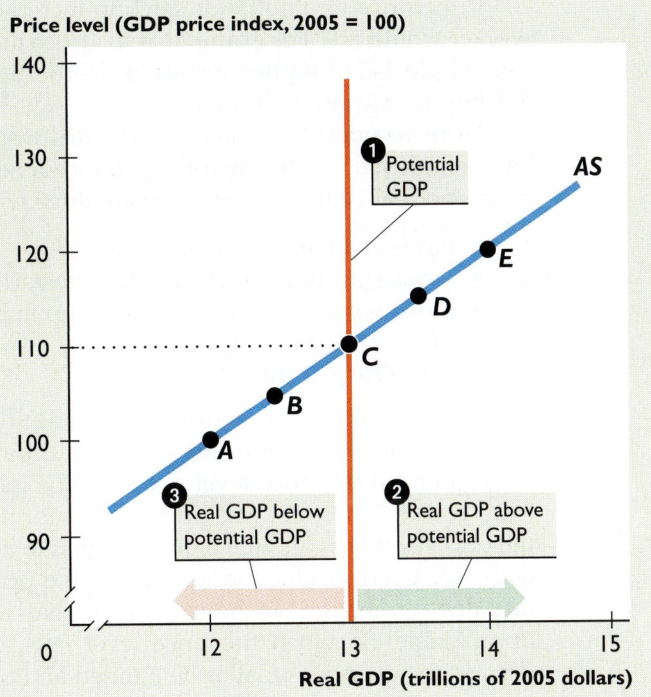

The aggregate supply schedule and aggregate supply curve, *AS*, show the relationship between the quantity of real GDP supplied and the price level when all other influences on production plans remain the same. Each point *A* through *E* on the *AS* curve corresponds to the row identified by the same letter in the schedule.

1. Potential GDP is \$13 trillion, and when the price level is 110, real GDP equals potential GDP.
2. If the price level is above 110, real GDP exceeds potential GDP.
3. If the price level is below 110, real GDP is less than potential GDP.

Among the other influences on production plans that remain constant along the *AS* curve are

- The money wage rate
- The money prices of other resources

In contrast, along the potential GDP line, when the price level changes, the money wage rate and the money prices of other resources change by the same percentage as the change in the price level to keep the real wage rate (and other real prices) at the full-employment equilibrium level.

Why the *AS* Curve Slopes Upward

Why does the quantity of real GDP supplied increase when the price level rises and decrease when the price level falls? The answer is that a movement along the *AS* curve brings a change in the real wage rate (and changes in the real cost of other resources whose money prices are fixed). If the price level rises, the real wage rate falls, and if the price level falls, the real wage rate rises. When the real wage rate changes, firms change the quantity of labor employed and the level of production.

Think about a concrete example. A ketchup producer has a contract with its workers to pay them \$20 an hour. The firm sells ketchup for \$1 a bottle. The real wage rate of a ketchup bottling worker is 20 bottles of ketchup. That is, the firm must sell 20 bottles of ketchup to buy one hour of labor. Now suppose the price of ketchup falls to 50 cents a bottle. The real wage rate of a bottling worker has increased to 40 bottles—the firm must now sell 40 bottles of ketchup to buy one hour of labor.

If the price of a bottle of ketchup increased, the real wage rate of a bottling worker would fall. For example, if the price increased to $2 a bottle, the real wage rate would be 10 bottles per worker—the firm needs to sell only 10 bottles of ketchup to buy one hour of labor.

Firms respond to a change in the real wage rate by changing the quantity of labor employed and the quantity produced. For the economy as a whole, employment and real GDP change. There are three ways in which these changes occur:

- Firms change their output rate.
- Firms shut down temporarily or restart production.
- Firms go out of business or start up in business.

Change in Output Rate

To change its output rate, a firm must change the quantity of labor that it employs. It is profitable to hire more labor if the additional labor costs less than the revenue it generates. If the price level rises and the money wage rate doesn't change, an extra hour of labor that was previously unprofitable becomes profitable. So when the price level rises and the money wage rate doesn't change, the quantity of labor demanded and production increase. If the price level falls and the money wage rate doesn't change, an hour of labor that was previously profitable becomes unprofitable. So when the price level falls and the money wage rate doesn't change, the quantity of labor demanded and production decrease.

Temporary Shutdowns and Restarts

A firm that is incurring a loss might foresee a profit in the future. Such a firm might decide to shut down temporarily and lay off its workers.

The price level relative to the money wage rate influences temporary shutdown decisions. If the price level rises relative to wages, fewer firms decide to shut down temporarily; so more firms operate and the quantity of real GDP supplied increases. If the price level falls relative to wages, a larger number of firms find that they cannot earn enough revenue to pay the wage bill and so temporarily shut down. The quantity of real GDP supplied decreases.

Business Failure and Startup

People create businesses in the hope of earning a profit. When profits are squeezed or when losses arise, more firms fail, fewer new firms start up, and the number of firms decreases. When profits are generally high, fewer firms fail, more firms start up, and the number of firms increases.

The price level relative to the money wage rate influences the number of firms in business. If the price level rises relative to wages, profits increase, the number of firms in business increases, and the quantity of real GDP supplied increases. If the price level falls relative to wages, profits fall, the number of firms in business decreases, and the quantity of real GDP supplied decreases.

In a severe recession, business failure can be contagious. The failure of one firm puts pressure on both its suppliers and its customers and can bring a flood of failures and a large decrease in the quantity of real GDP supplied.

Changes in Aggregate Supply

Aggregate supply changes when any influence on production plans other than the price level changes. In particular, aggregate supply changes when

- Potential GDP changes.
- The money wage rate changes.
- The money prices of other resources change.

Change in Potential GDP

Anything that changes potential GDP changes aggregate supply and shifts the aggregate supply curve. Figure 13.2 illustrates such a shift. You can think of point *C* as an anchor point. The *AS* curve and potential GDP line are anchored at this point, and when potential GDP changes, aggregate supply changes along with it. When potential GDP increases from $13 trillion to $14 trillion, point *C* shifts to point *C'*, and the *AS* curve and potential GDP line shift rightward together. The *AS* curve shifts from AS_0 to AS_1.

Change in Money Wage Rate

A change in the money wage rate changes aggregate supply because it changes firms' costs. The higher the money wage rate, the higher are firms' costs and the smaller is the quantity that firms are willing to supply at each price level. So an increase in the money wage rate decreases aggregate supply.

FIGURE 13.2

An Increase in Potential GDP

myeconlab Animation

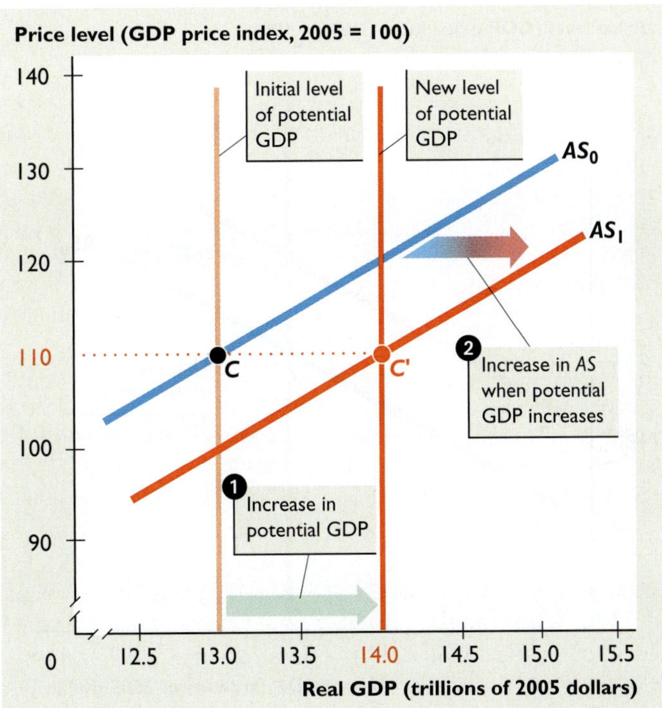

1. An increase in potential GDP increases aggregate supply.
2. When potential GDP increases from $13 trillion to $14 trillion, the aggregate supply curve shifts rightward from AS_0 to AS_1.

Suppose that the money wage rate is \$33 an hour and the price level is 110. Then the real wage rate is \$30 an hour (\$33 × 100 ÷ 110 = \$30)—see Chapter 7; page 182. If the full-employment equilibrium real wage rate is \$30 an hour, the economy is at full employment and real GDP equals potential GDP. In Figure 13.3, the economy is at point *C* on the aggregate supply curve AS_0. The money wage rate is \$33 an hour at all points on AS_0.

Now suppose the money wage rate rises to \$36 an hour but the full-employment equilibrium real wage rate remains at \$30 an hour. Real GDP now equals potential GDP when the price level is 120, at point *D* on the aggregate supply curve AS_2. (If the money wage rate is \$36 an hour and the price level is 120, the real wage rate is \$36 × 100 ÷ 120 = \$30 an hour.) The money wage rate is \$36 an hour at all points on AS_2. The rise in the money wage rate *decreases* aggregate supply and shifts the aggregate supply curve leftward from AS_0 to AS_2.

A change in the money wage rate does not change potential GDP. The reason is that potential GDP depends only on the economy's real ability to produce and on the full-employment quantity of labor, which occurs at the equilibrium *real* wage rate. The equilibrium real wage rate can occur at any money wage rate.

Change in Money Prices of Other Resources

A change in the money prices of other resources has a similar effect on firms' production plans to a change in the money wage rate. It changes firms' costs. At each price level, firms' real costs change and the quantity that firms are willing to supply changes so aggregate supply changes.

FIGURE 13.3

A Change in the Money Wage Rate

myeconlab Animation

A rise in the money wage rate decreases aggregate supply. The aggregate supply curve shifts leftward from AS_0 to AS_2. A rise in the money wage rate does not change potential GDP.

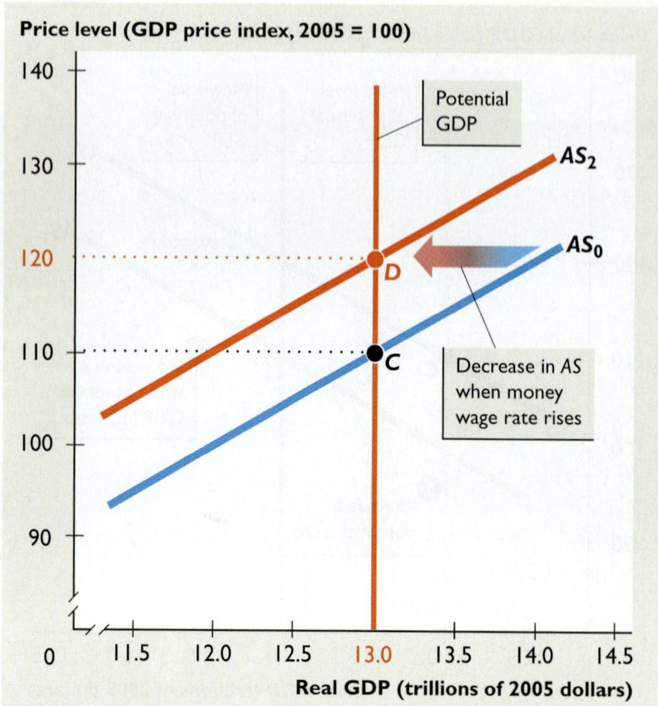

CHECKPOINT 13.1

Define and explain the influences on aggregate supply.

myeconlab

Work these problems in Study Plan 13.1 to get instant feedback.

Practice Problems

1. Explain the influence of each of the following events on the quantity of real GDP supplied and aggregate supply in India and use a graph to illustrate.
   - Fuel prices rise.
   - U.S. firms move their call handling, IT, and data functions to India.
   - Wal-Mart and Starbucks open in India.
   - Universities in India increase the number of engineering graduates.
   - The money wage rate in India rises.
   - The price level in India increases.
2. **Wages could hit steepest plunge in 18 years**

   A bad economy is starting to drag down wages for millions of workers. The average weekly wage of private-sector workers has fallen 1.4% this year through September. Colorado will become the first state to lower its minimum wage since the federal minimum wage law was passed in 1938, when the state cuts its rate by 4 cents an hour.

   Source: *USA Today*, October 16, 2009

   Explain how the fall in the average weekly wage and the minimum wage will influence aggregate supply.

Guided Solutions to Practice Problems

1. As fuel prices rise, the quantity of real GDP supplied at the current price level decreases. The *AS* curve shifts leftward (Figure 1).

   As businesses move their call handling, IT, and data functions to India, real GDP supplied at the current price level increases. The *AS* curve shifts rightward (Figure 2).

   As Wal-Mart and Starbucks open, the quantity of real GDP supplied at the current price level increases. The *AS* curve shifts rightward (Figure 2).

   With more graduates, the number of skilled workers increases, and production increases at the current price level. The *AS* curve shifts rightward (Figure 2).

   As the money wage rate rises, firms' costs increase and the quantity of real GDP supplied at the current price level decreases. The *AS* curve shifts leftward (Figure 1).

   As the price level increases, other things remaining the same, businesses became more profitable and increase the quantity of real GDP supplied along the *AS* curve (Figure 3). The *AS* curve does not shift.
2. The cut in the money wage rate decreases the real wage rate and increases aggregate supply. If the cut in the minimum wage decreases the natural unemployment rate, potential GDP increases and aggregate supply increases further.

FIGURE 1

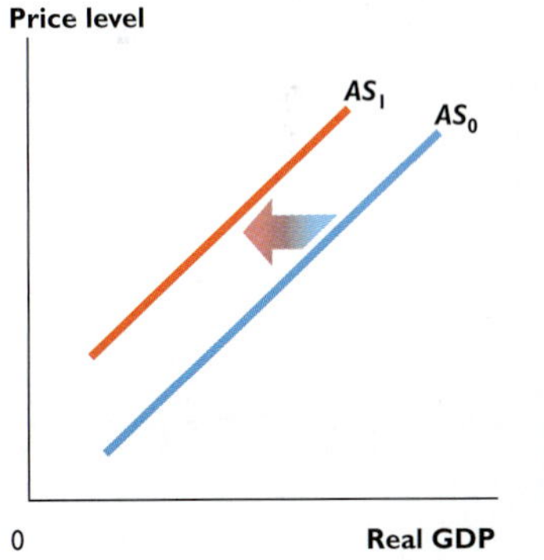

FIGURE 2

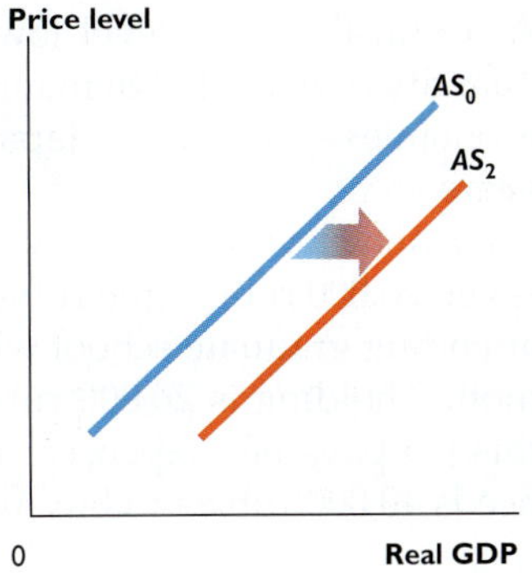

FIGURE 3

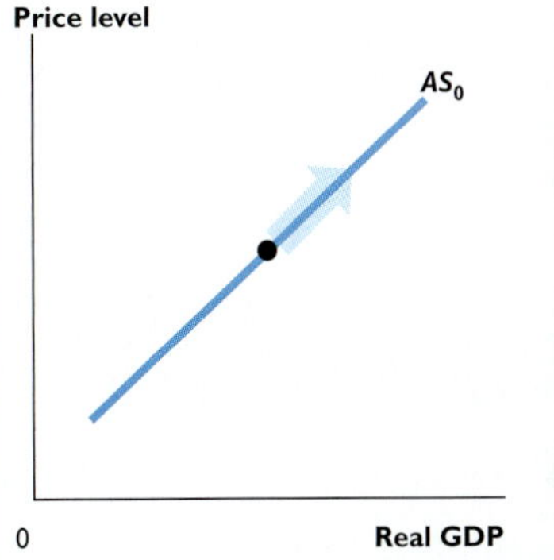

13.2 AGGREGATE DEMAND

The *quantity of real GDP demanded* (Y) is the total amount of final goods and services produced in the United States that people, businesses, governments, and foreigners plan to buy. This quantity is the sum of the real consumption expenditure (C), investment (I), government expenditure on goods and services (G), and exports (X) minus imports (M). That is,

$$Y = C + I + G + X - M$$

Many factors influence expenditure plans; to study aggregate demand, we divide them into two groups: the price level and everything else. We'll first consider the influence of the price level on expenditure plans and then consider the other influences.

Aggregate Demand Basics

Aggregate demand
The relationship between the quantity of real GDP demanded and the price level when all other influences on expenditure plans remain the same.

Aggregate demand is the relationship between the quantity of real GDP demanded and the price level when all other influences on expenditure plans remain the same. This relationship can be described as follows:

Other things remaining the same, the higher the price level, the smaller is the quantity of real GDP demanded; and the lower the price level, the greater is the quantity of real GDP demanded.

Figure 13.4 illustrates aggregate demand by using an aggregate demand schedule and aggregate demand curve. The aggregate demand schedule lists the quantities of real GDP demanded at each price level, and the downward-sloping *AD* curve graphs these points.

Along the aggregate demand curve, the only influence on expenditure plans that changes is the price level. A rise in the price level decreases the quantity of real GDP demanded and brings a movement up along the aggregate demand curve; a fall in the price level increases the quantity of real GDP demanded and brings a movement down along the aggregate demand curve.

The price level influences the quantity of real GDP demanded because a change in the price level brings a change in

- The buying power of money
- The real interest rate
- The real prices of exports and imports

The Buying Power of Money

A rise in the price level lowers the buying power of money and decreases the quantity of real GDP demanded. To see why, think about the buying plans in two economies—Russia and Japan—where the price level has changed a lot in recent years.

Anna lives in Moscow, Russia. She has worked hard all summer and has saved 20,000 rubles (the ruble is the currency of Russia), which she plans to spend attending graduate school when she has earned her economics degree. So Anna's money holding is 20,000 rubles. Anna has a part-time job, and her income from this job pays her expenses. The price level in Russia rises by 100 percent. Anna needs 40,000 rubles to buy what 20,000 rubles once bought. To make up some of

FIGURE 13.4

Aggregate Demand Schedule and Aggregate Demand Curve

myeconlab Animation

	Price level (GDP price index, 2005 = 100)	Quantity of real GDP demanded (trillions of 2005 dollars)
A	130	12.0
B	120	12.5
C	110	13.0
D	100	13.5
E	90	14.0

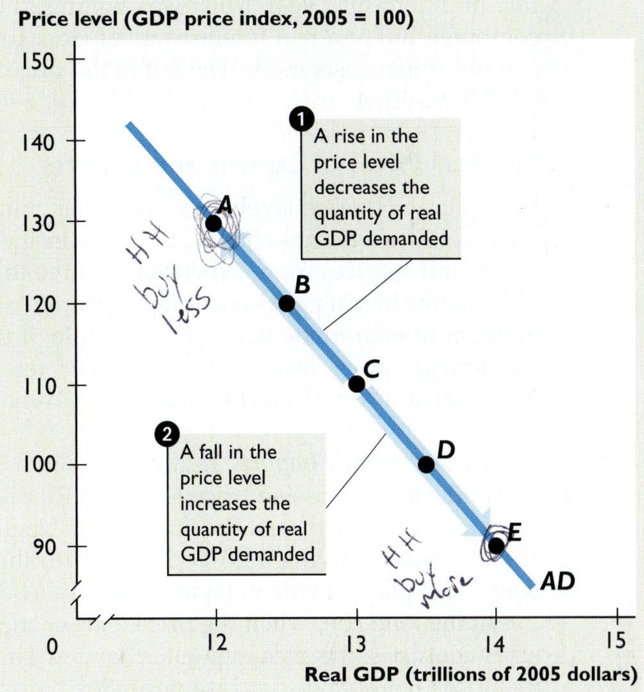

The aggregate demand schedule and aggregate demand curve, *AD*, show the relationship between the quantity of real GDP demanded and the price level when all other influences on expenditure plans remain the same. Each point *A* through *E* on the *AD* curve corresponds to the row identified by the same letter in the schedule.

The quantity of real GDP demanded

1. decreases when the price level rises and
2. increases when the price level falls.

the fall in the buying power of her money, Anna slashes her spending.

Similarly, a fall in the price level, other things remaining the same, brings an increase in the quantity of real GDP demanded. To see why, think about the buying plans of Mika, who lives in Tokyo, Japan. She too has worked hard all summer and has saved 200,000 yen (the yen is the currency of Japan), which she plans to spend attending school next year. The price level in Japan falls by 10 percent; now Mika needs only 180,000 yen to buy what 200,000 yen once bought. With a rise in what her money buys, Mika decides to buy a DVD player.

The Real Interest Rate

When the price level rises, the real interest rate rises. You saw in Chapter 12 (page 301) that an increase in the price level increases the amount of money that people want to hold—increases the demand for money. When the demand for money increases, the nominal interest rate rises. In the short run, the inflation rate does not change, so a rise in the nominal interest rate brings a rise in the real interest rate. Faced with a higher real interest rate, businesses and people delay plans to buy new capital and consumer durable goods and they cut back on spending. As the price level rises, the quantity of real GDP demanded decreases.

Anna and Mika Again Think about Anna and Mika again. Both of them want to buy a computer. In Moscow, a rise in the price level increases the demand for money and raises the real interest rate. At a real interest rate of 5 percent a year,

Anna was willing to borrow to buy the new computer. But at a real interest rate of 10 percent a year, she decides that the payments would be too high, so she delays buying it. The rise in the price level decreases the quantity of real GDP demanded.

In Tokyo, a fall in the price level lowers the real interest rate. At a real interest rate of 5 percent a year, Mika was willing to borrow to buy a low-performance computer. But at a real interest rate of close to zero, she decides to buy a fancier computer that costs more: The fall in the price level increases the quantity of real GDP demanded.

The Real Prices of Exports and Imports

When the U.S. price level rises and other things remain the same, the prices in other countries do not change. So a rise in the U.S. price level makes U.S.-made goods and services more expensive relative to foreign-made goods and services. This change in real prices encourages people to spend less on U.S.-made items and more on foreign-made items. For example, if the U.S. price level rises relative to the foreign price level, foreigners buy fewer U.S.-made cars (U.S. exports decrease) and Americans buy more foreign-made cars (U.S. imports increase).

Anna's and Mika's Imports In Moscow, Anna is buying some new shoes. With a sharp rise in the Russian price level, the Russian-made shoes that she planned to buy are too expensive, so she buys a less expensive pair imported from Brazil. In Tokyo, Mika is buying a DVD player. With the fall in the Japanese price level, a Sony DVD player made in Japan looks like a better buy than one made in Taiwan.

In the long run, when the price level changes by more in one country than in other countries, the exchange rate changes. The exchange rate change neutralizes the price level change, so this international price effect on buying plans is a short-run effect only. But in the short run, it is a powerful effect.

■ Changes in Aggregate Demand

A change in any factor that influences expenditure plans other than the price level brings a change in aggregate demand. When aggregate demand increases, the aggregate demand curve shifts rightward, which Figure 13.5 illustrates as the rightward shift of the *AD* curve from AD_0 to AD_1. When aggregate demand decreases, the aggregate demand curve shifts leftward, which Figure 13.5 illustrates as the leftward shift of the *AD* curve from AD_0 to AD_2. The factors that change aggregate demand are

- Expectations about the future
- Fiscal policy and monetary policy
- The state of the world economy

Expectations

An increase in expected future income increases the amount of consumption goods (especially big-ticket items such as cars) that people plan to buy now. Aggregate demand increases. An increase in expected future inflation increases aggregate demand because people decide to buy more goods and services now before their prices rise. An increase in expected future profit increases the investment that firms plan to undertake now. Aggregate demand increases.

A decrease in expected future income, future inflation, or future profit has the opposite effect and decreases aggregate demand.

FIGURE 13.5

Change in Aggregate Demand

myeconlab Animation

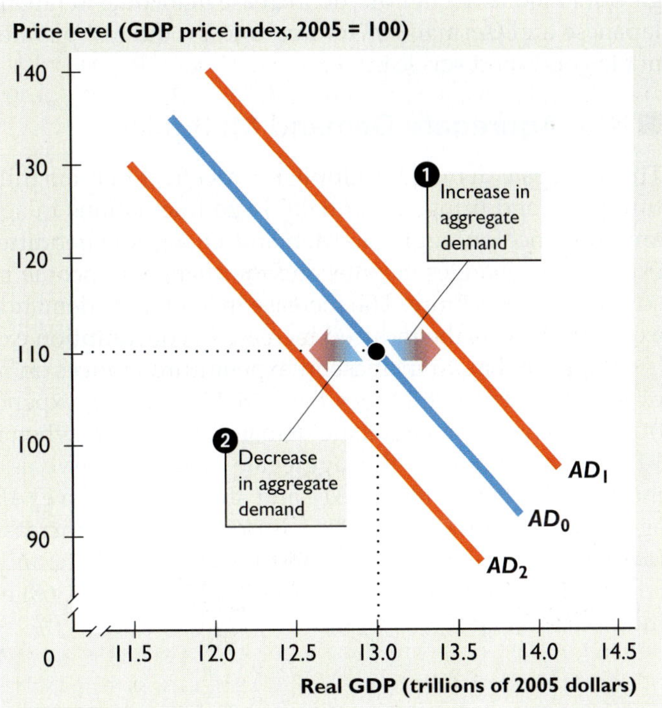

1 Aggregate demand *increases if*

- Expected future income, inflation, or profits increase.
- The government or the Federal Reserve takes steps that increase planned expenditure.
- The exchange rate falls or the global economy expands.

2 Aggregate demand *decreases if*

- Expected future income, inflation, or profits decrease.
- The government or the Federal Reserve takes steps that decrease planned expenditure.
- The exchange rate rises or the global economy contracts.

Fiscal Policy and Monetary Policy

We study the effects of policy actions on aggregate demand in Chapters 16 and 17. Here, we'll just briefly note that the government can use **fiscal policy**—changing taxes, transfer payments, and government expenditure on goods and services—to influence aggregate demand. The Federal Reserve can use **monetary policy**—changing the quantity of money and the interest rate—to influence aggregate demand. A tax cut or an increase in either transfer payments or government expenditure on goods and services increases aggregate demand. A cut in the interest rate or an increase in the quantity of money increases aggregate demand.

Fiscal policy
Changing taxes, transfer payments, and government expenditure on goods and services.

Monetary policy
Changing the quantity of money and the interest rate.

The World Economy

Two main influences that the world economy has on aggregate demand are the foreign exchange rate and foreign income. The foreign exchange rate is the amount of a foreign currency that you can buy with a U.S. dollar. Other things remaining the same, a rise in the foreign exchange rate decreases aggregate demand.

To see how the foreign exchange rate influences aggregate demand, suppose that \$1 exchanges for 100 Japanese yen. A Fujitsu phone made in Japan costs 12,500 yen, and an equivalent Motorola phone made in the United States costs \$110. In U.S. dollars, the Fujitsu phone costs \$125, so people around the world buy the cheaper U.S. phone. Now suppose the exchange rate rises to 125 yen per dollar. At 125 yen per dollar, the Fujitsu phone costs \$100 and is now cheaper than the Motorola phone. People will switch from the U.S. phone to the Japanese phone.

U.S. exports will decrease and U.S. imports will increase, so U.S. aggregate demand will decrease.

An increase in foreign income increases U.S. exports and increases U.S. aggregate demand. For example, an increase in income in Japan and Germany increases Japanese and German consumers' and producers' planned expenditures on U.S.-made goods and services.

The Aggregate Demand Multiplier

The aggregate demand multiplier is an effect that magnifies changes in expenditure plans and brings potentially large fluctuations in aggregate demand. When any influence on aggregate demand changes expenditure plans, the change in expenditure changes income; and the change in income induces a change in consumption expenditure. The increase in aggregate demand is the initial increase in expenditure plus the induced increase in consumption expenditure.

Suppose that an increase in expenditure induces an increase in consumption expenditure that is 1.5 times the initial increase in expenditure. Figure 13.6 illustrates the change in aggregate demand that occurs when investment increases by $0.4 trillion. Initially, the aggregate demand curve is AD_0. Investment then increases by $0.4 trillion ($\Delta I$) and the purple curve $AD_0 + \Delta I$ now describes aggregate spending plans at each price level. An increase in income induces an increase in consumption expenditure of $0.6 trillion, and the aggregate demand curve shifts rightward to AD_1. Chapter 14 (pp. 364–368) explains the expenditure multiplier in detail.

FIGURE 13.6

The Aggregate Demand Multiplier

myeconlab Animation

❶ An increase in investment increases aggregate demand and increases income.

❷ The increase in income induces an increase in consumption expenditure, so ❸ aggregate demand increases by more than the initial increase in investment.

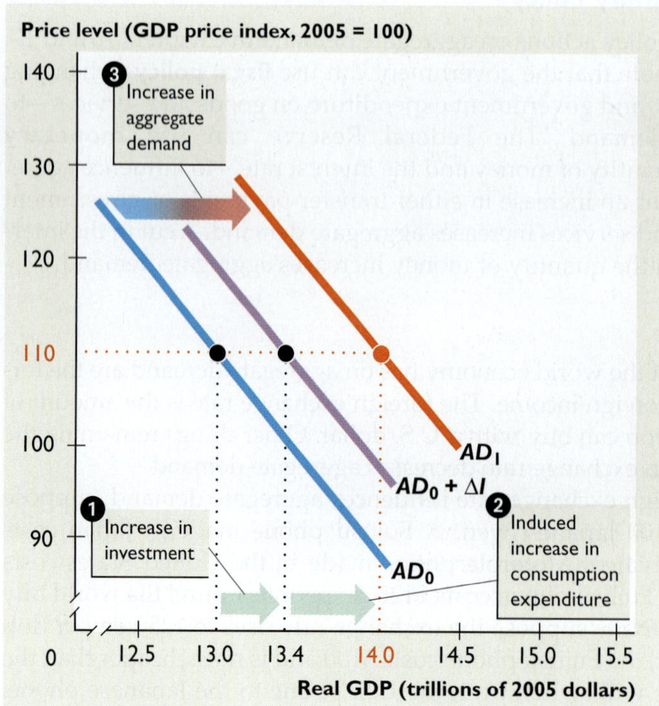

CHECKPOINT 13.2

Define and explain the influences on aggregate demand.

myeconlab
Work these problems in Study Plan 13.2 to get instant feedback.

Practice Problems

1. Mexico trades with the United States. Explain the effect of each of the following events on Mexico's aggregate demand.
   - The government of Mexico cuts income taxes.
   - The United States experiences strong economic growth.
   - Mexico sets new environmental standards that require factories to upgrade their production facilities.
2. Explain the effect of each of the following events on the quantity of real GDP demanded and aggregate demand in Mexico.
   - Europe trades with Mexico and goes into a recession.
   - The price level in Mexico rises.
   - Mexico increases the quantity of money.
3. **Durable goods orders surge in May, new-homes sales dip**
   The Commerce Department announced that demand for durable goods rose 1.8%, while new-home sales dropped 0.6% in May. U.S. companies suffered a sharp drop in exports as other countries struggle with recession.
   Source: *USA Today*, June 24, 2009
   Explain how the items in the news clip influence U.S. aggregate demand.

Guided Solutions to Practice Problems

1. A tax cut increases disposable income, which increases Mexico's aggregate demand. Strong U.S. growth increases the demand for Mexican-produced goods, which increases Mexico's aggregate demand. As factories upgrade their facilities, investment increases. Aggregate demand increases. In each case, the *AD* curve shifts rightward (Figure 1).
2. A recession in Europe decreases the demand for Mexico's exports, so aggregate demand decreases. The *AD* curve shifts leftward (Figure 2).
   A rise in the price level decreases the quantity of real GDP demanded along the *AD* curve, but the *AD* curve does not shift (Figure 3).
   An increase in the quantity of money increases aggregate demand, and the *AD* curve shifts rightward (Figure 1).
3. The purchase of durable goods and new homes is investment. Investment increased, which increased aggregate demand. The drop in U.S. exports is a decrease in the demand for U.S.-produced goods and services, so the drop in U.S. exports decreased U.S. aggregate demand.

FIGURE 1

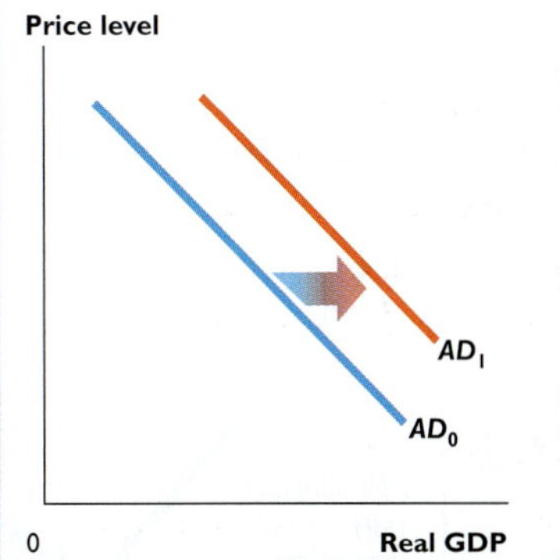

FIGURE 2

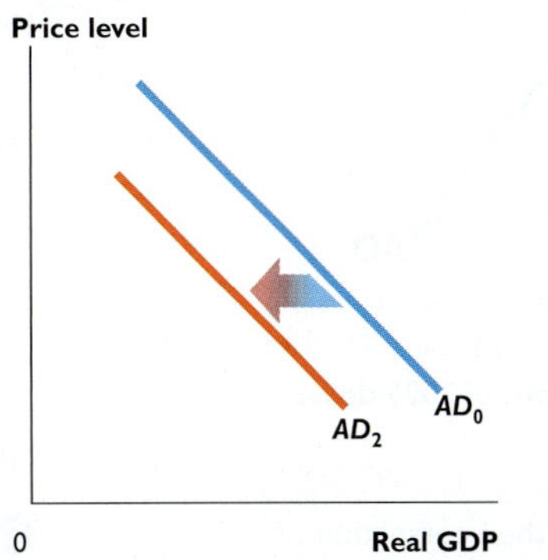

FIGURE 3

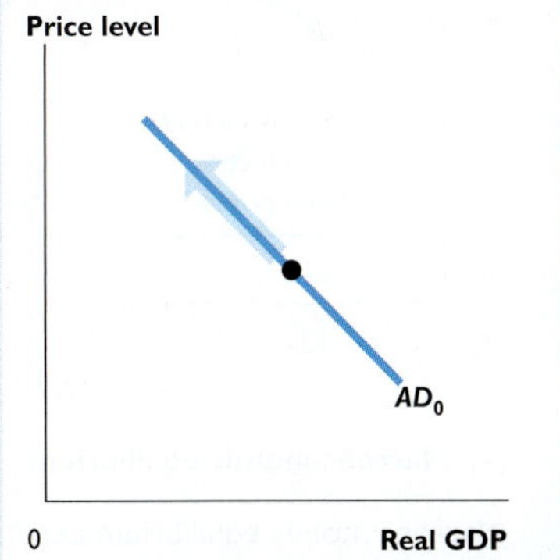

13.3 UNDERSTANDING THE BUSINESS CYCLE

Macroeconomic equilibrium
When the quantity of real GDP demanded equals the quantity of real GDP supplied at the point of intersection of the *AD* curve and the *AS* curve.

Aggregate supply and aggregate demand determine real GDP and the price level. **Macroeconomic equilibrium** occurs when the quantity of real GDP demanded equals the quantity of real GDP supplied at the point of intersection of the *AD* curve and the *AS* curve. Figure 13.7(a) shows such an equilibrium at a price level of 110 and real GDP of $13 trillion.

To see why this position is the equilibrium, think about what happens if the price level is something other than 110. Suppose that the price level is 120 and that real GDP is $14 trillion (point *E* on the *AS* curve). The quantity of real GDP demanded is less than $14 trillion, so firms are unable to sell all their output. Unwanted inventories pile up, and firms cut production and prices until they can sell all their output, which occurs only when real GDP is $13 trillion and the price level is 110.

Now suppose the price level is 100 and real GDP is $12 trillion (point *A* on the *AS* curve). The quantity of real GDP demanded exceeds $12 trillion, so firms are unable to meet the demand for their output. Inventories decrease, and customers clamor for goods and services. So firms increase production and raise prices until firms can meet demand, which occurs only when real GDP is $13 trillion and the price level is 110.

FIGURE 13.7

Macroeconomic Equilibrium

myeconlab Animation

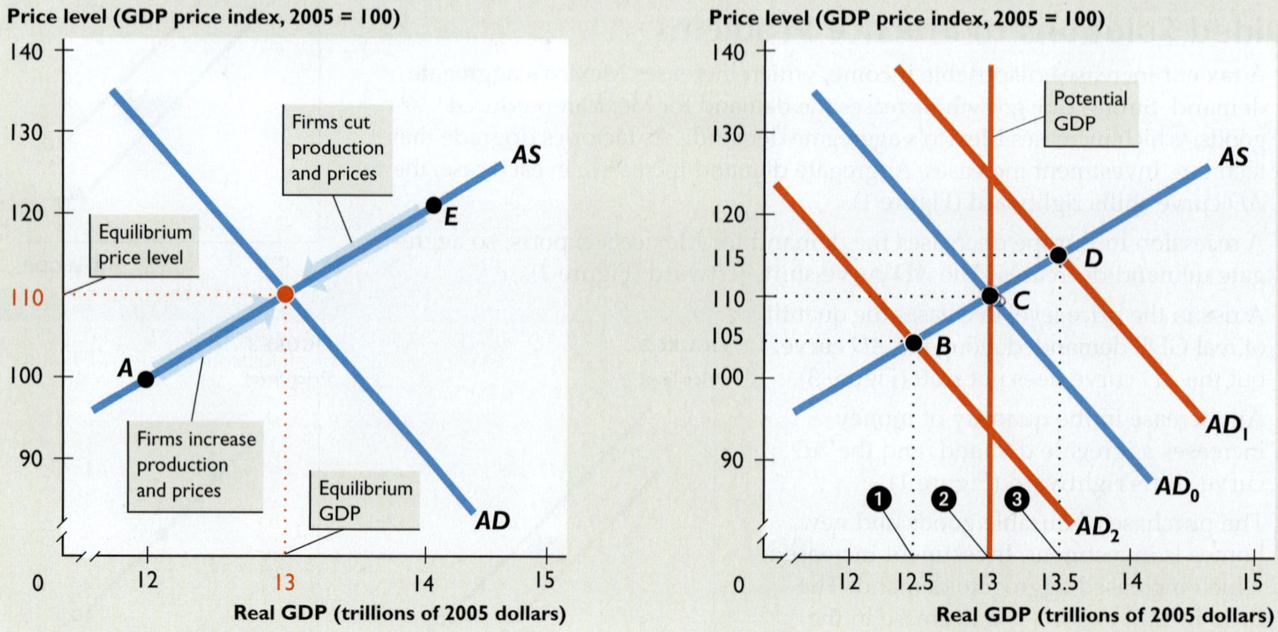

(a) Macroeconomic equilibrium

Macroeconomic equilibrium occurs at the intersection of the *AD* and *AS* curves. Macroeconomic equilibrium might be below full employment, at full employment, or above full employment.

(b) Three types of macroeconomic equilibrium

1. Below full-employment equilibrium
2. Full-employment equilibrium
3. Above full-employment equilibrium

In macroeconomic equilibrium, the economy might be at full employment or above or below full employment. Figure 13.7(b) shows these three possibilities. **Full-employment equilibrium**—when equilibrium real GDP equals potential GDP—occurs where AD_0 intersects the aggregate supply curve *AS*. Fluctuations in aggregate demand bring fluctuations in real GDP around potential GDP. If aggregate demand increases to AD_1, firms increase production and raise prices until they can meet the higher demand. Real GDP increases to $13.5 trillion and exceeds potential GDP in an **above full-employment equilibrium**. If aggregate demand decreases to AD_2, firms decrease production and cut prices until they can sell all their output. Real GDP decreases to $12.5 trillion and is less than potential GDP in a **below full-employment equilibrium**.

Full-employment equilibrium
When equilibrium real GDP equals potential GDP.

Above full-employment equilibrium
When equilibrium real GDP exceeds potential GDP.

Below full-employment equilibrium
When potential GDP exceeds equilibrium real GDP.

Aggregate Demand Fluctuations

Fluctuations in aggregate demand are one of the sources of the business cycle. To focus on the aggregate demand cycle, suppose that potential GDP and the full-employment price level remain constant. And suppose that aggregate demand fluctuates between AD_1 and AD_2 in Figure 13.7(b). The result of these fluctuations is the cycle in real GDP around potential GDP that Figure 13.8 shows.

In year 1, aggregate demand is AD_0 in Figure 13.7(b). The economy is at full employment with real GDP at $13 trillion. Then, in year 2, aggregate demand increases to AD_1. As aggregate demand increases, real GDP increases to $13.5 trillion at point *D* in Figure 13.7(b) and at a business cycle peak in Figure 13.8. In year 3, aggregate demand decreases to AD_0 in Figure 13.7(b). Real GDP now falls to $13 trillion, and the economy is back at full employment. Aggregate demand decreases further in year 4 to AD_2. Real GDP now decreases to $12.5 trillion at point *B* in Figure 13.7(b) and at a business-cycle trough in Figure 13.8. Finally, in year 5, aggregate demand increases to AD_0 and real GDP increases again to $13 trillion. The economy is again at full employment.

The sources of the fluctuations in aggregate demand could be any of the factors that we reviewed: Changes in expectations about the future, changes in fiscal policy and monetary policy, and changes in the world economy.

FIGURE 13.8

An Aggregate Demand Cycle

myeconlab Animation

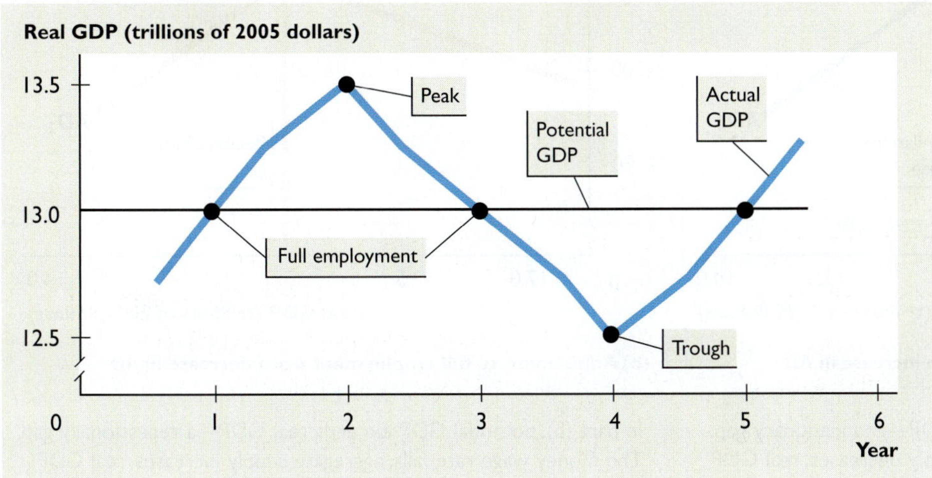

Fluctuations in aggregate demand bring fluctuations in real GDP around potential GDP.

In year 1, real GDP equals potential GDP. The economy is at full employment, such as at point *C* in Figure 13.7(b). In year 2, at a business cycle peak, real GDP exceeds potential GDP. The economy is operating above full employment, such as at point *D* in Figure 13.7(b). In year 3, there is full employment again. In year 4, at a business cycle trough, real GDP is below potential GDP. The economy is operating below full employment, such as at point *B* in Figure 13.7(b).

Adjustment Toward Full Employment

The cycle in real GDP that we've just described is modified by forces that begin to operate when the economy is away from full employment and that move real GDP toward potential GDP. Let's examine these forces.

In Figure 13.9(a), aggregate supply is AS_0 and aggregate demand increases from AD_0 to AD_1. Real GDP is above full employment. There is now an **inflationary gap**—a gap that brings a rising price level. Workers have experienced a fall in the buying power of their wages, and firms' profits have increased. Workers demand higher wages, and firms, anxious to maintain employment and output levels in the face of a labor shortage, meet those demands. As the money wage rate rises, aggregate supply decreases and the aggregate supply curve shifts leftward. Eventually, it reaches AS_1, where real GDP is back at potential GDP.

Inflationary gap
A gap that exists when real GDP exceeds potential GDP and that brings a rising price level.

In Figure 13.9(b), aggregate supply is AS_1 and aggregate demand decreases from AD_1 to AD_2. Real GDP is below full employment. There is a **recessionary gap**—a gap that brings a falling price level. The people who are lucky enough to have jobs see the buying power of their wages rise and firms' profits shrink. In these circumstances, and with a labor surplus, the money wage rate gradually falls and the aggregate supply curve gradually shifts rightward. Eventually, it reaches AD_2, where real GDP is back at potential GDP.

Recessionary gap
A gap that exists when potential GDP exceeds real GDP and that brings a falling price level.

FIGURE 13.9
Adjustment Toward Full Employment

myeconlab Animation

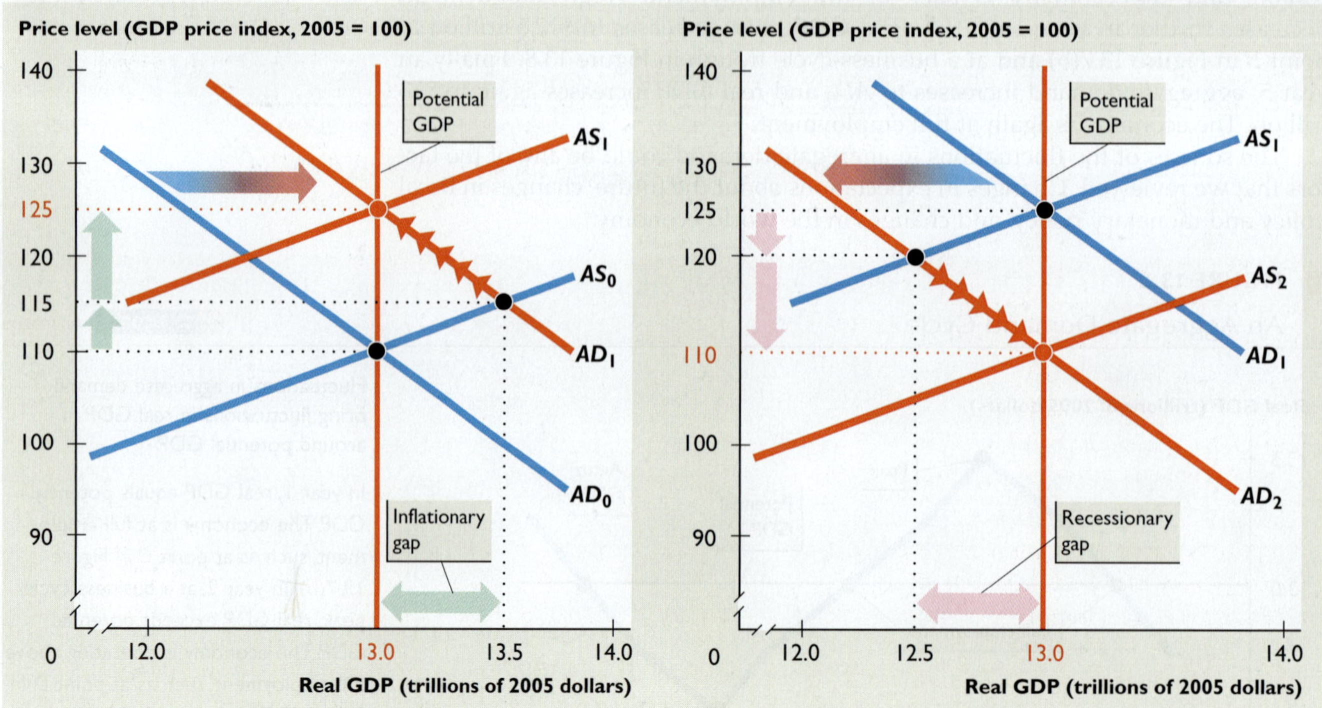

(a) Adjustment to full employment from increase in *AD*

(b) Adjustment to full employment from decrease in *AD*

In part (a), real GDP exceeds potential GDP—an inflationary gap. The money wage rate rises, aggregate supply decreases, real GDP decreases to $13 trillion and the price level rises to 125.

In part (b), potential GDP exceeds real GDP—a recessionary gap. The money wage rate falls, aggregate supply increases, real GDP increases to $13 trillion and the price level falls to 110.

Aggregate Supply Fluctuations

Aggregate supply can fluctuate for two types of reasons. First, potential GDP grows at an uneven pace. During a period of rapid technological change and capital accumulation, potential GDP grows rapidly and above its long-term trend. The second half of the 1990s experienced this type of expansion.

Second, the money price of a major resource, such as crude oil, might change. Oil is used so widely throughout the economy that a large change in its price affects almost every firm and impacts the aggregate economy.

EYE on the PAST

Oil Price Cycles in the U.S. and Global Economies

In 1970, a barrel of crude oil cost around $3.50—about $14 in 2005 dollars (see the figure). Most of the world's crude oil came from a handful of nations and the large producer nations were (and still are) members of an international cartel known as OPEC—the Organization of Petroleum Exporting Countries. (A cartel, illegal in the United States, is an organization that controls supply and manipulates the price of a commodity.)

In September 1973, OPEC cut the production of crude oil and raised its price to $10 a barrel—about $31 in 2005 dollars. This near tripling of the price of crude oil decreased aggregate supply and sent the United States, Europe, Japan, and the developing nations into recession.

In 1980, OPEC delivered a second jolt to the global economy by again cutting production and then raising the price to $37 a barrel—almost $80 in 2005 dollars. Aggregate supply decreased again and brought another recession. This recession was much more severe than that of the mid-1970s because the oil price shock was accompanied by a large decrease in aggregate demand that resulted from the Fed's monetary policy.

Faced with a high price of oil, the United States intensified exploration and increased domestic oil production. As additional supplies came onstream, the price of oil tumbled and through the rest of the 1980s and the 1990s, the U.S. and global economies entered a period of sustained expansion.

During the 2000s, rapid economic growth in Asia brought an increase in the demand for oil and its price began to rise again. By late 2007, the price of oil had surged to a new record high of more than $90 a barrel. This high price again decreased aggregate supply and was one of several influences that played a role in intensifying the 2008–2009 recession.

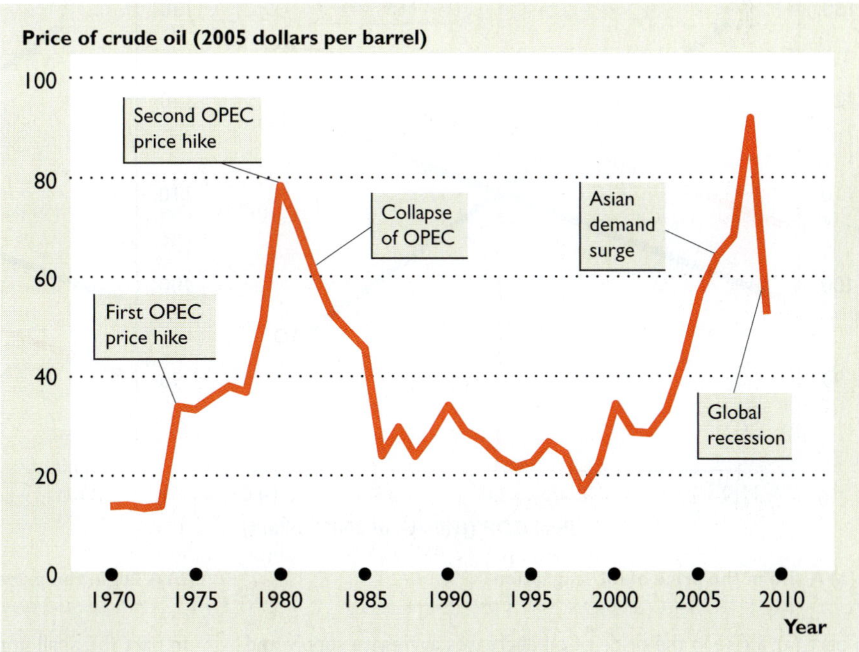

SOURCES OF DATA: Energy Information Administration and Bureau of Economic Analysis.

Eye on the Past on the previous page looks at the recent history of the price of crude oil, and Figure 13.10 illustrates how a rise in the price of oil brings recession and how a fall in the price of oil brings expansion.

In Figure 13.10(a), starting at full employment on aggregate demand curve *AD* and aggregate supply curve AS_0, the price of oil rises. Faced with higher energy costs, firms decrease production. Aggregate supply decreases, and the aggregate supply curve shifts leftward to AS_1. The price level rises and real GDP decreases. Because real GDP decreases, the economy experiences recession. Because the price level increases, the economy experiences inflation. A combination of recession and inflation, called **stagflation**, actually occurred in the United States and the global economy in the mid-1970s.

Stagflation
A combination of recession (falling real GDP) and inflation (rising price level).

In Figure 13.10(b), starting from the same full-employment equilibrium as before, the price of oil falls. With lower energy costs, firms increase production and the aggregate supply curve shifts rightward to AS_2. The price level falls and real GDP increases. The economy experiences expansion and moves above full employment. Similar events to these occurred in the United States and global economies during the mid-1980s, bringing strong economic expansion with a slowdown in the inflation rate.

FIGURE 13.10

An Oil Price Cycle

myeconlab Animation

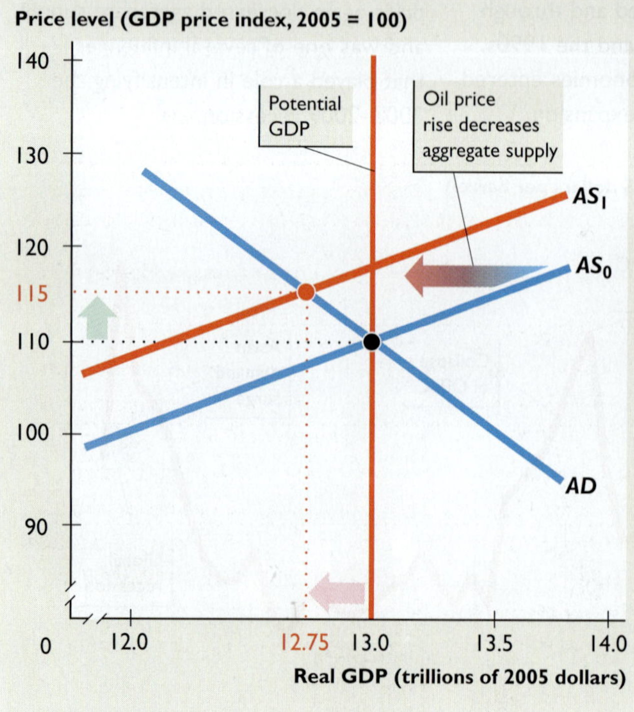

(a) A rise in the price of oil: stagflation

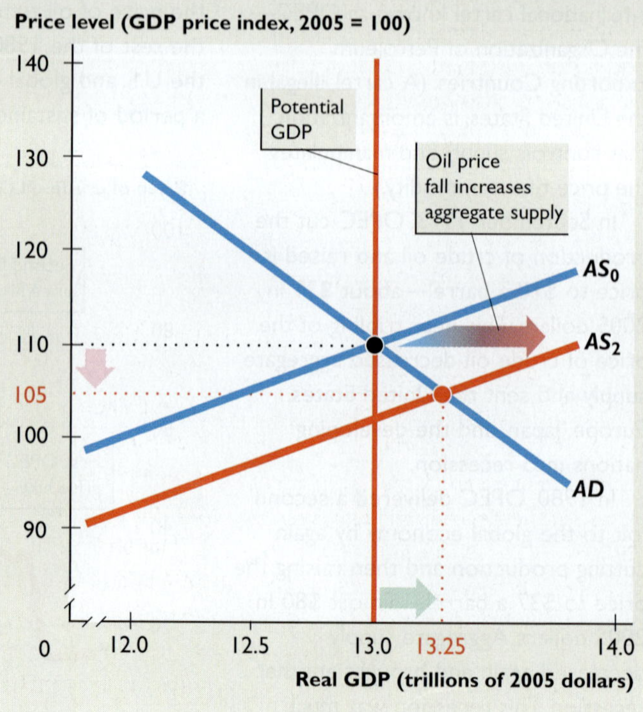

(b) A fall in the price of oil: expansion

In part (a), a rise in the price of oil decreases aggregate supply and shifts the *AS* curve leftward to AS_1. Real GDP decreases to $12.75 trillion, and the price level rises to 115.

In part (b), a fall in the price of oil increases aggregate supply and shifts the *AS* curve rightward to AS_2. Real GDP increases to $13.25 trillion, and the price level falls to 105.

EYE on the BUSINESS CYCLE

What Causes the Business Cycle?

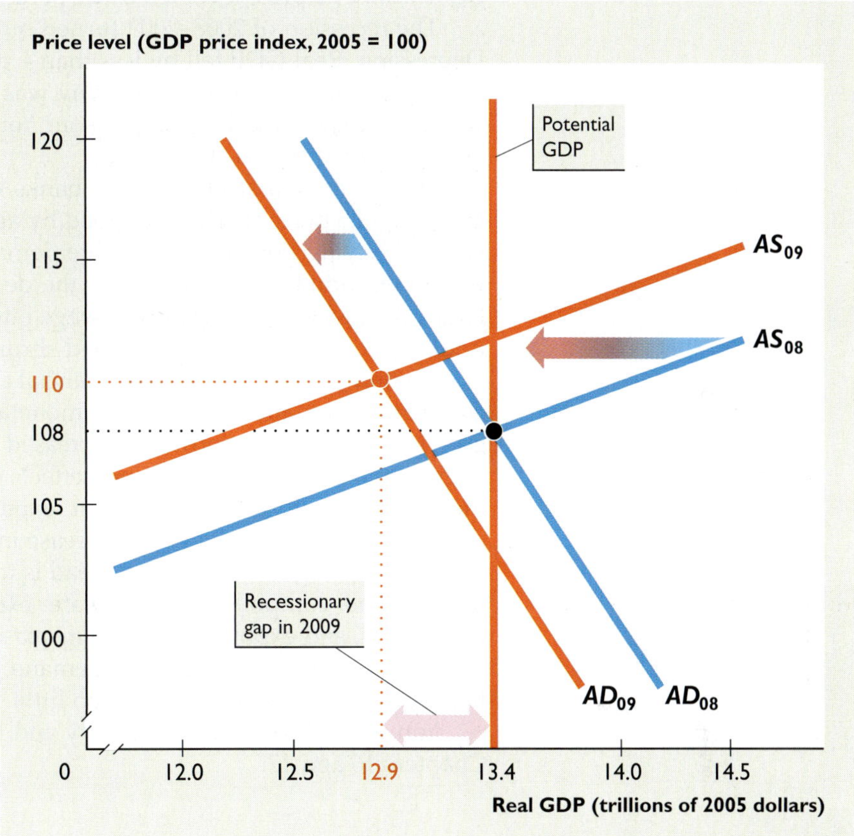

SOURCES OF DATA: Bureau of Economic Analysis and Congressional Budget Office.

What causes the business cycle and what in particular caused the 2008–2009 recession?

Business Cycle Theory

The mainstream business cycle theory is that potential GDP grows at a steady rate while aggregate demand grows at a fluctuating rate.

Because the money wage rate is slow to change, if aggregate demand grows more quickly than potential GDP, real GDP moves above potential GDP and an inflationary gap emerges. The inflation rate rises and real GDP is pulled back toward potential GDP.

If aggregate demand grows more slowly than potential GDP, real GDP moves below potential GDP and a recessionary gap emerges. The inflation rate slows, but the money wage rate responds very slowly to the recessionary gap and real GDP does not return to potential GDP until another increase in aggregate demand occurs.

Fluctuations in investment are the main source of aggregate demand fluctuations. Consumption expenditure responds to changes in income.

A recession can also occur if aggregate supply decreases to bring stagflation. Also, a recession might occur because both aggregate demand and aggregate supply decrease.

The 2008–2009 Recession

The 2008–2009 recession is an example of a recession caused by a decrease in both aggregate demand and aggregate supply. The figure illustrates these two contributing forces.

At the peak in 2008, real GDP was $13.4 trillion and the price level was 108. In the second quarter of 2009, real GDP had fallen to $12.9 trillion and the price level had risen to 110.

The financial crisis that began in 2007 and intensified in 2008 decreased the supply of loanable funds and lowered investment expenditure. In particular, construction investment collapsed.

Recession in the global economy lowered the demand for U.S. exports so this component of aggregate demand also decreased.

The decrease in aggregate demand was moderated by a large injection of spending by the U.S. government, but this move was not enough to stop aggregate demand from decreasing.

We cannot account for the combination of a rise in the price level and a fall in real GDP with a decrease in aggregate demand alone. Aggregate supply must also have decreased. The rise in oil prices in 2007 and a rise in the money wage rate were the two factors that brought about the decrease in aggregate supply.

Deflation and the Great Depression

When a financial crisis hit the United States in October 2008, many people feared a repeat of the dreadful events of the 1930s. From 1929 through 1933, the United States and most of the world experienced deflation and depression—the *Great Depression*. The price level fell by 22 percent and real GDP fell by 31 percent.

The recession of 2008–2009 turned out to be much less severe than the Great Depression. Real GDP fell by less than 4 percent and the price level continued to rise, although at a slower pace. Why was the Great Depression so bad and why was 2008–2009 so mild in comparison? You can answer these questions with what you've learned in this chapter.

During the Great Depression, banks failed and the quantity of money contracted by 25 percent. The Fed stood by and took no action to counteract the collapse of buying power so aggregate demand also collapsed. Because the money wage rate didn't fall immediately, the decrease in aggregate demand brought a large fall in real GDP. The money wage rate and price level fell eventually, but not until employment and real GDP had shrunk to 75 percent of their 1929 levels.

In contrast, during the 2008 financial crisis, the Fed bailed out troubled financial institutions and doubled the monetary base. The quantity of money kept growing. Also, the government increased its own expenditures, which added to aggregate demand. The combined effects of continued growth in the quantity of money and increased government expenditure limited the fall in aggregate demand and prevented a large decrease in real GDP.

The challenge that now lies ahead is to unwind the monetary and fiscal stimulus as the components of private expenditure—consumption expenditure, investment, and exports—begin to increase and return to more normal levels and so bring an increase in aggregate demand. Too much stimulus will bring an inflationary gap and faster inflation. Too little stimulus will leave a recessionary gap.

You will explore these monetary and fiscal policy actions and their effects in Chapters 16 and 17.

EYE on YOUR LIFE

Using the *AS-AD* Model

Using all the knowledge that you have accumulated over the term, and by watching or reading the current news, try to figure out where the U.S. economy is in its business cycle right now.

First, can you determine if real GDP is currently above, below, or at potential GDP? Second, can you determine if real GDP is expanding or contracting in a recession?

Next, try to form a view about where the U.S. economy is heading. What do you see as the main pressures on aggregate supply and aggregate demand, and in which directions are they pushing or pulling the economy?

Do you think that real GDP will expand more quickly or more slowly over the coming months? Do you think the gap between real GDP and potential GDP will widen or narrow?

How do you expect the labor market to be affected by the changes in aggregate supply and aggregate demand that you are expecting? Do you expect the unemployment rate to rise, fall, or remain constant?

Talk to your friends in class about where they see the U.S. economy right now and where it is heading. Is there a consensus or is there a wide range of opinion?

EYE on the U.S. ECONOMY

Real GDP Growth, Inflation, and the Business Cycle

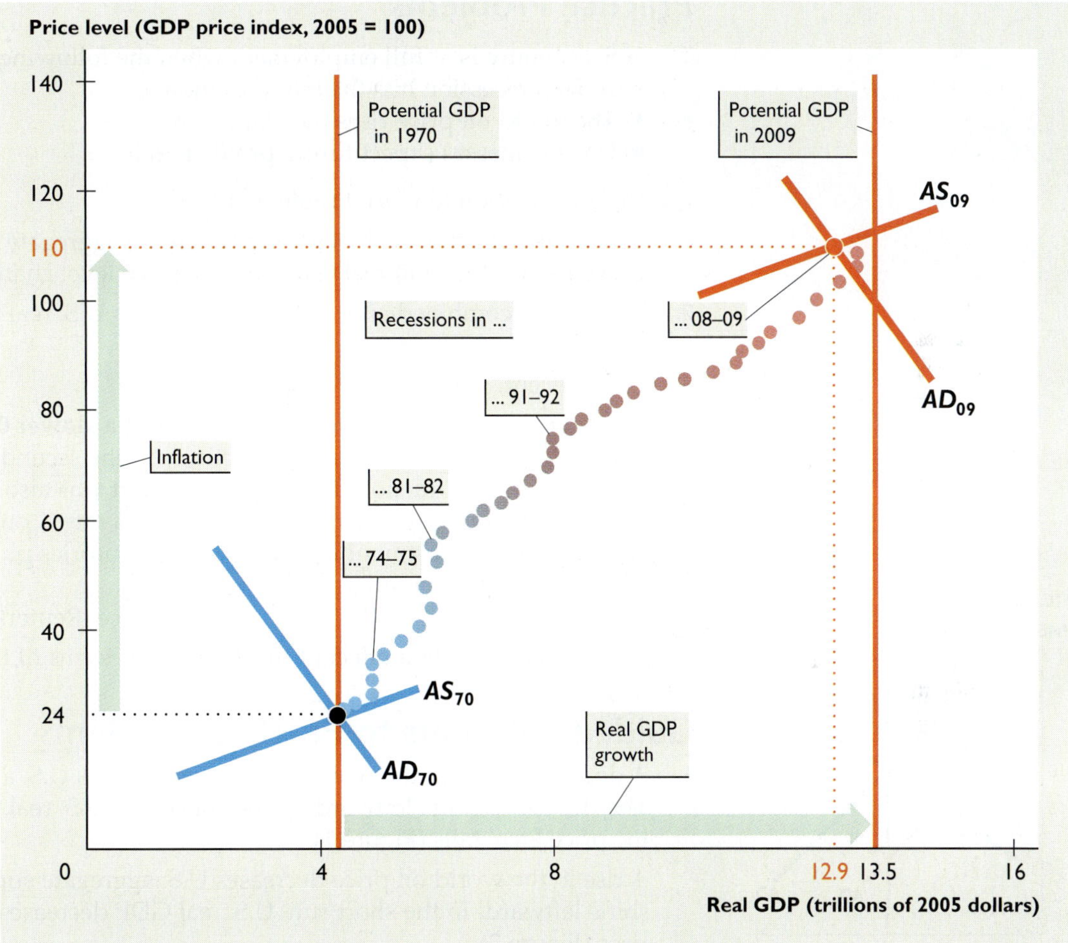

SOURCES OF DATA: Bureau of Labor Statistics, Bureau of Economic Analysis, and Congressional Budget Office.

Each dot in the figure represents the value of real GDP and the price level in a year from 1970 through 2009.

The figure interprets these data points as being generated by aggregate demand and aggregate supply.

The rightward movement in the dots shows increasing real GDP or economic growth, and a leftward movement shows recession.

The upward movement of the dots shows a rising price level or inflation.

When the path that the dots follow is steep, as it was during the 1970s, inflation is rapid and economic growth is slow.

When the dots follow a path that is gently rising, as it was during the 1990s, the inflation rate is low and real GDP growth is more rapid.

Notice that the dots move rightward and upward in waves and occasionally move leftward. These patterns show the business cycle expansions and recessions.

By comparing the dots with potential GDP, we can see that the economy was at full employment in 1970, and that the recessionary gap during the recession of 2008–2009 was large.

myeconlab

Work these problems in Study Plan 13.3 to get instant feedback.

CHECKPOINT 13.3

Explain how fluctuations in aggregate demand and aggregate supply create the business cycle.

Practice Problems

The U.S. economy is at full employment when the following events occur:

- A deep recession hits the world economy.
- The world oil price rises by a large amount.
- U.S. businesses expect future profits to fall.

Use this information to work Problems **1** to **3**.

1. Explain the effect of each event separately on aggregate demand and aggregate supply. How will real GDP and the price level change in the short run?
2. Explain the combined effect of these events on U.S. real GDP and the price level.
3. Which event, if any, brings stagflation?
4. **Stronger spending helps real GDP shrink at a slower 0.7%**
   The 0.7% decline in U.S. economic activity in the second quarter was better than the 1.2% contraction that was expected. It was also an improvement from the first quarter, when GDP fell at a 6.4% rate. Consumer spending fell 0.9%, business investment fell by 9.6% as inventories plunged, and exports fell in the last two months.

   Source: Reuters, September 30, 2009

   Explain the combined effect of these events in terms of the *AS-AD* model.

FIGURE 1

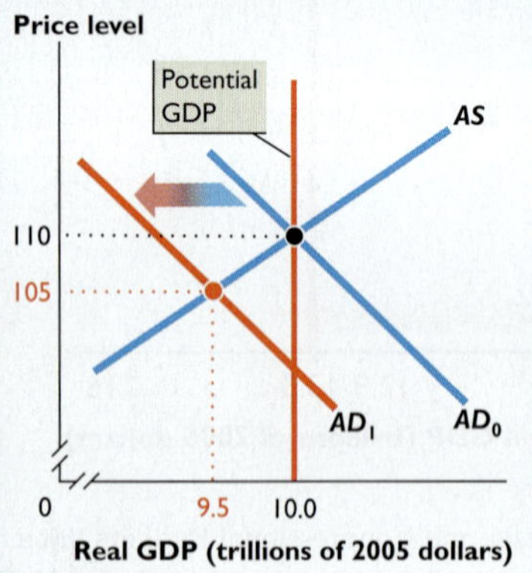

FIGURE 2

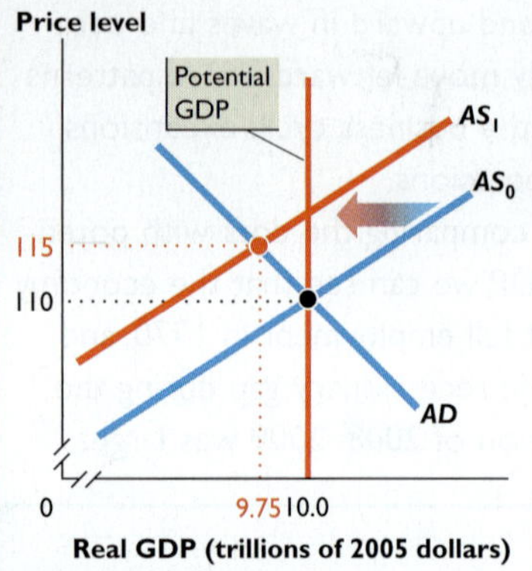

Guided Solutions to Practice Problems

1. A deep recession in the world economy decreases U.S. aggregate demand. The *AD* curve shifts leftward. In the short run, U.S. real GDP decreases and the price level falls (Figure 1).

   A rise in the world oil price decreases U.S. aggregate supply. The *AS* curve shifts leftward. In the short run, U.S. real GDP decreases and the price level rises (Figure 2).

   A fall in expected future profits decreases U.S. aggregate demand. The *AD* curve shifts leftward. In the short run, U.S. real GDP decreases and the price level falls (Figure 1).
2. All three events decrease U.S. real GDP (Figures 1 and 2). The deep world recession and the fall in expected future profits decrease the price level (Figure 1). The rise in the world oil price increases the price level (Figure 2). So the combined effect on the price level is ambiguous.
3. The rise in the world oil price brings stagflation because it decreases aggregate supply, decreases real GDP, and raises the price level (Figure 2). Stagflation occurs when the price level rises and real GDP decreases at the same time.
4. The news clip gives no information about aggregate supply. Consumer spending, business investment, and exports influence aggregate demand, so the news clip pins all the change in real GDP as arising from a slowing of the decrease in aggregate demand and a movement along the *AS* curve.

CHAPTER SUMMARY

Key Points

1 Define and explain the influences on aggregate supply.

- Aggregate supply is the relationship between the quantity of real GDP supplied and the price level when all other influences on production plans remain the same.
- The *AS* curve slopes upward because with a given money wage rate, a rise in the price level lowers the real wage rate, increases the quantity of labor demanded, and increases the quantity of real GDP supplied.
- A change in potential GDP, a change in the money wage rate, or a change in the money price of other resources changes aggregate supply.

2 Define and explain the influences on aggregate demand.

- Aggregate demand is the relationship between the quantity of real GDP demanded and the price level when all other influences on expenditure plans remain the same.
- The *AD* curve slopes downward because a rise in the price level decreases the buying power of money, raises the real interest rate, raises the real price of domestic goods compared with foreign goods, and decreases the quantity of real GDP demanded.
- A change in expected future income, inflation, and profits; a change in fiscal policy and monetary policy; and a change in the foreign exchange rate and foreign real GDP all change aggregate demand—the aggregate demand curve shifts.

3 Explain how fluctuations in aggregate demand and aggregate supply create the business cycle.

- Aggregate demand and aggregate supply determine real GDP and the price level.
- Business cycles occur because aggregate demand and aggregate supply fluctuate.
- Away from full employment, gradual adjustment of the money wage rate moves real GDP toward potential GDP.

Key Terms

Above full-employment equilibrium, 339
Aggregate demand, 332
Aggregate supply, 326
Below full-employment equilibrium, 339
Fiscal policy, 335
Full-employment equilibrium, 339
Inflationary gap, 340
Macroeconomic equilibrium, 338
Monetary policy, 335
Recessionary gap, 340
Stagflation, 342

myeconlab

Work these problems in Chapter 13 Study Plan to get instant feedback.

CHAPTER CHECKPOINT

Study Plan Problems and Applications

1. As more people in India have access to higher education, explain how potential GDP and aggregate supply will change in the long run.
2. Explain the effect of each of the following events on the quantity of U.S. real GDP demanded and the demand for U.S. real GDP:
   - The world economy goes into a strong expansion.
   - The U.S. price level rises.
   - Congress raises income taxes.
3. Table 1 sets out an economy's aggregate demand and aggregate supply schedules. What is the macroeconomic equilibrium? If potential GDP is $600 billion, what is the type of macroeconomic equilibrium? Explain how real GDP and the price level will adjust in the long run.

TABLE 1

Price level (GDP price index)	Real GDP demanded	Real GDP supplied
	(billions of 2005 dollars)	
90	900	600
100	850	700
110	800	800
120	750	900
130	700	1,000`

4. The United States is at full employment when the Fed cuts the quantity of money, and all other things remain the same. Explain the effect of the cut in the quantity of money on aggregate demand in the short run.
5. Suppose that the United States is at a below full-employment equilibrium when the world economy goes into an expansion. Explain the effect of the expansion on U.S. real GDP and unemployment in the short run.
6. Suppose that the Fed increases the quantity of money. On an *AS-AD* graph show the effect of the increased quantity of money on the macroeconomic equilibrium in the short run. Explain the adjustment process that restores the economy to full employment.

FIGURE 1

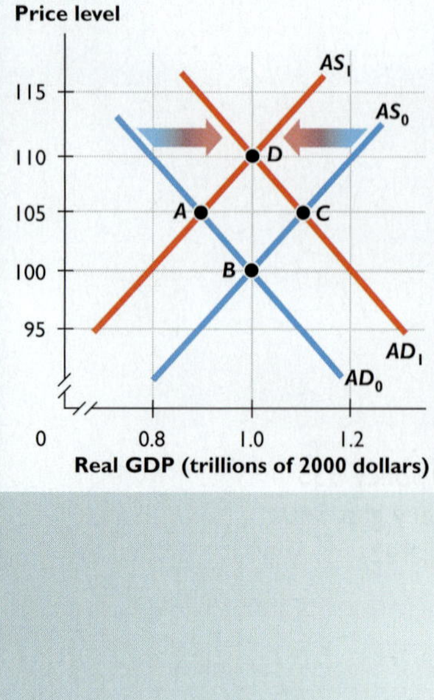

Use Figure 1 and the following information to work Problems 7 to 9. Initially, the aggregate supply is AS_0 and aggregate demand is AD_0.

7. Some events changed aggregate demand from AD_0 to AD_1. Describe two events that could have created this change in aggregate demand. What is the equilibrium after aggregate demand changed? If potential GDP is $1 trillion, the economy is at what the type of macroeconomic equilibrium?
8. Some events changed aggregate supply from AS_0 to AS_1. Describe two events that could have created this change in aggregate supply. What is the equilibrium after aggregate supply changed? If potential GDP is $1 trillion, does the economy have an inflationary gap, a recessionary gap, or no output gap?
9. Some events changed aggregate demand from AD_0 to AD_1 and aggregate supply from AS_0 to AS_1. What is the new macroeconomic equilibrium?
10. **Japan in a tail-spin?**

    Not long ago, Japan was "the economic miracle," but today unemployment is at a record high of 5.7 percent, and both prices and wages are falling fast. In the first quarter of 2009, Japan's economy shrank at an annualized rate of 11.7 percent, before recovering to a modest 2.3 percent annual rate of growth in the second quarter.

    Source: *The New York Times*, October 1, 2009

    On an *AS-AD* graph show the macroeconomic equilibrium in Japan at the start of 2009. Show why "prices and wages are falling fast."

Instructor Assignable Problems and Applications

Your instructor can assign these problems as homework, a quiz, or a test in **MyEconLab**.

1. What, according to the mainstream theory of the business cycle, is the most common source of recession: a decrease in aggregate demand, a decrease in aggregate supply, or both? Which is the most likely component of aggregate demand to start a recession? How does the aggregate demand multiplier influence a recession?
2. Suppose that the United States is at full employment. Explain the effect of each of the following events on aggregate supply:
   - Union wage settlements push the money wage rate up by 10 percent.
   - The price level increases.
   - Potential GDP increases.
3. Suppose that the United States is at full employment. Then the federal government cuts taxes, and all other influences on aggregate demand remain the same. Explain the effect of the tax cut on aggregate demand in the short run.

In 2009, the Japanese economy was at a below full-employment equilibrium. Use this information to work Problems 4 and 5.

4. Compare the amount of unemployment in Japan with Japan's natural unemployment and compare Japan's real GDP with its potential GDP.
5. What policies could Japan adopt to restore full employment? Would any of these policies create inflation? Explain.
6. Suppose that the world price of oil rises. On an *AS-AD* graph, show the effect of the world oil price rise on the macroeconomic equilibrium in the short run. Explain the adjustment process that restores the economy to full employment.
7. Explain the effects of a global recession on the U.S. macroeconomic equilibrium in the short run. Explain the adjustment process that restores the economy to full employment.

Use the following information to work Problems 8 and 9.

Recession puts wind power projects on hold

The wind-power industry will fall short of earlier growth projections for 2009 as many companies put projects on hold in 2008. The federal government provided about $950 million to the wind sector since August, helping bring some of the projects back. A slowdown in announcements of new facilities to manufacture the equipment to generate wind power has also occurred.

Source: *USA Today*, October 21, 2009

8. Explain the effect of the government's allocation of $950 million to the wind-power industry on U.S. aggregate demand and aggregate supply in 2009.
9. Use the *AS-AD* model to explain the effect on the U.S. economy as new facilities to manufacture the equipment to generate wind power and the planned wind-industry projects become completed.

TABLE 1

Price level (GDP price index)	Real GDP demanded	Real GDP supplied
	(trillions of 2000 yen)	
75	600	400
85	550	450
95	500	500
105	450	550
115	400	600
125	350	650
135	300	700

Table 1 sets out the aggregate demand and aggregate supply schedules in Japan. Potential GDP is 600 trillion yen. Use this information to work Problems 10 and 11.

10. What is the short-run macroeconomic equilibrium?

11. Does Japan have an inflationary gap or a recessionary gap and what is its magnitude?

Use the following information to work Problems 12 to 14.

Because fluctuations in the world oil price make the U.S. short-run macroeconomic equilibrium fluctuate, someone suggests that the government should vary the tax rate on oil, lowering the tax when the world oil price rises and increasing the tax when the world oil price falls, to stabilize the oil price in the U.S. market.

12. How do you think such an action would influence aggregate demand?

13. How do you think such an action would influence aggregate supply?

14. What are the arguments for and against such a policy?

Use the following information to work Problems 15 to 17.

Shoppers stimulate discount stores

As the economy remains weak, shoppers flock to discount stores for low prices. In June, Wal-mart's sales were up 5.8 percent and Costco Wholesale's sales were up 9 percent. Analysts attributed the increase in sales to the government's tax credits, which increased consumers' disposable incomes and consumers sought the biggest bang for their economic stimulus bucks.

Source: *CNN*, July 10, 2008

15. Explain and draw a graph to illustrate the effect of the government's tax credits on real GDP and the price level in the short run.

16. At what type of macroeconomic equilibrium would the government want to use such a policy?

17. If the government used this policy when the economy was at full employment, explain what would happen in the long run.

Use the following information to work Problems 18 and 19.

Still on the job, but at half the pay

In past recessions, firms have cut their labor costs by laying off workers. During this recession, many firms and state governments have trimmed labor costs by cutting pay or shortening the workweek, rather than laying off workers.

Source: *The New York Times*, October 13, 2009

18. Draw an *AS-AD* graph to illustrate an economy with a recessionary gap. Now as the recession continues, firms and governments trim their labor costs. In the graph, show the change in real GDP and the price level in the short run.

19. What effect might the strategy of cutting pay or the workweek rather than laying off workers have on the depth of the recession and the unemployment rate?

What is the expenditure multiplier?

How much income does a dollar of government expenditure generate?

Aggregate Expenditure Multiplier

14

CHAPTER CHECKLIST

When you have completed your study of this chapter, you will be able to

1. Distinguish between autonomous expenditure and induced expenditure and explain how real GDP influences expenditure plans.
2. Explain how real GDP adjusts to achieve equilibrium expenditure.
3. Explain the expenditure multiplier.
4. Derive the *AD* curve from equilibrium expenditure.

14.1 EXPENDITURE PLANS AND REAL GDP

When the government spends $1 million on a highway construction project, does that expenditure stimulate consumption expenditure in a multiplier effect? This question lies at the core of this chapter.

To answer the question, we use the *aggregate expenditure model*, a model that explains what determines the quantity of real GDP demanded and changes in that quantity *at a given price level.*

The aggregate expenditure model—also known as the *Keynesian model*—was originally designed to explain what happens in an economy in deep recession when firms can't cut their prices any further but can increase production without raising their prices, so the price level is actually fixed. The severity of the global recession of 2008–2009 gave the model a rebirth and the question of the size of the government expenditure multiplier became a hot issue.

You learned in Chapter 5 (pp. 115–117) that aggregate expenditure equals the sum of consumption expenditure, *C*, investment, *I*, government expenditure on goods and services, *G*, and net exports, *NX*. **Aggregate planned expenditure** is the sum of the spending plans of households, firms, and governments. We divide expenditure plans into autonomous expenditure and induced expenditure. *Autonomous expenditure* does not respond to changes in real GDP and *induced expenditure* does respond to changes in real GDP. We start by looking at induced expenditure and its main component, consumption expenditure.

Aggregate planned expenditure
Planned consumption expenditure plus planned investment, plus planned government expenditure, plus planned exports minus planned imports.

The Consumption Function

The **consumption function** is the relationship between consumption expenditure and disposable income, other things remaining the same. *Disposable income* is aggregate income—GDP—minus net taxes. (Net taxes are taxes paid to the government minus transfer payments received from the government.)

Consumption function
The relationship between consumption expenditure and disposable income, other things remaining the same.

Households must either spend their disposable income on consumption or save it. A decision to spend a dollar on consumption is a decision not to save a dollar. The consumption decision and the saving decision is one decision.

Consumption Plans

For households and the economy as a whole, as disposable income increases, planned consumption expenditure increases. But the increase in planned consumption is less than the increase in disposable income. The table in Figure 14.1 shows a consumption schedule. It lists the consumption expenditure that people plan to undertake at each level of disposable income.

Figure 14.1 shows a consumption function based on the consumption schedule. Along the consumption function, the points labeled *A* through *E* correspond to the columns of the table. For example, when disposable income is $9 trillion at point *D*, consumption expenditure is $8 trillion. Along the consumption function, as disposable income increases, consumption expenditure increases.

At point *A* on the consumption function, consumption expenditure is $2 trillion even though disposable income is zero. This consumption expenditure is called *autonomous consumption,* and it is the amount of consumption expenditure that would take place in the short run, even if people had no current income. This consumption expenditure would be financed either by spending past savings or by borrowing.

FIGURE 14.1

The Consumption Function

myeconlab Animation

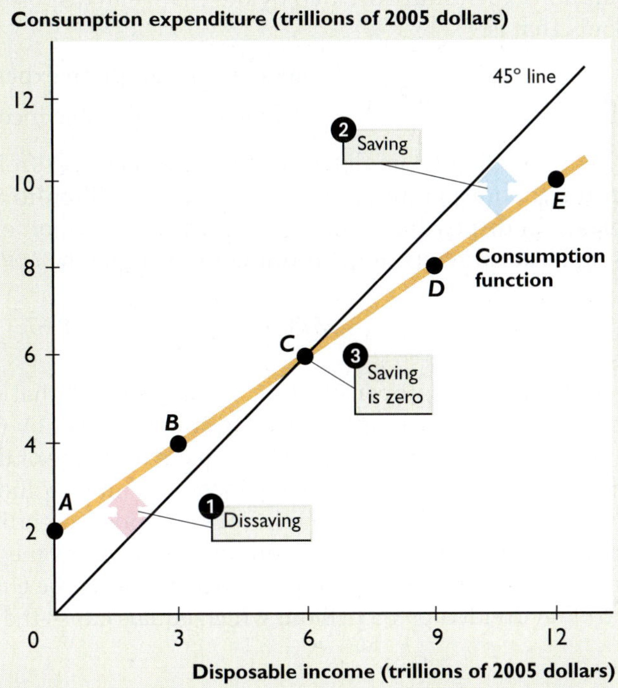

(trillions of 2005 dollars)					
Disposable income	0	3	6	9	12
Planned consumption expenditure	2	4	6	8	10
	A	***B***	***C***	***D***	***E***

The table shows consumption expenditure (and saving) plans at various levels of disposable income. The figure graphs these data as the consumption function. The figure also shows a 45° line along which consumption expenditure equals disposable income.

1. When the consumption function is above the 45° line, saving is negative (dissaving occurs).
2. When the consumption function is below the 45° line, saving is positive.
3. At the point where the consumption function intersects the 45° line, all disposable income is consumed and saving is zero.

Figure 14.1 also shows a 45° line. Because the scale on the x-axis measures disposable income and the scale on the y-axis measures consumption expenditure, and because the two scales are equal, along the 45° line consumption expenditure equals disposable income. So the 45° line serves as a reference line for comparing consumption expenditure and disposable income. Between *A* and *C*, consumption expenditure exceeds disposable income; between C and *E*, disposable income exceeds consumption expenditure; and at point *C*, consumption expenditure equals disposable income.

You can see saving in Figure 14.1. When consumption expenditure exceeds disposable income (and the consumption function is above the 45° line), saving is negative—called *dissaving*. When consumption expenditure is less than disposable income (the consumption function is below the 45° line), saving is positive. And when consumption expenditure equals disposable income (the consumption function intersects the 45° line), saving is zero.

When consumption expenditure exceeds disposable income, past savings are used to pay for current consumption. Such a situation cannot last forever, but it can and does occur if disposable income falls temporarily.

Marginal Propensity to Consume

Marginal propensity to consume
The fraction of a change in disposable income that is spent on consumption—the change in consumption expenditure divided by the change in disposable income that brought it about.

The **marginal propensity to consume** (*MPC*) is the fraction of a change in disposable income that is spent on consumption. It is calculated as the change in consumption expenditure divided by the change in disposable income that brought it about. That is,

$$MPC = \frac{\text{Change in consumption expenditure}}{\text{Change in disposable income}}.$$

Suppose that when disposable income increases from \$6 trillion to \$9 trillion, consumption expenditure increases from \$6 trillion to \$8 trillion. The \$3 trillion increase in disposable income increases consumption expenditure by \$2 trillion. Using these numbers in the formula to calculate the *MPC*,

$$MPC = \frac{\$2 \text{ trillion}}{\$3 \text{ trillion}} = \$0.67.$$

The marginal propensity to consume tells us that when disposable income increases by \$1, consumption expenditure increases by 67¢.

Figure 14.2 shows that the *MPC* equals the slope of the consumption function. A \$3 trillion increase in disposable income from \$6 trillion to \$9 trillion is the base of the red triangle. The increase in consumption expenditure that results from this increase in income is \$2 trillion and is the height of the triangle. The slope of the consumption function is given by the formula "slope equals rise over run" and is \$2 trillion divided by \$3 trillion, which equals 0.67—the *MPC*.

FIGURE 14.2

Marginal Propensity to Consume

myeconlab Animation

The marginal propensity to consume, *MPC*, is equal to the change in consumption expenditure divided by the change in disposable income, other things remaining the same.

The slope of the consumption function measures the *MPC*.

In the figure:

1. A \$3 trillion change in disposable income brings
2. A \$2 trillion change in consumption expenditure, so
3. The *MPC* equals \$2 trillion ÷ \$3 trillion = 0.67.

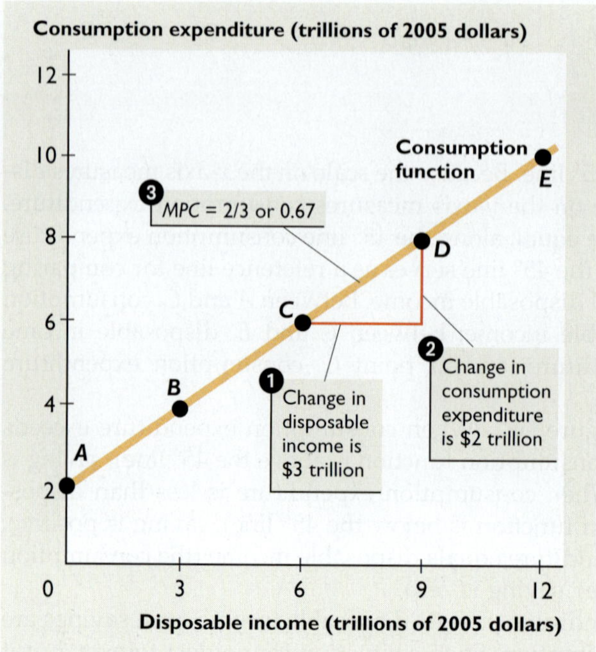

Other Influences on Consumption Expenditure

Consumption plans are influenced by many factors other than disposable income. The more important influences are:

- Real interest rate
- Wealth
- Expected future income

Real Interest Rate When the real interest rate falls, consumption expenditure increases (and saving decreases) and when the real interest rate rises, consumption expenditure decreases (and saving increases).

Wealth and Expected Future Income When either wealth or expected future income decreases, consumption expenditure also decreases and when wealth or expected future income increases, consumption expenditure also increases.

Figure 14.3 shows the effects of these influences on the consumption function. When the real interest rate falls or when wealth or expected future income increases, the consumption function shifts upward from CF_0 to CF_1. Such a shift occurs during the expansion phase of the business cycle if a stock market boom increases wealth and expected future income increases.

When the real interest rate rises, or when wealth or expected future income decreases, the consumption function shifts downward from CF_0 to CF_2. Such a shift occurs during a recession if a stock market crash decreases wealth and expected future income decreases.

FIGURE 14.3

Shifts in the Consumption Function

myeconlab Animation

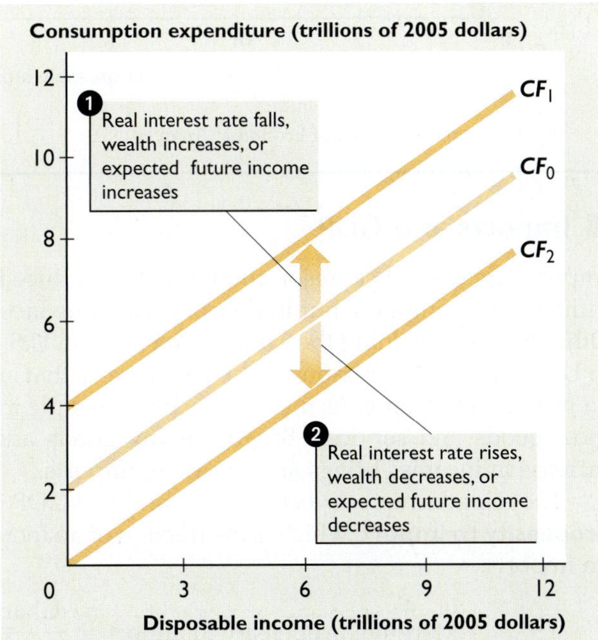

1 A fall in the real interest rate or an increase in either wealth or expected future income increases consumption expenditure and shifts the consumption function upward from CF_0 to CF_1.

2 A rise in the real interest rate or a decrease in either wealth or expected future income decreases consumption expenditure and shifts the consumption function downward from CF_0 to CF_2.

EYE on the U.S. ECONOMY

The U.S. Consumption Function

Each blue dot in the figure represents consumption expenditure and disposable income in the United States for a year between 1960 and 2009 (some labeled).

The lines labeled CF_0, CF_1, and CF_2 are estimates of the U.S. consumption function in 1960, 2008, and 2009, respectively.

The slope of these consumption functions—the marginal propensity to consume—is 0.87, which means that a $1 increase in disposable income brings an 87¢ increase in consumption expenditure.

The consumption function shifted upward from the 1960s to 2008 because economic growth brought higher expected future income and higher wealth.

The consumption function shifted downward in 2009 as the fall in home prices and stock prices lowered wealth and recession lowered expected future income.

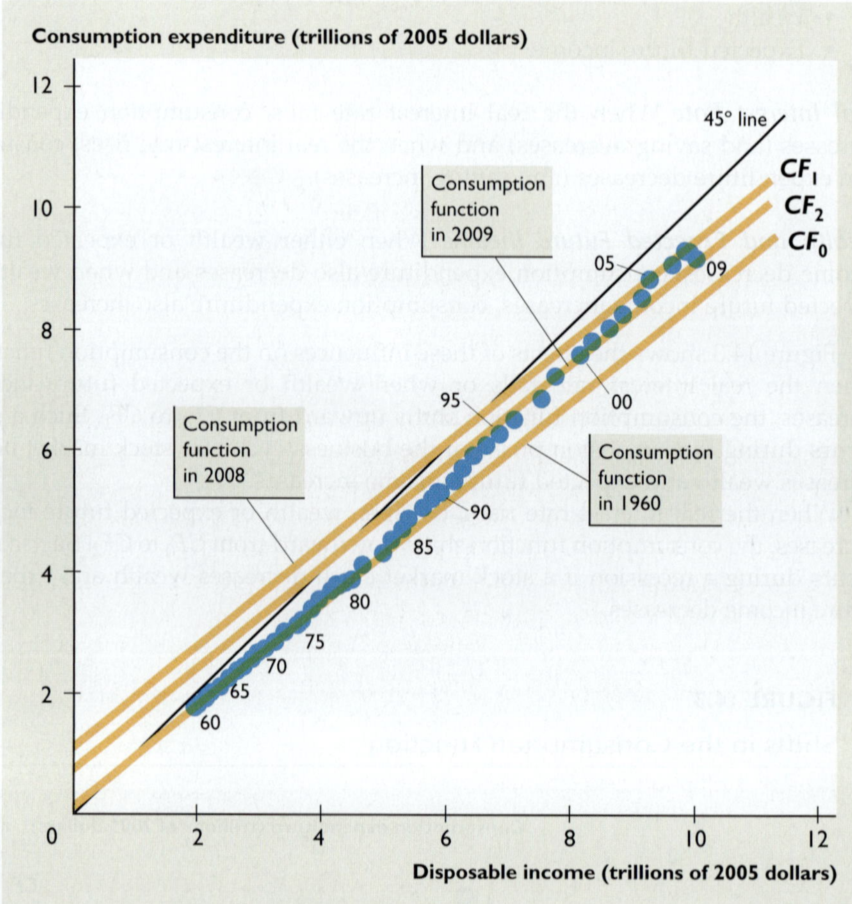

SOURCE OF DATA: Bureau of Economic Analysis.

Imports and GDP

Imports are the other major component of induced expenditure. Many factors influence U.S. imports, but in the short run, one factor dominates: U.S. real GDP. Other things remaining the same, an increase in U.S. real GDP brings an increase in U.S. imports. The reason for this influence is that an increase in real GDP is also an increase in income. As incomes increase, people increase their expenditures on most goods and services. Because many goods and services are imported, an increase in incomes brings an increase in imports.

Marginal propensity to import
The fraction of an increase in real GDP that is spent on imports—the change in imports divided by the change in real GDP.

The relationship between imports and real GDP is described by the **marginal propensity to import**, which is the fraction of an increase in real GDP that is spent on imports.

$$\text{Marginal propensity to import} = \frac{\text{Change in imports}}{\text{Change in real GDP}}.$$

For example, if, with other things remaining the same, a $1 trillion increase in real GDP increases imports by $0.2 trillion, then the marginal propensity to import is 0.2.

CHECKPOINT 14.1

Distinguish between autonomous expenditure and induced expenditure and explain how real GDP influences expenditure plans.

myeconlab

Work these problems in Study Plan 14.1 to get instant feedback.

Practice Problems

1. If the marginal propensity to consume is 0.8 and disposable income increases by $0.5 trillion, by how much will consumption expenditure change?
2. Explain how each of the following events influences the U.S. consumption function:
   - The marginal propensity to consume decreases.
   - U.S. autonomous consumption decreases.
   - Americans expect an increase in future income.
3. Figure 1 shows the consumption function. What is the marginal propensity to consume, and what is autonomous consumption?
4. **Americans cut back sharply on spending**

   In December 2007, consumer spending grew at the slowest rate in seven years. Despite the fact that average wages and salaries did not fall, consumer confidence, a barometer of economic health, plunged. Spending across the country dropped, but it was worse in states like Florida and California where home prices have fallen the most.

   Source: *The New York Times*, January 14, 2008

   Explain why consumers cut their spending when consumer confidence drops and house prices fall. Does the drop in consumer spending arise from a movement along the consumption function or a shift of the consumption function? Explain your answer.

FIGURE 1

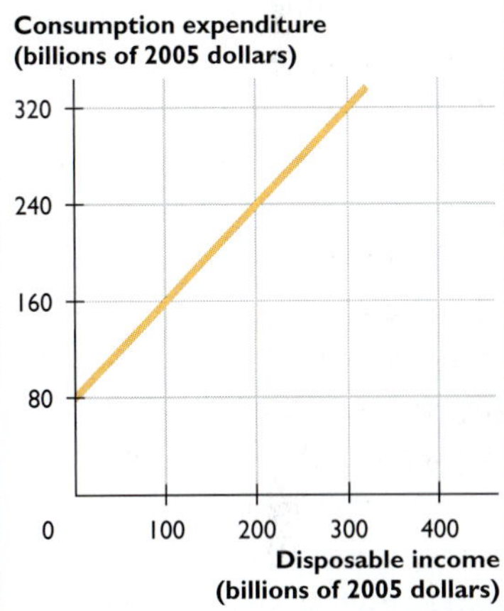

Guided Solutions to Practice Problems

1. Consumption expenditure will increase by $0.4 trillion, which is 0.8 multiplied by the change in disposable income of $0.5 trillion.
2. The marginal propensity to consume equals the slope of the consumption function. So when the marginal propensity to consume decreases, the consumption function becomes flatter.

   Autonomous consumption is the y-axis intercept of the consumption function. So when autonomous expenditure decreases, the consumption function shifts downward.

   When expected future income increases, current consumption expenditure increases and the consumption function shifts upward.
3. When disposable income increases by $100 billion, consumption expenditure increases by $80 billion. The *MPC* is $80 billion ÷ $100 billion = 0.8. Autonomous consumption (consumption expenditure that is independent of disposable income) equals the y-axis intercept and is $80 billion (Figure 2).
4. Consumer confidence drops when people become less certain about their future income. A fall in house prices decreases consumers' wealth. Both the fall in expected future income and the decrease in wealth shift the consumption function downward.

FIGURE 2

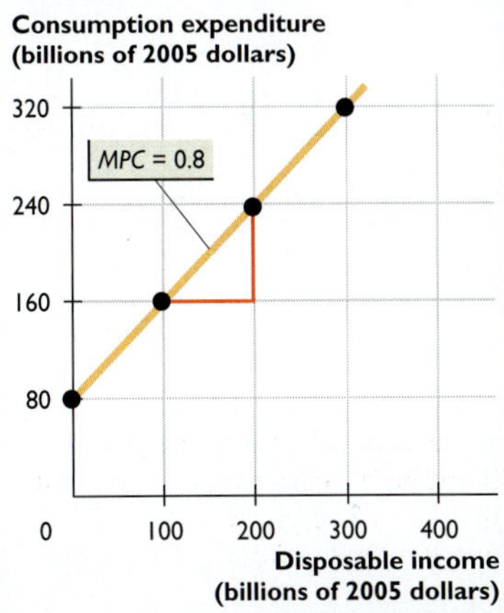

14.2 EQUILIBRIUM EXPENDITURE

You are now going to discover how, with a fixed price level, aggregate expenditure plans interact to determine real GDP. First we will study the relationship between aggregate planned expenditure and real GDP. Then we'll study the forces that make aggregate planned expenditure and actual expenditure equal.

An aggregate expenditure schedule and an aggregate expenditure curve describe the relationship between aggregate planned expenditure and real GDP.

Aggregate Planned Expenditure and Real GDP

You've seen that consumption expenditure increases when disposable income increases. Disposable income equals aggregate income—real GDP—minus net taxes, so disposable income and consumption expenditure increase when real GDP increases. We use this link between consumption expenditure and real GDP to determine equilibrium expenditure.

The table in Figure 14.4 sets out an aggregate expenditure schedule together with the components of aggregate planned expenditure. All the variables are measured in real (constant dollar) values. To calculate aggregate planned expenditure at a given real GDP, we add the various components together.

The first column of the table shows real GDP, and the second column shows the consumption expenditure generated by each level of real GDP. In this example, a $6 trillion increase in real GDP generates a $4.5 trillion increase in consumption expenditure—the *MPC* is 0.75. The next three columns show investment, government expenditure on goods and services, and exports. These items do not depend on real GDP. They are *autonomous expenditure*. Investment is $1.25 trillion, government expenditure is $1.0 trillion, and exports are $2.25 trillion.

The next column shows imports, which increase as real GDP increases. A $6 trillion increase in real GDP generates a $1.5 trillion increase in imports. The marginal propensity to import is 0.25.

The final column shows aggregate planned expenditure—the sum of planned consumption expenditure, investment, government expenditure on goods and services, and exports minus imports.

Figure 14.4 plots an aggregate expenditure curve. Real GDP is shown on the x-axis, and aggregate planned expenditure is shown on the y-axis. The aggregate expenditure curve is the red line *AE*. Points *A* through *F* on that curve correspond to the rows of the table. The *AE* curve is a graph of aggregate planned expenditure (the last column) plotted against real GDP (the first column).

Figure 14.4 also shows the components of aggregate expenditure. The horizontal lines show the components of autonomous expenditure—investment (I), government expenditure (G), and exports (X). The line labeled $C + I + G + X$ adds consumption expenditure to the autonomous expenditure.

Finally, to construct the *AE* curve, subtract imports (M) from the $C + I + G + X$ line. Aggregate expenditure is expenditure on U.S.-made goods and services. But $C + I + G + X$ includes expenditure on imports. For example, if a student buys a Honda motorbike made in Japan, the student's expenditure is part of C, but it is not an expenditure on a U.S.-produced good. To find the expenditure on U.S.-produced goods, we subtract the value of the imported motorbike.

Figure 14.4 shows that aggregate planned expenditure increases as real GDP increases. But notice that for each $1 increase in real GDP, aggregate planned

FIGURE 14.4

Aggregate Expenditure

myeconlab Animation

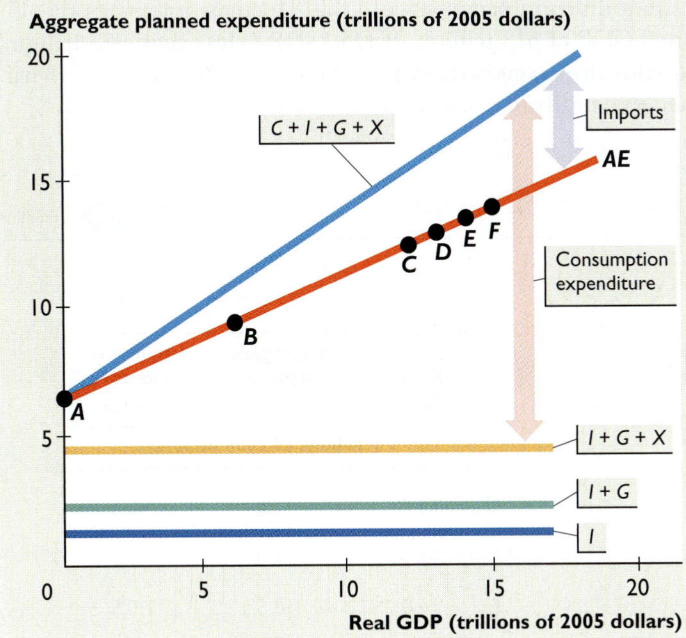

The aggregate expenditure schedule shows the relationship between aggregate planned expenditure and real GDP. For example, in row *B* of the table, when real GDP is $6 trillion, aggregate planned expenditure is $9.50 trillion ($6.50 + $1.25 + $1.00 + $2.25 – $1.50). As real GDP increases, aggregate planned expenditure increases.

This relationship is graphed as the aggregate expenditure curve *AE*. The components of aggregate expenditure that increase with real GDP are consumption expenditure and imports. The other components—investment, government expenditure, and exports—do not vary with real GDP.

	Real GDP (*Y*)	Consumption expenditure (*C*)	Investment (*I*)	Government expenditure (*G*)	Exports (*X*)	Imports (*M*)	Aggregate planned expenditure (*AE* = *C* + *I* + *G* + *X* – *M*)
		Planned expenditure					
	(trillions of 2005 dollars)						
A	0.00	2.00	1.25	1.00	2.25	0.00	6.50
B	**6.00**	**6.50**	**1.25**	**1.00**	**2.25**	**1.50**	**9.50**
C	12.00	11.00	1.25	1.00	2.25	3.00	12.50
D	13.00	11.75	1.25	1.00	2.25	3.25	13.00
E	14.00	12.50	1.25	1.00	2.25	3.50	13.50
F	15.00	13.25	1.25	1.00	2.25	3.75	14.00

expenditure increases by less than $1. For example, when real GDP increases from $12 trillion to $13 trillion (row *C* to row *D* of the table), aggregate planned expenditure increases from $12.5 trillion to $13 trillion. A $1 trillion increase in real GDP brings a $0.5 trillion increase in aggregate planned expenditure. This feature of the *AE* curve is important and plays a big role in determining equilibrium expenditure and the effect of a change in autonomous expenditure.

The *AE* curve summarizes the relationship between aggregate planned expenditure and real GDP. But what determines the point on the *AE* curve at which the economy operates? What determines actual aggregate expenditure?

Equilibrium Expenditure

Equilibrium expenditure
The level of aggregate expenditure that occurs when aggregate *planned* expenditure equals real GDP.

Equilibrium expenditure occurs when aggregate *planned* expenditure equals real GDP. In Figure 14.5(a) aggregate planned expenditure equals real GDP at all the points on the 45° line. Equilibrium occurs where the *AE* curve intersects the 45° line at point *D* with real GDP at $13 trillion. If real GDP is less than $13 trillion, aggregate planned expenditure exceeds real GDP; and if real GDP exceeds $13 trillion, aggregate planned expenditure is less than real GDP.

FIGURE 14.5
Equilibrium Expenditure

myeconlab Animation

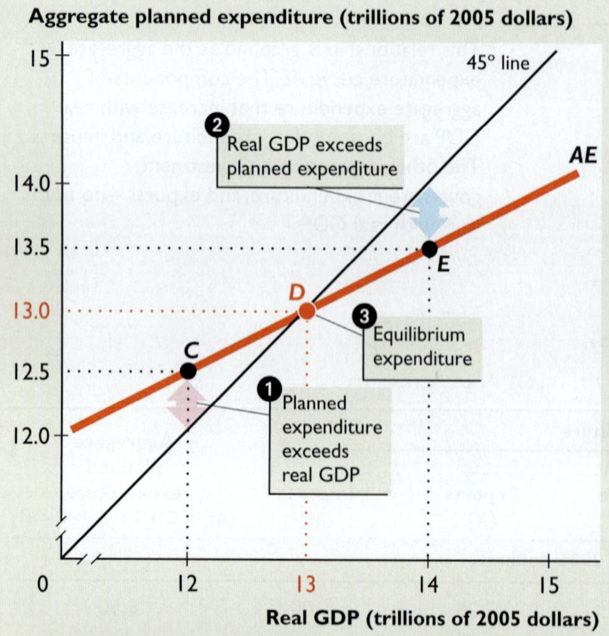

(a) Equilibrium expenditure

	Real GDP	Aggregate planned expenditure	Unplanned inventory change
	(trillions of 2005 dollars)		
C	12.0	12.5	–0.5
D	13.0	13.0	0.0
E	14.0	13.5	0.5

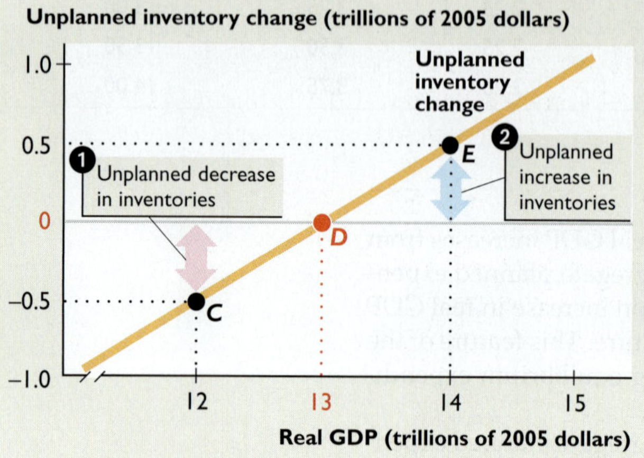

(b) Unplanned inventory change

The table shows expenditure plans and unplanned changes in inventories at different levels of real GDP. Part (a) illustrates equilibrium expenditure, and part (b) shows the unplanned inventory changes that bring changes in real GDP.

1. When aggregate planned expenditure exceeds real GDP, an unplanned decrease in inventories occurs. Firms increase production, and real GDP increases.
2. When real GDP exceeds aggregate planned expenditure, an unplanned increase in inventories occurs. Firms decrease production, and real GDP decreases.
3. When aggregate planned expenditure equals real GDP, there are no unplanned inventory changes and real GDP remains at its equilibrium level.

Convergence to Equilibrium

At equilibrium expenditure, production plans and spending plans agree, and there is no reason for production or spending to change. But when aggregate planned expenditure and actual aggregate expenditure are unequal, production plans and spending plans are misaligned, and a process of convergence toward equilibrium expenditure occurs. Throughout this convergence process, real GDP adjusts.

What are the forces that move aggregate expenditure toward equilibrium? To answer this question, we look at a situation in which aggregate expenditure is away from equilibrium.

Convergence from Below Equilibrium

Suppose that in Figure 14.5, real GDP is $12 trillion. At this level of real GDP, actual aggregate expenditure is also $12 trillion, but aggregate planned expenditure is $12.5 trillion—point *C* in Figure 14.5(a). Aggregate planned expenditure exceeds actual expenditure. When people spend $12.5 trillion and firms produce goods and services worth $12 trillion, firms' inventories decrease by $0.5 trillion—point *C* in Figure 14.5(b). This change in inventories is *unplanned.* Because the change in inventories is part of investment, the decrease in inventories decreases actual investment. So actual investment is $0.5 trillion less than planned investment.

Real GDP doesn't remain at $12 trillion for long. Firms have inventory targets based on their sales, and when inventories fall below target, firms increase production. Firms keep increasing production as long as unplanned decreases in inventories occur.

Eventually firms will have increased production by $1 trillion, so real GDP will have increased to $13 trillion. At this real GDP, aggregate planned expenditure rises to $13 trillion—point *D* in Figure 14.5(a). With aggregate planned expenditure equal to actual expenditure, the unplanned change in inventories is zero and firms hold production constant. The economy has converged on equilibrium expenditure.

Convergence from Above Equilibrium

Now suppose that in Figure 14.5, real GDP is $14 trillion. Actual aggregate expenditure is also $14 trillion, but aggregate planned expenditure is $13.5 trillion—point *E* in Figure 14.5(a). Actual expenditure exceeds planned expenditure and firms' inventories pile up by an unwanted $0.5 trillion—point *E* in Figure 14.5(b).

Real GDP doesn't remain at $14 trillion. Firms now want to lower their inventories, so they decrease production.

Eventually, firms will have decreased production by $1 trillion, so real GDP will have decreased to $13 trillion. At this real GDP, aggregate planned expenditure falls to $13 trillion—point *D* in Figure 14.5(a). With aggregate planned expenditure equal to actual expenditure, the unplanned change in inventories is zero and firms hold production constant. The economy has converged on equilibrium expenditure.

Starting from below equilibrium, unplanned decreases in inventories induce firms to increase production; starting from above equilibrium, unplanned increases in inventories induce firms to decrease production. In both cases, production is pulled toward the equilibrium level at which there are no unplanned inventory changes.

EYE on the PAST

Say's Law and Keynes' Principle of Effective Demand

During the Industrial Revolution, which began around 1760 and lasted for 70 years, technological change was rapid. People have talked about the "new economy" of the 1990s, but the 1990s was just another phase of a process that began in the truly new economy of the late 1700s. The pace of change in economic life during those years was unprecedented. Never before had old jobs been destroyed and new jobs created on such a scale. In this environment of rapid economic change, people began to wonder whether the economy could create enough jobs and a high enough level of demand to ensure that people would buy all the things that the new industrial economy could produce.

A French economist, Jean-Baptiste Say, provided the assurance that people were looking for. Born in 1767 (he was 9 years old when Adam Smith's *Wealth of Nations* was published—see Chapter 1, p. 17), Say suffered the wrath of Napoleon for his conservative call for smaller and leaner government and was the most famous economist of his era. His book *A Treatise on Political Economy (Traité d'économie politique)*, published in 1803, became the best-selling university economics textbook in both Europe and America.

In this book, Say reasoned that *supply creates its own demand*—an idea that came to be called *Say's Law*.

You've seen Say's Law at work in the full-employment economy. The real wage rate adjusts to ensure that the quantity of labor demanded equals the quantity of labor supplied and real GDP equals potential GDP. The real interest rate adjusts to ensure that the quantity of investment that firms plan equals the quantity of saving. Because saving equals income minus consumption expenditure, the equilibrium real interest rate ensures that consumption expenditure plus investment exactly equals potential GDP.

Say's Law came under attack at various times during the nineteenth century. But it came under an onslaught during the Great Depression of the 1930s. With a quarter of the labor force unemployed and real GDP at around three quarters of potential GDP, it seemed like a stretch to argue that supply creates its own demand. But there was no simple principle or slogan with which to replace Say's Law.

In the midst of the Great Depression, in 1936, a British economist, John Maynard Keynes, provided the catchphrase that the world was looking for: *effective demand.*

Born in England in 1883, Keynes was one of the outstanding people of the twentieth century. He was a prolific writer on economic issues, represented Britain at the Versailles peace conference at the end of World War I, and played a prominent role in creating the International Monetary Fund, which monitors the global macroeconomy today.

Keynes revolutionized macroeconomic thinking by turning Say's Law on its head. In Keynes' view, supply does *not* create its own demand, and *effective demand* determines real GDP. If businesses spend less on new capital than the amount that people save, equilibrium expenditure will be less than potential GDP. Prices and wages are sticky, and resources can become unemployed and remain unemployed indefinitely.

The aggregate expenditure model that you're studying in this chapter is the modern distillation of Keynes' idea.

Jean-Baptiste Say

John Maynard Keynes

CHECKPOINT 14.2

Explain how real GDP adjusts to achieve equilibrium expenditure.

myeconlab

Work these problems in Study Plan 14.2 to get instant feedback.

Practice Problems

Table 1 gives real GDP (Y) and its components in billions of dollars.

1. Calculate aggregate planned expenditure when real GDP is \$200 billion and when real GDP is \$600 billion.
2. Calculate equilibrium expenditure.
3. If real GDP is \$200 billion, explain the process that moves the economy toward equilibrium expenditure.
4. If real GDP is \$600 billion, explain the process that moves the economy toward equilibrium expenditure.
5. **Wholesale inventories decline, sales rise**
   The Commerce Department reported that wholesale inventories fell 1.3 percent in August for a record 12th consecutive month, evidence that companies are trimming orders to factories, which helped depress economic output during the recession. Economists hope that the rising sales will encourage businesses to begin restocking their inventories, which would boost factory production and help bolster broad economic growth in coming months.
   Source: *The New York Times*, October 8, 2009

   Explain why a fall in inventories is associated with recession and a restocking of inventories might bolster economic growth.

TABLE 1

	A	B	C	D	E	F	G
1		*Y*	*C*	*I*	*G*	*X*	*M*
2	*A*	100	110	50	60	60	15
3	*B*	200	170	50	60	60	30
4	*C*	300	230	50	60	60	45
5	*D*	400	290	50	60	60	60
6	*E*	500	350	50	60	60	75
7	*F*	600	410	50	60	60	90

Guided Solutions to Practice Problems

1. Aggregate planned expenditure equals $C + I + G + X - M$. When real GDP is \$200 billion (row *B* of Table 1), aggregate planned expenditure (in billions) equals \$170 + \$50 + \$60 + \$60 − \$30 = \$310 billion. When real GDP is \$600 billion (row *F* of Table 1), aggregate planned expenditure (in billions) equals \$410 + \$50 + \$60 + \$60 − \$90, which is \$490 billion.
2. Equilibrium expenditure occurs when aggregate planned expenditure equals real GDP. Equilibrium expenditure is \$400 billion (row *D* of Table 1).
3. If real GDP is \$200 billion, aggregate planned expenditure is \$310 billion, which exceeds real GDP. Firms' inventories decrease by \$110 billion. Firms' expenditure plans are not fulfilled, so they increase production to restore their inventories. Real GDP increases. As long as aggregate planned expenditure exceeds real GDP, firms will increase production to restore their inventories to their target level and real GDP will increase.
4. If real GDP is \$600 billion, aggregate planned expenditure is \$490 billion, which is less than real GDP. Firms' inventories increase by \$110 billion. Firms cut production and try to reduce their inventories. Real GDP decreases. As long as aggregate planned expenditure is less than real GDP, firms' inventories will increase. Firms will cut production as they try to reduce their inventories to their target level. Real GDP decreases.
5. When firms reduce their target level of inventories, planned investment falls and equilibrium expenditure and real GDP decrease—as occurred during the year to August 2009. When firms plan to restock their inventories, the reverse occurs. Equilibrium expenditure and real GDP increase.

14.3 EXPENDITURE MULTIPLIERS

Multiplier
The amount by which a change in any component of autonomous expenditure is magnified or multiplied to determine the change that it generates in equilibrium expenditure and real GDP.

When autonomous expenditure (investment, government expenditure, or exports) increases, aggregate expenditure and real GDP also increase. A **multiplier** determines the amount by which a change in autonomous expenditure is magnified or multiplied to determine the change in equilibrium expenditure and real GDP that it generates.

The Basic Idea of the Multiplier

An increase in investment increases real GDP, which increases disposable income and consumption expenditure. The increase in consumption expenditure adds to the increase in investment and a multiplier determines the magnitude of the resulting increase in aggregate expenditure.

Figure 14.6 illustrates the multiplier. The initial aggregate expenditure schedule graphs as AE_0. Equilibrium expenditure and real GDP are $13 trillion. You can see this equilibrium in row *B* of the table and where the curve AE_0 intersects the 45° line at point *B* in the figure.

Suppose that investment increases by $0.5 trillion. This increase in investment increases aggregate planned expenditure by $0.5 trillion at each level of real GDP. The new *AE* curve is AE_1. The new equilibrium expenditure (row *D'*) occurs where AE_1 intersects the 45° line and is $15 trillion (point *D'*). At this real GDP, aggregate planned expenditure equals real GDP. The increase in equilibrium expenditure ($2 trillion) is *larger* than the increase in investment ($0.5 trillion).

FIGURE 14.6
The Multiplier

myeconlab Animation

Real GDP (*Y*)		Aggregate planned expenditure: Original (AE_0)		Aggregate planned expenditure: New (AE_1)
(trillions of 2005 dollars)				
12.00	*A*	12.25	*A'*	12.75
13.00	*B*	**13.00**	*B'*	13.50
14.00	*C*	13.75	*C'*	14.25
15.00	*D*	14.50	*D'*	**15.00**
16.00	*E*	15.25	*E'*	15.75

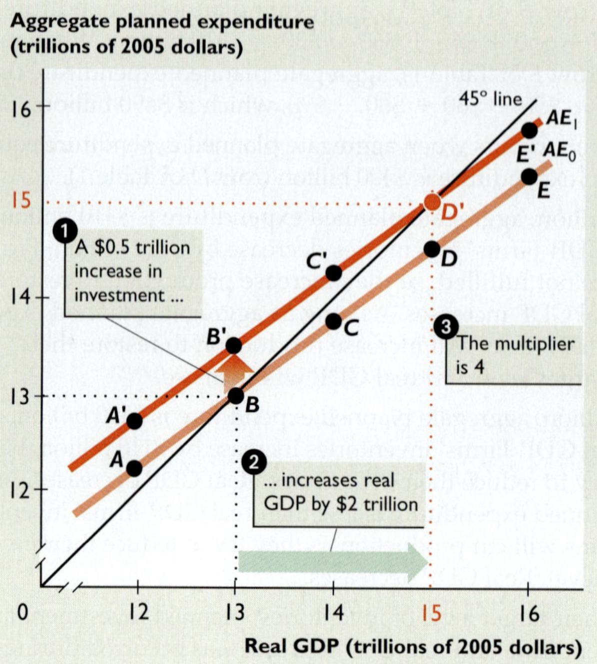

1. A $0.5 trillion increase in investment shifts the *AE* curve upward by $0.5 trillion from AE_0 to AE_1.
2. Equilibrium expenditure increases by $2 trillion from $13 trillion to $15 trillion.
3. The increase in equilibrium expenditure is 4 times the increase in autonomous expenditure, so the multiplier is 4.

The Size of the Multiplier

The multiplier is the amount by which a change in autonomous expenditure is multiplied to determine the change in equilibrium expenditure that it generates. To calculate the multiplier, we divide the change in equilibrium expenditure by the change in autonomous expenditure that generated it. That is,

$$\text{Multiplier} = \frac{\text{Change in equilibrium expenditure}}{\text{Change in autonomous expenditure}}.$$

The change in equilibrium expenditure also equals the change in real GDP, which we'll call ΔY. In Figure 14.6, the change in autonomous expenditure is a change in investment, which we'll call ΔI. The multiplier is

$$\text{Multiplier} = \frac{\Delta Y}{\Delta I}.$$

In Figure 14.6, equilibrium expenditure increases by \$2 trillion (ΔY = \$2 trillion) and investment increases by \$0.5 trillion (ΔI = \$0.5 trillion), so

$$\text{Multiplier} = \frac{\Delta Y}{\Delta I} = \frac{\$2 \text{ trillion}}{\$0.5 \text{ trillion}} = 4.$$

The multiplier is 4—real GDP changes by 4 times the change in investment.

Why is the multiplier greater than 1? It is because an increase in autonomous expenditure induces further increases in aggregate expenditure—induced expenditure increases. If the State of California spends \$10 million on a new highway, aggregate expenditure and real GDP immediately increase by \$10 million. Highway construction workers now have more income, and they spend part of it on cars, vacations, and other goods and services. Real GDP now increases by the initial \$10 million plus the extra consumption expenditure. The producers of cars, vacations, and other goods now have increased incomes, and they in turn spend part of the increase on consumption goods and services. Additional income induces additional expenditure, which creates additional income.

The Multiplier and the *MPC*

Ignoring imports and income taxes, the magnitude of the multiplier depends only on the marginal propensity to consume. To see why, let's do a calculation. The change in real GDP (ΔY) equals the change in consumption expenditure (ΔC) plus the change in investment (ΔI). That is,

$$\Delta Y = \Delta C + \Delta I.$$

But with no income taxes, the change in consumption expenditure is determined by the change in real GDP and the marginal propensity to consume. It is

$$\Delta C = MPC \times \Delta Y.$$

Now substitute $MPC \times \Delta Y$ for ΔC in the previous equation:

$$\Delta Y = MPC \times \Delta Y + \Delta I.$$

Now solve for ΔY as

$$(1 - MPC) \times \Delta Y = \Delta I,$$

and rearrange the equation:

$$\Delta Y = \frac{1}{(1 - MPC)}\Delta I.$$

Finally, divide both sides of the equation by ΔI to give

$$\text{Multiplier} = \frac{\Delta Y}{\Delta I} = \frac{1}{(1 - MPC)}.$$

In Figure 14.6, the *MPC* is 0.75. So if we use this value of *MPC*,

$$\text{Multiplier} = \frac{\Delta Y}{\Delta I} = \frac{1}{(1 - 0.75)} = \frac{1}{0.25} = 4.$$

The greater the marginal propensity to consume, the larger is the multiplier. For example, with a marginal propensity to consume of 0.9, the multiplier would be 10. Let's now look at the influence of imports and income taxes.

The Multiplier, Imports, and Income Taxes

The size of the multiplier depends on imports and income taxes, both of which make the multiplier smaller.

When an increase in investment increases consumption and real GDP, part of the increase in expenditure is on imports, not U.S.-produced goods and services. Only expenditure on U.S.-produced goods and services increases U.S. real GDP. The larger the marginal propensity to import, the smaller is the multiplier.

When an increase in investment increases real GDP, income tax payments increase so disposable income increases by less than the increase in real GDP, which means that consumption expenditure increases by less than it would if income tax payments had not changed. The marginal tax rate determines the extent to which income tax payments change when real GDP changes. The **marginal tax rate** is the fraction of a change in real GDP that is paid in income taxes. The larger the marginal tax rate, the smaller are the changes in disposable income and real GDP that result from a given change in autonomous expenditure.

Marginal tax rate
The fraction of a change in real GDP that is paid in income taxes—the change in tax payments divided by the change in real GDP.

The marginal propensity to import and the marginal tax rate together with the marginal propensity to consume determine the multiplier, and their combined influence determines the slope of the *AE* curve. The general formula for the multiplier is

$$\text{Multiplier} = \frac{\Delta Y}{\Delta I} = \frac{1}{(1 - \text{Slope of } AE \text{ curve})}.$$

Figure 14.7 compares two situations. In Figure 14.7(a), there are no imports and no income taxes. The slope of the *AE* curve equals *MPC*, which is 0.75, so the multiplier is 4 (as we calculated above). In Figure 14.7(b), imports and income taxes decrease the slope of the *AE* curve to 0.5. In this case,

$$\text{Multiplier} = \frac{\Delta Y}{\Delta I} = \frac{1}{(1 - 0.5)} = 2.$$

Over time, the value of the multiplier changes as the marginal tax rate, the marginal propensity to consume, and the marginal propensity to import change. These ongoing changes make the multiplier hard to predict.

FIGURE 14.7

The Multiplier and the Slope of the *AE* Curve

myeconlab Animation

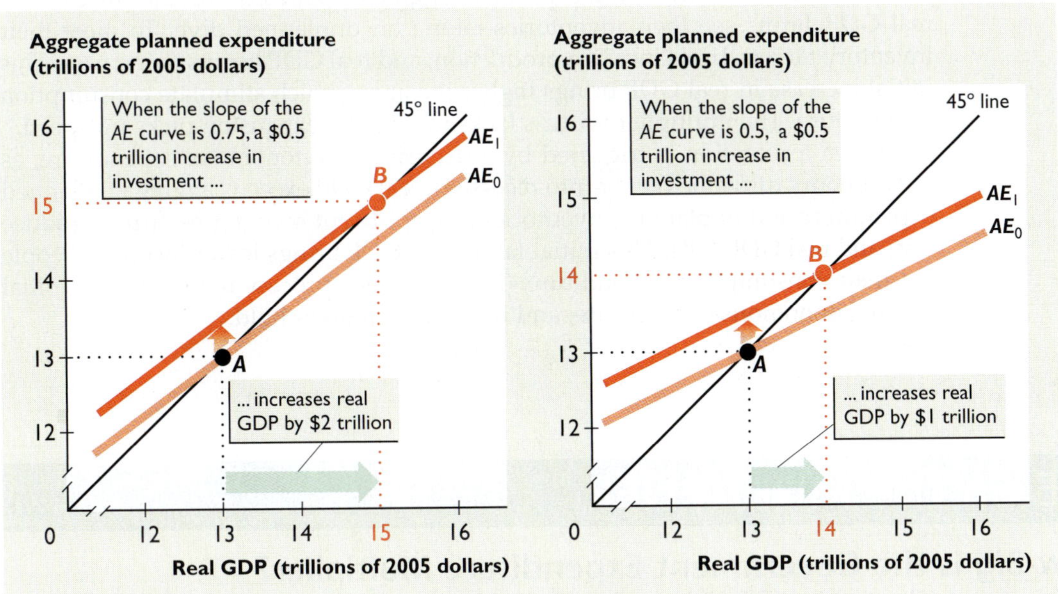

(a) Multiplier is 4 **(b) Multiplier is 2**

In part (a), with no imports and no income taxes, the slope of the *AE* curve equals the marginal propensity to consume, which in this example is 0.75. The multiplier is 4.

In part (b), with imports and income taxes, the slope of the *AE* curve is less than the marginal propensity to consume. In this example, the slope of the *AE* curve is 0.5 and the multiplier is 2.

EYE on YOUR LIFE

Looking for Multipliers

You can see multipliers in your daily life if you look in the right places and in the right way.

Look for an event in your home city or state that brings new economic activity. It might be a major construction project that is going on near your home or school. It might be a major sporting event that occurs infrequently and brings a large number of people to a city. Or it might be a major new business that moves into an area or expands its activity level.

What supplies do you see being delivered to the site, event, or new business? How many people do you estimate have jobs at this new activity? Where do the supplies and the workers come from?

This new economic activity sets off a multiplier process. What are the first round multiplier effects? Whose incomes are higher because of the purchase of these supplies and expenditure of the workers hired by the project?

Where do the workers buy their coffee and lunch? Do their purchases create new jobs for students and others in local coffee shops and fast-food outlets?

Where do the workers and suppliers spend the rest of their incomes?

Now think about the second round and subsequent round effects. Where do the students hired by coffee shops spend their incomes and what additional jobs do those expenditures create?

The process goes on and on.

Business-Cycle Turning Points

When an expansion is triggered by an increase in autonomous expenditure, as the economy turns the corner into expansion, aggregate planned expenditure exceeds real GDP. Firms see their inventories taking an unplanned dive. To meet their inventory targets, firms increase production, and real GDP begins to increase. This initial increase in real GDP brings higher incomes, which stimulate consumption expenditure. The multiplier process kicks in, and the expansion picks up speed.

When a recession is triggered by a decrease in autonomous expenditure, as the economy turns the corner into recession, real GDP exceeds aggregate planned expenditure and unplanned inventories pile up. To cut inventories, firms produce less, and real GDP falls. This initial fall in real GDP brings lower incomes. People cut their consumption expenditure. The multiplier process reinforces the initial cut in autonomous expenditure, and the recession takes hold.

EYE on the MULTIPLIER

How Big Is the Government Expenditure Multiplier?

Christina Romer, Chair of the President's Council of Economic Advisers, has estimated the government expenditure multiplier to be 1.6. This number led administration economists to predict that the stimulus plan that increased government expenditure would prevent the unemployment rate from rising much above 8 percent. This prediction turned out to be optimistic and one reason might be that the multiplier assumption is also too optimistic.

Robert Barro, a leading macroeconomist at Harvard University, has studied the effects of very large increases in government expenditure during wars. He finds that the multiplier is only 0.8, which means that real GDP increases by *less than* the increase in government expenditure. The reason is that some private expenditure, mainly investment, gets "crowded out" and real GDP falls.

John Taylor of Stanford University, another leading macroeconomist, agrees with Barro that the government expenditure multiplier is less than 1. He says that crowding out gets more severe as time passes, so the multiplier gets smaller after two years and smaller still after three years.

A big multiplier can occur only if there is substantial slack in the economy—when the recessionary gap is large.

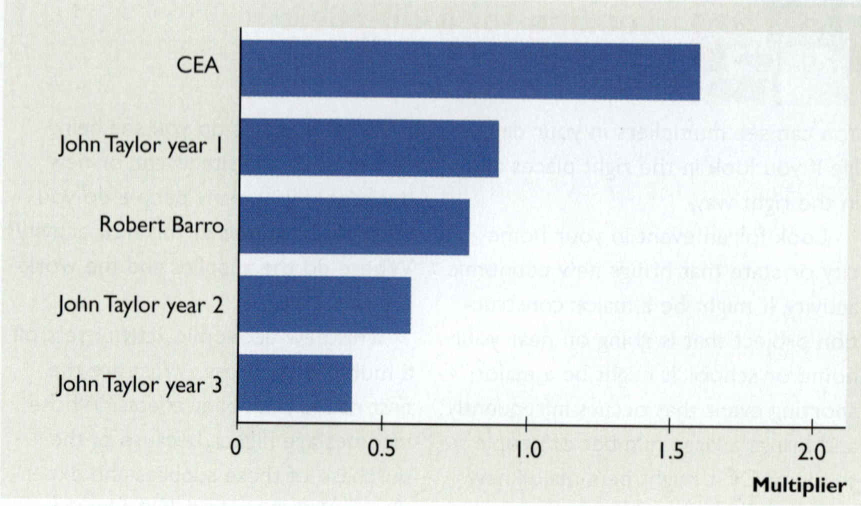

SOURCES OF DATA: Council of Economic Advisers (CEA), Christina Romer and Jared Bernstein, "The Job Impact of the American Recovery and Reinvestment Plan," January 2009; Robert J. Barro, "Government Spending is No Free Lunch," *The Wall Street Journal*, January 22, 2009; John F. Cogan, Tobias Cwik, John B. Taylor, Volker Wieland, "New Keynesian versus Old Keynesian Government Spending Multipliers," February 2009.

CHECKPOINT 14.3

Explain the expenditure multiplier.

myeconlab

Work these problems in Study Plan 14.3 to get instant feedback.

Practice Problems

An economy has no imports and no income taxes, *MPC* is 0.80, and real GDP is $150 billion. Businesses increase investment by $5 billion. Use this information to answer Problems **1** and **2**.

1. Calculate the multiplier and the change in real GDP.
2. Calculate the new level of real GDP and explain why real GDP increases by more than $5 billion.

An economy has no imports and no income taxes. An increase in autonomous expenditure of $2 trillion increases equilibrium expenditure by $8 trillion. Use this information to answer Problems **3** and **4**.

3. Calculate the multiplier and the marginal propensity to consume.
4. What happens to the multiplier if an income tax is introduced?
5. **And the winner is ...**

   The game of winning the Olympic games has become popular with cities around the world. To win the 2016 games, Rio de Janeiro in Brazil spent some $50 million. Now it will spend about $50 billion to build new stadiums, other sports facilities, new bridges and roads, to extend the metro, and to double the number of hotel rooms.

   Source: *The Economist*, October 8, 2009

   Use the multiplier to explain why cities want to stage the Olympic games.

Guided Solutions to Practice Problems

1. The multiplier equals $1/(1 - MPC)$. *MPC* is 0.8, so the multiplier is 5.

   Real GDP increases by $25 billion. The increase in investment increases real GDP by the multiplier (5) times the change in investment ($5 billion).
2. Real GDP increases from $150 billion to $175 billion. Real GDP increases by more than $5 billion because the increase in investment induces an increase in consumption expenditure.
3. The multiplier is the increase in equilibrium expenditure ($8 trillion) divided by the increase in autonomous expenditure ($2 trillion). The multiplier is 4.

   The marginal propensity to consume is 0.75. The multiplier is $1/(1 - MPC)$. So $4 = 1/(1 - MPC)$, and *MPC* is 0.75.
4. If the government introduces an income tax, the slope of the *AE* curve becomes smaller and the multiplier becomes smaller.
5. The expenditure of $50 billion will increase real GDP by more than $50 billion because the expenditure multiplier exceeds 1. When Rio embarks on its investment program (building new stadiums, sports facilities, roads, and bridges and extending the metro), new workers will be hired. These workers will earn an income and they will spend part of it on consumption goods and services.With the increase in demand for goods and services, the sellers of those goods and services will hire more workers, who earn an income, and so on. The $50 billion of investment will increase real GDP by a multiple of $50 billion.

14.4 THE *AD* CURVE AND EQUILIBRIUM EXPENDITURE

In this chapter, we've studied the aggregate expenditure model, in which firms change production when sales and inventories change but they don't change their prices. The aggregate expenditure model determines equilibrium expenditure and real GDP at a given price level. In Chapter 13, we studied the simultaneous determination of real GDP and the price level using the *AS–AD* model. The aggregate demand curve and equilibrium expenditure are related, and this section shows you how.

Deriving the *AD* Curve from Equilibrium Expenditure

The *AE* curve is the relationship between aggregate planned expenditure and real GDP when all other influences on expenditure plans remain the same. A movement along the *AE* curve arises from a change in real GDP.

The *AD* curve is the relationship between the quantity of real GDP demanded and the price level when all other influences on expenditure plans remain the same. A movement along the *AD* curve arises from a change in the price level.

Equilibrium expenditure depends on the price level. When the price level rises, other things remaining the same, aggregate planned expenditure decreases and equilibrium expenditure decreases. And when the price level falls, other things remaining the same, aggregate planned expenditure increases and equilibrium expenditure increases. The reason is that a change in the price level changes the buying power of money, the real interest rate, and the real prices of exports and imports (see Chapter 13, pp. 332–334).

When the price level rises, each of these effects decreases aggregate planned expenditure at each level of real GDP. So the *AE* curve shifts downward. A fall in the price level has the opposite effect. When the price level falls, the *AE* curve shifts upward.

Figure 14.8(a) shows the effects of a change in the price level on the *AE* curve and equilibrium expenditure. When the price level is 110, the *AE* curve is AE_0, and it intersects the 45° line at point *B*. Equilibrium expenditure is $14 trillion. If the price level rises to 130, aggregate planned expenditure decreases and the *AE* curve shifts downward to AE_1. Equilibrium expenditure decreases to $13 trillion at point *A*. If the price level falls to 90, aggregate planned expenditure increases and the *AE* curve shifts upward to AE_2. Equilibrium expenditure increases to $15 trillion at point *C*.

The price level changes that shift the *AE* curve and change equilibrium expenditure bring movements along the *AD* curve. Figure 14.8(b) shows these movements. At a price level of 110, the quantity of real GDP demanded is $14 trillion—point *B* on the *AD* curve. If the price level rises to 130, the quantity of real GDP demanded decreases along the *AD* curve to $13 trillion at point *A*. If the price level falls to 90, the quantity of real GDP demanded increases along the *AD* curve to $15 trillion at point *C*.

The two parts of Figure 14.8 are connected and illustrate the relationship between the *AE* curve and the *AD* curve. Each point of equilibrium expenditure corresponds to a point on the *AD* curve. The equilibrium expenditure points *A*, *B*, and *C* (part a) correspond to the points *A*, *B*, and *C* on the *AD* curve (part b).

FIGURE 14.8

Equilibrium Expenditure and Aggregate Demand

myeconlab Animation

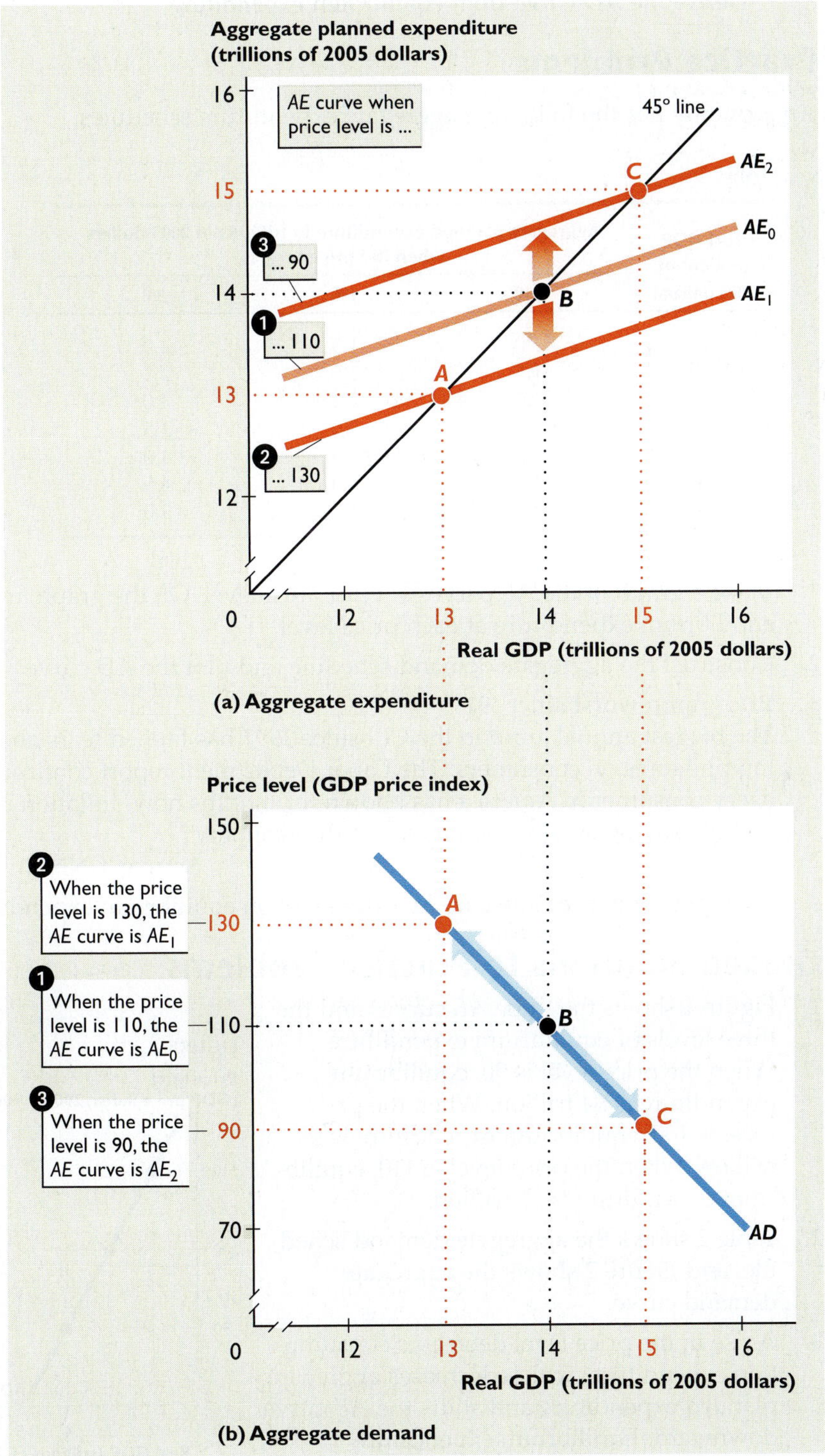

A change in the price level shifts the *AE* curve and results in a movement along the *AD* curve.

1. When the price level is 110, equilibrium expenditure is \$14 trillion at point *B* on the *AE* curve AE_0 and the quantity of real GDP demanded is \$14 trillion at point *B* on the *AD* curve.
2. When the price level rises to 130, the *AE* curve shifts downward to AE_1 and equilibrium expenditure decreases to \$13 trillion at point *A*. The quantity of real GDP demanded decreases along the *AD* curve to point *A*.
3. When the price level falls to 90, the *AE* curve shifts upward to AE_2 and equilibrium expenditure increases to \$15 trillion at point *C*. The quantity of real GDP demanded increases along the *AD* curve to point *C*.

Points *A*, *B*, and *C* on the *AD* curve in part (b) correspond to the equilibrium expenditure points *A*, *B*, and *C* in part (a).

myeconlab

Work these problems in Study Plan 14.4 to get instant feedback.

CHECKPOINT 14.4

Derive the *AD* curve from equilibrium expenditure.

Practice Problems

An economy has the following aggregate expenditure schedules:

TABLE 1

Real GDP (trillions of 2005 dollars)	Aggregate planned expenditure in trillions of 2005 dollars when the price level is		
	110	100	90
0	1.0	1.5	2.0
1.0	1.5	2.0	2.5
2.0	2.0	2.5	3.0
3.0	2.5	3.0	3.5
4.0	3.0	3.5	4.0
5.0	3.5	4.0	4.5
6.0	4.0	4.5	5.0

1. Make a graph of the *AE* curves at each price level. On the graph, mark the equilibrium expenditure at each price level.
2. Construct the aggregate demand schedule and plot the *AD* curve.
3. **Price jump worst since '91**
   The biggest annual jump in the CPI since 1991 has fanned fears about growing pressures on consumers. The Labor Department report confirms what every consumer in America has known for months now: Inflation is soaring and it's having an adverse impact on the economy.
   Source: CNN, July 16, 2008
   Explain the effect of a rise in the price level on equilibrium expenditure.

Guided Solutions to Practice Problems

1. Figure 1 shows the three *AE* curves and the three levels of equilibrium expenditure. When the price level is 90, equilibrium expenditure is \$4 trillion. When the price level is 100, equilibrium expenditure is \$3 trillion. When the price level is 110, equilibrium expenditure is \$2 trillion.
2. Table 2 shows the aggregate demand schedule, and Figure 2 shows the aggregate demand curve.
3. A rise in the price level decreases consumption expenditure, which decreases aggregate planned expenditure and shifts the *AE* curve downward. Equilibrium expenditure decreases.

FIGURE 1

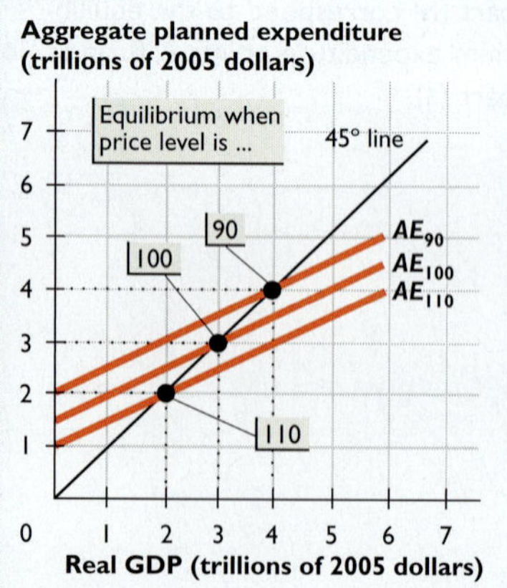

TABLE 2

Price level	Real GDP demanded (trillions of 2005 dollars)
90	4
100	3
110	2

FIGURE 2

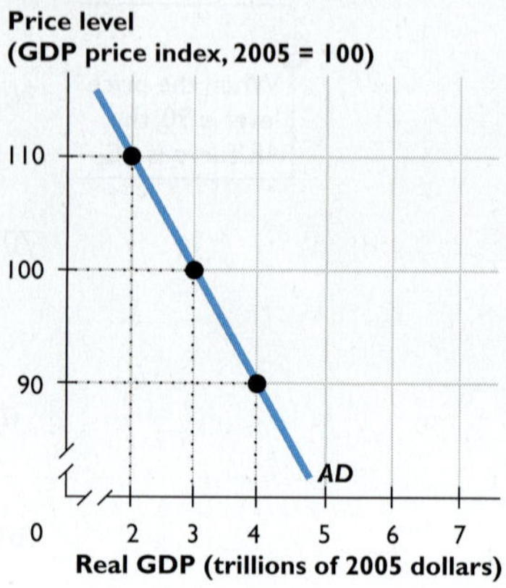

CHAPTER SUMMARY

Key Points

1 **Distinguish between autonomous expenditure and induced expenditure and explain how real GDP influences expenditure plans.**

- Autonomous expenditure is the sum of the components of aggregate expenditure that real GDP does not influence directly.
- Induced expenditure is the sum of the components of aggregate expenditure that real GDP influences.
- Consumption expenditure varies with disposable income and real GDP and depends on the marginal propensity to consume.
- Imports vary with real GDP and depend on the marginal propensity to import.

2 **Explain how real GDP adjusts to achieve equilibrium expenditure.**

- Actual aggregate expenditure equals real GDP, but when aggregate planned expenditure differs from real GDP, firms have unplanned inventory changes.
- If aggregate planned expenditure exceeds real GDP, firms increase production and real GDP increases. If real GDP exceeds aggregate planned expenditure, firms decrease production and real GDP decreases.
- Real GDP changes until aggregate planned expenditure equals real GDP.

3 **Explain the expenditure multiplier.**

- When autonomous expenditure changes, equilibrium expenditure changes by a larger amount: There is a multiplier.
- The multiplier is greater than 1 because a change in autonomous expenditure changes induced expenditure.
- The larger the marginal propensity to consume, the larger is the multiplier.
- Income taxes and imports make the multiplier smaller.

4 **Derive the *AD* curve from equilibrium expenditure.**

- The *AD* curve is the relationship between the quantity of real GDP demanded and the price level when all other influences on expenditure plans remain the same.
- The quantity of real GDP demanded on the *AD* curve is the equilibrium real GDP when aggregate planned expenditure equals real GDP.

Key Terms

myeconlab

Work these problems in Chapter 14 Study Plan to get instant feedback.

TABLE 1

Disposable income	Saving
(trillions of dollars)	
0	−5
10	−3
20	−1
30	1
40	3
50	5

CHAPTER CHECKPOINT

Study Plan Problems and Applications

Table 1 shows disposable income and saving in an economy. Use Table 1 to answer Problems **1** and **2**.

1. Calculate consumption expenditure at each level of disposable income. Over what range of disposable income is there dissaving? Estimate the level of disposable income at which saving is zero.

2. Calculate the marginal propensity to consume. If wealth increases by $10 trillion, in which direction will the consumption function change?

Table 2 shows real GDP, *Y*, consumption expenditure, *C*, investment, *I*, government expenditure on goods and services, *G*, exports, *X*, imports, *M*, and aggregate planned expenditure, *AE*, in millions of dollars. Taxes are constant. Use Table 2 to work Problems **3**, **4**, and **5**.

TABLE 2

	Planned expenditure					
Y	*C*	*I*	*G*	*X*	*M*	*AE*
0	2.0	1.75	1.0	1.25	0	6.0
2	**Q**	1.75	1.0	1.25	0.4	6.8
4	4.4	**R**	1.0	1.25	0.8	7.6
6	5.6	1.75	**S**	1.25	1.2	8.4
8	6.8	1.75	1.0	**T**	1.6	9.2
10	8.0	1.75	1.0	1.25	**U**	10.0
12	9.2	1.75	1.0	1.25	2.4	**V**

3. Find the value of Q, R, S, T, U, and V.

4. Calculate the marginal propensity to consume and the marginal propensity to import. What is equilibrium expenditure?

5. If investment crashes to $0.55 million but nothing else changes, what is equilibrium expenditure and what is the multiplier?

6. Figure 1 shows aggregate planned expenditure when the price level is 100. When the price level increases to 110, aggregate planned expenditure changes by $0.5 trillion. What is the quantity of real GDP demanded when the price level is 100 and 110?

FIGURE 1

Aggregate planned expenditure (trillions of 2005 dollars)

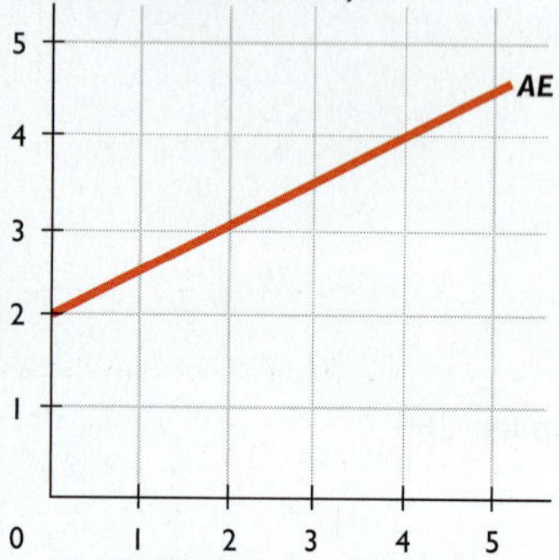

Real GDP (trillions of 2005 dollars)

Business spending looks up

Producers of equipment such as the bulldozer maker Caterpillar Inc. and hydraulic-parts maker Parker Hannifin Corp. say that there is an upturn in spending by businesses with companies raising their investment plans.

Source: *Wall Street Journal*, October 21, 2009

Use this information to work Problems **7** and **8**.

7. Explain how the increase in planned investment at a constant price level changes equilibrium expenditure.

8. What determines the increase in aggregate demand resulting from an increase in business investment?

Instructor Assignable Problems and Applications

Your instructor can assign these problems as homework, a quiz, or a test in **MyEconLab**.

1. The output gap in the second quarter of 2009 was \$0.8 trillion. How much fiscal stimulus would be required to close the output gap if the multiplier was as large as the Obama team believes? How much fiscal stimulus would be required if the multiplier was as large as Robert Barro believes?

Table 1 shows disposable income and consumption expenditure in an economy. Use Table 1 to work Problems 2 and 3.

2. Calculate saving at each level of disposable income. Over what range of disposable income does consumption expenditure exceed disposable income? Calculate autonomous consumption expenditure.
3. Calculate the marginal propensity to consume. At what level of disposable income will saving be zero? If expected future income increases, in which direction will the consumption function change?

TABLE 1

Disposable income (billions of dollars)	Consumption expenditure (billions of dollars)
200	350
400	500
600	650
800	800
1,000	950

Use the following information to work Problems 4 to 6.

In an economy with no exports and no imports, autonomous consumption is \$1 trillion, the marginal propensity to consume is 0.8, investment is \$5 trillion, and government expenditure on goods and services is \$4 trillion. Taxes are \$4 trillion and do not vary with real GDP.

4. If real GDP is \$30 trillion, calculate disposable income, consumption expenditure, and aggregate planned expenditure. What is equilibrium expenditure?
5. If real GDP is \$30 trillion, explain the process that takes the economy to equilibrium expenditure. If real GDP is \$40 trillion, explain the process that takes the economy to equilibrium expenditure.
6. If investment increases by \$0.5 trillion, calculate the change in equilibrium expenditure and the multiplier.

Use the following information to work Problems 7 and 8.

Figure 1 shows the aggregate demand curve in an economy. Suppose that aggregate planned expenditure increases by \$0.75 trillion for each \$1 trillion increase in real GDP.

7. If investment increases by \$1 trillion, calculate the change in the quantity of real GDP demanded if the price level is 100.
8. Compare the shift of the *AD* curve with the \$1 trillion increase in investment. Explain the magnitude of the shift of the *AD* curve.

FIGURE 1

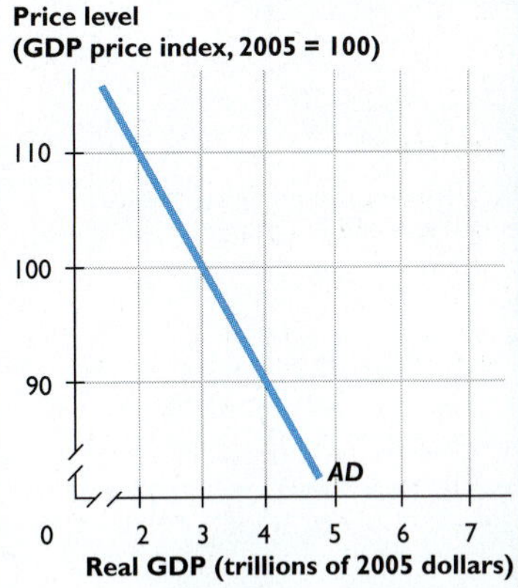

9. **Federal deficit hits record \$1.42 trillion**

   The 2009 federal budget deficit of \$1.42 trillion is more than three times as large as the deficit in any other single year. In September, the government spent \$46.6 billion more than it collected in tax revenue. The 2008 budget deficit was \$459 billion.

   Source: *USA Today*, October 16, 2009

   By how much did real GDP increase as a result of the government's additional \$46.6 billion of expenditure if the multiplier is what the Obama team believed it to be?

10. It is 2000 and the Japanese economy is in a recession. Economists suggested that the Japanese government increase its expenditure on goods and services but not change taxes. Explain how such a policy change would influence equilibrium expenditure. Would such a policy change help to turn the economy from recession to expansion?

Table 2 shows real GDP, *Y*, consumption expenditure, *C*, investment, *I*, government expenditure on goods and services, *G*, exports, *X*, imports, *M*, and aggregate planned expenditure, *AE*, in trillions of dollars. Taxes are constant. Use Table 2 to work Problems **11** to **14**.

TABLE 2

	Planned expenditure					
Y	***C***	***I***	***G***	***X***	***M***	***AE***
0	0.4	1.4	0.4	1.0	0	3.2
2	2.0	1.4	0.4	1.0	0.4	**T**
4	3.6	1.4	0.4	1.0	0.8	5.6
6	5.2	1.4	0.4	1.0	**S**	6.8
8	6.8	**R**	0.4	1.0	1.6	8.0
10	**Q**	1.4	0.4	1.0	2.0	9.2
12	10.0	1.4	0.4	1.0	2.4	10.4

11. Find the value of Q, R, S, and T.

12. Calculate autonomous expenditure and induced expenditure when real GDP is $4 trillion.

13. Calculate the marginal propensity to consume, the marginal propensity to import, and equilibrium expenditure.

14. If government expenditure increases to $1.2 trillion but other things remain the same, what is equilibrium expenditure and what is the multiplier?

Use the following information to work Problems **15** and **16**.

It is 2012, and real GDP in the U.S. economy is in an expansion phase of the business cycle. Consumption expenditure and other components of aggregate expenditure are increasing.

15. Explain how these events will influence the U.S. consumption function, the U.S. saving function, and the U.S. aggregate expenditure curve.

16. Explain how these events will influence equilibrium expenditure and the quantity of real GDP demanded in the United States.

17. Zimbabwe is in a deep recession. Use the aggregate expenditure model to illustrate the state of the economy. Then Zimbabwe's new platinum mine starts production and its exports increase. Explain how the increase in exports will influence Zimbabwe's aggregate expenditure and equilibrium expenditure.

18. In an economy in which the marginal propensity to consume is 0.7, real GDP increased by $11.2 trillion in 2009 while inventories fell by $13.4 billion, less than the fall of $16.6 billion in 2008. Describe the process that is going on in this economy: As real GDP grows, inventories continue to fall but at a slower pace.

Can we have low unemployment *and* low inflation?

Or must we pay for lower inflation with higher unemployment?

The Short-Run Policy Tradeoff

15

CHAPTER CHECKLIST

When you have completed your study of this chapter, you will be able to

1. Describe the short-run tradeoff between inflation and unemployment.
2. Distinguish between the short-run and the long-run Phillips curves and describe the shifting tradeoff between inflation and unemployment.
3. Explain how the Fed can influence the expected inflation rate and how expected inflation influences the short-run tradeoff.

15.1 THE SHORT-RUN PHILLIPS CURVE

Short-run Phillips curve
A curve that shows the relationship between the inflation rate and the unemployment rate when the natural unemployment rate and the expected inflation rate remain constant.

The **short-run Phillips curve** is a curve that shows the relationship between the inflation rate and the unemployment rate when the natural unemployment rate and the expected inflation rate remain constant.

Figure 15.1 illustrates the short-run Phillips curve. Here, the natural unemployment rate is 6 percent and the expected inflation rate is 3 percent a year. At full employment, the unemployment rate equals the natural unemployment rate and the inflation rate equals the expected inflation rate at point *B*. This point is the anchor point for the short-run Phillips curve.

In an expansion, the unemployment rate decreases and the inflation rate rises. For example, the economy might move to a point such as *A*, where the unemployment rate is 5 percent and the inflation rate is 4 percent a year.

In a recession, the unemployment rate increases and the inflation rate falls. For example, the economy might move to a point such as *C*, where the unemployment rate is 7 percent and the inflation rate is 2 percent a year.

The short-run Phillips curve presents a *tradeoff* between inflation and unemployment. Along a given short-run Phillips curve, a lower unemployment rate can be achieved only by paying the cost of a higher inflation rate, and a lower inflation rate can be achieved only by paying the cost of a higher unemployment rate. For example, in Figure 15.1, a decrease in the unemployment rate from 6 percent to 5 percent costs a 1-percentage point increase in the inflation rate from 3 percent a year to 4 percent a year.

FIGURE 15.1

A Short-Run Phillips Curve

myeconlab Animation

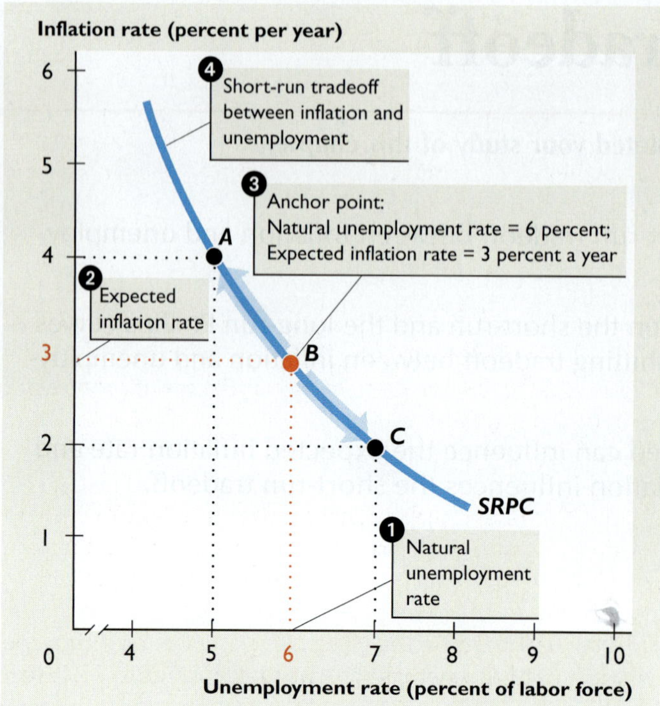

❶ If the natural unemployment rate is 6 percent, and ❷ the expected inflation rate is 3 percent a year, then ❸ point *B* is at full employment on a short-run Phillips curve.

❹ The short-run Phillips curve (*SRPC*) shows the tradeoff between inflation and unemployment at the given natural unemployment rate and expected inflation rate.

A higher unemployment rate brings a lower inflation rate, and a lower unemployment rate brings a higher inflation rate.

Aggregate Supply and the Short-Run Phillips Curve

The short-run Phillips curve is another way of looking at the upward-sloping aggregate supply curve that you learned about in Chapter 13—see pp. 326–329.

Both the short-run Phillips curve and the aggregate supply curve arise because the money wage rate is fixed in the short run.

Along an aggregate supply curve, the money wage rate is fixed. So when the price level rises, the *real wage rate* falls, and a fall in the real wage rate increases the quantity of labor employed and increases the quantity of real GDP supplied.

The events that we've just described also play out along a short-run Phillips curve. The rise in the price level means that the inflation rate has (perhaps temporarily) increased. The increase in the quantity of labor employed means a decrease in the number unemployed and a fall in the unemployment rate.

So a movement along an aggregate supply curve is equivalent to a movement along a short-run Phillips curve. Let's explore these connections between the aggregate supply curve and the short-run Phillips curve a bit more closely.

Unemployment and Real GDP

In a given period, with a fixed amount of capital and a given state of technology, real GDP depends on the quantity of labor employed. At full employment, the quantity of real GDP is *potential GDP* and the unemployment rate is the natural unemployment rate. If real GDP exceeds potential GDP, employment exceeds its full-employment level and the unemployment rate falls below the natural unemployment rate. Similarly, if real GDP is less than potential GDP, employment is less than its full-employment level and the unemployment rate rises above the natural unemployment rate.

The quantitative relationship between the unemployment rate and real GDP was first estimated by economist Arthur M. Okun and is called **Okun's Law**. Okun's Law states that for each percentage point that the unemployment rate is above the natural unemployment rate, real GDP is 2 percentage points below potential GDP. For example, if the natural unemployment rate is 6 percent and potential GDP is $10 trillion, then when the actual unemployment rate is 7 percent, real GDP is $9.8 trillion—98 percent of potential GDP, or 2 percentage points below potential GDP. And when the actual unemployment rate is 5 percent, real GDP is $10.2 trillion—102 percent of potential GDP, or 2 percentage points above potential GDP. Table 15.1 summarizes this relationship.

Okun's Law
For each percentage point that the unemployment rate is above the natural unemployment rate, real GDP is 2 percentage points below potential GDP.

TABLE 15.1

	Unemployment rate (percent)	Real GDP (trillions of 2005 dollars)
A	5	10.2
B	6	10.0
C	7	9.8

Inflation and the Price Level

The inflation rate is the percentage change in the price level. So starting from last period's price level, the higher the inflation rate, the higher is the current period's price level. Suppose that last year, the price level was 100. If the inflation rate is 2 percent, the price level rises to 102; if the inflation rate is 3 percent, the price level rises to 103; and if the inflation rate is 4 percent, the price level rises to 104.

With these relationships between the unemployment rate and real GDP (in Table 15.1) and between the inflation rate and the price level, we can establish the connection between the short-run Phillips curve and the aggregate supply curve. Figure 15.2 shows this connection.

First suppose that in the current year, real GDP equals potential GDP and the unemployment rate equals the natural unemployment rate. In Figure 15.2, real

GDP is $10 trillion and the unemployment rate is 6 percent. The economy is at point *B* on the short-run Phillips curve in part (a) and point *B* on the aggregate supply curve in part (b). The inflation rate is 3 percent a year (its expected rate) in part (a), and the price level is 103 (also its expected level) in part (b).

Next suppose that instead of being at full employment, the economy is above full employment with real GDP of $10.2 trillion at point *A* on the aggregate supply curve in Figure 15.2(b). In this case, the unemployment rate is 5 percent in Table 15.1 and the economy is at point *A* on the short-run Phillips curve in Figure 15.2(a). The inflation rate is 4 percent a year (higher than expected) in part (a), and the price level is 104 (also higher than expected) in part (b).

Finally, suppose that the economy is below full employment with real GDP of $9.8 trillion at point C on the aggregate supply curve in Figure 15.2(b). In this case, the unemployment rate is 7 percent in Table 15.1 and the economy is at point C on the short-run Phillips curve in Figure 15.2(a). The inflation rate is 2 percent a year (lower than expected) in part (a), and the price level is 102 (also lower than expected) in part (b).

FIGURE 15.2

The Short-Run Phillips Curve and the Aggregate Supply Curve

myeconlab Animation

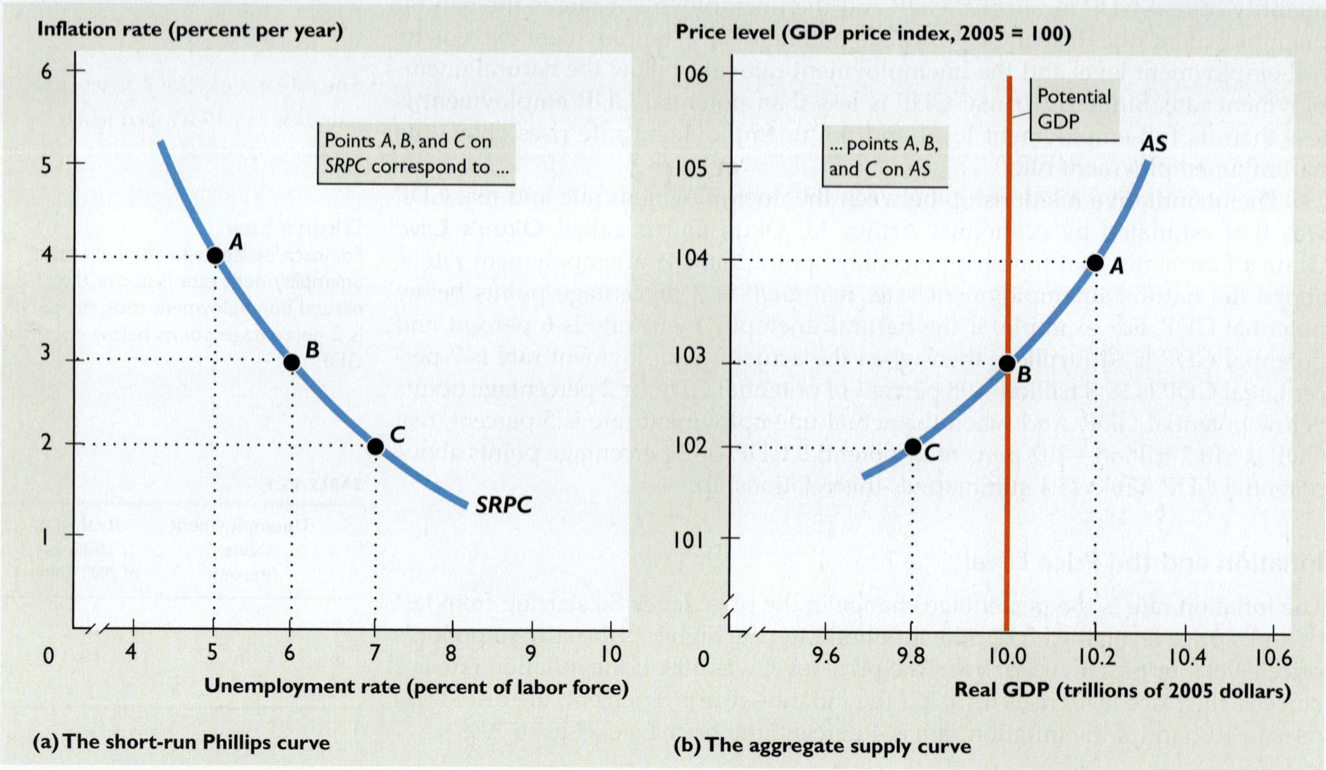

Point *A* on the Phillips curve corresponds to point *A* on the aggregate supply curve: The unemployment rate is 5 percent and the inflation rate is 4 percent a year in part (a), and real GDP is $10.2 trillion and the price level is 104 in part (b).

Point *B* on the Phillips curve corresponds to point *B* on the aggregate supply curve: The unemployment rate is 6 percent and the inflation rate is 3 percent a year in part (a), and real GDP is $10 trillion and the price level is 103 in part (b).

Point *C* on the Phillips curve corresponds to point *C* on the aggregate supply curve: The unemployment rate is 7 percent and the inflation rate is 2 percent a year in part (a), and real GDP is $9.8 trillion and the price level is 102 in part (b).

Aggregate Demand Fluctuations

A decrease in aggregate demand that brings a movement down along the aggregate supply curve from point *B* to point *C* lowers the price level and decreases real GDP. That same decrease in aggregate demand brings a movement down along the Phillips curve from point *B* to point *C*.

Similarly, an increase in aggregate demand that brings a movement up along the aggregate supply curve from point *B* to point *A* raises the price level and increases real GDP relative to what they would have been. That same increase in aggregate demand brings a movement up along the Phillips curve from point *B* to point *A*.

EYE on the GLOBAL ECONOMY

Inflation and Unemployment

The Phillips curve is so named because New Zealand economist A.W. (Bill) Phillips discovered the relationship in about 100 years of unemployment and wage inflation data for the United Kingdom.

The figure shows data on inflation and unemployment in the United Kingdom over most of the twentieth century—1900 to 1997. The data reveal no neat, tight tradeoff. The short-run tradeoff shifts around a great deal.

The highest inflation rate did not occur at the lowest unemployment rate, and the lowest inflation rate did not occur at the highest unemployment rate. But the lowest unemployment rate in 1917 did bring a high inflation rate. And the highest unemployment rate during the Great Depression of the 1930s brought a gently falling price level.

A.W. (Bill) Phillips

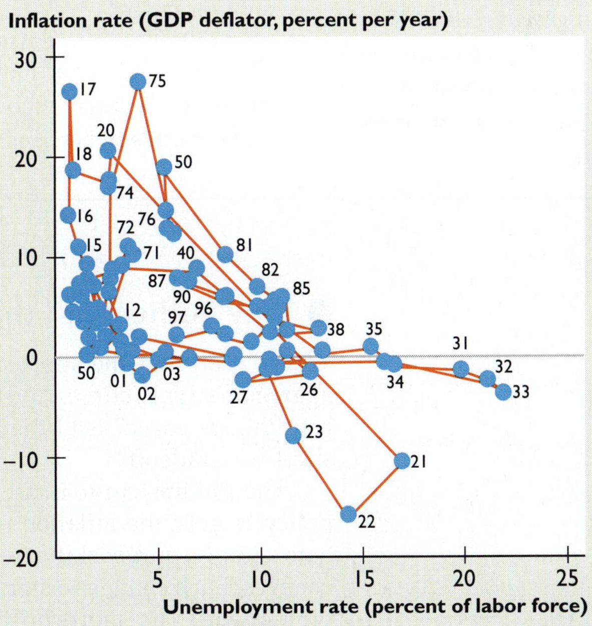

SOURCE: Michael Parkin, "Unemployment, Inflation, and Monetary Policy," *Canadian Journal of Economics*, November 1998.

EYE on the PAST

The U.S. Phillips Curve

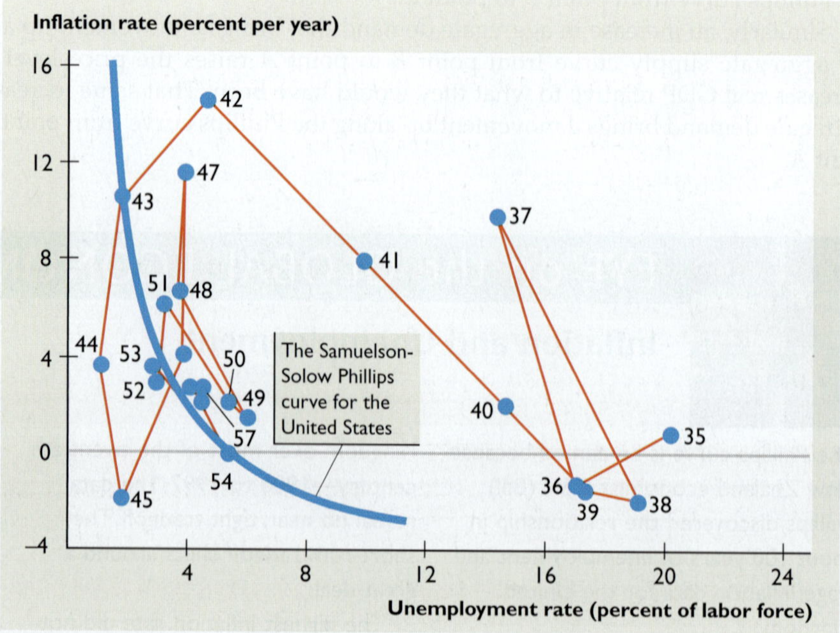

Source of data: Paul A. Samuelson and Robert M. Solow, "Problem of Achieving and Maintaining a Stable Price Level, Analytical Aspects of Anti-Inflation Policy." *American Economic Review*, 50(2), May 1960.

Phillips made his discovery in 1958, two years before the election of John F. Kennedy as President of the United States. Very soon thereafter, two young American economists, Paul A. Samuelson and Robert M. Solow, both at MIT and eager to help the new Kennedy administration to pursue a low-unemployment strategy, looked for a Phillips curve in the U.S. data. The figure shows what they found: The red line joining the blue dots shows no recognizable relationship between inflation and unemployment for the 20 or so years that they studied.

Giving more weight to the 1950s experience, Samuelson and Solow proposed the Phillips curve shown in the figure. They believed that the U.S. Phillips curve provided support for the then growing view that the new Kennedy administration could pursue a low unemployment policy with only a moderate rise in the inflation rate.

As the 1960s unfolded, the Samuelson-Solow version of the Phillips curve began to look like a permanent tradeoff between inflation and unemployment. But in the late 1960s and early 1970s, the relationship disappeared in the face of rising inflation expectations.

Why Bother with the Phillips Curve?

You've seen that the short-run Phillips curve is another way of looking at the aggregate supply curve. And you might be wondering, why bother with the short-run Phillips curve? Isn't the aggregate supply curve adequate for describing the short-run tradeoff?

The Phillips curve is useful for two reasons. First, it focuses directly on two policy targets: the inflation rate and the unemployment rate. Second, the aggregate supply curve shifts whenever the money wage rate or potential GDP changes. Such changes occur every day, so the aggregate supply curve is not a stable tradeoff. The short-run Phillips curve isn't a stable tradeoff either, but it is more stable than the aggregate supply curve. The short-run Phillips curve shifts only when the natural unemployment rate changes or when the expected inflation rate changes.

CHECKPOINT 15.1

Describe the short-run tradeoff between inflation and unemployment.

myeconlab

Work these problems in Study Plan 15.1 to get instant feedback.

Practice Problems

Table 1 describes five possible outcomes for 2010, depending on the level of aggregate demand in that year. Potential GDP is $10 trillion, and the natural unemployment rate is 5 percent. Use Table 1 to work Problems **1** to **5**.

1. Calculate the inflation rate for each possible outcome.
2. Use Okun's Law to find real GDP at each unemployment rate in Table 1.
3. What are the expected price level and the expected inflation rate in 2010?
4. Plot the short-run Phillips curve for 2010. Mark the points *A*, *B*, *C*, *D*, and *E* that correspond to the data in Table 1 and that you have calculated.
5. Plot the aggregate supply curve for 2010. Mark the points *A*, *B*, *C*, *D*, and *E* that correspond to the data in Table 1.
6. **Inflation at lowest rate in 5 years**
   In September, inflation in the United Kingdom fell to 1.1% a year, its lowest in 5 years. Analysts expected an inflation rate of 1.3% a year.
   Source: *The New York Times*, October 13, 2009

   With the unemployment rate at 8 percent and the natural unemployment rate at 6 percent, sketch the short-run Phillips curve and mark on your graph the point which shows the situation in September. Label the point *A*.

TABLE 1

	Price level (2009 = 100)	Unemployment rate (percentage)
A	102.5	9
B	105.0	6
C	106.0	5
D	107.5	4
E	110.0	3

FIGURE 1

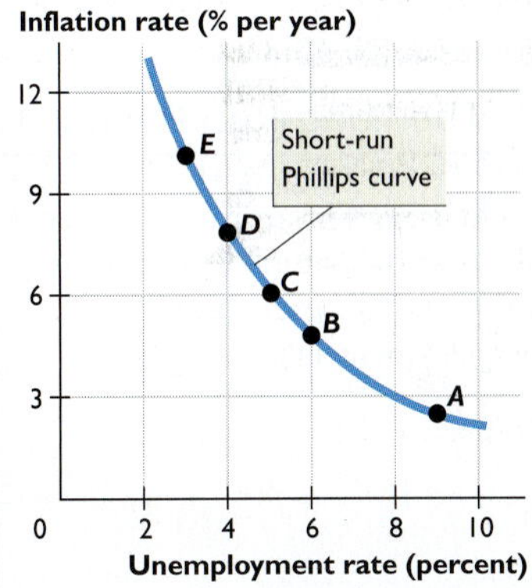

Guided Solutions to Practice Problems

1. The inflation rate equals the price level minus 100. So for *A*, the inflation rate is $102.5 - 100 = 2.5$. Calculate the other inflation rates in the same way.
2. Okun's law is that the output gap $= -2 \times (U - U^*)$ percent, where U is the unemployment rate and U^* is the natural unemployment rate. So for *A*, the output gap $= -2 \times (9 - 5) = -8$, which means that real GDP is 8 percent below potential GDP and equals $9.2 trillion. Calculate the other levels of real GDP in the same way.
3. The expected price level is 106 and the expected inflation rate is 6 percent—row *C* at full employment.
4. Plot the inflation rate (Problem 1) against the unemployment rate (Table 1) to get the short-run Phillips curve (Figure 1).
5. Plot the price level (Table 1) against real GDP (Problem 2) to get the aggregate supply curve (Figure 2).
6. With the natural unemployment rate of 6 percent and expected inflation of 1.3 percent the Phillips curve passes through point *B* on Figure 3. Point *A* lies on the Phillips curve at the unemployment rate of 8 percent and actual inflation rate of 1.1 percent a year.

FIGURE 2

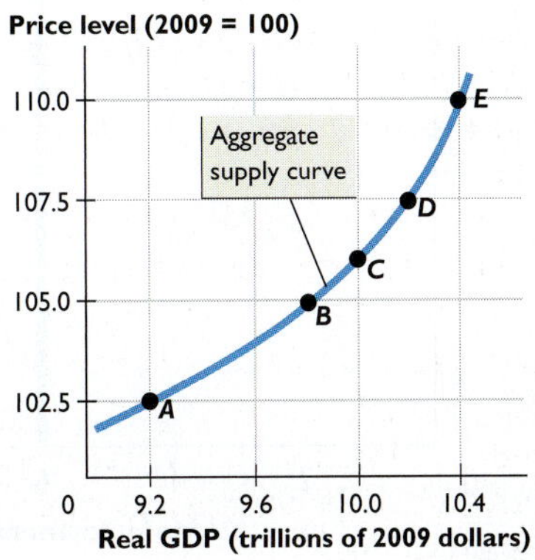

FIGURE 3

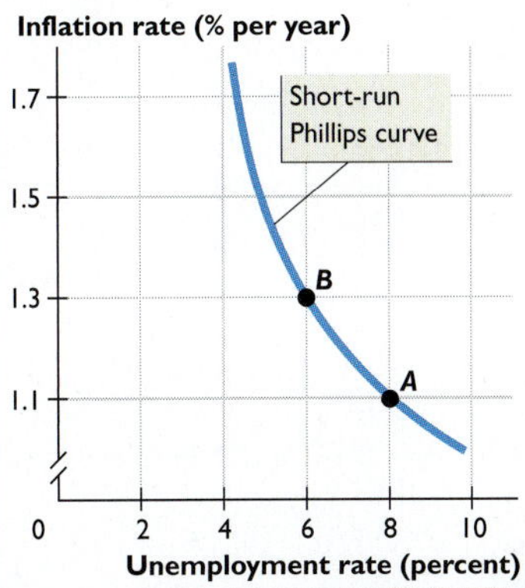

15.2 SHORT-RUN AND LONG-RUN PHILLIPS CURVES

The short-run Phillips curve shows the *tradeoff* between inflation and unemployment when the natural unemployment rate and expected inflation rate remain the same. Changes in the natural unemployment rate and the expected inflation rate change the short-run tradeoff and changes in the expected inflation rate give rise to a *long-run* Phillips curve that we'll now examine.

The Long-Run Phillips Curve

Long-run Phillips curve
The vertical line that shows the relationship between inflation and unemployment when the economy is at full employment.

The **long-run Phillips curve** shows the relationship between inflation and unemployment when the economy is at full employment. At full employment, the unemployment rate is the *natural unemployment rate*, so on the long-run Phillips curve, there is only one possible unemployment rate: the natural unemployment rate.

In contrast, the inflation rate can take on any value at full employment. You learned in Chapter 12 (pp. 310–313) that at full employment, for a given real GDP growth rate, the greater the money growth rate, the greater is the inflation rate.

This description of the economy at full employment tells us the properties of the long-run Phillips curve: It is a vertical line located at the natural unemployment rate. In Figure 15.3, the long-run Phillips curve is *LRPC* along which the unemployment rate equals the natural unemployment rate and any inflation rate is possible.

FIGURE 15.3
The Long-Run Phillips Curve

myeconlab Animation

The long-run Phillips curve is a vertical line at the natural unemployment rate. In the long run, there is no unemployment–inflation tradeoff.

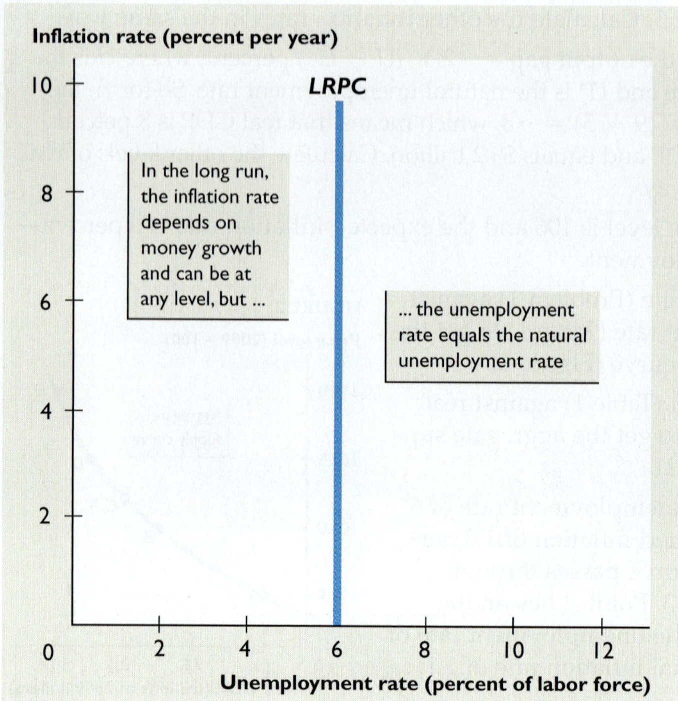

Expected Inflation

The **expected inflation rate** is the inflation rate that people forecast and use to set the money wage rate and other money prices. Suppose there is full employment and McDonald's servers earn $7 an hour. With no inflation, a money wage rate of $7 an hour keeps the market for servers in equilibrium. But with 10 percent inflation, a constant money wage rate means a falling real wage rate and a shortage of servers. Now, a 10 percent rise in the money wage rate to $7.70 is needed to keep the market for servers in equilibrium. If McDonald's and everyone else expect 10 percent inflation, the money wage rate will rise by 10 percent to prevent a labor shortage from arising.

If expectations about the inflation rate turn out to be correct, the price level rises by the 10 percent expected and the real wage rate remains constant at its full-employment equilibrium level and unemployment remains at the natural unemployment rate.

Because the actual inflation rate equals the expected inflation rate at full employment, we can interpret the long-run Phillips curve as the relationship between inflation and unemployment when the inflation rate equals the expected inflation rate.

Figure 15.4 shows short-run Phillips curves for two expected inflation rates. A short-run Phillips curve shows the tradeoff between inflation and unemployment at *a particular expected inflation rate.* When the expected inflation rate changes, the short-run Phillips curve shifts to intersect the long-run Phillips curve at the new expected inflation rate.

Expected inflation rate
The inflation rate that people forecast and use to set the money wage rate and other money prices.

FIGURE 15.4

Short-Run and Long-Run Phillips Curves

myeconlab Animation

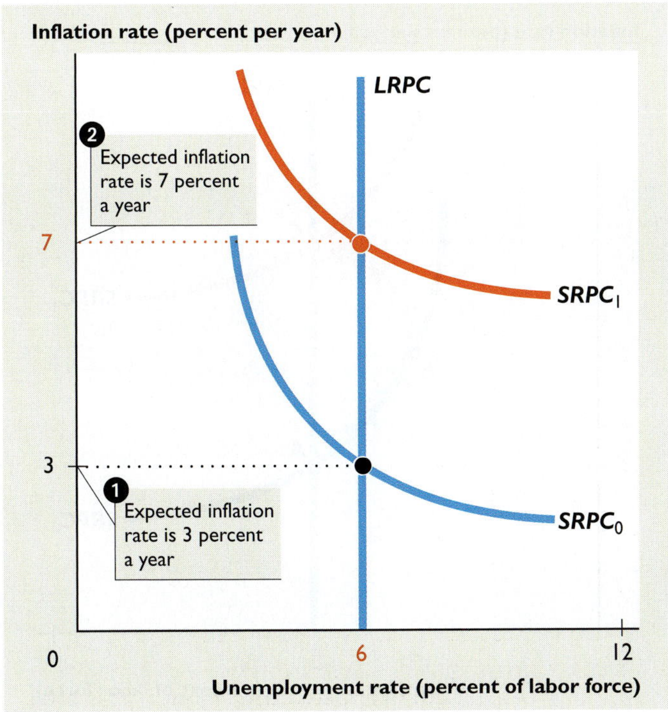

If the natural unemployment rate is 6 percent, the long-run Phillips curve is *LRPC*.

1. If the expected inflation rate is 3 percent a year, the short-run Phillips curve is $SRPC_0$.
2. If the expected inflation rate is 7 percent a year, the short-run Phillips curve is $SRPC_1$.

In Figure 15.4, when the expected inflation rate is 3 percent a year, the short-run Phillips curve is $SRPC_0$, and when the expected inflation rate is 7 percent a year, the short-run Phillips curve is $SRPC_1$.

The Natural Rate Hypothesis

Natural rate hypothesis
The proposition that when the inflation rate changes, the unemployment rate changes *temporarily* and eventually returns to the natural unemployment rate.

The **natural rate hypothesis** is the proposition that when the inflation rate changes, the unemployment rate changes *temporarily* and eventually returns to the natural unemployment rate. The temporary change in the unemployment rate occurs because the real wage rate changes, which leads to a change in the quantity of labor demanded. The unemployment rate returns to the natural rate because eventually, the money wage rate changes to catch up with the change in the price level and return the real wage rate to its full-employment level.

Figure 15.5 illustrates the natural rate hypothesis. Initially, the inflation rate is 3 percent a year and the economy is at full employment, at point *A*. Then the quantity of money grows more rapidly, at a rate that will generate inflation at 7 percent a year in the long run. In the short run, with a fixed money wage rate, the real wage rate falls, the quantity of labor employed increases and the unemployment rate falls. The inflation rate rises to 5 percent a year, and the economy moves from point *A* to point *B*. When the higher inflation rate is expected, the money wage rate increases. As the expected inflation rate increases from 3 percent to 7 percent a year, the short-run Phillips curve shifts upward from $SRPC_0$ to $SRPC_1$. Inflation speeds up and the unemployment rate returns to the natural unemployment rate. In Figure 15.5, the economy moves from point *B* to point *C*.

FIGURE 15.5
The Natural Rate Hypothesis

myeconlab Animation

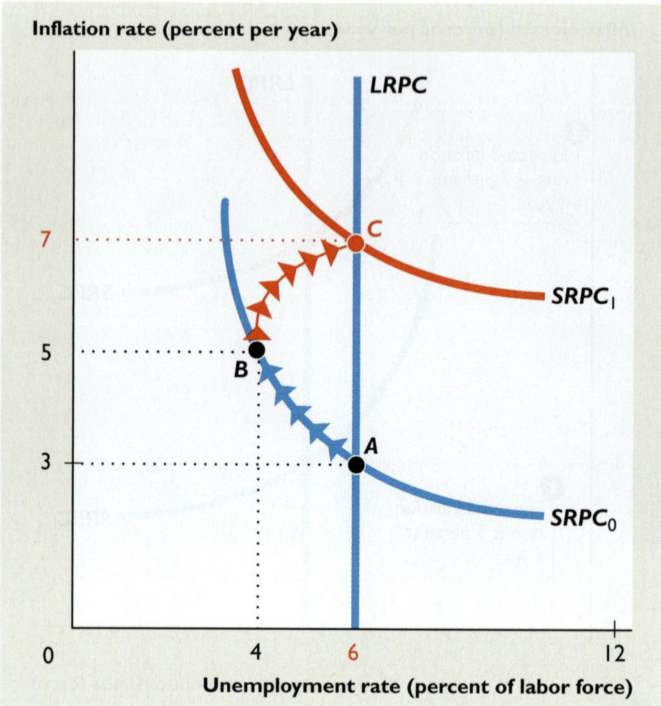

The inflation rate is 3 percent a year, and the economy is at full employment, at point *A*. Then the inflation rate increases.

In the short run, the money wage rate is fixed and the increase in the inflation rate brings a decrease in the unemployment rate—a movement along $SRPC_0$ to point *B*.

Eventually, the higher inflation rate is expected, the money wage rate rises, and the short-run Phillips curve shifts upward gradually to $SRPC_1$. At the higher expected inflation rate, unemployment returns to the natural unemployment rate—the natural rate hypothesis. The economy is at point *C*.

EYE on the PAST

A Live Test of the Natural Rate Hypothesis

The figure describes the U.S. economy from 1960 to 1971 and shows that the natural rate hypothesis describes these years well.

The natural unemployment rate was around 6 percent, so the long-run Phillips curve, *LRPC,* was located at that unemployment rate.

At the beginning of the period, the inflation rate and the expected inflation rate were around 1 percent a year. The short-run Phillips curve was $SRPC_0$.

Through 1966, the expected inflation rate remained at 1 percent a year but the actual inflation rate edged upward and the unemployment rate decreased below the natural unemployment rate. The economy moved up along $SRPC_0$ from point *A* to point *B*.

Then, from 1967 through 1969, the inflation rate increased and so did the expected inflation rate. By 1969, the economy had moved to point *C*. By 1970, the expected inflation rate was around 5 percent a year and the short-run Phillips curve had shifted upward to $SRPC_1$. As the higher inflation rate came to be expected, the unemployment rate increased; by 1971, it had returned to the natural unemployment rate and the economy had moved to point *D*.

Notice the similarity between the actual events of this period and the natural rate hypothesis, which Figure 15.5 illustrates.

Edmund S. Phelps of Columbia University and Milton Friedman of the University of Chicago proposed the natural rate hypothesis and predicted these events *before* they occurred.

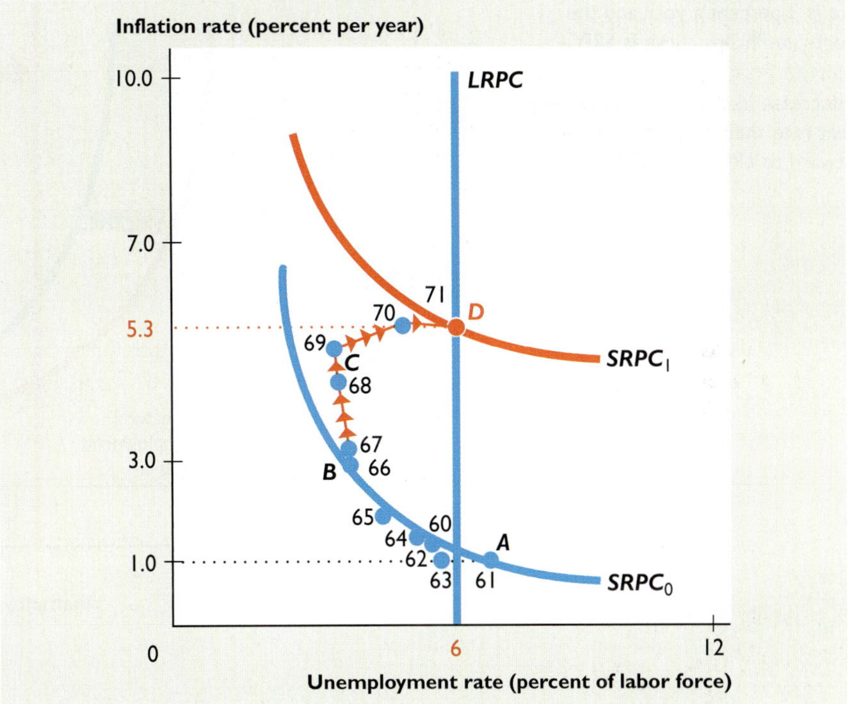

SOURCE OF DATA: Bureau of Labor Statistics and Bureau of Economic Analysis.

Changes in the Natural Unemployment Rate

If the natural unemployment rate changes, both the long-run Phillips curve and the short-run Phillips curve shift. When the natural unemployment rate increases, both the long-run Phillips curve and the short-run Phillips curve shift rightward; and when the natural unemployment rate decreases, both the long-run Phillips curve and the short-run Phillips curve shift leftward.

Figure 15.6 illustrates these changes. When the natural unemployment rate is 6 percent, the long-run Phillips curve is $LRPC_0$. If the expected inflation rate is 3 percent a year, the short-run Phillips curve is $SRPC_0$. A decrease in the natural

FIGURE 15.6

Changes in the Natural Unemployment Rate

myeconlab Animation

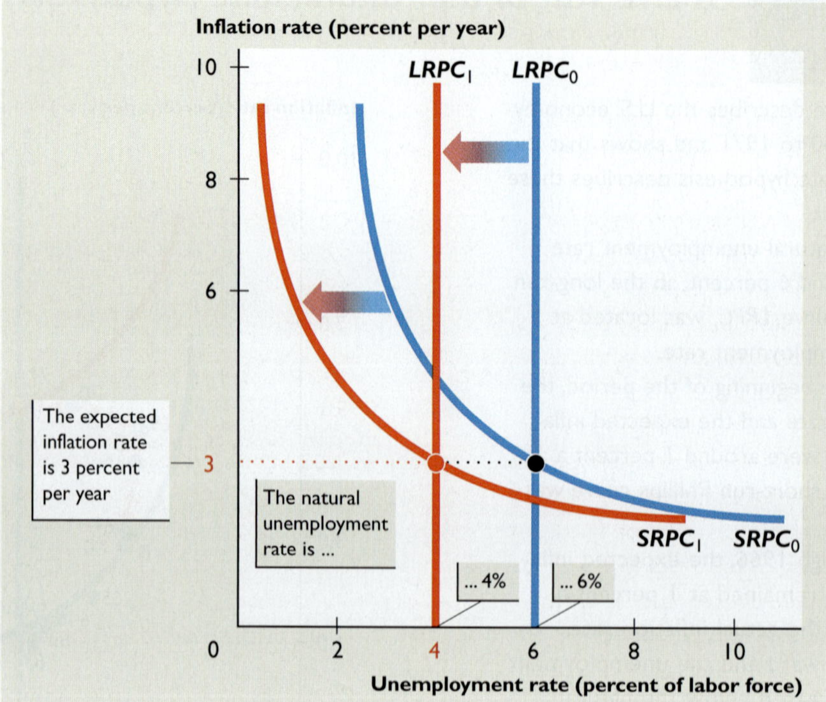

The natural unemployment rate is 6 percent, and the long-run Phillips curve is $LRPC_0$. The expected inflation rate is 3 percent a year, and the short-run Phillips curve is $SRPC_0$.

A decrease in the natural unemployment rate shifts both Phillips curves leftward to $LRPC_1$ and $SRPC_1$.

unemployment rate, with no change in the expected inflation rate, shifts both Phillips curves leftward to $LRPC_1$ and $SRPC_1$.

Have Changes in the Natural Unemployment Rate Changed the Tradeoff?

Changes in the natural unemployment rate have changed the tradeoff. According to the Congressional Budget Office, the natural unemployment rate increased from about 5 percent in 1950 to more than 6 percent in the mid-1970s and then decreased to 4.8 percent by 2000. It has been constant at this level through 2009.

You learned about the factors that influence the natural unemployment rate in Chapter 8 (pp. 204–209). Those factors divide into two groups: influences on job search and influences on job rationing. Job search is influenced by demographic change, unemployment compensation, and structural change. Job rationing arises from efficiency wages, the minimum wage, and union wages.

A bulge in the birth rate (known as the "baby boom") that occurred after World War II in the late 1940s and early 1950s, brought a bulge in the number of young people entering the labor force during the late 1960s and early 1970s. This bulge in the number of new entrants increased the amount of job search and increased the natural unemployment rate.

Structural change during the 1970s and 1980s, much of it a response to massive hikes in the world price of oil, also contributed to the increase in the natural unemployment rate during the 1970s and early 1980s.

EYE on the TRADEOFF

Can We Have Low Unemployment *and* Low Inflation?

The short-run Phillips curve describes the unemployment–inflation tradeoff that we face. In the short run, we can have low unemployment only if we permit the inflation rate to rise. And we can have low inflation only if we permit the unemployment rate to increase. But in the long run, we can improve that tradeoff.

We can have low unemployment if we can lower the natural unemployment rate, but that is hard to do.

We can have low inflation if we can lower the expected inflation rate. That, too, is hard to do, but it isn't as hard as lowering the natural unemployment rate. The expected inflation rate does change frequently and sometimes by large amounts.

The years 2000–2009 show how changes in the expected inflation rate change the short-run tradeoff.

During these years, the natural unemployment rate was constant at 4.8 percent, so the long-run Phillips curve remained fixed at *LRPC*.

The expected inflation rate was 1.5 percent a year in 2000 and 2001 and the short-run Phillips curve was $SRPC_0$.

The expected inflation rate then increased to 3.5 percent a year, where it remained until 2007, and the short-run Phillips curve shifted to $SRPC_1$.

In 2008, the expected inflation rate decreased to 1.5 percent a year and the short-run Phillips curve shifted back from $SRPC_1$ to $SRPC_0$. The tradeoff improved.

The next section explains how policy actions might lower the expected inflation rate and improve the tradeoff.

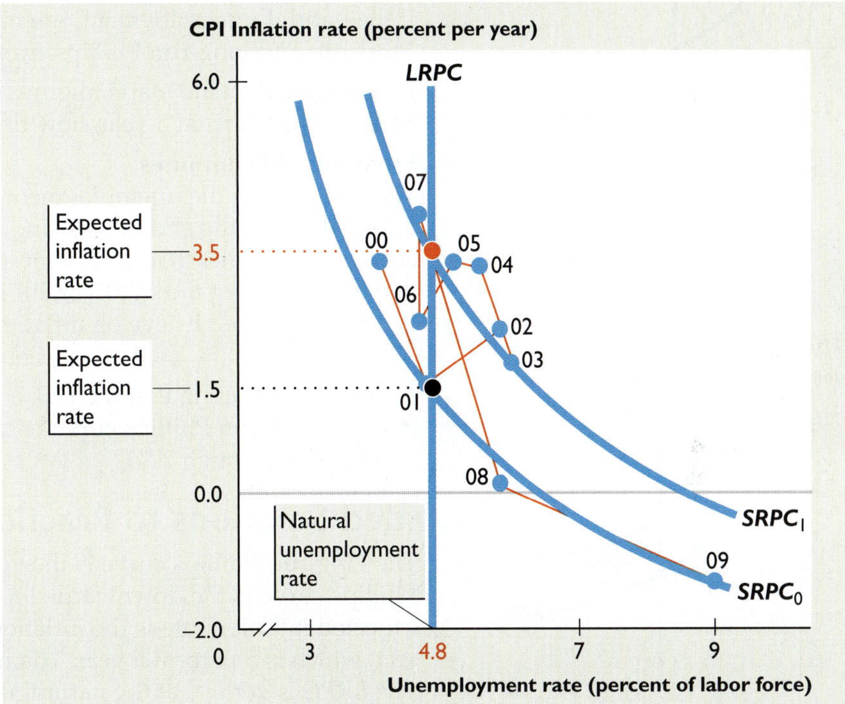

SOURCE OF DATA: Bureau of Labor Statistics and Congressional Budget Office.

As the baby boom generation approached middle age during the 1980s and 1990s, the number of new labor market entrants decreased and the natural unemployment rate decreased too. Also, during the 1990s, rapid technological change brought an increase in productivity and an increase in the demand for labor that shortened the time people spent in job search and lowered the natural unemployment rate yet further. During the 2000s, the natural unemployment rate remained steady.

The changes in the natural unemployment rate that we've just described shifted the short-run and long-run Phillips curves rightward during the 1960s and 1970s and shifted them leftward during the 1980s and 1990s.

myeconlab

Work these problems in Study Plan 15.2 to get instant feedback.

CHECKPOINT 15.2

Distinguish between the short-run and the long-run Phillips curves and describe the shifting tradeoff between inflation and unemployment.

Practice Problems

Use Figure 1, which shows a short-run Phillips curve and a long-run Phillips curve, to work Problems **1** to **4**.

1. Identify the curves and label them. What is the expected inflation rate and what is the natural unemployment rate?
2. If the expected inflation rate increases to 7.5 percent a year, show the new short-run and long-run Phillips curves.
3. If the natural unemployment rate increases to 8 percent, show the new short-run and long-run Phillips curves.
4. If aggregate demand starts to grow more rapidly and the inflation rate eventually hits 10 percent a year, how do unemployment and inflation change?
5. **From the Fed's minutes**

   The Fed expects the unemployment rate will drop from 9.8 percent today to 9.25 percent by the end of 2010 and to 8 percent by the end of 2011. Private economists predict that the unemployment rate won't drop to a more normal 5 or 6 percent until 2013 or 2014. Inflation should stay subdued, but the Fed needs to keep its eye on inflation expectations.

   Source: *The New York Times*, October 14, 2009

   Is the Fed predicting that the U.S. economy will move rightward or leftward along a short-run Phillips curve or that the short-run Phillips curve will shift up or down through 2011?

FIGURE 1

Guided Solutions to Practice Problems

1. The long-run Phillips curve is the vertical curve, *LRPC*, and the short-run Phillips curve is the downward-sloping curve, $SRPC_0$ (Figure 2). The expected inflation rate is the inflation rate at which *LRPC* and $SRPC_0$ intersect, which is 5 percent a year. The natural unemployment rate is 6 percent. The *LRPC* is vertical at the natural unemployment rate.
2. The short-run Phillips curve shifts upward, but the long-run Phillips curve does not change (Figure 2).
3. Both the short-run and long-run Phillips curves shift rightward (Figure 3).
4. Figure 4 shows that as expectations change, the inflation rate rises to 10 percent a year and unemployment falls and then gradually returns to its natural rate.
5. If inflation remains subdued and inflation expectations do not change, the economy is on a short-run Phillips curve to the right of the *LRPC* and is predicted to move leftward up along the *SRPC* toward the *LRPC*.

FIGURE 2

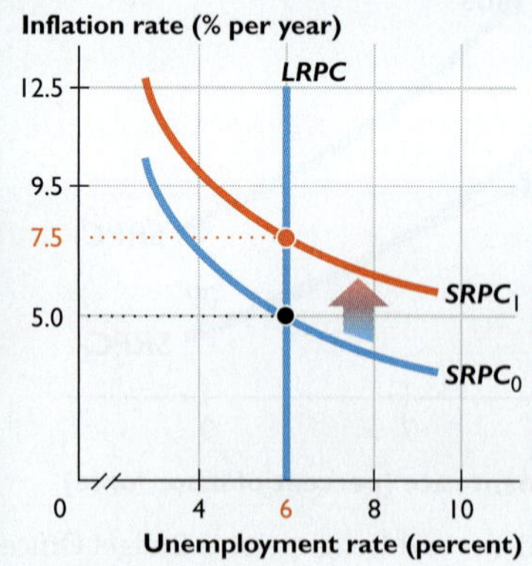

FIGURE 3

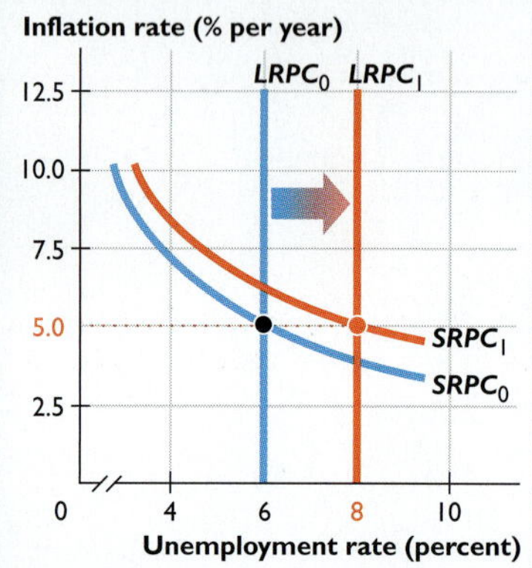

FIGURE 4

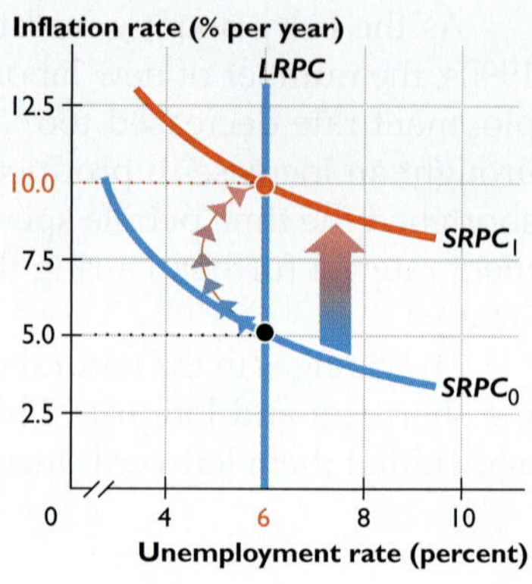

15.3 EXPECTED INFLATION

You've seen that expected inflation plays a big role in determining the position of the short-run tradeoff. When the expected inflation rate is low, as it was in 2000, the tradeoff is more favorable than when the expected inflation rate is high, as it was in 1980. The effect of expected inflation on the short-run tradeoff raises two questions:

- What determines the expected inflation rate?
- What can policy do to lower expected inflation?

What Determines the Expected Inflation Rate?

The *expected inflation rate* is the inflation rate that people forecast and use to set the money wage rate and other money prices. To forecast the inflation rate, people use the same basic method that they use to forecast other variables that affect their lives.

Data make up the first ingredient in forecasting—data about the past behavior of the phenomenon that we want to forecast. When people laid heavy bets that Tiger Woods would win the British Open in 2005, they based their forecast on the performance of Tiger and the other golfers in the months leading up to that event.

Science is the second ingredient in forecasting—the specific science that seeks to understand the phenomenon that we wish to forecast. If we want to know whether it is likely to rain tomorrow, we turn to the science of meteorology. Science is not a substitute for data. It is knowledge that tells people how to interpret data.

So to forecast inflation, people use data about past inflation and other relevant variables and the science of economics, which seeks to understand the forces that cause inflation.

You already know the relevant economics: the *AS-AD* model. You know that the money growth rate determines the growth of aggregate demand in the long run. And you know that the trend growth rate of real GDP is the growth rate of aggregate supply in the long run. So the trend money growth rate minus the trend real GDP growth rate determines the trend inflation rate.

The inflation rate fluctuates around its trend as the state of the economy changes over the business cycle. In an expansion, the inflation rate rises above trend, and in a recession, the inflation rate falls below trend as aggregate demand fluctuates to bring movements along the aggregate supply curve. And you know that the money growth rate is one of the influences on these aggregate demand fluctuations.

The Fed determines the money growth rate, so the major ingredient in a forecast of inflation is a forecast of the Fed's actions. Professional Fed watchers and economic forecasters use these ideas along with a lot of data and elaborate statistical models of the economy to forecast the inflation rate.

When all the relevant data and economic science are used to forecast inflation, the resulting forecast is called a **rational expectation**. The rational expectation of the inflation rate is a forecast based on the Fed's forecasted monetary policy along with forecasts of the other forces that influence aggregate demand and aggregate supply. But the dominant factor is the Fed's monetary policy.

Rational expectation
The forecast that results from the use of all the relevant data and economic science.

What Can Policy Do to Lower Expected Inflation?

If the Fed wants to lower the inflation rate, it can pursue two alternative lines of attack:

- A surprise inflation reduction
- A credible announced inflation reduction

A Surprise Inflation Reduction

In Figure 15.7, the economy is at full employment with inflation raging and expected to rage at 10 percent a year. Unemployment is at its natural rate, which is 6 percent. The economy is on its long-run Phillips curve, *LRPC*, and its short-run Phillips curve, $SRPC_0$, at point *A*.

No one is expecting the Fed to change its policy but the Fed does change its policy and starts to slow inflation to a target rate of 3 percent a year. The Fed raises interest rates and slows money growth. With no change in expected inflation, money wage rates continue to rise by the same amount as before but aggregate demand growth slows. The unemployment rate rises, and the inflation rate falls along $SRPC_0$. Gradually, the expected inflation rate falls and the short-run Phillips curve shifts downward toward $SRPC_1$. The Fed slows inflation but at the cost of recession. The economy follows the path of the red arrows—and unemployment remains above its natural rate until, eventually, the economy arrives at point *B*.

FIGURE 15.7

Slowing Inflation

myeconlab Animation

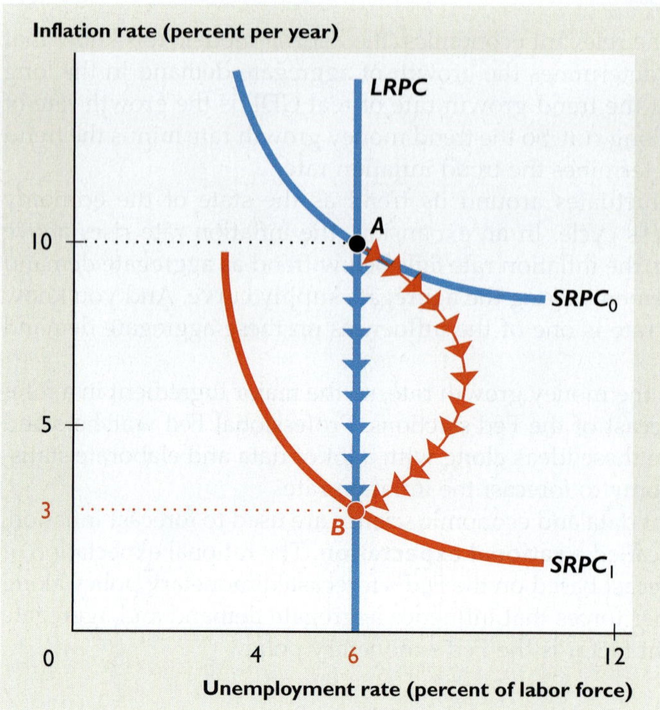

The economy is at point *A*. The natural unemployment rate is 6 percent, and inflation is 10 percent a year.

An unexpected slowdown in aggregate demand growth slows inflation and increases the unemployment rate as the economy slides down along $SRPC_0$. Eventually, the expected inflation rate falls and the short-run Phillips curve shifts toward $SRPC_1$ (red arrows). The unemployment rate remains above 6 percent through the adjustment to point *B*.

A credible, announced slowdown in aggregate demand growth lowers the expected inflation rate and shifts the short-run Phillips curve downward to $SRPC_1$ (blue arrows). Inflation slows to 3 percent a year, and unemployment remains at 6 percent as the economy moves along the *LRPC* curve to point *B*.

A Credible Announced Inflation Reduction

Suppose that instead of unexpectedly slowing inflation, the Fed announces its intention to bring the inflation rate down. Ahead of its action, the Fed convinces everyone that it has a credible plan, so its announcement is believed.

Because people believe that the Fed will lower the inflation rate, the expected inflation rate falls. And because the expected inflation rate falls, the rate of increase in the money wage rate slows.

The lower expected inflation rate shifts the short-run Phillips curve, in Figure 15.7, downward to $SRPC_1$. The inflation rate falls to 3 percent a year, while the unemployment rate remains at the natural rate of 6 percent. This announced inflation reduction lowers the inflation rate but with no accompanying loss of output or increase in unemployment. The economy moves directly from *A* to *B*.

Inflation Reduction in Practice

It was back in 1981 that the Fed was last faced with a high inflation rate, and to slow it, we paid a high price. The Fed's policy action was unexpected. Money wage rates had been set too high for the path that the Fed followed. The consequence was recession—a decrease in real GDP and increased unemployment. We followed a path like the red arrows in Figure 15.7. Because it is difficult to lower the inflation rate without bringing on a recession, the policy focus today is inflation avoidance. The Fed (and most economists) think that it is better to avoid inflation than to be faced with the challenge of curing it.

EYE on YOUR LIFE

The Short-Run Tradeoff in Your Life

The short-run tradeoff enters your life in three distinct ways:

1) It helps you to interpret and understand the current state of the U.S. economy.
2) It helps you to understand the policy decisions taken by the Fed.
3) It encourages you to take a stand on the relative weight that should be given to unemployment and inflation.

The Current State of the Economy

Consider the change in the U.S. unemployment rate and inflation rate over the past year. Did they change in the same direction or in opposite directions? Can you interpret the change as a movement along a short-run Phillips curve or as a shifting short-run Phillips curve? Can you think of reasons why the short-run Phillips curve might have shifted? Did the natural unemployment rate change? Did the expected inflation rate change?

Was your expected inflation rate the same as what people on the average expected?

The Fed's Recent Decisions

What has the Fed been doing to the interest rate over the past year? How do you think the changes in unemployment and inflation affected the Fed's policy decisions?

Unemployment or Inflation

You've seen that in the long run, there is no tradeoff between unemployment and inflation. But in the short run, there is a tradeoff. If the inflation rate is high, how much unemployment is worth putting up with, and for how long, to lower the inflation rate? Economists don't agree on the answer to this question. Some say that if inflation is too high, it must be lowered quickly. Some even say that no unemployment is worth enduring to lower inflation. What is your view? Which is worse, too much inflation or too much unemployment?

Work these problems in Study Plan 15.3 to get instant feedback.

CHECKPOINT 15.3

Explain how the Fed can influence the expected inflation rate and how expected inflation influences the short-run tradeoff.

Practice Problems

Figure 1 shows the Phillips curves. The current inflation rate is 5 percent a year. The Fed announces that it will slow the money growth rate so that inflation will fall to 2.5 percent a year. Use Figure 1 to work Problems **1** to **3**.

1. If no one believes the Fed and expected inflation remains at 5 percent a year, explain the effect of the Fed's action on inflation and unemployment next year.
2. If everyone believes the Fed, explain the effect of the Fed's action on inflation and unemployment next year.
3. If no one believes the Fed but the Fed keeps inflation at 2.5 percent for many years, explain the effect of the Fed's action on inflation and unemployment.
4. **FOMC Press Release, June 24, 2009**

   The FOMC anticipates a gradual resumption of sustainable growth in the context of price stability and substantial resource slack will keep inflation subdued for some time.

   Source: Board of Governors of the Federal Reserve System

   How might this press release influence the short-run Phillips curve? Where on that curve is the economy believed to be operating?

FIGURE 1

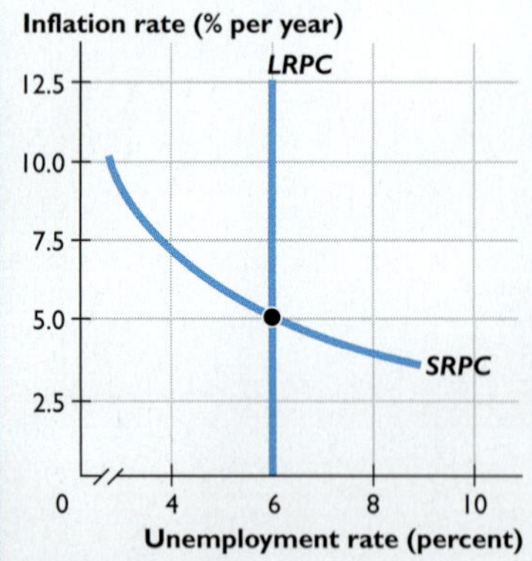

FIGURE 2

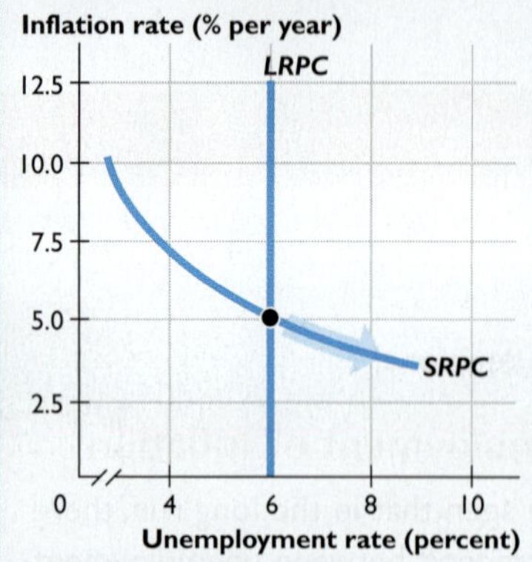

Guided Solutions to Practice Problems

1. The inflation rate falls and the unemployment rate rises as the economy moves down along its short-run Phillips curve (see Figure 2).
2. The inflation rate falls to 2.5 percent a year, and unemployment remains at 6 percent. People believe the Fed so expected inflation falls to 2.5 percent a year. The short-run Phillips curve shifts downward to $SRPC_1$ (Figure 3).
3. Initially, inflation falls below 5 percent a year and unemployment rises above 6 percent. The longer the Fed maintains this policy, the lower the expected inflation will be and the short-run Phillips curve will shift downward. The unemployment rate will decrease. Eventually, inflation will be 2.5 percent a year when the unemployment rate returns to 6 percent (Figure 4).
4. If the press release lowered inflation expectations, the short-run Phillips curve would shift downward and intersect the long-run Phillips curve at an expected inflation rate close to zero. The actual inflation rate is believed to be below the expected inflation rate and the unemployment rate to be above the natural rate.

FIGURE 3

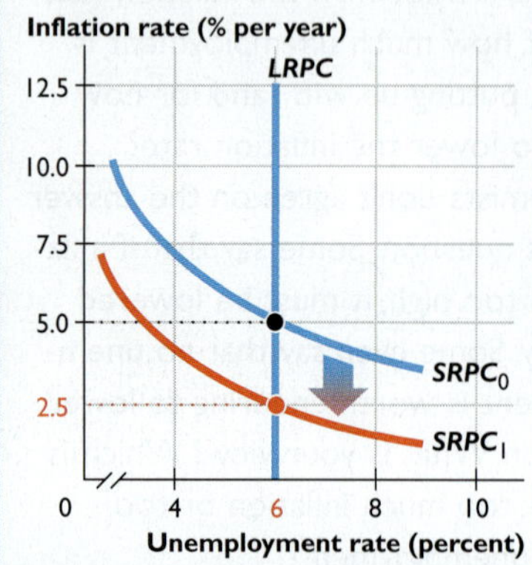

FIGURE 4

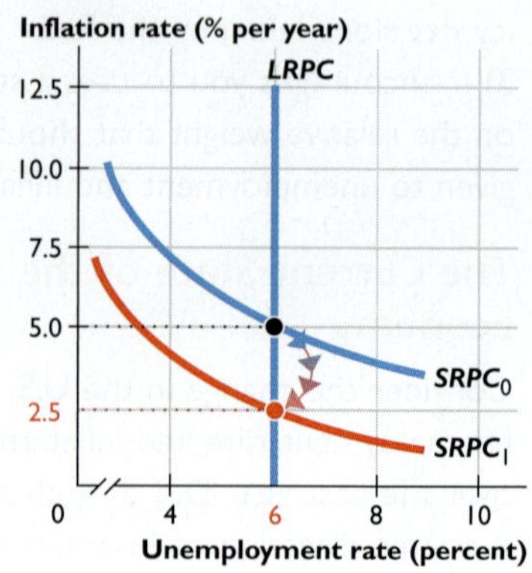

CHAPTER SUMMARY

Key Points

1 Describe the short-run tradeoff between inflation and unemployment.

- The short-run Phillips curve is the downward-sloping relationship between the inflation rate and the unemployment rate when all other influences on these two variables remain the same.
- The short-run Phillips curve presents a *tradeoff* between inflation and unemployment.
- The short-run Phillips curve is another way of looking at the aggregate supply curve.

2 Distinguish between the short-run and the long-run Phillips curves and describe the shifting tradeoff between inflation and unemployment.

- The long-run Phillips curve shows the relationship between inflation and unemployment when the unemployment rate equals the natural unemployment rate and the inflation rate equals the expected inflation rate.
- The long-run Phillips curve is vertical at the *natural unemployment rate,* and there is no long-run tradeoff between unemployment and inflation.
- When the expected inflation rate changes, the short-run Phillips curve shifts to intersect the long-run Phillips curve at the new expected inflation rate.
- When the money growth rate changes, the unemployment rate changes temporarily and eventually returns to the natural unemployment rate—the natural rate hypothesis.
- Changes in the natural unemployment rate shift both the *SRPC* and the *LRPC.*

3 Explain how the Fed can influence the expected inflation rate and how expected inflation influences the short-run tradeoff.

- The rational expectation of the inflation rate is based on the forecasted actions of the Fed's monetary policy and the other forces that influence aggregate demand and aggregate supply.
- A change in the expected inflation rate changes the short-run tradeoff gradually because the money wage rate responds only gradually to a change in the expected inflation rate.
- To lower the expected inflation rate, the Fed must take actions that will slow the actual inflation rate.

Key Terms

Expected inflation rate, 385
Long-run Phillips curve, 384
Natural rate hypothesis, 386
Okun's Law, 379
Rational expectation, 391
Short-run Phillips curve, 378

myeconlab

Work these problems in Chapter 15 Study Plan to get instant feedback.

TABLE 1 DATA 2011

	Price level (2010 = 100)	Real GDP (trillions of 2010 dollars)	Unemployment rate (percent)
A	102	11.0	9
B	104	11.1	7
C	106	11.2	5
D	110	11.4	3

TABLE 2 DATA 2012

	Price level (2010 = 100)	Real GDP (trillions of 2010 dollars)	Unemployment rate (percent)
A	108	11.1	9
B	110	11.2	7
C	112	11.3	5
D	116	11.5	3

CHAPTER CHECKPOINT

Study Plan Problems and Applications

Table 1 describes four situations that might arise in 2011, depending on the level of aggregate demand. Table 2 describes four situations that might arise in 2012. Use Tables 1 and 2 to work Problems **1** to **4**.

1. Plot the short-run Phillips curve and aggregate supply curve for 2011 and mark the points *A*, *B*, *C*, and *D* on each curve that correspond to the data in Table 1.

2. In 2011, the outcome turned out to be row C of Table 1. Plot the short-run Phillips curve for 2012 and mark the points *A*, *B*, *C*, and *D* that correspond to the data in Table 2.

3. Compare the short-run Phillips curve of 2012 with that of 2011.

4. What is Okun's Law? If the natural unemployment rate is 6 percent, does this economy behave in accordance with Okun's Law?

5. Suppose that the natural unemployment rate is 5 percent in 2010 and it increases to 6 percent in 2011 with no change in expected inflation. Explain how the short-run and long-run tradeoffs change.

6. Suppose that the natural unemployment rate is 5 percent and the expected inflation rate is 4 percent a year in 2010. If the inflation rate is expected to fall to 3 percent a year in 2011, explain how the short-run and the long-run Phillips curves will change.

7. The inflation rate is 2 percent a year, and the quantity of money is growing at a pace that will maintain that inflation rate. The natural unemployment rate is 5.5 percent, and the current unemployment rate is 9 percent. In what direction will the unemployment rate change? How will the short-run Phillips curve and the long-run Phillips curve shift?

8. Inflation in Brazil and Uruguay have repeatedly risen to levels unheard of in the United States. Explain how a history of rapid inflation might influence the short-run and long-run Phillips curves in these countries.

Use the following information to work Problems **9** to **11**.

Changing course, Australia raises interest rate

The Reserve Bank of Australia (the central bank) raised its overnight rate (equivalent to the U.S. federal funds rate) by a quarter of a percentage point, to 3.25 percent a year, amid concerns about rising inflation. The interest rate rise came earlier than many economists had expected.

Source: *New York Times*, October 6, 2009

9. Sketch the Phillips curves if expected inflation is 2 percent a year and the natural unemployment rate is 5 percent.

10. If with the Reserve bank's "concerns about rising inflation," people increase the expected inflation rate, explain how the short-run tradeoff will change.

11. If actual inflation had risen prior to the Reserve Bank raising the overnight rate, explain how the short-run tradeoff would change.

Instructor Assignable Problems and Applications

Your instructor can assign these problems as homework, a quiz, or a test in **MyEconLab**.

1. Suppose that as the U.S. economy recovers from the global financial crisis and recession the natural unemployment rate rises to its 1970s level and the expected inflation rate falls to zero. How would the short-run and long-run Phillips curves change? Would the tradeoff be more favorable or less favorable than that of 2009? Draw a graph to illustrate your answer.
2. In an economy, the natural unemployment rate is 4 percent and the expected inflation rate is 3 percent a year. Draw a graph of the short-run and long-run Phillips curves that display this information. Label each curve.

Table 1 describes four possible situations that might arise in 2011, depending on the level of aggregate demand in 2011. Table 2 describes four possible situations that might arise in 2012. Use Tables 1 and 2 to work Problems 3 and 4.

TABLE 1 DATA 2011

	Price level (2010 = 100)	Real GDP (trillions of 2010 dollars)	Unemployment rate (percent)
A	102	10.0	8
B	104	10.1	6
C	106	10.2	4
D	110	10.4	2

TABLE 2 DATA 2012

	Price level (2010 = 100)	Real GDP (trillions of 2010 dollars)	Unemployment rate (percent)
A	108	10.3	8
B	110	10.4	6
C	112	10.5	4
D	116	10.7	2

3. Plot the short-run Phillips curve and aggregate supply curve for 2011 and mark the points *A, B, C,* and *D* on each curve that correspond to the data in Table 1.
4. In 2011, the outcome turned out to be row *D* of Table 1. Plot the short-run Phillips curve for 2012 and mark the points *A, B, C,* and *D* that correspond to the data in Table 2.
5. Explain the relationship between the long-run Phillips curve and potential GDP and the short-run Phillips curve and the aggregate supply curve.
6. The inflation rate is 3 percent a year, and the quantity of money is growing at a pace that will maintain the inflation rate at 3 percent a year. The natural unemployment rate is 4 percent, and the current unemployment rate is 3 percent. In what direction will the unemployment rate change? How will the short-run Phillips curve and the long-run Phillips curve shift?
7. The inflation rate is 6 percent a year, the unemployment rate is 4 percent, and the economy is at full employment. The Fed announces that it intends to slow the money growth rate to keep the inflation rate at 3 percent a year for the foreseeable future. People believe the Fed. Explain how unemployment and inflation change in the short run and in the long run.

Use the following information to work Problems 8 and 9.

U.S. consumer confidence hits a 9-month high

The Reuters/University of Michigan Surveys of Consumers reported a rise in June of consumer confidence that exceeded economists' expectations and a rise in expected inflation to 3.1 percent a year. Such a rise should be a concern to the Federal Reserve, which has been pumping money into the economy in an attempt to contain the recession and spur a recovery.

Source: *The New York Times*, June 12, 2009

8. Show on a graph the effect of an increase in the expected inflation rate on the Phillips curves if there is no change in the natural unemployment rate.
9. If the Fed is concerned about inflation and unexpectedly slows money growth, explain how unemployment will change in the short run and in the long run.

10. The inflation rate is 1.5 percent a year, the unemployment rate is 4 percent, and the economy is at full employment. Unexpectedly, the Fed increases the money growth rate to raise the inflation rate to 3 percent a year. Explain how unemployment and inflation change in the short run.
11. In light of the fact that whenever the inflation rate is lowered, the unemployment rate increases, is lowering inflation ever a good policy? Would it be better to simply live with the inflation rate we've currently got?
12. In light of the fact that whenever the inflation rate is lowered, the unemployment rate increases, do you think we should ever permit the inflation rate to rise to an unacceptable level? Would it be better to nip an increase in inflation in the bud even if it meant a small and brief recession?
13. Looking at the data on inflation and unemployment, it is very difficult to see any sign of a short-run tradeoff. Explain why it is difficult to see the short-run tradeoff. Does the fact that the short-run tradeoff is hard to see in the data mean that we can ignore it? Why or why not?
14. Explain why the Phillips curve is a useful model and describe how it relates to and supplements the *AS-AD* model.

Use the following information to work Problems 15 and 16.

Because the Fed doubled the monetary base in 2008 and because the government has spent billions of dollars bailing out troubled banks, insurance companies, and auto producers, some people are concerned that a serious upturn in the inflation rate will occur, not immediately but in a few years' time. At the same time, massive changes in the global economy might bring the need for structural change in the United States.

15. Explain how the Fed's doubling of the monetary base and government bailouts might influence the short-run and long-run unemployment–inflation tradeoffs. Will the influence come from changes in the expected inflation rate, the natural unemployment rate, or both?
16. Explain how large-scale structural change might influence the short-run and long-run unemployment–inflation tradeoffs. Will the influence come from changes in the expected inflation rate, the natural unemployment rate, or both?
17. Describe the changes in inflation and unemployment in the United States between 1935 and 1957 and explain how these changes might have resulted from shifts of the short-run and long-run Phillips curves and from movements along the short-run Phillips curve.
18. Describe the changes in inflation and unemployment in the United States since 2000 and explain how these changes have resulted from shifts of the short-run and long-run Phillips curves and from movements along the short-run Phillips curve.
19. How would you expect an increase in unemployment benefits and a rise in the minimum wage to influence the short-run and long-run Phillips curves?

Did fiscal stimulus end the recession?

In the global recession of 2008 and 2009 most countries engaged in massive fiscal stimulus programs. Did these policies help to moderate the recession and speed the recovery?

16

Fiscal Policy

CHAPTER CHECKLIST

When you have completed your study of this chapter, you will be able to

1 Describe the federal budget process and the recent history of revenues, outlays, deficits, and debts.

2 Explain the demand-side effects of fiscal policy on employment and real GDP.

3 Explain the supply-side effects of fiscal policy on employment, potential GDP, and the economic growth rate.

16.1 THE FEDERAL BUDGET

Federal budget
An annual statement of the revenues, outlays, and surplus or deficit of the government of the United States.

The **federal budget** is an annual statement of the revenues, outlays, and surplus or deficit of the government of the United States, together with the laws and regulations that authorize these revenues and outlays.

The federal budget has two purposes:

1. To finance the activities of the federal government
2. To achieve macroeconomic objectives

The first purpose of the federal budget was its only purpose before the Great Depression years of the 1930s. The second purpose evolved as a response to the Great Depression and was initially based on the ideas of *Keynesian macroeconomics* (described in Chapter 8, pp. 192–193).

Fiscal policy
The use of the federal budget to achieve the macroeconomic objectives of high and sustained economic growth and full employment.

The use of the federal budget to achieve macroeconomic objectives is **fiscal policy**. During the 1960s, in the heyday of Keynesian macroeconomics, full employment was the main macroeconomic objective of fiscal policy. But as economics has advanced and ideas have changed, productivity and economic growth have assumed an increasingly prominent place in the objectives of fiscal policy. So today, fiscal policy is concerned with achieving *both* full employment and high and sustained economic growth.

The Institutions and Laws

Fiscal year
A year that begins on October 1 and ends on September 30. Fiscal 2011 *begins* on October 1, 2010.

The President and Congress make the budget and develop fiscal policy on a fixed annual time line and fiscal year. The U.S. **fiscal year** runs from October 1 to September 30 in the next calendar year. Fiscal 2011 is the fiscal year that begins on October 1, 2010.

The Roles of the President and Congress

The President *proposes* a budget to Congress each February. After Congress has passed the budget acts in September, the President either signs those acts into law or vetoes the entire budget bill. The President does not have the veto power to eliminate specific items in a budget bill and approve others—known as a line-item veto. Many state governors have long had line-item veto authority, and Congress attempted to grant these powers to the President of the United States in 1996. But a 1998 Supreme Court ruling declared the line-item veto for the President to be unconstitutional. Although the President proposes and ultimately approves the budget, the task of making the tough decisions on spending and taxes rests with Congress.

Congress begins its work on the budget with the President's proposal. The House of Representatives and the Senate develop their own budget ideas in their respective House and Senate Budget Committees. Formal conferences between the two houses eventually resolve differences of view, and a series of spending acts and an overall budget act are usually passed by both houses before the start of the fiscal year.

During a fiscal year, Congress often passes supplementary budget laws, and the budget outcome is influenced by the evolving state of the economy. For example, if a recession begins, tax revenues fall and welfare payments increase.

Figure 16.1 summarizes the budget time line and the roles of the President and Congress in the budget process.

FIGURE 16.1

The Federal Budget Time Line for Fiscal 2011

myeconlab Animation

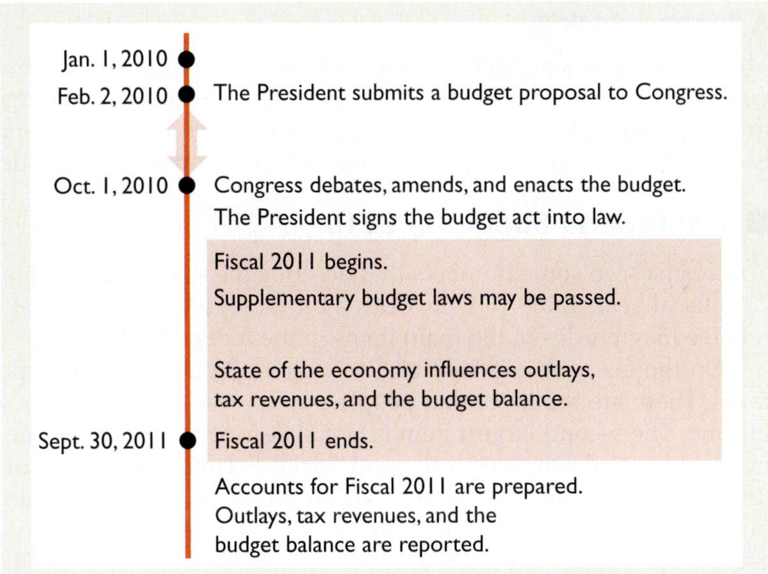

The federal budget process begins with the President's proposals in February. Congress debates and amends these proposals and enacts a budget before the start of the fiscal year on October 1. The President signs the budget act into law. Throughout the fiscal year, Congress might pass supplementary budget laws. The budget outcome is calculated after the end of the fiscal year.

Budget Surplus, Deficit

You've seen that the federal budget is the annual statement of the outlays and tax revenues of the government of the United States. The government's budget balance is equal to tax revenues minus outlays. That is,

$$\text{Budget balance} = \text{Tax revenues} - \text{Outlays.}$$

If tax revenues equal outlays, the government has a **balanced budget**. The government has a **budget surplus** if tax revenues exceed outlays. The government has a **budget deficit** if outlays exceed tax revenues.

Balanced budget
The budget balance when tax revenues equal outlays.

Budget surplus
The positive budget balance when tax revenues exceed outlays.

Budget deficit
The negative budget balance when outlays exceed tax revenues.

The budget projections for the 2010 fiscal year were tax revenues of \$2,703 billion, outlays of \$3,973 billion, and a budget deficit of \$1,270 billion. You can see that \$2,703 billion − \$3,973 billion = −\$1,270 billion.

Surplus, Deficit, and Debt

The government budget balance is equal to government saving, which might be zero (balanced budget), positive (budget surplus), or negative (budget deficit). When the government has a budget deficit, it incurs debt. That is, the government borrows to finance a budget deficit. When the government has a budget surplus, it repays some of its debt. The amount of government debt outstanding—debt that has arisen from past budget deficits—is called **national debt**.

National debt
The amount of government debt outstanding–debt that has arisen from past budget deficits.

The national debt at the end of a fiscal year equals the national debt at the end of the previous fiscal year plus the budget deficit or minus the budget surplus. For example,

$$\text{Debt at end of 2010} = \text{Debt at end of 2009} + \text{Budget deficit in 2010.}$$

At the end of the 2009 fiscal year, national debt was $8,531 billion. With a deficit of $1,270 billion in 2010, national debt at the end of the 2010 fiscal year becomes $9,801 billion. That is, $8,531 billion + $1,270 billion = $9,801 billion.

A Personal Analogy

The government's budget and debt are like your budget and debt, only bigger. If you take a student loan each year to go to school, you have a budget deficit and a growing debt. After graduating, if you have a job and repay some of your loan each year, you have a budget surplus each year and a shrinking debt.

The Federal Budget in 2010

You've just seen some numbers that describe the scale of the federal budget in the 2010 fiscal year. Table 16.1 provides a bit more detail and enables you to see the relative magnitudes of the main items in the federal budget.

On the tax revenues side of the budget, the largest item is personal income taxes. These are the taxes that people pay on wages and salaries and on interest income. The second largest item is Social Security taxes. These are the taxes paid by workers and employers to fund Social Security benefits. Corporate income taxes, which are the taxes paid by corporations on their profits, are the next item but they are much smaller than the two largest ones. Indirect taxes are the smallest revenue source. These are sales taxes and customs and excise taxes.

Transfer payments
Social Security benefits, Medicare and Medicaid benefits, unemployment benefits, and other cash benefits.

On the outlays side of the budget, **transfer payments**—Social Security benefits, Medicare and Medicaid benefits, unemployment benefits, and other cash benefits paid to individuals and firms—take the largest share of the government's financial resources. Expenditure on goods and services includes the government's defense and homeland security budgets. Debt interest is the interest on the national debt.

We've described the budget process and are now ready to study the effects on the economy. We begin in the next section with the demand-side effects.

TABLE 16.1

The Federal Budget in Fiscal 2010

The federal budget for 2010 was expected to be in a large deficit. Tax revenues of $2,703 billion were expected to be $1,270 billion less than outlays of $3,973 billion.

Personal income taxes are the largest revenue source and transfer payments are the largest outlay.

Item	Projections (billions of dollars)	
Tax Revenues	**2,703**	
Personal income taxes		1,068
Social Security taxes		1,026
Corporate income taxes		233
Indirect taxes		376
Outlays	**3,973**	
Transfer payments		2,322
Expenditure on goods and services		1,244
Debt interest		407
Balance	**–1,270**	

SOURCE OF DATA: *Budget of the United States Government, Fiscal Year 2010*, Table 14.1.

EYE on the PAST

Federal Revenues, Outlays, Deficits, and Debt

In 1940, in the first year of World War II, for every dollar earned, the federal government collected 6.5 cents in taxes and spent 9.3 cents. By 1943, at the depth of the most terrible war in history, the government was spending 40 cents of every dollar earned and collecting 12 cents in taxes. The government deficit in 1943 and 1944 was almost 30 percent of GDP.

The result of these enormous deficits was a mushrooming government debt. By 1946, when the debt-to-GDP ratio (debt as a percentage of GDP) peaked, the government owed more than a year's GDP.

During the 1950s and 1960s, the government's debt-to-GDP ratio tumbled as balanced budgets combined with rapid real GDP growth. By 1974, the debt-to-GDP ratio had fallen to a low of 23 percent.

Budget deficits returned during the 1980s as the defense budget swelled and some tax rates were cut. The result was a growing debt-to-GDP ratio that climbed to almost 50 percent by 1995.

Expenditure restraint combined with sustained real GDP growth lowered the debt-to-GDP ratio during the 1990s, but a surge in expenditures on defense and homeland security, further tax cuts, and a spending surge in 2009 and 2010 to fight global financial crisis and recession, all combined to swell the debt-to-GDP ratio again.

SOURCE OF DATA: *Budget of the U.S. Government, Fiscal Year 2010*, Historical Tables, Tables 7.1 and 14.1.

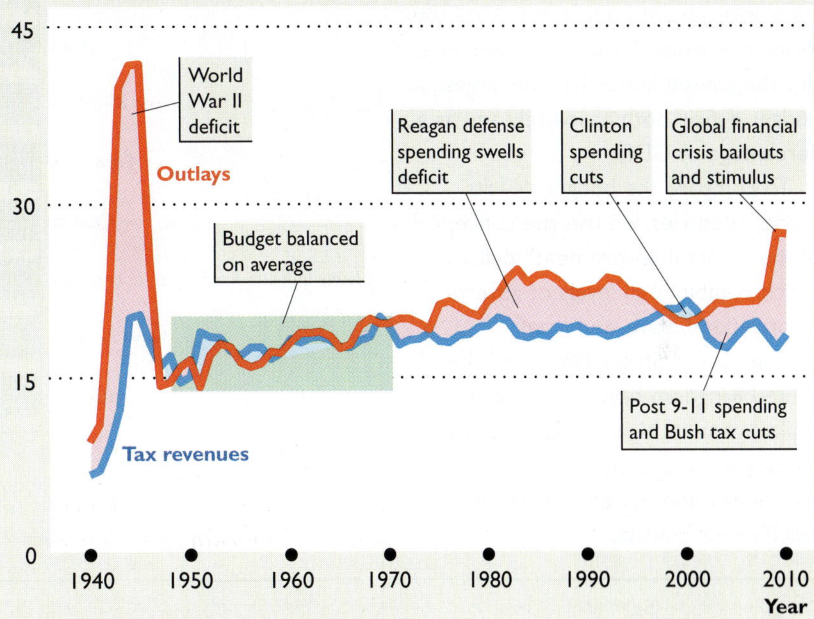

(a) Tax revenues, outlays, and deficits

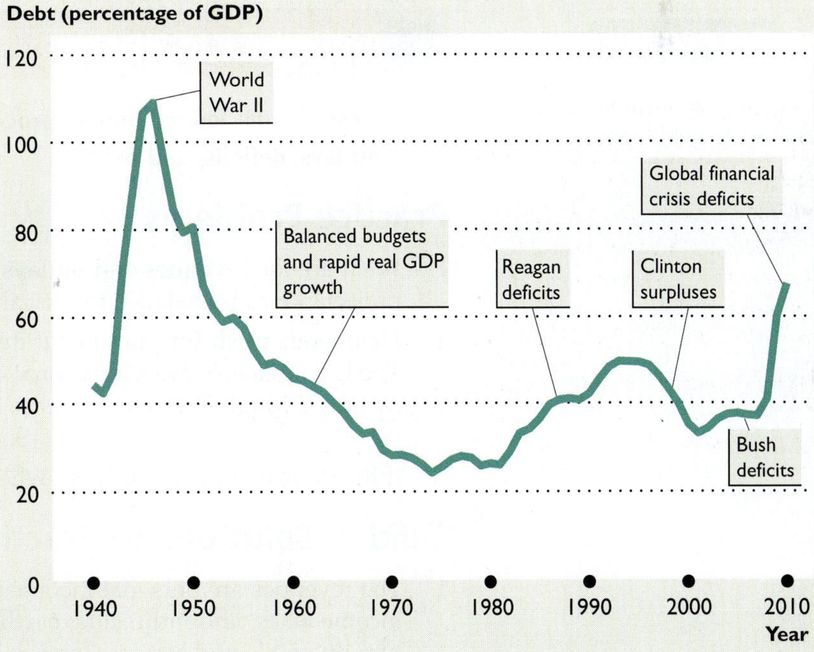

(b) Debt

EYE on the GLOBAL ECONOMY

The U.S. Budget in Global Perspective

The United States is not alone in having a government budget deficit. All the major countries share this experience. But the United States has the largest budget deficit, both absolutely and as a percentage of GDP.

To compare the budget deficits across countries, we use the concept of the "general government" deficit, which combines all levels of government: federal, state, and local.

The United States, Japan, and the United Kingdom have large deficits while Australia, New Zealand, Canada, the newly industrialized Asian economies, and the Euro area have much lower deficits.

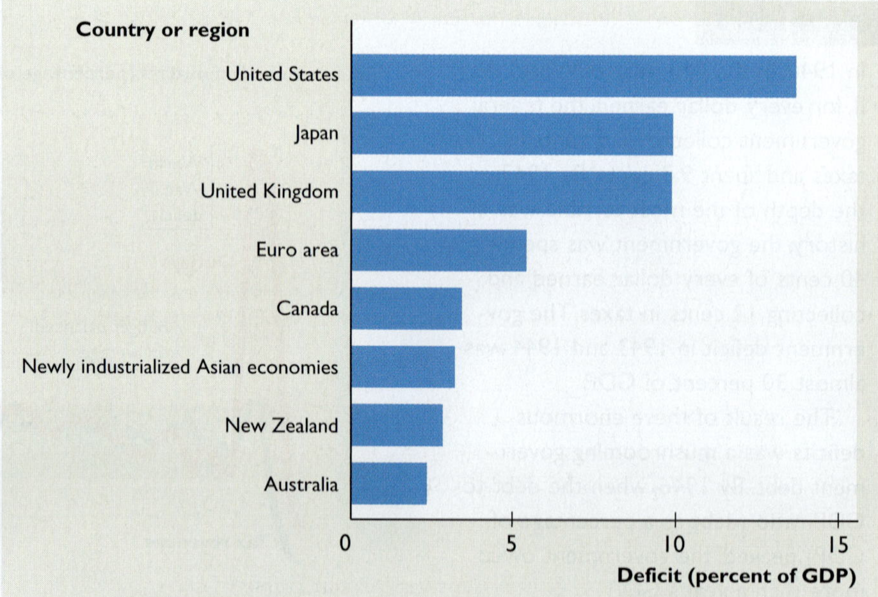

SOURCE OF DATA: International Monetary Fund, *World Economic Outlook*, April 2009.

myeconlab

Work these problems in Study Plan 16.1 to get instant feedback.

CHECKPOINT 16.1

Describe the federal budget process and the recent history of revenues, outlays, deficits, and debts.

Practice Problems

1. What are the revenues and outlays in the federal budget, and what was the projected budget balance for Fiscal 2010?
2. **Democrats push for plan to cut deficit**
   The U.S. Treasury faces a national-debt limit of $12 trillion and projected deficits through 2019 will increase the national debt by $9 trillion.
   Source: *The New York Times*, October 31, 2009
   If the deficits remain constant, when will the national-debt limit be hit?

Guided Solutions to Practice Problems

1. The revenues are personal income taxes, Social Security taxes, corporate income taxes, and indirect taxes; the outlays are transfer payments, expenditure on goods and services, and debt interest. The projected budget balance for Fiscal 2010 was a deficit of $1,270 billion.
2. Current national debt is about $10 trillion. By adding an average of $0.9 trillion ($9 trillion/10 year) per year to the current national debt, the limit of $12 trillion will be hit during 2012.

16.2 THE DEMAND SIDE: STABILIZING REAL GDP

We've described the federal budget and the institutions that make fiscal policy, and now we're going to study the *effects* of fiscal policy. In doing so, we move from describing facts to explaining theories, and the theory of fiscal policy is controversial.

Schools of Thought and Cracks in Today's Consensus

We described the three main schools of macroeconomic thought—*classical*, *Keynesian*, and *monetarist* macroeconomics—in Chapter 8 (see pp. 192–193). We also described today's consensus as one that takes insights from each of the schools. While there is a consensus, the macroeconomic events of 2008 and 2009 have placed the consensus under some stress and cracks are emerging. Some of these cracks have become so public, with economists debating in the pages of *The New York Times*, *The Wall Street Journal*, and *The Economist*, that in discussing the theory of fiscal policy, we must explain the divergent views. The main crack is between the views of Keynesian economists and others and it is on this divide that we will focus. Before digging deeper into the details, we'll provide a quick overview of the two sides of the debate.

The Keynesian View

The Keynesian view is that **fiscal stimulus**—an increase in government outlays or a decrease in tax revenues—boosts real GDP and creates or saves jobs. The leading economists who advance this view include the 2008 Nobel Prize Winner Paul Krugman (Princeton University) and President Obama's chief economic adviser Christina Romer (on leave from University of California, Berkeley).

Fiscal stimulus
An increase in government outlays or a decrease in tax revenues designed to boost real GDP and create or save jobs.

Keynesians say that fiscal stimulus boosts real GDP and employment by increasing aggregate demand. Further, the fiscal stimulus has a multiplier effect: A $1 increase in government outlays or decrease in tax revenues brings a greater than $1 increase in aggregate demand and real GDP.

These positive effects of fiscal stimulus, say the Keynesians, make it a vital and powerful tool in the fight against deep recession and depression.

The Mainstream View

The mainstream view is that Keynesians over-estimate the multiplier effects of fiscal stimulus and that these effects are small, short-lived, and incapable of working fast enough to be useful. Among the leading economists who advance this view are Robert J. Barro (Harvard University), the 1995 Nobel Prize Winner Robert E. Lucas Jr. (University of Chicago), and John B. Taylor (Stanford University).

Mainstream economists say that government stimulus does not provide a "free lunch" and instead "crowds out" private consumption expenditure and investment. The durable results of a fiscal stimulus are bigger government, lower potential GDP, a slower real GDP growth rate, and a greater burden of government debt on future generations.

We begin our more detailed look at fiscal policy by explaining the mechanisms that Keynesians emphasize and believe operate to influence aggregate demand. Later in the chapter, we return to the mainstream view and look at supply-side and "crowding out" effects.

Fiscal Policy and Aggregate Demand

Fiscal policy can take the form of a change in government outlays or a change in tax revenues. And a change in government outlays can take the form of a change in expenditure on goods and services or a change in transfer payments. *Other things remaining the same*, a change in any of the items in the government budget changes aggregate demand and has a multiplier effect— aggregate demand changes by a greater amount than the initial change in the item in the government budget. These multiplier effects are similar to the ones that you studied in Chapters 13 and 14. (Other things might not remain the same, and we'll look at some possible offsetting factors after we've explained the basic Keynesian idea.)

The Government Expenditure Multiplier

Government expenditure multiplier
The effect of a change in government expenditure on goods and services on aggregate demand.

The **government expenditure multiplier** is the effect of a change in government expenditure on goods and services on aggregate demand. Government expenditure is a component of aggregate expenditure, so when government expenditure increases, aggregate demand increases. Real GDP increases and induces an increase in consumption expenditure, which brings a further increase in aggregate expenditure. A multiplier process like the one described in Chapter 14 (pp. 364–368) ensues.

The Tax Multiplier

Tax multiplier
The effect of a change in taxes on aggregate demand.

The **tax multiplier** is the magnification effect of a change in taxes on aggregate demand. A *decrease* in taxes *increases* disposable income, which increases consumption expenditure. A decrease in taxes works like an increase in government expenditure. But the magnitude of the tax multiplier is smaller than the government expenditure multiplier because a $1 tax cut generates *less than* $1 of additional expenditure. The marginal propensity to consume determines the initial increase in expenditure induced by a tax cut and the magnitude of the tax multiplier. For example, if the marginal propensity to consume is 0.75, then the initial increase in consumption expenditure induced by a $1 tax cut is only 75 cents. In this case, the tax multiplier is 0.75 times the magnitude of the government expenditure multiplier.

The Transfer Payments Multiplier

Transfer payments multiplier
The effect of a change in transfer payments on aggregate demand.

The **transfer payments multiplier** is the effect of a change in transfer payments on aggregate demand. This multiplier works like the tax multiplier but in the opposite direction. An *increase* in transfer payments *increases* disposable income, which *increases* consumption expenditure. The magnitude of the transfer payments multiplier is similar to that of the tax multiplier. Just as a $1 tax cut generates *less than* $1 of additional expenditure, so also does a $1 increase in transfer payments. Again, it is the marginal propensity to consume that determines the increase in expenditure induced by an increase in transfer payments.

The Balanced Budget Multiplier

Balanced budget multiplier
The effect on aggregate demand of a *simultaneous* change in government expenditure and taxes that leaves the budget balance unchanged.

The **balanced budget multiplier** is the magnification effect on aggregate demand of a *simultaneous* change in government expenditure and taxes that leaves the budget balance unchanged. The balanced budget multiplier is not zero. It is greater than zero because a $1 increase in government expenditure injects a dollar more into aggregate demand while a $1 tax rise (or decrease in transfer payments) takes less than $1 from aggregate demand. So when both government expenditure and taxes increase by $1, aggregate demand increases.

A Successful Fiscal Stimulus

If real GDP is below potential GDP, the government might pursue a fiscal stimulus by increasing its expenditure on goods and services, increasing transfer payments, cutting taxes, or doing some combination of all three. Figure 16.2 shows us how these actions increase aggregate demand for a successful stimulus package.

In Figure 16.2(a), potential GDP is \$13 trillion but real GDP is only \$12 trillion. The economy is at point *A* and there is a *recessionary gap* (see Chapter 13, p. 340).

To eliminate the recessionary gap and restore full employment, the government introduces a fiscal stimulus. An increase in government expenditure or a tax cut increases aggregate expenditure by ΔE. If this were the only change in spending plans, the *AD* curve would become $AD_0 + \Delta E$ in Figure 16.2(b). But the initial increase in expenditure sets off a multiplier process, which increases consumption expenditure. As the multiplier process plays out, aggregate demand increases and the *AD* curve shifts rightward to AD_1.

With no change in the price level, the economy would move from the initial point *A* to point *B* on AD_1. But the increase in aggregate demand combined with the upward-sloping aggregate supply curve brings a rise in the price level, and the economy moves to a new equilibrium at point *C*. The price level rises to 110, real GDP increases to \$13 trillion, and the economy returns to full employment.

Cash for Clunkers stimulated aggregate demand.

FIGURE 16.2

Fiscal Stimulus

myeconlab Animation

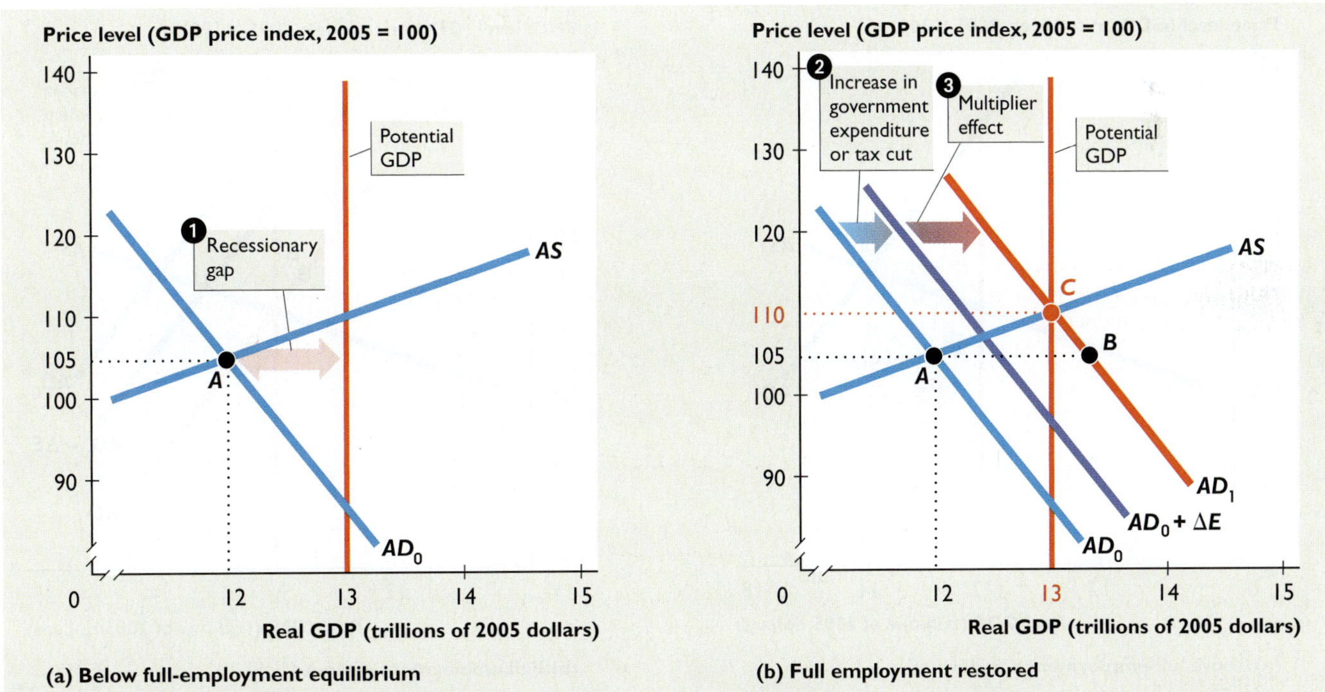

Potential GDP is \$13 trillion. At point *A*, real GDP is \$12 trillion, and ❶ there is a \$1 trillion recessionary gap. ❷ An increase in government expenditure or a tax cut increases expenditure by ΔE.

❸ The multiplier increases induced expenditure. The *AD* curve shifts rightward to AD_1, the price level rises to 110, real GDP increases to \$13 trillion, and the recessionary gap is eliminated.

A Successful Contractionary Fiscal Policy

Contractionary fiscal policy
A decrease in government expenditure on goods and services, a decrease in transfer payments, or an increase in taxes designed to decrease aggregate demand.

If real GDP is above potential GDP, the government might pursue a **contractionary fiscal policy**—decrease its expenditure on goods and services, decrease transfer payments, raise taxes, or do some combination of all three. Figure 16.3 shows us how these actions decrease aggregate demand.

In Figure 16.3(a), potential GDP is \$13 trillion but real GDP is \$14 trillion. The economy is at point *A* and there is an *inflationary gap* (see Chapter 13, p. 340).

To eliminate the inflationary gap and restore full employment, the government takes a contractionary fiscal policy action. A decrease in government expenditure or a rise in taxes decreases aggregate expenditure by ΔE. If this were the only change in spending plans, the *AD* curve would become $AD_0 - \Delta E$. But the initial decrease in aggregate expenditure sets off a multiplier process, which decreases consumption expenditure. As the multiplier process plays out, aggregate demand decreases and the *AD* curve shifts leftward to AD_1.

With no change in the price level, the economy would move from the initial point *A* to point *B* on AD_1. But the decrease in aggregate demand combined with the upward-sloping *AS* curve brings a fall in the price level, and the economy moves to a new equilibrium at point C. The price level falls to 110, real GDP decreases to \$13 trillion, and the inflationary gap is eliminated.

FIGURE 16.3

Contractionary Fiscal Policy

myeconlab Animation

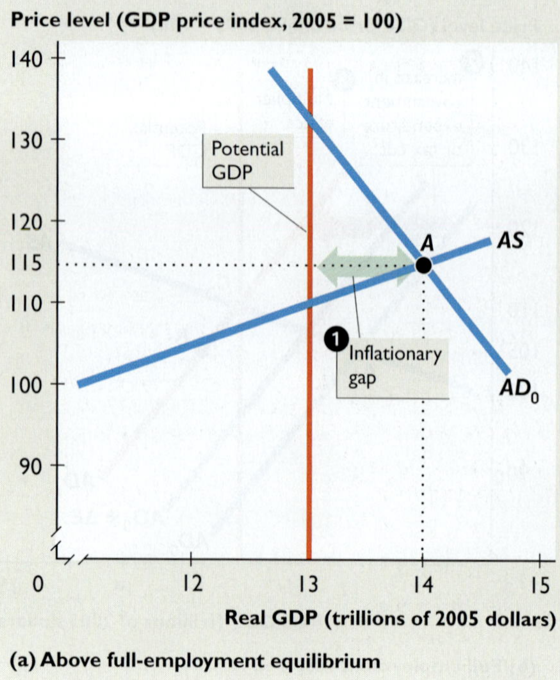

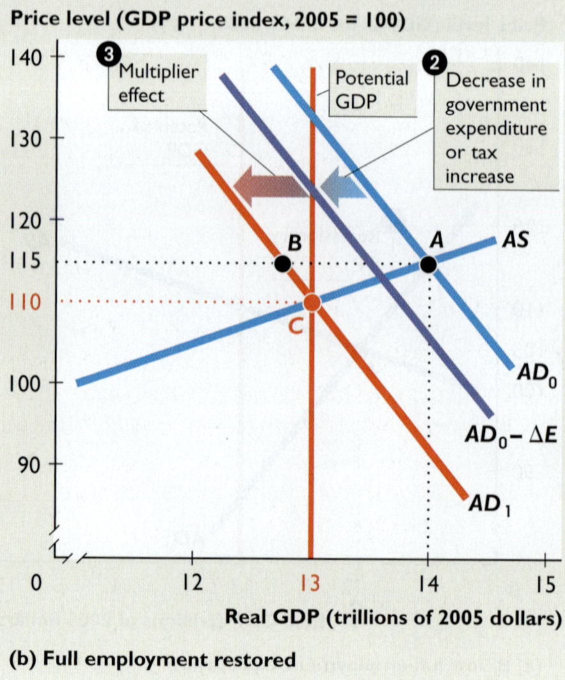

Potential GDP is \$13 trillion, real GDP is \$14 trillion, and ❶ there is a \$1 trillion inflationary gap. ❷ A decrease in government expenditure or a tax increase decreases expenditure by ΔE.

❸ The multiplier decreases induced expenditure. The *AD* curve shifts leftward to AD_1, the price level falls to 110, real GDP decreases to \$13 trillion, and the inflationary gap is eliminated.

Automatic and Discretionary Fiscal Stimulus

Fiscal policy actions that are aimed at stimulating aggregate demand can be automatic or discretionary.

Automatic Fiscal Policy

A fiscal policy action that is triggered by the state of the economy is called an **automatic fiscal policy**. For example, an increase in unemployment induces an increase in transfer payments, and a fall in incomes induces a decrease in tax revenues.

Automatic fiscal policy
A fiscal policy action that is triggered by the state of the economy.

Discretionary Fiscal Policy

A fiscal policy action that is initiated by an act of Congress is called a **discretionary fiscal policy**. A discretionary fiscal policy action requires a change in a spending program or in a tax law. Increases in defense spending or cuts in the income tax rate are examples of discretionary fiscal policy.

Discretionary fiscal policy
A fiscal policy action that is initiated by an act of Congress.

Automatic Fiscal Policy

Automatic fiscal policy is a consequence of tax revenues and outlays that fluctuate with real GDP. These features of fiscal policy are called **automatic stabilizers** because they work to stabilize real GDP without explicit action by the government.

Automatic stabilizers
Features of fiscal policy that stabilize real GDP without explicit action by the government.

Induced Taxes

On the revenue side of the budget, tax laws define tax *rates*, not tax *dollars*. Tax dollars paid depend on tax rates and incomes. But incomes vary with real GDP, so tax revenues depend on real GDP. Taxes that vary with real GDP are called **induced taxes**. When real GDP increases in an expansion, wages and profits rise, so the taxes on these incomes—induced taxes—rise. When real GDP decreases in a recession, wages and profits fall, so the induced taxes on these incomes fall.

Induced taxes
Taxes that vary with real GDP.

Needs-Tested Spending

On the expenditure side of the budget, the government creates programs that entitle suitably qualified people and businesses to receive benefits. The spending on such programs is called **needs-tested spending**, and it results in transfer payments that depend on the economic state of individual citizens and businesses. When the economy is in a recession, the number of people experiencing unemployment and economic hardship increases, but needs-tested spending on unemployment benefits and food stamps increases. When the economy expands, the number of people experiencing unemployment and economic hardship decreases, and needs-tested spending decreases.

Needs-tested spending
Spending on programs that entitle suitably qualified people and businesses to receive transfer payments that vary with need and with the state of the economy.

Induced taxes and needs-tested spending decrease the multiplier effects of changes in investment or exports, so they moderate both expansions and recessions and make real GDP more stable. They achieve this outcome by weakening the link between real GDP and disposable income and so reduce the effect of a change in real GDP on consumption expenditure. When real GDP increases, induced taxes increase and needs-tested spending decreases, so disposable income does not increase by as much as the increase in real GDP. As a result, consumption expenditure does not increase by as much as it otherwise would have done and the multiplier effect is reduced.

Discretionary Fiscal Policy

Discretionary fiscal stabilization policy looks easy. Calculate the output gap and the multiplier, and determine the direction and size of the change in government expenditure or taxes that will eliminate the gap. In reality, discretionary fiscal policy is seriously hampered by many factors, four of which are:

- Law-making time lag
- Shrinking area of law-maker discretion
- Estimating potential GDP
- Economic forecasting

Law-Making Time Lag

The law-making time lag is the amount of time it takes Congress to pass the laws needed to change taxes or spending. This process takes time because each member of Congress has a different idea about what is the best tax or spending program to change, so long debates and committee meetings are needed to reconcile conflicting views. The economy might benefit from fiscal stimulation today, but by the time Congress acts, a different fiscal medicine might be needed.

Shrinking Area of Law-Maker Discretion

During the 2000s, federal spending increased faster than in any other peacetime period. This growth in spending was driven by two forces: increased security threats and an aging population.

The increased security threat resulted in a large increase in expenditure on the military and homeland security. The aging population brought a very large increase in expenditure on entitlement programs such as Medicare.

The growth of this spending has reduced the areas in which Congress can act to change either taxes or outlays. Around 80 percent of the federal budget is effectively off limits for discretionary policy action, and the remaining 20 percent of items are very hard to cut.

So even if the state of the economy calls for a change in fiscal policy, Congress's room to maneuver is severely limited.

Estimating Potential GDP

Potential GDP is not directly observed, so it must be estimated. Because it is not easy to tell whether real GDP is below, above, or at potential GDP, a discretionary fiscal action might move real GDP *away* from potential GDP instead of toward it. This problem is a serious one because too large a fiscal stimulus brings inflation and too little might bring recession.

Economic Forecasting

Fiscal policy changes take a long time to enact in Congress and yet more time to become effective. So fiscal policy must target forecasts of where the economy will be in the future. Economic forecasting has improved enormously in recent years, but it remains inexact and subject to error. So for a second reason, discretionary fiscal action might move real GDP *away* from potential GDP and create the very problems that it seeks to correct.

Further problems with discretionary fiscal policy arise from their supply-side effects that we will examine in the next section.

CHECKPOINT 16.2

Explain the demand-side effects of fiscal policy on employment and real GDP.

myeconlab

Work these problems in Study Plan 16.2 to get instant feedback.

Practice Problems

1. Classify the following items as automatic fiscal policy, discretionary fiscal policy, or not part of fiscal policy.
   - A decrease in tax revenues in a recession
   - Additional expenditure to upgrade highways
   - An increase in the public education budget
   - A cut in funding for NASA during a boom
2. Explain how aggregate demand changes when government expenditure on national defense increases by $100 billion.
3. Explain how aggregate demand changes when the government increases taxes by $100 billion.
4. Explain how aggregate demand changes when the government increases both expenditure and taxes by $100 billion.
5. **How to curb the deficit**

   Senator Evan Bayh, Democrat of Indiana, noted that Democrats want to spend more than we can afford; Republicans tend to want to cut taxes more than we can afford. So we are stuck with large deficits.

   Source: *The New York Times*, October 31, 2009

   What policy will change aggregate demand the most: Democrats agreeing to cut the budget outlays or Republicans agreeing to raise taxes?

Guided Solutions to Practice Problems

1. A decrease in tax revenues in a recession is an automatic fiscal policy. Expenditure to upgrade highways is a discretionary fiscal policy. An increase in the public education budget is a discretionary fiscal policy. A cut in funding for NASA is a discretionary fiscal policy.
2. Aggregate demand increases by more than $100 billion because government expenditure increases induced expenditure.
3. Aggregate demand decreases by more than $100 billion because the tax increase has a multiplier effect that decreases induced expenditure.
4. An increase in government expenditure of $100 billion increases aggregate demand by more than $100 billion. An increase in taxes of $100 billion decreases aggregate demand by more than $100 billion. The increase is greater than the decrease, so together aggregate demand increases.
5. The effect of a cut in budget outlays on aggregate demand depends on whether the items cut are expenditures on goods and services (government expenditure multiplier) or transfer payments (transfer payments multiplier). An increase in taxes will decrease aggregate demand (tax multiplier). The magnitude of the government expenditure multiplier exceeds the other two multipliers, so a cut in government expenditure on goods and services will decrease aggregate demand the most.

16.3 THE SUPPLY SIDE: POTENTIAL GDP AND GROWTH

Supply-side effects
The effects of fiscal policy on potential GDP and the economic growth rate.

You've seen how fiscal policy can influence the output gap by changing aggregate demand and real GDP relative to potential GDP. But fiscal policy also influences potential GDP and the growth rate of potential GDP. These influences on potential GDP and economic growth arise because the government provides public goods and services that increase productivity and because taxes change the incentives the people face. These influences, called **supply-side effects**, operate more slowly than the demand-side effects emphasized by Keynesians. Supply-side effects are often ignored in times of recession when the focus is on fiscal stimulus and restoring full employment. But in the long run, the supply-side effects of fiscal policy dominate and determine potential GDP.

We'll begin an account of the supply side with a brief explanation of how full employment and potential GDP are determined in the absence of government services and taxes. Then we'll see how government services and taxes change employment and potential GDP.

Full Employment and Potential GDP

The quantity of labor demanded and the quantity of labor supplied depend on the real wage rate. The higher the real wage rate, other things remaining the same, the smaller is the quantity of labor demanded and the greater is the quantity of labor supplied. When the real wage rate has adjusted to make the quantity of labor demanded equal to the quantity of labor supplied, there is full employment. And when the quantity of labor is the full-employment quantity, real GDP equals potential GDP.

This brief description of how potential GDP and the full-employment quantity of labor are determined is a summary of the more detailed account in Chapter 8 (pp. 195–201).

How do taxes and the provision of government services—the elements of fiscal policy—influence employment and potential GDP?

Fiscal Policy, Employment, and Potential GDP

Both sides of the government budget influence potential GDP. The expenditure side provides public goods and services that enhance productivity and make labor more productive. The revenue side levies taxes that modify incentives that change the full-employment quantities of labor, as well as the amount of saving and investment.

Public Goods and Productivity

Governments provide a legal system and other infrastructure services such as roads and highways, fire-fighting and policing services, and national security, all of which increase the nation's productive potential. Today's world provides a vivid demonstration of the role that good government plays in enhancing productivity. Compare the chaos and absence of productivity in parts of the Middle East and Africa with the order and calm and the productivity that they permit in the United States and other industrialized countries.

Public goods and services, financed by the government budget, increase the real GDP that a given amount of labor can produce. So the provision of public goods and services increases potential GDP.

Taxes and Incentives

A tax drives a wedge—called the **tax wedge**—between the price paid by a buyer and the price received by a seller. In the labor market, the income tax drives a wedge between the cost of labor to employers and the take-home pay of workers and decreases the equilibrium quantity of labor employed. A smaller quantity of labor produces a smaller amount of real GDP, so taxes lower potential GDP.

The income tax wedge is only a part of the tax wedge that affects labor-supply decisions. Taxes on expenditure also create a tax wedge that affects employment and potential GDP.

Taxes on consumption expenditure add to the tax wedge that lowers potential GDP. The reason is that a tax on consumption expenditure raises the prices paid for consumption goods and services and is equivalent to a cut in the real wage rate. The incentive to supply labor depends on the goods and services that an hour of labor can buy. The higher the tax on consumption expenditure, the smaller is the quantity of goods and services that an hour of labor buys and the weaker is the incentive to supply labor.

The expenditure tax rate must be added to the income tax rate to find the total tax wedge. If the income tax rate is 25 percent and the tax rate on consumption expenditure is 10 percent, a dollar earned buys only 65 cents worth of goods and services. The tax wedge is 35 percent.

Tax wedge
The gap created by a tax between what a buyer pays and what a seller receives. In the labor market, it is the gap between the before-tax wage rate and the after-tax wage rate.

EYE on the GLOBAL ECONOMY

Some Real-World Tax Wedges

Edward C. Prescott of the Arizona State University, who shared the 2004 Nobel Prize for Economic Science, has estimated the tax wedges for a number of countries. The U.S. tax wedge is a combination of consumption taxes, income taxes, and Social Security taxes.

Among the industrial countries, the U.S. tax wedge is relatively small. Prescott estimates that in France, (marginal) taxes on consumption are 33 percent and taxes on incomes are 49 percent. The estimates for the United Kingdom fall between those for France and the United States. The figure shows these components of the tax wedges in the three countries.

According to Prescott's estimates, the tax wedge has a powerful effect on employment and potential GDP. Potential GDP per person in France is lower than that of the United States, and the entire difference can be attributed to the difference in the tax wedge in the two countries.

Potential GDP per person in the United Kingdom is lower than that of the United States, and about a third of the difference arises from the different tax wedges. (The rest is due to different productivities.)

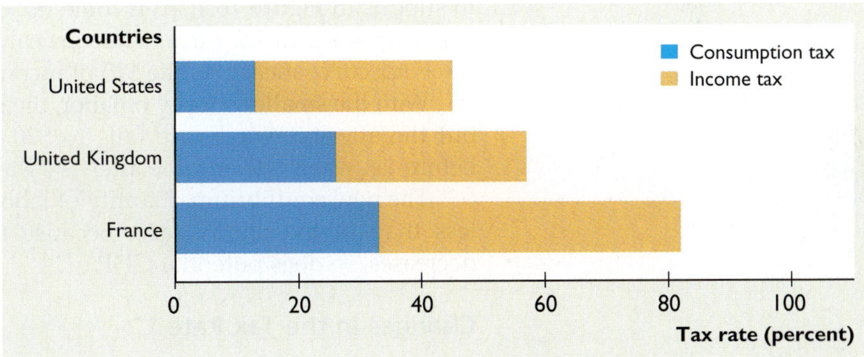

SOURCE OF DATA: Edward C. Prescott, *American Economic Review*, 2003.

Fiscal Policy and Potential GDP: A Graphical Analysis

Figure 16.4 illustrates the effects of fiscal policy on potential GDP. It begins with the economy at full employment and with no income tax.

Full Employment With No Income Tax

In part (a), the demand for labor curve is *LD*, and the supply of labor curve is *LS*. The equilibrium real wage rate is $30 an hour, and 250 billion hours of labor a year are employed. The economy is at full employment. In Figure 16.4(b), the production function is *PF*. (This production function incorporates the productivity of an efficient provision of public services.) When 250 billion hours of labor are employed, real GDP—which is also potential GDP—is $14 trillion.

Let's now see how an income tax changes potential GDP.

The Effects of the Income Tax

The tax on labor income influences potential GDP by changing the full-employment quantity of labor. The income tax weakens the incentive to work and drives a wedge between the take-home wage of workers and the cost of labor to firms. The result is a smaller quantity of labor employed and a smaller potential GDP. Figure 16.4 shows this outcome.

In the labor market in part (a), the income tax has no effect on the demand for labor because the quantity of labor that firms plan to hire depends only on how productive labor is and what labor costs—the real wage rate. The demand for labor remains at *LD*.

But the income tax changes the supply of labor. With no income tax, the real wage rate is $30 an hour and 250 billion hours of labor a year are employed. An income tax weakens the incentive to work. Workers must pay the government part of each dollar of the before-tax wage rate, as determined by the income tax code. Workers look at the after-tax wage rate when they decide how much labor to supply. In Figure 16.4, an income tax of $15 an hour shifts the supply of labor curve leftward to *LS* + *tax*. The vertical distance between the *LS* curve and the *LS* + *tax* curve measures the $15 of income tax.

With the smaller supply of labor, the before-tax wage rate rises to $35 an hour but the after-tax wage rate falls to $20 an hour. The gap created between the before-tax wage rate and the after-tax wage rate is the *tax wedge*.

The new equilibrium quantity of labor employed is 200 billion hours a year—less than in the no-tax case. Because the full-employment quantity of labor decreases, so does potential GDP.

Changes in the Tax Rate

A change in the income tax rate changes equilibrium employment and potential GDP. In the example that you've just worked through, the tax rate is about 43 percent—a $15 tax on a $35 wage rate. If the income tax rate is increased, the supply of labor decreases yet more and the *LS* + *tax* curve shifts farther leftward. Equilibrium employment and potential GDP decrease.

If the income tax rate is decreased, the supply of labor increases and the *LS* + *tax* curve shifts rightward. Equilibrium employment and potential GDP increase.

You can now see that a tax cut has two effects: It increases aggregate demand by boosting consumption expenditure and it increases potential GDP.

FIGURE 16.4

Fiscal Policy and Potential GDP

myeconlab Animation

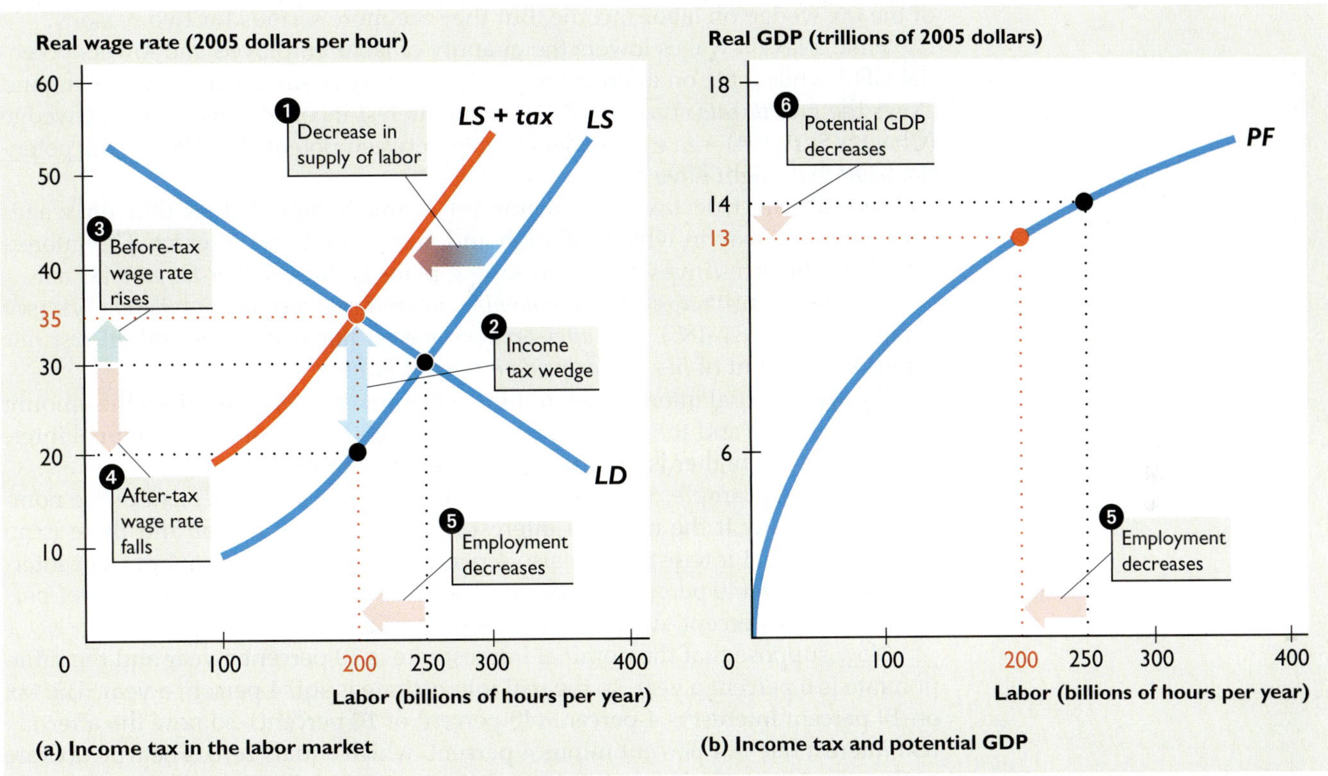

In part (a), the demand for labor is *LD* and the supply of labor is *LS*. With no income tax, the equilibrium real wage rate is $30 an hour and employment is 250 billion hours. In part (b), the production function, *PF*, tells us that 250 billion hours of labor (full employment of labor) produces a potential GDP of $14 trillion.

An income tax ❶ decreases the supply of labor and creates ❷ an income tax wedge between the wage that firms pay and the wage that workers receive. ❸ The before-tax wage rate paid by employers rises and ❹ the after-tax wage rate received by workers falls. ❺ Employment decreases and ❻ potential GDP decreases.

Taxes, Deficits, and Economic Growth

You've just seen how taxes can change incentives in the labor market and influence potential GDP. Taxes also affect the market for financial capital, which influences the amount of saving and investment; and saving and investment in turn affect the pace of capital accumulation and the economic growth rate.

Fiscal policy influences the economic growth rate in two ways:

First, taxes drive a wedge between the interest rate paid by borrowers and the interest rate received by lenders. This wedge lowers the amount of saving and investment and slows the economic growth rate.

Second, if the government has a budget deficit, then government borrowing to finance the deficit competes with firms' borrowing to finance investment and to some degree, government borrowing "crowds out" private investment.

Let's examine these two influences on economic growth a bit more closely.

Interest Rate Tax Wedge

Lenders pay an income tax on the interest they receive from borrowers, which creates an interest rate tax wedge. The effects of this tax wedge are analogous to those of the tax wedge on labor income. But they are more serious for two reasons.

First, a tax on wages lowers the quantity of labor employed and lowers potential GDP, while a tax on interest lowers the quantity of saving and investment and slows the *growth rate of real GDP*. A tax on interest income creates a Lucas wedge (Chapter 8, p. 194)—an ever widening gap between potential GDP and the potential GDP that might have been.

Second, the true tax rate on interest is much higher than that on wages because of the way in which inflation and taxes on interest interact. The interest rate that influences investment and saving plans is the *real after-tax interest rate*.

The *real interest rate* equals the *nominal interest rate* minus the *inflation rate* (see Chapter 7, pp. 184–185). The *after-tax real interest rate* equals the *real interest rate* minus the amount of *income tax paid on interest income*.

But the nominal interest rate, not the real interest rate, determines the amount of tax to be paid; and the higher the inflation rate, the higher is the nominal interest rate, and the higher is the true tax rate on interest income.

Here is an example. Suppose the tax rate on interest is 40 percent of the nominal interest rate. If the nominal interest rate is 4 percent a year and there is no inflation, the real interest rate is also 4 percent a year. The tax on 4 percent interest is 1.6 percent (40 percent of 4 percent), so the after-tax real interest rate is 4 percent minus 1.6 percent, which equals 2.4 percent a year.

Now suppose that the nominal interest rate is 10 percent a year and the inflation rate is 6 percent a year, so the real interest rate is still 4 percent a year. The tax on 10 percent interest is 4 percent (40 percent of 10 percent), so now the after-tax real interest rate is 4 percent minus 4 percent, which equals zero. The true tax rate in this case is not 40 percent but 100 percent!

Even modest inflation makes the true tax rate on interest income extremely high and results in a smaller equilibrium quantity of saving and investment, a slower rate of capital accumulation, and a slower growth rate of real GDP.

Deficits and Crowding Out

With no change in the government's outlays, a tax cut that increases the budget deficit brings an increase in the demand for loanable funds. (You learned about this effect of a government budget deficit in Chapter 10, pp. 258–260.) An increase in the demand for loanable funds raises the real interest rate and crowds out private investment. There is uncertainty about the magnitude of the crowding-out effect but no doubt about its presence.

You can see that this effect of an income tax cut works against the incentive effect. A lower income tax rate shrinks the tax wedge and stimulates employment, saving, and investment, but a higher budget deficit decreases investment.

■ The Supply-Side Debate

Before 1980, few economists paid attention to the supply-side effects of taxes on employment and potential GDP. Then, when Ronald Reagan took office as President, a group of supply-siders began to argue the virtues of cutting taxes. Arthur Laffer was one of them. Laffer and his supporters were not held in high esteem among mainstream economists, but they did become influential for a period. They correctly argued that tax cuts would increase employment and

EYE on FISCAL STIMULUS

Did Fiscal Stimulus End the Recession?

In February 2009, in the depths of the 2008–2009 recession, Congress passed the American Recovery and Reinvestment Act, a $787 billion fiscal stimulus package that the President signed at an economic forum in Denver.

This Act of Congress is an example of discretionary fiscal policy. Did this action by Congress contribute to ending the 2008–2009 recession and making the recession less severe than it might have been?

The Obama Administration economists are confident that the answer is yes: The stimulus package made a significant contribution to easing and ending the recession.

But many, and perhaps most, economists think that the stimulus package played a small role and that the truly big story is not discretionary fiscal policy but the role played by automatic stabilizers.

Let's take a closer look at the fiscal policy actions and their likely effects.

Discretionary Fiscal Policy

In a number of speeches, President Obama promised that fiscal stimulus would save or create 650,000 jobs by the end of the 2009 summer. In October 2009, the Administration economists declared the promise fulfilled. Fiscal stimulus had saved or created the promised 650,000 jobs.

This claim of success might be correct but it isn't startling and it isn't a huge claim. To see why, start by asking how much GDP 650,000 people would produce. In 2009, each employed person produced $100,000 of real GDP on average. So 650,000 people would produce $65 billion of GDP.

Although the fiscal stimulus passed by Congress totalled $787 billion, by October 2009 only 20 percent of the stimulus had been spent (or taken in tax breaks). So the stimulus was about $160 billion.

If government outlays of $160 billion created $65 billion of GDP, the multiplier was 0.4 (65/160 = 0.4).

This multiplier is much smaller than the 1.6 that the Obama economists say will eventually occur. They believe, like Keynes, that the multiplier starts out small and gets larger over time as spending plans respond to rising incomes. An initial increase in expenditure increases aggregate expenditure. But the increase in aggregate expenditure generates higher incomes, which in turn induces greater consumption expenditure.

Automatic Fiscal Policy

Government revenue is sensitive to the state of the economy. When personal incomes and corporate profits fall, income tax revenues fall too. When unemployment increases, outlays on unemployment benefits and other social welfare benefits increase. These fiscal policy changes are automatic. They occur with speed and without help from Congress.

The scale of automatic fiscal policy changes depends of the depth of recession. In 2009, real GDP sank to 6 percent below potential GDP—a recessionary gap of $800 billion.

Responding to this deep recession, tax revenues crashed and transfer payments skyrocketed. The figure below shows the magnitudes as percentages of GDP. You can see that the automatic stabilizers were much bigger than the discretionary actions—six times as large. This automatic action, not the stimulus package, played the major role in limiting job losses.

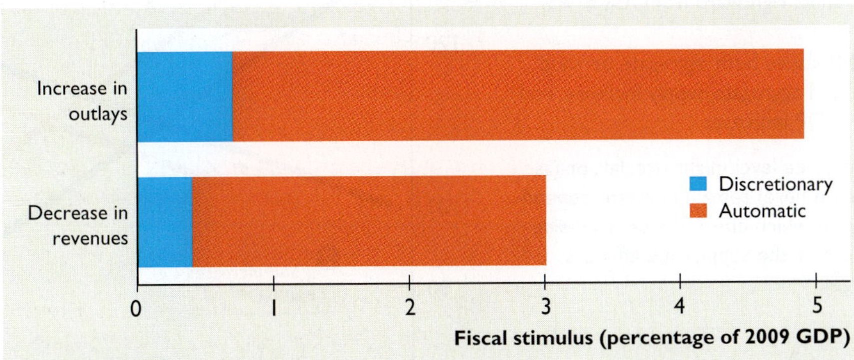

SOURCES OF DATA: Budget of the United States, 2010, Bureau of Economic Analysis, and White House press releases.

increase output. But they incorrectly argued that tax cuts would increase tax revenues by enough to decrease the budget deficit. Given that U.S. tax rates are among the lowest in the industrial world, it is unlikely that tax cuts would increase tax revenues. When the Reagan administration did cut taxes, the budget deficit increased, a fact that reinforces this view.

Supply-side economics became tarnished because of its association with Laffer and came to be called "voodoo economics." But mainstream economists, including Martin Feldstein, a Harvard professor who was Reagan's chief economic advisor, recognized the power of tax cuts as incentives but took the standard view that tax cuts without spending cuts would swell the budget deficit and bring a crowding-out effect. This view is now widely accepted by economists on both sides of the political debate.

Combined Demand-Side and Supply-Side Effects

You've seen that a fiscal stimulus increases aggregate demand and potential GDP. What is the combined demand-side and supply-side effect? When potential GDP increases, aggregate supply also increases (see Chapter 13, p. 329). When both aggregate demand and aggregate supply increase, we know that equilibrium real GDP increases, but the price level might rise, fall, or remain the same.

Figure 16.5 illustrates this last, neutral case. A fiscal stimulus increases aggregate demand and shifts the *AD* curve rightward from AD_0 to AD_1. The same fis-

FIGURE 16.5

The Combined Demand-Side and Supply-Side Effects of a Fiscal Stimulus

myeconlab Animation

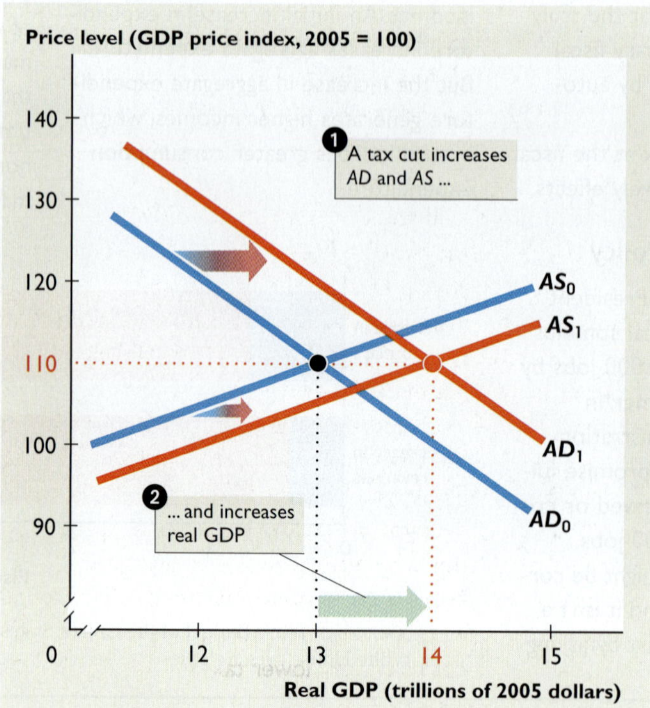

1 A tax cut increases disposable income, which increases aggregate demand and shifts the *AD* curve from AD_0 to AD_1. A tax cut also strengthens the incentives to work, save, and invest, which increases potential GDP and aggregate supply. The *AS* curve shifts rightward from AS_0 to AS_1.

2 Because both aggregate demand and aggregate supply increase, real GDP increases.

The price level might rise, fall, or (as shown here) remain constant depending on which effect, the demand-side effect or the supply-side effect, is larger.

cal action increases aggregate supply and shifts the *AS* curve rightward from AS_0 to AS_1. In this example, the increase in aggregate supply equals the increase in aggregate demand. This combination increases real GDP and leaves the price level unchanged.

If a fiscal stimulus increases aggregate supply by more than it increases aggregate demand, real GDP would still increase but the price level would fall. (Draw a figure like Figure 16.5 to show this case.) Similarly, if the increase in aggregate supply were smaller than the increase in aggregate demand, again real GDP would increase but the price level would rise. (Draw another figure like Figure 16.5 to show this case.)

Long-Run Fiscal Policy Effects

The long-run consequences of fiscal policy are the most profound ones. If investment is crowded out by a large budget deficit, the economic growth rate slows and potential GDP gets ever farther below what it might have been as the Lucas wedge widens. If a large budget deficit persists so that debt increases, confidence in the value of money is eroded and inflation erupts. History provides many examples of this consequence of a fiscal stimulus that gets out of control. It is these long-run effects of fiscal policy that make it vital to keep government outlays and budget deficits under control and to have a plan for restoring a balanced budget at full employment.

EYE on YOUR LIFE

Your Views on Fiscal Policy and How Fiscal Policy Affects You

Consider the U.S. economy right now. Using all the knowledge that you have accumulated during your course and by reading or watching the current news, try to determine the macroeconomic policy issues that face the U.S. economy today.

Do we have a business-cycle problem? Does the economy have a recessionary gap or an inflationary gap, or is the economy back at full employment?

Do we have a productivity problem? Is potential GDP either too low or growing too slowly?

In light of your assessment of the current state of the U.S. economy, what type of fiscal policy would you recommend and vote for?

Are you more concerned about the provision of public services, the size of the budget deficit, or the size of the tax wedge?

If you are more concerned about the provision of public services, would your preferred package include increased spending? If so, on what programs? Again, how would you pay for the expenditure?

If you are more concerned about the size of the budget deficit, how would you propose lowering it?

If you are more concerned about the tax wedge, would your preferred fiscal package include tax cuts? If it would, what public services would you cut to achieve lower taxes?

Consider recent changes in fiscal policy that you have seen reported in the media. What do you think these changes say about the federal government's views of the state of the economy? Do these views agree with yours?

Thinking further about the recent changes in fiscal policy: How do you expect these changes to affect you? How might your spending, saving, and labor supply decisions change?

Using your own responses to fiscal policy changes as an example, are these policy changes influencing aggregate demand, aggregate supply, or both? How do you think they will change real GDP?

myeconlab

Work these problems in Study Plan 16.3 to get instant feedback.

CHECKPOINT 16.3

Explain the supply-side effects of fiscal policy on employment, potential GDP, and the economic growth rate.

Practice Problems

1. The government cuts the income tax rate. Explain the effects of this action on the supply of labor, the demand for labor, the equilibrium level of employment, the real wage rate, and potential GDP.
2. What is the true income tax rate on interest income if the nominal interest rate is 8 percent a year, the inflation rate is 5 percent a year, and the tax rate on nominal interest is 25 percent?
3. The government cuts its outlays but keeps tax revenue unchanged. Explain the effects of this action on saving, investment, the real interest rate, and the growth rate of real GDP.
4. **Support builds for tax credit to help hiring**
   With about 10 percent of the labor force unemployed, the idea of a tax credit for businesses that create new jobs is gaining support. The current proposal is for the tax credit scheme to run for about 2 years.
   Source: *The New York Times*, October 6, 2009

   Explain how the tax credit will influence employment and potential GDP.

Guided Solutions to Practice Problems

1. When the government cuts the income tax rate, the supply of labor increases but the demand for labor does not change. The equilibrium level of employment increases. The real wage rate paid by employers decreases and the real wage rate received by workers increases—the tax wedge shrinks. With increased employment, potential GDP increases.
2. The true tax is 66.67 percent. With a nominal interest rate of 8 percent a year and a tax rate of 25 percent, the tax paid is 25 percent of 8 percent, which is 2 percent. The before-tax real interest rate is 8 percent minus 5 percent, which is 3 percent a year. The true tax paid is 2 percent tax divided by 3 percent before-tax real interest, which is 66.67 percent.
3. If the government cuts outlays but keeps tax revenue unchanged, the budget deficit decreases or the budget surplus increases. Either way, the supply of loanable funds to private borrowers increases. The real interest rate falls and private saving decreases, but total saving increases and investment increases. With greater investment, capital grows more quickly, and so does real GDP.
4. The tax credit will lower the cost of employing a new worker, so businesses will increase their current demand for labor. Given the supply of labor, the quantity of labor employed will increase and real GDP will increase. Once the tax credit scheme comes to an end, the cost of employing the new workers will rise and the demand for labor will return to its original level. Employment will return to the market equilibrium quantity. Potential GDP will not change.

CHAPTER SUMMARY

Key Points

1 Describe the federal budget process and the recent history of revenues, outlays, deficits, and debts.

- The federal budget is an annual statement of the outlays, tax revenues, and budget surplus or deficit of the government of the United States.
- Fiscal policy is the use of the federal budget to finance the federal government and to influence macroeconomic performance.

2 Explain the demand-side effects of fiscal policy on employment and real GDP.

- Fiscal policy became controversial during the 2008–2009 recession: Keynesians advocated aggressive fiscal stimulus and others urged a more cautious approach.
- Fiscal policy can be either discretionary or automatic.
- Changes in government expenditure and changes in taxes have multiplier effects on aggregate demand and can be used to try to keep real GDP at potential GDP.
- In practice, law-making time lags, a shrinking area of law-maker discretion, the difficulty of estimating potential GDP, and the limitations of economic forecasting seriously hamper discretionary fiscal policy.
- Automatic stabilizers arise because tax revenues and outlays fluctuate with real GDP.

3 Explain the supply-side effects of fiscal policy on employment, potential GDP, and the economic growth rate.

- The provision of public goods and services increases productivity and increases potential GDP.
- Income taxes create a wedge between the wage rate paid by firms and received by workers and lower both employment and potential GDP.
- Income taxes create a wedge between the interest rate paid by firms and received by lenders and lower saving and investment and the growth rate of real GDP.
- A government budget deficit raises the real interest rate and crowds out some private investment, which slows real GDP growth.

Key Terms

myeconlab

Work these problems in Chapter 16 Study Plan to get instant feedback.

CHAPTER CHECKPOINT

Study Plan Problems and Applications

1. Suppose that in an economy, investment is $400 billion, saving is $400 billion, tax revenues are $500 billion, exports are $300 billion, and imports are $200 billion. Calculate government expenditure and the government's budget balance.
2. Classify the following items as automatic fiscal policy actions, discretionary fiscal policy actions, or neither.
   - An increase in expenditure on homeland security
   - An increase in unemployment benefits paid during a recession
   - Decreased expenditures on national defense during peace time
   - An increase in Medicaid expenditure brought about by a flu epidemic
   - A cut in farm subsidies
3. The U.S. economy is in recession and has a large recessionary gap. Describe what automatic fiscal policy might occur. Describe a fiscal stimulus that could be used that would not increase the budget deficit.

OilPatch is a mineral rich economy in which the government gets most of its tax revenue from oil royalties. But OilPatch has an income tax. Table 1 describes the labor market in OilPatch and Table 2 describes the economy's production function. The government introduces an income tax of $2 per hour worked. Use Tables 1 and 2 to work Problems 4 to 6.

TABLE 1 LABOR MARKET

Real wage rate (dollars per hour)	Quantity of labor demanded (thousands of hours)	Quantity of labor supplied (thousands of hours)
10	6	2
11	5	3
12	4	4
13	3	5
14	2	6
15	1	7

TABLE 2 PRODUCTION FUNCTION

Employment (thousands of hours)	Real GDP (millions of dollars)
2	6
3	11
4	15
5	18
6	20
7	21

4. What are the levels of employment and potential GDP in OilPatch, what is the real wage rate paid by employers, and what is the after-tax real wage rate received by workers?
5. If OilPatch eliminates its income tax, what then are the levels of employment and potential GDP and what is the real wage rate in OilPatch?
6. If OilPatch doubles its income tax to $4 an hour, what then are the levels of employment and potential GDP? What is the real wage rate paid by employers and the after-tax real wage rate received by workers?
7. The income tax rate on all forms of income is 40 percent and there is a tax of 10 percent on all consumption expenditure. The nominal interest rate is 7 percent a year and the inflation rate is 5 percent a year. What is the size of the tax wedge on wages and what is the true tax rate on interest?

Use the following information to work Problems 8 and 9.

IMF urges global stimulus

The IMF forecasted that world growth in 2009 would fall to 2.2 percent. Olivier Blanchard (IMF Chief Economist) said that a coordinated G-20 fiscal stimulus is needed and needed soon.

Source: IMF Survey Online, November 6, 2008

8. Explain the effects of fiscal stimulus if it is implemented well.
9. The Canadian Prime Minister Stephen Harper warned on November 6, 2008 that if policy makers adopt too large a fiscal stimulus then long-term growth might be jeopardized. Explain what he meant.

Instructor Assignable Problems and Applications

Your instructor can assign these problems as homework, a quiz, or a test in **MyEconLab**.

1. From the peak in 1929 to the Great Depression trough in 1933, government tax revenues fell by 1.9 percent of GDP and government expenditure increased by 0.3 percent. Real GDP fell by 25 percent. Compare and contrast this experience with the fiscal policy that accompanied the 2008–2009 recession. What did fiscal policy do to moderate the last recession that was largely absent during the Great Depression?
2. Suppose that the U.S. government increases its expenditure on highways and bridges by $100 billion. Explain the effect that this expenditure would have on aggregate demand and real GDP.
3. Suppose that the U.S. government increases its expenditure on highways and bridges by $100 billion. Explain the effect that this expenditure would have on needs-tested spending and the government's budget surplus.

Table 1 describes the labor market in LowTaxLand and Table 2 describes the economy's production function. LowTaxLand introduces an income tax of $1 per hour worked. Use Tables 1 and 2 to work Problems 4 to 6.

TABLE 1 LABOR MARKET

Real wage rate (dollars per hour)	Quantity of labor demanded (thousands of hours)	Quantity of labor supplied (thousands of hours)
10.00	18	6
10.50	15	9
11.00	12	12
11.50	9	15
12.00	6	18
12.50	3	21

TABLE 2 PRODUCTION FUNCTION

Employment (thousands of hours)	Real GDP (millions of dollars)
6	7
9	12
12	16
15	19
18	21
21	22

4. What are the levels of employment and potential GDP in LowTaxLand, what is the real wage rate paid by employers, and what is the after-tax real wage rate received by workers?
5. If LowTaxLand eliminates its income tax, what then are the levels of employment and potential GDP and what is the real wage rate in LowTaxLand?
6. If LowTaxLand doubles its income tax to $2 an hour, what then are the levels of employment and potential GDP? What is the real wage rate paid by employers and the after-tax real wage rate received by workers?
7. Describe the supply-side effects of a fiscal stimulus and explain how a tax cut will influence potential GDP.
8. Use an aggregate supply–aggregate demand graph to illustrate the effects on real GDP and the price level of a fiscal stimulus when the economy is in recession.

Use the following information to work Problems 9 and 11.

Federal deficit hits record $1.42 trillion

In 2009, the government collected $2.10 trillion in revenues, a drop of 16.6 percent while government spending jumped to $3.52 trillion, up 18.2 percent over 2008. The Obama administration has pledged to include a deficit-reduction plan in its 2011 budget, which will go to Congress in February 2010.

Source: *Charleston Daily Mail*, October 16, 2009

9. If the deficit-reduction plan includes a cut in transfer payments and a rise in taxes of the same amount, how will this policy influence the budget deficit and real GDP?
10. If the deficit-reduction plan includes an increase in taxes on the wealthy, explain how this policy might have serious supply-side consequences for both potential GDP and the growth rate of real GDP.

11. If the deficit-reduction plan includes an increase in the tax rate on interest income and a decrease in the tax rate on wage income, how will this policy influence the labor market and the equilibrium amount of loanable funds? Also explain how this policy will influence potential GDP.

Use the following information to work Problems 12 and 13.

Suppose that in an economy, investment is $160 billion, saving is $140 billion, government expenditure on goods and services is $150 billion, exports are $200 billion, and imports are $250 billion.

12. Calculate the tax revenue and the budget balance.
13. What fiscal policy action might increase investment and speed economic growth? Explain how the policy would work.
14. Suppose that the output gap in an economy becomes a large recessionary gap. Describe the automatic fiscal policy actions that might occur. Explain how they would work.
15. Suppose that an economy is in a boom and the inflationary gap is large. Describe the discretionary fiscal policy that the government might introduce. Explain how it would work.

Use the following information to work Problems 16 and 17.

Suppose that the tax on interest income is levied on the nominal interest rate, the tax rate is 20 percent, and the real interest rate is 3 percent a year.

16. If there is no inflation, calculate the after-tax real interest rate and the true tax rate on interest income.
17. If there is 5 percent inflation, calculate the after-tax real interest rate and the true tax rate on interest income.
18. **Australian GDP to grow faster than expected**

    The Australian economy will grow faster than previously forecast. Growth was driven by a surge in consumer spending after the government distributed more than $20 billion in cash to households and the government has begun spending $22 billion on roads, railways, and schools. The current deficit is $57 billion.

    Source: Bloomberg.com, November 3, 2009

    The economy is no longer in recession. Explain why the faster than expected growth might have pushed the economy into an inflationary gap.

Did the Fed save us from another Great Depression?

When banks stopped lending, the Fed flooded them with reserves. Did that action avoid a financial meltdown and depression?

17

Monetary Policy

CHAPTER CHECKLIST

When you have completed your study of this chapter, you will be able to

1 Describe the objectives of U.S. monetary policy, the framework for achieving those objectives, and the Fed's monetary policy actions.

2 Explain the transmission channels through which the Fed influences real GDP and the inflation rate.

3 Explain and compare alternative monetary policy strategies.

17.1 HOW THE FED CONDUCTS MONETARY POLICY

A nation's monetary policy objectives and the framework for setting and achieving those objectives stem from the relationship between the central bank and the government. We'll describe the objectives of U.S. monetary policy and the framework and assignment of responsibility for achieving those objectives.

Monetary Policy Objectives

The objectives of monetary policy are ultimately political. In the United States, these objectives are set out in the mandate of the Board of Governors of the Federal Reserve System, which is defined by the Federal Reserve Act of 1913 and its subsequent amendments.

Federal Reserve Act

The Fed's mandate was most recently clarified in an amendment to the Federal Reserve Act passed by Congress in 2000, which states that

> The Board of Governors of the Federal Reserve System and the Federal Open Market Committee shall maintain long-run growth of the monetary and credit aggregates commensurate with the economy's long-run potential to increase production, so as to promote effectively the goals of maximum employment, stable prices, and moderate long-term interest rates.

Goals and Means

This description of the Fed's monetary policy objectives has two distinct parts: a statement of goals and a prescription of the means by which to pursue the goals.

Goals of Monetary Policy

The Fed's goals are "maximum employment, stable prices, and moderate long-term interest rates." In the *long run*, these goals are in harmony and reinforce each other.

The goal of "maximum employment" means attaining the maximum sustainable growth rate of potential GDP, keeping real GDP close to potential GDP, and keeping the unemployment rate close to the natural unemployment rate. The goal of "stable prices" means keeping the inflation rate low. Achieving the goal of "moderate long-term interest rates" means keeping long-term *nominal* interest rates close to the long-term *real* interest rate.

Price stability is the key goal. It provides the best available environment for households and firms to make the saving and investment decisions that bring economic growth. So price stability encourages the maximum sustainable growth rate of potential GDP.

Price stability delivers moderate long-term interest rates because the nominal interest rate equals the real interest rate plus the inflation rate. With stable prices, the nominal interest rate is close to the real interest rate, and most of the time, this rate is likely to be moderate.

While the Fed's goals are in harmony in the long run, in the short run, the Fed faces a tradeoff. You saw in Chapter 15 that taking an action that is designed to lower the inflation rate and achieve stable prices lowers employment and real GDP and increases the unemployment rate in the short run.

Means for Achieving the Goals

The 2000 law instructs the Fed to pursue its goals by "maintain[ing] long-run growth of the monetary and credit aggregates commensurate with the economy's long-run potential to increase production." You can perhaps recognize this statement as being consistent with the quantity theory of money that you studied in Chapter 12 (see pp. 310–313). The "economy's long-run potential to increase production" is the growth rate of potential GDP. The "monetary and credit aggregates" are the quantities of money and loans. By keeping the growth rate of the quantity of money in line with the growth rate of potential GDP, the Fed is expected to be able to maintain full employment and keep the price level stable.

Prerequisite for Achieving the Goals

The financial crisis that started in the summer of 2007 and intensified in the fall of 2008 brought the problem of financial instability to the top of the Fed's agenda. The focus of policy became the single-minded pursuit of **financial stability**—of enabling financial markets and institutions to resume their normal functions of allocating capital resources and risk.

Financial stability
A situation in which financial markets and institutions function normally to allocate capital resources and risk.

The pursuit of financial stability by the Fed is not an abandonment of the mandated goals of maximum employment and stable prices. Rather, it is a prerequisite for attaining those goals. Financial instability has the potential to bring severe recession and deflation—falling prices—and undermine the attainment of the mandated goals.

To pursue its mandated monetary policy goals, the Fed must make the general concepts of maximum employment and stable prices precise and operational.

Operational "Maximum Employment" Goal

The Fed pays close attention to the business cycle and tries to steer a steady course between inflation and recession. To gauge the state of output and employment relative to full employment, the Fed looks at a large number of indicators that include the labor force participation rate, the unemployment rate, measures of capacity utilization, activity in the housing market, the stock market, and regional information gathered by the regional Federal Reserve Banks. All these data are summarized in the Fed's *Beige Book.*

The *output gap*—the percentage deviation of real GDP from potential GDP—summarizes the state of aggregate demand relative to potential GDP. A positive output gap—an *inflationary gap*—brings rising inflation. A negative output gap—a *recessionary gap*—results in lost output and unemployment above the natural unemployment rate. The Fed tries to minimize the output gap.

Operational "Stable Prices" Goal

The Fed believes that core inflation provides the best indication of whether price stability is being achieved. The *core inflation rate* is the annual percentage change in the Personal Consumption Expenditure deflator (PCE deflator) *excluding* the prices of food and fuel (see Chapter 7, pp. 177–178).

The Fed has not defined price stability but many economists regard it as meaning a core inflation rate of between 1 and 2 percent a year. Former Fed Chairman Alan Greenspan said that "price stability is best thought of as an environment in which inflation is so low and stable over time that it does not materially enter into the decisions of households and firms."

Responsibility for Monetary Policy

Who is responsible for monetary policy in the United States? What are the roles of the Fed, Congress, and the President?

The Role of the Fed

The Federal Reserve Act makes the Board of Governors of the Federal Reserve System and the Federal Open Market Committee (FOMC) responsible for the conduct of monetary policy. We described the composition of the FOMC in Chapter 11 (see p. 280). The FOMC makes a monetary policy decision at eight scheduled meetings a year and publishes its minutes three weeks after each meeting.

The Role of Congress

Congress plays no role in making monetary policy decisions, but the Federal Reserve Act requires the Board of Governors to report on monetary policy to Congress. The Fed makes two reports each year, one in February and another in July. These reports, along with the Fed Chairman's testimony before Congress and the minutes of the FOMC, communicate the Fed's thinking on monetary policy to lawmakers and the public.

The Role of the President

The formal role of the President of the United States is limited to appointing the members and the Chairman of the Board of Governors. But some Presidents—Richard Nixon was one—have tried to influence Fed decisions.

You now know the objectives of monetary policy and can describe the framework and assignment of responsibility for achieving those objectives. Your next task is to see how the Fed conducts its monetary policy.

Choosing a Policy Instrument

Monetary policy instrument
A variable that the Fed can directly control or closely target and that influences the economy in desirable ways.

To conduct its monetary policy, the Fed must select a **monetary policy instrument**, a variable that the Fed can directly control or closely target and that influences the economy in desirable ways.

As the sole issuer of the *monetary base*, the Fed is a monopoly. A monopoly can fix the quantity of its product and leave the market to determine the price; or it can fix the price of its product and leave the market to choose the quantity. The "price" of monetary base is the **federal funds rate**, the interest rate at which banks can borrow and lend reserves in the federal funds market. The Fed can target the monetary base or the federal funds rate, but not both. If the Fed wants to decrease the monetary base, the federal funds rate must rise; and if the Fed wants to raise the federal funds rate, the monetary base must decrease.

Federal funds rate
The interest rate at which banks can borrow and lend reserves in the federal funds market.

The Federal Funds Rate

The Fed's choice of monetary policy instrument is the federal funds rate. Given this choice, the Fed permits the monetary base and the quantity of money to find their own equilibrium values and has no preset targets for them.

Figure 17.1 shows the federal funds rate since 2000. You can see that the federal funds rate was 5.5 percent at the beginning of 2000 and during 2000 and 2001, the Fed increased the rate to 6.5 percent. The Fed raised the interest rate to this high level to lower the inflation rate.

FIGURE 17.1

The Fed's Key Monetary Policy Instrument: The Federal Funds Rate

myeconlab Animation

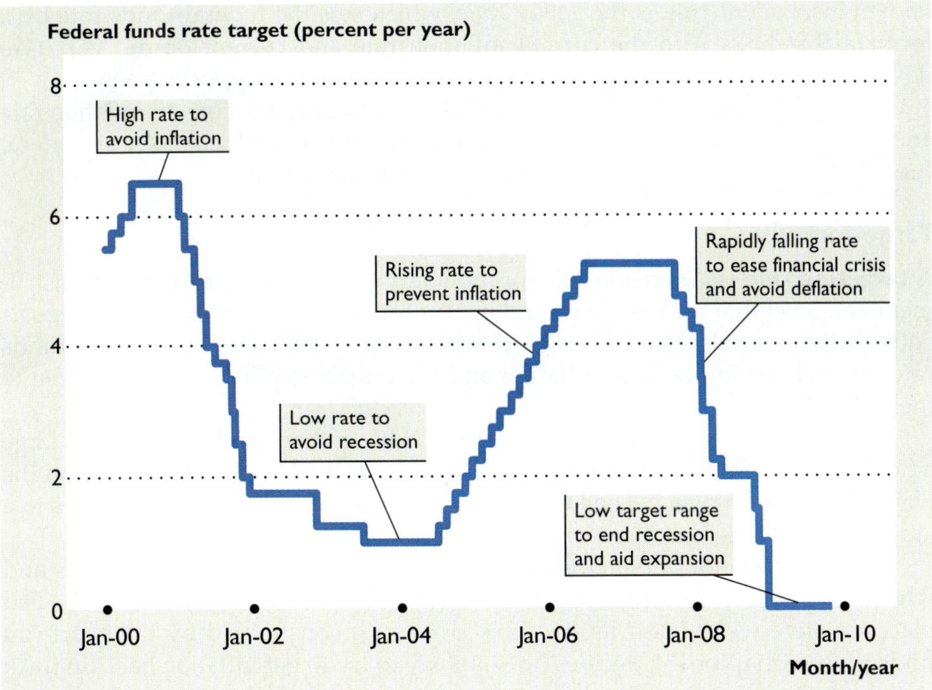

The Fed sets a target for the federal funds rate and then takes actions to keep the rate close to target.

When the Fed wants to slow inflation, it raises the federal funds rate target.

When the inflation rate is below target and the Fed wants to avoid recession, it lowers the federal funds rate target.

When the Fed focussed on restoring financial stability, it cut the federal funds rate target aggressively to almost zero.

SOURCE OF DATA: Board of Governors of the Federal Reserve System.

Between 2002 and 2004, the federal funds rate was set at historically low levels. The reason is that with inflation well anchored at close to 2 percent a year, the Fed was less concerned about inflation than it was about recession so it wanted to lean in the direction of avoiding recession.

From mid-2004 through early 2006, the Fed was increasingly concerned about the build-up of inflation pressures and it raised the federal funds rate target on 17 occasions to take it to 5.25 percent, a level that was held until September 2007.

When the global financial crisis began, the Fed acted cautiously in cutting the federal funds rate target. But as the crisis intensified, rate cuts became more frequent and larger, ending in December 2008 with an interest rate close to zero. The normal changes of a quarter of a percentage point (also called 25 *basis points*) were abandoned as the Fed slashed the rate, first by an unusual 50 basis points and finally, in December 2008, by an unprecedented 100 basis points.

How does the Fed decide the appropriate level for the federal funds rate? And how, having made that decision, does the Fed move the federal funds rate to its target level?

The Fed's Decision-Making Strategy

Two alternative decision-making strategies might be used by a central bank and they are summarized as two alternative *rules*:

- Instrument rule
- Targeting rule

Instrument Rule

Instrument rule
A decision rule for monetary policy that sets the policy instrument by a formula based on the current state of the economy.

An **instrument rule** is a decision rule for monetary policy that sets the policy instrument by a formula based on the current state of the economy. The best-known instrument rule is the *Taylor Rule*, which sets the federal funds rate by a formula that links it to the current inflation rate and current output gap. (We describe the Taylor Rule in *Eye on the U.S. Economy* on the opposite page.)

To implement the Taylor rule, the FOMC would plug the current inflation rate and output gap into the formula and calculate the level at which to set the federal funds rate. A computer would make the interest rate decision.

Targeting Rule

Targeting rule
A decision rule for monetary policy that sets the policy instrument at a level that makes the central bank's forecast of the ultimate policy goals equal to their targets.

A **targeting rule** is a decision rule for monetary policy that sets the policy instrument at a level that makes the central bank's forecast of the ultimate policy goals equal to their targets. The Fed employs such a rule. The Fed sets the federal funds rate that gets its forecasts of inflation and the output gap as close as possible to their target levels.

To implement its targeting rule, the FOMC gathers and processes a large amount of information about the economy, the way it responds to shocks, and the way it responds to policy. The FOMC then processes all these data and comes to a judgment about the best level for the federal funds rate.

The Fed does not pursue formal published targets: It has implicit targets and when the economy deviates from these targets, as it does most of the time, the Fed places relative weights on its two objectives and, constrained by the short-run tradeoff (see Chapter 15), decides how quickly to try to get inflation back on track or the economy back to full employment.

We've now described the Fed's monetary policy instrument and the FOMC's strategy for setting it. We next see what the Fed does to make the federal funds rate hit its target.

Hitting the Federal Funds Rate Target

The federal funds rate is the interest rate that banks earn (or pay) when they lend (or borrow) reserves. The federal funds rate is also the opportunity cost of holding reserves. Holding a larger quantity of reserves is the alternative to lending reserves to another bank, and holding a smaller quantity of reserves is the alternative to borrowing reserves from another bank. So the quantity of reserves that banks are willing to hold varies with the federal funds rate: The higher the federal funds rate, the smaller is the quantity of reserves that the banks plan to hold.

The Fed controls the quantity of reserves supplied, and the Fed can change this quantity by conducting an open market operation. You learned in Chapter 11 (pp. 285–288) how an open market purchase increases reserves and an open market sale decreases reserves. To hit the federal funds rate target, the New York Fed conducts open market operations until the supply of reserves is at just the right quantity to hit the target federal funds rate.

Figure 17.2 illustrates this outcome in the market for bank reserves. The x-axis measures the quantity of bank reserves on deposit at the Fed, and the y-axis measures the federal funds rate. The demand for reserves—the willingness of the banks to hold reserves—is the curve labeled *RD*.

The Fed's open market operations determine the supply of reserves, which is the supply curve *RS*. To decrease reserves, the Fed conducts an open market sale.

FIGURE 17.2

Equilibrium in the Market for Bank Reserves

myeconlab Animation

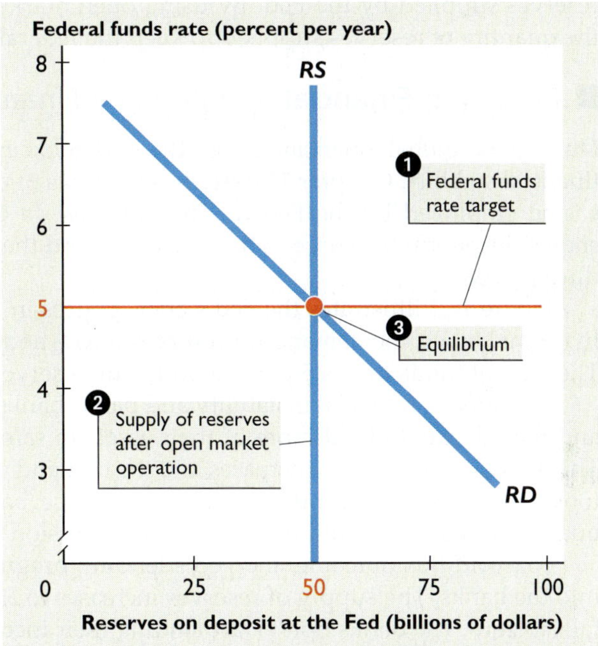

The federal funds rate (on the y-axis) is the opportunity cost of holding reserves: The higher the federal funds rate, the smaller is the quantity of reserves that banks want to hold. The demand curve for bank reserves is *RD*.

1. The FOMC sets the federal funds rate target at 5 percent a year.
2. The New York Fed conducts open market operations to make the quantity of reserves supplied equal to $50 billion and the supply of reserves curve is *RS*.
3. Equilibrium in the market for bank reserves occurs at the target federal funds rate.

EYE on the U.S. ECONOMY

The Fed's Interest Rate Decisions and the Taylor Rule

John B. Taylor (Stanford University) has proposed a formula for setting the federal funds rate—the *Taylor Rule*.

If the inflation rate is 2 percent a year and there is no output gap, the Taylor rule sets the federal funds rate to neutral at 4 percent a year.

A 1 percent deviation of the inflation rate from target and a 1 percent deviation of real GDP from potential GDP moves the federal funds rate up or down by 0.5 percent.

The Taylor Rule was derived by crunching a large amount of U.S. macroeconomic data to construct a statistical model of the economy.

The figure shows the Fed's decision and the Taylor rule since 2000. Taylor thinks the Fed moved the interest rate too low and kept it too low for too long and then raised the interest rate too fast and by too much. He believes the Fed's deviation from his rule contributed to the global financial crisis.

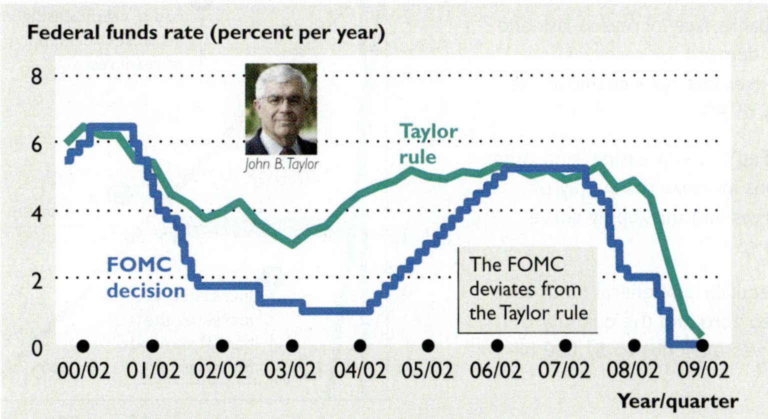

SOURCES OF DATA: Federal Reserve Board and Federal Reserve Bank of St Louis.

To increase reserves, the Fed conducts an open market purchase.

Equilibrium in the market for bank reserves determines the federal funds rate where the quantity of reserves demanded by the banks equals the quantity of reserves supplied by the Fed. By using open market operations, the Fed adjusts the quantity of reserves supplied to keep the federal funds rate on target.

Restoring Financial Stability in a Financial Crisis

During the global financial crisis, the Fed took extraordinary steps to restore financial stability. Chapter 11 describes the tools of quantitative easing and credit easing employed by the Fed (p. 281) and *Eye on Creating Money* (pp. 290–291) shows the enormous surge in bank reserves and the monetary base that occurred during 2008.

Figure 17.3 illustrates the Fed's crisis polices in the market for bank reserves. In normal times, the demand for reserves is RD_0 and the supply of reserves is RS_0. The federal funds rate is 5 percent and bank reserves are $50 billion.

At a time of financial instability and panic, banks' assessments of risk increase and they decide to hold more of their assets in safe, reserve deposits at the Fed. The demand for reserves increases and the demand curve becomes RD_1. If the Fed took no actions, the federal funds rate would rise, bank lending would shrink, the quantity of money would decrease, and a recession would intensify.

To avoid this outcome, the Fed's lending programs pump billions of dollars into the banks. The supply of reserves increases to RS_1, and the federal funds rate falls to zero. The banks don't start lending their increased reserves. They hang on to them. But flush with reserves, banks don't call in loans and deepen the recession. The Fed's action averted a worsening credit crisis and worsening recession.

FIGURE 17.3

The Market for Bank Reserves in a Financial Crisis

myeconlab Animation

In a normal time, the demand for bank reserves is RD_0 and the supply of reserves is RS_0. The federal funds rate is 5 percent per year.

In a financial crisis:

1. The banks face increased risk and their demand for reserves increases and the demand curve shifts to RD_1.
2. The Fed's "credit easing" and other actions increase the supply of reserves and the supply curve shifts to RS_1.
3. The equilibrium federal funds rate falls to zero and the quantity of reserves explodes to $1,000 billion.

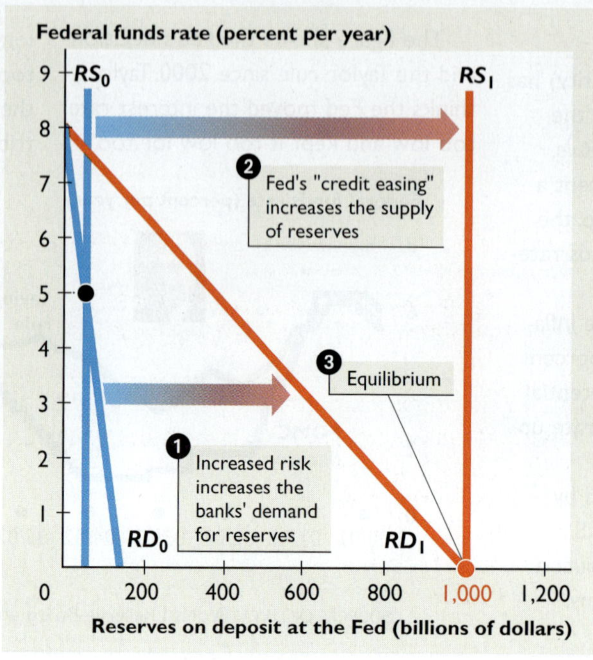

CHECKPOINT 17.1

Describe the objectives of U.S. monetary policy, the framework for achieving those objectives, and the Fed's monetary policy actions.

myeconlab

Work these problems in Study Plan 17.1 to get instant feedback.

Practice Problems

1. What are the objectives of U.S. monetary policy?
2. What is core inflation and how does it differ from total PCE inflation?
3. What is the Fed's monetary policy instrument and what influences the level at which the Fed sets it?
4. Figure 1 shows the demand curve for bank reserves, *RD*. The current quantity of reserves supplied is $20 billion. The Fed wants to set the federal funds rate at 4 percent a year. Illustrate the target on the graph and show the supply of reserves that will achieve the target. Does the Fed conduct an open market operation and if so, does it buy or sell securities?
5. **Money on autopilot**
   In the third quarter of 2009, GDP grew at 3.5% a year. With no risk of inflation, the FOMC is mainly focused on the output gap.
   Source: *The Wall Street Journal*, November 5, 2009

   Explain whether this description of the Fed's focus in the third quarter of 2009 is consistent with its monetary policy objectives.

FIGURE 1

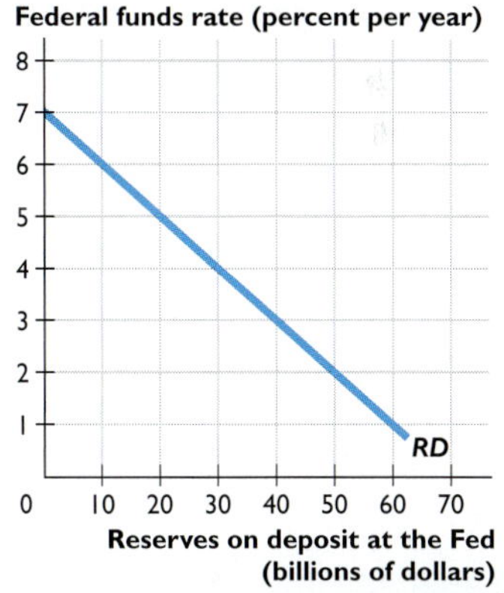

Guided Solutions to Practice Problems

1. The objectives of U.S. monetary policy are to achieve stable prices (interpreted at a core inflation rate of about 2 percent per year) and maximum employment (interpreted as full employment).
2. Core inflation excludes the changes in the prices of food and fuel. The total PCE inflation rate includes the changes in all consumer prices. The core inflation rate fluctuates less than the total PCE inflation rate.
3. The federal funds rate is the Fed's monetary policy instrument and the inflation rate and output gap are two of the influences on the level at which the Fed sets the federal funds rate.
4. Figure 2 shows the market for bank reserves. If the initial quantity of reserves supplied was $20 billion, the federal funds rate must have been 5 percent a year at point *A*. To set the federal funds rate at 4 percent a year, the Fed must conduct an open market purchase of securities to increase the supply of reserves to *RS*. With supply *RS*, the equilibrium federal funds rate equals the 4 percent target rate.
5. The objectives of monetary policy are maximum employment and stable prices. The maximum-employment goal means keeping the economy as close as possible to potential GDP. The stable-prices goal means keeping the inflation rate low. In 2009, the inflation rate was low but the unemployment rate and the output gap were high. By focusing on the output gap, the Fed was seeking to re-establish "maximum employment." The Fed believed that inflation would remain low, so its focus was consistent with its monetary policy objectives.

FIGURE 2

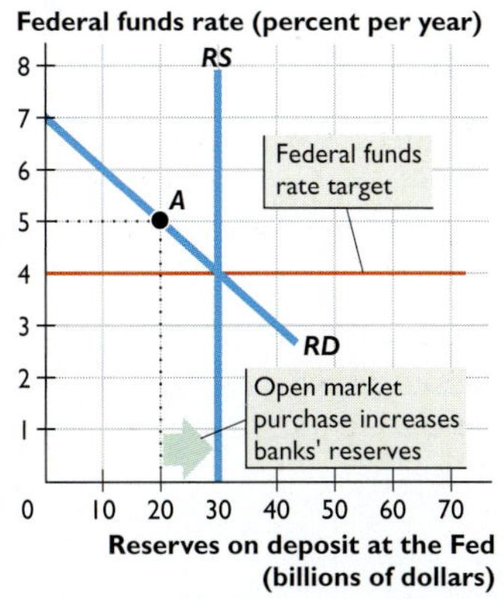

17.2 MONETARY POLICY TRANSMISSION

You've seen that the Fed's goal is to keep the inflation rate around 2 percent a year and to keep the output gap close to zero. You've also seen how the Fed uses its market power to set the federal funds rate at the level that is designed to achieve these objectives. We're now going to trace the events that follow a change in the federal funds rate and see how those events lead to the ultimate policy goals. We'll begin with a quick overview of the transmission process and then look a bit more closely at each step.

Quick Overview

When the Fed lowers the federal funds rate, other short-term interest rates and the exchange rate also fall. The quantity of money and the supply of loanable funds increase. The long-term real interest rate falls. The lower real interest rate increases consumption expenditure and investment. The lower exchange rate makes U.S. exports cheaper and imports more costly, so net exports increase. Easier bank loans reinforce the effect of lower interest rates on aggregate expenditure. Aggregate demand increases, which increases real GDP and the price level relative to what they would have been. Real GDP growth and inflation speed up.

When the Fed raises the federal funds rate, as the sequence of events that we've just reviewed plays out, the effects are in the opposite directions.

Figure 17.4 provides a schematic summary of these ripple effects for both a cut and a rise in the federal funds rate. These ripple effects stretch out over a period of between one and two years. The interest rate and exchange rate effects are immediate. The effects on money and bank loans follow in a few weeks and run for a few months. Real long-term interest rates change quickly and often in anticipation of the short-term rate changes. Spending plans change and real GDP growth changes after about one year. The inflation rate changes between one year and two years after the change in the federal funds rate. But these time lags are not entirely predictable and can be longer or shorter. We're going to look at each stage in the transmission process, starting with the interest rate effects.

Interest Rate Changes

The first effect of a monetary policy decision by the FOMC is a change in the federal funds rate. Other interest rates then change. These interest rate effects occur quickly and relatively predictably.

The interest rates on U.S. government 3-month Treasury bills is immediately affected by a change in the federal funds rate. A powerful substitution effect keeps these two rates close to each other. Banks have a choice about how to hold their short-term liquid assets and a loan to another bank is a close substitute for holding Treasury bills. If the interest rate on Treasury bills is higher than the federal funds rate, the banks increase the quantity of Treasury bills held and decrease loans to other banks. The price of a Treasury bill rises and the interest rate falls. Similarly, if the interest rate on Treasury bills is lower than the federal funds rate, the banks decrease the quantity of Treasury bills held and increase loans to other banks. The price of a Treasury bill falls, and the interest rate rises. When the interest rate on Treasury bills is close to the federal funds rate, there is no incentive for a bank to switch between making loans to other banks and holding Treasury bills. Both the Treasury bill market and the federal funds market are in equilibrium.

FIGURE 17.4
Ripple Effects of the Fed's Actions

myeconlab Animation

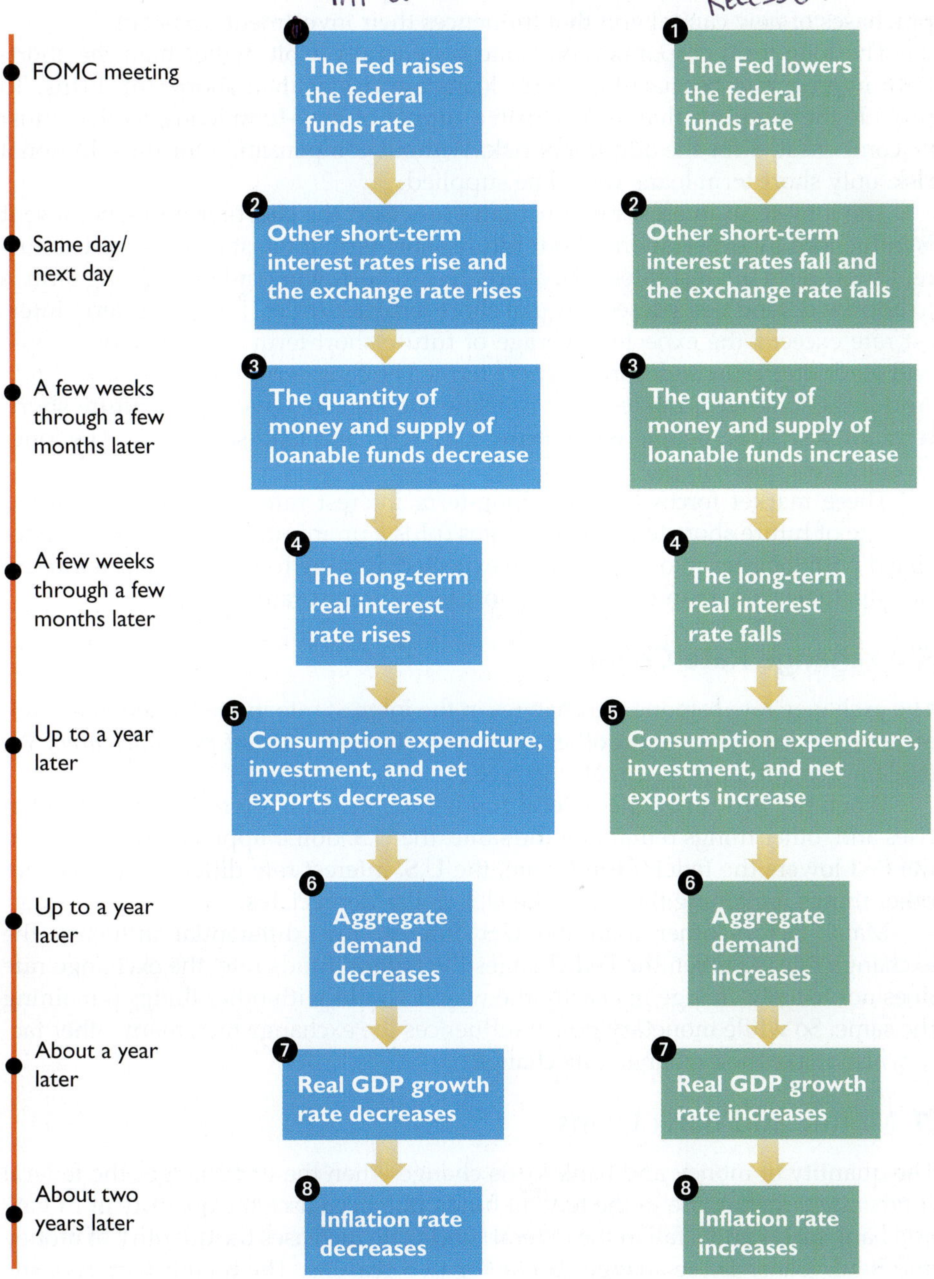

(a) The Fed tightens **(b) The Fed eases**

The Fed changes its interest rate target and conducts open market operations to ❶ change the federal funds rate. The same day ❷ other short-term interest rates change and so does the exchange rate. A few weeks through a few months after the FOMC meeting, ❸ the quantity of money and supply of loanable funds changes, which ❹ changes the long-term real interest rate.

Up to a year after the FOMC meeting, ❺ consumption, investment, and net exports change, so ❻ aggregate demand changes. Eventually, the change in the federal funds rate has ripple effects that ❼ change real GDP and about two years after the FOMC meeting, ❽ the inflation rate changes.

Long-term interest rates also change, but not by as much as short-term rates. The long-term corporate bond rate, the interest rate paid on bonds issued by large corporations, is the most significant interest rate to be influenced by the federal funds rate. It is this interest rate that businesses pay on the loans that finance their purchases of new capital and that influences their investment decisions.

The long-term corporate bond rate is generally a bit higher than the short-term interest rate because long-term loans are riskier than short-term loans. To provide the incentive that brings forth a supply of long-term loans, lenders must be compensated for the additional risk. Without compensation for the additional risk, only short-term loans would be supplied.

The long-term interest rate fluctuates less than the short-term rate because it is influenced by expectations about future short-term interest rates as well as current short-term interest rates. The alternative to borrowing or lending long term is to borrow or lend using a sequence of short-term securities. If the long-term interest rate exceeds the expected average of future short-term interest rates, people will lend long term and borrow short term. The long-term interest rate will fall. And if the long-term interest rate is below the expected average of future short-term interest rates, people will borrow long term and lend short term. The long-term interest rate will rise.

These market forces keep the long-term interest rate close to the expected average of future short-term interest rates (plus a premium for the extra risk associated with long-term loans). And the expected average future short-term interest rate fluctuates less than the current short-term interest rate.

Exchange Rate Changes

The exchange rate responds to changes in the interest rate in the United States relative to the interest rates in other countries—the *U.S. interest rate differential.* We explain this influence in Chapter 19 (see pp. 488, 491, 493).

When the Fed raises the federal funds rate, the U.S. interest rate differential rises and, other things remaining the same, the U.S. dollar appreciates. And when the Fed lowers the federal funds rate, the U.S. interest rate differential falls and, other things remaining the same, the U.S. dollar depreciates.

Many factors other than the U.S. interest rate differential influence the exchange rate, so when the Fed changes the federal funds rate, the exchange rate does not usually change in exactly the way it would with other things remaining the same. So while monetary policy influences the exchange rate, many other factors also make the exchange rate change.

Money and Bank Loans

The quantity of money and bank loans change when the Fed changes the federal funds rate target. A rise in the federal funds rate decreases the quantity of money and bank loans; and a fall in the federal funds rate increases the quantity of money and bank loans. These changes occur for two reasons: The quantity of deposits and loans created by the banking system changes and the quantity of money demanded changes.

You've seen that to change the federal funds rate, the Fed must change the quantity of bank reserves. A change in the quantity of bank reserves changes the monetary base, which in turn changes the quantity of deposits and loans that the banking system can create. A rise in the federal funds rate decreases reserves and decreases the quantity of deposits and bank loans created; and a fall in the federal funds rate increases reserves and increases the quantity of deposits and bank loans created.

The quantity of money created by the banking system must be held by households and firms. The change in the interest rate changes the quantity of money demanded. A fall in the interest rate increases the quantity of money demanded and a rise in the interest rate decreases the quantity of money demanded.

A change in the quantity of money and the supply of bank loans directly affects consumption and investment plans. With more money and easier access to loans, consumers and firms spend more. With less money and loans harder to get, consumers and firms spend less.

The Long-Term Real Interest Rate

Demand and supply in the market for loanable funds determine the long-term real interest rate, which equals the long-term nominal interest rate minus the expected inflation rate. The long-term real interest rate influences expenditure decisions.

In the long run, demand and supply in the loanable funds market depend only on real forces—on saving and investment decisions. But in the short run, when the price level is not fully flexible, the supply of loanable funds is influenced by the supply of bank loans. Changes in the federal funds rate change the supply of bank loans, which changes the supply of loanable funds and changes the real interest rate in the loanable funds market.

A fall in the federal funds rate that increases the supply of bank loans increases the supply of loanable funds and lowers the equilibrium real interest rate. A rise in the federal funds rate that decreases the supply of bank loans decreases the supply of loanable funds and raises the equilibrium real interest rate.

These changes in the real interest rate, along with the other factors we've just described, change expenditure plans.

Expenditure Plans

The ripple effects that follow a change in the federal funds rate change three components of aggregate expenditure:

- Consumption expenditure
- Investment
- Net exports

Other things remaining the same, the lower the real interest rate, the greater is the amount of consumption expenditure and the smaller is the amount of saving.

Again, other things remaining the same, the lower the real interest rate, the greater is the amount of investment.

Finally, and again other things remaining the same, the lower the interest rate, the lower is the exchange rate and the greater are exports and the smaller are imports.

A cut in the federal funds rate increases all the components of aggregate expenditure; a rise in the federal funds rate decreases all the components of aggregate expenditure. These changes in aggregate expenditure plans change aggregate demand, which in turn changes real GDP and the inflation rate.

The Fed Fights Recession

We're now going to pull all the steps in the transmission story together. We'll start with inflation below target and real GDP below potential GDP. The Fed takes actions that are designed to restore full employment. Figure 17.5 shows the effects of the Fed's actions, starting in the market for bank reserves and ending in the market for real GDP.

In Figure 17.5(a), which shows the market for bank reserves, the FOMC lowers the target federal funds rate from 5 percent to 4 percent a year. To achieve the new target, the New York Fed buys securities and increases the supply of reserves in the banking system from RS_0 to RS_1.

With increased reserves, the banks create deposits by making loans and the supply of money increases. The short-term interest rate falls and the quantity of money demanded increases. In Figure 17.5(b), the supply of money increases from MS_0 to MS_1, the interest rate falls from 5 percent to 4 percent a year, and the quantity of money increases from \$3 trillion to \$3.1 trillion. The interest rate in the money market and the federal funds rate are kept close to each other by the powerful substitution effect described on page 434.

FIGURE 17.5

The Fed Fights Recession

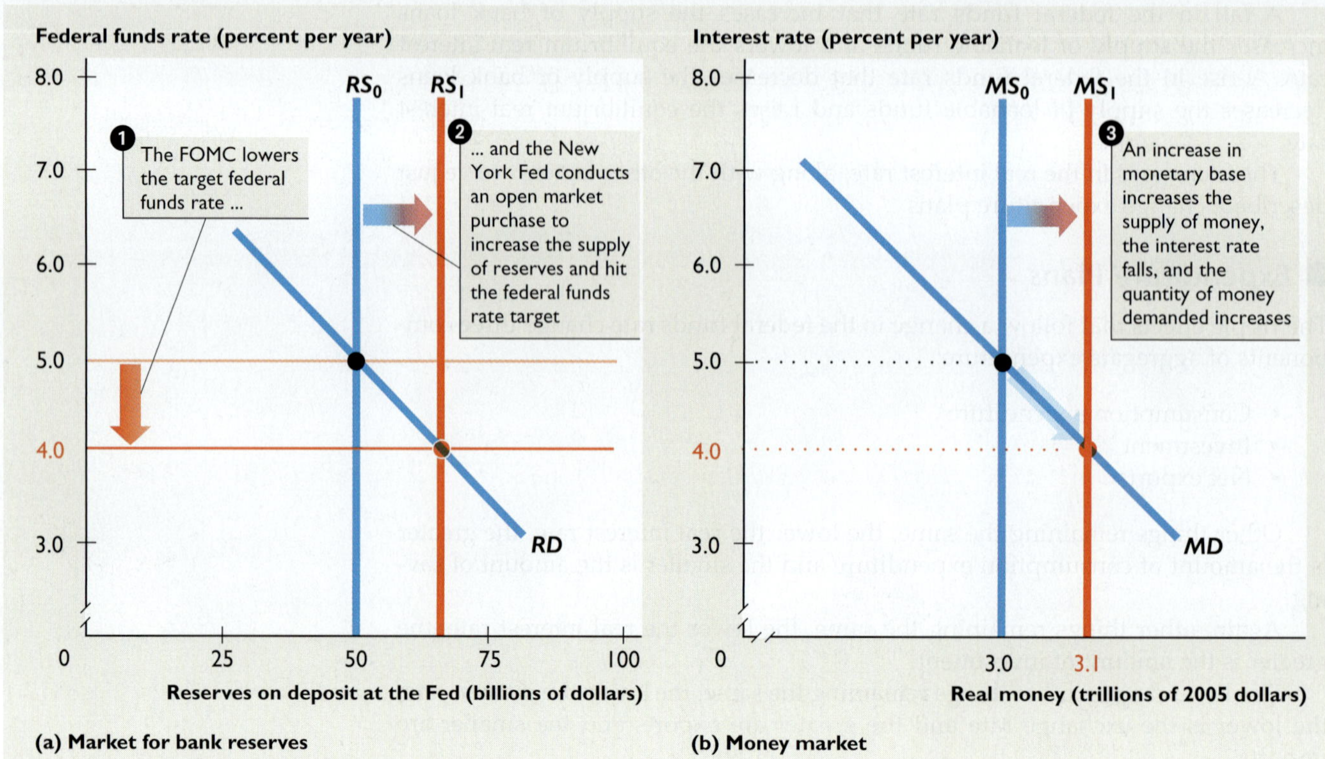

1 The FOMC lowers the federal funds rate target from 5 percent to 4 percent a year. **2** The New York Fed buys securities in an open market operation and increases reserves from RS_0 to RS_1 to hit the new federal funds rate target.

3 The supply of money increases from MS_0 to MS_1, the short-term interest rate falls, and the quantity of money demanded increases. The short-term interest rate and the federal funds rate change by similar amounts.

Banks create money by making loans. In the long run, an increase in the supply of bank loans is matched by a rise in the price level and the quantity of real loans is unchanged. But in the short run, with a sticky price level, an increase in the supply of bank loans increases the supply of (real) loanable funds. In Figure 17.5(c), the supply of loanable funds curve shifts rightward from SLF_0 to SLF_1. With the demand for loanable funds at *DLF*, the real interest rate falls from 6 percent to 5.5 percent a year.

Figure 17.5(d) shows aggregate demand and aggregate supply and the recessionary gap that triggered the Fed's action. The increase in money and loans and the decrease in the real interest rate increase aggregate planned expenditure. (Not shown in the figure, a fall in the interest rate lowers the exchange rate, which increases net exports and aggregate planned expenditure.) The increase in aggregate expenditure, ΔE, increases aggregate demand and shifts the aggregate demand curve rightward to $AD_0 + \Delta E$. A multiplier process begins. The increase in expenditure increases income, which induces an increase in consumption expenditure. Aggregate demand increases further, and the aggregate demand curve eventually shifts rightward to AD_1. The new equilibrium is at full employment but with a higher price level (and faster inflation).

myeconlab Animation

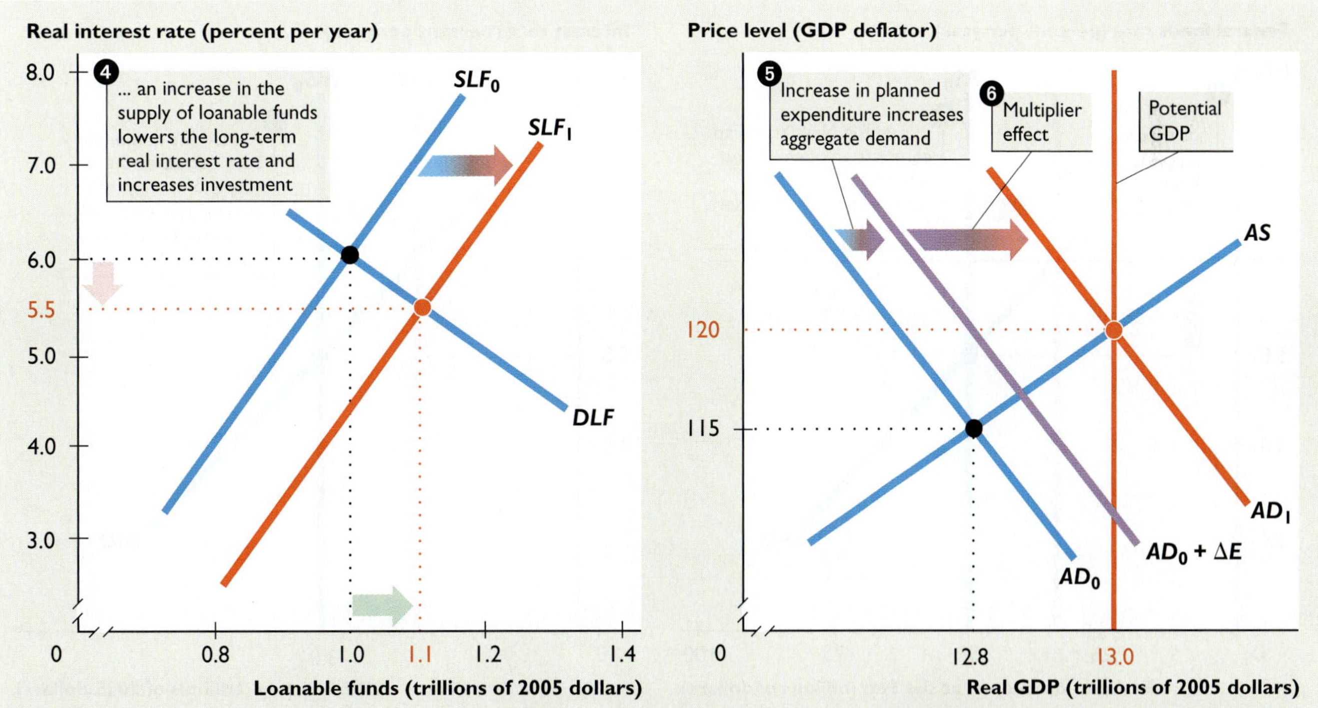

(c) Market for loanable funds

(d) Real GDP and the price level

❹ An increase in the supply of bank loans increases the supply of loanable funds from SLF_0 to SLF_1 and the real interest rate falls. Investment increases.

❺ Aggregate planned expenditure increases and the aggregate demand curve shifts to $AD_0 + \Delta E$. ❻ A multiplier effect increases aggregate demand to AD_1. Real GDP increases and the price level rises (inflation speeds up).

The Fed Fights Inflation

If the inflation rate is too high and real GDP is above potential GDP, the Fed takes actions that are designed to lower the inflation rate and restore price stability. Figure 17.6 shows the effects of the Fed's actions starting in the market for reserves and ending in the market for real GDP.

In Figure 17.6(a), which shows the market for bank reserves, the FOMC raises the target federal funds rate from 5 percent to 6 percent a year. To achieve the new target, the New York Fed sells securities and decreases the supply of reserves in the banking system from RS_0 to RS_1.

With decreased reserves, the banks shrink deposits by decreasing loans and the supply of money decreases. The short-term interest rate rises and the quantity of money demanded decreases. In Figure 17.6(b), the supply of money decreases from MS_0 to MS_1, the interest rate rises from 5 percent to 6 percent a year, and the quantity of money decreases from $3 trillion to $2.9 trillion.

With a decrease in reserves, banks must decrease the supply of loans. The supply of (real) loanable funds decreases, and the supply of loanable funds curve shifts leftward in Figure 17.6(c) from SLF_0 to SLF_1. With the demand for loanable

FIGURE 17.6

The Fed Fights Inflation

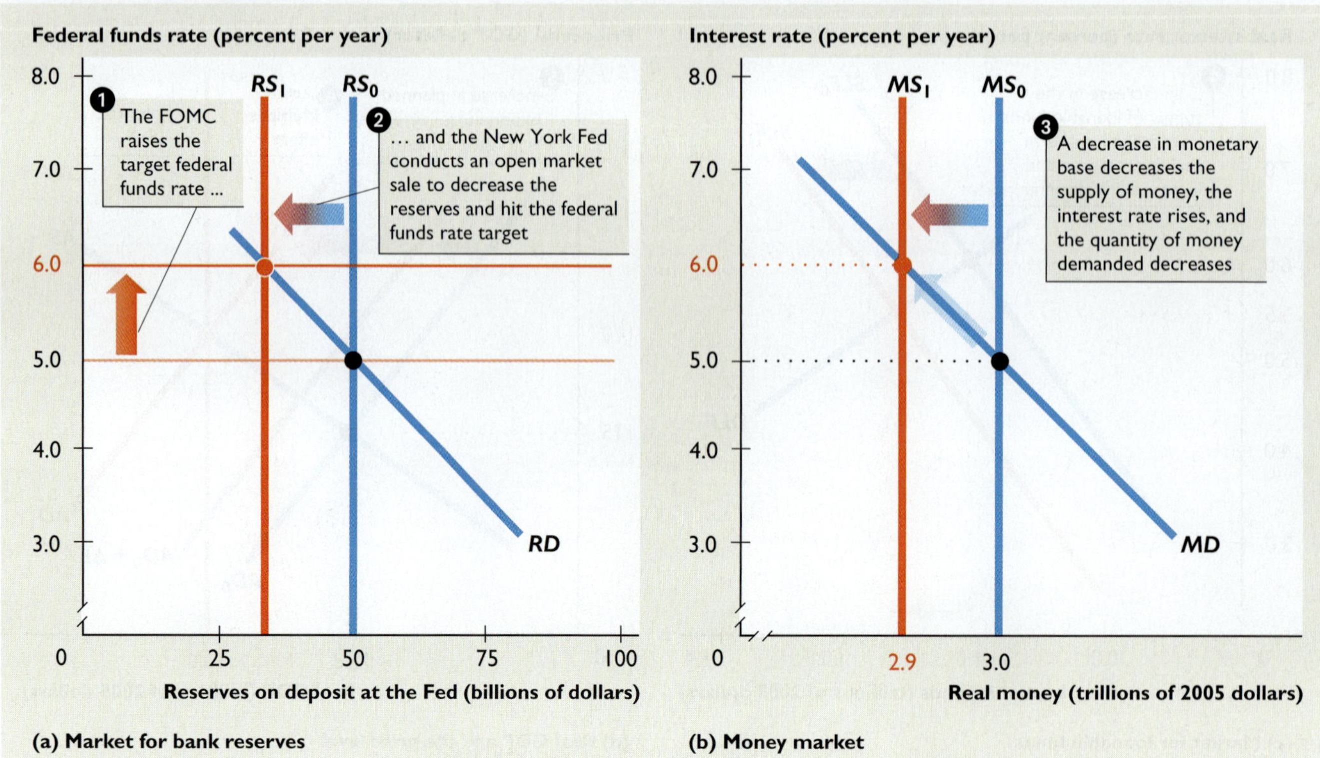

❶ The FOMC raises the federal funds rate target from 5 percent to 6 percent a year. ❷ The New York Fed sells securities in an open market operation and decreases reserves from RS_0 to RS_1 to hit the new federal funds rate target.

❸ The supply of money decreases from MS_0 to MS_1, the short-term interest rate rises, and the quantity of money demanded decreases. The short-term interest rate and the federal funds rate change by similar amounts.

funds at *DLF*, the real interest rate rises from 6 percent to 6.5 percent a year.

Figure 17.6(d) shows aggregate demand and aggregate supply in the market for real GDP and the inflationary gap to which the Fed is reacting. The decrease in the quantity of money and loans and the rise in the real interest rate decrease aggregate planned expenditure. The decrease in aggregate expenditure, ΔE, decreases aggregate demand and shifts the aggregate demand curve leftward to $AD_0 - \Delta E$. A multiplier process begins. The decrease in expenditure decreases income, which induces a decrease in consumption expenditure. Aggregate demand decreases further, and the aggregate demand curve eventually shifts leftward to AD_1. The economy returns to full employment. Real GDP is equal to potential GDP. The price level falls (the inflation rate slows).

In both of the examples, we have given the Fed a perfect hit at achieving full employment and keeping the price level stable. If the Fed changed aggregate demand by too little and too late, or by too much and too early, the economy would not have returned to full employment. Too little action would leave a recessionary or an inflationary gap. Too much action would overshoot the objective. If the Fed hits the brakes too hard, it pushes the economy from inflation to recession. If it stimulates too much, it turns recession into inflation.

myeconlab Animation

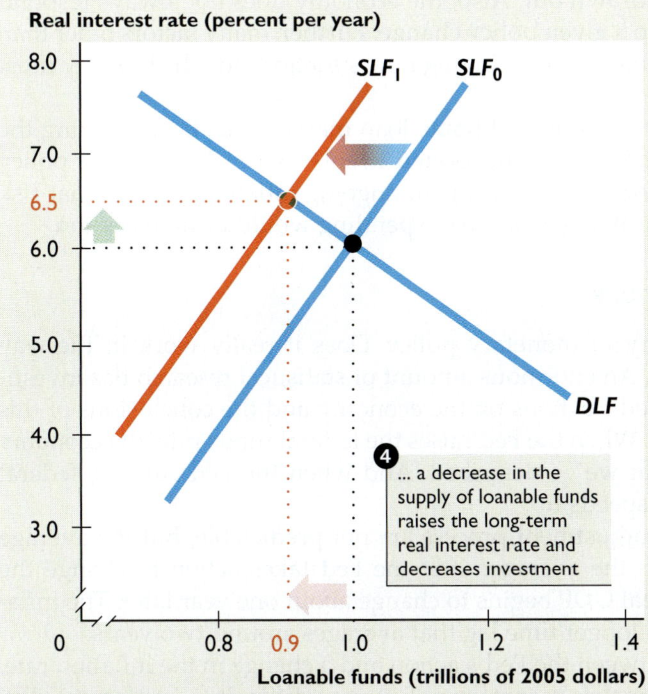

(c) Market for loanable funds

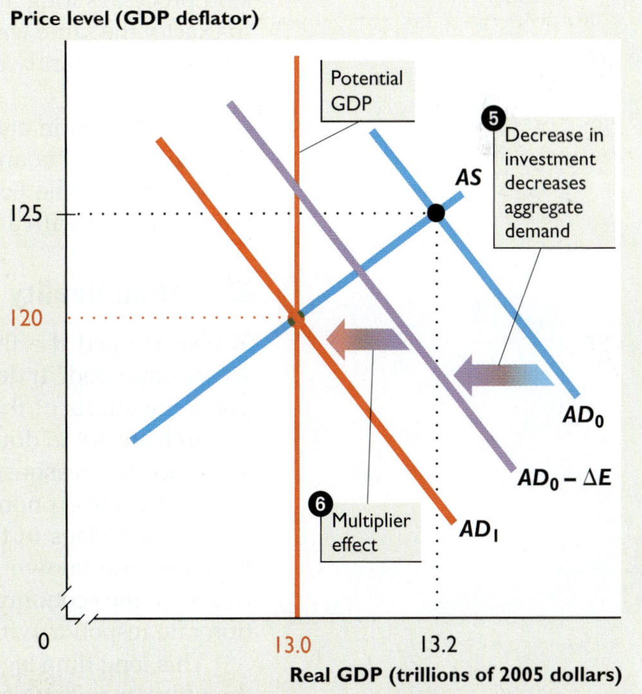

(d) Real GDP and the price level

❹ A decrease in the supply of bank loans decreases the supply of loanable funds from SLF_0 to SLF_1 and the real interest rate rises. Investment decreases.

❺ Aggregate planned expenditure decreases and the aggregate demand curve shifts to $AD_0 - \Delta E$. ❻ A multiplier decreases aggregate demand to AD_1. Real GDP decreases and the price level falls (inflation slows down).

Loose Links and Long and Variable Lags

The ripple effects of monetary policy that we've just analyzed with the precision of an economic model are, in reality, very hard to predict and anticipate.

To achieve its goals of price stability and full employment, the Fed needs a combination of good judgment and good luck. Too large an interest rate cut in an underemployed economy can bring inflation, as it did during the 1970s. And too large an interest rate rise in an inflationary economy can create unemployment, as it did in 1981 and 1991.

Loose links in the chain that runs from the federal funds rate to the ultimate policy goals make unwanted policy outcomes inevitable. And time lags that are both long and variable add to the Fed's challenges.

Loose Links from Federal Funds Rate to Spending

The long-term real interest rate that influences spending plans is linked only loosely to the federal funds rate. Also, the response of the long-term real interest rate to a change in the nominal rate depends on how inflation expectations change. The response of expenditure plans to changes in the real interest rate depends on many factors that make the response hard to predict.

Time Lags in the Adjustment Process

The Fed is especially handicapped by the fact that the monetary policy transmission process is long and drawn out. Also, the economy does not always respond in exactly the same way to a given policy change. Further, many factors other than policy are constantly changing and bringing new situations to which policy must respond.

The turmoil in credit markets and home loan markets that began during the summer of 2007 is an example of unexpected events to which monetary policy must respond. The Fed found itself facing an ongoing inflation risk but that risk was combined with a fear that a collapse of spending would bring recession.

A Final Reality Check

You've studied the theory of monetary policy. Does it really work in the way we've described? It does. An enormous amount of statistical research has investigated the effects of the Fed's actions on the economy and the conclusions of this research are not in doubt. When the Fed raises the federal funds rate, the economy slows for the reasons that we've described. And when the Fed cuts the federal funds rate, the economy speeds up.

The time lags in the adjustment process are not predictable, but the average time lags are known. On the average, after the Fed takes action to change the course of the economy, real GDP begins to change about one year later. The inflation rate responds with a longer time lag that averages around two years.

This long time lag between the Fed's action and a change in the inflation rate, the ultimate policy goal, makes monetary policy very difficult to implement. The state of the economy two years in the future cannot be predicted, so the Fed's actions might turn out to be exactly the opposite of what is needed to steer a steady course between recession and inflation.

You've now seen how the Fed operates and studied the effects of its actions. We close this chapter by looking at alternative approaches to monetary policy.

CHECKPOINT 17.2

Explain the transmission channels through which the Fed influences real GDP and the inflation rate.

Practice Problems

1. List the sequence of events in the transmission from a rise in the federal funds rate to a change in the inflation rate.

The economy has slipped into recession and the Fed takes actions to lessen its severity. Use this information to work Problems **2** and **3**.

2. What action does the Fed take? Illustrate the effects of the Fed's actions in the money market and the loanable funds market.
3. Explain how the Fed's actions change aggregate demand and real GDP.
4. **The Fed's tricky balancing act**
   The FOMC was a bit more optimistic about the economy recovering, but said that policy tightening was not going to happen any time soon.
   Source: *Business Week*, June 6, 2009

   What are the ripple effects and time lags that the Fed must consider in deciding when to start raising the federal funds rate?

Guided Solutions to Practice Problems

1. When the Fed raises the federal funds rate, other short-term interest rates rise and the exchange rate rises; the quantity of money and supply of loanable funds decrease and the long-term real interest rate rises; consumption, investment, and net exports decrease; aggregate demand decreases; and eventually the real GDP growth rate and the inflation rate decrease.
2. The Fed lowers the federal funds rate, which lowers other short-term interest rates, and increases the supply of money (Figure 1). The lower federal funds rate increases the supply of bank loans, which increases the supply of loanable funds. The real interest rate falls (Figure 2).
3. A lower real interest rate (and lower exchange rate) and greater quantity of money and loans increase aggregate expenditure. Aggregate demand increases and the *AD* curve shifts to $AD_0 + \Delta E$. A multiplier effect increases aggregate demand and the *AD* curve shifts rightward to AD_1. Real GDP increases and recession is avoided (Figure 3).
4. Figure 17.4 (p. 435) describes the ripple effects and the time lags. The Fed can influence interest rates quickly but several months pass before the quantity of money and loans respond, up to a year before expenditure plans respond, and up to two years before the inflation rate responds to the Fed's interest rate actions.

FIGURE 1

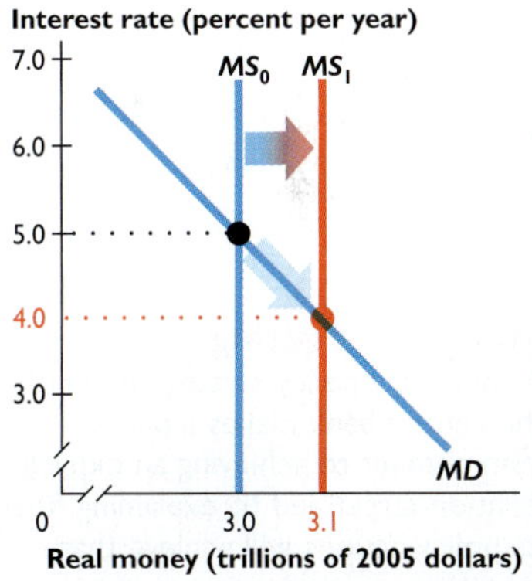

FIGURE 2

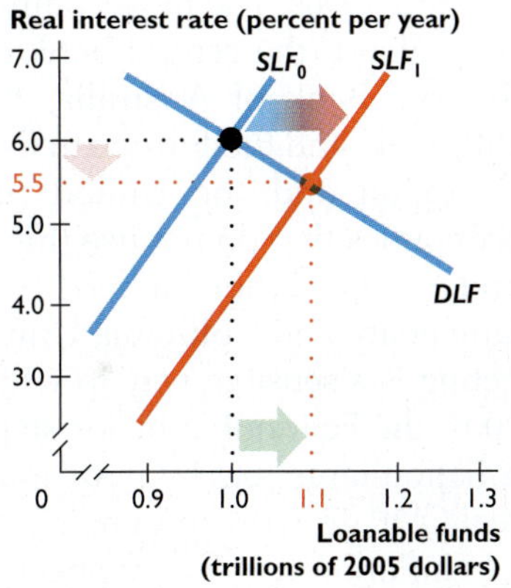

FIGURE 3

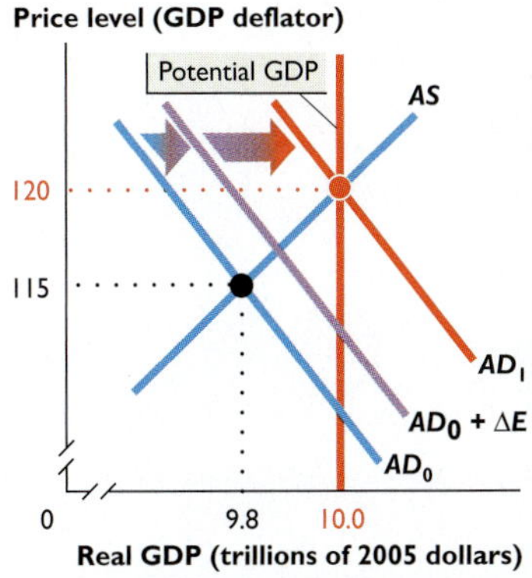

17.3 ALTERNATIVE MONETARY POLICY STRATEGIES

So far in this chapter, we've described and analyzed the Fed's method of conducting monetary policy. But the Fed does have choices among alternative monetary policy strategies. We're going to end our discussion of monetary policy by examining the alternatives and explaining why the Fed has rejected them in favor of the interest rate strategy that we've described.

You've seen that we can summarize monetary policy strategies in two broad categories: *instrument rules* and *targeting rules*.

Why Rules?

Discretionary monetary policy
A monetary policy that is based on an expert assessment of the current economic situation.

You might be wondering why all monetary policy strategies involve *rules*. Why doesn't the Fed pursue a **discretionary monetary policy** and just do what seems best every day, month, and year, based on its expert assessment of the current economic situation? The answer is that monetary policy must keep inflation expectations anchored close to the target inflation rate. In both financial markets and labor markets, people must make long-term commitments. These markets work best when plans are based on correctly anticipated inflation outcomes. A well-understood monetary policy rule helps to create an environment in which inflation is easier to forecast and manage.

Although rules beat discretion, there are three alternative rules that the Fed might have chosen. They are

- An inflation targeting rule
- A money targeting rule
- A gold price targeting rule (gold standard)

Inflation Targeting Rule

Inflation targeting
A monetary policy strategy in which the central bank makes a public commitment to achieving an explicit inflation target and to explaining how its policy actions will achieve that target.

Inflation targeting is a monetary policy strategy in which the central bank makes a public commitment to achieving an explicit inflation target and to explaining how its policy actions will achieve that target.

Of the alternatives to the Fed's current strategy, inflation targeting is the most likely to be considered. In fact, some economists see it as a small step from what the Fed currently does.

Several major central banks practice inflation targeting and have done so since the mid-1990s. The most committed inflation-targeting central banks are the Bank of England (the central bank of the United Kingdom), the Bank of Canada, the Reserve Bank of Australia, the Reserve Bank of New Zealand, the Swedish Riksbank, and the European Central Bank (the central bank of the euro countries).

Japan and the United States are the most prominent major industrial economies that do not use this monetary policy strategy. But when Ben Bernanke and Fed Governor Frederic S. Mishkin were economics professors (at Princeton University and Columbia University, respectively) they argued that inflation targeting is a sensible way in which to conduct monetary policy. And in November 2007, the Fed took a major step toward greater transparency, a central feature of inflation targeting, by publishing FOMC members' detailed forecasts of inflation, real GDP growth, and unemployment through 2010.

Inflation targets are specified in terms of a range for the CPI inflation rate. This range is typically between 1 percent and 3 percent a year, with an aim to

EYE on the GLOBAL ECONOMY

Inflation Targeting Around the World

Five advanced economies and the Eurozone have inflation targets (shown by the green bars) designed to anchor inflation expectations.

Most inflation targets have been achieved (orange lines), which makes it easier for the central bank to stabilize both the inflation rate and real GDP.

High-quality central bank inflation reports encourage an enhanced level of public discussion about inflation and awareness of each central bank's views.

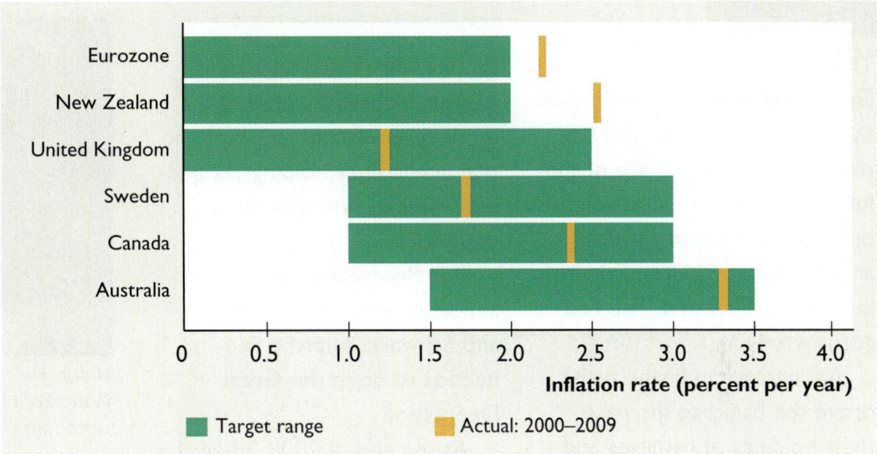

SOURCES OF DATA: National central banks and World Economic Outlook database, April 2009.

achieve an average inflation rate of 2 percent a year. Because the lags in the operation of monetary policy are long, if the inflation rate falls outside the target range, the expectation is that the central bank will move the inflation rate back on target over the next two years.

The idea of inflation targeting is to state clearly and publicly the goals of monetary policy, to establish a framework of accountability, and to keep the inflation rate low and stable while maintaining a high and stable level of employment.

There is wide agreement that inflation targeting achieves its first two goals. It's also clear that the inflation reports of inflation targeters have raised the level of discussion and understanding of the monetary policy process.

It is less clear whether inflation targeting does better than the implicit targeting that the Fed currently pursues in achieving low and stable inflation. The Fed's own record, without a formal inflation target, had been impressive until the global financial crisis called into question its neglect of a potential bubble and bust.

Money Targeting Rule

As long ago as 1948, Nobel Laureate Milton Friedman proposed a targeting rule for the quantity of money. Friedman's ***k*-percent rule** makes the quantity of money grow at a rate of *k* percent a year, where *k* equals the growth rate of potential GDP. Friedman's *k*-percent rule relies on a stable demand for money, which translates to a stable velocity of circulation. Friedman had examined data on money and nominal GDP and argued that the velocity of circulation of money was one of the most stable macroeconomic variables and that it could be exploited to deliver a stable price level and small business cycle fluctuations.

***k*-percent rule**
A monetary policy rule that makes the quantity of money grow at *k* percent per year, where *k* equals the growth rate of potential GDP.

Friedman's idea remained just that until the 1970s, when inflation increased to more than 10 percent a year in the United States and to much higher rates in some other major countries.

EYE on THE FED in a CRISIS

Did the Fed Save Us From Another Great Depression?

The story of the Great Depression is complex and even today, after almost 80 years of research, economists are not in full agreement on its causes. But one part of the story is clear and it is told by Milton Friedman and Anna J. Schwartz: The Fed got it wrong.

An increase in financial risk drove the banks to increase their holdings of reserves and everyone else to lower their bank deposits and hold more currency.

Between 1929 and 1933, (Figure 1) the banks' desired reserve ratio increased from 8 percent to 12 percent and the currency drain ratio increased from 9 percent to 19 percent.

The money multiplier (Figure 2) fell from 6.5 to 3.8.

The quantity of money (Figure 3) crashed by 35 percent.

This massive contraction in the quantity of money was accompanied by a similar contraction of bank loans and by the failure of a large number of banks.

Friedman and Schwartz say that this contraction of money and bank loans and failure of banks could (and should) have been avoided by a more alert and wise Fed.

The Fed could have injected reserves into the banks to accommodate their desire for greater security by holding more reserves and to offset the rise in currency holdings as people switched out of bank deposits.

Ben Bernanke's Fed did almost exactly what Friedman and Schwartz said the Fed needed to do in the Great Depression.

At the end of 2008, when the banks faced increased financial risk, the Fed flooded them with the reserves that they wanted to hold (Figure 1).

The money multiplier fell from 9.1 in 2008 to 4.6 in 2009 (Figure 2)—much more than it had fallen between 1929 and 1933—but there was no contraction of the quantity of money (Figure 3). Rather, the quantity of M2 increased by 8 percent in the year to August 2009.

We can't be sure that the Fed averted a Great Depression in 2009, but we can be confident that the Fed's actions helped to limit the depth and duration of the 2008–2009 recession.

The Fed's next challenge will be to reverse the monetary policy stimulus when the economy begins to build momentum, and investment and exports begin to increase more quickly.

Milton Friedman and Anna J. Schwartz, authors of A Monetary History of the United States, *who say the Fed turned an ordinary recession into the Great Depression.*

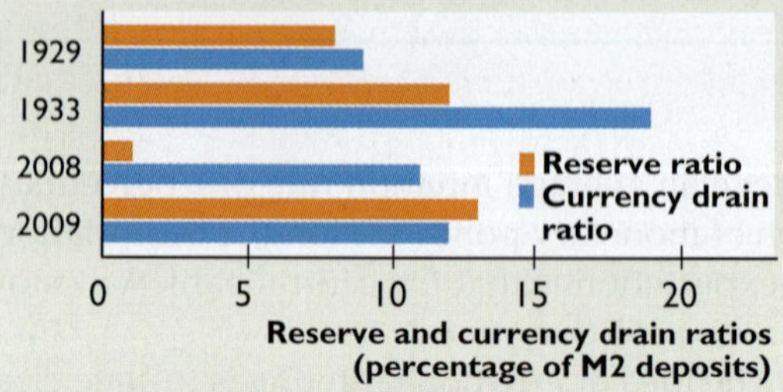

Figure 1 The flight to safety: Reserve and currency ratios increase

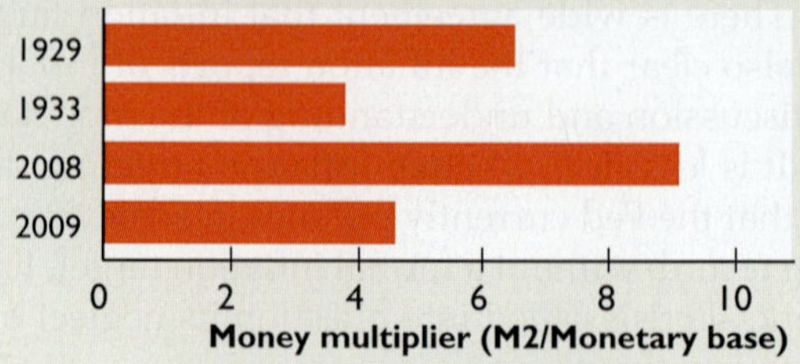

Figure 2 The collapsing money multiplier

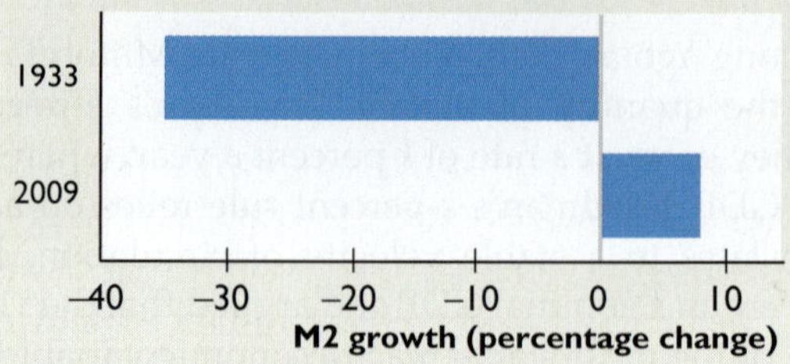

Figure 3 Money contraction versus growth

SOURCE OF DATA: Federal Reserve Board.

During the mid-1970s, in a bid to end the inflation, the central banks of most major countries adopted the *k*-percent rule for the growth rate of the quantity of money. The Fed, too, began to pay close attention to the growth rates of money aggregates, including M1 and M2.

Inflation rates fell during the early 1980s in the countries that had adopted a *k*-percent rule. But one by one, these countries abandoned the *k*-percent rule.

Money targeting works when the demand for money curve is stable and predictable—when the velocity of circulation is stable. But in the world of the 1980s, and possibly in the world of today, technological change in the banking system leads to large and unpredictable shifts in the demand for money curve, which make the use of monetary targeting unreliable.

With monetary targeting, aggregate demand fluctuates because the demand for money fluctuates. With interest rate targeting, aggregate demand is insulated from fluctuations in the demand for money (and the velocity of circulation).

Gold Price Targeting Rule

The Fed could intervene in the market for gold and keep the dollar price of gold at a specified level. This monetary policy regime is called a **gold standard** and it was operated for much of the nineteenth and early twentieth centuries. At that time, this monetary regime was regarded as the only one that could be trusted to deliver price stability. Also, it had the virtue of providing one monetary standard for the world, for it was an *international* gold standard.

Gold standard
A monetary policy rule that fixes the dollar price of gold.

Under the gold standard, a country has no direct control over its inflation rate. And the inflation that occurs is determined by changes in the prices of consumption goods and services relative to the (fixed) price of gold. Historically, under the gold standard, prices were stable on the average but swung between periods of inflation (when new gold was discovered) and deflation (when economic growth outpaced the discovery of gold).

Today, most economists regard the gold standard as an outmoded system, but advocates continue to regret its passing.

EYE on YOUR LIFE

Your Views on Monetary Policy and How Monetary Policy Affects You

Using the knowledge that you have accumulated during your course and by reading or watching the current news, try to determine the monetary policy issues that face the U.S. economy today.

What is the greater monetary policy risk: inflation or recession? If the risk is inflation, what action do you expect the Fed to take? If the risk is recession, what do you expect the Fed to do?

Which of these problems, inflation or recession, do you care most about? Do you want the Fed to be more cautious about inflation and keep the interest rate high, or more cautious about recession and keep the interest rate low?

When Ben Bernanke was an economics professor at Princeton, he studied inflation targeting and found that it works well.

Do you think the United States should join the ranks of inflation targeters? Should the Fed announce an inflation target?

Watch the media for commentary on the Fed's interest rate decisions and evolving monetary policy strategy.

myeconlab

Work these problems in Study Plan 17.3 to get instant feedback.

CHECKPOINT 17.3

Explain and compare alternative monetary policy strategies.

Practice Problems

1. What are the three alternative monetary policy strategies that the Fed could have adopted and why is discretionary monetary policy not one of them?
2. Why does the Fed not target the quantity of money?
3. Which countries practice inflation targeting? How does this monetary policy strategy work and does it achieve a lower inflation rate?
4. **One tool, one target**

   The one-tool, one-target rule by which central banks operated has gone. Monetary policy is now a messier business.

   Source: *The Economist*, April 25, 2009

   What is the tool and the target that the news clip says is gone and what is the problem with "messy" monetary policy?

Guided Solutions to Practice Problems

1. The Fed could have adopted three alternative monetary policy strategies: an inflation targeting rule, a *k*-percent money targeting rule, and a gold price targeting rule (gold standard). A rule-based monetary policy beats discretionary monetary policy because it provides a more secure anchor for inflation expectations, which in turn makes long-term contracts in labor and capital markets more efficient.
2. The Fed does not target the quantity of money because it believes that the demand for money is too unstable and fluctuations in demand would bring unwanted fluctuations in interest rates, aggregate demand, real GDP, and the inflation rate.
3. The countries that practice inflation targeting are the United Kingdom, Canada, Australia, New Zealand, Sweden, and the European countries that use the euro. Inflation targeting works by announcing a target inflation rate, setting the overnight interest rate (equivalent to the federal funds rate) to achieve the target, and publishing reports that explain how and why the central bank believes that its current policy actions will achieve its ultimate policy goals. Eurozone and New Zealand have missed their inflation targets, but the other inflation targeters have achieved their goals.
4. The tool is the overnight interest rate (the federal funds rate in the United States). There never has been one target. The Fed targets the inflation rate and the output gap and even the central banks that have formal inflation targets also pay attention to the output gap. The problem with "messy" monetary policy is that it might fail to anchor inflation expectations and lead to a worsening of the short-run policy tradeoff.

CHAPTER SUMMARY

Key Points

1 Describe the objectives of U.S. monetary policy, the framework for achieving those objectives, and the Fed's monetary policy actions.

- The Federal Reserve Act requires the Fed to use monetary policy to achieve maximum employment, stable prices, and moderate long-term interest rates.
- The Fed's goals can come into conflict in the short run.
- The Fed translates the goal of stable prices as a core inflation rate of between 1 and 2 percent a year.
- The Fed's monetary policy instrument is the federal funds rate.
- The Fed sets the federal funds rate at the level that makes its forecast of inflation and other goals equal to their targets.
- The Fed hits its federal funds rate target by using open market operations and in times of financial crisis by quantitative easing and credit easing.

2 Explain the transmission channels through which the Fed influences real GDP and the inflation rate.

- A change in the federal funds rate changes other interest rates, the exchange rate, the quantity of money and loans, aggregate demand, and eventually real GDP and the inflation rate.
- Changes in the federal funds rate change real GDP about one year later and change the inflation rate with an even longer time lag.

3 Explain and compare alternative monetary policy strategies.

- The main alternatives to setting the federal funds rate are an inflation targeting rule, a money targeting rule, or a gold standard.
- Rules dominate discretion in monetary policy because they better enable the central bank to manage inflation expectations.

Key Terms

Discretionary monetary policy, 444
Federal funds rate, 428
Financial stability, 427
Gold standard, 447
Inflation targeting, 444
Instrument rule, 430
k-percent rule, 445
Monetary policy instrument, 428
Targeting rule, 430

myeconlab

Work these problems in Chapter 17 Study Plan to get instant feedback.

CHAPTER CHECKPOINT

Study Plan Problems and Applications

1. **Bernanke raises alarm on spending**
   Federal Reserve Chairman Ben Bernanke warned that government spending and budget deficits threaten financial stability and might be setting the scene for the next crisis.

   Source: *The Globe and Mail*, June 4, 2009

   How might a large increase in government spending and the government's budget deficit threaten financial stability and make the Fed's job harder?

Use the following information to work Problems 2 to 4.

The U.S. economy is at full employment when strong economic growth in Asia increases the demand for U.S.-produced goods and services.

2. Explain how the U.S. price level and real GDP will change in the short run.
3. Explain how the U.S. price level and real GDP will change in the long run if the Fed takes monetary policy actions that are consistent with its objectives as set out in the Federal Reserve Act of 2000.
4. Explain whether the Fed faces a tradeoff in the short run.

Use the following information to work Problems 5 to 7.

Figure 1 shows the aggregate demand curve, *AD*, and the short-run aggregate supply curve, *AS*, in the economy of Artica. Potential GDP is $300 billion.

FIGURE 1

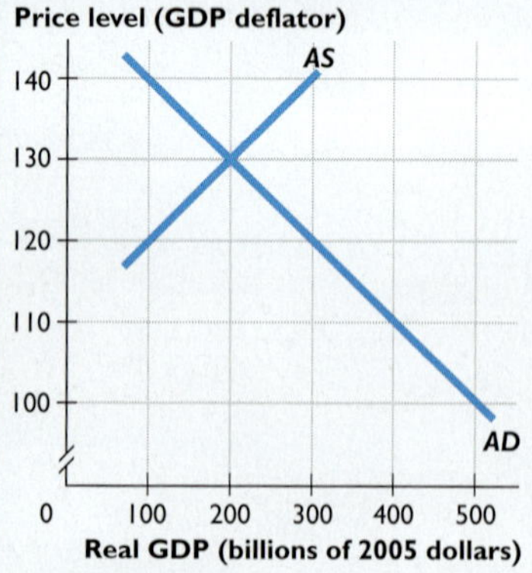

5. What are the price level and real GDP? Does Artica have an unemployment problem or an inflation problem? Why?
6. What do you predict will happen if the central bank takes no monetary policy actions? What monetary policy action would you advise the central bank to take and what do you predict will be the effect of that action?
7. Suppose that a drought decreases potential GDP in Artica to $250 billion. Explain what happens if the central bank lowers the federal funds rate. Do you recommend that the central bank lower the interest rate? Why?

Use the following information to work Problems 8 and 9.

Fed sees no need to raise interest rates soon

The Fed has consistently said that it will not raise the federal funds rate any time soon. The Fed's challenge will be how to get monetary policy back to normal over the next several years. The Fed has to make a judgment about timing—tightening too early could send the economy back into recession, as happened during the late 1930s; waiting too long would set the stage for inflation.

Source: *The New York Times*, November 5, 2009

8. If the recovery continues and inflation starts to rise, what effect will the Fed's decision to not change the federal funds rate have on the U.S. economy?
9. If the economic recovery slows and the economy slips back into recession, what effect will the Fed's no-change decision have on the economy?

Instructor Assignable Problems and Applications

Your instructor can assign these problems as homework, a quiz, or a test in **MyEconLab**.

1. In which episode, the Great Depression or the 2008–2009 recession, did the banks' desired reserve ratio and the currency drain ratio increase by the larger amount and the money multiplier fall by the larger amount?
2. Compare and contrast the Fed's monetary policy response to the surge in desired reserves and currency holdings in the Great Depression and the 2008–2009 recession.

Use the following information to work Problems 3 to 5.

The U.S. economy is at full employment when the world price of oil begins to rise sharply. Short-run aggregate supply decreases.

3. Explain how the U.S. price level and real GDP will change in the short run.
4. Explain how the U.S. price level and real GDP will change in the long run if the Fed takes monetary policy actions that are consistent with its objectives as set out in the Federal Reserve Act of 2000.
5. Does the Fed face a tradeoff in the short run? Explain why or why not.

Use the following information to work Problems 6 to 9.

Figure 1 shows the aggregate demand curve, *AD*, and the short-run aggregate supply curve, *AS*, in the economy of Freezone. Potential GDP is $300 billion.

FIGURE 1

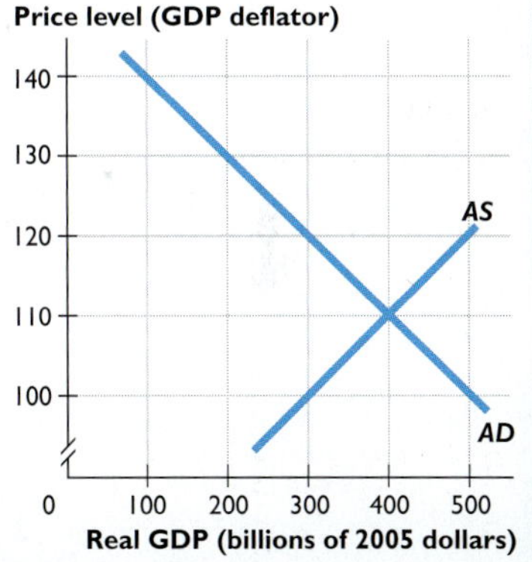

6. What are the price level and real GDP? Does Freezone have an unemployment problem or an inflation problem? Why?
7. What do you predict will happen in Freezone if the central bank takes no monetary policy actions? What monetary policy action would you advise the central bank to take and what do you predict will be the effect of that action?
8. What happens in Freezone if the central bank lowers the federal funds rate? Do you recommend that the central bank lower the interest rate? Why?
9. What happens in Freezone if the central bank conducts an open market sale of securities? How will the interest rate change? Do you recommend that the central bank conduct an open market sale of securities? Why?

Use the following information to work Problems 10 and 11.

Many ways to blow up an economy

Excessive stimulus could bring inflation in the United States in the long term, but for now, inflation is falling. Bond interest rates reflect inflation expectations that are within the Fed's long-term target levels.

Source: *Australian Financial Review*, May 9, 2009

10. Explain why inflation was falling in 2009 and how excessive stimulus could bring inflation in the long term.
11. What does it mean to say that inflation expectations are within the Fed's target levels?

Use the following information to work Problems 12 and 13.

Fed Is Split Over Timing of Rate Rise

In October 2009, the Fed was forecasting that unemployment will average 9.8 percent in 2010 and said the federal funds rate will remain "exceptionally low" for "an extended period." But some officials were beginning to worry about unwinding the $2 trillion in special credits that have boosted the monetary base and to wonder if the interest rate might need to start rising soon.

Source: *The New York Times*, October 9, 2009

12. Describe the time lags in the operation of monetary policy and explain why they pose a challenge for the Fed in deciding when to start raising the federal funds rate target in a recession.

13. Explain why unwinding the $2 trillion in special credits that have boosted the monetary base and the federal funds rate target are linked.

14. Bernanke warns against meddling with Fed

Testifying on Capitol Hill, Fed chairman Bernanke warned that if Congress limits the Fed's independence, financial markets will send interest rates higher.

Source: *The Independent*, July 22, 2009

How might limiting the Fed's independence make interest rates rise?

15. In the summer of 2007, the Fed conducted aggressive open market operations to increase the monetary base but didn't change the federal funds rate target. Then, a few weeks later, the Fed cut the federal funds rate by 50 basis points. Why did the Fed need to increase the monetary base if it didn't want to change the interest rate?

16. Inflation is rising toward 5 percent a year, and the Fed, Congress, and the White House are discussing ways of containing inflation without damaging employment and output. The President wants to cut aggregate demand but to do so in a way that will give the best chance of keeping investment high to encourage long-term economic growth. Explain which of the following actions would best meet the President's objectives and which would present the greatest obstacles to those objectives.

- A rise in the federal funds rate.
- A fall in the federal funds rate.
- No change in the federal funds rate and some fiscal policy action.

17. In a deep recession, the Fed, Congress, and the White House are discussing ways of restoring full employment. The President wants to stimulate aggregate demand but to do so in a way that will give the best chance of boosting investment and long-term economic growth. Explain which of the following actions would best meet the President's objectives and which would present the greatest obstacles to those objectives.

- A rise in the federal funds rate.
- A fall in the federal funds rate.
- No change in the federal funds rate and some fiscal policy action.

Who wins and who loses from globalization?

iPods, Wii games, and Nike shoes are just three of the many things you might buy that are not produced in the United States. Why don't we make these things here and by doing so, create more American jobs?

18

International Trade Policy

CHAPTER CHECKLIST

When you have completed your study of this chapter, you will be able to

1. Explain how markets work with international trade and identify the gains from international trade and its winners and losers.
2. Explain the effects of international trade barriers.
3. Explain and evaluate arguments used to justify restricting international trade.

18.1 HOW GLOBAL MARKETS WORK

Imports
The goods and services that firms in one country buy from households and firms in other countries.

Exports
The goods and services that firms in one country sell to households and firms in other countries.

Because we trade with people in other countries, the goods and services that we buy and consume are not limited by what we produce. The goods and services that we buy from firms in other countries are our **imports**; the goods and services that we sell to people in other countries are our **exports**.

International Trade Today

Global trade today is enormous. In 2009, global exports and imports (the two numbers are the same because what one country exports another imports) were about \$15 trillion, which is 27 percent of the value of global production. The United States is the world's largest international trader and accounts for 10 percent of world exports and 15 percent of world imports. Germany and China, which rank 2 and 3 behind the United States, lag by a large margin.

In 2009, total U.S. exports were \$1.5 trillion, which is about 11 percent of the value of U.S. production. Total U.S. imports were \$1.9 trillion, which is about 13 percent of the value of total expenditure in the United States.

The United States trades both goods and services. In 2009, exports of services were \$0.5 trillion (33 percent of total exports) and imports of services were \$0.4 trillion (21 percent of total imports).

Our largest exports are services such as banking, insurance, business consulting, and other private services. Our largest exports of goods are airplanes. Our largest imports are crude oil and automobiles. *Eye on the U.S. Economy* (p. 455) provides a bit more detail on our ten largest exports and imports.

What Drives International Trade?

Comparative advantage is the fundamental force that drives international trade. We defined comparative advantage in Chapter 3 (p. 75) as the ability of a person to perform an activity or produce a good or service at a lower opportunity cost than anyone else. This same idea applies to nations. We can define *national comparative advantage* as the ability of a *nation* to perform an activity or produce a good or service at a lower opportunity cost than *any other nation*.

The opportunity cost of producing a T-shirt is lower in China than in the United States, so China has a comparative advantage in producing T-shirts. The opportunity cost of producing an airplane is lower in the United States than in China, so the United States has a comparative advantage in producing airplanes.

You saw in Chapter 3 how Liz and Joe reaped gains from trade by specializing in the production of the good at which they have a comparative advantage and then trading. Both were better off. This same principle applies to trade among nations. Because China has a comparative advantage at producing T-shirts and the United States has a comparative advantage at producing airplanes, the people of both countries can gain from specialization and trade. China can buy airplanes from the United States at a lower opportunity cost than that at which it can produce them. And Americans can buy T-shirts from China for a lower opportunity cost than that at which U.S. firms can produce them. Also, through international trade, Chinese producers can get higher prices for their T-shirts and Boeing can sell airplanes for a higher price. Both countries gain from international trade.

Let's now illustrate the gains from trade that we've just described by studying demand and supply in the global markets for T-shirts and airplanes.

EYE on the U.S. ECONOMY

U.S. Exports and Imports

The blue bars in part (a) of the figure show the ten largest U.S. exports and the red bars in part (b) show the ten largest U.S. imports. The values are graphed as *net exports* and *net imports* because we both export and import items in most of the categories.

Six of our top ten exports are services—private services (such as the sale of advertising by Google to Adidas, a European sports-wear maker), royalties and license fees (such as fees received by Hollywood movie producers on films shown abroad), business services, financial services, travel (such as the expenditure on a Florida vacation by a visitor from England), and education services (foreign students in our colleges and universities).

Automobiles and the fuel that runs them are our largest imports. We also import large quantities of clothing, furniture, TV sets, DVD players, and computers. Insurance and freight services also feature in our ten largest imports.

Although we import a large quantity of computers, we export many of the semiconductors (computer chips) inside those computers. The Intel chip in a Lenovo laptop built in China and imported into the United States is an example. This chip was made in the United States and previously exported to China.

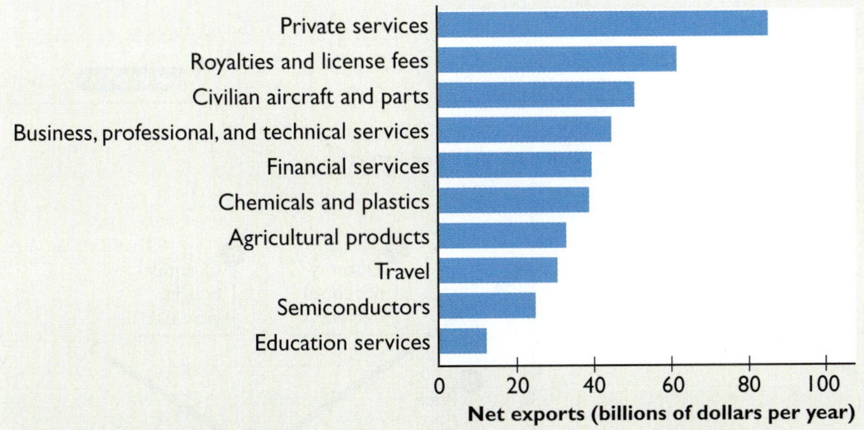

(a) The 10 largest U.S. exports

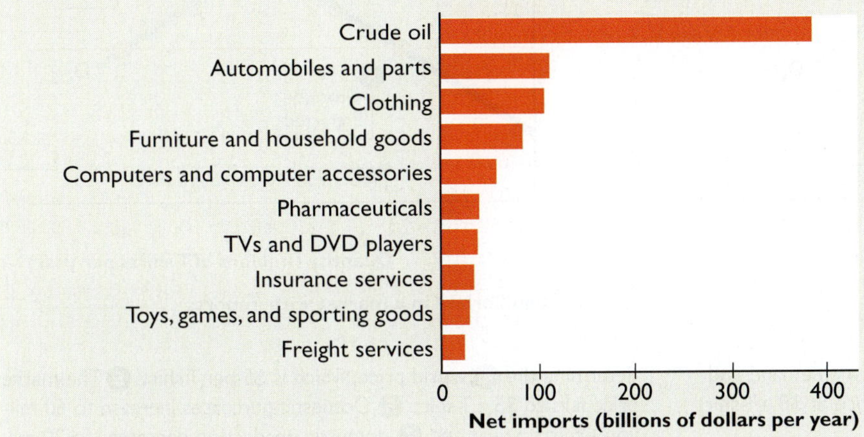

(b) The 10 largest U.S. imports

SOURCE OF DATA: Bureau of Economic Analysis.

The United States exports airplanes ...

and imports crude oil.

Why the United States Imports T-Shirts

Figure 18.1 illustrates the effects of international trade in T-shirts. The demand curve D_{US} and the supply curve S_{US} show the demand and supply in the U.S. domestic market only. The demand curve tells us the quantity of T-shirts that Americans are willing to buy at various prices. The supply curve tells us the quantity of T-shirts that U.S. garment makers are willing to sell at various prices.

Figure 18.1(a) shows what the U.S. T-shirt market would be like with no international trade. The price of a T-shirt would be \$8 and 40 million T-shirts a year would be produced by U.S. garment makers and bought by U.S. consumers.

Figure 18.1(b) shows the market for T-shirts *with* international trade. Now the price of a T-shirt is determined in the world market, not the U.S. domestic market. The world price is *less than* \$8 a T-shirt, which means that the rest of the world has a comparative advantage in producing T-shirts. The world price line shows the world price as \$5 a T-shirt.

The U.S. demand curve, D_{US}, tells us that at \$5 a T-shirt, Americans buy 60 million T-shirts a year. The U.S. supply curve, S_{US}, tells us that at \$5 a T-shirt, U.S. garment makers produce 20 million T-shirts. To buy 60 million T-shirts when only 20 million are produced in the United States, we must import T-shirts from the rest of the world. The quantity of T-shirts imported is 40 million a year.

FIGURE 18.1

A Market With Imports

myeconlab Animation

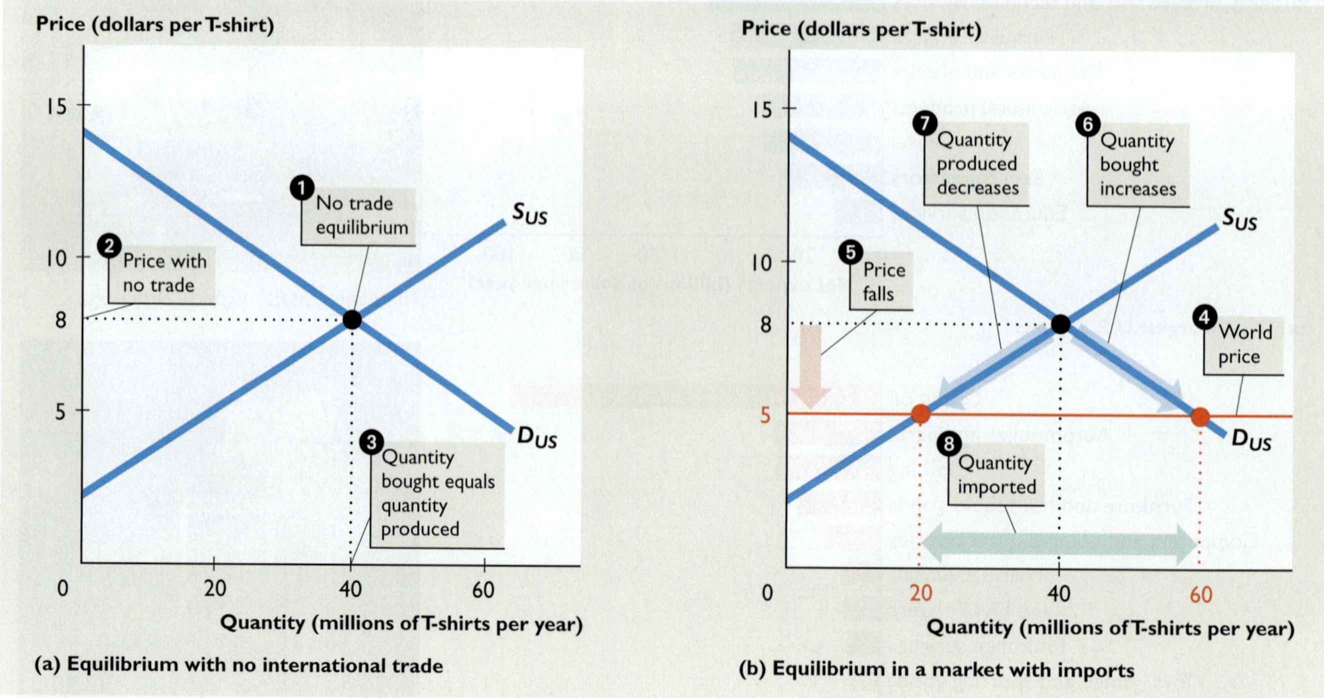

With no international trade, in part (a), ❶ domestic demand and domestic supply determine ❷ the equilibrium price at \$8 a T-shirt and ❸ the quantity at 40 million T-shirts a year.
With international trade, in part (b), world demand and world supply determine the ❹ world price, which is \$5 per T-shirt. ❺ The market price falls to \$5 a T-shirt. ❻ Domestic purchases increase to 60 million T-shirts a year, and ❼ domestic production decreases to 20 million T-shirts a year. ❽ 40 million T-shirts a year are imported.

Why the United States Exports Airplanes

Figure 18.2 illustrates the effects of international trade in airplanes. The demand curve D_{US} and the supply curve S_{US} show the demand and supply in the U.S. domestic market only. The demand curve tells us the quantity of airplanes that U.S. airlines are willing to buy at various prices. The supply curve tells us the quantity of airplanes that U.S. aircraft makers are willing to sell at various prices.

Figure 18.2(a) shows what the U.S. airplane market would be like with no international trade. The price of an airplane would be $100 million and 400 airplanes a year would be produced by U.S. aircraft makers and bought by U.S. airlines.

Figure 18.2(b) shows the U.S. airplane market *with* international trade. Now the price of an airplane is determined in the world market, not the U.S. domestic market. The world price is *higher than* $100 million, which means that the United States has a comparative advantage in producing airplanes. The world price line shows the world price as $150 million.

The U.S. demand curve, D_{US}, tells us that at $150 million an airplane, U.S. airlines buy 200 airplanes a year. The U.S. supply curve, S_{US}, tells us that at $150 million an airplane, U.S. aircraft makers produce 700 airplanes a year. The quantity produced in the United States (700 a year) minus the quantity purchased by U.S. airlines (200 a year) is the quantity of U.S. exports, which is 500 airplanes a year.

FIGURE 18.2

A Market With Exports

myeconlab Animation

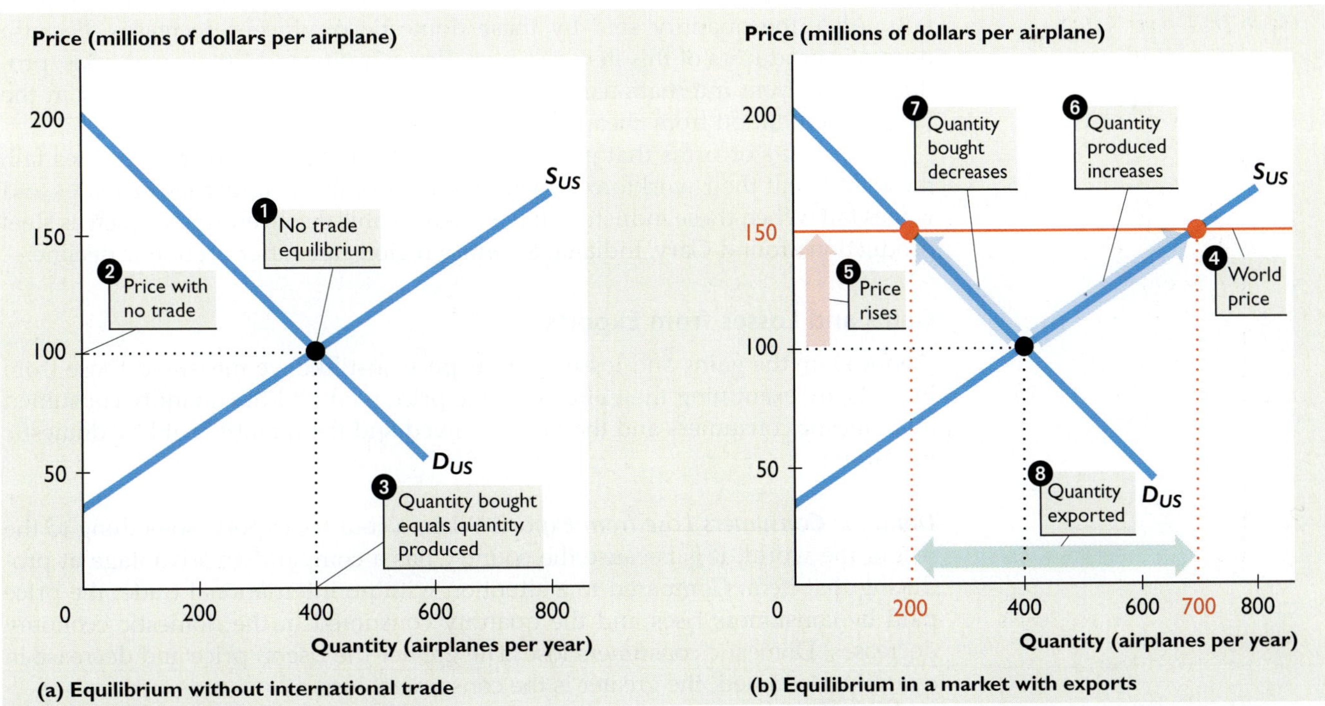

With no international trade, in part (a), ❶ domestic demand and domestic supply determine ❷ the equilibrium price at $100 million an airplane and ❸ the quantity at 400 airplanes a year.

With international trade, in part (b), world demand and world supply determine ❹ the world price, which is $150 million an airplane. ❺ The price rises. ❻ Domestic production increases to 700 airplanes a year, ❼ domestic purchases decrease to 200 airplanes a year, and ❽ 500 airplanes a year are exported.

Winners, Losers, and Net Gains from Trade

International trade has winners and it has losers. It is because some people lose that we often hear complaints about international competition. We're now going to see who wins and who loses from international trade. You will then be able to understand who complains about international competition and why. You will learn why we hear producers complaining about cheap foreign imports. You will also see why we never hear consumers of imported goods and services complaining and why we never hear exporters complaining except when they want greater access to foreign markets.

Gains and Losses from Imports

We can measure the gains and losses from imports by examining their effect on the price paid and quantity consumed by domestic consumers and their effect on the price received and quantity sold by domestic producers.

Domestic Consumers Gain from Imports When a country freely imports something from the rest of the world, it is because the rest of the world has a comparative advantage at producing that item. Compared to a situation with no international trade, the price paid by the consumer falls and the quantity consumed increases. It is clear that the consumer gains. The greater the fall in price and increase in quantity consumed, the greater is the gain to the consumer.

Domestic Producers Lose from Imports Compared to a situation with no international trade, the price received by domestic producers of an item that is imported falls. Also, the quantity sold by these domestic producers decreases. Because domestic producers of this item sell a smaller quantity and for a lower price, producers lose from international trade. Import-competing industries shrink in the face of competition from cheaper foreign-produced imports.

The profits of firms that produce import-competing goods and services fall, these firms cut their workforce, unemployment in these industries increases and wages fall. When these industries have a geographical concentration, such as steel production around Gary, Indiana, an entire region can suffer economic decline.

Gains and Losses from Exports

We measure the gains and losses from exports just like we measured those from imports, by examining their effects on the price paid and the quantity consumed by domestic consumers and the price received and the quantity sold by domestic producers.

Domestic Consumers Lose from Exports When a country exports something to the rest of the world, it is because the country has a comparative advantage at producing that item. Compared to a situation with no international trade, the price paid by consumers rises and the quantity consumed in the domestic economy decreases. Domestic consumers lose. The greater the rise in price and decrease in quantity consumed, the greater is the consumers' loss.

Domestic Producers Gain from Exports Compared to a situation with no international trade, the price received by a domestic producer of an item that is exported rises. Also, the quantity sold by domestic producers of this good or service increases. Because these domestic producers sell a larger quantity and for a higher

EYE on GLOBALIZATION

Who Wins and Who Loses from Globalization?

Economists generally agree that the gains from globalization vastly outweigh the losses. But there are both winners and losers.

The U.S. consumer is a big winner. Globalization has brought iPods, Wii games, Nike shoes, and a wide range of other products to our shops at ever lower prices.

The Indian (and Chinese and other Asian) worker is another big winner. Globalization has brought a wider range of more interesting jobs and higher wages.

The U.S. (and European) textile workers and furniture makers are big losers. Their jobs have disappeared and many of them have struggled to find new jobs even when they've been willing to take a pay cut.

But one of the *biggest* losers is the African farmer. Blocked from global food markets by trade restrictions and subsidies in the United States and Europe, globalization is leaving much of Africa on the sidelines.

The U.S. consumer ...

and the Indian worker gain from globalization.

But some U.S. workers ...

and African farmers lose.

price, producers gain from international trade. Export industries expand in the face of global demand for their product.

The profits of firms that produce exports rise, these firms expand their workforce, unemployment in these industries decreases and wages rise. When these industries have a geographical concentration, such as software production in Silicon Valley, an entire region can boom.

Net Gain

Export producers and import consumers gain, and export consumers and import producers lose, but the gains are greater than the losses. In the case of imports, consumers gain what producers lose and then even more from the cheaper imports. In the case of exports, producers gain what consumers lose and then even more from the items exported. So international trade provides a net gain for a country.

myeconlab

Work these problems in Study Plan 18.1 to get instant feedback.

CHECKPOINT 18.1

Explain how markets work with international trade and identify the gains from international trade and its winners and losers.

Practice Problems

Before the 1980s, China did not trade internationally. When China opened up to trade, the world price of coal was less than China's domestic price and the world price of shoes was higher than its domestic price. Use this information to work Problems **1** to **4**.

1. Does China import or export coal? Who, in China, gains and who loses from international trade in coal? Does China gain from this trade in coal?
2. Draw a graph to illustrate the market for coal in China and use your graph to show who gains and who loses from international trade in coal.
3. Does China import or export shoes? Who, in China, gains and who loses from international trade in shoes? Does China gain from this trade in shoes?
4. Draw a graph to illustrate the market for shoes in China and use your graph to show who gains and who loses from international trade in shoes.
5. **Underwater oil discovery to transform Brazil into a major exporter**
   This discovery will turn Brazil from an importer of oil into an exporter.
   Source: *New York Times*, January 11, 2008
   What is Brazil's comparative advantage in producing oil? What changed it?

FIGURE 1

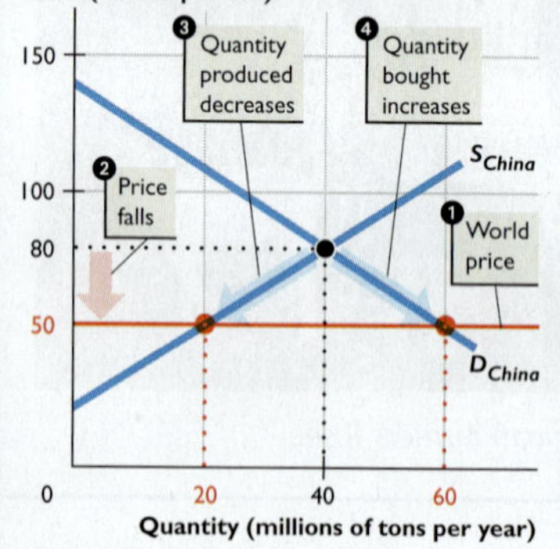

FIGURE 2

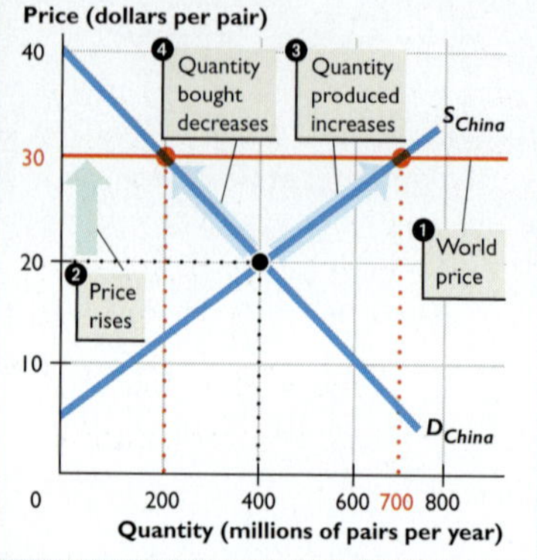

Guided Solutions to Practice Problems

1. The rest of the world has a comparative advantage in producing coal. China imports coal, Chinese coal consumers gain, and Chinese coal producers lose. The gains exceed the losses: China gains from international trade in coal.
2. Figure 1 shows the market for coal in China with international trade. The price falls to the world price, the quantity produced in China decreases, and the quantity bought increases. Producers lose from the lower price and smaller quantity produced. Consumers gain from the lower price what the producers lose but also gain more from the larger quantity consumed, so the gains to consumers exceed the losses to producers.
3. China has a comparative advantage in producing shoes. China exports shoes, Chinese shoe producers gain, and Chinese shoe consumers lose. The gains exceed the losses. China gains from international trade in shoes.
4. Figure 2 shows the market for shoes in China with international trade. The price rises to the world price, the quantity produced in China increases, and the quantity bought decreases. Consumers lose from the higher price and smaller quantity bought. Producers gain from the higher price what the consumers lose but also gain more from the larger quantity produced, so the gains to producers exceed the losses to consumers.
5. Before the discovery, the cost of producing oil in Brazil was higher than the world price, so Brazil imported oil. With the discovery of new oil, the cost of producing oil in Brazil has fallen below the world price, so Brazil has a comparative advantage in producing oil and will become an oil exporter.

18.2 INTERNATIONAL TRADE RESTRICTIONS

Governments use three sets of tools to influence international trade and protect domestic industries from foreign competition. They are

- Tariffs
- Import quotas
- Other import barriers

Tariffs

A **tariff** is a tax that is imposed on a good when it is imported. For example, the government of India imposes a 100 percent tariff on wine imported from California. When an Indian firm imports a $10 bottle of Californian wine, it pays the Indian government a $10 import duty.

Tariff
A tax imposed on a good when it is imported.

The incentive for governments to impose tariffs is strong. First, they provide revenue to the government. Second, they enable the government to satisfy the self-interest of people who earn their incomes in import-competing industries. As you will see, tariffs and other restrictions on free international trade decrease the gains from trade and are not in the social interest. Let's see how.

EYE on the PAST

The History of U.S. Tariffs

The figure shows the average tariff rate on U.S. imports since 1930. Tariffs peaked during the 1930s when Congress passed the Smoot-Hawley Act. With other nations, the United States signed the General Agreement on Tariffs and Trade (GATT) in 1947. In a series of rounds of negotiations, GATT achieved widespread tariff cuts for the United States and many other nations. Today, the World Trade Organization (WTO) continues the work of GATT and seeks to promote unrestricted trade among all nations.

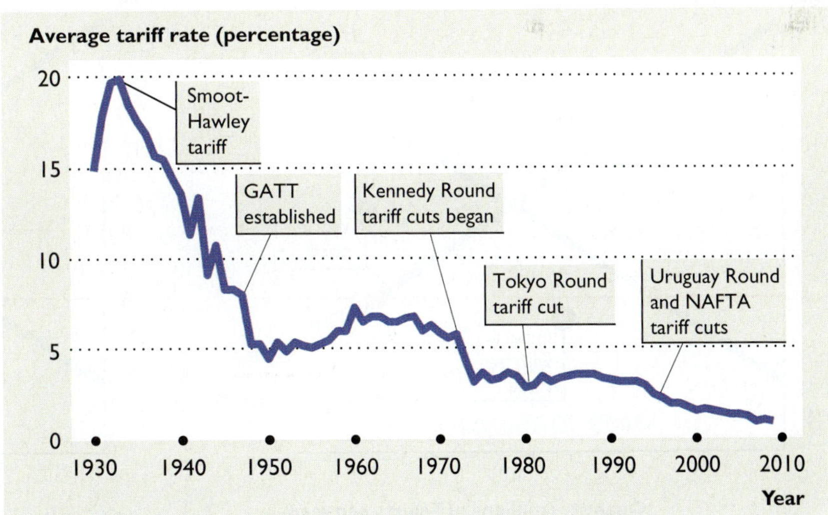

SOURCES OF DATA: The Budget for Fiscal Year 2006, Historical Tables, Table 2.5 and Bureau of Economic Analysis.

The United States is a party to many trade agreements with individual countries or regions. These include the North American Free Trade Agreement (NAFTA) and the Central American Free Trade Agreement (CAFTA). These agreements have eliminated tariffs on most goods traded between the United States and the countries of Central and North America.

The Effects of a Tariff

To see the effects of a tariff, let's return to the example in which, with international free trade, the United States imports T-shirts. The T-shirts are imported and sold at the world price. Then, under pressure from U.S. garment makers, the U.S. government imposes a tariff on imported T-shirts. Buyers of T-shirts must now pay the world price plus the tariff. Several consequences follow in the market for T-shirts. Figure 18.3 illustrates these consequences.

Figure 18.3(a) is the same as Figure 18.1(b) and shows the situation with free international trade. The United States produces 20 million T-shirts and imports 40 million T-shirts a year at the world price of $5 a T-shirt.

Figure 18.3(b) shows what happens with a tariff, which is set at $2 per T-shirt. The following changes occur in the U.S. market for T-shirts:

- The price of a T-shirt in the United States rises by $2.
- The quantity of T-shirts bought in the United States decreases.
- The quantity of T-shirts produced in the United States increases.
- The quantity of T-shirts imported into the United States decreases.
- The U.S. government collects a tariff revenue.

FIGURE 18.3

The Effects of a Tariff

myeconlab Animation

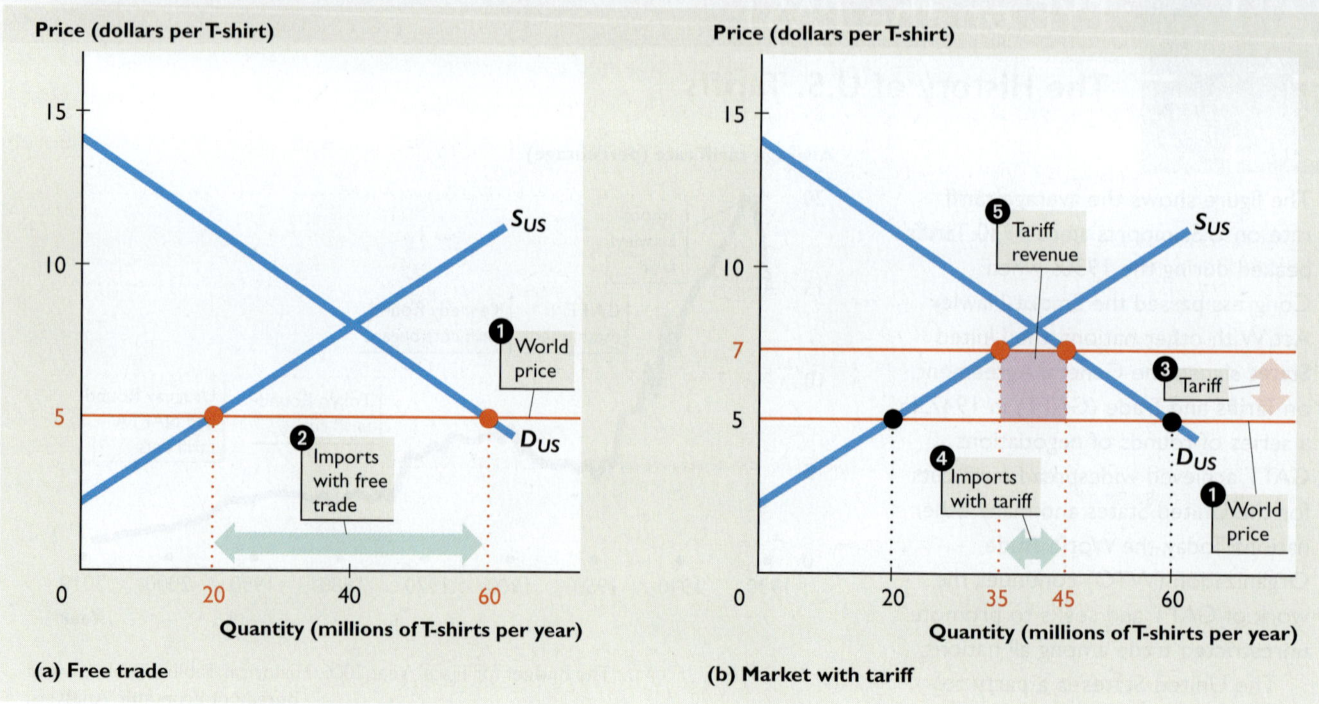

❶ The world price of a T-shirt is $5. With free trade, in part (a), Americans buy 60 million T-shirts. The United States produces 20 million T-shirts and ❷ imports 40 million T-shirts. ❸ With a tariff of $2 per T-shirt in part (b), the domestic price rises to $7 a T-shirt. Domestic production increases, purchases decrease, and ❹ the quantity imported decreases. ❺ The U.S. government collects tariff revenue of $2 on each T-shirt imported, which is shown by the purple rectangle.

Rise in Price of a T-Shirt To buy a T-shirt, Americans must pay the world price plus the tariff, so the price of a T-shirt rises by $2 to $7. Figure 18.3(b) shows the new domestic price line, which lies $2 above the world price line.

Decrease in Purchases The higher price of a T-shirt brings a decrease in the quantity demanded, which Figure 18.3(b) shows as a movement along the demand curve from 60 million T-shirts at $5 a T-shirt to 45 million T-shirts at $7 a T-shirt.

Increase in Domestic Production The higher price of a T-shirt stimulates domestic production, which Figure 18.3(b) shows as a movement along the supply curve from 20 million T-shirts at $5 a T-shirt to 35 million T-shirts at $7 a T-shirt.

Decrease in Imports T-shirt imports decrease by 30 million from 40 million to 10 million a year. Both the decrease in purchases and the increase in domestic production contribute to this decrease in imports.

Tariff Revenue The government's tariff revenue is $20 million—$2 per T-shirt on 10 million imported T-shirts—shown by the purple rectangle.

Winners, Losers, and the Social Loss from a Tariff

A tariff on an imported good creates winners and losers. When the U.S. government imposes a tariff on an imported good,

- U.S. consumers of the good lose.
- U.S. producers of the good gain.
- U.S. consumers lose more than U.S. producers gain: Society loses.

U.S. Consumers of the Good Lose Because the price of a T-shirt in the United States rises, the quantity of T-shirts demanded decreases. The combination of a higher price and smaller quantity bought makes the consumer worse off.

U.S. Producers of the Good Gain Because the price of an imported T-shirt rises by the tariff, U.S. T-shirt producers are now able to sell their T-shirts for a higher price—the world price plus the tariff. As the price of a T-shirt rises, U.S. producers increase the quantity supplied. The combination of a higher price and larger quantity produced increases producers' profits, so the U.S. producers gain from the tariff.

U.S. Consumers Lose More Than U.S. Producers Gain Consumers lose from a tariff for three reasons:

- They pay a higher price to domestic producers.
- They consume a smaller quantity of the good.
- They pay tariff revenue to the government.

The tariff revenue is a loss to consumers of T-shirts but a gain to consumers of public services paid for by the tariff revenue. The higher price paid to domestic producers pays for the higher cost of domestic production. The increased domestic production could have been obtained at lower cost as an import. Consumers lose and no one gains from decreased quantity of T-shirts consumed.

Import Quotas

Import quota
A quantitative restriction on the import of a good that limits the maximum quantity of a good that may be imported in a given period.

An **import quota** is a quantitative restriction on the import of a good that limits the maximum quantity of a good that may be imported in a given period. The United States imposes quotas on many items, including sugar, bananas, and textiles. Quotas enable the government to satisfy the self-interest of people who earn their incomes in import-competing industries. You will see that like a tariff, a quota on imports decreases the gains from trade and is not in the social interest.

The Effects of an Import Quota

Figure 18.4 shows the effects of an import quota. Figure 18.4(a) shows the situation with free international trade. Figure 18.4(b) shows what happens with a quota that limits imports to 10 million T-shirts a year. The U.S. supply curve of T-shirts becomes the domestic supply curve, S_{US}, plus the quantity that the quota permits to be imported. So the U.S. supply curve becomes the curve labeled S_{US} + *quota*.

The price of a T-shirt rises to $7, the quantity of T-shirts bought in the United States decreases to 45 million a year, the quantity of T-shirts produced in the United States increases to 35 million a year, and the quantity of T-shirts imported into the United States decreases to the quota quantity of 10 million a year. All these effects of a quota are identical to the effects of a $2 per T-shirt tariff, as you can check in Figure 18.3(b).

FIGURE 18.4

The Effects of an Import Quota

myeconlab Animation

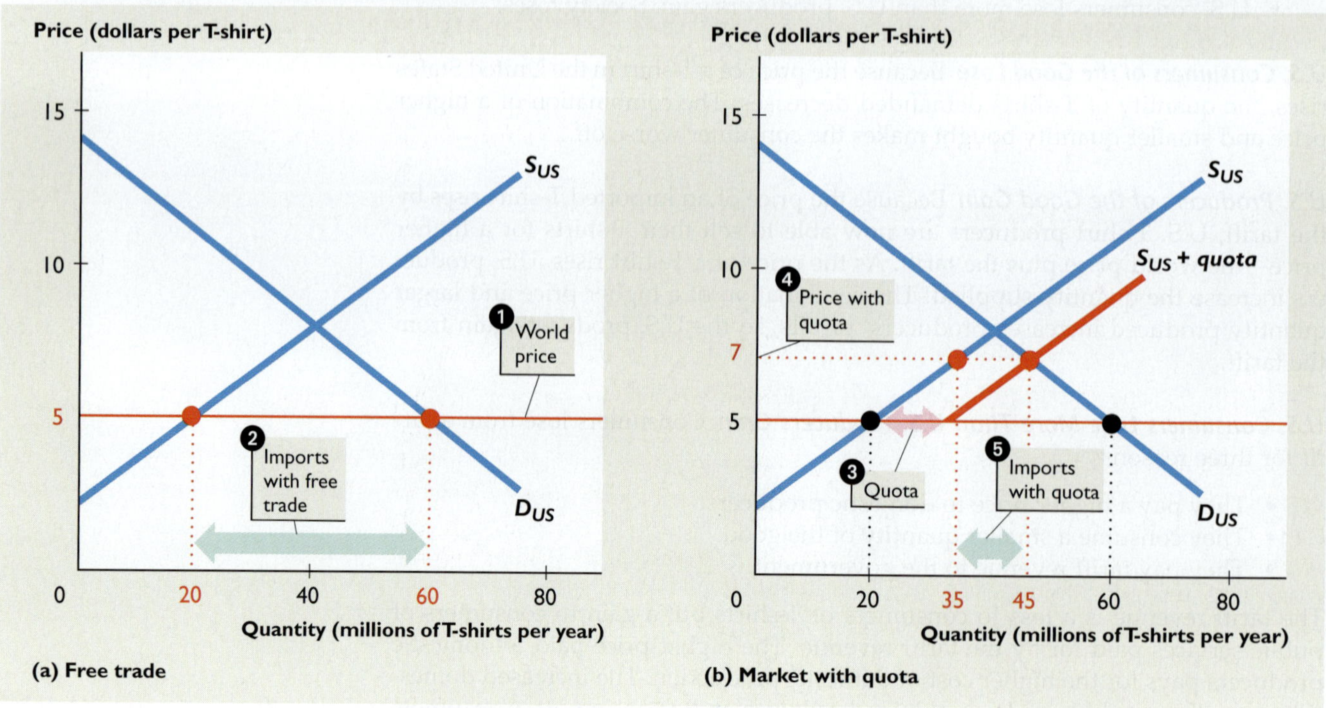

With free trade, in part (a), Americans buy 60 million T-shirts at ❶ the world price. The United States produces 20 million T-shirts and ❷ imports 40 million T-shirts. ❸ With an import quota of 10 million T-shirts, in part (b), the U.S. supply curve becomes S_{US} + *quota*. ❹ The price rises to $7 a T-shirt. Domestic production increases, purchases decrease, and ❺ the quantity imported decreases.

Winners, Losers, and the Social Loss from an Import Quota

An import quota creates winners and losers that are similar to those of a tariff but with an interesting difference. When the government imposes an import quota,

- U.S. consumers of the good lose.
- U.S. producers of the good gain.
- Importers of the good gain.
- Society loses.

U.S. Consumers of the Good Lose Because the price of a T-shirt in the United States rises, the quantity of T-shirts demanded decreases. The combination of a higher price and smaller quantity bought makes the consumer worse off. So the U.S. consumers lose when a quota is imposed.

U.S. Producers of the Good Gain Because the price of a T-shirt rises, U.S. T-shirt producers increase production. The combination of a higher price and larger quantity produced increases producers' profits. So the U.S. producers gain from the quota.

Importers of the Good Gain The importer is able to buy T-shirts on the world market at the world price and sell them in the domestic market at the domestic price. Because the domestic price exceeds the world price, the importer gains.

Society Loses Society loses because the loss to consumers exceeds the gains of domestic producers and importers. Just like the social loss from a tariff, there is a social loss because part of the higher price paid to domestic producers pays the higher cost of domestic production and because the quantity of the good consumed at the higher price decreases.

Other Import Barriers

Two sets of policies that influence imports are

- Health, safety, and regulation barriers
- Voluntary export restraints

Health, Safety, and Regulation Barriers

Thousands of detailed health, safety, and other regulations restrict international trade. For example, U.S. food imports are examined by the Food and Drug Administration to determine whether the food is "pure, wholesome, safe to eat, and produced under sanitary conditions." The European Union bans imports of most genetically modified foods, such as U.S.-produced soybeans. Although regulations of the type we've just described are not designed to limit international trade, they have that effect.

Voluntary Export Restraints

A *voluntary export restraint* is like a quota allocated to a foreign exporter of the good. A voluntary export restraint decreases imports just like an import quota does, but the foreign exporter gets the profit from the gap between the domestic price and the world price.

myeconlab

Work these problems in Study Plan 18.2 to get instant feedback.

CHECKPOINT 18.2

Explain the effects of international trade barriers.

Practice Problems

Before 1995, the United States imposed tariffs on imports from Mexico and Mexico imposed tariffs on imports from the United States. Both countries gradually removed these tariffs after Mexico joined the North American Free Trade Agreement (NAFTA) in 1995. Use this information to work Problems **1** to **3**.

1. Explain how the price that U.S. consumers pay for goods imported from Mexico and the quantity of U.S. imports from Mexico have changed. Who, in the United States, are the winners and losers from this free trade?
2. Explain how the quantity of U.S. exports to Mexico and the U.S. government's tariff revenue from trade with Mexico have changed.
3. Suppose that tomato growers in Florida lobby the U.S. government to impose an import quota on Mexican tomatoes. Explain who, in the United States, would gain and who would lose from such a quota.
4. **U.S. tariff angers French**

   Just days before Obama took office, the United States raised the tariff on imports of French sheep's-milk cheese to 300% from 100%—with the hope that the domestic price will be so high that imports of the cheese will cease.

   Source: *The Guardian*, January 17, 2009

   Explain how this tariff influences the price that U.S. consumers pay for sheep's-milk cheese, the quantity of sheep's-milk cheese produced in the United States, and the effect of the tariff on U.S. gains from trade with France. Who, in the United States, gains from the tariff and who loses?

Guided Solutions to Practice Problems

1. The price that U.S. consumers pay for goods imported from Mexico has fallen and the quantity of U.S. imports from Mexico has increased. The winners are U.S. consumers of goods imported from Mexico and the losers are U.S. producers of goods imported from Mexico.
2. The quantity of U.S. exports to Mexico has increased and the U.S. government's tariff revenue from trade with Mexico has fallen.
3. With an import quota, the price of tomatoes in the United States would rise and the quantity bought would decrease. Tomato consumers would lose. Growers would receive a higher price, produce a larger quantity, and their profits would increase. The U.S. consumers of tomatoes would lose more than the U.S. producers of tomatoes gained.
4. The tariff raises the price of sheep's-milk cheese in the United States to 400 percent of the world price (world price + 300 percent of the world price). U.S. imports decrease, U.S. production of sheep's-milk cheese increases, and the U.S. government collects a tariff revenue. With the higher U.S. domestic price, consumers lose and producers gain. Some of the consumers' loss goes to the government as tariff revenue, but some of the consumers' loss is no one's gain— consumers pay a higher price for a smaller quantity.

18.3 THE CASE AGAINST PROTECTION

For as long as nations and international trade have existed, people have debated whether free international trade or protection from foreign competition is better for a country. The debate continues, but most economists believe that free trade promotes prosperity for all countries while protection reduces the potential gains from trade. We've seen the most powerful case for free trade: All countries benefit from their comparative advantage. But there is a broader range of issues in the free trade versus protection debate. Let's review these issues.

Three Traditional Arguments for Protection

Three traditional arguments for protection and restricting international trade are

- The national security argument
- The infant-industry argument
- The dumping argument

Let's look at each in turn.

The National Security Argument

The national security argument is that a country must protect industries that produce defense equipment and armaments and those on which the defense industries rely for their raw materials and other intermediate inputs. This argument for protection can be taken too far.

First, it is an argument for international isolation, for in a time of war, there is no industry that does not contribute to national defense. Second, if the case is made for boosting the output of a strategic industry—say aerospace—it is more efficient to achieve this outcome with a subsidy financed out of taxes than with a tariff or quota. A subsidy would keep the industry operating at the scale that is judged appropriate, and free international trade would keep the prices faced by consumers at their world market levels.

The Infant-Industry Argument

Infant-industry argument
The argument that it is necessary to protect a new industry to enable it to grow into a mature industry that can compete in world markets.

The **infant-industry argument** is that it is necessary to protect a new industry to enable it to grow into a mature industry that can compete in world markets. The argument is based on an idea called *learning-by-doing*. By working repeatedly at a task, workers become better at that task and can increase the amount they produce in a given period.

There is nothing wrong with the idea of learning-by-doing. It is a powerful engine of human capital accumulation and economic growth. Learning-by-doing can change comparative advantage. If on-the-job experience lowers the opportunity cost of producing a good, a country might develop a comparative advantage in producing that good. Learning-by-doing does not justify protection.

It is in the self-interest of firms and workers who benefit from learning-by-doing to produce the efficient quantities. If the government protected these firms to boost their production, there would be an overproduction of these items.

The historical evidence is against the protection of infant industries. Countries in East Asia that have not given such protection have performed well. Countries that have protected infant industries, as India once did, have performed poorly.

The Dumping Argument

Dumping
When a foreign firm sells its exports at a lower price than its cost of production.

Dumping occurs when a foreign firm sells its exports at a lower price than its cost of production. You might be wondering why a firm would ever want to sell any of its output at a price below the cost of production. Wouldn't such a firm be better off either selling nothing, or, if it could do so, raising its price to at least cover its costs? Two possible reasons why a firm might sell at a price below cost and therefore engage in dumping are

- Predatory pricing
- Subsidy

Predatory Pricing A firm that engages in *predatory pricing* sets its price below cost in the hope that it can drive its competitors out of the market. If a firm in one country tries to drive out competitors in another country, it will be *dumping* its product in the foreign market. The foreign firm sells its output at a price below its cost to drive domestic firms out of business. When the domestic firms have gone, the foreign firm takes advantage of its monopoly position and charges a higher price for its product. The higher price will attract new competitors, which makes it unlikely that this strategy will be profitable. For this reason, economists are skeptical that this type of dumping occurs.

Subsidy A *subsidy* is a payment by the government to a producer. A firm that receives a subsidy is able to sell profitably for a price below cost. Subsidies are very common in almost all countries. The United States and the European Union subsidize the production of many agricultural products and dump their surpluses on the world market. This action lowers the prices that farmers in developing nations receive and weakens the incentive to expand farming in poor countries. India and Europe have been suspected of dumping steel in the United States.

Whatever its source, dumping is illegal under the rules of the WTO, NAFTA, and CAFTA and is regarded as a justification for temporary tariffs. Consequently, anti-dumping tariffs have become important in today's world.

But there are powerful reasons to resist the dumping argument for protection. First, it is virtually impossible to detect dumping because it is hard to determine a firm's costs. As a result, the test for dumping is whether a firm's export price is below its domestic price. This test is a weak one because it can be rational for a firm to charge a lower price in markets in which the quantity demanded is highly sensitive to price and a higher price in a market in which demand is less price-sensitive.

Second, it is hard to think of a good that is produced by a single firm. Even if all the domestic firms were driven out of business in some industry, it would always be possible to find several and usually many alternative foreign sources of supply and to buy at prices determined in competitive markets.

Third, if a good or service were a truly global natural monopoly, the best way to deal with it would be by regulation—just as in the case of domestic monopolies. Such regulation would require international cooperation.

The three arguments for protection that we've just examined have an element of credibility. The counterarguments are in general stronger, so these arguments do not make the case for protection. They are not the only arguments that you might encounter. There are many others, four of which we'll now examine.

Four Newer Arguments for Protection

Four newer and commonly made arguments for restricting international trade are that protection

- Saves jobs
- Allows us to compete with cheap foreign labor
- Brings diversity and stability
- Penalizes lax environmental standards

Saves Jobs

When Americans buy imported goods such as shoes from Brazil, U.S. workers who produce shoes lose their jobs. With no earnings and poor prospects, these workers become a drain on welfare and spend less, which creates a ripple effect of further job losses. The proposed solution is to protect U.S. jobs by banning imports of cheap foreign goods. The proposal is flawed for the following reasons.

First, free trade does cost some jobs, but it also creates other jobs. It brings about a global rationalization of labor and allocates labor resources to their highest-valued activities. Because of international trade in textiles, tens of thousands of workers in the United States have lost jobs because textile mills and other factories have closed. Tens of thousands of workers in other countries now have jobs because textile mills have opened there. And tens of thousands of U.S. workers now have better-paying jobs than as textile workers because other export industries have expanded and created more jobs than have been destroyed.

Second, imports create jobs. They create jobs for retailers that sell imported goods and for firms that service those goods. They also create jobs by creating incomes in the rest of the world, some of which are spent on imports of U.S.-made goods and services.

Protection saves some particular jobs, but it does so at a high cost. For example, until 2005, textile jobs in the United States were protected by quotas imposed under an international agreement called the Multifiber Arrangement (or MFA). The U.S. International Trade Commission (ITC) estimated that because of quotas, 72,000 jobs existed in textiles that would otherwise disappear and annual clothing expenditure in the United States was $15.9 billion ($160 per family) higher than it would be with free trade. An implication of the ITC estimate is that each textile job saved cost consumers $221,000 a year. The end of the MFA led to the destruction of a large number of textile jobs in the United States and Europe in 2005.

Allows Us to Compete with Cheap Foreign Labor

With the removal of protective tariffs in U.S. trade with Mexico, some people said that jobs would be sucked into Mexico and that the United States would not be able to compete with its southern neighbor. Let's see what's wrong with this view.

Labor costs depend on the wage rate and the quantity a worker produces. For example, if a U.S. auto worker earns $30 an hour and produces 15 units of output an hour, the average labor cost of a unit of output is $2. If a Mexican auto worker earns $3 an hour and produces 1 unit of output an hour, the average labor cost of a unit of output is $3. Other things remaining the same, the greater the output a worker produces, the higher is the worker's wage rate. High-wage workers produce a large output. Low-wage workers produce a small output.

Although high-wage U.S. workers are more productive, on the average, than lower-wage Mexican workers, there are differences across industries. U.S. labor is relatively more productive in some activities than in others. For example, the productivity of U.S. workers in producing movies, financial services, and customized computer chips is relatively higher than their productivity in the production of metals and some standardized machine parts. The activities in which U.S. workers are relatively more productive than their Mexican counterparts are those in which the United States has a comparative advantage. By engaging in free trade, increasing our production and exports of the goods and services in which we have a comparative advantage, and decreasing our production and increasing our imports of the goods and services in which our trading partners have a comparative advantage, we can make ourselves and the citizens of other countries better off.

Brings Diversity and Stability

A diversified investment portfolio is less risky than one that has all of its eggs in one basket. The same is true for an economy's production. A diversified economy fluctuates less than an economy that produces only one or two goods.

Most economies, whether the advanced United States, Japan, and Europe or the developing China and Brazil, have diversified production and do not have this type of stability problem. A few economies, such as Saudi Arabia, have a comparative advantage that leads to the specialized production of only one good. But even these economies can stabilize their income and consumption by investing in a wide range of production activities in other countries.

Penalizes Lax Environmental Standards

A new argument for protection is that many poorer countries, such as Mexico, do not have the same environmental standards that we have, and because they are willing to pollute and we are not, we cannot compete with them without tariffs. If these countries want free trade with the richer and "greener" countries, then they must raise their environmental standard.

This argument for trade restrictions is not entirely convincing. A poor country is less able than a rich one to devote resources to achieving high environmental standards. If free trade helps a poor country to become richer, then it will also help that country to develop the means to improve its environment. But there probably is a case for using the negotiation of free trade agreements such as NAFTA and CAFTA to hold member countries to higher environmental standards. There is an especially large payoff from using such bargaining to try to avoid irreversible damage to resources such as tropical rainforests.

So the four common arguments that we've just considered do not provide overwhelming support for protection. They all have flaws and leave the case for free international trade a strong one.

■ Why Is International Trade Restricted?

Why, despite all the arguments against protection, is international trade restricted? One reason that applies to developing nations is that the tariff is a convenient source of government revenue, but this reason does not apply to the United States where the government has access to income taxes and sales taxes.

Political support for international trade restrictions in the United States and most other developed countries arises from rent seeking. **Rent seeking** is lobbying and other political activity that seeks to capture the gains from trade. You've seen that free trade benefits consumers but shrinks the producer surplus of firms that compete in markets with imports.

Rent seeking
Lobbying and other political activity that aims to capture the gains from trade.

The winners from free trade are the millions of consumers of low-cost imports, but the benefit per individual consumer is small. The losers from free trade are the producers of import-competing items. Compared to the millions of consumers, there are only a few thousand producers.

Now think about imposing a tariff on clothing. Millions of consumers will bear the cost in the form of a smaller consumer surplus and a few thousand garment makers and their employees will share the gain in producer surplus.

Because the gain from a tariff is large, producers have a strong incentive to incur the expense of lobbying *for* a tariff and *against* free trade. On the other hand, because each consumer's loss is small, consumers have little incentive to organize and incur the expense of lobbying *for* free trade. The gain from free trade for any one person is too small for that person to spend much time or money on a political organization to lobby for free trade. The loss from free trade will be seen as being so great by those bearing that loss that they will find it profitable to join a political organization to prevent free trade. Each group weighs benefits against costs and chooses the best action for themselves, but the anti-free-trade group will undertake more political lobbying than will the pro-free-trade group.

EYE on YOUR LIFE

International Trade

International trade plays an extraordinarily large role in your life in three broad ways. It affects you as a

- Consumer
- Producer
- Voter

As a *consumer*, you benefit from the availability of a wide range of low-cost, high-quality goods and services that are produced in other countries.

Look closely at the labels on the items you buy. Where was your computer made? Where were your shirt and your shoes made? Where are the fruits and vegetables that you buy, especially in winter, grown?

The answers to all these questions are most likely Asia, Mexico, or South America. A few items were produced in Europe, Canada, and the United States.

As a *producer* (or as a potential producer if you don't yet have a job), you benefit from huge global markets for U.S. products. Your job prospects would be much dimmer if the firm for which you work didn't have global markets in which to sell its products.

People who work in the aircraft industry, for example, benefit from the huge global market for large passenger jets. Airlines from Canada to China are buying Boeing 777 aircraft as fast as they can be pushed out of the production line.

Even if you were to become a college professor, you would benefit from international trade in education services when your school admits foreign students.

As a *voter*, you have a big stake in the politics of free trade versus protection. As a buyer, your self-interest is hurt by tariffs and quotas on imported goods. Each time you buy a $20 sweater, you contribute $5 to the government in tariff revenue. But as a worker, your self-interest might be hurt by offshoring and by freer access to U.S. markets for foreign producers.

So as you decide how to vote, you must figure out what trade policy serves your self-interest and what best serves the social interest.

myeconlab

Work these problems in Study Plan 18.3 to get instant feedback.

CHECKPOINT 18.3

Explain and evaluate arguments used to justify restricting international trade.

Practice Problems

1. Japan sets quotas on imports of rice. California rice growers would like to export more rice to Japan. What are Japan's arguments for restricting imports of Californian rice? Are these arguments correct? Who loses from this restriction in trade?
2. The United States has, from time to time, limited imports of steel from Europe. What argument has the United States used to justify this quota? Who wins from this restriction? Who loses?
3. The United States maintains a quota on imports of sugar. What is the argument for this quota? Is this argument flawed? If so, explain why.
4. **U.S., China agree on free farm trade**

   Despite the failure of the Doha Round, the United States and China agree on the need to resist protectionist farm tariffs even in the face of the world economic crisis. In 2007, the United States exported $18.4 billion of farm and processed food products to China and imported $8 billion of farm products from China.

   Source: *USA Today*, December 6, 2008

   With the world in a global economic crisis, what arguments against free trade might U.S. producers of the farm products put forward? What would be wrong with the argument you suggest?

Guided Solutions to Practice Problems

1. The main arguments are that Japanese rice is a better quality rice and that the quota limits competition faced by Japanese farmers. The arguments are not correct. If Japanese consumers do not like the quality of Californian rice, they will not buy it. The quota does limit competition and the quota allows Japanese farmers to use their land less efficiently. The big losers are the Japanese consumers who pay about three times the U.S. price for rice.
2. The U.S. argument is that European producers dump steel on the U.S. market. With a quota, U.S. producers will face less competition in the market for steel and U.S. jobs will be saved. Workers in the steel industry and owners of steel companies will win at the expense of U.S. buyers of steel.
3. The argument is that the quota protects the jobs of U.S. workers. The argument is flawed because the United States does not have a comparative advantage in producing sugar and so a quota allows the U.S. sugar industry to be inefficient. With free international trade in sugar, the U.S. sugar industry would exist but it would be much smaller and more efficient.
4. With the United States in recession, a likely argument against free trade with China in farm products would be "impose restrictions to save U.S. jobs." By reducing imports of farm products, U.S. growers will receive a larger producer surplus, but U.S. total surplus will decrease.

CHAPTER SUMMARY

Key Points

1 Explain how markets work with international trade and identify the gains from international trade and its winners and losers.

- Comparative advantage drives international trade.
- When the world price of a good is lower than the price that balances domestic demand and supply, a country gains by decreasing production and importing the good.
- When the world price of a good is higher than the price that balances domestic demand and supply, a country gains by increasing production and exporting the good.
- Compared to a no-trade situation, in a market with imports, consumers gain and producers lose but the gains exceed the losses.
- Compared to a no-trade situation, in a market with exports, producers gain and consumers lose but the gains exceed the losses.

2 Explain the effects of international trade barriers.

- Countries restrict international trade by imposing tariffs, quotas, and other import barriers.
- Trade restrictions raise the domestic price of imported goods, lower the quantity imported, make consumers worse off, make producers better off, and damage the social interest.

3 Explain and evaluate arguments used to justify restricting international trade.

- The arguments that protection is necessary for national security, for infant industries, and to prevent dumping are weak.
- Arguments that protection saves jobs, allows us to compete with cheap foreign labor, makes the economy diversified and stable, and is needed to penalize lax environmental standards are flawed.
- Trade is restricted because protection brings small losses to a large number of people and large gains to a small number of people.

Key Terms

myeconlab

Work these problems in Chapter 18 Study Plan to get instant feedback.

FIGURE 1 U.S. SHOE MARKET

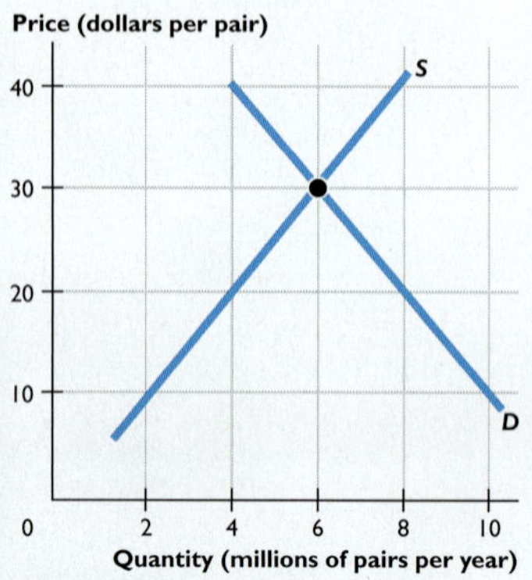

FIGURE 2 BRAZIL'S SHOE MARKET

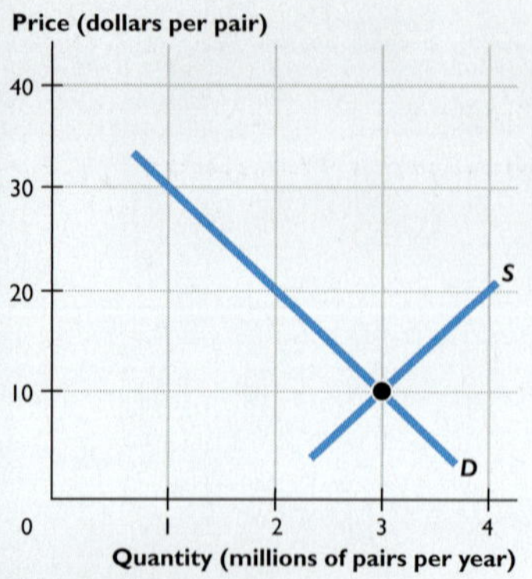

CHAPTER CHECKPOINT

Study Plan Problems and Applications

Use the information in Figures 1 and 2 to work Problems 1 to 4. Figure 1 shows the U.S. market for shoes and Figure 2 shows Brazil's market for shoes if there is no international trade in shoes between the United States and Brazil.

1. Which country has a comparative advantage in producing shoes? With international trade between Brazil and the United States, explain which country would export shoes and how the price of shoes in the importing country and the quantity produced by the importing country would change. Explain which country gains from this trade.
2. With international trade, the world price of a pair of shoes is $20. Explain how consumers and producers in the United States gain or lose as a result of international trade. Show the change in U.S. consumption, production, and price.
3. The world price of a pair of shoes is $20. Explain how consumers and producers in Brazil gain or lose as a result of international trade. Show the change in Brazil's consumption, production, and price.
4. Who in the United States loses from free trade in shoes with Brazil? Explain why.

Use the following information to work Problems 5 to 7.

The supply of roses in the United States is made up of U.S. grown roses and imported roses. Draw a graph to illustrate the U.S. rose market with free international trade in roses. On your graph, mark the price of roses and the quantities of roses bought, produced, and imported into the United States.

5. Who in the United States loses from this trade in roses and would lobby for a restriction on the quantity of imported roses? If the U.S. government put a tariff on rose imports, show on your graph the effects on U.S. consumers and U.S. producers. Show the government's tariff revenue.
6. Suppose that the U.S. government puts an import quota on roses. Show on your graph the effects on the quantity bought by consumers, the quantity produced, and the quantity imported.
7. Suppose that the U.S. government bans rose imports. Show on your graph the effects on the price and quantity produced and consumed. Who gains and who loses from this ban?
8. **Mexico to raise tariffs on 90 U.S. exports**

   Mexico plans to impose tariffs on 90 U.S. industrial and agricultural products imported into Mexico in retaliation for the cancellation earlier this year of a commercial trucking project that allowed small trucks to travel further inside each other's country.

   Source: CNNMoney.com, March 16, 2009

   Explain who in Mexico gains and who loses from these new tariffs on imported U.S. goods. Who in the United States gains and loses?

Instructor Assignable Problems and Applications

Your instructor can assign these problems as homework, a quiz, or a test in **MyEconLab**.

Use the following information to work Problems 1 and 2.

The future of U.S.–India relations

In May 2009, Secretary of State Hillary Clinton gave a major speech covering all the issues in U.S.–India relations. On economic and trade relations she noted that India maintains significant barriers to U.S. trade. The United States also maintains barriers against Indian imports such as textiles. Mrs. Clinton, President Obama, and Anand Sharma, the Indian Minister of Commerce and Industry say they want to dismantle these trade barriers.

Source: www.state.gov

1. Explain who in the United States would gain and who might lose from dismantling trade barriers between the United States and India.
2. Draw a graph of the U.S. market for textiles and show how removing a tariff would change the quantities produced, consumed, and imported. Explain why the gains exceed the losses.
3. The United States exports wheat. Draw a graph of the U.S. wheat market if there is free international trade in wheat. On your graph, mark the price of wheat and the quantities bought, produced, and exported by the United States.

Use Figure 1 and the following information to work Problems 4 to 6. Figure 1 shows the car market in Mexico when Mexico places no restriction on the quantity of cars imported. The world price of a car is $10,000.

FIGURE 1

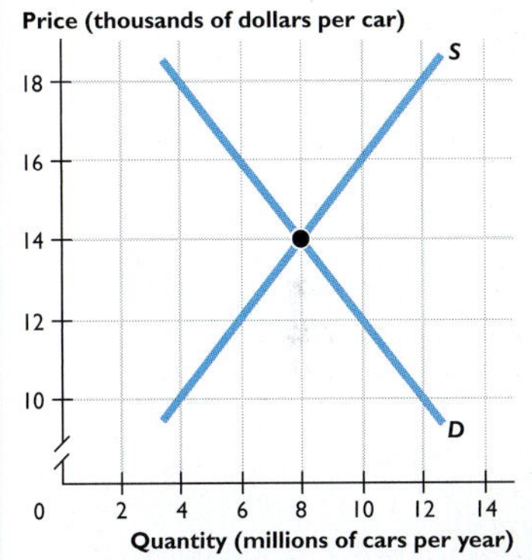

4. If the government of Mexico introduces a $2,000 tariff on car imports, what will be the price of a car in Mexico, the quantity of cars produced in Mexico, the quantity imported into Mexico, and the government's tariff revenue?
5. If the government of Mexico introduces a quota of 4 million cars a year, what will be the price of a car in Mexico, the quantity of cars produced in Mexico, and the quantity imported?
6. What argument might be used to encourage the government of Mexico to introduce a $2,000 tariff on car imports from the United States? Who will gain and who will lose as a result of Mexico's tariff?
7. Suppose that the world price of sugar is 10 cents a pound, the United States does not trade internationally, and the price of sugar in the United States is 20 cents a pound. The United States then begins to trade internationally.
   - How does the U.S. price of sugar change? Do U.S. consumers buy more or less sugar? Do U.S. sugar growers produce more or less sugar?
   - Does the United States export or import sugar and why?
8. In the 1950s, Ford and General Motors established a car-producing industry in Australia and argued for a high tariff on car imports. The tariff remained through the years and until 2000, it was 22.5 percent. What might have been Ford's and General Motors' argument for the high tariff? Is the tariff the best way to achieve the goals of the argument?
9. The United States exports services and imports coffee. Why does the United States gain from exporting services and importing coffee? How do economists measure the net gain from this international trade?

TABLE 1

Price (dollars per unit)	Quantity demanded	Quantity supplied
	(billions of units per year)	
10	25	0
12	20	20
14	15	40
16	10	60
18	5	80
20	0	100

10. A semiconductor is a key component in your laptop, cell phone, and iPod. Table 1 provides information about the market for semiconductors in the United States. Producers of semiconductors can get $18 a unit on the world market. With no international trade, what would be the price of a semiconductor and how many semiconductors a year would be bought and sold in the United States? At $18 a unit, does the United States have a comparative advantage in producing semiconductors? If U.S. producers of semiconductors sell at the highest possible price, how many do they sell in the United States and how many do they export?
11. In 1845, French economist Frédéric Bastiat wrote a satirical "petition of the candlemakers" in which he argued that competition from the sun was unfair to the makers of artificial lighting. He suggested that to level the playing field, boost the production of artificial light, and create much employment and economic activity, the government should pass a law ordering the shutting up of all windows, openings, and chinks through which sunlight may enter buildings. Explain why the argument presented in Bastiat's petition is similar to that of people who argue for protection from foreign competition.

Use the following information to work Problems 12 to 14.

U.S. expands China paper anti-dumping tariff

The U.S. Commerce Department has raised the tariff on imports of glossy paper from China up to 918.65 percent, as a result of complaints by NewPage Corp. of Dayton, Ohio. Imports from China increased 166 percent from 2005 to 2006. This glossy paper is used in art books, high-end magazines, and textbooks.

Source: *Reuters*, May 30, 2007

12. What is dumping? Who in the United States loses from China's dumping of glossy paper?
13. Explain what an anti-dumping tariff is. What argument might NewPage Corp. have used to persuade the U.S. Commerce Department to impose a 99.65 percent tariff?
14. Explain who, in the United States, will gain and who will lose from the tariff on glossy paper. How do you expect the prices of magazines and textbooks that you buy to change?
15. **Halved tariffs cut imported car prices by thousands**

    Prices of imported cars in Australia are set to plunge after a government review called for tariffs to be cut from 10 percent to 5 percent. The price of a small imported car will drop by $1,000 and the price of basic BMWs by more than $2,000. But the proposed tariff cut could be bad news for local car makers and a major union has demanded a "tariff freeze" to protect local industry and jobs.

    Source: *Courier Mail*, August 16, 2008

    Explain why the tariff cut is "bad news for local car makers." Why is the union demanding a tariff freeze? Who will gain from the tariff freeze?

Why has our dollar been sinking?

One U.S. dollar was worth 1.17 euros in 2001 but only 68 euro cents in 2009. Why?

19

International Finance

CHAPTER CHECKLIST

When you have completed your study of this chapter, you will be able to

1. Describe a country's balance of payments accounts and explain what determines the amount of international borrowing and lending.
2. Explain how the exchange rate is determined and why it fluctuates.

19.1 FINANCING INTERNATIONAL TRADE

When Apple Computer, Inc. imports iPods that it manufactures in Taiwan, it pays for them using Taiwanese dollars. When a French construction company buys an earthmover from Caterpillar, Inc., it uses U.S. dollars. Whenever we buy things from another country, we pay in the currency of that country. It doesn't make any difference what the item being traded is; it might be a consumption good or a service or a capital good, a building, or even a firm.

We're going to study the markets in which different types of currency are bought and sold. But first we're going to look at the scale of international trading and borrowing and lending and at the way in which we keep our records of these transactions. These records are called the balance of payments accounts.

Balance of Payments Accounts

Balance of payments accounts
The accounts in which a nation records its international trading, borrowing, and lending.

A country's **balance of payments accounts** record its international trading, borrowing, and lending. There are in fact three balance of payments accounts:

- Current account
- Capital account
- Official settlements account

Current account
Record of receipts from the sale of goods and services to other countries (exports), minus payments for goods and services bought from other countries (imports), plus the net amount of interest and transfers received from and paid to other countries.

Capital account
Record of foreign investment in the United States minus U.S. investment abroad.

Official settlements account
Record of the change in U.S. official reserves.

U.S. official reserves
The government's holdings of foreign currency.

The **current account** records receipts from the sale of goods and services to other countries (exports), minus payments for goods and services bought from other countries (imports), plus the net amount of interest and transfers (such as foreign aid payments) received from and paid to other countries. The **capital account** records foreign investment in the United States minus U.S. investment abroad. The **official settlements account** records the change in U.S. official reserves. **U.S. official reserves** are the government's holdings of foreign currency. If U.S. official reserves increase, the official settlements account balance is negative. The reason is that holding foreign money is like investing abroad and U.S. investment abroad is a minus item in the capital account. (By the same reasoning, if official reserves decrease, the official settlements account balance is positive.)

The sum of the balances on the three accounts always equals zero. That is, to pay for our current account deficit, we must either borrow more from abroad than we lend abroad or use our official reserves to cover the shortfall.

Table 19.1 shows the U.S. balance of payments accounts in 2008. Items in the current account and capital account that provide foreign currency to the United States have a plus sign; items that cost the United States foreign currency have a minus sign. The table shows that in 2008, U.S. imports exceeded U.S. exports and the current account deficit was $706 billion. We paid for imports that exceeded the value of our exports by borrowing from the rest of the world. The capital account tells us by how much. We borrowed $534 billion (foreign investment in the United States) and, net, made no loans to the rest of the world (no U.S. investment abroad). Other net foreign borrowing of –$29 billion and a statistical discrepancy of $206 billion made our capital account balance $711 billion. Our official reserves increased by $5 billion and are shown in Table 19.1 as a negative $5 billion, a convention that makes the three accounts sum to zero.

You might better understand the balance of payments accounts and the way in which they are linked if you think about the income and expenditure, borrowing and lending, and bank account of an individual.

EYE on the PAST

The U.S. Balance of Payments

The numbers in Table 33.1 provide a snapshot of the U.S. balance of payments in 2008. The figure puts this snapshot into perspective by showing how the balance of payments evolved from 1980 to 2008.

A current account deficit emerged during the 1980s but briefly disappeared with a near-zero balance in the recession of the early 1990s.

As the economy resumed its expansion during the 1990s the current account deficit increased. It continued to increase through the 2000s.

The current account deficit has decreased only in recessions and increased again once a recovery gets going.

The capital account balance is almost a mirror image of the current account balance and the reason is that the official settlements balance—the change in gold and foreign exchange reserves—is very small in comparison with the balances on the other two accounts.

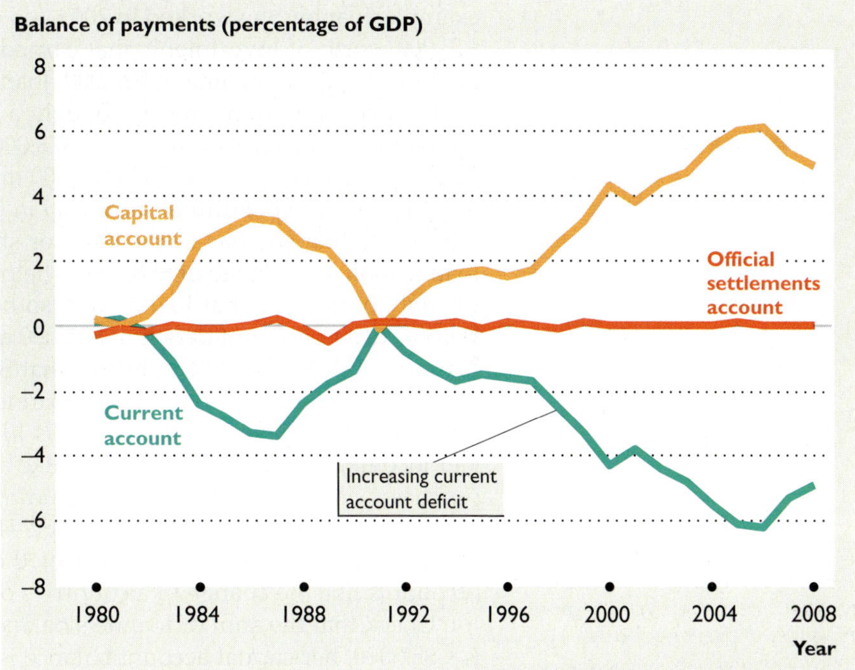

SOURCE OF DATA: Bureau of Economic Analysis.

TABLE 19.1

The U.S. Balance of Payments Accounts in 2008

Current account	**(billions of dollars)**
Exports of goods and services	+1,827
Imports of goods and services	–2,524
Net interest	+119
Net transfers	–128
Current account balance	**–706**
Capital account	
Foreign investment in the United States	+534
U.S. investment abroad	0
Other net foreign investment in the United States	–29
Statistical discrepancy	206
Capital account balance	**+711**
Official settlements account	
Official settlements account balance	**–5**

SOURCE OF DATA: Bureau of Economic Analysis.

Personal Analogy

You have a set of personal balance of payments accounts that parallel those of a nation. You have a current account, a capital account, and a settlements account.

Your current account records your income from supplying the services of factors of production and your expenditure on goods and services. Consider, for example, Joanne. She worked in 2009 and earned an income of $25,000. Joanne has $10,000 worth of investments that earned her interest of $1,000. Joanne's current account shows an income of $26,000. Joanne spent $18,000 buying goods and services for consumption. She also bought a new apartment, which cost her $60,000. So Joanne's total expenditure was $78,000. The difference between her expenditure and her income is $52,000 ($78,000 minus $26,000).

To pay for expenditure of $52,000 in excess of her income, Joanne has to use the money that she has in the bank or she has to take out a loan. Suppose that Joanne took a mortgage of $50,000 to help buy her apartment. This mortgage was the only borrowing that Joanne did, so her capital account surplus was $50,000. With a current account deficit of $52,000 and a capital account surplus of $50,000, Joanne is still $2,000 short. She got that $2,000 from her own bank account. Her cash holdings decreased by $2,000. Joanne's settlements balance was $2,000.

Joanne's income from her work is like a country's income from its exports. Her income from her investments is like a country's interest from foreigners. Her purchases of goods and services, including her purchase of an apartment, are like a country's imports. Joanne's mortgage—borrowing from someone else—is like a country's borrowing from the rest of the world. The change in Joanne's bank account is like the change in a country's official reserves.

Check that the sum of Joanne's balances is zero. Her current account balance is −$52,000, her capital account balance is +$50,000, and her settlements account balance is +$2,000, so the sum of the three balances is zero.

Borrowers and Lenders, Debtors and Creditors

Net borrower
A country that is borrowing more from the rest of the world than it is lending to the rest of the world.

Net lender
A country that is lending more to the rest of the world than it is borrowing from the rest of the world.

A country that is borrowing more from the rest of the world than it is lending to the rest of the world is called a **net borrower**. Similarly, a **net lender** is a country that is lending more to the rest of the world than it is borrowing from it.

The United States is a net borrower, but it is a relative newcomer to the ranks of net borrower nations. Throughout the 1960s and most of the 1970s, the United States was a net lender. It had a surplus on its current account and a deficit on its capital account. It was not until 1983 that the United States became a significant net borrower. Between 1983 and 1987, U.S. borrowing increased each year. Then it decreased and was briefly zero in 1991. After 1991, U.S. borrowing started to increase again. The average net foreign borrowing by the United States between 1983 and 2009 was $286 billion a year.

Most countries are net borrowers like the United States. But a small number of countries, including Japan and oil-rich Saudi Arabia, are net lenders.

Debtor nation
A country that during its entire history has borrowed more from the rest of the world than it has lent to the rest of the world.

Creditor nation
A country that during its entire history has invested more in the rest of the world than other countries have invested in it.

A net borrower might be reducing its net assets held in the rest of the world, or it might be going deeper into debt. A nation's total stock of foreign investment determines whether the nation is a debtor or creditor. A **debtor nation** is a country that during its entire history has borrowed more from the rest of the world than it has lent to the rest of the world. It has a stock of outstanding debt to the rest of the world that exceeds the stock of its own claims on the rest of the world. A **creditor nation** is a country that during its entire history has invested more in the rest of the world than other countries have invested in it.

Flows and Stocks

At the heart of the distinction between a net borrower and a net lender on the one hand and between a debtor nation and a creditor nation on the other hand is the distinction between flows and stocks, which you have encountered many times in your study of macroeconomics. Borrowing and lending are flows—amounts borrowed or lent per unit of time. Debts are stocks—amounts owed at a point in time. The flow of borrowing and lending changes the stock of debt.

The United States was a debtor nation through the nineteenth century as we borrowed from Europe to finance our westward expansion, railroads, and industrialization. The United States paid off its debt and became a creditor nation for most of the twentieth century. But following a string of current account deficits, the United States became a debtor nation again in 1989.

Since 1989, the total stock of U.S. borrowing from the rest of the world has exceeded U.S. lending to the rest of the world. The largest debtor nations are the capital-hungry developing countries (as the United States was during the nineteenth century). The international debt of these countries grew from less than a third to more than a half of their gross domestic product during the 1980s and created what is called the "Third World debt crisis."

Should we be concerned that the United States is a net borrower? The answer to this question depends mainly on what the net borrower is doing with the borrowed money. If the borrowed money is financing investment that in turn is generating economic growth and higher income, then the borrowing is not a problem. If the borrowed money is being used to finance consumption, then higher interest payments are being incurred, and consequently, consumption will eventually have to be reduced. In this case, the more the borrowing and the longer it goes on, the greater is the reduction in consumption that will eventually be necessary. We'll see below whether the United States is borrowing for investment or consumption.

Current Account Balance

What determines a country's current account balance and net foreign borrowing? You've seen in Table 19.1 that exports of goods and services (X) and imports of goods and services (M) are the largest items in the current account. We call exports minus imports net exports (NX). So net exports is the main component of the current account. We can define the current account balance (CAB) as

$$CAB = NX + \text{Net interest and transfers from abroad.}$$

Fluctuations in net exports are the main source of fluctuations in the current account balance. Net interest and transfers from abroad are small and have trends, but they do not fluctuate much. So we can study the current account balance by looking at what determines net exports.

Net Exports

The government budget and private saving and investment determine net exports. To see how they determine net exports, we need to recall some of the things that we learned about the national income accounts in Chapter 5. Table 19.2 will refresh your memory and summarize some calculations.

TABLE 19.2

Net Exports, the Government Budget, Saving, and Investment

	Symbols and equations	United States in 2008 (billions of dollars)
(a) Variables		
Exports	X	1,831
Imports	M	2,539
Investment	I	2,136
Saving	S	2,362
Government expenditure on goods and services	G	2,883
Net taxes	NT	1,940
(b) Balances		
Net exports	$X - M$	1,831 – 2,539 = –708
Private sector balance	$S - I$	2,362 – 2,136 = 226
Government sector balance	$NT - G$	1,950 – 2,883 = –934
(c) Relation among balances		
National accounts	$Y = C + I + G + X - M = C + S + NT$	
Rearranging:	$X - M = S - I + NT - G$	
Net exports	$X - M$	–708
Equals:		
Private sector balance	$S - I$	226
Plus:		
Government sector balance	$NT - G$	–934

SOURCE OF DATA: Bureau of Economic Analysis, 2009. (The National Income and Product Accounts measures of exports and imports are slightly different from the Balance of Payments Accounts measures in Table 19.1 on p. 479. The government sector includes state and local governments.)

Part (a) of Table 19.2 lists the national income variables with their symbols. Part (b) defines three balances. *Net exports* are exports of goods and services minus imports of goods and services.

Private sector balance
Saving minus investment.

The **private sector balance** is saving minus investment. If saving exceeds investment, a private sector surplus is lent to other sectors. If investment exceeds saving, borrowing from other sectors finances a private sector deficit.

Government sector balance
Net taxes minus government expenditure on goods and services.

The **government sector balance** is equal to net taxes minus government expenditure on goods and services. If that number is positive, a government sector surplus is lent to other sectors; if that number is negative, borrowing from other sectors must finance a government deficit. The government sector is the sum of the federal, state, and local governments.

Part (b) also shows the values of these balances for the United States in 2008. As you can see, net exports were –\$708 billion, a deficit. The private sector saved \$2,362 billion and invested \$2,136 billion, so it had a surplus of \$226 billion. The government sector's revenue from net taxes was \$1,950 billion, and its expenditure was \$2,883 billion, so the government sector balance was –\$934 billion, a deficit.

Part (c) of Table 19.2 shows the relationship among the three balances. From the national income accounts, we know that real GDP, Y, is the sum of consumption expenditure, C; investment, I; government expenditure on goods and services, G; and net exports, $X - M$. Real GDP also equals the sum of consumption expenditure, C, saving, S, and net taxes, NT. Rearranging these equations tells us that net exports equals $(S - I)$, the private sector balance, plus $(NT - G)$, the government sector balance. That is,

$$\text{Net exports} = (S - I) + (NT - G).$$

Should we be concerned that the United States is a net borrower? The answer is probably not. Our international borrowing finances the purchase of new capital goods. In 2006, businesses spent $2,136 billion on new buildings, plant, and equipment. Government spent $496 billion on defense equipment and public structures. All these purchases added to the nation's capital, and much of it increased productivity. Governments also purchased education and health care services, which increased human capital.

Our international borrowing is financing private and public investment, not consumption.

EYE on the GLOBAL ECONOMY

Current Account Balances Around the World

The U.S. current account deficit in 2008 is the major international payments deficit. No other country has a deficit remotely similar to that of the United States.

For every deficit, there must be a corresponding surplus. The figure shows that the U.S. deficit is reflected in a large number of surpluses spread around the world. No single country has a surplus to match the U.S. deficit.

But China and the oil-exporting countries of the Middle East have surpluses that in total equal the U.S. deficit.

Japan, other advanced economies, and the newly industrialized Asian economies also have surpluses.

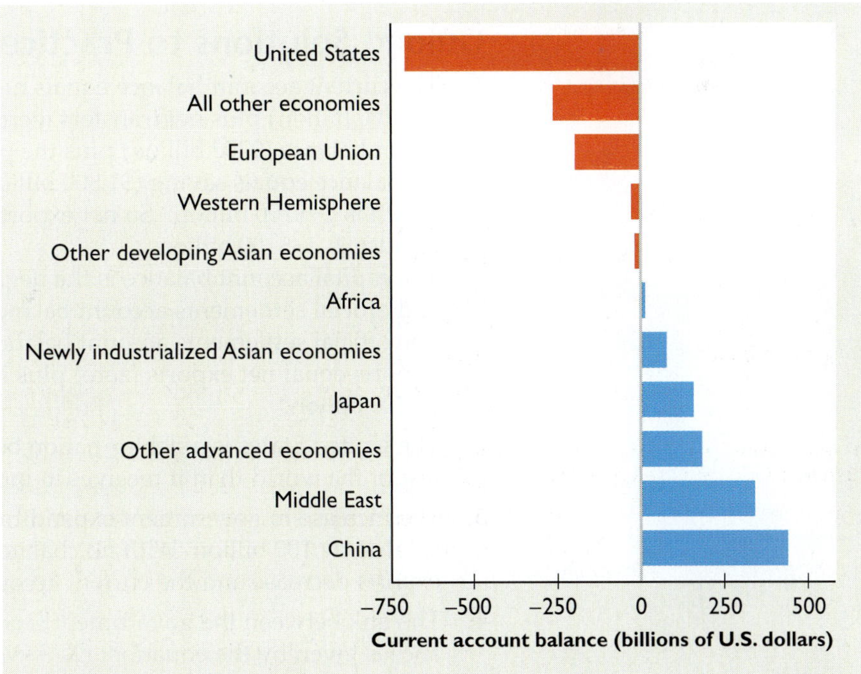

SOURCE OF DATA: International Monetary Fund, *World Economic Outlook*, April 2009.

myeconlab

Work these problems in Study Plan 19.1 to get instant feedback.

CHECKPOINT 19.1

Describe a country's balance of payments accounts and explain what determines the amount of international borrowing and lending.

Practice Problems

Use the following information about the United States to work Problems **1** to **3**.

Imports of goods and services: $2,000 billion; interest paid to the rest of the world: $500 billion; interest received from the rest of the world: $400 billion; decrease in U.S. official reserves: $10 billion; government sector balance: $200 billion; saving: $1,800 billion; investment: $2,000 billion; net transfers: zero.

1. Calculate the current account balance, the capital account balance, the official settlements account balance, and exports of goods and services.
2. Is the United States a debtor or a creditor nation?
3. If government expenditure on goods and services increases by $100 billion, how does the current account balance change?
4. **Something has got to give**

   As the recovery takes hold, the U.S. government must reduce its expenditure to trim its huge budget deficit. To keep aggregate demand growing, consumption, investment, or exports must grow. U.S. consumers are burdened with debt, U.S. firms have unused capital, so exports must grow.

   Source: *USA Today*, September 3, 2009

   Explain why a cut in government expenditure to trim the budget deficit will require exports to grow.

Guided Solutions to Practice Problems

1. The current account balance equals net exports plus net interest from abroad (−$100 billion) plus net transfers (zero). Net exports equal the government sector balance ($200 billion) plus the private sector balance. The private sector balance equals saving ($1,800 billion) minus investment ($2,000 billion), which is −$200 billion. So net exports are zero, and the current account balance is −$100 billion.

   The capital account balance is the negative of the sum of the current account and official settlements account balances, which is $90 billion.

   The official settlements account balance is a *surplus* of $10 billion.

   Exports equal net exports (zero) plus imports ($2,000 billion), which equals $2,000 billion.
2. The United States is a debtor nation because it pays more in interest to the rest of the world than it receives in interest from the rest of the world.
3. The increase in government expenditure decreases the government sector balance by 100 billion. With no change in the private sector balance, net exports decrease and the current account deficit increases by $100 billion.
4. The link between the government sector balance and the private sector balance is given by the equation: $(X - M) = (S - I) + (NT - G)$. Rewrite the equation as $(G - NT) = (S - I) - (X - M)$. A cut in G will decrease the left side of the equation. If consumption does not increase, then S will increase. To make the right side of the equation decrease, X must increase.

19.2 THE EXCHANGE RATE

When we buy foreign goods or invest in another country, we pay using that country's currency. When foreigners buy U.S.-made goods or invest in the United States, they pay in U.S. dollars. We get foreign currency, and foreigners get U.S. dollars in the foreign exchange market. The **foreign exchange market** is the market in which the currency of one country is exchanged for the currency of another. The foreign exchange market is not a place like a downtown flea market or produce market. It is made up of thousands of people: importers and exporters, banks, and specialist traders of foreign exchange, called foreign exchange brokers. The foreign exchange market opens on Monday morning in Hong Kong, which is still Sunday evening in New York. As the day advances, markets open in Singapore, Tokyo, Bahrain, Frankfurt, London, New York, Chicago, and San Francisco. As the U.S. West Coast markets close, Hong Kong is only an hour away from opening for the next business day. Dealers around the world are in continual contact, and on a typical day in 2009, more than $3 trillion changed hands.

Foreign exchange market
The market in which the currency of one country is exchanged for the currency of another.

The price at which one currency exchanges for another is called a **foreign exchange rate**. For example, in October 2009, one U.S. dollar bought 68 euro cents. The exchange rate was 68 euro cents per dollar. We can also express the exchange rate in terms of dollars (or cents) per euro, which in October 2009 was $1.48 per euro.

Foreign exchange rate
The price at which one currency exchanges for another.

Currency appreciation is the rise in the value of one currency in terms of another currency. For example, when the dollar rose from 86 euro cents in 1999 to 1.17 euros in 2001, the dollar appreciated by 36 percent.

Currency appreciation
The rise in the value of one currency in terms of another currency.

EYE on the PAST

The Dollar and the Euro Since 1999

From 1999 to 2001, the value of the dollar rose against the euro—the dollar *appreciated*. From 2002 to 2009, the value of the dollar fell against the euro—the dollar *depreciated*.

The rate of the dollar's depreciation was rapid during 2003, but it slowed during 2004 and for a few months the dollar appreciated again.

The dollar's slide resumed in 2006 and aside from another brief appreciation in 2008, the dollar kept on falling against the euro. The overall fall was from a high of 1.17 euros to a low of 0.68 euros.

SOURCE OF DATA: PACIFIC FX Service, University of British Columbia.

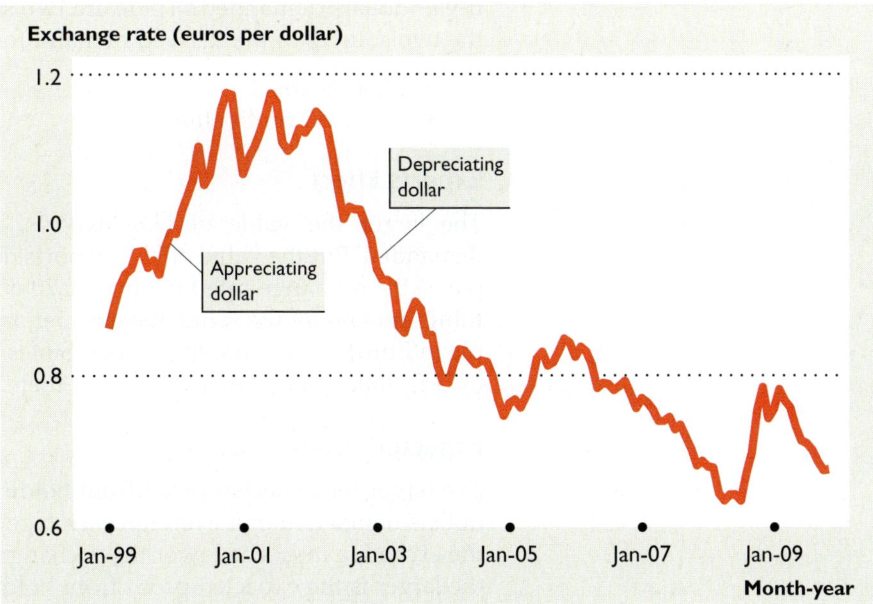

Currency depreciation
The fall in the value of one currency in terms of another currency.

Currency depreciation is the fall in the value of one currency in terms of another currency. For example, when the dollar fell from 1.17 euros in 2001 to 0.68 euros in 2009, the dollar depreciated by 42 percent. Why does the U.S. dollar fluctuate in value? Why does it sometimes depreciate and sometimes appreciate?

The exchange rate is a price. And like all prices, demand and supply determine the exchange rate. So to understand the forces that determine the exchange rate, we need to study demand and supply in the foreign exchange market. We'll begin by looking at the demand side of the market.

Demand in the Foreign Exchange Market

The quantity of U.S. dollars demanded in the foreign exchange market is the amount that traders plan to buy during a given time period at a given exchange rate. This quantity depends on many factors, but the main ones are

- The exchange rate
- Interest rates in the United States and other countries
- The expected future exchange rate

Let's look first at the relationship between the quantity of dollars demanded in the foreign exchange market and the exchange rate.

The Law of Demand for Foreign Exchange

People do not buy dollars because they enjoy them. The demand for dollars is a *derived demand.* People demand dollars so that they can buy U.S.-made goods and services (U.S. exports). They also demand dollars so that they can buy U.S. assets such as bank accounts, bonds, stocks, businesses, and real estate. Nevertheless, the law of demand applies to dollars just as it does to anything else that people value.

Other things remaining the same, the higher the exchange rate, the smaller is the quantity of dollars demanded. For example, if the price of the U.S. dollar rises from 0.70 euros to 0.80 euros but nothing else changes, the quantity of U.S. dollars that people plan to buy decreases. Why does the exchange rate influence the quantity of dollars demanded? There are two separate reasons, and they are related to the two sources of the derived demand for dollars. They are

- Exports effect
- Expected profit effect

Exports Effect

The larger the value of U.S. exports, the larger is the quantity of dollars demanded. But the value of U.S. exports depends on the exchange rate. For example, if the exchange rate falls from 0.70 euros to 0.60 euros per U.S. dollar, other things remaining the same, the cheaper are U.S.-made goods and services to people in Europe, the more the United States exports, and the greater is the quantity of U.S. dollars demanded to pay for them.

Expected Profit Effect

The larger the expected profit from holding dollars, the greater is the quantity of dollars demanded in the foreign exchange market. But expected profit depends on the exchange rate. The lower the exchange rate, other things remaining the same, the larger is the expected profit from holding dollars and the greater is the quantity of dollars demanded on the foreign exchange market.

FIGURE 19.1

The Demand for Dollars

myeconlab Animation

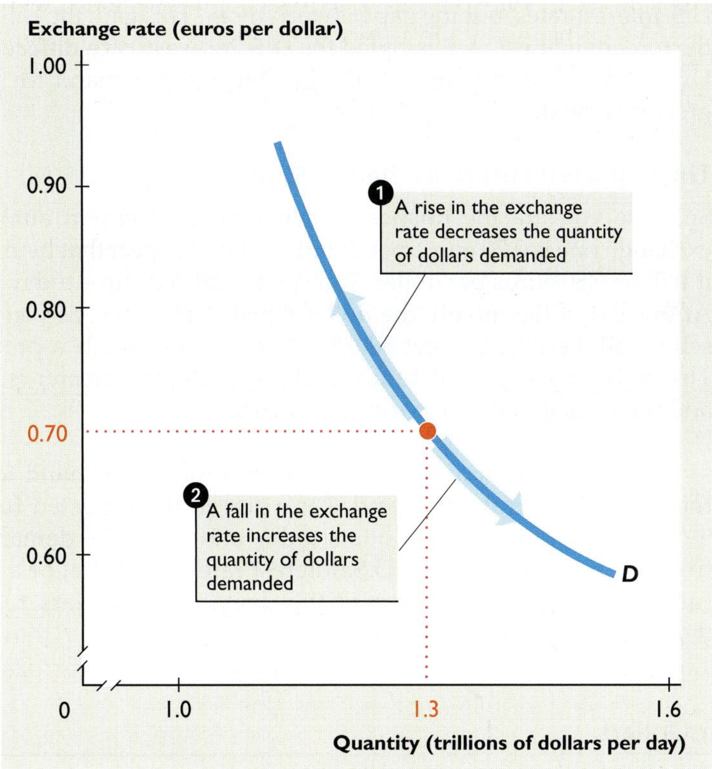

Other things remaining the same, the quantity of dollars that people plan to buy depends on the exchange rate.

1. If the exchange rate rises, the quantity of dollars demanded decreases and there is a movement up along the demand curve for dollars.
2. If the exchange rate falls, the quantity of dollars demanded increases and there is a movement down along the demand curve for dollars.

To understand this effect, suppose that you think the dollar will be worth 0.80 euros by the end of the month. If a dollar costs 0.75 euros today, you buy dollars. But a person who thinks that the dollar will be worth 0.75 euros at the end of the month does not buy dollars. Now suppose that the exchange rate falls to 0.65 euros per dollar. More people think that they can profit from buying dollars, so the quantity of dollars demanded today increases.

Figure 19.1 shows the demand curve for U.S. dollars in the foreign exchange market. For the two reasons we've just reviewed, when the foreign exchange rate rises, other things remaining the same, the quantity of dollars demanded decreases and there is a movement up along the demand curve, as shown by the arrow. When the exchange rate falls, other things remaining the same, the quantity of dollars demanded increases and there is a movement down along the demand curve, as shown by the arrow.

Changes in the Demand for Dollars

A change in any other influence on the quantity of U.S. dollars that people plan to buy in the foreign exchange market brings a change in the demand for dollars. These other influences are

- Interest rates in the United States and other countries
- The expected future exchange rate

Interest Rates in the United States and Other Countries

U.S. interest rate differential
The U.S. interest rate minus the foreign interest rate.

If you can borrow in another country and lend in the United States at a higher interest rate, you will make a profit. What matters is not the level of foreign and U.S. interest rates, but the gap between them. This gap, the U.S. interest rate minus the foreign interest rate, is called the **U.S. interest rate differential**. The larger the U.S. interest rate differential, the greater is the demand for U.S. assets and the greater is the demand for dollars.

The Expected Future Exchange Rate

Suppose you are the finance manager of the German auto maker BMW. The exchange rate is 0.70 euros per dollar, and you expect that by the end of the month, it will be 0.80 euros per dollar. You spend 700,000 euros today and buy $1,000,000. At the end of the month, the dollar equals 0.80 euros, as you predicted, and you sell the $1,000,000. You get 800,000 euros. You've made a profit of 100,000 euros. The higher the expected future exchange rate, the greater is the expected profit and the greater is the demand for dollars.

Figure 19.2 summarizes the influences on the demand for dollars. A rise in the U.S. interest rate differential or a rise in the expected future exchange rate increases the demand for dollars today and shifts the demand curve rightward from D_0 to D_1. A fall in the U.S. interest rate differential or a fall in the expected future exchange rate decreases the demand for dollars today and shifts the demand curve leftward from D_0 to D_2.

FIGURE 19.2

Changes in the Demand for Dollars

myeconlab Animation

❶ The demand for dollars increases if:

- The U.S. interest rate differential increases.
- The expected future exchange rate rises.

❷ The demand for dollars decreases if:

- The U.S. interest rate differential decreases.
- The expected future exchange rate falls.

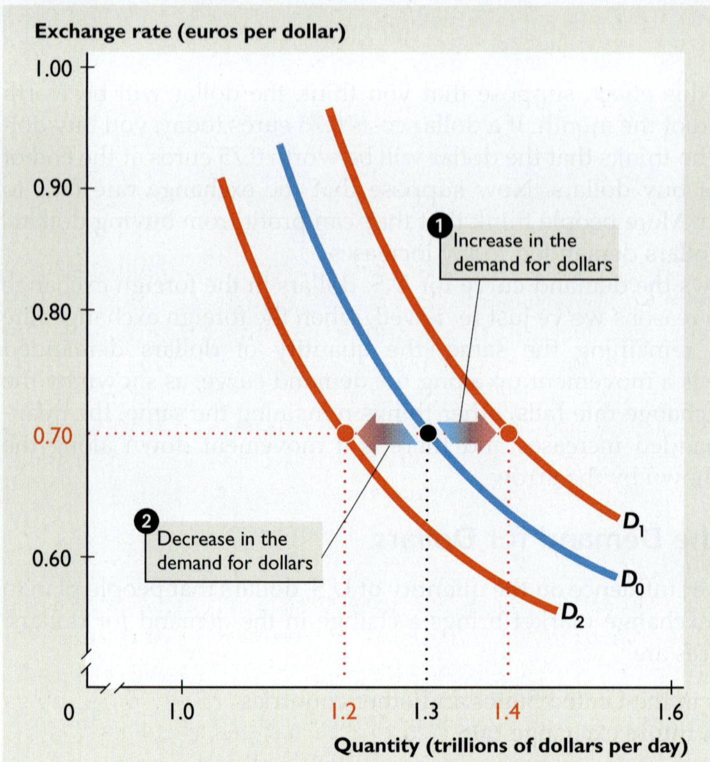

Supply in the Foreign Exchange Market

The quantity of U.S. dollars supplied in the foreign exchange market is the amount that traders plan to sell during a given time period at a given exchange rate. This quantity depends on many factors, but the main ones are

- The exchange rate
- Interest rates in the United States and other countries
- The expected future exchange rate

Does this list of factors seem familiar? It should: It is the same list as that for demand. The demand side and the supply side of the foreign exchange market are influenced by all the same factors. But the ways in which these three factors influence supply are the opposite of the ways in which they influence demand.

Let's look first at the relationship between the quantity of dollars supplied in the foreign exchange market and the exchange rate.

The Law of Supply of Foreign Exchange

Traders supply U.S. dollars in the foreign exchange market when people and businesses buy other currencies. They buy other currencies so that they can buy foreign-made goods and services (U.S. imports). Traders also supply dollars and buy foreign currencies so that people and businesses can buy foreign assets such as bank accounts, bonds, stocks, businesses, and real estate. The law of supply applies to dollars just as it does to anything else that people plan to sell.

Other things remaining the same, the higher the exchange rate, the greater is the quantity of dollars supplied in the foreign exchange market. For example, if the price of the U.S. dollar rises from 0.70 euros to 0.80 euros but nothing else changes, the quantity of U.S. dollars that people plan to sell in the foreign exchange market increases. Why does the exchange rate influence the quantity of dollars supplied?

There are two reasons, and they parallel the two reasons on the demand side of the market. They are

- Imports effect
- Expected profit effect

Imports Effect

The larger the value of U.S. imports, the larger is the quantity of foreign currency demanded to pay for these imports. And when people buy foreign currency, they supply dollars. So the larger the value of U.S. imports, the greater is the quantity of dollars supplied on the foreign exchange market. But the value of U.S. imports depends on the exchange rate. The higher the exchange rate, other things remaining the same, the cheaper are foreign-made goods and services to Americans. So the more the United States imports, the greater is the quantity of U.S. dollars supplied on the foreign exchange market to pay for these imports.

Expected Profit Effect

The larger the expected profit from holding a foreign currency, the greater is the quantity of that currency demanded and the greater is the quantity of dollars supplied in the foreign exchange market. But the expected profit from holding a foreign currency depends on the exchange rate. The higher the exchange rate, other things remaining the same, the larger is the expected profit from selling dollars and the greater is the quantity of dollars supplied on the foreign exchange market.

FIGURE 19.3

The Supply of Dollars

myeconlab Animation

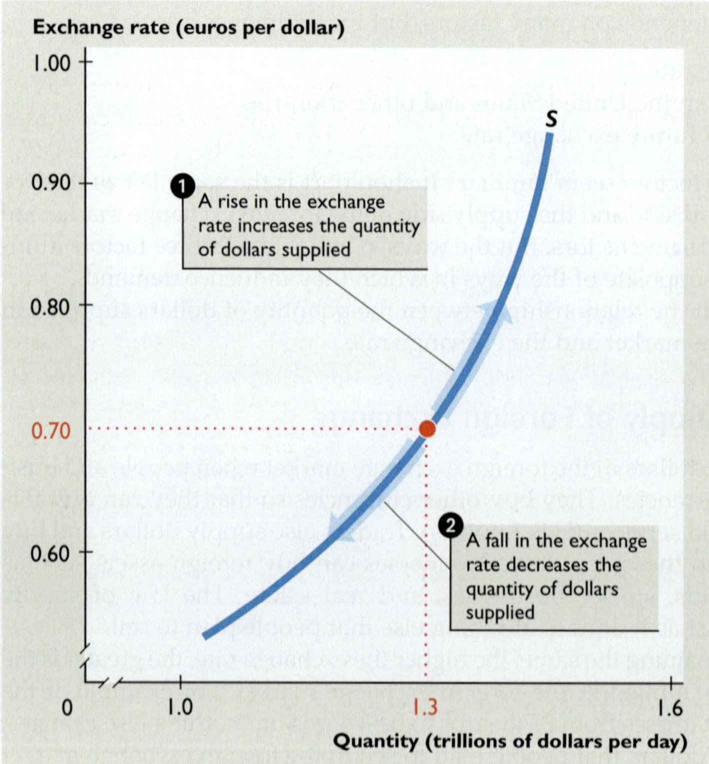

Other things remaining the same, the quantity of dollars that people plan to sell depends on the exchange rate.

1. If the exchange rate rises, the quantity of dollars supplied increases and there is a movement up along the supply curve of dollars.
2. If the exchange rate falls, the quantity of dollars supplied decreases and there is a movement down along the supply curve of dollars.

For the two reasons we've just reviewed, other things remaining the same, when the foreign exchange rate rises, the quantity of dollars supplied increases, and when the foreign exchange rate falls, the quantity of dollars supplied decreases. Figure 19.3 shows the supply curve of U.S. dollars in the foreign exchange market. In this figure, when the foreign exchange rate rises, other things remaining the same, there is an increase in the quantity of dollars supplied and a movement up along the supply curve, as shown by the arrow. When the exchange rate falls, other things remaining the same, there is a decrease in the quantity of dollars supplied and a movement down along the supply curve, as shown by the arrow.

Changes in the Supply of Dollars

A change in any other influence on the quantity of U.S. dollars that people plan to sell in the foreign exchange market brings a change in the supply of dollars, and the supply curve of dollars shifts. Supply either increases or decreases. These other influences on supply parallel the other influences on demand but have exactly the opposite effects. These influences are

- Interest rates in the United States and other countries
- The expected future exchange rate

Interest Rates in the United States and Other Countries

The larger the U.S. interest rate differential, the smaller is the demand for foreign assets and the smaller is the supply of dollars on the foreign exchange market.

The Expected Future Exchange Rate

Other things remaining the same, the higher the expected future exchange rate, the smaller is the supply of dollars. To see why, suppose that the dollar is trading at 0.70 euros per dollar today and you think that by the end of the month, the dollar will trade at 0.80 euros per dollar. You were planning on selling dollars today, but you decide to hold off and wait until the end of the month. If you supply dollars today, you get only 0.70 euros per dollar. But at the end of the month, if the dollar is worth 0.80 euros as you predict, you'll get 0.80 euros for each dollar you supply. You'll make a profit of 0.10 euros per dollar. So the higher the expected future exchange rate, other things remaining the same, the smaller is the expected profit from selling U.S. dollars and the smaller is the supply of dollars today.

Figure 19.4 summarizes the influences on the supply of dollars. A rise in the U.S. interest rate differential or the expected future exchange rate decreases the supply of dollars today and shifts the supply curve leftward from S_0 to S_1. A fall in the U.S. interest rate differential or the expected future exchange rate increases the supply of dollars today and shifts the supply curve rightward from S_0 to S_2.

FIGURE 19.4

Changes in the Supply of Dollars

myeconlab Animation

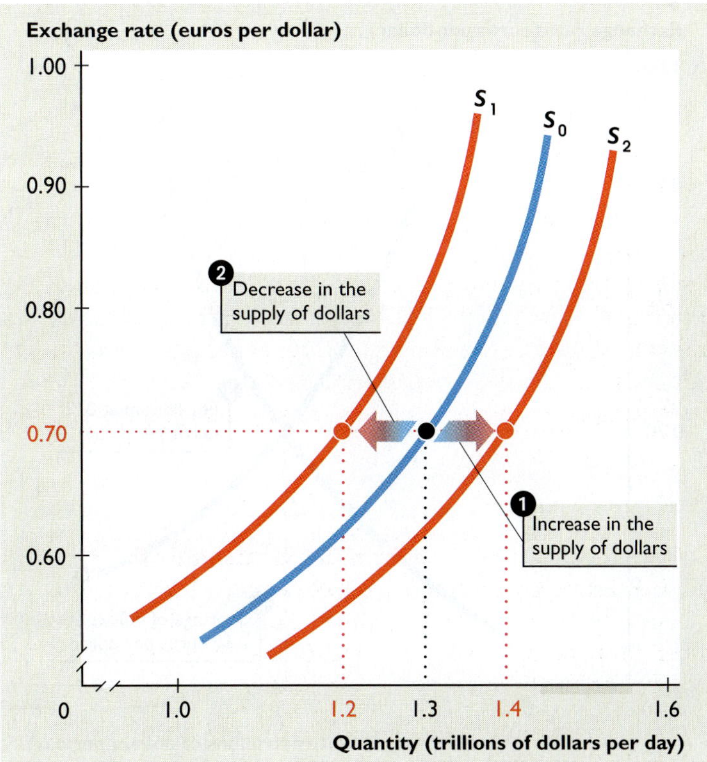

1. The supply of dollars increases if:
   - The U.S. interest rate differential decreases.
   - The expected future exchange rate falls.
2. The supply of dollars decreases if:
   - The U.S. interest rate differential increases.
   - The expected future exchange rate rises.

Market Equilibrium

Demand and supply in the foreign exchange market determine the exchange rate. Just as in all the other markets you've studied, the price (the exchange rate) acts as a regulator. If the exchange rate is too high, there is a surplus—the quantity supplied exceeds the quantity demanded. If the exchange rate is too low, there is a shortage—the quantity supplied is less than the quantity demanded. At the equilibrium exchange rate, there is neither a shortage nor a surplus. The quantity supplied equals the quantity demanded.

Figure 19.5 illustrates market equilibrium. The demand for dollars is *D*, and the supply of dollars is *S*. The equilibrium exchange rate is 0.70 euros per dollar. At this exchange rate, the quantity demanded equals the quantity supplied and is \$1.3 trillion a day. If the exchange rate is above 0.70 euros, for example, 0.80 euros per dollar, there is a surplus of dollars and the exchange rate falls. If the exchange rate is below 0.70 euros, for example, 0.60 euros per dollar, there is a shortage of dollars and the exchange rate rises.

The foreign exchange market is constantly pulled to its equilibrium by the forces of supply and demand. Foreign exchange dealers are constantly looking for the best price they can get. If they are selling, they want the highest price available. If they are buying, they want the lowest price available. Information flows from dealer to dealer through the worldwide computer network, and the price adjusts second by second to keep buying plans and selling plans in balance. That is, price adjusts second by second to keep the market at its equilibrium.

FIGURE 19.5

Equilibrium Exchange Rate

myeconlab Animation

The demand curve for dollars is *D*, and the supply curve is *S*.

1. If the exchange rate is 0.80 euros per dollar, there is a surplus of dollars and the exchange rate falls.
2. If the exchange rate is 0.60 euros per dollar, there is a shortage of dollars and the exchange rate rises.
3. If the exchange rate is 0.70 euros per dollar, there is neither a shortage nor a surplus of dollars and the exchange rate remains constant. The market is in equilibrium.

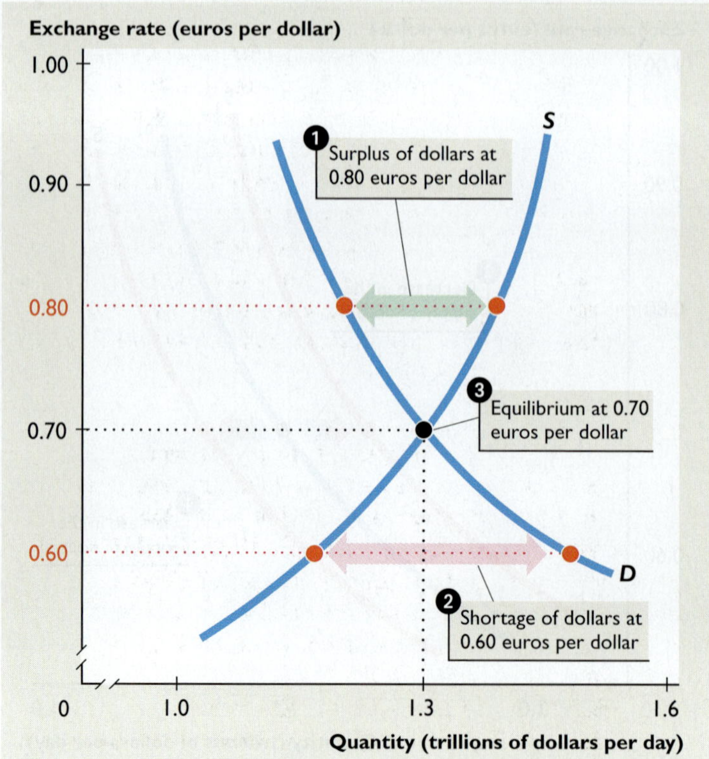

EYE on the DOLLAR

Why Has Our Dollar Been Sinking?

Our dollar has been on a falling trend since the early 2000s but it hasn't always been sinking. Let's start by looking at a rising dollar.

A Rising Dollar: 1999–2001

Between 1999 and 2001, the dollar appreciated against the euro. It rose from 0.86 euros to 1.17 euros per dollar. Figure 1 explains why this happened.

In 1999, the demand and supply curves were those labeled D_{99} and S_{99}. The equilibrium exchange rate was 0.86 euros per dollar—where the quantity of dollars supplied equaled the quantity of dollars demanded.

During the next two years, the U.S. economy expanded faster than the European economy. Interest rates in Europe were 2 percentage points lower than in the United States, and the euro was expected to depreciate and the dollar was expected to appreciate.

With a positive U.S. interest rate differential and an expected dollar appreciation, the demand for dollars increased and the supply of dollars decreased. The demand curve shifted from D_{99} to D_{01} and the supply curve shifted from S_{99} to S_{01}. These two reinforcing shifts made the exchange rate rise to 1.17 euros per dollar.

A Falling Dollar: 2001–2009

Between 2001 and 2009, the dollar fell from 1.17 euros to 0.68 euros per dollar. Figure 2 explains this fall.

In 2001, the demand and supply curves were those labeled D_{01} and S_{01}. The exchange rate was 1.17 euros per dollar. During the next few years, U.S. economic growth slipped below the European growth rate, European inflation fell, interest rates in Europe exceeded those in the United States, and the U.S. current account deficit continued to increase.

Under these conditions, currency traders expected the exchange rate to fall. The demand for dollars decreased and the supply of dollars increased. The demand curve shifted leftward to D_{09} and the supply curve shifted rightward to S_{09}. The exchange rate fell to 0.68 euros per dollar.

Will the dollar keep falling? No one knows, but while U.S. interest rates remain low and the current account deficit remains high, a falling dollar is not unlikely.

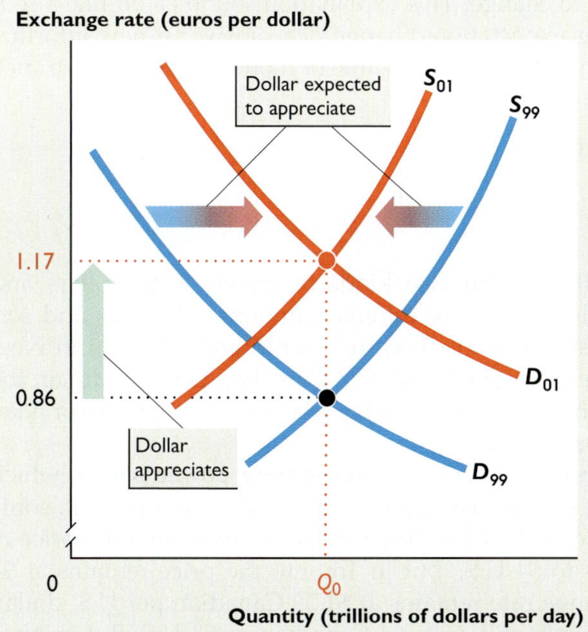

Figure 1 1999 to 2001

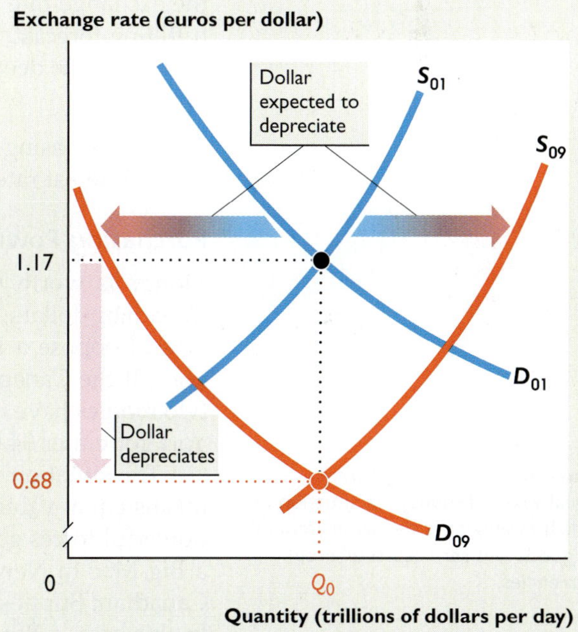

Figure 2 2001 to 2009

Why Exchange Rates Are Volatile

You've seen that sometimes the dollar depreciates and at other times it appreciates. The exchange rates of other currencies are similarly volatile. The Japanese yen, Canadian dollar, and Mexican peso along with most currencies swing between appreciation and depreciation. Yet the quantity of dollars (and other currencies) traded on the foreign exchange market each day barely changes. Why?

A large part of the answer is that everyone in the foreign exchange market is potentially either a buyer or a seller—a demander or a supplier. Each has a price above which he or she will sell and below which he or she will buy.

This fact about the participants in the foreign exchange market means that supply and demand are not independent. The same shocks to the market that change the demand for a currency also change its supply. Demand and supply change in *opposite directions*, and result is large price changes and small quantity changes.

The two key influences that change both demand and supply in the foreign exchange market are the interest rate differential and the expected future exchange rate.

A rise in the U.S. interest rate differential *increases* the *demand* for U.S. dollars on the foreign exchange market and *decreases* the *supply.* A rise in the expected future exchange rate also increases the demand for U.S. dollars and decreases the supply.

These common influences that change demand and supply in *opposite directions* bring changes in the exchange rate and little change in the quantities of currencies traded. They can bring cumulative movements in the exchange rate or frequent changes of direction—volatility.

Exchange Rate Expectations

The changes in the exchange rate that we've just considered occur in part because the exchange rate is expected to change. This explanation sounds a bit like a self-fulfilling forecast. What makes expectations change? The answer is new information about the deeper forces that influence the value of money. There are two such forces:

- Purchasing power parity
- Interest rate parity

Purchasing Power Parity

Money is worth what it will buy. But two kinds of money, U.S. dollars and Canadian dollars, for example, might buy different amounts of goods and services. Suppose a Big Mac costs $4 (Canadian) in Toronto and $3 (U.S.) in New York. If the Canadian dollar exchange rate is $1.33 Canadian per U.S. dollar, the two monies have the same value. You can buy a Big Mac in either Toronto or New York for either $4 Canadian or $3 U.S.

Purchasing power parity
Equal value of money—a situation in which money buys the same amount of goods and services in different currencies.

The situation we've just described is called **purchasing power parity**, which means equal value of money. If purchasing power parity does not prevail, some powerful forces go to work. To understand these forces, suppose that the price of a Big Mac in New York rises to $4 U.S., but in Toronto the price remains at $4 Canadian. Suppose the exchange rate remains at $1.33 Canadian per U.S. dollar. In this case, a Big Mac in Toronto still costs $4 Canadian or $3 U.S. But in New

York, it costs $4 U.S. or $5.32 Canadian. Money buys more in Canada than in the United States. Money is not of equal value in both countries.

If all (or most) prices have increased in the United States and not increased in Canada, then people will generally expect that the U.S. dollar exchange rate is going to fall. The demand for U.S. dollars decreases, and the supply of U.S. dollars increases. The U.S. dollar exchange rate falls, as expected. If the U.S. dollar falls to $1.00 Canadian and there are no further price changes, purchasing power parity is restored. A Big Mac now costs $4 in either U.S. dollars or Canadian dollars in both New York and Toronto.

If prices increase in Canada and other countries but remain constant in the United States, then people will generally expect that the value of the U.S. dollar on the foreign exchange market is too low and that the U.S. dollar exchange rate will rise. The demand for U.S. dollars increases, and the supply of U.S. dollars decreases. The U.S. dollar exchange rate rises, as expected.

Ultimately, the value of money is determined by prices. So the deeper forces that influence the exchange rate have tentacles that spread throughout the economy. If prices in the United States rise faster than those in other countries, the exchange rate falls. And if prices in the United States rise more slowly than those in other countries, the exchange rate rises.

EYE on the GLOBAL ECONOMY

Purchasing Power Parity

Purchasing power parity (PPP) is a long-run phenomenon. In the short run, deviations from PPP can be large.

The figure shows the range of deviations from PPP in October 2009. At that time, the Danish krone was overvalued by more than 70 percent and the Swiss franc by 60 percent. An overvalued currency is one that, according to PPP, will depreciate at some point in the future.

The most undervalued currencies in October 2009 were the Mexican peso and Russian ruble. An undervalued currency is one that, according to PPP, will appreciate at some time in the future.

PPP theory predicts that a currency might depreciate or appreciate but not *when* it will depreciate or appreciate.

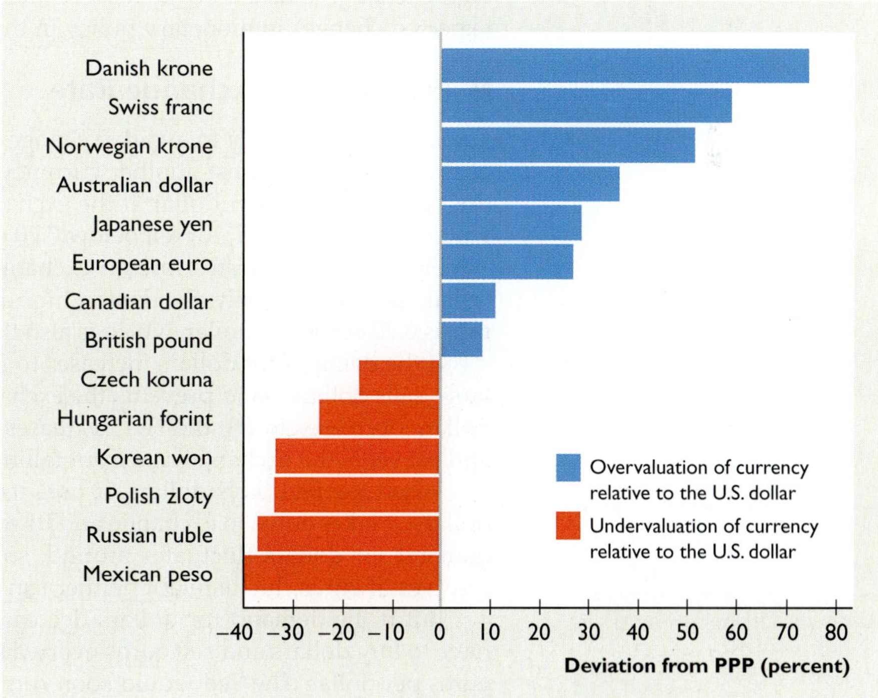

SOURCE OF DATA: PACIFIC FX Service, University of British Columbia, November 6, 2009.

Interest Rate Parity

Suppose a Canadian dollar bank deposit in a Toronto bank earns 5 percent a year and a U.S. dollar bank deposit in a New York bank earns 3 percent a year. Why does anyone deposit money in New York? Why doesn't all the money flow to Toronto? The answer is: Because of exchange rate expectations. Suppose people expect the Canadian dollar to depreciate by 2 percent a year. This 2 percent depreciation must be subtracted from the 5 percent interest to obtain the net return of 3 percent a year that an American can earn by depositing funds in a Toronto bank. The two returns are equal. This situation is one of **interest rate parity**—equal interest rates when exchange rate changes are taken into account.

Interest rate parity
Equal interest rates—a situation in which the interest rate in one currency equals the interest rate in another currency when exchange rate changes are taken into account.

Interest rate parity always prevails. Funds move to get the highest return available. If interest rate parity did not hold because the Canadian dollar had too high a value on the foreign exchange market, the expected return in Toronto would be lower than in New York. In seconds, traders would sell the Canadian dollar, its exchange rate would fall, and the expected return from lending in Toronto would rise to equal that in New York.

Monetary Policy and the Exchange Rate

Monetary policy influences the interest rate (see Chapter 12, pp. 302–305), so monetary policy also influences the interest rate differential and the exchange rate. If the Fed increases the U.S. interest rate and other central banks keep interest rates in other countries unchanged, the value of the U.S. dollar rises on the foreign exchange market. If other central banks increase their interest rates and the Fed keeps the U.S. interest rate unchanged, the value of the U.S. dollar falls on the foreign exchange market. So exchange rates fluctuate in response to changes and expected changes in monetary policy in the United States and around the world.

Pegging the Exchange Rate

Some central banks try to avoid exchange rate fluctuations by pegging the value of their currency against another currency. Suppose the Fed wanted to keep the dollar at 0.70 euros per dollar. If the exchange rate rose above 0.70 euros, the Fed would sell dollars and if it fell below 0.70 euros, the Fed would buy dollars.

Figure 19.6 illustrates foreign exchange market intervention. The supply of dollars is S, and initially, the demand for dollars is D_0. The equilibrium exchange rate is 0.70 euros per dollar, which is also the Fed's target—the horizontal red line.

If the demand for dollars increases to D_1, the Fed increases the supply of dollars—sells dollars—and prevents the exchange rate from rising. If the demand for dollars decreases to D_2, the Fed decreases the supply of dollars—buys dollars—and prevents the exchange rate from falling.

When the Fed buys dollars, it uses its reserves of euros; when the Fed sells dollars, it takes euros in exchange and its reserves of euros increase. As long as the demand for dollars fluctuates around, so on average remains at, D_0, the Fed's reserves of euros fluctuate but neither run dry nor persistently increase.

But if the demand for dollars decreased permanently to D_2, the Fed would have to buy dollars and sell euros every day to maintain the exchange rate at 0.70 euros per dollar. The Fed would soon run out of euros, and when it did, the dollar would sink. If the demand for dollars increased permanently to D_1, the Fed would have to sell dollars and buy euros every day. The Fed would be piling up unwanted euros and at some point would let the dollar rise.

FIGURE 19.6

Foreign Exchange Market Intervention

myeconlab Animation

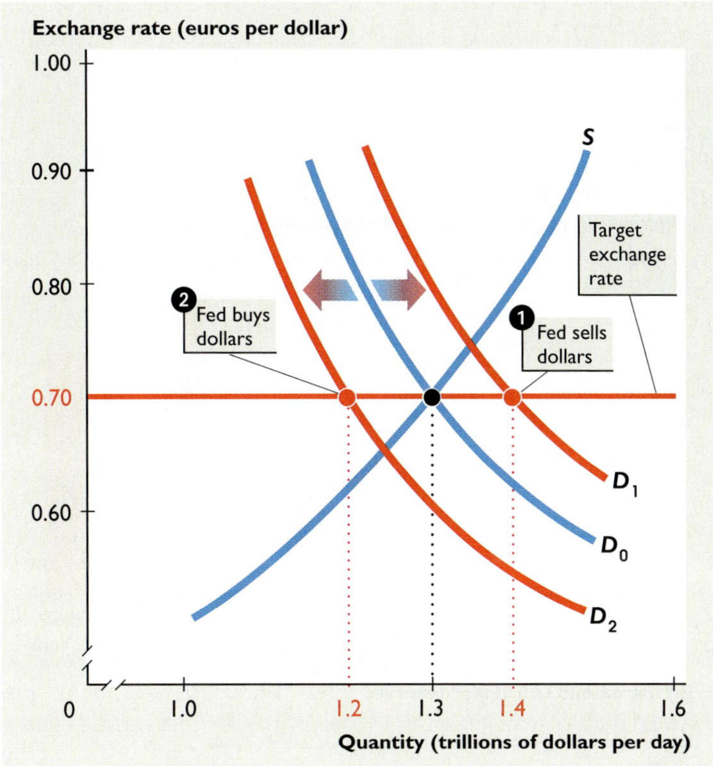

Initially, the demand for dollars is D_0, the supply of dollars is S, and the exchange rate is 0.70 euros per dollar. The Fed can intervene in the foreign exchange market to keep the exchange rate close to its target rate (0.70 euros per dollar in this example).

1. If demand increases from D_0 to D_1, the Fed sells dollars to increase the supply of dollars and maintain the exchange rate.

2. If demand decreases from D_0 to D_2, the Fed buys dollars to decrease the supply of dollars and maintain the exchange rate.

Persistent intervention on one side of the market cannot be sustained.

The People's Bank of China in the Foreign Exchange Market

Although the Fed could peg the value of the dollar, it chooses not to do so. But China's central bank, the People's Bank of China, does intervene to peg the value of its currency—the yuan. *Eye on the Global Economy* on page 499 shows the result of this intervention.

During much of the period that the yuan has been pegged to the U.S. dollar, China has piled up U.S. dollar reserves. Figure 19.7(a) shows the numbers. During 2007 to 2009, China's reserves increased by more than $1 trillion.

Figure 19.7(b), which shows the market for U.S. dollars priced in terms of the yuan, explains why China's reserves increased. The demand curve *D* and supply curve *S* intersect at 5 yuan per dollar. If the People's Bank of China took no actions in the foreign exchange market, this exchange rate would be the equilibrium rate. (This particular value is only an example. No one knows what the yuan-dollar exchange rate would be with no intervention.)

By intervening in the market and buying U.S. dollars, the People's Bank can peg the yuan at 6.80 yuan per dollar. But to do so, it must keep holding the dollars that it buys. In Figure 19.7(b), the People's Bank buys $250 billion a year.

Only by allowing the yuan to appreciate can China stop accumulating dollars. That is what the People's Bank decided to do in July 2005. But China continues to intervene in the foreign exchange market to manage the rate of appreciation of the yuan. Eventually, when China's foreign exchange market becomes more accustomed to a floating yuan, it is likely that the People's Bank will lessen its intervention and the value of the yuan will be determined by market forces.

FIGURE 19.7

China's Foreign Exchange Market Intervention

myeconlab Animation

China has been piling up reserves of U.S. dollars since 2000. In 2007 through 2009, the build-up of reserves was very large. Part (a) shows the numbers.

Part (b) shows the market for the U.S. dollar in terms of the Chinese yuan. Note that a higher exchange rate (yuan per dollar) means a lower value of the yuan and a higher value of the dollar. The yuan appreciates when the number of yuan per dollar decreases.

1. With demand curve *D* and supply curve *S*, the equilibrium exchange rate is 5 yuan per dollar. (The actual equilibrium value is not known, and the value assumed is only an example.)
2. The People's Bank of China has a target exchange rate of 6.80 yuan per dollar. At this exchange rate, the yuan is *undervalued.*
3. To keep the exchange rate pegged at its target level, the People's Bank of China must buy U.S. dollars in exchange for yuan, and China's reserves of dollars pile up.

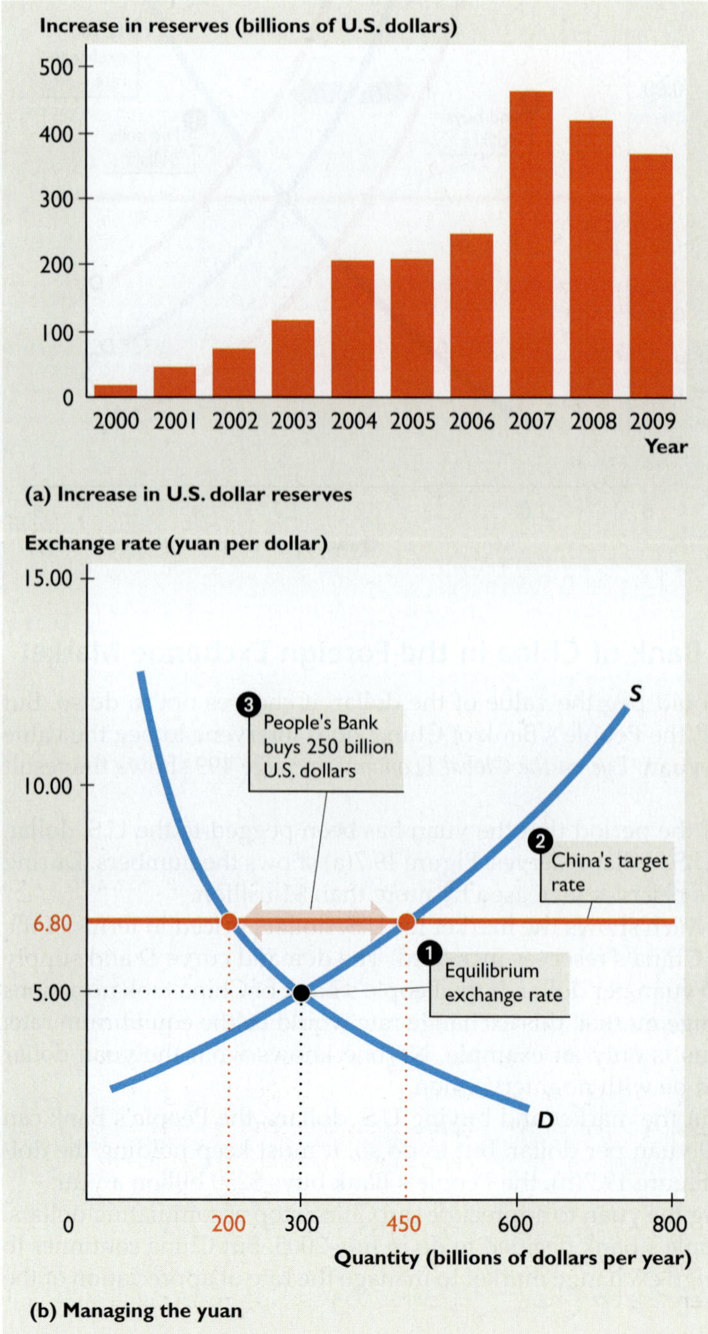

SOURCE OF DATA: The People's Bank of China.

EYE on the GLOBAL ECONOMY

The Fixed Yuan

The Chinese central bank, the People's Bank of China, has pegged the value of the yuan in terms of the U.S. dollar for more than 10 years.

The figure shows the value of the yuan (yuan per U.S. dollar) from the early 1990s to 2009.

The yuan was devalued in January 1994. It appreciated a bit during 1994 and 1995. But it was then pegged at 8.28 yuan per U.S. dollar, a value that the People's Bank of China maintained for more than 10 years. In July 2005, the yuan began a managed float—a managed appreciation of the yuan. Then, in July 2008, the exchange rate was again pegged, this time at 6.8 yuan per dollar.

SOURCE OF DATA: PACIFIC FX Service, University of British Columbia.

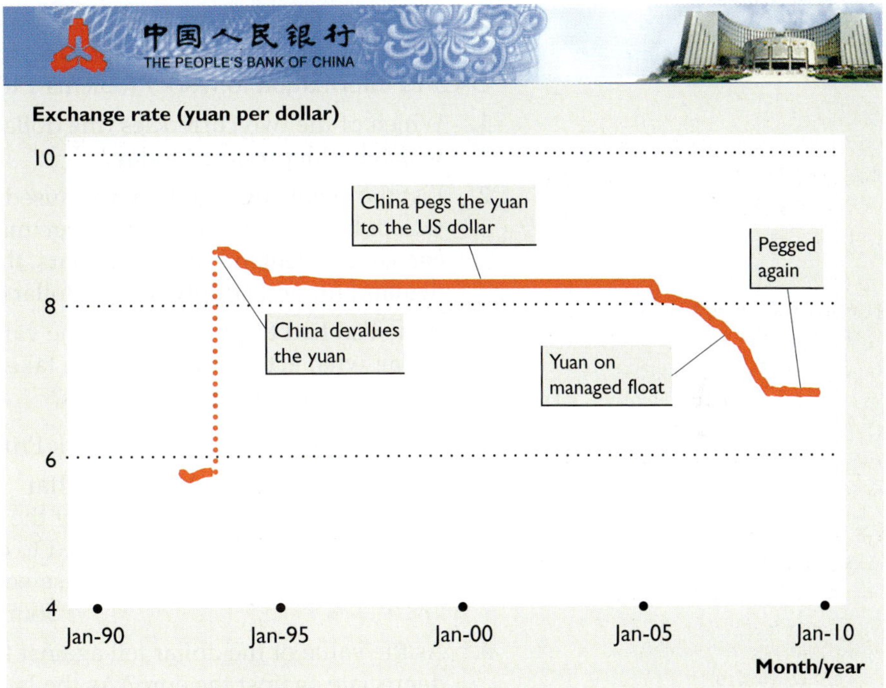

EYE on YOUR LIFE

Your Foreign Exchange Transactions

If you plan to go to Europe for a vacation next summer, you will need some euros. What is the best way to get euros?

You could just take your ATM/debit card or credit card and use an ATM in Europe. You'll get euros from the cash machine, and your bank account in the United States will get charged for the cash you obtain.

When you get euros, the number of euros you request is multiplied by the exchange rate to determine how many dollars to take from your bank account.

You have just made a transaction in the foreign exchange market. You have exchanged dollars for euros.

The exchange rate that you paid was probably costly. Your bank took a commission for helping you get euros. Some banks charge as much as 5 percent. Check in advance. It might be better to buy euros from your bank before you leave on your trip.

Another question has possibly occurred to you: How many euros will your budget buy next summer? Should you get the euros now at a price that is certain or would it be better to wait until closer to your travel date and take a chance on the value of the dollar then?

No one can answer this question. But you can buy euros today at a fixed price for delivery at a later date. (This transaction is made in a market called the forward exchange market.) Again, though, you'll end up paying a big commission for the service.

myeconlab

Work these problems in Study Plan 19.2 to get instant feedback.

CHECKPOINT 19.2

Explain how the exchange rate is determined and why it fluctuates.

Practice Problems

Suppose that yesterday, the U.S. dollar was trading on the foreign exchange market at 100 yen per dollar. Today, the U.S. dollar is trading at 105 yen per dollar. Use this information to work Problems **1** to **3**.

1. Which of the two currencies (the dollar or the yen) has appreciated and which has depreciated today?
2. List the events that could have caused today's change in the value of the U.S. dollar on the foreign exchange market. Did these events on your list change the demand for U.S. dollars, the supply of U.S. dollars, or both the demand for and supply of U.S. dollars?
3. If the Fed had tried to stabilize the value of the U.S. dollar at 100 yen per dollar, what action would it have taken? What effect would the Fed's actions have had on U.S. official reserves?

Use the following information to work Problems **4** and **5**.

Gold gains as investors shun the dollar

In the past seven months, the value of the dollar has slid by 15 percent against major currencies as investors migrated to other markets. Today, the dollar fell to $1.47 against the euro and the Japanese yen fell from 89 to 88.83 yen per dollar.

Source: *The New York Times*, October 6, 2009

4. As the value of the dollar fell against the euro, did the dollar appreciate or depreciate against the euro? As the Japanese yen strengthened against the dollar, did the dollar appreciate or depreciate against the yen?
5. What actions in the foreign exchange market lowered the dollar?

Guided Solutions to Practice Problems

1. Because the price of the U.S. dollar is a larger number of yen, the U.S. dollar has appreciated. The yen has depreciated because it buys fewer dollars.
2. The main events might be an increase in the U.S. interest rate, a decrease in the Japanese interest rate, or a rise in the expected future exchange rate of the U.S. dollar.

   The events listed change both the demand for and supply of U.S. dollars. The events increase the demand for and decrease the supply of U.S. dollars.
3. To stabilize the value of the U.S. dollar, the Fed would have sold U.S. dollars to increase the supply of U.S. dollars in the foreign exchange market.

   When the Fed sells U.S. dollars, it buys foreign currency. U.S. official reserves would have increased.
4. Because the euro buys fewer dollars, the euro has appreciated and the dollar has depreciated. Because the dollar buys fewer yen, the dollar depreciated against the yen.
5. As investors increased their demand for gold, the demand for U.S. dollars decreased. As some holders of U.S. dollars wanted to switch to gold, the supply of dollars increased. The result was a depreciation of the U.S. dollar.

CHAPTER SUMMARY

Key Points

1 Describe a country's balance of payments accounts and explain what determines the amount of international borrowing and lending.

- Foreign currency is used to finance international trade and the purchase of foreign assets.
- A country's balance of payments accounts record its international transactions.
- Historically, the United States has been a net lender to the rest of the world, but in 1983 that situation changed and the United States became a net borrower, and in 1989 the United States became a debtor nation.
- Net exports are equal to the private sector balance plus the government sector balance.

2 Explain how the exchange rate is determined and why it fluctuates.

- Foreign currency is obtained in exchange for domestic currency in the foreign exchange market.
- The exchange rate is determined by demand and supply in the foreign exchange market.
- The lower the exchange rate, the greater is the quantity of dollars demanded. A change in the exchange rate brings a movement along the demand curve for dollars.
- Changes in the expected future exchange rate and the U.S. interest rate differential change the demand for dollars and shift the demand curve.
- The lower the exchange rate, the smaller is the quantity of dollars supplied. A change in the exchange rate brings a movement along the supply curve of dollars.
- Changes in the expected future exchange rate and the U.S. interest rate differential change the supply of dollars and shift the supply curve.
- Fluctuations in the exchange rate occur because fluctuations in the demand for and supply of dollars are not independent.
- A central bank can intervene in the foreign exchange market to smooth fluctuations in the exchange rate.

Key Terms

Balance of payments accounts, 478
Capital account, 478
Creditor nation, 480
Currency appreciation, 485
Currency depreciation, 486
Current account, 478
Debtor nation, 480
Foreign exchange market, 485
Foreign exchange rate, 485
Government sector balance, 482
Interest rate parity, 496
Net borrower, 480
Net lender, 480
Official settlements account, 478
Private sector balance, 482
Purchasing power parity, 494
U.S. interest rate differential, 488
U.S. official reserves, 478

myeconlab

Work these problems in Chapter 19 Study Plan to get instant feedback.

CHAPTER CHECKPOINT

Study Plan Problems and Applications

Table 1 gives some data that describe the economy of Antarctica in 2050:

TABLE 1

Item	(billions of Antarctica dollars)
Imports of goods and services	150
Exports of goods and services	50
Net interest	−10
Net transfers	35
Foreign investment in Antarctica	125
Antarctica's investment abroad	55

Use Table 1 to answer Problems 1 and 2.

1. Calculate Antarctica's current account balance, capital account balance, and the increase in Antarctica's official reserves.
2. Is Antarctica a debtor nation or a creditor nation? Are its international assets increasing or decreasing? Is Antarctica borrowing to finance investment or consumption? Explain.
3. The U.S. dollar depreciates. Explain which of the following events could have caused the depreciation and why.
   - The Fed intervened in the foreign exchange market. Did the Fed buy or sell U.S. dollars?
   - People began to expect that the U.S. dollar would depreciate.
   - The U.S. interest rate differential increased.
   - Foreign investment in the United States increased.

Suppose that the inflation rate is lower in Japan than it is in the United States, and that the difference in the inflation rates persists for some years. Use this information to answer Problems 4 to 6.

4. Will the U.S. dollar appreciate or depreciate against the yen and will purchasing power parity be violated? Why or why not?
5. Will U.S. interest rates be higher or lower than Japanese interest rates and will interest rate parity hold? Why or why not?
6. Explain how the expected future exchange rate will change.
7. **Aussie dollar hit by interest rate talk**

   The Australian dollar fell against the U.S. dollar to its lowest value in the past two weeks. CPI inflation was reported to be generally as expected, but not strong enough to justify expectations for an aggressive interest rate rise by Australia's central bank next week.

   Source: Reuters, October 28, 2009

   Explain why the expected rise of the Australian interest rate with no change in the U.S. interest rate lowered the current value of the Australian dollar against the U.S. dollar.

Instructor Assignable Problems and Applications

Your instructor can assign these problems as homework, a quiz, or a test in **MyEconLab**.

1. If the European Central Bank starts to raise its policy interest rate before the Fed starts to raise the federal funds rate target, what do you predict will happen to the dollar/euro exchange rate? Illustrate your answer with an appropriate graphical analysis.
2. Table 2 gives some data that describe the economy of Atlantis in 2020:

TABLE 2

Item	(billions of Atlantis dollars)
Government expenditure	200
Saving	100
Increase in official reserves of Atlantis	5
Net foreign investment in Atlantis	50
Net taxes	150
Investment	125

   Calculate the current account balance, the capital account balance, the government budget balance, and the private sector balance.
3. The U.S. dollar appreciates, and U.S. official reserves increase. Explain which of the following events might have caused these changes to occur and why.
   - The Fed intervened in the foreign exchange market and sold U.S. dollars.
   - The Fed conducted an open market operation and sold bonds.
   - People began to expect that the U.S. dollar would appreciate.
   - The U.S. interest rate differential narrowed.
4. Which of the following events might have caused the euro to appreciate and why?
   - The European Central Bank sold euros in the foreign exchange market.
   - The Fed intervened in the foreign exchange market and bought U.S. dollars.
   - The EU interest rate differential increased.
   - Profits increased in Europe, and U.S. investment in Europe surged.

Use the following information to work Problems 5 and 6.

Brazil's overvalued real

This year the Brazilian real appreciated 33 percent against the dollar and has pushed up the price of a Big Mac in Sao Paulo to $US4.60, higher than the New York price of $US3.99. Brazil's interest rate is 8.75 percent a year compared to the U.S. interest rate at near zero, and foreign funds flowing into Brazil surged.

Source: *Bloomberg News*, October 27, 2009

5. Does purchasing power parity (PPP) hold between Brazil and the United States? If not, does PPP predict that the real will appreciate further or depreciate against the U.S. dollar?
6. Does interest rate parity hold between Brazil and the United States? If interest rate parity does hold, what is the expected rate of appreciation or depreciation of the Brazilian real against the U.S. dollar? If the Fed raised the interest rate while the Brazilian interest remained at 8.75 percent a year, how would the expected appreciation or depreciation of the real change?

Use the following information to work Problems 7 and 8.

Suppose that the euro keeps appreciating against the U.S. dollar. The Fed decides to stop the euro from appreciating (stop the U.S. dollar from depreciating) and intervenes in the foreign exchange market.

7. What actions might the Fed take in the foreign exchange market? Could these actions persist in the long run? Would the Fed's actions prevent interest rate parity from being achieved? Why or why not?
8. Are there any other actions that the Fed could take to raise the foreign exchange value of the dollar? Explain your answer.
9. Many people think that a current account deficit is a sign that a nation is not able to compete in international markets. Explain why this view is incorrect and describe the factors that create a current account deficit.

Use the following information to work Problems 10 to 12.

For most of the 1990s, Argentina pegged the value of its currency, the peso, to the U.S. dollar: 1 peso equaled 1 U.S. dollar. Then, at the end of 2001, the peso was allowed to find its own value on the foreign exchange market and it fell dramatically.

10. Why might it be difficult for Argentina to peg the value of its currency to the U.S. dollar?
11. Why, nonetheless, might it be a good idea for Argentina to peg the value of its currency to the U.S. dollar? What are the potential benefits to Argentina?
12. On balance, do you think a country such as Argentina should peg its currency to the U.S. dollar?

Use the following information to work Problems 13 and 14.

Suppose that the U.K. pound is trading at 1.82 U.S. dollars per U.K. pound and at this exchange rate purchasing power parity holds. The U.S. interest rate is 2 percent a year and the U.K. interest rate is 4 percent a year.

13. Calculate the U.S. interest rate differential. What is the U.K. pound expected to be worth in terms of U.S. dollars one year from now?
14. Which country more likely has the lower inflation rate? How can you tell?
15. You can purchase a laptop in Mexico City for 12,960 Mexican pesos. If the exchange rate is 10.8 Mexican pesos per U.S. dollar and if purchasing power parity prevails, at what price can you buy an identical computer in Dallas, Texas?

Glossary

Above full-employment equilibrium When equilibrium real GDP exceeds potential GDP. (p. 339)

Absolute advantage When one person is more productive than another person in several or even all activities. (p. 76)

Aggregate demand The relationship between the quantity of real GDP demanded and the price level when all other influences on expenditure plans remain the same. (p. 332)

Aggregate planned expenditure Planned consumption expenditure plus planned investment plus planned government expenditure plus planned exports minus planned imports. (p. 352)

Aggregate supply The relationship between the quantity of real GDP supplied and the price level when all other influences on production plans remain the same. (p. 326)

Automatic fiscal policy A fiscal policy action that is triggered by the state of the economy. (p. 409)

Automatic stabilizers Features of fiscal policy that stabilize real GDP without explicit action by the government. (p. 409)

Balance of payments accounts The accounts in which a nation records its international trading, borrowing, and lending. (p. 478)

Balanced budget The budget balance when revenues equal outlays. (p. 401)

Balanced budget multiplier The effect on aggregate demand of a *simultaneous* change in government expenditure and taxes that leaves the budget balanced unchanged. (p. 406)

Banking system The Federal Reserve and the banks and other institutions that accept deposits and provide the services that enable people and businesses to make and receive payments. (p. 274)

Barter The direct exchange of goods and services for other goods and services, which requires a double coincidence of wants. (p. 269)

Below full-employment equilibrium When potential GDP exceeds equilibrium real GDP. (p. 339)

Benefit The benefit of something is the gain or pleasure that it brings. (p. 11)

Bond A promise to pay specified sums of money on specified dates. (p. 244)

Budget deficit The negative budget balance when outlays exceed revenues. (p. 401)

Budget surplus The positive budget balance when revenues exceed outlays. (p. 401)

Business cycle A periodic but irregular up-and-down movement of total production and other measures of economic activity. (p. 128)

Capital Tools, instruments, machines, buildings, and other items that have been produced in the past and that businesses now use to produce goods and services. (pp. 37, 242)

Capital account Record of foreign investment in the United States minus U.S. investment abroad. (p. 478)

Capital goods Goods that are bought by businesses to increase their productive resources. (p. 34)

Central bank A public authority that provides banking services to banks and governments and regulates financial institutions and markets. (p. 279)

Ceteris paribus Other things remaining the same (often abbreviated as *cet. par.*). (p. 15)

Chained-dollar real GDP The measure of real GDP calculated by the Bureau of Economic Analysis. (p. 139)

Change in demand A change in the quantity that people plan to buy when any influence on buying plans other than the price of the good changes. (p. 88)

Change in the quantity demanded A change in the quantity of a good that people plan to buy that results from a change in the price of the good. (p. 90)

Change in the quantity supplied A change in the quantity of a good that suppliers plan to sell that results from a change in the price of the good. (p. 97)

Change in supply A change in the quantity that suppliers plan to sell when any influence on selling plans other than the price of the good changes. (p. 95)

Circular flow model A model of the economy that shows the circular flow of expenditures and incomes that result from decision makers' choices and the way those choices interact to determine what, how, and for whom goods and services are produced. (p. 48)

Classical growth theory The theory that the clash between an exploding population and limited resources will eventually bring economic growth to an end. (p. 225)

Classical macroeconomics The view that the market economy works well, that aggregate fluctuations are a natural consequence of an expanding economy, and that government intervention cannot improve the efficiency of the market economy. (p. 192)

Commercial bank A firm that is chartered by the Comptroller of the Currency in the U.S. Treasury (or by a state agency) to accept deposits and make loans. (p. 274)

Comparative advantage The ability of a person to perform an activity or produce a good or service at a lower opportunity cost than someone else. (p. 75)

Complement A good that is consumed with another good. (p. 88)

Complement in production A good that is produced along with another good. (p. 95)

Consumer Price Index A measure of the average of the prices paid by urban consumers for a fixed market basket of consumption goods and services. (p. 168)

Consumption expenditure The expenditure by households on consumption goods and services. (p. 115)

Consumption function The relationship between consumption expenditure and disposable income, other things remaining the same. (p. 352)

Consumption goods and services Goods and services that are bought by individuals and used to provide personal enjoyment and contribute to a person's standard of living. (p. 34)

Contractionary fiscal policy A decrease in government expenditure on goods and services, a decrease in transfer payments, or an increase in taxes designed to decrease aggregate demand. (p. 408)

Core inflation rate The annual percentage increase in the PCE price index excluding the prices of food and energy. (p. 177)

Correlation The tendency for the values of two variables to move in a predictable and related way. (p. 16)

Cost of living index A measure of the change in the amount of money that people need to spend to achieve a given standard of living. (p. 174)

Creditor nation A country that during its entire history has invested more in the rest of the world than other countries have invested in it. (p. 480)

Cross-section graph A graph that shows the values of an economic variable for different groups in a population at a point in time. (p. 24)

Crowding-out effect The tendency for a government budget deficit to raise the real interest rate and decrease investment. (p. 260)

Currency Notes (dollar bills) and coins. (p. 270)

Currency appreciation The rise in the value of one currency in terms of another currency. (p. 485)

Currency depreciation The fall in the value of one currency in terms of another currency. (p. 486)

Current account Record of receipts from the sale of goods and services to other countries (exports), minus payments for goods and services bought from other countries (imports), plus the net amount of interest and transfers received from and paid to other countries. (p. 478)

Cyclical unemployment The fluctuating unemployment over the business cycle that increases during a recession and decreases during an expansion. (p. 158)

Debtor nation A country that during its entire history has borrowed more from the rest of the world than it has lent to the rest of the world. (p. 480)

Deflation A situation in which the price level is *falling* and the inflation rate is *negative*. (p. 171)

Demand The relationship between the quantity demanded and the price of a good when all other influences on buying plans remain the same. (p. 85)

Demand curve A graph of the relationship between the quantity demanded of a good and its price when all the other influences on buying plans remain the same. (p. 86)

Demand for labor The relationship between the quantity of labor demanded and the real wage rate when all other influences on firms' hiring plans remain the same. (p. 197)

Demand for loanable funds The relationship between the quantity of loanable funds demanded and the real interest rate when all other influences on borrowing plans remain the same. (p. 249)

Demand for money The relationship between the quantity of money demanded and the nominal interest rate, when all other influences on the amount of money that people wish to hold remain the same. (p. 300)

Demand schedule A list of the quantities demanded at each different price when all the other influences on buying plans remain the same. (p. 86)

Depreciation The decrease in the value of capital that results from its use and from obsolescence. (p. 122)

Diminishing returns The tendency for each additional hour of labor employed to produce a successively smaller additional amount of real GDP. (p. 196)

Direct relationship A relationship between two variables that move in the same direction. (p. 26)

Discount rate The interest rate at which the Fed stands ready to lend reserves to commercial banks. (p. 281)

Discouraged worker A marginally attached worker who has not made specific efforts to find a job within the past four weeks because previous unsuccessful attempts to find a job were discouraging. (p. 146)

Discretionary fiscal policy A fiscal policy action that is initiated by an act of Congress. (p. 409)

Discretionary monetary policy Monetary policy that is based on expert assessment of the current economic situation. (p. 444)

Disposable personal income Income received by households minus personal income taxes paid. (p. 123)

Dumping When a foreign firm sells its exports at a lower price than its cost of production. (p. 468)

Economic freedom A condition in which people are able to make personal choices, their private property is protected by the rule of law, and they are free to buy and sell in markets. (p. 232)

Economic growth The sustained expansion of production possibilities. (p. 73)

Economic growth rate The annual percentage change of real GDP. (p. 216)

Economics The social science that studies the choices that individuals, businesses, government, and entire societies make as they cope with *scarcity* and the *incentives* that influence and reconcile them. (p. 3)

Efficiency wage A real wage rate that is set above the full-employment equilibrium wage rate to induce greater work effort. (p. 207)

Entrepreneurship The human resource that organizes labor, land, and capital. (p. 38)

Equation of exchange An equation that states that the quantity of money multiplied by the velocity of circulation equals the price level multiplied by real GDP. (p. 311)

Equilibrium expenditure The level of aggregate expenditure that occurs when aggregate *planned* expenditure equals real GDP. (p. 360)

Equilibrium price The price at which the quantity demanded equals the quantity supplied. (p. 99)

Equilibrium quantity The quantity bought and sold at the equilibrium price. (p. 99)

Excess demand A situation in which the quantity demanded exceeds the quantity supplied. (p. 99)

Excess reserves A bank's actual reserves minus its desired reserves. (p. 284)

Excess supply A situation in which the quantity supplied exceeds the quantity demanded. (p. 99)

Expected inflation rate The inflation rate that people forecast and use to set the money wage rate and other money prices. (p. 385)

Export goods and services Goods and services that are produced in one country and sold in other countries. (p. 34)

Exports The goods andservices that firms in one country sell to households and firms in other countries. (pp. 54, 454)

Exports of goods and services Items that firms in the United States produce and sell to the rest of the world. (p. 116)

Factor markets The markets in which the services of the factors of production are bought and sold. (p. 48)

Factors of production The productive resources that are used to produce goods and services—land, labor, capital, and entrepreneurship. (p. 36)

Federal budget An annual statement of the revenues, outlays, and surplus or deficit of the government of the United States. (p. 400)

Federal funds rate The interest rate at which banks can borrow and lend reserves (interbank loans) in the federal funds market. (pp. 276, 428)

Federal Open Market Committee The Fed's main policy-making committee. (p. 280)

Federal Reserve System (The Fed) The central bank of the United States. (p. 279)

Fiat money Objects that are money because the law decrees or orders them to be money. (p. 270)

Final good or service A good or service that is produced for its final user and not as a component of another good or service. (p. 114)

Financial institution A firm that operates on both sides of the market for financial capital: It borrows on one market and lends in another. (p. 245)

Financial stability A situation in which financial markets and institutions function normally to allocate capital resources and risk. (p. 427)

Firms The institutions that organize the production of goods and services. (p. 48)

Fiscal policy Changing taxes, transfer payments, and government expenditure on goods and services. (p. 335) The use of the federal budget to achieve the macroeconomic objectives of high and sustained economic growth and full employment. (p. 400)

Fiscal stimulus An increase in government outlays or a decrease in tax revenues designed to boost real GDP and create or save jobs. (p. 405)

Fiscal year A year that begins on October 1 and ends on September 30. Fiscal 2011 begins on October 1, 2010. (p. 400)

Foreign exchange market The market in which the currency of one country is exchanged for the currency of another. (p. 485)

Foreign exchange rate The price at which one currency exchanges for another. (p. 485)

Frictional unemployment The unemployment that arises from normal labor turnover—from people entering and leaving the labor force, from quitting jobs to find better ones, and from the ongoing creation and destruction of jobs. (p. 157)

Full employment When there is no cyclical unemployment or, equivalently, when all the unemployment is frictional, structural, or seasonal. (p. 159)

Full-employment equilibrium When equilibrium real GDP equals potential GDP. (p. 339)

Full-time workers People who usually work 35 hours or more a week. (p. 147)

Functional distribution of income The distribution of income among the factors of production. (p. 39)

GDP price index An average of the current prices of all the goods and services included in GDP expressed as a percentage of base-year prices. (p. 177)

Gold standard A monetary policy rule that fixes the dollar price of gold. (p. 447)

Goods and services The objects (goods) and the actions (services) that people value and produce to satisfy human wants. (p. 3)

Goods markets Markets in which goods and services are bought and sold. (p. 48)

Government expenditure multiplier The effect of a change in government expenditure on goods and services on aggregate demand. (p. 406)

Government expenditure on goods and services The expenditure by all levels of government on goods and services. (p. 116)

Government goods and services Goods and services that are bought by governments. (p. 34)

Government sector balance Net taxes minus government expenditure on goods and services. (p. 482)

Great Depression A period of high unemployment, low incomes, and extreme economic hardship that lasted from 1929 to 1939. (p. 149)

Gross domestic product (GDP) The market value of all the final goods and services produced within a country within a given time period. (p. 114)

Gross investment The total amount spent on new capital goods. (p. 242)

Gross national product (GNP) The market value of all the final goods and services produced anywhere in the world in a given time period by the factors of production supplied by the residents of the country. (p. 123)

Households Individuals or groups of people living together. (p. 48)

Household production The production of goods and services in the home. (p. 131)

Human capital The knowledge and skill that people obtain from education, on-the-job training, and work experience. (p. 37)

Hyperinflation Inflation at a rate that exceeds 50 percent a *month* (which translates to 12,875 percent a year). (p. 314)

Import quota A quantitative restriction on the import of a good that limits the maximum quantity of a good that may be imported in a given period. (p. 464)

Imports The goods and services that households and firms in one country buy from firms in other countries. (pp. 54, 454)

Imports of goods and services Items that households, firms, and governments in the United States buy from the rest of the world. (p. 116)

Incentive A reward or a penalty—a "carrot" or a "stick"—that encourages or discourages an action. (p. 13)

Induced taxes Taxes that vary with real GDP. (p. 409)

Infant-industry argument The argument that it is necessary to protect a new industry to enable it to grow into a mature industry that can compete in world markets. (p. 467)

Inferior good A good for which demand decreases when income increases. (p. 89)

Inflationary gap A gap that exists when real GDP exceeds potential GDP and that brings a rising price level. (p. 340)

Inflation rate The percentage change in the price level from one year to the next. (p. 171)

Inflation targeting A monetary policy strategy in which the central bank makes a public commitment to achieving an explicit inflation target and to explaining how its policy actions will achieve that target. (p. 444)

Instrument rule A decision rule for monetary policy that sets the policy instrument by a formula based on the current state of the economy. (p. 430)

Interest Income paid for the use of capital. (p. 39)

Interest rate parity Equal interest rates—a situation in which the interest rate in one currency equals the interest rate in another currency when exchange rate changes are taken into account. (p. 496)

Intermediate good or service A good or service that is used as a component of a final good or service. (p. 114)

Inverse relationship A relationship between two variables that move in opposite directions. (p. 27)

Investment The purchase of new *capital goods*—tools, instruments, machines, buildings, and additions to inventories. (p. 115)

Job rationing A situation that arises when the real wage rate is above the full-employment equilibrium level. (p. 206)

Job search The activity of looking for an acceptable vacant job. (p. 205)

Keynesian macroeconomics The view that the market economy is inherently unstable and needs active government intervention to achieve full employment and sustained economic growth. (p. 192)

***k*-percent rule** A monetary policy rule that makes the quantity of money grow at *k* percent per year, where *k* equals the growth rate of potential GDP. (p. 445)

Labor The work time and work effort that people devote to producing goods and services. (p. 37)

Labor force The number of people employed plus the number unemployed. (p. 144)

Labor force participation rate The percentage of the working-age population who are members of the labor force. (p. 146)

Labor productivity The quantity of real GDP produced by one hour of labor. (p. 220)

Land The "gifts of nature," or *natural resources*, that we use to produce goods and services. (p. 36)

Law of demand Other things remaining the same, if the price of a good rises, the quantity demanded of that good decreases; and if the price of a good falls, the quantity demanded of that good increases. (p. 85)

Law of market forces When there is a shortage, the price rises; when there is a surplus, the price falls. (p. 99)

Law of supply Other things remaining the same, if the price of a good rises, the quantity supplied of that good increases; and if the price of a good falls, the quantity supplied that good decreases. (p. 92)

Linear relationship A relationship that graphs as a straight line. (p. 26)

Long-run Phillips curve The vertical line that shows the relationship between inflation and unemployment when the economy is at full employment. (p. 384)

Loss Income earned by an entrepreneur for running a business when that income is negative. (p. 39)

M1 Currency, traveler's checks, and checkable deposits owned by individuals and businesses. (p. 270)

M2 M1 plus savings deposits and small time deposits, money market funds, and other deposits. (p. 270)

Macroeconomic equilibrium When the quantity of real GDP demanded equals the quantity of real GDP supplied at the point of intersection of the *AD* curve and the *AS* curve. (p. 338)

Macroeconomics The study of the aggregate (or total) effects on the national economy and the global economy of the choices that individuals, businesses, and governments make. (p. 14)

Malthusian theory Another name for classical growth theory—named for Thomas Robert Malthus. (p. 225)

Margin A choice on the margin is a choice that is made by comparing *all* the relevant alternatives systematically and incrementally. (p. 12)

Marginal benefit The benefit that arises from a one-unit increase in an activity. The marginal benefit of something is measured by what you *are willing to* give up to get *one additional* unit of it. (p. 12)

Marginal cost The opportunity cost that arises from a one-unit increase in an activity. The marginal cost of something is what you *must* give up to get one more unit of it. (p. 12) The marginal cost of producing a good is the change in total cost that results from a one-unit increase in output. (p. 332)

Marginally attached worker A person who does not have a job, is available and willing to work, has not made specific efforts to find a job within the previous four weeks, but has looked for work sometime in the recent past. (p. 146)

Marginal propensity to consume The fraction of a change in disposable income that is spent on consumption—the change in consumption expenditure divided by the change in disposable income that brought it about. (p. 354)

Marginal propensity to import The fraction of an increase in real GDP that is spent on imports—the change in imports divided by the change in real GDP. (p. 356)

Marginal tax rate The fraction of a change in real GDP that is paid in income taxes—the change in tax payments divided by the change in real GDP. (p. 366)

Market Any arrangement that brings buyers and sellers together and enables them to get information and do business with each other. (p. 48)

Market demand The sum of the demands of all the buyers in a market. (p. 87)

Market equilibrium When buyers' and sellers' plans are in balance—the quantity demanded equals the quantity supplied. (p. 99)

Market for loanable funds The aggregate of all the individual financial markets. (p. 248)

Market supply The sum of the supplies of all the sellers in the market. (p. 94)

Means of payment A method of settling a debt. (p. 268)

Medium of exchange An object that is generally accepted in return for goods and services. (p. 269)

Microeconomics The study of the choices that individuals and businesses make and the way these choices interact and are influenced by governments. (p. 14)

Minimum wage law A government regulation that makes hiring labor for less than a specified wage illegal. (p. 207)

Monetarist macroeconomics The view that the market economy works well, that aggregate fluctuations are the natural consequence of an expanding economy, but that fluctuations in the quantity of money also bring the business cycle. (p. 193)

Monetary base The sum of coins, Federal Reserve notes, and banks' reserves at the Fed. (p. 281)

Monetary policy Changing the quantity of money and the interest rate. (p. 335)

Monetary policy instrument A variable that the Fed can directly control or closely target and that influences the economy in desirable ways. (p. 428)

Money Any commodity or token that is generally accepted as a means of payment. (p. 268)

Money multiplier The number by which a change in the monetary base is multiplied to find the resulting change in the quantity of money. (p. 289)

Multiplier The amount by which a change in any component of autonomous expenditure is magnified or multiplied to determine the change that it generates in equilibrium expenditure and real GDP. (p. 364)

National debt The amount of government debt outstanding—

the debt that has arisen from past budget deficits. (pp. 52, 401)

Natural rate hypothesis The proposition that when the inflation rate changes, the unemployment rate changes *temporarily* and eventually returns to the natural unemployment rate. (p. 386)

Natural unemployment rate The unemployment rate when the economy is at full employment. (p. 159)

Needs-tested spending Spending on programs that entitle suitably qualified people and businesses to receive transfer payments that vary with need and with the state of the economy. (p. 409)

Negative relationship A relationship between two variables that move in opposite directions. (p. 27)

Neoclassical growth theory The theory that real GDP per person will increase as long as technology keeps advancing. (p. 227)

Net borrower A country that is borrowing more from the rest of the world than it is lending to the rest of the world. (p. 480)

Net domestic product at factor cost The sum of wages, interest, rent, and profit. (p. 121)

Net exports of goods and services The value of exports of goods and services minus the value of imports of goods and services. (p. 116)

Net investment The change in the quantity of capital—equals gross investment minus depreciation. (p. 242)

Net lender A country that is lending more to the rest of the world than it is borrowing from the rest of the world. (p. 480)

Net taxes Taxes paid minus cash benefits received from governments. (p. 116)

Net worth The total market value of what a financial institution has lent minus the market value of what it has borrowed. (p. 246)

New growth theory The theory that our unlimited wants will lead us to ever greater productivity and perpetual economic growth. (p. 227)

Nominal GDP The value of the final goods and services produced in a given year expressed in terms of the prices of that same year. (p. 124)

Nominal interest rate The dollar amount of interest expressed as a percentage of the amount loaned. (p. 184)

Nominal wage rate The average hourly wage rate measured in *current* dollars. (p. 182)

Normal good A good for which demand increases when income increases. (p. 89)

Official settlements account Record of the change in U.S. official reserves. (p. 478)

Okun's Law For each percentage point that the unemployment rate is above the natural unemployment rate, real GDP is 2 percentage points below potential GDP. (p. 379)

Open market operation The purchase or sale of government securities—U.S. Treasury bills and bonds—by the New York Fed in the open market. (p. 281)

Opportunity cost The opportunity cost of something is the best thing you *must* give up to get it. (p. 11)

Output gap Real GDP minus potential GDP expressed as a percentage of potential GDP. (p. 160)

Part time for economic reasons People who work 1 to 34 hours per week but are looking for full-time work and cannot find it because of unfavorable business conditions. (p. 147)

Part-time workers People who usually work less than 35 hours a week. (p. 147)

PCE price index An average of the current prices of the goods and services included in the consumption expenditure component of GDP expressed as a percentage of base-year prices. (p. 177)

Personal distribution of income The distribution of income among households. (p. 39)

Physical capital The tools, instruments, machines, buildings, and other items that have been produced in the past and that are used to produce goods and services. (p. 242)

Positive relationship A relationship between two variables that move in the same direction. (p. 26)

Potential GDP The value of real GDP when all the economy's factors of production—labor, capital, land, and entrepreneurial ability—are fully employed. (pp. 127, 160, 195)

Private sector balance Saving minus investment. (p. 482)

Production function A relationship that shows the maximum quantity of real GDP that can be produced as the quantity of labor employed changes and all other influences on production remain the same. (p. 196)

Production possibilities frontier The boundary between the combinations of goods and services that can be produced and the combinations that cannot be produced, given the available factors of production and the state of technology. (p. 62)

Profit Income earned by an entrepreneur for running a business. (p. 39)

Property rights Social arrangements that govern the protection of private property—legally established titles to the ownership, use, and disposal of factors of production and goods and services that are enforceable in the courts. (p. 232)

Purchasing power parity Equal value of money—a situation in which money buys the same amount of goods and services in different currencies. (p. 494)

Quantity demanded The amount of any good, service, or resource that people are willing and able to buy during a specified period at a specified price. (p. 85)

Quantity of labor demanded The total labor hours that all the firms in the economy plan to hire during a given time period at a given real wage rate. (p. 197)

Quantity of labor supplied The number of labor hours that all the households in the economy plan to work during a given time period at a given real wage rate. (p. 199)

Quantity of money demanded The amount of money that households and firms choose to hold. (p. 299)

Quantity supplied The amount of any good, service, or resource that people are willing and able to sell during a specified period at a specified price. (p. 92)

Quantity theory of money The proposition that when real GDP equals potential GDP, an increase in the quantity of money brings an equal percentage increase in the price level. (p. 310)

Rational choice A choice that uses the available resources to most effectively satisfy the wants of the person making the choice. (p. 10)

Rational expectation The inflation forecast resulting from use of all the relevant data and economic science. (p. 391)

Real GDP The value of the final goods and services produced in a given year expressed in terms of the prices in a *base year*. (p. 124)

Real GDP per person Real GDP divided by the population. (pp. 127, 216)

Real interest rate The goods and services forgone in interest expressed as a percentage of the amount loaned and calculated as the nominal interest rate minus the inflation rate. (p. 184)

Real wage rate The average hourly wage rate measured in the dollars of a given reference base year. (p. 182)

Recession A period during which real GDP decreases for at least two successive quarters; or defined by the NBER as "a period of significant decline in total output, income, employment, and trade, usually lasting from six months to a year, and marked by contractions in many sectors of the economy." (p. 128)

Recessionary gap A gap that exists when potential GDP exceeds real GDP and that brings a falling price level. (p. 340)

Reference base period A period for which the CPI is defined to equal 100. Currently, the reference base period is 1982–1984. (p. 168)

Rent Income paid for the use of land (p. 39)

Rent-seeking Lobbying and other political activity that aims to capture the gains from trade. (p. 471)

Required reserve ratio The minimum percentage of deposits that the Fed requires banks and other financial institutions to hold in reserves. (p. 275)

Reserves The currency in the bank's vaults plus the balance on its reserve account at a Federal Reserve Bank. (p. 275)

Rule of 70 The number of years it takes for the level of any variable to double is approximately 70 divided by the annual percentage growth rate of the variable. (p. 217)

Saving The amount of income that is not paid in net taxes or spent on consumption goods and services. (p. 116)

Scarcity The condition that arises because wants exceed the ability of resources to satisfy them. (p. 2)

Scatter diagram A graph of the value of one variable against the value of another variable. (p. 24)

Seasonal unemployment The unemployment that arises because of seasonal patterns. (p. 158)

Self-interest The choices that are best for the individual who makes them. (p. 4)

Shortage A situation in which the quantity demanded exceeds the quantity supplied. (p. 99)

Short-run Phillips curve A curve that shows the relationship between the inflation rate and the unemployment rate when the natural unemployment rate and the expected inflation rate remain constant. (p. 378)

Slope The change in the value of the variable measured on the *y*-axis divided by the change in the value of the variable measured on the *x*-axis. (p. 29)

Social interest The choices that are best for society as a whole. (p. 4)

Stagflation A combination of recession (falling real GDP) and inflation (rising price level). (p. 342)

Standard of living The level of consumption of goods and services that people enjoy, *on average*; it is measured by average income per person. (p. 127)

Statistical discrepancy The discrepancy between the expenditure approach and the income approach estimates of GDP, calculated as the GDP expenditure total minus GDP income total. (p. 122)

Stock A certificate of ownership and claim to the profits that a firm makes. (p. 244)

Store of value Any commodity or token that can be held and exchanged later for goods and services. (p. 269)

Structural unemployment The unemployment that arises when changes in technology or international competition change the skills needed to perform jobs or change the locations of jobs. (p. 157)

Substitute A good that can be consumed in place of another good. (p. 88)

Substitute in production A good that can be produced in place of another good. (p. 95)

Sunk cost A previously incurred and irreversible cost. (p. 11)

Supply The relationship between the quantity supplied and the price of a good when all other influences on selling plans remain the same. (p. 92)

Supply curve A graph of the relationship between the quantity supplied of a good and its price when all the other influences on selling plans remain the same. (p. 93)

Supply of labor The relationship between the quantity of labor supplied and the real wage rate when all other influences on work plans remain the same. (p. 199)

Supply of loanable funds The relationship between the quantity of loanable funds supplied and the real interest rate when all other influences on lending plans remain the same. (p. 251)

Supply of money The relationship between the quantity of money supplied and the nominal interest rate. (p. 302)

Supply schedule A list of the quantities supplied at each different price when all the other influences on selling plans remain the same. (p. 93)

Supply-side effects The effects of fiscal policy on potential GDP and the economic growth rate. (p. 412)

Surplus A situation in which the quantity supplied exceeds the quantity demanded. (p. 99)

Targeting rule A decision rule for monetary policy that sets the policy instrument at a level that makes the central bank's forecast of the ultimate policy goals equal to their targets. (p. 430)

Tariff A tax imposed on a good when it is imported. (p. 461)

Tax multiplier The effect of a change in taxes on aggregate demand. (p. 406)

Tax wedge The gap created by a tax between what a buyer pays and what a seller receives. In the labor market, it is the gap between the before-tax wage rate and the after-tax wage rate. (p. 413)

Time-series graph A graph that measures time on the *x*-axis and the variable or variables in which we are interested on the *y*-axis. (p. 24)

Tradeoff An exchange—giving up one thing to get something else. (p. 65)

Transfer payments Social Security benefits, Medicare and Medicaid benefits, unemployment benefits, and other cash transfers. (p. 402)

Transfer payments multiplier The effect of a change in transfer payments on aggregate demand. (p. 406)

Trend A general tendency for the value of a variable to rise or fall over time. (p. 24)

Underground production The production of goods and services hidden from the view of government. (p. 131)

Unemployment rate The percentage of the people in the labor force who are unemployed. (p. 145)

Union wage A wage rate that results from collective bargaining between a labor union and a firm. (p. 207)

Unit of account An agreed-upon measure for stating the prices of goods and services. (p. 269)

U.S. interest rate differential The U.S. interest rate minus the foreign interest rate. (p. 488)

U.S. official reserves The government's holdings of foreign currency. (p. 478)

Velocity of circulation The average number of times in a year that each dollar of money gets used to buy final goods and services. (p. 310)

Wages Income paid for the services of labor. (p. 39)

Wealth The value of all the things that people own. (p. 242)

Working-age population The total number of people aged 16 years and over who are not in jail, hospital, or some other form of institutional care or in the U.S. Armed Forces. (p. 144)

Index

Key terms and pages on which they are defined appear in **boldface**.

Credits

(continuation from page ii)

Chapter 1: p. 1: David Shankbone/Wikimedia Commons; p. 3 top: Owen Franken/Stone Allstock/Getty Images; p. 3 bottom: George Rose/Getty Images; p. 4: Photodisc/Getty Images; p. 5 top: Feverpitch/Shutterstock.; p. 5 bottom: Library of Congress; p. 6 top: Courtesy REA Agency; p. 6 bottom: Getty Images; p. 7 top: Getty Images/Digital Vision; p. 7 center: Lakov Kalinin/Shutterstock; p. 7 bottom: Getty Images/Digital Vision; p. 8 top: Getty Images/Digital Vision; p. 8 bottom: Wally McNamee/CORBIS; p. 11 left: Scott T. Baxter/Getty Images, Inc.-Photodisc; p. 11 right: Getty Images, Inc.; p. 13 left: Yuri Arcurs/Shutterstock; p. 13 right: John Eder/Image Bank/Getty Images; p. 14: Jim Young/Reuters Limited; p. 15: Getty Images/Digital Vision; p. 17: CORBIS-NY.

Chapter 2: p. 33 TONY AVELAR/AFP/Getty Images; p. 35 top: Getty Images/Digital Vision; p. 35 top center: Monkey Business Images/Shutterstock; p. 35 bottom center: Photodisc/Getty Images; p. 35 bottom: Joe Sohm/VisionsofAmerica/Getty Images/Digital Vision; p. 38 top left: EyeWire Collection/Getty Images-Photodisc-Royalty Free; p. 38 top right: Jean Schweitzer/Shutterstock; p. 38 bottom left: Photodisc/Getty Images; p. 38 bottom right: Getty Images/Digital Vision; p. 44: Tatiana Markow/Sygma/Corbis-NY; p. 45 top: Bruce Connolly/CORBIS All Rights Reserved; p. 45 bottom: Earl & Nazima Kowall/CORBIS All Rights Reserved.

Chapter 3: p. 61: Greg Randles/Shutterstock; p. 75 top: Courtesy Sara Piaseczynski; p. 75 bottom: Jack Hollingsworth/Corbis Royalty Free.

Chapter 4: p. 83: Getty Images; p. 84 left: Steven Rubin/The Image Works; p. 84 center: Howard Grey/Getty Images/Digital Vision; p. 84 right: Prentice Hall School Division; p. 106: Yuri Arcurs/Shutterstock; p. 107: Shutterstock.

Chapter 5: p. 113: Andy Sacks/Stone/Getty Images; p. 120: Jeff Christensen/Reuters/Corbis.

Chapter 6: p. 143: Robyn Beck/AFP/Getty Images; p. 144: Sokolovsky/Shutterstock; p. 147: Courtesy of U.S. Census Bureau; p. 155: Sokolovsky/Shutterstock; P. 157 top: Dmitry Yashkin/Shutterstock; p. 157 bottom: ©Jim Sugar Photography/CORBIS All Rights Reserved.

Chapter 7: p. 167: Emmanuel Faure/Stone/Getty Images; p. 174: AVAVA/Shutterstock; p. 175 top: Fedor Selivanov/Shutterstock; p. 175 center: Monkey Business Images/Shutterstock; p. 175 bottom: Ioana Drutu/Shutterstock; p. 180 top: Brendan Howard/Shutterstock; p. 180 bottom: Kirsten Sims.

Chapter 8: p. 191 top: Richard Passmore/Stone/Getty Images; p. 191 bottom: Jerome Tisne/Photographer's Choice/Getty Images; p. 209: PhotoDisc/Getty Images.

Chapter 9: p. 215: MAYSKYPHOTO/Shutterstock; p. 222 top: Minnesota Historical Society/Corbis; p. 222 bottom: TONGRO IMAGE STOCK/BRAND X/Corbis Royalty Free.

Chapter 10: p. 241: Frances Roberts/Alamy; p. 256 top: Frontpage/Shutterstock; p. 256 bottom: Frontpage/Shutterstock.

Chapter 11: p. 267: Alex Wong/Getty Images; p. 275: Scala/Art Resource, NY; p. 279: Win McNamee/Getty Images, Inc.; p. 285: Reuters/HO/Landov.

Chapter 12: p. 297: Getty Images; p. 314: Bettmann/CORBIS.

Chapter 13: p. 325 top: Susan Yates/Alamy; p. 325 bottom: ©Bob Krist/CORBIS All Rights Reserved.

Chapter 14: p. 351 top: Purestock/Getty Royalty Free; p. 351 bottom: iStockphoto; p. 362 top: ©Bibliotheque Nationale, Paris, France/Giraudon—Bridgeman Art Library; p. 362 bottom: ©Bettmann/CORBIS.

Chapter 15: p. 377: Jim Young/Reuters; p. 381: Courtesy of MIT Museum.

Chapter 16: p. 399: Scott J. Ferrell/Congressional Quarterly/Getty Images, Inc; p. 407: Gabriel Bouys/AFP/Getty Images.

Chapter 17: p. 425: Leon Neal/AFP/Getty Images; p. 446 left: Staff/AFP/Getty Images; p. 446 right: Courtesy of Anna J. Schwartz.

Chapter 18: p. 453: Getty Images; p. 455 top: John Froschauer/AP Wide World Photos; p. 455 bottom: Anna Sheveleva/Shutterstock; p. 4591 top left: Chris O'Meara/AP Wide World Photos; p. 459 top right: Amy Waldman/The New York Times; p. 459 bottom left: Sokolovsky/Shutterstock; p. 459 bottom right: Lucian Coman/Shutterstock.

Chapter 19: p. 477: Rob Walls/Alamy.

The Pearson Series in Economics

Abel/Bernanke/Croushore
*Macroeconomics**

Bade/Parkin
*Foundations of Economics**

Bierman/Fernandez
Game Theory with Economic Applications

Blanchard
Macroeconomics

Blau/Ferber/Winkler
The Economics of Women, Men and Work

Boardman/Greenberg/Vining/Weimer
Cost-Benefit Analysis

Boyer
Principles of Transportation Economics

Branson
Macroeconomic Theory and Policy

Brock/Adams
The Structure of American Industry

Bruce
Public Finance and the American Economy

Carlton/Perloff
Modern Industrial Organization

Case/Fair/Oster
*Principles of Economics**

Caves/Frankel/Jones
World Trade and Payments: An Introduction

Chapman
Environmental Economics: Theory, Application, and Policy

Cooter/Ulen
Law & Economics

Downs
An Economic Theory of Democracy

Ehrenberg/Smith
Modern Labor Economics

Ekelund/Ressler/Tollison
*Economics**

Farnham
Economics for Managers

Folland/Goodman/Stano
The Economics of Health and Health Care

Fort
Sports Economics

Froyen
Macroeconomics

Fusfeld
The Age of the Economist

Gerber
International Economics

Gordon
Macroeconomics

Greene
Econometric Analysis

Gregory
Essentials of Economics

Gregory/Stuart
Russian and Soviet Economic Performance and Structure

Hartwick/Olewiler
The Economics of Natural Resource Use

Heilbroner/ Milberg
The Making of the Economic Society

Heyne/ Boettke / Prychitko
The Economic Way of Thinking

Hoffman/Averett
Women and the Economy: Family, Work, and Pay

Holt
Markets, Games and Strategic Behavior

Hubbard
Money, the Financial System, and the Economy

Hubbard/OBrien
*Economics**

Hughes/Cain
American Economic History

Husted/Melvin
International Economics

Jehle/Reny
Advanced Microeconomic Theory

Johnson-Lans
A Health Economics Primer

Keat/Young
Managerial Economics

Klein
Mathematical Methods for Economics

Krugman/Obstfeld
*International Economics: Theory & Policy**

Laidler
The Demand for Money

Leeds/von Allmen
The Economics of Sports

Leeds/von Allmen/Schiming
*Economics**

Lipsey/Ragan/Storer
*Economics**

Lynn
Economic Development: Theory and Practice for a Divided World

Melvin
International Money and Finance

Miller
*Economics Today**

Understanding Modern Economics

Miller/Benjamin
The Economics of Macro Issues

Miller/Benjamin/North
The Economics of Public Issues

Mills/Hamilton
Urban Economics

Mishkin
*The Economics of Money, Banking, and Financial Markets**

*The Economics of Money, Banking, and Financial Markets, Business School Edition**

Murray
Econometrics: A Modern Introduction

Nafziger
The Economics of Developing Countries

O'Sullivan/Sheffrin/Perez
*Economics: Principles, Applications and Tools**

Parkin
*Economics**

Perloff
*Microeconomics**

Microeconomics: Theory and Applications with Calculus

Perman/Common/McGilvray/Ma
Natural Resources and Environmental Economics

Phelps
Health Economics

Pindyck/Rubinfeld
*Microeconomics**

Riddell/Shackelford/Stamos/Schneider
Economics: A Tool for Critically Understanding Society

Ritter/Silber/Udell
*Principles of Money, Banking & Financial Markets**

Roberts
The Choice: A Fable of Free Trade and Protection

Rohlf
Introduction to Economic Reasoning

Ruffin/Gregory
Principles of Economics

Sargent
Rational Expectations and Inflation

Sawyer/Sprinkle
International Economics

Scherer
Industry Structure, Strategy, and Public Policy

Schiller
The Economics of Poverty and Discrimination

Sherman
Market Regulation

Silberberg
Principles of Microeconomics

Stock/Watson
Introduction to Econometrics

Introduction to Econometrics, Brief Edition

Studenmund
Using Econometrics: A Practical Guide

Tietenberg/Lewis
Environmental and Natural Resource Economics

Environmental Economics and Policy

Todaro/Smith
Economic Development

Waldman
Microeconomics

Waldman/Jensen
Industrial Organization: Theory and Practice

Weil
Economic Growth

Williamson
Macroeconomics

Macroeconomic Data

These macroeconomic data series show some of the trends in GDP and its components, the price level, and other variables that provide information about changes in the standard of living and the cost of living—the central questions of macroeconomics. You will find these data in a spreadsheet that you can download from your MyEconLab Web site.

	NATIONAL INCOME AND PRODUCT ACCOUNTS	1963	1964	1965	1966	1967	1968	1969	1970	1971	1972
	EXPENDITURES APPROACH										
the sum of	1 Personal consumption expenditures	383	412	444	481	508	558	605	648	702	770
	2 Gross private domestic investment	94	102	118	131	129	141	156	152	178	208
	3 Government expenditures	136	143	151	172	193	209	221	234	246	263
	4 Exports	31	35	37	41	44	48	52	60	63	71
less	5 Imports	26	28	32	37	40	47	51	56	62	74
equals	6 Gross domestic product	618	664	719	788	832	910	984	1,038	1,127	1,238
	INCOMES APPROACH										
	7 Compensation of employees	345	371	400	443	475	524	578	617	659	725
plus	8 Net operating surplus	159	171	190	203	206	219	226	219	243	275
equals	9 Net domestic product at factor cost	504	542	589	646	681	743	803	837	902	1,001
plus	10 Indirect taxes less subsidies	51	55	58	59	64	72	79	87	96	101
	11 Depreciation (capital consumption)	63	66	71	77	83	90	99	108	118	127
	12 GDP (income approach)	619	663	718	782	828	906	982	1,031	1,116	1,229
	13 Statistical discrepancy	–1	1	2	6	5	4	3	7	11	9
equals	14 GDP (expenditure approach)	618	664	719	788	832	910	985	1,038	1,127	1,238
	15 Real GDP (billions of 2005 dollars)	3,207	3,392	3,610	3,845	3,943	4,133	4,262	4,270	4,413	4,648
	16 Real GDP growth rate (percent per year)	4.4	5.8	6.4	6.5	2.5	4.8	3.1	0.2	3.4	5.3
	OTHER DATA										
	17 Population (millions)	189.3	191.9	194.3	196.6	198.8	200.7	202.7	205.1	207.7	209.9
	18 Labor force (millions)	71.8	73.1	74.5	75.8	77.3	78.7	80.7	82.8	84.4	87.0
	19 Employment (millions)	67.8	69.3	71.1	72.9	74.4	75.9	77.9	78.7	79.4	82.2
	20 Unemployment (millions)	4.1	3.8	3.4	2.9	3.0	2.8	2.8	4.1	5.0	4.9
	21 Labor force participation rate (percent of working-age population)	58.7	58.7	58.9	59.2	59.6	59.6	60.1	60.4	60.2	60.4
	22 Unemployment rate (percent of labor force)	5.7	5.2	4.5	3.8	3.8	3.6	3.5	4.9	5.9	5.6
	23 Real GDP per person (2005 dollars per year)	16,940	17,675	18,576	19,559	19,836	20,590	21,021	20,820	21,249	22,140
	24 Growth rate of real GDP per person (percent per year)	2.9	4.3	5.1	5.3	1.4	3.8	2.1	–1.0	2.1	4.2
	25 Quantity of money (M2, billions of dollars)	393.2	424.7	459.2	480.2	524.8	566.8	587.9	626.5	710.3	802.3
	26 GDP deflator (2005 = 100)	19.3	19.6	19.9	20.5	21.1	22.0	23.1	24.3	25.5	26.6
	27 GDP deflator inflation rate (percent per year)	1.1	1.5	1.8	2.8	3.1	4.3	5.0	5.3	5.0	4.3
	28 Consumer price index (1982–1984 = 100)	30.6	31.0	31.5	32.4	33.4	34.8	36.7	38.8	40.5	41.8
	29 CPI inflation rate (percent per year)	1.3	1.3	1.6	2.9	3.1	4.2	5.5	5.7	4.4	3.2
	30 Current account balance (billions of dollars)	4.4	6.8	5.4	3.0	2.6	0.6	0.4	2.3	–1.4	–5.8

	1973	1974	1975	1976	1977	1978	1979	1980	1981	1982	1983	1984	1985
	852	933	1,034	1,151	1,278	1,428	1,591	1,756	1,940	2,076	2,289	2,501	2,718
	245	249	230	292	361	438	493	479	572	517	564	736	736
	282	318	358	383	414	454	501	566	628	680	733	797	879
	95	127	139	150	159	187	230	281	305	283	277	302	302
	91	128	123	151	182	212	253	294	318	303	329	405	417
	1,382	1,500	1,638	1,825	2,030	2,294	2,562	2,788	3,127	3,253	3,535	3,931	4,218
	811	890	949	1,059	1,181	1,336	1,498	1,648	1,820	1,920	2,036	2,246	2,412
	310	314	351	392	444	509	546	561	653	669	756	911	971
	1,121	1,204	1,300	1,452	1,625	1,844	2,045	2,208	2,473	2,589	2,792	3,156	3,383
	112	122	131	141	153	162	172	191	224	226	242	269	287
	141	164	190	208	232	261	299	344	393	434	451	474	505
	1,374	1,490	1,621	1,801	2,009	2,268	2,515	2,743	3,090	3,248	3,485	3,899	4,175
	8	10	16	24	21	26	47	45	37	5	50	32	42
	1,382	1,500	1,638	1,825	2,030	2,294	2,562	2,788	3,127	3,253	3,535	3,931	4,217
	4,917	4,890	4,880	5,141	5,378	5,678	5,855	5,839	5,987	5,871	6,136	6,577	6,849
	5.8	−0.6	−0.2	5.4	4.6	5.6	3.1	−0.3	2.5	−1.9	4.5	7.2	4.1
	211.9	213.9	216.0	218.1	220.3	222.6	225.1	227.7	230.0	232.2	234.3	236.4	238.5
	89.4	91.9	93.8	96.2	99.0	102.3	105.0	106.9	108.7	110.2	111.6	113.5	115.5
	85.1	86.8	85.8	88.8	92.0	96.0	98.8	99.3	100.4	99.5	100.8	105.0	107.2
	4.4	5.2	7.9	7.4	7.0	6.2	6.1	7.6	8.3	10.7	10.7	8.5	8.3
	60.8	61.3	61.2	61.6	62.3	63.2	63.7	63.8	63.9	64.0	64.0	64.4	64.8
	4.9	5.6	8.5	7.7	7.1	6.1	5.8	7.1	7.6	9.7	9.6	7.5	7.2
	23,200	22,861	22,592	23,575	24,412	25,503	26,010	25,640	26,030	25,282	26,186	27,823	28,718
	4.8	−1.5	−1.2	4.3	3.6	4.5	2.0	−1.4	1.5	−2.9	3.6	6.3	3.2
	855.5	902.1	1,016.2	1,152.0	1,270.3	1,366.0	1,473.7	1,599.8	1,755.4	1,910.3	2126.5	2309.9	2,495.7
	28.1	30.7	33.6	35.5	37.8	40.4	43.8	47.8	52.2	55.4	57.6	59.8	61.6
	5.6	9.0	9.4	5.8	6.4	7.0	8.3	9.1	9.4	6.1	4.0	3.8	3.0
	44.4	49.3	53.8	56.9	60.6	65.2	72.6	82.4	90.9	96.5	99.6	103.9	107.6
	6.2	11.0	9.1	5.8	6.5	7.6	11.3	13.5	10.3	6.2	3.2	4.3	3.6
	7.1	2.0	18.1	4.3	−14.3	−15.1	−0.3	2.3	5.0	−5.5	−38.7	−94.3	−118.2